THE MICRO ECONOMY TODAY

Tenth Edition

BRADLEY R. SCHILLER

American University

 **McGraw-Hill**
Irwin

Boston   Burr Ridge, IL   Dubuque, IA   Madison, WI   New York   San Francisco   St. Louis
Bangkok   Bogotá   Caracas   Kuala Lumpur   Lisbon   London   Madrid   Mexico City
Milan   Montreal   New Delhi   Santiago   Seoul   Singapore   Sydney   Taipei   Toronto

**McGraw-Hill
Irwin**

THE MICRO ECONOMY TODAY

Published by McGraw-Hill/Irwin, a business unit of The McGraw-Hill Companies, Inc., 1221 Avenue of the Americas, New York, NY, 10020. Copyright © 2006, 2003, 2000, 1997, 1994, 1991, 1989, 1986, 1983, 1980 by The McGraw-Hill Companies, Inc. All rights reserved. No part of this publication may be reproduced or distributed in any form or by any means, or stored in a database or retrieval system, without the prior written consent of The McGraw-Hill Companies, Inc., including, but not limited to, in any network or other electronic storage or transmission, or broadcast for distance learning.

Some ancillaries, including electronic and print components, may not be available to customers outside the United States.

This book is printed on acid-free paper.

1 2 3 4 5 6 7 8 9 0 DOW/DOW 0 9 8 7 6 5 4

ISBN   0-07-297964-X

Publisher: *Gary Burke*
Executive sponsoring editor: *Paul Shensa*
Developmental editor: *Rebecca Hicks*
Editorial coordinator: *Heila Hubbard*
Senior marketing manager: *Martin D. Quinn*
Lead producer, Media technology: *Kai Chiang*
Project manager: *Harvey Yep*
Senior production supervisor: *Rose Hepburn*
Photo research coordinator: *Lori Kramer*
Lead media project manager: *Becky Szura*
Senior supplement producer: *Carol Loreth*
Developer, Media technology: *Brian Nacik*
Cover design: *Kami Carter*
Interior design: *Kami Carter*
Typeface: *10/12 Times New Roman*
Compositor: *GTS–York, PA Campus*
Printer: *R. R. Donnelley*
Cover image: © David Parker/Photo Researchers, Inc./Description: Simulated detection of Higgs boson. Computer simulation of an event in which the decay of a Higgs boson particle produces four muons. Two of these muons are seen here (green tracks). The muons, along with countless other particles (red and blue tracks), are produced in a head-on collision between two protons. The Higgs boson is a localized clustering in the Higgs Field. This field permeates space, and local distortions of the Higgs Field are thought to be the way that particles gain mass. This image shows how the Higgs boson might be seen in the CMS detector on the Large Hadron Collider at CERN, the European particle physics laboratory.

Library of Congress Control Number: 2004116602

www.mhhe.com

Bradley R. Schiller has over three decades of experience teaching introductory economics at American University, the University of California (Berkeley and Santa Cruz), and the University of Maryland. He has given guest lectures at more than 300 colleges ranging from Fresno, California, to Istanbul, Turkey. Dr. Schiller's unique contribution to teaching is his ability to relate basic principles to current socioeconomic problems, institutions, and public policy decisions. This perspective is evident throughout *The Micro Economy Today.*

Dr. Schiller derives this policy focus from his extensive experience as a Washington consultant. He has been a consultant to most major federal agencies, many congressional committees, and political candidates. In addition, he has evaluated scores of government programs and helped design others. His studies of discrimination, training programs, tax reform, pensions, welfare, Social Security, and lifetime wage patterns have appeared in both professional journals and popular media. Dr. Schiller is also a frequent commentator on economic policy for television, radio, and newspapers.

Dr. Schiller received his Ph.D. from Harvard in 1969. He earned a B.A. degree, with great distinction, from the University of California (Berkeley) in 1965. He is now a professor of economics in the School of Public Affairs at American University in Washington, D.C.

THE 24/7 ECONOMY

24/7. That's the way the economy works. While you're sleeping, workers at the Texas Instrument plant in Kuala Lumpur are assembling the electronic circuits that will instruct your alarm clock to go off, relay the news via satellite TV or radio, enable video presentations in class or at remote locations, and help retrieve music files on the iPod you carry around. Venezuelan oil workers are pumping oil that will fuel your drive to class. Ethiopian farmers are harvesting the coffee beans that will help keep you alert. Traders in London, Hong Kong, and Tokyo are pushing the value of the dollar up or down, changing the cost of travel and trade. In an increasingly globalized economy, the economy truly never sleeps. It's in motion 24 hours a day, 7 days a week.

All of this perpetual motion makes teaching economics increasingly difficult. The parameters of the economy are constantly changing. Interest rates are up one day, down the next. The same with oil prices. Inflation looks worrisome one month and benign the next. Job growth looks great one month, then dismal the next. Even such famous prognosticators as Alan Greenspan have trouble keeping track of all these (changing) data, much less divining the implied direction of the economy.

At the micro level, incessant changes in the economy create similar problems. Market structures are continuously evolving. Products are always changing. With those changes, even market boundaries are on the move. Is your local cable franchise really a monopoly when satellite and Internet companies offer virtually identical products? Will Apple Computer, Inc., with a 70 percent market share in the portable MP3-player market, behave more like a monopolist or like a perfect competitor? With the Internet creating *global* shopping malls, how should industry concentration ratios be calculated? The Federal Trade Commission and the Antitrust Division of the U.S. Justice Department are vexed by ever-changing market boundaries and structures.

Coping with Change

So how do we cope with all this flux in the classroom? Or, for that matter, in a textbook that will be in print for three years? We could ignore the complexities of the real world and focus exclusively on abstract principles, perhaps "enlivening" the presentation with fables about the Acme Widget Company or the Jack and Jill Water Company. That approach not only bores students, but it also solidifies the misperception that economics is irrelevant to their daily life. Alternatively, we could spend countless hours reporting and discussing the economic news of the day. But that approach transforms the principles course into a current-events symposium.

The Micro Economy Today pursues a different strategy. I am convinced that economics is an exciting and very relevant field of study. I have felt this way since I attended my first undergraduate principles course. Despite an overbearing, boring textbook and a super-sized class (over 1,000 students!), I somehow discerned that economics could be an interesting topic. All it needed was a commitment to merging theoretical insights with the daily realities of shopping malls, stock markets, global integration, and policy development. Whew!

What Makes Economies Tick

How does this lofty ambition translate into the nuts and bolts of teaching? It starts by infusing the textbook and the course with a purposeful theme. Spotlighting scarcity and the necessity for choice is not enough; there's a much bigger picture. It's really about why some nations prosper while others languish. As we look around the world, how can we explain why millionaires abound in the United States, Hong Kong, the United Kingdom, and Australia, while 2.8 *billion* earthlings live on less than $2 a day? How is it that affluent consumers in developed nations carry around videophones while one-fourth of the world's population has never made a phone call? Surely, the

EFFECTIVE PEDAGOGY

Despite the abundance of real-world applications, this is at heart a *principles* text, not a compendium of issues. Good theory and interesting applications are not mutually exclusive. This is a text that wants to *teach microeconomics,* not just increase awareness of policy issues. To that end, *The Micro Economy Today* provides a logically organized and uncluttered theoretical structure for macro, micro, and international theory. What distinguishes this text from others on the market is that it conveys theory in a lively, student-friendly manner.

Clean, Clear Theory

Student comprehension of core theory is facilitated with careful, consistent, and effective pedagogy. This distinctive pedagogy includes the following features:

Concept Reinforcement

Graphs are *completely* labeled, colorful, and positioned on background grids. Because students often enter the principles course as graph-phobics, graphs are frequently accompanied by synchronized tabular data. Every table is also annotated. This shouldn't be a product-differentiating feature but, sadly, it is. Putting a table in a textbook without an annotation is akin to writing a cluster of numbers on the board, then leaving the classroom without any explanation.

Self-Explanatory Graphs and Tables

FIGURE 3.3
Shifts vs. Movements

A demand curve shows how a consumer responds to price changes. If the determinants of demand stay constant, the response is a *movement* along the curve to a new quantity demanded. In this case, the quantity demanded increases from 5 (point d_1), to 12 (point g_1), when price falls from $35 to $20 per hour.

If the determinants of demand change, the entire demand curve *shifts.* In this case, an increase in income increases demand. With more income, Tom is willing to buy 12 hours at the initial price of $35 (point d_2), not just the 5 hours he demanded before the lottery win.

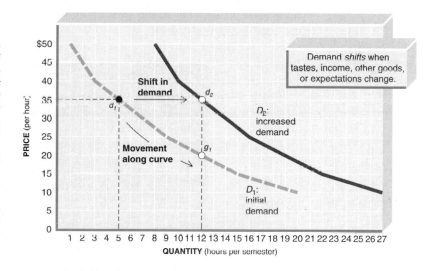

		Quantity Demanded (hours per semester)	
	Price (per hour)	Initial Demand	After Increase in Income
A	$50	1	8
B	45	2	9
C	40	3	10
D	35	5	12
E	30	7	14
F	25	9	16
G	20	12	19
H	15	15	22
I	10	20	27

Key terms are defined in the margin when they first appear and, unlike in other texts, redefined as necessary in subsequent chapters. Web site references are directly tied to the book's content, not hung on like ornaments. End-of-chapter discussion questions use tables, graphs, and boxed news stories from the text, reinforcing key concepts.

Reinforced Key Concepts

Boxed and Annotated Applications

In addition to the real-world applications that run through the body of the text, *The Micro Economy Today* intersperses boxed domestic (In the News) and global (World View) case studies. Although nearly every text on the market now offers boxed applications, *The Micro Economy Today's* presentation is distinctive. First, the sheer number of In the News (70) and World View (35) boxes is unique. Second, and more important, *every* boxed application is referenced in the body of the text. Third, *every* News and World View comes with a brief, self-contained explanation. Fourth, the News and World View boxes are the subject of the end-of-chapter Discussion Questions and Student Problem Set exercises. In combination, these distinctive features assure that students will actually read the boxed applications and discern their economic content. The *Test Bank* and *DiscoverEcon with Paul Solman videos* also provide subsets of questions tied to the News and World View boxes so that instructors can confirm student use of this feature.

Photos and Cartoons

The text presentation is also enlivened with occasional photos and cartoons that reflect basic concepts. The photos on page 40 are much more vivid testimony to the extremes of inequality than the data in Figure 2.6 (p. 39). The contrasting photos of the original Apple I (p. 180) and the iMac (p. 189) underscore how the "animal spirits" of competitive markets spur innovation. The cartoon on page ix reminds students that not all economists are of the same mind. Every photo and cartoon is annotated and referenced in the body of the text. These visual features are an integral part of the presentation, not diversions.

© Alan Schein Photography/CORBIS

© Wolfgang Spunbarg/Photo Edit

Analysis: The market distributes income (and, in turn, goods and services) according to the resources an individual owns and how well they are used. If the resulting inequalities are too great, some redistribution via government intervention may be desired.

Readability

The one adjective invariably used to describe *The Micro Economy Today* is "readable." Professors often express a bit of shock when they realize that students actually enjoy reading the book. (Well, not as much as a Stephen King novel, but a whole lot better than most textbooks they've had to plow through.) The writing style is lively and issue-focused. Unlike any other textbook on the market, every boxed feature, every graph, every table, and every cartoon is explained and analyzed. Every feature is also referenced in the text, so students actually learn the material rather than skipping over it. Because readability is ultimately in the eye of the beholder, you might ask a couple of students to read and compare an analogous chapter in *The Micro Economy Today* and in another text. This is a test *The Micro Economy Today* usually wins.

I firmly believe that students must *work* with key concepts in order to really learn them. Weekly homework assignments are *de rigueur* in my own classes. To facilitate homework assignments, I have prepared the *Student Problem Set,* which includes built-in numerical and graphing problems that build on the tables, graphs, and boxed material in each chapter. Grids for drawing graphs are also provided. Each chapter's problem set is detachable and includes answer boxes that facilitate grading. (Answers are available in the *Instructor's Resource Manual,* in print, or in downloadable form on the book's Web site). The *Student Problem Set* is behind the tab at the end of this book.

All of these pedagogical features add up to an unusually supportive learning context for students. With this support, students will learn and retain more economic concepts—and maybe even enjoy the educational process.

DISTINCTIVE MICRO

The Micro Economy Today focuses on the performance of specific companies and government programs to showcase the principles of market structure, labor-market functioning, redistribution, and regulation.

The real power of the market originates in competitive forces that breed innovation in products and technology. Other texts treat the competitive firm as a lifeless agent buffeted by larger market forces, but this book provides a very different perspective. *The Micro Economy Today* is the only principles text that has two chapters on perfect competition: Chapter 7 on firm behavior and Chapter 8 on industry behavior. Chapter 8 traces the actual evolution of the computer industry from the 1976 Apple I to the iMac. It gives students a real-world sense of how market structure changes over time and lets them see how dynamic, even revolutionary, competitive markets can be. The rise and fall of "dot.coms" and the ongoing plunge in MP3 player (iPod) prices reinforce the notion that competitive markets move with lightning speed to satisfy consumer demand.

As mentioned earlier, Chapter 12 focuses on the (de)regulation of private industry. The chapter first examines the qualities of natural monopoly and the rationale for regulating its behavior. The trade-offs inherent in any regulatory strategy are highlighted in the review of the railroad, cable TV, airline, telephone, and electricity industries. As in so many areas, the choice between imperfect markets and imperfect regulation is emphasized.

The Micro Economy Today offers parallel chapters on taxes and transfers. Chapters 18 and 19 emphasize the central trade-offs between equity and efficiency that plague tax and transfer policies. The varying distributional effects of specific taxes and transfers are highlighted. Examples are drawn from the Bush tax-cut packages of 2001–2004, President Bush's own 2003 tax return (p. 380), as well as the tax and benefit sides of Social Security. Taken together, the two chapters underscore the government's role in reshaping the market's answer to the FOR WHOM question.

Chapter 17 emphasizes the *economic* rather than the institutional role of financial markets, a topic rarely found in competing texts. The stock and bond markets are viewed as arbiters of risk and mechanisms of resource allocation. The mechanisms of present value discounting are also covered. The chapter starts with the financing of Columbus's New World expedition and ends with a look at the role today's venture capitalists play in promoting growth and technology.

Although real-world content is a general attribute of *The Micro Economy Today,* the level of detail in the micro section is truly exceptional. Table 10.2 (p. 220) offers concentration ratios for specific *products* (e.g., video game consoles), not the abstract industries

Student Problem Set

By MAL, Associated Features, Inc. Reprinted with permission.

Analysis: There are different theories about when and how the government should "fix" the economy. Policymakers must decide which advice to follow in specific situations.

Competitive Market Dynamics

(De)Regulation

Taxes and Transfers

Financial Markets

Real Companies, Real Products

IN THE NEWS

The President's Taxes

President and Mrs. Bush received over $800,000 of income in 2003. Taxable income was reduced by deductions, however. Their $227,494 tax bill represented 31.3 percent of *taxable* income (the *nominal* tax rate) but only 27.7 percent of *total* income (the *effective* rate).

Income	
Wages	$397,264
Interest	401,803
Dividends	23,471
Capital gain (loss)	1–3,000
Partnership gain	2,588
Adjusted gross income	$822,126

Deductions	
Charitable contributions	68,360
Investment expenses	22,990
Tax preparation fee	2,820
Other deductions	873
Total deductions	$ 95,043
Taxable income	$727,083
Tax	$227,494

Source: The White House. www.whitehouse.gov

Analysis: Taxes are levied on *taxable* income, not total income. Various deductions and exemptions reduce taxable income and *effective* tax rates.

(e.g., electronic equipment) that inhabit other texts. No other text provides such specific data, though this is the kind of detail that students can relate to. The oligopoly chapter (10) reviews a slew of recent price-fixing cases (music CD's, laser eye surgery, auction houses) and mergers. The chapter on monopolistic competition (11) starts with an examination of Starbucks and ends with a look at the growing market for "branded" bottled waters. Students will recognize these names and absorb the principles of market structure. Baseball fans will gain a greater appreciation of labor-demand principles after examining the multimillion-dollar salary of New York Yankees third baseman Alex Rodriguez.

DISTINCTIVE INTERNATIONAL

The global economy runs through every chapter of *The Micro Economy Today.*

World Views

The most visible evidence of this globalism is in the 35 World View boxes that are distributed throughout the text. As noted earlier, these boxed illustrations offer specific global illustrations of basic principles. To facilitate their use, every World View has a brief caption that highlights the theoretical relevance of the example. The *Test Bank* and Student Problem Set also offer questions based on the World Views.

Vested Interests

Consistent with the reality-based content of the entire text, the discussions of trade and finance theory go beyond basic principles to policy trade-offs and constraints. It's impossible to make sense of trade policy without recognizing the vested interests that battle trade principles. Chapters 20 and 21 emphasize that there are both winners and losers associated with every change in trade flows or exchange rates. Because vested interests are typically highly concentrated and well organized, they can often bend trade rules and flows to their advantage. Trade disputes over Mexican trucks, "dumped" steel, and sugar quotas help illustrate the realities of trade policy. The ongoing protest against the World Trade Organization is also assessed in terms of competing interests.

DISTINCTIVE WEB SUPPORT

The tenth edition of *The Micro Economy Today* continues to set the pace for Web applications and support of the principles course.

A mini Web site directory is provided in each chapter's marginal WebNotes. These URLs aren't random picks; they were selected because they let students extend and update adjacent in-text discussions.

WebNotes

The Micro Economy Today's Web site now includes even more features that both instructors and students will find engaging and instructive. The Online Learning Center is user-friendly. Upon entering the site at **www.mhhe.com/economics/schiller10,** students and instructors will find three separate book covers: one for *The Economy Today,* one for *The Macroeconomy Today,* and one for *The Microeconomy Today.* By clicking on the appropriate cover, users will link to a specific site for the version of the book they are using.

www.mhhe.com/ economics/schiller10

Proceeding into the Student Center, students will find lots of brand-new interactive study material. Diane Keenan of Cerritos College has prepared 15 self-grading multiple-choice and five true-or-false questions per chapter, which are ideal for self-quizzing before a test. Solomon Namala, also of Cerritos College, has created a supplementary Student Problem Set for the site. Professors can assign the additional five problems per chapter as homework or students can access them for additional skills practice. Answers can be found on the password-protected Instructor's Edition of the Web site. Mark Maier of Glendale College has created two Web Activities per chapter and 15 Collaborative Activities, unique to the site. On top of all that, students have access to my periodic NewsFlashes, a User's Manual for the site, and links to Econ Graph Kit, *DiscoverEcon with Paul Solman* videos, Economics on the Web, and Career Opportunities. They will also have the option of purchasing PowerWeb access with their book, which supplies them with three to five news articles per week on the topics they are studying.

The password-protected Instructor Center includes some wonderful resources for instructors who want to include more interactive student activities in their courses. The downloadable *Instructor's Manual* and PowerPoints, auxiliary Student Problem Set and answers, and Instructor's Notes for the Collaborative Activities and Web Activities are available to provide guidance for instructors who collect these assignments and grade them. John Min of Northern Virginia Community College has created Online Lecture Launchers. These interactive PowerPoint presentations highlight current events relevant to key macro, micro, and international topics. They serve as excellent "jumping-off points" for in-class discussion and lectures and will be updated quarterly to provide the most current information.

(www.mhhe.com/schiller10.com/discoverecon) A video and software program, this student online tutorial with accompanying videos is provided with every new copy of the tenth edition of *The Micro Economy Today.* It contains a fully updated and enhanced version of Discover-Econ, developed by Gerald C. Nelson of the University of Illinois at Urbana-Champaign, featuring new learning opportunities for the students and easy integration into existing courses for the instructor. The software is like an interactive text: software chapters parallel text chapters and software pages include specific page references to the text. With Discover-Econ's e-submission, professors can manage the Discover-Econ exercise results of their students electronically. These results are available at anytime to the student and the instructor can easily set up a course management site to make this information available to them. The program provides links to related videos for key topics on the accompanying Web-streamed videos. Paul Solman, economics correspondent for the *Newsttour with Jim Lehrer* is the creator of the video component, which consists of over 250 minutes of video, broken down into segments ranging from 7 to 10 minutes in length. These video segments

DiscoverEcon with Paul Solman Videos

explain the key economic ideas such as economic growth, elasticity, and production possibilities in a memorable, accessible way.

Opportunities for active learning abound. All DiscoverEcon chapters contain a multiple-choice quiz, discussion questions with online links, and match-the-terms exercises. Interactive graphs, animated charts, and live tables let your students manipulate variables and study the outcomes. Links to the glossary and text references clarify key concepts, and Web-based exercises give students a direct link to the site in question. With the addition of a new syllabus development tool, instructors can create interactive syllabi by linking DiscoverEcon exercises, special Web sites, and Solman videos to their class syllabus. Access to DiscoverEcon is available online, via a password code card supplied with each new book. Link to *DiscoverEcon with Paul Solman* videos at **www.mhhe.com/schiller10/discoverecon.**

WHAT'S NEW IN THE TENTH

To previous users of *The Micro Economy Today,* all of its distinctive features have become familiar—and hopefully, welcome. For those instructors already familiar with *The Micro Economy Today,* the more urgent question is, What's new? The answer is *a lot.* By way of brief summary, you may want to note the following:

New "Economy Tomorrow"s

The chapter-ending "Economy Tomorrow" sections continue to challenge students with future-looking applications of core concepts. In Chapter 1, the "Journey to Mars" highlights opportunity costs. In Chapter 2, the new "A Better Tomorrow" ponders the prospects of fulfilling the World Bank's ambitious Millennium Declaration. In Chapter 6, the threat of "Outsourcing Jobs" is confronted. Chapter 8 explains why iPods are likely to cost only $49 in a very short time.

New In the News

There are at least 20 all-new In the News applications in *The Micro Economy Today.* These cover everything from Google's August 2004 IPO (p. 362) to the 2004 Supreme Court rejection of regulated network-access fees for the Baby Bells (pp. 267–268).

New World Views

World Views have also been updated throughout the test of the new World Views. New World Views include the EU's antitrust pursuit of Microsoft (p. 215), OPEC price hikes (p. 230), and urban pollution (p. 278).

Built-in Student Problem Set

The Micro Economy Today's set of arithmetic and graphing problems has proven to be an extremely valuable tool for homework and quizzes. In fact, it has become so widely used that it is now packaged in the text itself, at the back. As before, it offers quantitative and graphing problems (with grids!) explicitly tied to the text, including each chapter's figures, tables, In the News, and World Views. There are 45 new problems, as well as improvements to old ones. Answers are in the print *Instructor's Resource Manual,* also available on the password-protected instructor's section of the Web site.

New Questions for Discussion

There are at least 20 new end-of-chapter Questions for Discussion. As always these draw explicitly on the content of their respective chapters, including boxed applications and figures.

New Data on Endcovers

The data displayed on the inside cover pages and immediately preceding the Problem Sets have not only been updated but refocused as well. Tables now include series on household income and poverty status by race (1980–2003); productivity and related data (1959–2003); stock and bond prices and yields (1969–2003); corporate profits (1959–2003); and international transactions (1946–2002).

New WebNotes

Previous WebNotes have been checked for currency and edited as needed, and a score of new WebNotes have been added as well. These are designed to enable students to update and extend in-text discussions.

Besides all these salient updates, the entire text has been rendered up-to-date with the latest statistics and case studies. ***This unparalleled currency is a distinctive feature of*** The Micro Economy Today.

NEW AND IMPROVED SUPPLEMENTS

Test Bank. Linda Wilson and Jane Himarios of the University of Texas at Arlington have thoroughly revised the *Test Bank* for the tenth edition. This team assures a high level of quality and consistency of the test questions and the greatest possible correlation with the content of the text as well as the *Study Guide,* which was prepared by Linda Wilson with Mark Maier. All questions are coded according to level of difficulty and have a text-page reference where the student will find a discussion of the concept on which the question is based. The computerized *Test Bank* is available in Brownstone Diploma, a flexible and easy-to-use electronic testing program. Diploma systems can produce high-quality graphs from the test banks and feature the ability to generate multiple tests, with versions "scrambled" to be distinctive. This software will meet the various needs of the widest spectrum of computer users. Both the print and computerized test banks are offered in micro and macro versions, each of which contains nearly 4,000 questions including over 200 essay questions.

PowerPoint Presentations. Anthony Zambelli of Cuyamaca College created new presentation slides for the tenth edition. Developed using Microsoft PowerPoint software, these slides are a step-by-step review of the key points in each of the book's 36 chapters. They are equally useful to the student in the classroom as lecture aids or for personal review at home or the computer lab. The slides use animation to show students how graphs build and shift.

Overhead Transparencies. All of the text's tables and graphs have been reproduced as full-color overhead transparency acetates.

Instructor's Resource Manual. Mark Maier of Glendale College has prepared the *Instructor's Resource Manual* as well as much of the original content for the Web site. This has allowed him to integrate the two in a way that will make online Web resources easier than ever for instructors to use in class.

The *Instructor's Resource Manual* is available in book form or online, and it includes chapter summaries and outlines, "lecture launchers" to stimulate class discussion, and media exercises to extend the analysis. New features include a section that details common misconceptions regarding the material in a particular chapter; an annotated outline of the chapter; and answers to the Questions for Discussion and the Student Problem Sets. Rae Jean Goodman of the United States Naval Academy has worked with Mark to update the debate projects found in the *Instructor's Resource Manual.* In addition, there is a photocopy-ready Print Media Exercise for each chapter.

News Flashes. As up-to-date as *The Micro Economy Today* is, it can't foretell the future. As the future becomes the present, however, I write two-page News Flashes describing major economic events and relating them to specific text references. These News Flashes provide good lecture material and can be copied for student use. Adopters of *The Micro Economy Today* have the option of receiving News Flashes via fax or mail. They're also available on the Schiller Web site. Four to six News Flashes are sent to adopters each year. (Contact your local McGraw-Hill/Irwin sales representative to get on the mailing list.)

At the instructor's discretion, students have access to the News Flashes described above. In addition, the following supplements can facilitate learning.

Built-in Student Problem Set. The built-in *Student Problem Set* is found at the back of every copy of *The Micro Economy Today*. Each chapter has 8 to 10 numerical and graphing problems tied to the content of the text. Graphing grids are provided. The answer blanks are formatted to facilitate grading and all answers are contained in the *Instructor's Resource Manual*. For convenience, the *Student Problem Set* pages are also perforated.

Study Guide. The new *Study Guide* has been completely updated by Linda Wilson and Mark Maier. The *Study Guide* develops quantitative skills and the use of economic terminology, and enhances critical thinking capabilities. Each chapter includes a Quick Review which lists the key points in an easy-to-read bulleted format, Learning Objectives for the chapter, a crossword puzzle using key terms, 10 true-false questions with explanations, 20 multiple-choice questions, problems and applications that relate directly back to the text, and common student errors. Answers to all problems, exercises, and questions are provided at the end of each chapter.

A NOTE ABOUT THE COVER

The tenth edition cover image is a theoretical representation of the Higgs boson. Dubbed the "God Particle" by Nobel Prize-wining physicist Leon Lederman, the Higgs boson is an, as yet, undiscovered elementary particle. Scientists believe that Higgs particles generate a thick firmament through which other particles move, distorting the field and picking up drag that constitutes that particle's mass.

Scientists have spent years and millions of dollars in their quest to isolate the "God Particle". Perhaps the most ambitious of labs is the Centre Européen de Recherche Nucléaire (CERN), where they are constructing a $3 billion Large Hadron Collider (LHC). Two hundred feet under ground, the LHC sends particles zooming around its 17-mile circumference, smashing them into one another to create dozens of tinier particles whose data is calculated by the LHC's large computer grid system.

The LHC Computing Grid, created to process the 12-14 PetaBytes of data generated by the LHC each year (equivalent to 20 million CDs), incorporates over 200 scientists in 36 countries into a massive virtual computing organization. The Grid has the capacity to revolutionize the way we use the Internet, making it a more reliable way to quickly transmit large quantities of data. While the discovery of the Higgs boson could be years away, the LHC's computer grid has already provided real-world improvements for the economy today and a glimpse of the effects it could have on the economy tomorrow.

ACKNOWLEDGMENTS

This tenth edition is unquestionably the finest edition of *The Micro Economy Today,* and I am deeply grateful to all those people who helped develop it. Paul Shensa, my editor for the last thirty years, again picked a first-rate team and supported it well with budgets cajoled from Gary Burke, the economics publisher. The stand-out player was Becca Hicks, who as Development Editor not only kept the whole package together but also made many independent contributions to the text's content and style. Harvey Yep, the Project Manager, did an exceptional job in assuring that every page of the text was visually pleasing, properly formatted, error-free, and timely produced. The design team, led by Kami Carter, created a lively pallette of colors and features that enhanced *The Micro Economy Today's* readability. My thanks to all of them and their supporting staff. I also expect to be eternally grateful to Martin Quinn, who is in charge of marketing *The Micro Economy Today*. I trust he is already out knocking on office doors and setting new sales records.

I also want to express my heartfelt thanks to the professors who have shared their reactions (both good and bad) with me. Direct feedback from these users and reviewers has been a great source of continuing improvements in *The Micro Economy Today:*

James L. Allen, Jr.,
Wharton County Junior College
Louis Amato,
University of North Carolina—Charlotte
Janice C. Baldon,
University of Louisville
Nancy Brooks,
University of Vermont, Burlington
Bill Burrows,
Lane Community College
Mike Cohick,
Collin County Community College
Amy S. Cramer,
Pima Community College
Michael Ellis,
Texas Wesleyan College
Robert Eyler,
Sonoma State University
Kaya Ford,
Northern Virginia Community College
Alan Frishman,
Hobart and William Smith Colleges
Melissa A. Groves,
Towson University
Katherine M. Huger,
Charlestown Southern University
Marcha L. Hunley,
Cincinnati State University
Anisul M. Islam,
University of Houston—Downtown
Miren Ivankovic,
Southern Wesleyan University
James A. Janke,
Dakota State University
Paul E. Jorgensen,
Linn-Benton Community College
Emil Koren,
Hillsborough Community College
Ellen Lindeman,
Raritan Valley Community College
Cecil Mackey,
Michigan State University
Tom Masterson,
Westfield State College

Frederick W. May,
Trident Technical College
John Min,
North Virginia Community College
Stan Mitchell,
McLennan Community College
George L. Nagy,
Hudson Valley Community College
Michael L. Palmer,
Maplewood Community College
Norman Paul,
San Jacinto College
Peggy Pelt,
Gulf Coast Community College
Bob Potter,
University of Central Florida
Joe Prinzinger,
Lynchburg College
Taghi Ramin,
William Patterson University
John Romps,
St. Anselm College
Werner Sichel,
Western Michigan University
Noel S. Smith,
Palm Beach Community College
Carol O. Stivender,
University of North Carolina—Charlotte
Geetha Suresh,
Purdue University
Daniel A. Talley,
Dakota State University
Michael M. Tansey,
Rockhurst University
Deborah Thorsen,
Palm Beach Community College
Marjolein van der Veen,
Shoreline Community College
Richard D. Wolff,
University of Massachusetts
Virginia York,
Gulf Coast Community College
Andrea Zanter,
Hillsborough Community College

Gayla B. Ashford,
Calhoun Community College
Josiah Baker,
University of Central Florida
Millica Z. Bookman,
Saint Joseph's University
Wesley F. Booth,
San Antonio College
Nancy Brooks,
University of Vermont

Tim Burson,
Queens College (North Carolina)
James L. Butkiewitz,
University of Delaware
Suparna Chakraborty,
University of Minnesota
J. M. Cypher,
California State University—Fresno
Julie Edwards,
Blinn College

Harry Ellis, Jr.,
University of North Texas
Robert Eyler,
Sonoma State University
Indranil Ghosh,
Pennsylvania State University—Erie
Doug Greer,
San Jose State University
Rick Hirschi,
Brigham Young University (Idaho)
Jayvanath Ishwaran,
Stephen F. Austin State University
Kevin Klein,
Illinois College
Norman Knaub,
Pennsylvania State University—Altoona
Nazma Latif-Zaman,
Providence College
Tony Lima,
California State University—Hayward
Cathleen Leue,
University of Oregon
Jessica McCraw,
Texas Christian University
Carrie A. Meyer,
George Mason University
Francis D. Mummery,
Fullerton College

Sheila Amin Gutierrez de Piñeres,
University of Texas—Dallas
Judith E. Pasch,
University of Wisconsin
David R. Poma,
St. Francis College
Edward Price,
Oklahoma State University
Paddy Quick,
St. Francis College
George D. Santopietro,
Radford University
Reza Sepassi,
McLennan Community College
Mohamed Sharif,
University of Rhode Island
David J. St. Clair,
California State University
Carol O. Stivender,
University of North Carolina—Charlotte
Michael Stroup,
Stephen F. Austin State University
Geetha Suresh,
Purdue University
Kamal Upadhyaya,
University of New Haven

Finally, I'd like to thank all the professors and students who are going to use *The Micro Economy Today* as an introduction to economics principles. I welcome any responses (even the bad ones) you'd like to pass on for future editions.

—Bradley R. Schiller

CONTENTS IN BRIEF

CONTENTS

WORLD VIEW:
Cloudy Days in Tomorrowland 2 •
Food Shortages Plague N. Korea 9 •
North Korea Expanding Missile
Programs 9 • India's Economy Gets a
Jolt from Mr. Shourie 11 • Index of
Economic Freedom 15 • China's
Leaders Back Private Property 17

WORLD VIEW:
Comparative Output 28 • GDP Per
Capita around the World 29 • The
Education Gap between Rich and Poor
Nations 35 • Income Share of the
Rich 41

WORLD VIEW:
Dining on the Downtick 64

IN THE NEWS:
PC Prices Fall with Demand 50 • Prices
Soar As Cold Snap Shreds Iceberg
Lettuce Supply 58 • For Fans, What's 4
Nights for U2? 61 • Demand for Cipro
Rising 63 • Federal Price Limits
Backfire 67

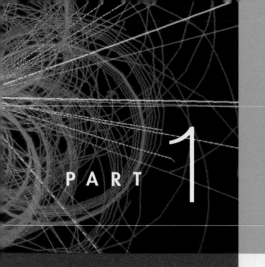

PART 1

The "God Particle"

The image on the cover is a theoretical depiction of a deteriorating "God Particle"—the most elusive speck of matter in the universe. Physicists believe that the God Particle, formally known as the Higgs boson, is the glue that holds the universe together. The God Particle is thought to emit a kind of soupy ether through which other particles move, picking up drag that turns matter into mass.

What does the God Particle have to do with economics? In their quest to isolate the God Particle, researchers are developing a supercomputing grid. The LHC Computing Grid will integrate computing resources from around the globe, creating a superpowerful *computation* network, similar in design to the Internet's global *communications* network. The LHC (for the Swiss-based $3-billion Large Hadron Collider) computer grid will allow individual users to tap into supercomputing power. The resultant computer power will vastly increase our technological abilities to process and interpret data. This will create new investment opportunities and enhance productivity in industries as diverse as film editing, drug design, and earthquake detection. In other words, pursuit of the God Particle, like the Internet, will expand the economy's production capacity and bring us still more goods and services in the economy tomorrow.

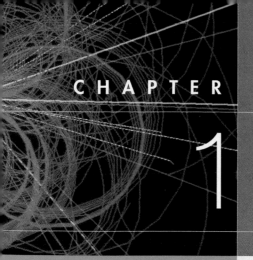

Economics: The Core Issues

I n February 2004, Intel Corporation announced a research breakthrough that stunned the high-tech industry. The company's engineers had created a new processor with 125 million transistors—the tiny parts that regulate the flow of electricity on a silicon chip. The new transistors are so small (90 nanometers, or less than one thousandth the width of a human hair) that 1 billion of them can be packed onto a single chip. That's a gargantuan leap from the 42-million-transistor Pentium 4 chip that now dominates the market and light-years away from the 2,300-transistor chip that powered IBM computers in 1972. What does all this have to do with you? For starters, it means that all electronic goods and services will be able to operate faster and with more options. In other words, the extraordinary array of goods we now confront in the marketplace will continue to expand and improve.

Maybe more isn't always better, but the history of humankind reveals a relentless quest for more and better output. To a large extent, the quest for more output has been driven by necessity. The world's population keeps growing, but the amount of land doesn't. That's why the English economist Thomas Malthus predicted in 1778 that the world would run out of food long before the nineteenth century ended. He didn't know that a few years later someone would invent the iron plow (1808), the reaper (1826), or the milking machine (1878). And Malthus had no conception of what biotechnology's "green revolution" might become and no clues at all about electronic circuits. So his prediction of global starvation turned out to be unduly pessimistic.

Although we've managed to increase global food output faster than the population has grown, we can't be complacent. The United Nations predicts that the world's population, now at 6.4 billion, will increase by another billion every 10 years. Even if we find ways for food output to keep pace, we can't be satisfied. Our future goals are much more ambitious. We want an ever higher standard of living, not just enough food on the table. No matter how fast our incomes grow, we always want more. The living standards earlier generations dreamed of we now take for granted. Today's luxuries—plasma TVs, camera phones, satellite radio—will most likely be viewed as necessities in a few years, but only if we keep squeezing more and more output out of available resources.

Ironically, some people fear we will do exactly that—and end up destroying the environment in the process. They foresee a Doomsday in which greenhouse gases generated by ever-rising production levels will overheat the earth, melt the solar icecaps, flood coastal areas, and destroy crops.

As the accompanying World View illustrates, no one really knows how the future will unfold. Even some of history's greatest minds have made predictions that turned out to be ludicrous. In gazing into the future, however, we can be certain of some fundamental principles. The first principle is that resources will always be scarce, relative to our desires. Second, how we use those scarce resources will shape our future. If we use resources today to miniaturize electronic circuits, we'll

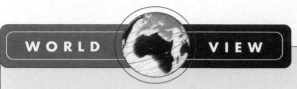

Cloudy Days in Tomorrowland

We'd like to think all *our* predictions will prove right. But the highways of history are littered with wrong calls, false insights and bad guesses. Here's a sampler of twentieth-century futurology that flopped.

I confess that in 1901, I said to my brother Orville that man would not fly for 50 years . . . Ever since, I have distrusted myself and avoided all predictions.

> —Wilbur Wright, *U.S. aviation pioneer, 1908*

I must confess that my imagination . . . refuses to see any sort of submarine doing anything but suffocating its crew and floundering at sea.

> —H. G. Wells, *British novelist, 1901*

Airplanes are interesting toys but of no military value.

> —Marshal Ferdinand Foch, *French military strategist and future World War 1 commander, 1911*

The horse is here to stay, but the automobile is only a novelty—a fad.

> —*A president of the Michigan Savings Bank advising* Horace Rackham *(Henry Ford's lawyer) not to invest in the Ford Motor Co., 1903. Rackham ignored the advice, bought $5,000 worth of stock and sold it several years later for $12.5 million.*

Radio has no future.

> —Lord Kelvin, *Scottish mathematician and physicist, former president of the Royal Society, 1897*

Everything that can be invented has been invented.

> —Charles H. Duell, *U.S. commissioner of patents, 1899*

Who the hell wants to hear actors talk?

> —Harry M. Warner, *Warner Brothers, 1927*

There is no reason for any individual to have a computer in their home.

> —Kenneth Olsen, *president and founder of Digital Equipment Corp., 1977*

[Man will never reach the moon] regardless of all future scientific advances.

> —Dr. Lee De Forest, *inventor of the Audion tube and a father of radio, February 25, 1967*

We don't like their sound. Groups of guitars are on the way out.

> —Decca Records, *rejecting the Beatles, 1962*

What use could this company make of an electrical toy?

> —*Western Union president* William Orton, *rejecting Alexander Graham Bell's offer to sell his struggling telephone company to Western Union for $100,000*

Computers in the future may . . . perhaps only weigh 1.5 tons.

> —Popular Mechanics, *forecasting the development of computer technology, 1949*

Stocks have reached what looks like a permanently high plateau.

> —Irving Fisher, *professor of economics, Yale University, October 17, 1929*

[Television] won't be able to hold on to any market it captures after the first six months. People will soon get tired of staring at a plywood box every night.

> —Darryl F. Zanuck, *head of 20th Century-Fox, 1946*

Analysis: No one predicts the future well. But the economic choices we make today about the use of scarce resources will determine the kind of future we have.

WEBNOTE

Intel Corporation showcases its latest technology at www.intel.com/research/silicon.

economics: The study of how best to allocate scarce resources among competing uses.

be able to produce more and better products in the future. Likewise, if we build more factories and cyber networks today, we'll be able to produce more output tomorrow. If we install more pollution controls in cars, power plants, and factories today, we'll even have cleaner air tomorrow.

The science of economics helps us frame these choices. In a nutshell, **economics** is the study of how people use scarce resources. How do you decide how much time to spend studying? How does Amazon.com decide how many workers to hire? How does DaimlerChrysler decide whether to use its factories to produce sports utility vehicles or sedans? What share of a nation's resources should be devoted to space exploration, the delivery of health care services, or pollution control? In every instance, alternative ways of using scarce labor, land, and building resources are available, and we have to choose one use over another.

In this first chapter we explore the nature of scarcity and the kinds of choices it forces us to make. As we'll see, ***three core issues must be resolved:***

- ***WHAT to produce with our limited resources.***
- ***HOW to produce the goods and services we select.***
- ***FOR WHOM goods and services are produced;*** that is, who should get them.

We also have to decide who should answer these questions. Should the marketplace decide what gets produced and how and for whom? Or should the government dictate output choices, regulate production processes, and redistribute incomes? Should Microsoft decide what features get included in a computer's operating system, or should the government make that decision? Should private companies provide airport security or should the government assume that responsibility? Should interest rates be set by private banks alone, or should the government try to control interest rates? The battle over *who* should answer the core questions is often as contentious as the questions themselves.

THE ECONOMY IS US

To learn how the economy works, let's start with a simple truth: *The economy is us.* "The economy" is simply an abstraction referring to the grand sum of all our production and consumption activities. What we collectively produce is what the economy produces; what we collectively consume is what the economy consumes. In this sense, the concept of "the economy" is no more difficult than the concept of "the family." If someone tells you that the Jones family has an annual income of $42,000, you know that the reference is to the collective earnings of all the Joneses. Likewise, when someone reports that the nation's income is $11 trillion per year—as it now is—we should recognize that the reference is to the grand total of everyone's income. If we work fewer hours or get paid less, both family income *and* national income decline. The "meaningless statistics" (see accompanying cartoon) often cited in the news are just a summary of our collective market behavior.

The same relationship between individual behavior and aggregate behavior applies to specific outputs. If we as individuals insist on driving cars rather than taking public transportation, the economy will produce millions of cars each year and consume vast quantities of oil. In a slightly different way, the economy produces billions of dollars

"Meaningless statistics were up one-point-five per cent this month over last month."

Analysis: Many people think of economics as dull statistics. But economics is really about human behavior—how people decide to use scarce resources and how those decisions affect market outcomes.

of military hardware to satisfy our desire for national defense. In each case, the output of the economy reflects the collective behavior of the 300 million individuals who participate in the economy.

We may not always be happy with the output of the economy. But we can't ignore the link between individual action and collective outcomes. If the highways are clogged and the air is polluted, we can't blame someone else for the transportation choices we made. If we're disturbed by the size of our military arsenal, we must still accept responsibility for our choices (or nonchoices, if we failed to vote). In either case, we continue to have the option of reallocating our resources. We can create a different outcome the next day, month, or year.

SCARCITY: THE CORE PROBLEM

Although we can change economic outcomes, we can't have everything we want. If you go to the mall with $20 in your pocket, you can only buy so much. The money in your pocket sets a *limit* to your spending.

The output of the entire economy is also limited. The limits in this case are set not by money but by the resources available for producing goods and services. Everyone wants more housing, new schools, better transit systems, and a new car. But even a country as rich as the United States can't produce everything people want. So, like every other nation, we have to grapple with the core problem of **scarcity**—the fact that there aren't enough resources available to satisfy all our desires.

scarcity: Lack of enough resources to satisfy all desired uses of those resources.

Factors of Production

factors of production: Resource inputs used to produce goods and services, such as land, labor, capital, and entrepreneurship.

The resources used to produce goods and services are called **factors of production.** *The four basic factors of production are*

- *Land*
- *Labor*
- *Capital*
- *Entrepreneurship*

These are the *inputs* needed to produce desired *outputs.* To produce this textbook, for example, we needed paper, printing presses, a building, and lots of labor. We also needed people with good ideas who could put it together. To produce the education you're getting in this class, we need not only a textbook but a classroom, a teacher, and a blackboard as well. Without factors of production, we simply can't produce anything.

Land. The first factor of production, land, refers not just to the ground but to all natural resources. Crude oil, water, air, and minerals are all included in our concept of "land."

Labor. Labor too has several dimensions. It's not simply a question of how many bodies there are. When we speak of labor as a factor of production, we refer to the skills and abilities to produce goods and services. Hence, both the quantity and the quality of human resources are included in the "labor" factor.

capital: Final goods produced for use in the production of other goods, e.g., equipment, structures.

Capital. The third factor of production is capital. In economics the term **capital** refers to final goods produced for use in further production. The residents of fishing villages in southern Thailand, for example, braid huge fishing nets. The sole purpose of these nets is to catch more fish. The nets themselves become a factor of production in obtaining the final goods (fish) that people desire. Thus, they're regarded as *capital.* Blast furnaces used to make steel and desks used to equip offices are also capital inputs.

Entrepreneurship. The more land, labor, and capital available, the greater the amount of potential output. A farmer with 10,000 acres, 12 employees, and six tractors can grow more crops than a farmer with half those resources. But there's no guarantee that he will. The farmer with fewer resources may have better ideas about what to plant, when to irrigate, or how to harvest the crops. *It's not just a matter of what resources you have but also of how well you use them.* This is where the fourth factor of production—**entrepreneurship**—comes in. The entrepreneur is the person who sees the opportunity for new or better products and brings together the resources needed for producing them. If it weren't for entrepreneurs, Thai fishermen would still be using sticks to catch fish. Without entrepreneurship, farmers would still be milking their cows by hand. If someone hadn't thought of a way to miniaturize electronic circuits, you wouldn't have a cell phone.

The role of entrepreneurs in economic progress is a key issue in the market versus government debate. The Austrian economist Joseph Schumpeter argued that free markets unleash the "animal spirits" of entrepreneurs, propelling innovation, technology, and growth. Critics of government regulation argue that government interference in the marketplace, however well intentioned, tends to stifle those very same animal spirits.

No matter how an economy is organized, there's a limit to how fast it can grow. The most evident limit is the amount of resources available for producing goods and services. These resource limits imply that we can't produce everything we want. When President Bush announced an ambitious plan to colonize the Moon and explore Mars, people were excited. But then people wondered how we'd pay for a trillion-dollar Mars expedition. In *dollar* terms, the money would have to come from other programs. In *economic* terms, the resources used for space exploration would be unavailable for producing more earthly goods like education, health care, and highways.

The earthly sacrifices implied by an expedition to Mars go to the heart of the scarcity problem. *Every time we use scarce resources in one way, we give up the opportunity to use them in other ways.* If we use more resources to explore space, we have fewer resources available for producing earthly goods. The forgone earthly goods represent the **opportunity costs** of a Mars expedition. *Opportunity cost is what is given up to get something else.* Even a so-called free lunch has an opportunity cost (see cartoon). The resources used to produce the lunch could have been used to produce something else. A trip to Mars has a much higher opportunity cost.

Your economics class also has an opportunity cost. The building space used for your economics class can't be used to show movies at the same time. Your professor can't lecture (produce education) and repair motorcycles simultaneously. The decision to use these scarce resources (capital, labor) for an economics class implies producing less of other goods.

> **entrepreneurship:** The assembling of resources to produce new or improved products and technologies.

Limits to Output

Opportunity Costs

> **opportunity cost:** The most desired goods or services that are forgone to obtain something else.

"There's no such thing as a free lunch."

Analysis: All goods and services have an opportunity cost. Even the resources used to produce a "free lunch" could have been used to produce something else.

Even reading this book is costly. That cost is not measured in dollars and cents. The true (economic) cost is, instead, measured in terms of some alternative activity. What would you like to be doing right now? The more time you spend reading this book, the less time you have available for that alternative use of your time. The opportunity cost of reading this text is the best alternative use of your scarce time. If you are missing your favorite TV show, we'd say that show is the opportunity cost of reading this book. It is what you gave up to do this assignment. Hopefully, the benefits you get from studying will outweigh that cost. Otherwise this wouldn't be the best way to use your scarce time.

Guns vs. Butter

WEBNOTE

To see how the share of output allocated to national defense has changed in recent decades, visit the Congressional Budget Office web site at www.cbo.gov and search for "discretionary outlays."

One of the persistent national choices about resource use entails defense spending. After the September 11, 2001, terrorist attacks on the World Trade Center and Pentagon, American citizens overwhelmingly favored an increase in military spending. But where were the extra resources going to come from? Any resources employed in national defense must be taken from other industries. The 1.4 million men and women already serving in the armed forces aren't available to build schools, program computers, or teach economics. Similarly, the land, labor, capital, and entrepreneurship devoted to producing military hardware aren't available for producing civilian goods. An *increase* in national defense would imply still more sacrifices of civilian goods and services. This is the "guns versus butter" dilemma that all nations confront.

After the end of the Cold War in 1989, the United States had chosen to produce far fewer "guns." The defense budget declined from a high of 6.3 percent of total output in 1986 to only 3 percent in 2001. In the process, the armed forces had been cut by 500,000 men and women. These defense cutbacks freed up scarce resources that produced more civilian goods ("butter"). This is referred to as the "peace dividend" from military downsizing. The post-terrorist military buildup and the war in Iraq reversed part of that dividend.

PRODUCTION POSSIBILITIES

The opportunity costs implied by our every choice can be illustrated easily. Suppose a nation can produce only two goods, trucks and tanks. To keep things simple, assume that labor (workers) is the only factor of production needed to produce either good. Although other factors of production (land, machinery) are also needed in actual production, ignoring them for the moment does no harm. Let us assume further that we have a total of only 10 workers available per day to produce either trucks or tanks. Our initial problem is to determine the *limits* of output. How many trucks or tanks *can* be produced in a day with available resources?

Before going any further, notice how opportunity costs will affect the answer. If we use all 10 workers to produce trucks, no labor will be available to assemble tanks. In this case, forgone tanks would become the *opportunity cost* of a decision to employ all our resources in truck production.

We still don't know how many trucks could be produced with 10 workers or exactly how many tanks would be forgone by such a decision. To get these answers, we need more details about the production processes involved—specifically, how many workers are required to manufacture trucks or tanks.

The Production Possibilities Curve

production possibilities: The alternative combinations of final goods and services that could be produced in a given time period with all available resources and technology.

Table 1.1 summarizes the hypothetical choices, or **production possibilities,** that we confront in this case. Row *A* of the table shows the consequences of a decision to produce trucks only. With 10 workers available and a labor requirement of 2 workers per truck, we can manufacture a maximum of five trucks per day. By so doing, however, we use all available workers, leaving none for tank assembly. If we want tanks, we have to cut back on truck production; this is the essential choice we must make.

The remainder of Table 1.1 describes the full range of production choices. By cutting back truck production from five to four trucks per day (row *B*), we reduce labor use from 10 workers to 8. That leaves 2 workers available for other uses.

TABLE 1.1
Production Possibilities Schedule

As long as resources are limited, their use entails an opportunity cost. In this case, resources (labor) used to produce trucks can't be used for tank assembly at the same time. Hence, the forgone tanks are the opportunity cost of additional trucks. If all our resources were used to produce trucks (row A), no tanks could be assembled.

| | Total Available Labor | Truck Production | | | | Tank Production | | |
		Output of Trucks per Day	×	Labor Needed per Truck =	Total Labor Required for Trucks	Labor Not Used for Trucks	Potential Output of Tanks per Day	Increase in Tank Output
A	10	5		2	10	0	0	
B	10	4		2	8	2	2.0 >	2.0
C	10	3		2	6	4	3.0 >	1.0
D	10	2		2	4	6	3.8 >	0.8
E	10	1		2	2	8	4.5 >	0.7
F	10	0		2	0	10	5.0 >	0.5

If we employ these remaining 2 workers to assemble tanks, we can build two tanks a day. We would then end up with four trucks and two tanks per day. What's the opportunity cost of these two tanks? It's the one additional truck (the fifth truck) that we could have produced but didn't.

As we proceed down the rows of Table 1.1, the nature of opportunity costs becomes apparent. Each additional tank built implies the loss (opportunity cost) of truck output. Likewise, every truck produced implies the loss of some tank output.

These trade-offs between truck and tank production are illustrated in the production possibilities curve of Figure 1.1. *Each point on the production possibilities curve depicts an alternative mix of output* that could be produced. In this case, each point represents a different combination of trucks and tanks that we could produce in a single day using all available resources (labor in this case).

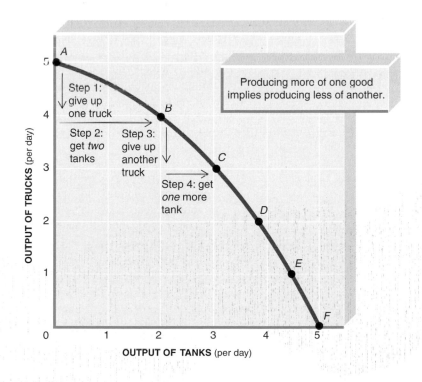

FIGURE 1.1
A Production Possibilities Curve

A production possibilities curve describes the various output combinations that could be produced in a given time period with available resources and technology. It represents a menu of output choices an economy confronts. Point *B* indicates that we could produce a *combination* of four trucks and two tanks per day. By producing one less truck, we could assemble a third tank, and thus move to point *C*. Points *A, D, E,* and *F,* illustrate still other output combinations that could be produced. This curve is a graphic illustration of the production possibilities schedule in Table 1.1.

Notice in particular how points *A* through *F* in Figure 1.1 represent the choices described in each row of Table 1.1. At point *A*, we're producing five trucks per day and no tanks. As we move down the curve from point *A* to point *B*, truck production drops from five to four vehicles per day while tank assembly increases from zero to two. In other words, we're giving up one truck to get two tanks assembled. The opportunity cost of those tanks is one truck that is given up. A production possibilities curve, then, is simply a graphic summary of production possibilities, as described in Table 1.1. It illustrates the alternative goods and services we could produce and the implied opportunity costs of each choice. In other words, *the production possibilities curve illustrates two essential principles:*

- *Scarce resources.* There's a limit to the amount we can produce in a given time period with available resources and technology.
- *Opportunity costs.* We can obtain additional quantities of any desired good only by reducing the potential production of another good.

Increasing Opportunity Costs

The shape of the production possibilities curve reflects another limitation on our choices. Notice how opportunity costs increase as we move along the production possibilities curve. When we cut truck output from five to four (step 1, Figure 1.1), we get two tanks (step 2). When we cut truck production further, however (step 3), we get only one tank per truck given up (step 4). The opportunity cost of tank production is increasing. This process of increasing opportunity cost continues. By the time we give up the last truck (row *F*), tank output increases by only 0.5: We get only half a tank for the last truck given up. These increases in opportunity cost are reflected in the outward bend of the production possibilities curve.

Why do opportunity costs increase? Mostly because it's difficult to move resources from one industry to another. It's easy to transform trucks to tanks on a blackboard. In the real world, however, resources don't adapt so easily. Workers who assemble trucks may not have the same skills for tank assembly. As we continue to transfer labor from one industry to the other, we start getting fewer tanks for every truck we give up.

The difficulties entailed in transferring labor skills, capital, and entrepreneurship from one industry to another are so universal that we often speak of the *law* of *increasing opportunity cost.* This law says that we must give up ever-increasing quantities of other goods and services in order to get more of a particular good. The law isn't based solely on the limited versatility of individual workers. The *mix* of factor inputs makes a difference as well. Truck assembly requires less capital than tank assembly. In a pinch, wheels can be mounted on a truck almost completely by hand, whereas tank treads require more sophisticated machinery. As we move labor from truck assembly to tank assembly, available capital may restrict our output capabilities.

The Cost of North Korea's Military

WEBNOTE

The International Institute for Strategic Studies compiles data on national military forces (www.iiss.org). To determine what percentage of a nation's population is in the armed forces, try the Central Intelligence Agency (www.odci.gov/cia/publications/factbook).

The kind of opportunity costs that arise in truck production or tank assembly takes on even greater significance in the broader decisions nations make about WHAT to produce. Consider, for example, North Korea's decision to maintain a large military. North Korea is a relatively small country: Its population of 24 million ranks fortieth in the world. Yet North Korea maintains the fourth-largest army in the world. To do so, it must allocate 16 percent of all its resources to feeding, clothing, and equipping its military forces. As a consequence, there aren't enough resources available to produce food. Without adequate machinery, seeds, fertilizer, or irrigation, Korea's farmers can't produce enough food to feed the population (see World View). As Figure 1.2 illustrates, the opportunity cost of "guns" in Korea is a lot of needed "butter."

During World War II, the United States confronted a similar trade-off. In 1944, nearly 40 percent of all U.S. output was devoted to the military. Civilian goods were so scarce that they had to be rationed. Staples like butter, sugar, and gasoline were doled out in small quantities. Even golf balls were rationed. In North Korea, golf balls would be a luxury even without a military buildup. As the share of North Korea's output devoted to the military increased, even basic food production became more difficult.

WORLD VIEW

Food Shortages Plague N. Korea

BEIJING, Feb. 13—A severe food shortage has crippled the U.N. feeding program that sustains North Korea's most vulnerable and undernourished people, according to Masood Hyder, the U.N. humanitarian aid coordinator and World Food Program representative in Pyongyang.

He said his organization can now feed fewer than 100,000 of the 6.5 million people it normally does, many of them kindergarten-age children and pregnant women who cannot get what they need to stay healthy from the country's distribution system. . . .

Food shortages already produce stunted growth in four out of 10 North Korean students and allow pregnant women to gain only half of the 22 pounds they are expected to gain to give birth to healthy babies.

Some orphanages have started serving two meals a day instead of three because of the shortages, Masood said.

—Edward Cody

Source: *Washington Post*, February 14, 2004. © 2004 The Washington Post. Reprinted with permission. www.washingtonpost.com

North Korea Expanding Missile Programs

Despite international pressure to curtail its missile program, North Korea is building at least two new launch facilities for the medium-range Taepo Dong 1 and has stepped up production of short-range missiles, according to U.S. intelligence and diplomatic sources.

The projects, and a conclusion by U.S. intelligence agencies that North Korea intends to test-fire a second missile capable of striking Japan, are inflaming regional tensions, U.S. officials and Korea experts said.

—Dana Priest and Thomas W. Lippman

Source: *Washington Post*, November 20, 1998. © 1998 The Washington Post. Reprinted with permission. www.washingtonpost.com

Analysis: North Korea's inability to feed itself is partly due to maintaining its large army: Resources used for the military aren't available for producing food.

Russia confronted a similarly difficult trade-off. In September 2000, Russia decided it could no longer afford to devote such a large share of its resources to the military. It decided to shrink its armed forces by more than a fourth, releasing over 300,000 workers to produce civilian goods and services. As a result, Russia now has a smaller armed force than North Korea but also a lot more food. Figure 1.3 illustrates how other nations divide up available resources between military and civilian production. The $420 billion the United States now spends on national defense absorbs only 3.8 percent of total output. This made the opportunity costs of the war in Iraq and post-terrorist military buildup less painful.

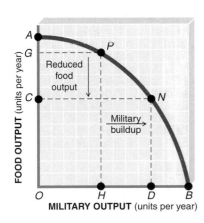

FIGURE 1.2
The Cost of War

North Korea devotes 16 percent of its output to the military. The opportunity cost of this decision is reduced output of food. As the military expands from *OH* to *OD,* food output drops from *OG* to *OC.*

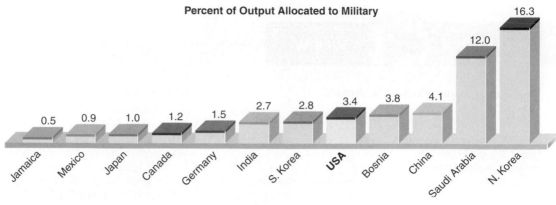

Percent of Output Allocated to Military

FIGURE 1.3
The Military Share of Output

The share of output allocated to the military is an indication of the opportunity cost of maintaining an army. North Korea has the highest cost, using 16 percent of its resources for military pur-

poses. Although China and the United States have much larger armies, their military *share* of output is much smaller.
Source: International Institute of Strategic Studies (2002 data).

Efficiency

Not all of the choices on the production possibilities curve are equally desirable. They are, however, all *efficient*. Efficiency means squeezing *maximum* output out of available resources. Every point of the production possibilities curve satisfies this condition. Although the *mix* of output changes as we move around the production possibilities curve (Figures 1.1 and 1.2), at every point we are getting as much *total* output as physically possible. Since **efficiency** in production means simply "getting the most from what you've got," every point on the production possibilities curve is efficient. At any point on the curve we are using all available resources in the best way we know how.

> **efficiency:** Maximum output of a good from the resources used in production.

Inefficiency

There's no guarantee, of course, that we'll always use resources so efficiently. *A production possibilities curve shows* **potential** *output, not necessarily* **actual** *output.* If we're inefficient, actual output will be less than that potential. This happens. In the real world, workers sometimes loaf on the job. Or they call in sick and go to a baseball game instead of working. Managers don't always give the clearest directions or stay in touch with advancing technology. Even students sometimes fail to put forth their best effort on homework assignments. This kind of slippage can prevent us from achieving maximum production. When that happens, we end up *inside* the production possibilities curve rather than *on* it.

Point *Y* in Figure 1.4 illustrates the consequences of inefficient production. At point *Y*, we're producing only three trucks and two tanks. This is less than our potential. We could assemble a third tank without cutting back truck production (point *C*). Or

FIGURE 1.4
Points Inside and Outside the Curve

Points outside the production possibilities curve (point *X*) are unattainable with available resources and technology. Points inside the curve (point *Y*) represent the incomplete use of available resources. Only points on the production possibilities curve (*A, B, C*) represent maximum use of our production capabilities.

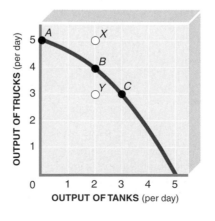

WORLD VIEW

India's Economy Gets a New Jolt From Mr. Shourie

NEW DELHI—In March 2001, strikers opposed to the Indian government's sale of an aluminum company threatened to fast until they died, an act of civil disobedience made famous by the nation's founding father, Mahatma Gandhi. India's privatization czar, Arun Shourie, was unmoved. "I said you can do what you want," recalls Mr. Shourie, photos of Mr. Gandhi hanging on the office wall in front of him. "But we're still not going to talk to you." The strike folded weeks later.

The sale of Bharat Aluminum Co. was a big test of Mr. Shourie's three-year campaign to sell off the almost 250 companies owned by India's central government. . . .

Since becoming minister of disinvestment in 2000, Mr. Shourie has taken state-owned companies once thought sacrosanct, such as India's long-distance telephone company and its biggest auto maker, and placed them in private hands. . . .

In India, state-owned companies provide a vast patronage system to ministers, party officials, and even petty bureaucrats.

For that system's beneficiaries, privatization represents a "loss of control, prestige, and money," says a banker who has advised the government on privatizations. . . .

What Mr. Shourie learned about the condition of many state-owned companies shocked him. On one fact-finding trip, he toured a state-owned airport hotel in New Delhi that had only a 3% occupancy rate and inoperable toilets. A state-owned tourist hotel in the south of the country had a crematorium and two burial grounds on its land. And a fertilizer company in West Bengal hadn't produced an ounce of product in 14 years. "The employees just sat around all day playing carrom," says Mr. Shourie, referring to an Indian board game.

—Jay Solomon and Joanna Slater

Source: *The Wall Street Journal*, January 9, 2004. Reprinted by permission of the Wall Street Journal, © 2004 Dow Jones & Company. All rights reserved worldwide.

Analysis: When resources are used inefficiently, a nation's output lies *inside* its production possibilities. By privatizing inefficient state enterprises, India hopes to increase total output and reach its production possibilities.

---

we could get an extra truck without sacrificing any tank output (point *B*). Instead, we're producing *inside* the production possibilities curve at point *Y*. Such inefficiencies plagued centrally planned economies. Government-run factories guaranteed everyone a job regardless of how much output he or she produced. They became bloated bureaucracies; as much as 40 percent of the workers were superfluous. When communism collapsed, many of these factories were "privatized," that is, sold to private investors. The privatized companies were able to fire thousands of workers and *increase* output. Governments in Europe and Latin America have also sold off many of their state-owned enterprises in the hopes of increasing efficiency and reaching the production possibilities curve. India's "Minister of Disinvestment" has been pursuing the same strategy, as the World View attests.

Unemployment

Countries may also end up inside their production possibilities curve if all available resources aren't used. In 2003, for example, as many as 8 million Americans were looking for work each week, but no one hired them. As a result, we were stuck *inside* the production possibilities curve, producing less output than we could have. A basic challenge for policymakers is to eliminate unemployment and keep the economy on its production possibilities curve. In 2004, the United States was closer to this goal.

Economic Growth

Figure 1.4 also illustrates an output mix that everyone would welcome. Point *X* lies *outside* the production possibilities curve. It suggests that we could get *more* goods than we're capable of producing! Unfortunately, point *X* is only a mirage: All output combinations that lie outside the production possibilities curve are unattainable with available resources and technology.

Things change, however. Every year, population growth and immigration increase our supply of labor. As we continue building factories and machinery, the stock of available capital also increases. The *quality* of labor and capital also increase when we train workers and pursue new technologies. Entrepreneurs may discover new products or better ways of producing old ones (e.g., Intel's latest chips). All these changes

FIGURE 1.5
Growth: Increasing Production Possibilities

A production possibilities curve is based on *available* resources and technology. If more resources or better technology becomes available, production possibilities will increase. This economic growth is illustrated by the *shift* from PP_1 to PP_2.

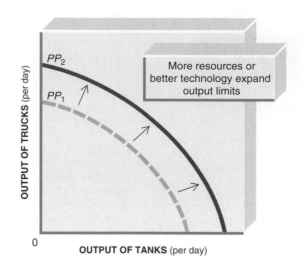

economic growth: An increase in output (real GDP); an expansion of production possibilities.

increase potential output. This is illustrated in Figure 1.5 by the outward *shift* of the production possibilities curve. Before the appearance of new resources or better technology, our production possibilities were limited by the curve PP_1. **With more resources or better technology, our production possibilities increase.** This greater capacity to produce is represented by curve PP_2. This outward shift of the production possibilities curve is the essence of **economic growth.** With economic growth, countries can have more guns *and* more butter. Without economic growth, living standards decline as the population grows. This is the problem that plagues some of the world's poorest nations, where population increases every year but output often doesn't.

BASIC DECISIONS

Production possibilities define the output choices that a nation confronts. From these choices every nation must make some basic decisions. As we noted at the beginning of this chapter, the three core economic questions are

- *WHAT to produce*
- *HOW to produce*
- *FOR WHOM to produce*

WHAT

There are millions of points along a production possibilities curve, and each one represents a different mix of output. We can choose only *one* of these points at any time. The point we choose determines what mix of output gets produced. That choice determines how many guns are produced, and how much butter.

The production possibilities curve doesn't tell us which mix of output is best; it just lays out a menu of available choices. It's up to us to pick out the one and only mix of output that will be produced at a given time. This WHAT decision is a basic decision every nation must make.

HOW

Decisions must also be made about HOW to produce. Should we generate electricity by burning coal, smashing atoms, or transforming solar power? Should we harvest ancient forests even if that destroys endangered owls or other animal species? Should we dump municipal and industrial waste into nearby rivers, or should we dispose of it in some other way? There are lots of different ways of producing goods and services, and someone has to make a decision about which production methods to use. The HOW decision is a question not just of efficiency but of social values as well.

FOR WHOM

After we've decided what to produce and how, we must address a third basic question: FOR WHOM? Who is going to get the output produced? Should everyone get an equal share? Should everyone wear the same clothes and drive identical cars? Should some people get to enjoy seven-course banquets while others forage in garbage cans for food scraps? How should the goods and services an economy produces be distributed? Are we satisfied with the way output is now distributed?

THE MECHANISMS OF CHOICE

Answers to the questions of WHAT, HOW, and FOR WHOM largely define an economy. But who formulates the answers? Who actually decides which goods are produced, what technologies are used, or how incomes are distributed?

Adam Smith had an answer back in 1776. In his classic work *The Wealth of Nations,* Smith said the "invisible hand" determines what gets produced, how, and for whom. The invisible hand he referred to wasn't a creature from a science fiction movie but, instead, a characterization of the way markets work.

Consider the decision about how many cars to produce in the United States. Who decides to produce over 16 million cars and trucks, a year? There's no "auto czar" who dictates production. Not even General Motors can make such a decision. Instead, the *market* decides how many cars to produce. Millions of consumers signal their desire to have a car by browsing the Internet, visiting showrooms, and buying cars. Their purchases flash a green light to producers, who see the potential to earn more profits. To do so, they'll increase auto output. If consumers stop buying cars, profits will disappear. Producers will respond by reducing output, laying off workers, and even closing factories. These interactions between consumers and producers determine how many cars are produced.

Notice how the invisible hand moves us along the production possibilities curve. If consumers demand more cars, the mix of output will include more cars and less of other goods. If auto production is scaled back, the displaced autoworkers will end up producing other goods and services, which will change the mix of output in the opposite direction.

Adam Smith's invisible hand is now called the **market mechanism.** Notice that it doesn't require any direct contact between consumers and producers. Communication is indirect, transmitted by market prices and sales. Indeed, *the essential feature of the market mechanism is the price signal.* If you want something and have sufficient income, you can buy it. If enough people do the same thing, the total sales of that product will rise, and perhaps its price will as well. Producers, seeing sales and prices rise, will want to exploit this profit potential. To do so, they'll attempt to acquire a larger share of available resources and use it to produce the goods we desire. That's how the "invisible hand" works.

The market mechanism can also answer the HOW question. To maximize their profits, producers will seek to use the lowest-cost method of producing a good. By observing prices in the marketplace, they can identify the cheapest method and adopt it.

The market mechanism can also resolve the FOR WHOM question. A market distributes goods to the highest bidder. Individuals who are willing and able to pay the most for a good tend to get it in a pure market economy.

Adam Smith was so impressed with the ability of the market mechanism to answer the basic WHAT, HOW, and FOR WHOM questions that he urged government to "leave it alone" (**laissez faire**). In his view, the price signals and responses of the marketplace were likely to do a better job of allocating resources than any government could.

The laissez-faire policy Adam Smith favored has always had its share of critics. Karl Marx emphasized how free markets tend to concentrate wealth and power in the hands of the few, at the expense of the many. As he saw it, unfettered markets permit the capitalists (those who own the machinery and factories) to enrich themselves while the proletariat (the workers) toil long hours for subsistence wages. Marx argued that the government not only had to intervene but had to *own* all the means of production—the

The Invisible Hand of a Market Economy

market mechanism: The use of market prices and sales to signal desired outputs (or resource allocations).

laissez faire: The doctrine of "leave it alone," of nonintervention by government in the market mechanism.

Government Intervention and Command Economies

factories, the machinery, the land—in order to avoid savage inequalities. In *Das Kapital* (1867) and the *Communist Manifesto* (1848), he laid the foundation for a communist state in which the government would be the master of economic outcomes.

The British economist John Maynard Keynes seemed to offer a less drastic solution. The market, he conceded, was pretty efficient in organizing production and building better mousetraps. However, individual producers and workers had no control over the broader economy. The cumulative actions of so many economic agents could easily tip the economy in the wrong direction. A completely unregulated market might veer off in one direction and then another as producers all rushed to increase output at the same time or throttled back production in a herdlike manner. The government, Keynes reasoned, could act like a pressure gauge, letting off excess steam or building it up as the economy needed. With the government maintaining overall balance in the economy, the market could live up to its performance expectations. While assuring a stable, full-employment environment, the government might also be able to redress excessive inequalities. In Keynes's view, government should play an active but not all-inclusive role in managing the economy.

Continuing Debates

These historical views shed perspective on today's political debates. The core of most debates is some variation of the WHAT, HOW, or FOR WHOM questions. Much of the debate is how these questions should be answered. Conservatives favor Adam Smith's laissez-faire approach, while liberals tend to think government intervention is likely to improve the answers. Conservatives resist workplace regulation, affirmative action, and minimum wages because such interventions might impair market efficiency. Liberals argue that such interventions temper the excesses of the market and promote both equity and efficiency.

The debate over how best to manage the economy is not unique to the United States. Countries around the world confront the same choice, between reliance on the market and reliance on the government. Few countries have ever relied exclusively on either one or the other to manage their economy. Even the former Soviet Union, where the government owned all the means of production and central planners dictated how they were to be used, made limited use of free markets. In Cuba, the government still manages the economy's resources but encourages farmers' markets and some private trade and investment. As a previous World View indicated, India is now letting the market play a larger role in deciding what is produced, how it is produced, and who gets the resulting output.

The World View below categorizes nations by the extent of their market reliance. Hong Kong scores high on this "Index of Economic Freedom" because its tax rates are relatively low, the public sector is comparatively small, and there are few restrictions on private investment or trade. By contrast, North Korea scores extremely low because the government owns all property, directly allocates resources, sets wages, and limits trade.

The rankings shown in the World View are neither definitive nor stable. In 1989, Russia began a massive transformation from a state-controlled economy to a more market-oriented economy. Some of the former republics (e.g., Estonia) became relatively free, while others (e.g., Turkmenistan) still rely on extensive government control of the economy. China has greatly expanded the role of private markets and Cuba is moving in the same direction in fits and starts. Even Libya—the second "least-free" nation on the Heritage list—is just now experimenting with some market reforms.

In the United States, the changes have been less dramatic. The most notable shift was President Franklin Roosevelt's New Deal, which greatly expanded the government's role in the economy. In more recent times, the tug-of-war between laissez faire and government intervention has been much less decisive. Although President Reagan often said that "government *is* the problem," he hardly made a dent in government growth during the eight years of his presidency. Likewise, President Clinton's very different conviction that the government can *fix* problems, not cause them, had only

WEBNOTE

For more information on Smith, Malthus, Keynes, and Marx, visit the Federal Reserve Bank of San Francisco at www.frbsf.org/econedu and click on "Great Economists and Their Times" under "Publications and Resources."

WEBNOTE

To learn how the Heritage Foundation defines economic freedom, visit its Web site at www.heritage.org.

WORLD   VIEW

Index of Economic Freedom

Hong Kong ranks number one among the world's nations in economic freedom. It achieves that status with low tax rates, free-trade policies, minimal government regulation, and secure property rights. These and other economic indicators place Hong Kong at the top of the Heritage Foundation's 2004 country rankings by the degree of "economic freedom." The "most free" and the "least free" (repressed) economies on the list of 155 countries are

Greatest Economic Freedom	Least Economic Freedom
Hong Kong	North Korea
Singapore	Libya
New Zealand	Zimbabwe
Luxembourg	Laos
Ireland	Burma
Estonia	Turkmenistan
United Kingdom	Uzbekistan
Denmark	Iran
Switzerland	Venezuela
United States	Tajikstan

Source: Heritage Foundation, *2004 Index of Economic Freedom*, Washington, DC, 2004.
www.heritage.org

Analysis: All nations must decide whether to rely on market signals or government directives to determine economic outcomes. Nations that rely the least on government intervention score highest on this Index of Economic Freedom.

minor effects on the size and scope of government activity. President George W. Bush has sought to not only lower taxes but also lessen government regulation of HOW goods are produced.

Even if President Bush got all the tax cuts and deregulation he wanted, the government would still play a large role in the U.S. economy. No one wants to rely exclusively on Adam Smith's invisible hand. Nor is anyone willing to have the economy steered exclusively by the highly visible hand of the government. *The United States, like most nations, uses a combination of market signals and government directives to select economic outcomes.* The resulting compromises are called **mixed economies.**

The reluctance of countries around the world to rely exclusively on either market signals or government directives is due to the recognition that both mechanisms can and do fail on occasion. As we've seen, market signals are capable of answering the three core questions of WHAT, HOW, and FOR WHOM. But the answers may not be the best possible ones.

When market signals don't give the best possible answers to the WHAT, HOW, and FOR WHOM questions, we say that the market mechanism has *failed.* Specifically, **market failure** means that the invisible hand has failed to achieve the best possible outcomes. If the market fails, we end up with the wrong (*sub*optimal) mix of output, too much unemployment, polluted air, or an inequitable distribution of income.

In a market-driven economy, for example, producers will select production methods based on cost. Cost-driven production decisions, however, may lead a factory to spew pollution into the environment rather than to use cleaner but more expensive

A Mixed Economy

mixed economy: An economy that uses both market signals and government directives to allocate goods and resources.

Market Failure

market failure: An imperfection in the market mechanism that prevents optimal outcomes.

methods of production. The resulting pollution may be so bad that society ends up worse off as a result of the extra production. In such a case we may need government intervention to force better answers to the WHAT and HOW questions.

We could also let the market decide who gets to consume cigarettes. Anyone who had enough money to buy a pack of cigarettes would then be entitled to smoke. What if, however, children aren't experienced enough to balance the risks of smoking against the pleasures? What if nonsmokers are harmed by secondhand smoke? In this case as well, the market's answer to the FOR WHOM question might not be optimal.

Government Failure

government failure: Government intervention that fails to improve economic outcomes.

Government intervention may move us closer to our economic goals. If so, the resulting mix of market signals and government directives would be an improvement over a purely market-driven economy. But government intervention may fail as well. **Government failure** occurs when government intervention fails to improve market outcomes or actually makes them worse.

The collapse of communism revealed how badly government directives can fail. But government failure also occurs in less spectacular ways. For example, the government may intervene to force an industry to clean up its pollution. The government's directives may impose such high costs that the industry closes factories and lays off workers. Some cutbacks in output might be appropriate, but they could also prove excessive. The government might also mandate pollution control technologies that are too expensive or even obsolete. None of this has to happen, but it might. If it does, government failure will have worsened economic outcomes.

The government might also fail if it interferes with the market's answer to the FOR WHOM question. For 50 years, communist China distributed goods by government directive, not market performance. Incomes were more equal, but uniformly low. To increase output and living standards, China has turned to market incentives (see World View on the next page). As entrepreneurs respond to these incentives, everyone may become better off—even while inequality increases.

Excessive taxes and transfer payments can also worsen economic outcomes. If the government raises taxes on the rich to pay welfare benefits for the poor, neither the rich nor the poor may see much purpose in working. In that case, the attempt to give everybody a "fair" share of the pie might end up shrinking the size of the pie. If that happened, society could end up worse off.

Seeking Balance

None of these failures has to occur, but each might. The challenge for society is to minimize failures by selecting the appropriate balance of market signals and government directives. This isn't an easy task. It requires that we know how markets work and why they sometimes fail. We also need to know what policy options the government has and how and when they might work.

WHAT ECONOMICS IS ALL ABOUT

Understanding how economies function is the basic purpose of studying economics. We seek to know how an economy is organized, how it behaves, and how successfully it achieves its basic objectives. Then, if we're lucky, we can discover better ways of attaining those same objectives.

End vs. Means

Economists don't formulate an economy's objectives. Instead, they focus on the *means* available for achieving given *goals*. In 1978, for example, the U.S. Congress identified "full employment" as a major economic goal. Congress then directed future presidents (and their economic advisers) to formulate policies that would enable us to achieve full employment. The economist's job is to help design policies that will best achieve this and other economic goals.

Macro vs. Micro

The study of economics is typically divided into two parts: macroeconomics and microeconomics. Macroeconomics focuses on the behavior of an entire economy—the "big picture." In macroeconomics we worry about such national goals as full employment, control of inflation, and economic growth, without worrying about the

WORLD VIEW

China's Leaders Back Private Property

SHANGHAI, Dec. 22—China's Communist Party leaders on Monday proposed amendments to the nation's constitution that would enshrine a legal right to private property while broadening the focus of the party to represent private businesses.

Virtually assured of adoption in the party-controlled National People's Congress, the amendments constitute a significant advance in China's ongoing transition from communism to capitalism. They amount to recognition that the economic future of the world's most populous country rests with private enterprise—a radical departure from the political roots of this land still known as the People's Republic of China.

Not since the Communist Party swept to power in 1949 in a revolution built on antipathy toward landowners and industrialists have Chinese been legally permitted to own property. Under the leadership of Chairman Mao, millions of people suffered persecution for being tainted with "bad" class backgrounds that linked them to landowning pasts.

But in present-day China the profit motive has come to pervade nearly every area of life. The site in Shanghai where the Communist Party was founded is now a shopping and entertainment complex anchored by a Starbucks coffee shop. From the poor villages in which most Chinese still live to the cities now dominated by high-rises, the market determines the price of most goods and decisions about what to produce. Business is widely viewed as a favored, even noble, undertaking.

The state-owned firms that once dominated China's economy have traditionally been sustained by credit from state banks, regardless of their balance sheets. Today, many are bankrupt, and banks are burdened by about $500 billion in bad loans, according to private economists. The government has cast privatization as the prescription for turning them around, creating management incentives to make them profitable.

— Peter S. Goodman

Source: *Washington Post*, December 23, 2003. © 2003 The Washington Post. Reprinted with permission. www.washingtonpost.com

Analysis: Government-directed production, prices, and incomes may increase equalities but blunt incentives. Private property and market-based incomes motivate higher productivity and growth.

well-being or behavior of specific individuals or groups. The essential concern of **macroeconomics** is to understand and improve the performance of the economy as a whole.

Microeconomics is concerned with the details of this big picture. In microeconomics we focus on the individuals, firms, and government agencies that actually compose the larger economy. Our interest here is in the behavior of individual economic actors. What are their goals? How can they best achieve these goals with their limited resources? How will they respond to various incentives and opportunities?

A primary concern of macroeconomics, for example, is to determine how much money, *in total,* consumers will spend on goods and services. In microeconomics, the focus is much narrower. In micro, attention is paid to purchases of *specific* goods and services rather than just aggregated totals. Macro likewise concerns itself with the level of *total* business investment, while micro examines how *individual* businesses make their investment decisions.

Although they operate at different levels of abstraction, macro and micro are intrinsically related. Macro (aggregate) outcomes depend on micro behavior, and micro (individual) behavior is affected by macro outcomes. One can't fully understand how an economy works until one understands how all the participants behave and why they behave as they do. But just as you can drive a car without knowing how its engine is constructed, you can observe how an economy runs without completely disassembling it. In macroeconomics we observe that the car goes faster when the accelerator is depressed and that it slows when the brake is applied. That's all we need to know in most situations. At times, however, the car breaks down. When it does, we have to know something more about how the pedals work. This leads us into micro studies. How does each part work? Which ones can or should be fixed?

Our interest in microeconomics is motivated by more than our need to understand how the larger economy works. The "parts" of the economic engine are people. To

macroeconomics: The study of aggregate economic behavior, of the economy as a whole.

microeconomics: The study of individual behavior in the economy, of the components of the larger economy.

the extent that we care about the welfare of individuals in society, we have a fundamental interest in microeconomic behavior and outcomes. In this regard, we examine how individual consumers and business firms seek to achieve specific goals in the marketplace. The goals aren't always related to output. Gary Becker won the 1992 Nobel Prize in economics for demonstrating how economic principles also affect decisions to marry, to have children, or to engage in criminal activities.

Theory vs. Reality

The distinction between macroeconomics and microeconomics is one of many simplifications we make in studying economic behavior. The economy is much too vast and complex to describe and explain in one course (or one lifetime). Accordingly, we focus on basic relationships, ignoring annoying detail. In so doing, we isolate basic principles of economic behavior and then use those principles to predict economic events and develop economic policies. This means that we formulate theories, or *models,* of economic behavior and then use those theories to evaluate and design economic policy.

Our model of consumer behavior assumes, for example, that people buy less of a good when its price rises. In reality, however, people *may* buy *more* of a good at increased prices, especially if those high prices create a certain snob appeal or if prices are expected to increase still further. In predicting consumer responses to price increases, we typically ignore such possibilities by *assuming* that the price of the good in question is the *only* thing that changes. This assumption of "other things remaining equal" (unchanged) (in Latin, **ceteris paribus**) allows us to make straightforward predictions. If instead we described consumer responses to increased prices in any and all circumstances (allowing everything to change at once), every prediction would be accompanied by a book full of exceptions and qualifications. We'd look more like lawyers than economists.

ceteris paribus: The assumption of nothing else changing.

Although the assumption of *ceteris paribus* makes it easier to formulate economic theory and policy, it also increases the risk of error. If other things do change in significant ways, our predictions (and policies) may fail. But, like weather forecasters, we continue to make predictions, knowing that occasional failure is inevitable. In so doing, we're motivated by the conviction that it's better to be approximately right than to be dead wrong.

Politics. Politicians can't afford to be quite so complacent about economic predictions. Policy decisions must be made every day. And a politician's continued survival may depend on being more than approximately right. George H. Bush's loss in the 1992 election resulted in part from his repeated predictions that the economy was "turning around." When this optimistic forecast proved wrong, voters lost faith in President Bush's ability to direct the economy. Ironically, his son gained a critical advantage in the superclose 2000 presidential election because of another economic slowdown and a slumping stock market. Once again, voters sought a new economic policy team.

After he took office, President George W. Bush immediately sought to change the mix of output. Even before the September 11, 2001, terrorist attacks, he wanted more "guns," as reflected in added defense spending. He also secured tax cuts to boost private consumption and investment. Were these the right choices? Economic theory can't completely answer that question. Choices about the mix of output are ultimately political—decisions that must take into account not only economic trade-offs (opportunity costs) but also social values. "Politics"—the balancing of competing interests—is an inevitable ingredient of economic policy.

Comparative data on the percentage of goods and services the various national governments provide is available from the Penn World Tables at www.pwt.econ.upenn.edu.

Imperfect Knowledge. One last word of warning before you read further. Economics claims to be a science, in pursuit of basic truths. We want to understand and explain how the economy works without getting tangled up in subjective value judgments. This may be an impossible task. First, it's not clear where the truth lies. For more than 200 years economists have been arguing about what makes the economy tick. None of the competing theories has performed spectacularly well. Indeed, few economists have successfully predicted major economic events with any consistency. Even annual forecasts of inflation, unemployment, and output are regularly in error. Worse still, never-ending arguments about what caused a major economic event continue long after it occurs. In fact, economists are still arguing over the primary causes of the Great Depression of the 1930s!

In part, this enduring controversy reflects diverse sociopolitical views on the appropriate role of government. Some people think a big public sector is undesirable, even if it improves economic performance. But the controversy has even deeper roots. Major gaps in our understanding of the economy persist. We know how much of the economy works, but not all of it. We're adept at identifying all the forces at work, but not always successful in gauging their relative importance. In point of fact, we may *never* find an absolute truth, because the inner workings of the economy change over time. When economic behavior changes, our theories must be adapted.

In view of all these debates and uncertainties, don't expect to learn everything there is to know about the economy today in this text or course. Our goals are more modest. We want to develop a reasonable perspective on economic behavior, an understanding of basic principles. With this foundation, you should acquire a better view of how the economy works. Daily news reports on economic events should make more sense. Congressional debates on tax and budget policies should take on more meaning. You may even develop some insights that you can apply toward running a business or planning a career, or—if the Nobel prize-winning economist Gary Becker is right—developing a lasting marriage.

THE ECONOMY TOMORROW

January 3, 2004, was a milestone in space exploration. That was the day the first robotic space vehicle—*Spirit*—landed on Mars. The pictures *Spirit* transmitted back to Earth unveiled a whole new boundary for human exploration. It created a challenge President Bush was quick to confront. Within days he announced an ambitious new agenda for America's space program:

The Journey to Mars

AFP/Getty Images

- By 2010 the United States is to complete the International Space Station.
- By 2008, a new Crew Exploration Vehicle, capable of ferrying astronauts and scientists to the Space Station, will be developed and ready for use.
- By 2015, the Crew Exploration Vehicle will begin extended human missions to the Moon.
- After 2015, human missions to Mars will begin.

Scientists and ordinary citizens around the world cheered both *Spirit's* accomplishments and President Bush's vision. People heard echoes of President Kennedy's May 1961 promise that mankind would soon set foot on the Moon—a promise that seemed equally implausible at the time, but ultimately proved to be attainable.

The journey to Mars is not only a technological commitment but an economic commitment as well. The resources used to complete the Space Station, to colonize the Moon, and to journey onto Mars and worlds beyond all have alternative uses here on Earth. Some of the same scientists could be developing high-speed *rail* systems, safer domestic flights, or more eco-friendly technologies. The technological resources being poured into space exploration could be perfecting cell phone quality or simply accelerating online data transmissions. If we devoted as many resources to medical research as space research, we might find more ways to extend and improve life here on Earth. In other words, the journey to Mars will entail opportunity costs, that is, the sacrifice of earthly goods and services that could be produced with those same resources.

Opportunity Costs

The journey to Mars won't be cheap. President Kennedy's *Apollo* program cost over $100 billion in today's dollars. Cost estimates for the journey to Mars run as high as $1 *trillion,* spread out over 20 years. That much money would fund a lot of earthly programs.

Earthly Benefits

WEBNOTE

Review NASA's budget at www.whitehouse.gov or www.cbo.gov. For more information on the space program, visit www.nasa.gov.

NASA says the benefits of the Mars journey would outweigh those opportunity costs. Space exploration has already generated tangible benefits for us earthlings. NASA cites advances in weather forecasting, in communications technology, in robotics, in computing and electronics, and in search and rescue technology. The research behind the space program has also helped create the satellite telecommunications network and the Global Positioning System. Medical technologies such as the image processing used in CAT scanners and MRI machines also trace their origins to engineering work for space exploration. President Bush said we should expect still further benefits from the journey to Mars: not only tangible benefits like new resources and technological advance but also intangibles like the spiritual uplifting and heightened quest for knowledge that exploration promotes.

Resource Allocations

As a society, we're going to have to make important choices about the economy tomorrow. Do we want to take the journey to Mars? If so, how fast do we want to get there? How many earthly goods and services do we want to give up to pay for the journey? Every year, the President and the U.S. Congress have to answer these questions. Their answers are reflected in the funds allocated to NASA (rather than other programs) in each year's federal budget. Would you allocate scarce resources for the economy tomorrow in the same way?

SUMMARY

- Scarcity is a basic fact of economic life. Factors of production (land, labor, capital, entrepreneurship) are scarce in relation to our desires for goods and services.
- All economic activity entails opportunity costs. Factors of production (resources) used to produce one output cannot simultaneously be used to produce something else. When we choose to produce one thing, we forsake the opportunity to produce some other good or service.
- A production possibilities curve illustrates the limits to production and the opportunity costs associated with different output combinations. It shows the alternative combinations of final goods and services that could be produced in a given period if all available resources and technology are used efficiently.
- The bent shape of the production possibilities curve reflects the law of increasing opportunity costs. This law states that increasing quantities of any good can be obtained only by sacrificing ever-increasing quantities of other goods.
- Inefficient or incomplete use of resources will fail to attain production possibilities. Additional resources or better

technologies will expand them. This is the essence of economic growth.
- Every country must decide WHAT to produce, HOW to produce, and FOR WHOM to produce with its limited resources.
- The choices of WHAT, HOW, and FOR WHOM can be made by the market mechanism or by government directives. Most nations are mixed economies, using a combination of these two choice mechanisms.
- Market failure exists when market signals generate suboptimal outcomes. Government failure occurs when government intervention worsens economic outcomes. The challenge for economic theory and policy is to find the mix of market signals and government directives that best fulfills our social and economic goals.
- The study of economics focuses on the broad question of resource allocation. Macroeconomics is concerned with allocating the resources of an entire economy to achieve aggregate economic goals (e.g., full employment). Microeconomics focuses on the behavior and goals of individual market participants.

Key Terms

economics

scarcity

factors of production

capital

entrepreneurship

opportunity cost

production possibilities

efficiency

economic growth

market mechanism

laissez faire

mixed economy

market failure

government failure

macroeconomics

microeconomics

ceteris paribus

Questions for Discussion

1. What opportunity costs did you incur in reading this chapter? If you read four more chapters of this book today, would your opportunity cost (per chapter) increase? Explain.
2. How much time could you spend on homework in a day? How much do you spend? How do you decide?
3. What's the real cost of the food in the free lunch cartoon?
4. What economic benefits might India get from privatizing state enterprises (World View, p. 11)?
5. How might a nation's production possibilities be affected by the following?
    a. A decrease in taxes.
    b. An increase in government regulation.
    c. An increase in military spending.
    d. An increase in college tuition.
    e. Faster, more powerful electronic chips.
6. Markets reward individuals according to their output; communism rewards people according to their needs. How might these different systems affect work effort?
7. How does government intervention affect college admissions? Who would go to college in a completely private (market) college system?
8. How will the Chinese economy benefit from private property? (See World View, page 17.) Is there any downside to greater entrepreneurial freedom?
9. How many resources should we allocate to space exploration? How will we make this decision?

PROBLEMS   The Student Problem Set at the back of this book contains numerical and graphing problems for this chapter.

WEB ACTIVITIES   to accompany this chapter can be found on the Online Learning Center.
http://www.mhhe.com/economics/schiller10

A P P E N D I X

USING GRAPHS

Economists like to draw graphs. In fact, we didn't even make it through the first chapter without a few graphs. This appendix looks more closely at the way graphs are drawn and used. The basic purpose of a graph is to illustrate a relationship between two *variables*. Consider, for example, the relationship between grades and studying. In general, we expect that additional hours of study time will lead to higher grades. Hence, we should be able to see a distinct relationship between hours of study time and grade-point average.

Suppose that we actually surveyed all the students taking this course with regard to their study time and grade-point averages. The resulting information can be compiled in a table such as Table A.1.

TABLE A.1
Hypothetical Relationship of
Grades to Study Time

Study Time (hours per week)	Grade-Point Average
16	4.0 (A)
14	3.5 (B+)
12	3.0 (B)
10	2.5 (C+)
8	2.0 (C)
6	1.5 (D+)
4	1.0 (D)
2	0.5 (F+)
0	0.0 (F)

According to the table, students who don't study at all can expect an F in this course. To get a C, the average student apparently spends 8 hours a week studying. All those who study 16 hours a week end up with an A in the course.

These relationships between grades and studying can also be illustrated on a graph. Indeed, the whole purpose of a graph is to summarize numerical relationships.

We begin to construct a graph by drawing horizontal and vertical boundaries, as in Figure A.1. These boundaries are called the *axes* of the graph. On the vertical axis (often called the *y*-axis) we measure one of the variables; the other variable is measured on the horizontal axis (the *x*-axis).

In this case, we shall measure the grade-point average on the vertical axis. We start at the *origin* (the intersection of the two axes) and count upward, letting the distance between horizontal lines represent half (0.5) a grade point. Each horizontal line is numbered, up to the maximum grade-point average of 4.0.

The number of hours each week spent doing homework is measured on the horizontal axis. We begin at the origin again, and count to the right. The *scale* (numbering) proceeds in increments of 1 hour, up to 20 hours per week.

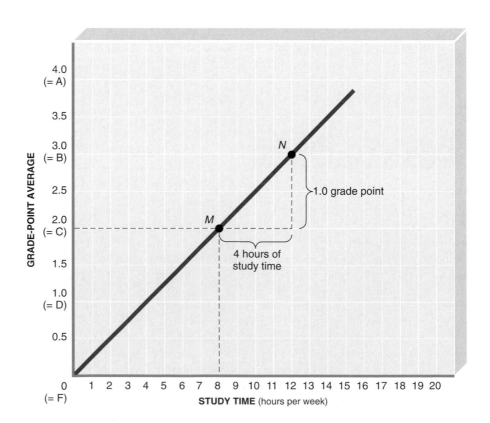

FIGURE A.1
The Relationship of Grades to Study Time

The upward (positive) slope of the curve indicates that additional studying is associated with higher grades. The average student (2.0, or C grade) studies 8 hours per week. This is indicated by point *M* on the graph.

When both axes have been labeled and measured, we can begin illustrating the relationship between study time and grades. Consider the typical student who does 8 hours of homework per week and has a 2.0 (C) grade-point average. We illustrate this relationship by first locating 8 hours on the horizontal axis. We then move up from that point a distance of 2.0 grade points, to point *M*. Point *M* tells us that 8 hours of study time per week is typically associated with a 2.0 grade-point average.

The rest of the information in Table A.1 is drawn (or *plotted*) on the graph the same way. To illustrate the average grade for people who study 12 hours per week, we move upward from the number 12 on the horizontal axis until we reach the height of 3.0 on the vertical axis. At that intersection, we draw another point (point *N*).

Once we've plotted the various points describing the relationship of study time to grades, we may connect them with a line or curve. This line (curve) is our summary. In this case, the line slopes upward to the right—that is, it has a *positive* slope. This slope indicates that more hours of study time are associated with *higher* grades. Were higher grades associated with *less* study time, the curve in Figure A.1 would have a *negative* slope (downward from left to right).

Slopes

The upward slope of Figure A.1 tells us that higher grades are associated with increased amounts of study time. That same curve also tells us *by how much* grades tend to rise with study time. According to point *M* in Figure A.1, the average student studies 8 hours per week and earns a C (2.0 grade-point average). To earn a B (3.0 average), students apparently need to study an average of 12 hours per week (point *N*). Hence an increase of 4 hours of study time per week is associated with a 1-point increase in grade-point average. This relationship between *changes* in study time and *changes* in grade-point average is expressed by the steepness, or *slope,* of the graph.

The slope of any graph is calculated as

$$\text{Slope} = \frac{\text{vertical distance between two points}}{\text{horizontal distance between two points}}$$

In our example, the vertical distance between *M* and *N* represents a change in grade-point average. The horizontal distance between these two points represents the change in study time. Hence the slope of the graph between points *M* and *N* is equal to

$$\text{Slope} = \frac{3.0\ \text{grade} - 2.0\ \text{grade}}{12\ \text{hours} - 8\ \text{hours}} = \frac{1\ \text{grade point}}{4\ \text{hours}}$$

In other words, a 4-hour increase in study time (from 8 to 12 hours) is associated with a 1-point increase in grade-point average (see Figure A.1).

Shifts

The relationship between grades and studying illustrated in Figure A.1 isn't inevitable. It's simply a graphical illustration of student experiences, as revealed in our hypothetical survey. The relationship between study time and grades could be quite different.

Suppose that the university decided to raise grading standards, making it more difficult to achieve every grade other than an F. To achieve a C, a student now would need to study 12 hours per week, not just 8 (as in Figure A.1). Whereas students could previously expect to get a B by studying 12 hours per week, now they'd have to study 16 hours to get that grade.

Figure A.2 illustrates the new grading standards. Notice that the new curve lies to the right of the earlier curve. We say that the curve has *shifted* to reflect a change in the relationship between study time and grades. Point *R* indicates that 12 hours of study time now "produces" a C, not a B (point *N* on the old curve). Students who now study only 4 hours per week (point *S*) will fail. Under the old grading policy, they could have at least gotten a D. ***When a curve shifts, the underlying relationship between the two variables has changed.***

FIGURE A.2
A Shift

When a relationship between two variables changes, the entire curve *shifts*. In this case a tougher grading policy alters the relationship between study time and grades. To get a C, one must now study 12 hours per week (point *R*), not just 8 hours (point *M*).

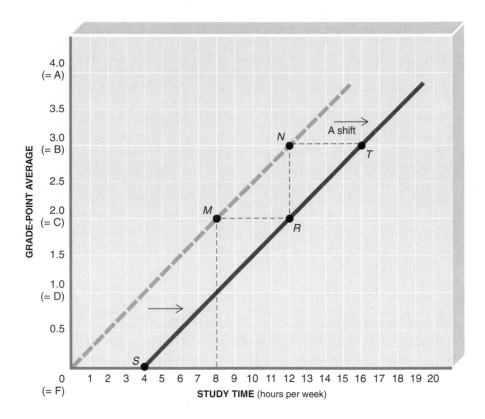

A shift may also change the slope of the curve. In Figure A.2, the new grading curve is parallel to the old one; it therefore has the same slope. Under either the new grading policy or the old one, a 4-hour increase in study time leads to a 1-point increase in grades. Therefore, the slope of both curves in Figure A.2 is

$$\text{Slope} = \frac{\text{vertical change}}{\text{horizontal change}} = \frac{1}{4}$$

This too may change, however. Figure A.3 illustrates such a possibility. In this case, zero study time still results in an F. But now the payoff for additional studying is reduced. Now it takes 6 hours of study time to get a D (1.0 grade point), not 4 hours as before. Likewise, another 4 hours of study time (to a total of 10) raises the grade by only two-thirds of a point. It takes 6 hours to raise the grade a full point. The slope of the new line is therefore

$$\text{Slope} = \frac{\text{vertical change}}{\text{horizontal change}} = \frac{1}{6}$$

The new curve in Figure A.3 has a smaller slope than the original curve and so lies below it. What all this means is that it now takes a greater effort to *improve* your grade.

Linear vs. Nonlinear Curves

In Figures A.1–A.3 the relationship between grades and studying is represented by a straight line—that is, a *linear curve*. A distinguishing feature of linear curves is that they have the same (constant) slope throughout. In Figure A.1, it appears that *every* 4-hour increase in study time is associated with a 1-point increase in average grades. In Figure A.3, it appears that every 6-hour increase in study time leads to a 1-point increase in grades. But the relationship between studying and grades may not be linear. Higher grades may be more difficult to attain. You may be able to raise a C to a B by studying 4 hours more per week. But it may be harder to raise a B to an A.

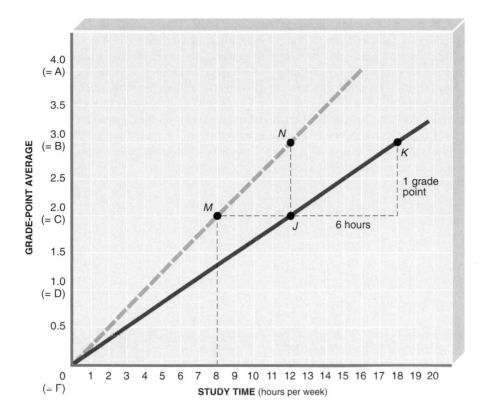

FIGURE A.3
A Change in Slope

When a curve shifts, it may change its slope as well. In this case, a new grading policy makes each higher grade more difficult to reach. To raise a C to a B, for example, one must study 6 additional hours (compare points *J* and *K*). Earlier it took only 4 hours to move the grade scale up a full point. The slope of the line has declined from 0.25(= 1 ÷ 4) to 0.17(= 1 ÷ 6).

According to Figure A.4, it takes an additional 8 hours of studying to raise a B to an A. Thus the relationship between study time and grades is *nonlinear* in Figure A.4; the slope of the curve changes as study time increases. In this case, the slope decreases as study time increases. Grades continue to improve, but not so fast, as more and more time is devoted to homework. You may know the feeling.

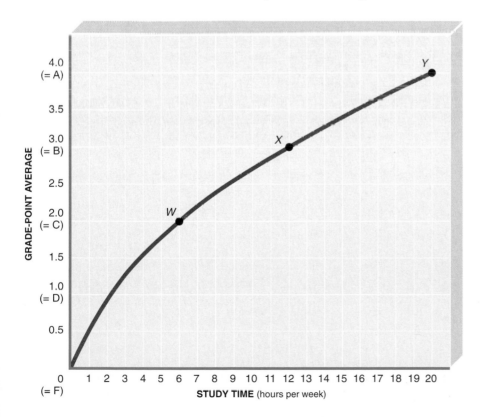

FIGURE A.4
A Nonlinear Relationship

Straight lines have a constant slope, implying a constant relationship between the two variables. But the relationship (and slope) may vary. In this case, it takes 6 extra hours of study to raise a C (point *W*) to a B (point *X*) but 8 extra hours to raise a B to an A (point *Y*). The slope decreases as we move up the curve.

Causation

For online practice with graphs, visit "Math Skills for Introductory Economics" at syllabus.syr.edu/cid/graph/book.html.

Figure A.4 doesn't by itself guarantee that your grade-point average will rise if you study 4 more hours per week. In fact, the graph drawn in Figure A.4 doesn't prove that additional study ever results in higher grades. The graph is only a summary of empirical observations. It says nothing about cause and effect. It could be that students who study a lot are smarter to begin with. If so, then less-able students might not get higher grades if they studied harder. In other words, the *cause* of higher grades is debatable. At best, the empirical relationship summarized in the graph may be used to support a particular theory (e.g., that it pays to study more). Graphs, like tables, charts, and other statistical media, rarely tell their own story; rather, they must be *interpreted* in terms of some underlying theory or expectation.

The U.S. Economy: A Global View

All nations must confront the central economic questions of WHAT to produce, HOW to produce, and FOR WHOM to produce it. However, the nations of the world approach these issues with vastly different production possibilities. China, Canada, the United States, and Brazil each has more than *3 million* acres of land. All that land gives them far greater production possibilities than Dominica, Tonga, Malta, or Lichtenstein, each of which has less than 500 acres of land. The population of China totals more than 1.3 billion people, five times that of the United States, and 25,000 times the population of Greenland. Obviously, these nations confront very different output choices.

In addition to vastly uneven production possibilities, the nations of the world use different mechanisms for deciding WHAT, HOW, and FOR WHOM to produce. Belarus, Romania, North Korea, and Cuba still rely heavily on central planning. By contrast, Singapore, New Zealand, Ireland, and the United States permit the market mechanism to play a dominant role in shaping economic outcomes.

With different production possibilities and mechanisms of choice, you'd expect economic outcomes to vary greatly across nations. And they do. This chapter assesses how the U.S. economy stacks up. Specifically,

* **WHAT goods and services does the United States produce?**
* **HOW is that output produced?**
* **FOR WHOM is the output produced?**

In each case, we want to see not only how the United States has answered those questions but also how America's answers compare with those of other nations.

WHAT AMERICA PRODUCES

The United States has less than 5 percent of the world's population and only 12 percent of the world's arable land, yet it produces more than 20 percent of the world's output.

GDP Comparisons

The World View shows how total U.S. production compares with other nations. These comparisons are based on the total market value of all the goods and services a nation produces—what we call **gross domestic product (GDP).**

In 2002, the U.S. economy produced about $10 trillion worth of output. The second-largest economy, China, produced only half that much. Japan came in third, with about a third of U.S. output. Cuba, by contrast, produced only $1.6 billion of output, less than the state of South Dakota. Russia, which was once regarded as a superpower, produced only $1.1 trillion, about as much as New York state. The entire 25-member European Union produces less than the United States.

> **gross domestic product (GDP):** The total market value of all final goods and services produced within a nation's borders in a given time period.

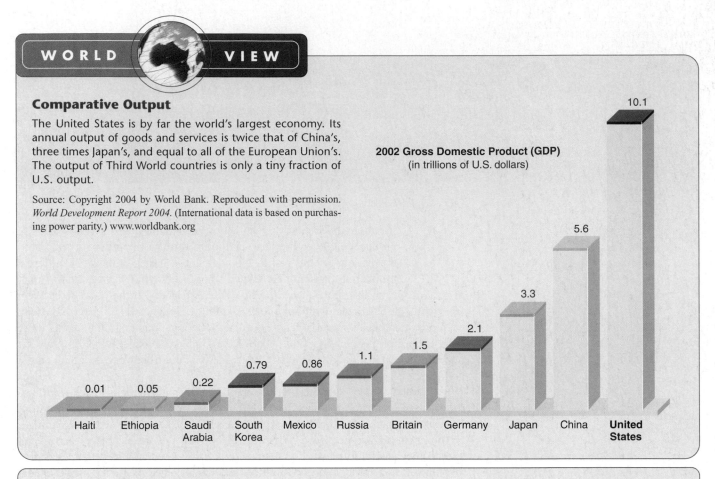

WORLD VIEW

Comparative Output

The United States is by far the world's largest economy. Its annual output of goods and services is twice that of China's, three times Japan's, and equal to all of the European Union's. The output of Third World countries is only a tiny fraction of U.S. output.

Source: Copyright 2004 by World Bank. Reproduced with permission. *World Development Report 2004.* (International data is based on purchasing power parity.) www.worldbank.org

2002 Gross Domestic Product (GDP)
(in trillions of U.S. dollars)

Haiti	0.01	
Ethiopia	0.05	
Saudi Arabia	0.22	
South Korea	0.79	
Mexico	0.86	
Russia	1.1	
Britain	1.5	
Germany	2.1	
Japan	3.3	
China	5.6	
United States	10.1	

Analysis: The market value of output (GDP) is a basic measure of an economy's size. The U.S. economy is far larger than any other and accounts for over one-fifth of the entire world's output.

per capita GDP: The dollar value of GDP divided by total population; average GDP.

Per Capita GDP. What makes the U.S. share of world output so noteworthy is that with only 5 percent of the world's population, the United States produces far more output *per person* than other countries do. This people-based measure of economic performance is called **per capita GDP.** Per capita GDP is simply total output divided by total population. Per capita GDP doesn't tell us how much any specific person gets. *Per capita GDP is an indicator of how much output the average person would get if all output were divided up evenly among the population.*

In 2002, per capita GDP in the United States was more than $35,000—nearly five times as much as the average in the rest of the world. The following World View provides a global perspective on just how "rich" America is. Some of the country-specific comparisons are startling. China, which has the world's second-largest GDP, also contains one-fifth of the world's population. Hence, China has such a relatively low per capita income that most of its citizens would be considered "poor" by official American standards. Yet people in other nations (e.g., Haiti, Ethiopia) don't even come close to that low standard. According to the World Bank, nearly half of the people on Earth subsist on incomes of less than $2 a day. Seen in this context, it's

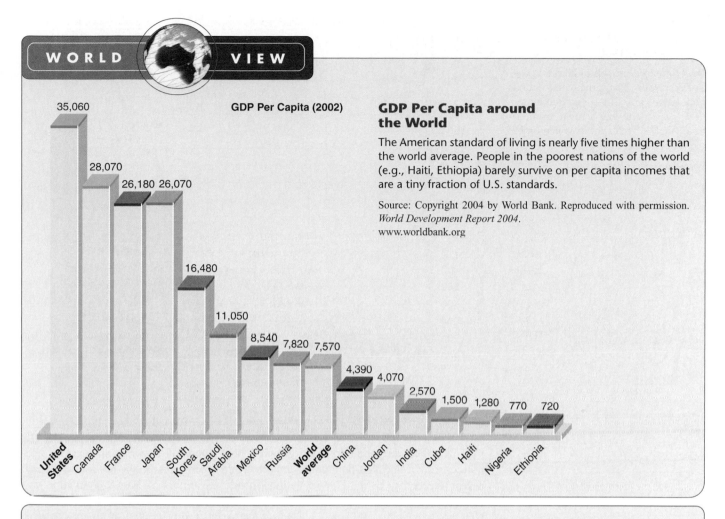

WORLD VIEW

GDP Per Capita around the World

The American standard of living is nearly five times higher than the world average. People in the poorest nations of the world (e.g., Haiti, Ethiopia) barely survive on per capita incomes that are a tiny fraction of U.S. standards.

Source: Copyright 2004 by World Bank. Reproduced with permission. *World Development Report 2004.* www.worldbank.org

GDP Per Capita (2002)

United States 35,060
Canada 28,070
France 26,180
Japan 26,070
South Korea 16,480
Saudi Arabia 11,050
Mexico 8,540
Russia 7,820
World average 7,570
China 4,390
Jordan 4,070
India 2,570
Cuba 1,500
Haiti 1,280
Nigeria 770
Ethiopia 720

Analysis: Per capita GDP is a measure of output that reflects average living standards. America's exceptionally high GDP per capita implies access to far more goods and services than people in other nations have.

easy to understand why the rest of the world envies (and sometimes resents) America's prosperity.

GDP Growth. What's even more startling about global comparisons is that the GDP gap between the United States and the world's poor nations keeps growing. The reason for that is **economic growth.** With few exceptions, U.S. output increases nearly every year. *On average, U.S. output has grown by roughly 3 percent a year, nearly three times faster than population growth (1 percent).* Hence, not only does *total* output keep rising, but *per capita* output keeps rising as well (see Figure 2.1).

Poor Nations. People in the world's poorest countries aren't so fortunate. China's economy has grown exceptionally fast in the last 20 years, propelling it to second place in the global GDP rankings. But in many other nations total output has actually *declined* year after year, further depressing living standards. Notice in Table 2.1, for example, what's been happening in Haiti. From 1990 to 2002, Haiti's output of

WEBNOTE

Data on the output of different nations are available from the Central Intelligence Agency at www.odci.gov/cia/publications/factbook.

economic growth: An increase in output (real GDP): an expansion of production possibilities.

U.S. Output and Population Growth Since 1900

Over time, the growth of output in the United States has greatly exceeded population growth. As a consequence, GDP per capita has grown tremendously. GDP per capita was five times higher in 2000 than in 1900.

Source: U.S. Department of Labor.

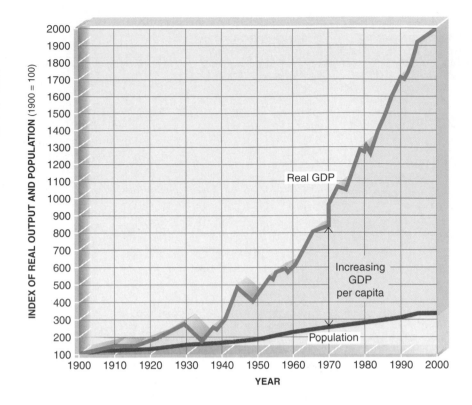

goods and services (GDP) declined by an average of 1.0 percent a year. As a result, total Haitian output in 2002 was 14 percent *smaller* than in 1990. During those same years, the Haitian population kept growing—by 2 percent a year. With *negative* economic growth and fast population growth, Haiti's per capita GDP fell below $1,300 a year. According to the United Nations, nearly two-thirds of Haiti's population was undernourished. As Table 2.1 shows, even some poor nations that had *positive* GDP growth in the 1990s (e.g., Kenya, Venezuela) didn't grow fast enough to raise

TABLE 2.1
Growth Rates in Selected Countries, 1990–2002

The relationship between GDP growth and population growth is very different in rich and poor countries. The populations of rich countries are growing very slowly, and gains in per capita GDP are easily achieved. In the poorest countries, population is still increasing rapidly, making it difficult to raise living standards. Notice how per capita incomes are *declining* in many poor countries (such as Kenya, Venezuela, Zimbabwe, and Haiti).

	Average Growth Rate (1990–2002) of		
	GDP	**Population**	**Per Capita GDP**
High-income countries			
United States	3.3	1.1	2.2
Canada	3.2	1.1	2.1
France	1.9	0.4	1.5
Japan	1.3	0.4	0.9
Low-income countries			
China	9.7	1.2	8.5
India	5.8	1.1	4.7
Ethiopia	4.6	2.6	2.0
Nigeria	2.4	2.8	−0.4
Kenya	1.9	2.9	−1.0
Venezuela	1.1	2.3	−1.2
Zimbabwe	1.1	2.7	−1.6
Haiti	−1.0	2.0	−3.0

Source: Copyright 2004 by World Bank. Reproduced with permission. *World Development Indicators, 2004.*

living standards. As a result, they fell even further behind America's (rising) level of prosperity.

Regardless of how much output a nation produces, the *mix* of output always includes both *goods* (such as cars, plasma TVs, potatoes) and *services* (like this economics course, visits to a doctor, or a professional baseball game). A century ago, about two-thirds of U.S. output consisted of farm goods (37 percent), manufactured goods (22 percent), and mining (9 percent). Since then, over 25 *million* people have left the farms and sought jobs in other sectors. As a result, today's mix of output is reversed: **Nearly 75 percent of U.S. output consists of services, not goods.** According to the U.S. Bureau of Labor Statistics, that trend is increasing. Over 98 percent of future job growth will be in service-producing industries such as health care, engineering, education, social services, and accounting. This trend will accelerate the change in the mix of output that has been underway for a long time (see Figure 2.2).

The *relative* decline in goods production (manufacturing, farming) doesn't mean that we're producing *fewer* goods today than in earlier decades. Quite the contrary. While some industries such as iron and steel have shrunk, others, such as chemicals, publishing, and telecommunications equipment, have grown tremendously. The result is that manufacturing output has increased fourfold since 1950. The same kind of thing has happened in the farm sector; where output keeps rising even though agriculture's *share* of total output has declined. It's just that output of *services* has increased so much faster.

Development Patterns. The transformation of the United States into a service economy is a reflection of our high incomes. In Ethiopia, where the most urgent concern is still to keep people from starving, over 50 percent of output comes from the farm sector. Poor people don't have enough income to buy dental services, vacations, or even an education, so the mix of output in poor countries is weighted toward goods, not services.

Services have become such a dominant share of the economy's output that we can say that **America is primarily a service economy and will become increasingly so in the future.** This generalization doesn't provide much detail, however, about exactly WHAT America produces. What kinds of services are being produced? Which goods?

We can develop a clearer picture of our answer to the WHAT question by examining the uses to which our output is put. *The four major uses of total output (GDP) are:*

- *Consumption*
- *Investment*
- *Government services*
- *Net exports*

The Mix of Output

WEBNOTE

Data on the mix of output in different nations are compiled in the World Bank's annual World Development Report, available at www.worldbank.org.

Today's Mix of Output

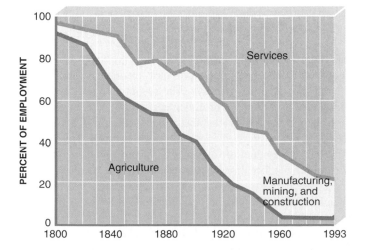

FIGURE 2.2
The Changing Mix of Output

Two hundred years ago, almost all U.S. output came from farms. Today, 75 percent of output consists of services, not farm or manufactured goods.

Source: US Department of Commerce.

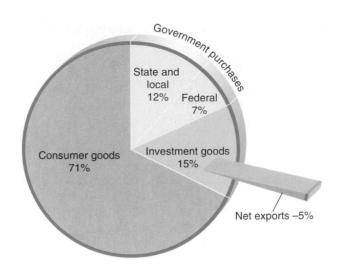

FIGURE 2.3
WHAT America Produces

Two-thirds of America's output consists of consumer goods and services. Investment (such as plant, equipment, buildings) claims about 15 percent of total output. The public sector gets nearly 19 percent. Although we export more than 10 percent of domestic output, we import an even larger share of goods and services; *net* exports are negative.

Source: *Economic Report of the President, 2004.*

investment: Expenditures on (production of) new plant, equipment, and structures (capital) in a given time period, plus changes in business inventories.

income transfers: Payments to individuals for which no current goods or services are exchanged, e.g., Social Security, welfare, unemployment benefits.

Consumer Goods and Services. Most of America's output consists of consumer goods and services. This output includes everything from breakfast cereals (a good) to movie rentals (a service) and college education (another service)—anything and everything households buy for their own use. As Figure 2.3 illustrates, such consumption goods and services account for over two-thirds of all output.

Investment Goods and Services. Investment goods are a completely different type of output. **Investment** goods are the plant, machinery, equipment, and structures that are produced for the business sector. These investment goods are used to (1) replace worn-out equipment and factories, thus *maintaining* our production possibilities, and (2) increase and improve our stock of capital, thereby *expanding* our production possibilities.

Presently the United States devotes 15 percent of output to investment. The opportunity cost of building more plants and equipment is the extra consumer goods we could have produced instead. There's a payoff, however. New factories, buildings, and machinery allow us to produce *more* of all goods and services in the future.

Poor countries need capital investment desperately. Their incomes are so low, however, that they can't afford to cut back much on consumer goods. When Stalin wanted to make Russia an industrial power, he cut output of consumer goods and forced Russian households to scrape by with meager supplies of food, clothing, and even shelter for decades. Today, most poor nations have to depend on foreign aid and other capital inflows to finance needed investment. Without more investment, they run the risk of continuing stagnation or even a decline of living standards.

Government Services. The third type of output every nation produces is government services. Federal, state, and local governments purchase resources to police the streets, teach classes, write laws, and build highways. The resources the government sector uses for these purposes are unavailable for either consumption or investment. At present, the production of government services absorbs roughly one-fifth of total U.S. output (see Figure 2.3).

Notice the emphasis again on the production of real goods and services. The federal government now *spends* about $2.5 trillion a year. Much of that spending, however, consists of income transfers, not resource purchases. **Income transfers** are payments to individuals for which no direct service is provided. Social Security benefits, welfare checks, food stamps, and unemployment benefits are all transfer payments. This spending is *not* part of our output of goods and services. ***Only that part of federal spending used to acquire resources and produce services is counted in GDP.***

Federal purchases (production) of goods and services account for only 7 percent of total output.

State and local governments are large providers of public services. What state and local governments lack in size, they make up for in sheer numbers. In addition to the 50 state governments, there are 3000 counties, 18,000 cities, 17,000 townships, 21,000 school districts, and over 20,000 special districts. These are the government entities that build roads; provide schools, police, and firefighters; administer hospitals; and provide social services. The output of all these state and local governments accounts for roughly 12 percent of total GDP.

Net Exports. Finally, we should note that some of the goods and services we produce each year are used abroad rather than at home. In other words, we **export** some of our output to other countries.

International trade isn't a one-way street. While we export some of our own output, we also **import** goods and services from other countries. These imports may be used for consumption (sweaters from New Zealand, Japanese DVDs, travel), investment (German ball bearings, Lloyds of London insurance), or government (French radar screens). Theoretically, imports wouldn't affect the value of GDP since GDP includes only goods and services produced within a nation's borders. In practice, however, estimates of GDP are based on market *purchases,* not surveys of production. As a result, consumption, investment, and government purchases include imports as well as domestically produced goods. To get an accurate reading of *domestic* production, imports must be subtracted out.

Figure 2.4 summarizes America's trade. In 2003, we exported $726 billion worth of goods (e.g., airplanes, farm machinery, tobacco, food) and another $320 billion of services (e.g., movies, travel, engineering). These exports amounted to approximately 10 percent of total output. We imported even more goods and services, however, and so ended up with negative **net exports** (a trade deficit).

exports: Goods and services sold to foreign buyers.

imports: Goods and services purchased from foreign sources.

net exports: The value of exports minus the value of imports.

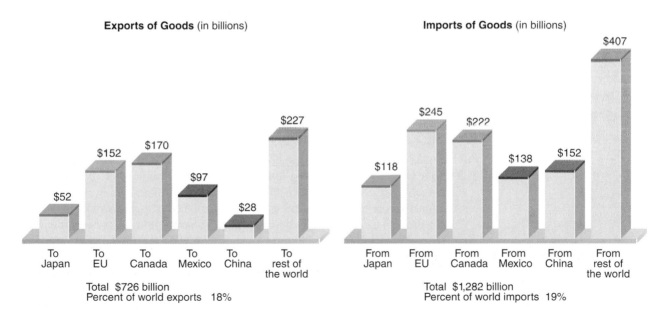

Exports of Goods (in billions)

Total $726 billion
Percent of world exports   18%

Imports of Goods (in billions)

Total $1,282 billion
Percent of world imports 19%

FIGURE 2.4
U.S. Exports and Imports

The United States is the world's largest exporter and importer. One-third of all U.S. trade is with Canada and Mexico. The European Union, Japan, and China account for another third. In 2003, U.S. merchandise (goods) imports exceeded exports by $556 billion. This merchandise trade gap was partially offset by net *service* exports, leaving $498 billion of *net imports* (of goods and services).

Comparative Advantage

> **comparative advantage:** The ability of a country to produce a specific good at a lower opportunity cost than its trading partners.

The motivation for this international trade originates in our quest for more output. Most of the goods we import could be produced in the United States. In fact, most imported goods have domestically produced substitutes, for example, cars, computers, and tomatoes. Our decision to import them is not based on our inability to produce them but on the efficiency of importing them. International trade allows a nation to produce goods in which it has a cost advantage and then trade them for imported goods in which it has a cost disadvantage. This principle of **comparative advantage** entails exporting goods with low opportunity cost and importing goods with high opportunity cost. In other words, **international trade allows countries to produce and export what they do best and import goods they don't produce as efficiently.**

Although all nations gain from international trade, smaller countries are most in need of specialization. With few resources, a small economy can't produce the whole array of goods and services consumers want. So they need to *specialize*—producing goods they can sell (export) in world markets. Saudi Arabia, for example, exports 40 percent of its total output, mostly in the form of crude oil. It then uses its export earnings to buy desired cars, engineering services, and food that it can't produce efficiently itself.

HOW AMERICA PRODUCES

All the goods and services included in gross domestic product are produced within the borders of the United States. The production process absorbs not only American-owned **factors of production** but also any foreign-owned land, labor, or capital used to produce goods or services in the United States. With the globalization of business ownership, it's often difficult to even identify who owns which factors of production. It's easy, however, to observe where the factors of production are. So GDP focuses on geographical boundaries. Japanese investors may *own* the Honda factory in Ohio, but the cars *produced* there are part of U.S. output. By contrast, all the shoes produced at Nike's Malaysian factories are counted as part of that nation's GDP.

> **factors of production:** Resource inputs used to produce goods and services, such as land, labor, capital, entrepreneurship.

Productivity

> **productivity:** Output per unit of input, such as output per labor-hour.

A lot of people worry that the Nike factory in Malaysia is stealing U.S. jobs. Workers in Malaysia and other poor nations are willing to work for extremely low wages (recall that nearly half the world's population has incomes of less than $2 a day). But low foreign wages aren't as great a threat as they just appear. We also have to consider how much a worker *produces*. One reason wages are so low in the Third World is that workers produce so little. U.S. workers get paid an average of over $16 an hour because they *produce* so much.

If the sheer number of workers was the decisive factor for a nation's output, China would have the world's largest economy. In reality, **productivity**—the amount of output a worker produces—is at least as important as the number of available workers. In fact, high productivity explains how the United States, with 300 million people, produces more goods and services than the combined output of China, India, Indonesia, and Brazil—nations with a combined population 10 times larger than the U.S.'s!

Factors of Production

> **capital-intensive:** Production processes that use a high ratio of capital to labor inputs.

Capital Stock. The exceptional productivity of U.S. workers is due in large part to an abundance of capital. America has accumulated a massive stock of capital—over $11 *trillion* worth of machinery, factories, and buildings. As a result of all this prior investment, U.S. production tends to be very **capital-intensive.** The contrast with *labor-intensive* production in poorer countries is striking. A Chinese farmer mostly works with his hands and crude implements, whereas a U.S. farmer works with computers, automated irrigation systems, and mechanized equipment (see photos on page 36). Russian business managers don't have the computer networks or telecommunications systems that make U.S. business so efficient. In Haiti and Ethiopia, even telephones, indoor plumbing, and dependable sources of power are scarce.

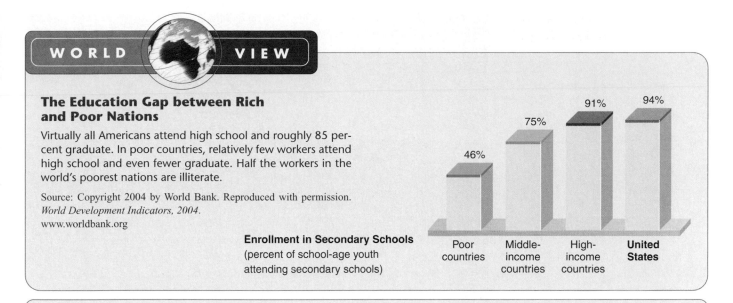

WORLD VIEW

The Education Gap between Rich and Poor Nations

Virtually all Americans attend high school and roughly 85 percent graduate. In poor countries, relatively few workers attend high school and even fewer graduate. Half the workers in the world's poorest nations are illiterate.

Source: Copyright 2004 by World Bank. Reproduced with permission. *World Development Indicators, 2004.*
www.worldbank.org

Enrollment in Secondary Schools
(percent of school-age youth attending secondary schools)

- Poor countries: 46%
- Middle-income countries: 75%
- High-income countries: 91%
- United States: 94%

Analysis: The high productivity of the American economy is explained in part by the quality of its labor resources. Workers in poorer, less developed countries get much less education or training.

Human Capital. Indoor plumbing and fiber-optic networks aren't the only kinds of capital a nation can accumulate. **Human capital**—the knowledge and skills workers possess—can also be accumulated. In the Stone Age, one's productive capacity was largely determined by physical strength and endurance. In today's economy, human capital is largely a product of education, training, and experience. Hence, a country can acquire more human capital even without more bodies.

Over time, the United States has invested heavily in human capital. In 1940, only 1 out of 20 young Americans graduated from college; today, over 30 percent of young people are college graduates. High school graduation rates have jumped from 38 percent to over 85 percent in the same time period. In the less developed countries, only 1 out of 2 youth ever *attend* high school, much less graduate (see World View). As a consequence, the United Nations estimates that 1.2 billion people—a fifth of humanity—are unable to read a book or even write their own names. Without even functional literacy, such workers are doomed to low-productivity jobs. Despite low wages, they are not likely to "steal" many jobs from America's highly educated and trained workforce.

The huge output of the United States is thus explained not only by a wealth of resources but by their quality as well. ***The high productivity of the U.S. economy results from using highly educated workers in capital-intensive production processes.***

Factor Mobility. Our continuing ability to produce the goods and services that consumers demand also depends on our agility in *reallocating* resources from one industry to another. Every year, some industries expand and others contract. Thousands of new firms start up each year and almost as many others disappear. In the process, land, labor, capital, and entrepreneurship move from one industry to another in response to changing demands and technology. In 1975, Federal Express, Compaq Computer, Staples, Oracle, and Amgen didn't even exist. Today these companies employ 200,000 people. These workers came from other firms and industries that weren't growing as fast.

Technological Advance. One of the forces that keeps shifting resources from one industry to another is continuing advances in technology. On the first page of this text we noted Intel's breakthrough in nanoelectronics. The discovery of new technology for microscopic miniaturization of electronic circuits expanded our production possibilities.

> human capital: The knowledge and skills possessed by the workforce.

© Richard Hamilton Smith/CORBIS

© Philippe Giraud/CORBIS SYGMA

Analysis: An abundance of capital equipment and advanced technology make American farmers and workers far more productive than workers in poor nations.

In the process, the productivity of workers in the electronics industry will rise, as will per capita GDP. A similar phenomenon happened when the fax machine was invented. That discovery not only made communication a lot faster and easier but it also released thousands of workers from the courier (bike messenger) business. Those workers moved to new industries where their productivity was higher. As e-mail replaces faxes, a similar transformation occurs. *Whenever technology advances, an economy can produce more output with existing resources.*

Outsourcing and Trade. The same technological advances that fuel economic growth also facilitate *global* resource use. Telecommunications has become so sophisticated and inexpensive that phone workers in India or Grenada can answer calls directed to

U.S. companies. Likewise, programmers in India can work online to write computer code, develop software, or perform accounting chores for U.S. corporations. Although such "outsourcing" is often viewed as a threat to U.S. jobs, it is really another source of increased U.S. output. By outsourcing routine tasks to foreign workers, U.S. workers are able to focus on higher-value jobs. U.S. computer engineers do less routine programming and more systems design. U.S. accountants do less cost tabulation and more cost analysis. By utilizing foreign resources in the production process, U.S. workers are able to pursue their *comparative advantage* in high-skill, capital-intensive jobs. In this way, both productivity and total output increase. Although some U.S. workers suffer temporary job losses in this process, the economy overall gains.

In assessing HOW goods are produced and economies grow, we must also take heed of the role the government plays. As we noted in Chapter 1, the amount of economic freedom varies greatly among the 200-plus nations of the world. Moreover, the Heritage Foundation has documented a positive relationship between the degree of economic freedom and economic growth (see Figure 2.5). Quite simply, when entrepreneurs are unfettered by regulation or high taxes, they are more likely to design and produce better mousetraps. When the government owns the factors of production, imposes high taxes, or tightly regulates output, there is little opportunity or incentive to design better products or pursue new technology.

Recognizing the productive value of economic freedom isn't tantamount to rejecting all government intervention. No one really advocates the complete abolition of government. On the contrary, the government plays a critical role in establishing a framework in which private businesses can operate.

- *Providing a legal framework.* One of the most basic functions of government is to establish and enforce the rules of the game. In some bygone era maybe a person's word was sufficient to guarantee delivery or payment. Businesses today, however, rely more on written contracts. The government gives legitimacy to contracts by establishing the rules for such pacts and by enforcing their provisions. In the absence of contractual rights, few companies would be willing to ship goods without prepayment (in cash). Even the incentive to write textbooks would disappear if government copyright laws didn't forbid unauthorized photocopying.

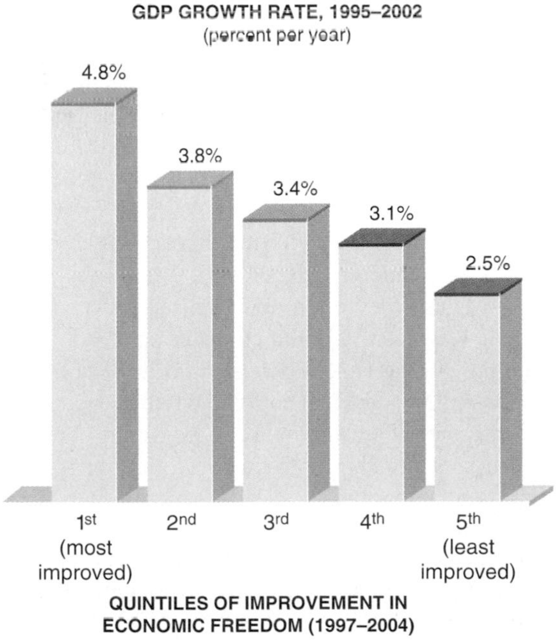

Role of Government

GDP GROWTH RATE, 1995–2002
(percent per year)

4.8%
3.8%
3.4%
3.1%
2.5%

1st
(most
improved)
2nd
3rd
4th
5th
(least
improved)

**QUINTILES OF IMPROVEMENT IN
ECONOMIC FREEDOM (1997–2004)**

FIGURE 2.5
Economic Freedom and Growth

The extent of economic freedom (market reliance) affects a nation's ability to grow. The Heritage Foundation shows that as nations become "freer" (rely more on markets and less on government), output (real GDP) grows more quickly.

Source: Heritage Foundation, *2004 Index of Economic Freedom* (Washington, DC: 2004).

By establishing ownership rights, contract rights, and other rules of the game, the government lays the foundation for market transactions.

- *Protecting the environment.* The government also intervenes in the market to protect the environment. The legal contract system is designed to protect the interests of a buyer and a seller who wish to do business. What if, however, the business they contract for harms third parties? How are the interests of persons who *aren't* party to the contract to be protected?

Numerous examples abound of how unregulated production may harm third parties. Earlier in the century, the steel mills around Pittsburgh blocked out the sun with clouds of sulfurous gases that spewed out of their furnaces. Local residents were harmed every time they inhaled. In the absence of government intervention, such side effects would be common. Decisions on how to produce would be based on costs alone, not on how the environment is affected. However, such **externalities**—spillover costs imposed on the broader community—affect our collective well-being. To reduce the external costs of production, the government limits air, water, and noise pollution and regulates environmental use.

> **externalities:** Costs (or benefits) of a market activity borne by a third party.

In poor countries, environmental protection often gets much less priority. In Haiti, residents keep cutting down newly planted saplings, destroying any hope of reforestation. They need the firewood *now* and can't afford to take the long-run view of economic growth. The Brazilian rain forests that are critical to the earth's ecosystem suffer the same fate. In the Caspian Sea, people poach so many sturgeon that the entire caviar industry is on the verge of destruction. In all these cases, the unbridled pursuit of individual gain has damaged broader economic welfare. More government regulation might both protect the environment and promote long-run growth.

- *Protecting consumers.* The government also uses its power to protect the interests of consumers. One way to do this is to prevent individual business firms from becoming too powerful. In the extreme case, a single firm might have a **monopoly** on the production of a specific good. As the sole producer of that good, a monopolist could dictate the price, the quality, and the quantity of the product. In such a situation, consumers would likely end up with the short end of the stick—paying too much for too little.

> **monopoly:** A firm that produces the entire market supply of a particular good or service.

To protect consumers from monopoly exploitation, the government tries to prevent individual firms from dominating specific markets. Antitrust laws prohibit mergers or acquisitions that would threaten competition. The U.S. Department of Justice and the Federal Trade Commission also regulate pricing practices, advertising claims, and other behavior that might put consumers at an unfair disadvantage in product markets.

Government regulates the safety of many products. Consumers don't have enough expertise to assess the safety of various medicines, for example. If they rely on trial and error to determine drug safety, they might not get a second chance. To avoid this calamity, the government requires rigorous testing of new drugs, food additives, and other products.

- *Protecting labor.* The government also regulates how labor resources are used in the production process. In most poor nations, children are forced to start working at very early ages, often for minuscule wages. They often don't get the chance to go to school or to stay healthy. In Africa, 40 percent of children under age 14 work to survive or to help support their families. In the United States, child labor laws and compulsory schooling prevent minor children from being exploited. Government regulations also set standards for workplace safety, minimum wages, fringe benefits, and overtime provisions. After decades of bloody confrontations, the government also established the right of workers to organize and set rules for union-management relations. The introduction of unemployment insurance, Social Security, and disability insurance, and guarantees for private pension benefits also protect workers from the vagaries of the marketplace. These social benefits have profoundly affected how much people work, when they retire, and even how long they live.

All these government interventions are designed to change the way resources are used. Such interventions reflect the conviction that the market alone might not select the best possible way of producing goods and services. There's no guarantee, however, that government regulation of HOW goods are produced always makes us better off. Excessive regulation may inhibit production, raise product prices, and limit consumer choices. As noted in Chapter 1, *government* failure might replace *market* failure, leaving us no better off—possibly even worse off. This possibility underscores the importance of striking the right balance between market reliance and government regulation. The balance attained in the United States is surely not perfect, but it appears to be much more effective than the balances of regulation and free enterprise in most poor countries.

FOR WHOM AMERICA PRODUCES

As we've seen, America produces a huge quantity of output, using high-quality labor and capital resources. That leaves one basic question unanswered: FOR WHOM is all this output produced?

How many goods and services one gets largely depends on how much income one has to spend. The U.S. economy uses the market mechanism to distribute most goods and services. Those who receive the most income get the most goods. This goes a long way toward explaining why millionaires live in mansions and homeless people seek shelter in abandoned cars. This is the kind of stark inequality that fueled Karl Marx's denunciation of capitalism. Even today, people wonder how some Americans can be so rich while others are so poor.

Figure 2.6 illustrates the actual distribution of income in the United States. For this illustration the entire population is sorted into five groups of equal size, ranked by income. In this depiction, all the rich people are in the top **income quintile;** the

income quintile: One-fifth of the population, rank-ordered by income (e.g., top fifth).

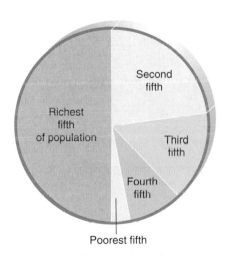

Income Quintile	2002 Income	Average Income	Share of Total Income (%)
Highest fifth	above $87,000	$147,000	49.8
Second fifth	$54,000–87,000	$ 69,000	23.4
Third fifth	$34,000–54,000	$ 44,000	14.8
Fourth fifth	$18,000–34,000	$ 26,000	8.7
Lowest fifth	$0–18,000	$ 10,000	3.4

Source: U.S. Department of Commerce, Bureau of the Census (averages rounded to thousands of dollars; 2002 data).

FIGURE 2.6
The U.S. Distribution of Income

The richest fifth of U.S. households gets nearly half of all the income— a huge slice of the income pie. By contrast, the poorest fifth gets only a sliver.

Global Inequality

poor are in the lowest quintile. To be in the top quintile in 2003, a household needed at least $87,000 of income. All the households in the lowest quintile had incomes under $18,000.

The most striking feature of Figure 2.6 is how large a slice of the income pie rich people get: ***The top 20 percent (quintile) of U.S. households gets nearly half of all U.S. income.*** By contrast, the poorest 20 percent (quintile) of U.S. households gets only a sliver of the income pie—less than 4 percent. Those grossly unequal slices explain why nearly half of all Americans believe the nation is divided into "haves" and "have nots."

As unequal as U.S. incomes are, income disparities are actually greater in many other countries. Ironically, income inequalities are often greatest in the poorest countries. In Brazil, Guatemala, Zimbabwe, and South Africa, the richest *tenth* of the population has a far larger share of income than the richest 10 percent of Americans have. These and other comparisons of the FOR WHOM resolution are illustrated in the World View on the next page.

Comparisons across countries would manifest even greater inequality. As we saw earlier, Third World GDP per capita is far below U.S. levels. As a consequence, even **poor people in the United States receive far more goods and services than the average household in most low-income countries.**

© Alan Schein Photography/CORBIS

© Wolfgang Spunbarg/Photo Edit

Analysis: The market distributes income (and, in turn, goods and services) according to the resources an individual owns and how well they are used. If the resulting inequalities are too great, some redistribution via government intervention may be desired.

Income Share of the Rich

Inequality tends to diminish as a country develops. In poor, developing nations, the richest tenth of the population typically gets 40 to 50 percent of all income. In developed countries, the richest tenth gets 20 to 30 percent of total income.

Source: Copyright 2004 by World Bank. Reproduced with permission. *World Development Indicators, 2004.*
www.worldbank.org

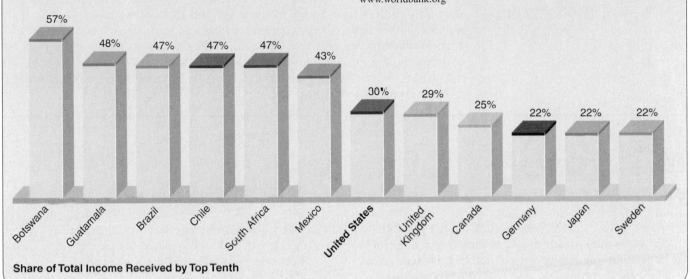

Share of Total Income Received by Top Tenth

Analysis: The FOR WHOM question is reflected in the distribution of income. Although the U.S. distribution is very unequal, inequalities loom even larger in most Third World countries.

THE ECONOMY TOMORROW

A Better Tomorrow?

Global answers to the basic questions of WHAT, HOW, and FOR WHOM have been shaped by market forces and government intervention. Obviously, the answers aren't yet fully satisfactory. Over 3 billion people around the world live in abject poverty—with incomes of less than $2 a day. Over a fourth of the world's population is illiterate, nearly half have no access to sanitation facilities, and a fifth are chronically malnourished. In view of these problems, the World Bank has set ambitious goals for the economy tomorrow. In the Millennium Declaration of October 2000, the 180 nation-members of the World Bank set specific goals for world development. By 2015, they agreed to

- Reduce extreme poverty and hunger by at least half.
- Achieve universal primary education.
- Reduce child and maternal mortality by two-thirds.
- Reduce by half the number of people without access to potable water.

Achieving these goals would obviously help billions of people. But how will we fulfill them?

People in rich nations also aspire to higher living standards in the economy tomorrow. They already enjoy more comforts than people in poor nations even dream of. But that doesn't stop us from wanting more consumer goods, better schools, improved health care, a cleaner environment, and greater economic security. How will we get them?

A magic wand could transform the economy tomorrow into utopia. But short of that, we're saddled with economic reality. All nations have limited resources and technology. To get to a better place tomorrow, we've got to put those resources to even better uses. Will the market alone head us down the right path? As we've observed, (Figure 2.5), economies that have relied more on market mechanisms than on government directives have prospered the most. But that doesn't mean we must fully embrace laissez faire. Government intervention still has potential to accelerate economic growth, reduce poverty, raise health and education standards, and protect the environment. The challenge for the economy both today and tomorrow is to find the right balance of market and government forces. We'll explore this quest in more detail as the text proceeds.

SUMMARY

- Answers to the core WHAT, HOW, and FOR WHOM questions vary greatly across nations. These differences reflect varying production possibilities, choice mechanisms, and values.

- Gross domestic product (GDP) is the basic measure of how much an economy produces. The United States produces over $11 trillion of output per year, more than one-fifth of the world's total. The U.S. GDP per capita is five times the world average.

- The high level of U.S. per capita GDP reflects the high productivity of U.S. workers. Abundant capital, education, technology, training, and management all contribute to high productivity. The relatively high degree of U.S. economic freedom (market reliance) is also an important cause of superior economic growth.

- Over 75 percent of U.S. output consists of services, including government services. This is a reversal of historical ratios and reflects the relatively high incomes in the United States. Poor nations produce much higher proportions of food and manufactured goods.

- Most of America's output consists of consumer goods and services. Investment goods account for only 15 percent of total output, and government purchases almost 20 percent.

- Incomes are distributed very unequally among households, with households in the highest income class (quintile) receiving over 10 times more income than low-income households. Incomes are even less equally distributed in many poor nations.

- The mix of output, production methods, and the income distribution continue to change. The WHAT, HOW, and FOR WHOM answers in tomorrow's economy will depend on the continuing interplay of (changing) market signals and (changing) government policy.

Key Terms

gross domestic product (GDP)
per capita GDP
economic growth
investment
income transfers
exports

imports
net exports
comparative advantage
factors of production
productivity
capital-intensive

human capital
externalities
monopoly
income quintile

Questions for Discussion

1. Americans already enjoy living standards that far exceed world averages. Do we have enough? Should we even try to produce more?
2. Why is per capita GDP so much higher in the United States than in Mexico?
3. Why do people suggest that the United States needs to devote more output to investment goods? Why not produce just consumption goods?
4. The U.S. farm population has shrunk by over 25 million people since 1900. Where did all the people go? Why did they move?
5. How might the following government interventions affect a nation's economic growth?
   a. Mandatory school attendance.
   b. High income taxes.
   c. Copyright and patent protection.
   d. Political corruption.
6. How many people are employed by your local or state government? What do they produce? What is the opportunity cost of that output?
7. Why should the government regulate how goods are produced? Can regulation ever be excessive?
8. Should the government try to equalize incomes more by raising taxes on the rich and giving more money to the poor? How might such redistribution affect total output and growth?
9. Do we need more or less government intervention to achieve the World Bank's Millennium goals? Provide specific examples.

PROBLEMS   The Student Problem Set at the back of this book contains numerical and graphing problems for this chapter.

WEB ACTIVITIES   to accompany this chapter can be found on the Online Learning Center:
http://www.mhhe.com/economics/schiller10

Supply and Demand

The lights went out in California in January 2001. With only minutes of warning, sections of high-tech Silicon Valley, San Francisco, the state capital of Sacramento, and a host of smaller cities went dark. Schools closed early, traffic signals malfunctioned, ATM machines shut down, and elevators abruptly stopped. "It's like we're living in Bosnia," said Michael Mischer, an Oakland, California baker. "How could this happen?"[1]

California's governor, Gray Davis, had a ready answer. He said out-of-state power company "pirates" were gouging California residents with exorbitant prices they could not pay. As he saw it, the electricity crisis was just an example of market-driven greed. To resolve the crisis, the governor proposed stiff price controls, the state purchase of transmission lines, and state-ordered customer refunds from "profiteering" power companies. As he saw it, only the state government could keep the lights on.

Critics said the governor's explanation made for good politics but bad economics. Government intervention, not the market, was the cause of the electricity crisis, they said. Supply and demand were out of balance in California and only *higher* prices and *less* government intervention could keep the lights on. U.S. Treasury Secretary Paul O'Neill criticized the governor for trying "to defeat economics. . . I mean, you don't have to have an economics degree to understand that this is an unworkable situation." One of UC–Berkeley's Nobel-winning economists, Daniel McFadden, echoed that sentiment, blaming the state's "rigid regulation" for its energy woes. President Bush was equally adamant that "price controls will not solve the problem" and urged the state to rely more on the market than on state legislators to avoid future blackouts.

California's 2001 energy crisis is a classic illustration of why the choice between market reliance and government intervention is so critical and often so controversial. The goal of this chapter is to put that choice into a coherent framework. To do so, we'll focus on how unregulated markets work. How does the market mechanism decide WHAT to produce, HOW to produce, and FOR WHOM to produce? Specifically,

- **What determines the price of a good or service?**
- **How does the price of a product affect its production and consumption?**
- **Why do prices and production levels often change?**

Once we've seen how unregulated markets work, we'll observe how government intervention may alter market outcomes—for better or worse. Hopefully, the lights won't go off before we finish.

---

[1]Rene Sanchez and William Booth, "California Forced to Turn the Lights Off," *Washington Post,* January 18, 2001, p. 1.

MARKET PARTICIPANTS

A good way to start figuring out how markets work is to see who participates in them. The answer is simple: just about every person and institution on the planet. Domestically, over 300 million consumers, about 20 million business firms, and tens of thousands of government agencies participate directly in the U.S. economy. Millions of international buyers and sellers also participate in U.S. markets.

Maximizing Behavior

All these market participants come into the marketplace to satisfy specific goals. Consumers, for example, come with a limited amount of income to spend. Their objective is to buy the most desirable goods and services that their limited budgets will permit. We can't afford *everything* we want, so we must make *choices* about how to spend our scarce dollars. Our goal is to *maximize* the utility (satisfaction) we get from our available incomes.

Businesses also try to maximize in the marketplace. In their case, the quest is for maximum *profits*. Business profits are the difference between sales receipts and total costs. To maximize profits, business firms try to use resources efficiently in producing products that consumers desire.

The public sector also has maximizing goals. The economic purpose of government is to use available resources to serve public needs. The resources available for this purpose are limited too. Hence, local, state, and federal governments must use scarce resources carefully, striving to maximize the general welfare of society. International consumers and producers pursue these same goals when participating in our markets.

Market participants sometimes lose sight of their respective goals. Consumers sometimes buy impulsively and later wish they'd used their income more wisely. Likewise, a producer may take a two-hour lunch, even at the sacrifice of maximum profits. And elected officials sometimes put their personal interests ahead of the public's interest. In all sectors of the economy, however, **the basic goals of utility maximization, profit maximization, and welfare maximization explain most market activity.**

Specialization and Exchange

The notion that buying and selling goods and services in the market might maximize our well-being originates in two simple observations. First, most of us are incapable of producing everything we desire to consume. Second, even if we *could* produce all our own goods and services, it would still make sense to specialize, producing only one product and trading it for other desired goods and services.

Suppose you were capable of growing your own food, stitching your own clothes, building your own shelter, and even writing your own economics text. Even in this little utopia, it would still make sense to decide how *best* to expend your limited time and energy and to rely on others to fill in the gaps. If you were *most* proficient at growing food, you would be best off spending your time farming. You could then exchange some of your food output for the clothes, shelter, and books you wanted. In the end, you'd be able to consume *more* goods than if you'd tried to make everything yourself.

Our economic interactions with others are thus necessitated by two constraints:

1. Our absolute inability as individuals to produce all the things we need or desire.
2. The limited amount of time, energy, and resources we have for producing those things we could make for ourselves.

Together, these constraints lead us to specialize and interact. Most of the interactions that result take place in the market.

THE CIRCULAR FLOW

Figure 3.1 summarizes the kinds of interactions that occur among market participants. Note first that the figure identifies four separate groups of participants. Domestically, the rectangle labeled "Consumers" includes all 300 million consumers in the United

Business firms supply goods and services to product markets (point *A*) and purchase factors of production in factor markets (*B*). Individual consumers supply factors of production such as their own labor (*C*) and purchase final goods and services (*D*). Federal, state, and local governments acquire resources in factor markets (*E*) and provide services to both consumers and business (*F*). International participants also take part by supplying imports, purchasing exports (*G*), and buying and selling factors of production (*H*).

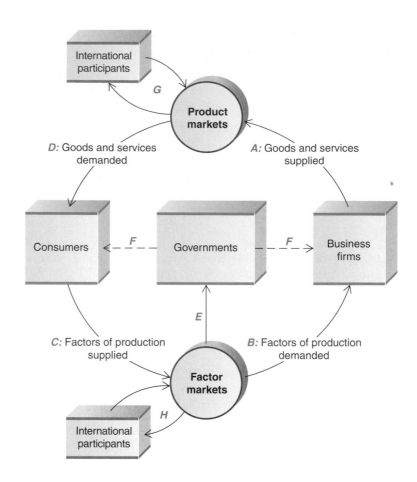

States. In the "Business firms" box are grouped all the domestic business enterprises that buy and sell goods and services. The third participant, "Governments," includes the many separate agencies of the federal government, as well as state and local governments. Figure 3.1 also illustrates the role of global actors.

The Two Markets

The easiest way to keep track of all this market activity is to distinguish two basic markets. Figure 3.1 makes this distinction by portraying separate circles for product markets and factor markets. In **factor markets,** factors of production are exchanged. Market participants buy or sell land, labor, or capital that can be used in the production process. When you go looking for work, for example, you're making a factor of production—your labor—available to producers. The producers will hire you—purchase your services in the factor market—if you're offering the skills they need at a price they're willing to pay. The same kind of interaction occurs in factor markets when the government enlists workers into the armed services or when the Japanese buy farmland in Montana.

factor market: Any place where factors of production (e.g., land, labor, capital) are bought and sold.

Interactions within factor markets are only half the story. At the end of a hard day's work, consumers go to the grocery store (or to a virtual store online) to buy desired goods and services—that is, to buy *products*. In this context, consumers again interact with business firms, this time purchasing goods and services those firms have produced. These interactions occur in **product markets.** Foreigners also participate in the product market by supplying goods and services (imports) to the United States and buying some of our output (exports).

product market: Any place where finished goods and services (products) are bought and sold.

The government sector also supplies services. (e.g., education, national defense, highways.) In California, Governor Davis even wanted the state to supply electricity to households and businesses. Most government services aren't explicitly sold in product markets, however. Typically, they're delivered "free," without an explicit price (e.g., public elementary schools, highways). This doesn't mean government services are truly free, though. There's still an opportunity cost associated with every service the government provides. Consumers and businesses pay that cost indirectly through taxes rather than directly through market prices.

In Figure 3.1, the arrow connecting product markets to consumers (point *D*) emphasizes the fact that consumers, by definition, don't supply products. When individuals produce goods and services, they do so within the government or business sector. For instance, a doctor, a dentist, or an economic consultant functions in two sectors. When selling services in the market, this person is regarded as a "business"; when away from the office, he or she is regarded as a "consumer." This distinction is helpful in emphasizing that *the consumer is the final recipient of all goods and services produced.*

Locating Markets. Although we refer repeatedly to two kinds of markets in this book, it would be a little foolish to go off in search of the product and factor markets. Neither market is a single, identifiable structure. The term *market* simply refers to a place or situation where an economic exchange occurs—where a buyer and seller interact. The exchange may take place on the street, in a taxicab, over the phone, by mail, or in cyberspace. In some cases, the market used may in fact be quite distinguishable, as in the case of a retail store, the Chicago Commodity Exchange, or a state employment office. But whatever it looks like, *a market exists wherever and whenever an exchange takes place.*

Dollars and Exchange

Figure 3.1 provides a useful summary of market activities, but it neglects one critical element of market interactions: dollars. Each arrow in the figure actually has two dimensions. Consider again the arrow linking consumers to product markets: It's drawn in only one direction because consumers, by definition, don't provide goods and services directly to product markets. But they do provide something: dollars. If you want to obtain something from a product market, you must offer to pay for it (typically, with cash, check, or credit card). Consumers exchange dollars for goods and services in product markets.

The same kinds of exchange occur in factor markets. When you go to work, you exchange a factor of production (your labor) for income, typically a paycheck. Here again, the path connecting consumers to factor markets really goes in two directions: one of real resources, the other of dollars. Consumers receive wages, rent, and interest for the labor, land, and capital they bring to the factor markets. Indeed, nearly *every market transaction involves an exchange of dollars for goods (in product markets) or resources (in factor markets).* Money is thus critical in facilitating market exchanges and the specialization the exchanges permit.

Supply and Demand

In every market transaction there must be a buyer and a seller. The seller is on the **supply** side of the market; the buyer is on the **demand** side. As noted earlier, we *supply* resources to the market when we look for a job—that is, when we offer our labor in exchange for income. We *demand* goods when we shop in a supermarket—that is, when we're prepared to offer dollars in exchange for something to eat. Business firms may *supply* goods and services in product markets at the same time they're *demanding* factors of production in factor markets. Whether one is on the supply side or the demand side of any particular market transaction depends on the nature of the exchange, not on the people or institutions involved.

supply: The ability and willingness to sell (produce) specific quantities of a good at alternative prices in a given time period, *ceteris paribus.*

demand: The ability and willingness to buy specific quantities of a good at alternative prices in a given time period, *ceteris paribus.*

DEMAND

To get a sense of how the demand side of market transactions work, we'll focus first on a single consumer. Then we'll aggregate to illustrate *market* demand.

Individual Demand

We can begin to understand how market forces work by looking more closely at the behavior of a single market participant. Let us start with Tom, a senior at Clearview

College. Tom has majored in everything from art history to government in his three years at Clearview. He didn't connect to any of those fields and is on the brink of academic dismissal. To make matters worse, his parents have threatened to cut him off financially unless he gets serious about his course work. By that, they mean he should enroll in courses that will lead to a job after graduation. Tom thinks he has found the perfect solution: Web design. Everything associated with the Internet pays big bucks. Plus, the girls seem to think Webbies are "cool." Or at least so Tom thinks. And his parents would definitely approve. So Tom has enrolled in Web-design courses.

Unfortunately for Tom, he never developed computer skills. Until he got to Clearview College, he thought mastering Sony's latest alien-attack video game was the pinnacle of electronic wizardry. His parents gave him a Wi-Fi laptop, but he used it only for surfing hot video sites. The concept of using his computer for course work, much less developing some Web content, was completely foreign to him. To compound his problems, Tom didn't have a clue about "streaming," "interfacing," "animation," or the other concepts the Web-design instructor outlined in the first lecture.

Given his circumstances, Tom was desperate to find someone who could tutor him in Web design. But desperation is not enough to secure the services of a Web architect. In a market-based economy, you must also be willing to *pay* for the things you want. Specifically, ***a demand exists only if someone is willing and able to pay for the good***—that is, exchange dollars for a good or service in the marketplace. Is Tom willing and able to *pay* for the Web-design tutoring he so obviously needs?

Let us assume that Tom has some income and is willing to spend some of it to get a tutor. Under these assumptions, we can claim that Tom is a participant in the *market* for Web-design services.

But how much is Tom willing to pay? Surely, Tom is not prepared to exchange *all* his income for help in mastering Web design. After all, Tom could use his income to buy more desirable goods and services. If he spent all his income on a Web tutor, that help would have an extremely high **opportunity cost.** He would be giving up the opportunity to spend that income on other goods and services. He'd pass his Web-design class but have little else. It doesn't sound like a good idea to Tom. Even though Tom says he would be willing to pay *anything* to pass the Web-design course, he probably has lower prices in mind. Indeed, it would be more reasonable to assume that there are *limits* to the amount Tom is willing to pay for any given quantity of Web-design tutoring. These limits will be determined by how much income Tom has to spend and how many other goods and services he must forsake in order to pay for a tutor.

Tom also knows that his grade in Web design will depend in part on how much tutoring service he buys. He can pass the course with only a few hours of design help. If he wants a better grade, however, the cost is going to escalate quickly.

Naturally, Tom wants it all: an A in Web design and a ticket to higher-paying jobs. But here again the distinction between *desire* and *demand* is relevant. He may *desire* to master Web design, but his actual proficiency will depend on how many hours of tutoring he is willing to *pay* for.

We assume, then, that when Tom starts looking for a Web-design tutor he has in mind some sort of **demand schedule,** like that described in Figure 3.2. According to row *A* of this schedule, Tom is willing and able to buy only 1 hour of tutoring service per semester if he must pay $50 an hour. At such an outrageous price he will learn minimal skills and pass the course. Just the bare minimum is all Tom is willing to buy at that price.

At lower prices, Tom would behave differently. According to Figure 3.2, Tom would purchase more tutoring services if the price per hour were less. At lower prices, he would not have to give up so many other goods and services for each hour of technical help. The reduced opportunity costs implied by lower service prices increase the attractiveness of professional help. Indeed, we see from row *I* of the demand schedule that Tom is willing to purchase 20 hours per semester—the whole bag of design tricks—if the price of tutoring is as low as $10 per hour.

opportunity cost: The most desired goods or services that are forgone in order to obtain something else.

demand schedule: A table showing the quantities of a good a consumer is willing and able to buy at alternative prices in a given time period, *ceteris paribus*.

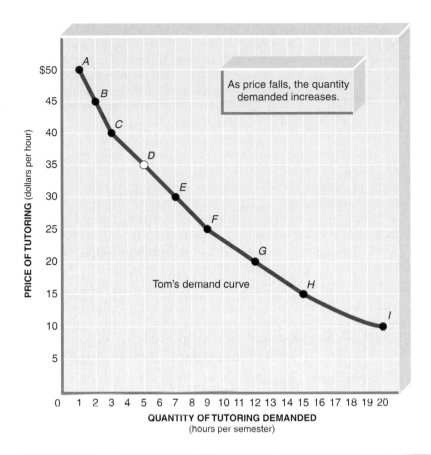

As price falls, the quantity demanded increases.

Tom's demand curve

PRICE OF TUTORING (dollars per hour)

QUANTITY OF TUTORING DEMANDED
(hours per semester)

FIGURE 3.2
A Demand Schedule and Curve

A demand schedule indicates the quantities of a good a consumer is able and willing to buy at alternative prices (*ceteris paribus*). The demand schedule below indicates that Tom would buy 5 hours of Web tutoring per semester if the price were $35 per hour (row *D*). If Web tutoring were less expensive (rows *E–I*), Tom would purchase a larger quantity.

A demand curve is a graphical illustration of a demand schedule. Each point on the curve refers to a specific quantity that will be demanded at a given price. If, for example, the price of Web tutoring were $35 per hour, this curve tells us the consumer would purchase 5 hours per semester (point *D*). If Web tutoring cost $30 per hour, 7 hours per semester would be demanded (point *E*). Each point on the curve corresponds to a row in the schedule.

	Tom's Demand Schedule	
	Price of Tutoring (per hour)	Quantity of Tutoring Demanded (hours per semester)
A	$50	1
B	45	2
C	40	3
D	35	5
E	30	7
F	25	9
G	20	12
H	15	15
I	10	20

Notice that the demand schedule doesn't tell us anything about *why* this consumer is willing to pay specific prices for various amounts of tutoring. Tom's expressed willingness to pay for Web-design tutoring may reflect a desperate need to finish a Web-design course, a lot of income to spend, or a relatively small desire for other goods and services. All the demand schedule tells us is what the consumer is *willing and able* to buy, for whatever reasons.

Also observe that the demand schedule doesn't tell us how many hours of design help the consumer will *actually* buy. Figure 3.2 simply states that Tom is *willing and able* to pay for one hour of tutoring per semester at $50 per hour, for two hours at $45 each, and so on. How much tutoring he purchases will depend on the actual price of such services in the market. Until we know that price, we cannot tell how much service will be purchased. Hence **"demand" is an expression of consumer buying intentions, of a willingness to buy, not a statement of actual purchases.**

demand curve: A curve describing the quantities of a good a consumer is willing and able to buy at alternative prices in a given time period, *ceteris paribus.*

A convenient summary of buying intentions is the **demand curve,** a graphical illustration of the demand schedule. The demand curve in Figure 3.2 tells us again that this consumer is willing to pay for only one hour of tutoring per semester if the price is $50 per hour (point *A*), for two if the price is $45 (point *B*), for three at $40 an hour (point *C*), and so on. Once we know what the market price of tutoring actually is, a glance at the demand curve tells us how much service this consumer will buy.

What the notion of *demand* emphasizes is that the amount we buy of a good depends on its price. We seldom if ever decide to buy only a certain quantity of a good at whatever price is charged. Instead, we enter markets with a set of desires and a limited amount of money to spend. How much we actually buy of any good will depend on its price.

law of demand: The quantity of a good demanded in a given time period increases as its price falls, *ceteris paribus.*

A common feature of demand curves is their downward slope. As the price of a good falls, people purchase more of it. In Figure 3.2 the quantity of Web-tutorial services demanded increases (moves rightward along the horizontal axis) as the price per hour decreases (moves down the vertical axis). This inverse relationship between price and quantity is so common we refer to it as the **law of demand.** Compaq used this law to increase computer sales in 2000 (see News).

Determinants of Demand

The demand curve in Figure 3.2 has only two dimensions—quantity demanded (on the horizontal axis) and price (on the vertical axis). This seems to imply that the amount of tutoring demanded depends only on the price of that service. This is surely not the case. A consumer's willingness and ability to buy a product at various prices depend on a variety of forces. *The determinants of market demand include*

- *Tastes* (desire for this and other goods).
- *Income* (of the consumer).
- *Other goods* (their availability and price).
- *Expectations* (for income, prices, tastes).
- *Number of buyers.*

PC Prices Fall with Demand

Retailers Try to Minimize Losses with Big Rebates

Compaq Computer became the latest casualty of the weakening personal computer market, warning Tuesday that its fourth-quarter sales and profit will fall short of Wall Street's expectations.

The world's biggest PC maker blamed softening consumer and small-business demand—heightening expectations that PC makers may have to resort to price cuts to move excess inventory.

"We're seeing some of the biggest rebates we've ever seen in the PC industry," says Kevin Knox, a Gartner analyst in Stamford, Conn.

- Consumers can get rebates of $100 to $400 on PCs by Compaq, Hewlett-Packard and eMachines at Circuit City, Best Buy and other retailers.

If sales don't pick up, bigger rebates are likely in January, analysts say.

- In a typical holiday bargain at Circuit City, shoppers can snap up a Compaq Presario computer, originally priced at $1,099, for $649. . . .

Analysts say PC makers and retail chains have inventory backlogs of eight to 12 weeks. The industry likes to see a backlog of three to four weeks. . . .

Worldwide, fourth-quarter PC shipments will be up 20 percent over the same period a year ago, says market research firm IDC.

—Edward Iwata

Source: *USA Today,* December 13, 2000. USA TODAY. Copyright 2000. Reprinted with permission. www.usatoday.com

Analysis: The law of demand predicted that Compaq would sell more computers if it reduced their price. That is exactly what happened.

Tom's "taste" for tutoring has nothing to do with taste buds. *Taste* is just another word for desire. In this case Tom's taste for Web-design services is clearly acquired. If he didn't have to pass a Web-design course, he would have no desire for related services, and thus no demand. If he had no income, he couldn't *demand* any Web-design tutoring either, no matter how much he might *desire* it.

Other goods also affect the demand for tutoring services. Their effect depends on whether they're *substitute* goods or *complementary* goods. A **substitute good** is one that might be purchased instead of tutoring services. In Tom's simple world, pizza is a substitute for tutoring. If the price of pizza fell, Tom would use his limited income to buy more pizzas and cut back on his purchases of Web tutoring. When the price of a substitute good falls, the demand for tutoring services declines.

A **complementary good** is one that's typically consumed with, rather than instead of, tutoring. If textbook prices or tuition increases, Tom might take fewer classes and demand *less* Web-design assistance. In this case, a price increase for a complementary good causes the demand for tutoring to decline.

Expectations also play a role in consumer decisions. If Tom expected to flunk his Web-design course anyway, he probably wouldn't waste any money getting tutorial help; his demand for such services would disappear. On the other hand, if he expects a Web tutor to determine his college fate, he might be more willing to buy such services.

If demand is in fact such a multidimensional decision, how can we reduce it to only the two dimensions of price and quantity? In Chapter 1 we first encountered this *ceteris paribus* trick. To simplify their models of the world, economists focus on only one or two forces at a time and *assume* nothing else changes. We know a consumer's tastes, income, other goods, and expectations all affect the decision to hire a tutor. But we want to focus on the relationship between quantity demanded and price. That is, we want to know what *independent* influence price has on consumption decisions. To find out, we must isolate that one influence, price, and assume that the determinants of demand remain unchanged.

The *ceteris paribus* assumption is not as farfetched as it may seem. People's tastes, income, and expectations do not change quickly. Also, the prices and availability of other goods don't change all that fast. Hence, a change in the *price* of a product may be the only factor that prompts a change in quantity demanded.

The ability to predict consumer responses to a price change is important. What would happen, for example, to enrollment at your school if tuition doubled? Must we guess? Or can we use demand curves to predict how the quantity of applications will change as the price of college goes up? *Demand curves show us how changes in market prices alter consumer behavior.* We used the demand curve in Figure 3.2 to predict how Tom's Web-design ability would change at different tutorial prices.

Although demand curves are useful in predicting consumer responses to market signals, they aren't infallible. The problem is that *the determinants of demand can and do change.* When they do, a specific demand curve may become obsolete. A *demand curve (schedule) is valid only so long as the underlying determinants of demand remain constant.* If the *ceteris paribus* assumption is violated—if tastes, income, other goods, or expectations change—the ability or willingness to buy will change. When this happens, the demand curve will **shift** to a new position.

Suppose, for example, that Tom won $1,000 in the state lottery. This increase in his income would greatly increase his ability to pay for tutoring services. Figure 3.3 shows the effect of this windfall on Tom's demand. The old demand curve, D_1, is no longer relevant. Tom's lottery winnings enable him to buy more tutoring at any price, as illustrated by the new demand curve, D_2. According to this new curve, lucky Tom is now willing and able to buy 12 hours per semester at the price of $35 per hour

substitute goods: Goods that substitute for each other; when the price of good *x* rises, the demand for good *y* increases, *ceteris paribus.*

complementary goods: Goods frequently consumed in combination; when the price of good *x* rises, the demand for good *y* falls, *ceteris paribus.*

Ceteris Paribus

ceteris paribus: The assumption of nothing else changing.

Shifts in Demand

shift in demand: A change in the quantity demanded at any (every) given price.

FIGURE 3.3
Shifts vs. Movements

A demand curve shows how a consumer responds to price changes. If the determinants of demand stay constant, the response is a *movement* along the curve to a new quantity demanded. In this case, the quantity demanded increases from 5 (point d_1), to 12 (point g_1), when price falls from $35 to $20 per hour.

If the determinants of demand change, the entire demand curve *shifts*. In this case, an increase in income increases demand. With more income, Tom is willing to buy 12 hours at the initial price of $35 (point d_2), not just the 5 hours he demanded before the lottery win.

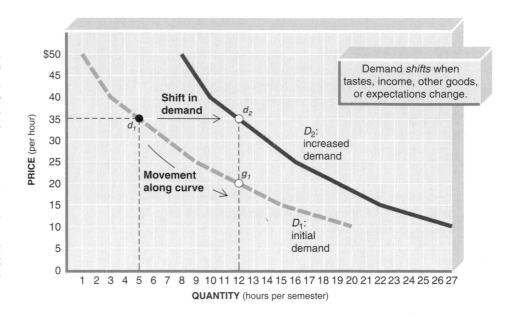

		Quantity Demanded (hours per semester)	
	Price (per hour)	Initial Demand	After Increase in Income
A	$50	1	8
B	45	2	9
C	40	3	10
D	35	5	12
E	30	7	14
F	25	9	16
G	20	12	19
H	15	15	22
I	10	20	27

(point d_2). This is a large increase in demand; previously (before winning the lottery) he demanded only 5 hours at that price (point d_1).

With his higher income, Tom can buy more tutoring services at every price. Thus, *the entire demand curve shifts to the right when income goes up.* Figure 3.3 illustrates both the old (prelottery) and the new (postlottery) demand curves.

Income is only one of the basic determinants of demand. Changes in any of the other determinants of demand would also cause the demand curve to shift. Tom's taste for Web tutoring might increase dramatically, for example, if his parents promised to buy him a new car for passing Web design. In that case, he might be willing to forgo other goods and spend more of his income on tutors. *An increase in taste (desire) also shifts the demand curve to the right.*

Pizza and Politics. A similar demand shift occurs at the White House when a political crisis erupts. On an average day, White House staffers order about $180 worth of pizza from the nearby Domino's. When a crisis hits, however, staffers work well into the night and their demand for pizza soars. On the days preceeding the March 2003 invasion of Iraq, White House staffers ordered more than $1,000 worth of pizza per day!

It's important to distinguish shifts of the demand curve from movements along the demand curve. ***Movements along a demand curve are a response to price changes for that good.*** Such movements assume that determinants of demand are unchanged. By contrast, ***shifts of the demand curve occur when the determinants of demand change.*** When tastes, income, other goods, or expectations are altered, the basic relationship between price and quantity demanded is changed (shifts).

For convenience, movements along a demand curve and shifts of the demand curve have their own labels. Specifically, take care to distinguish

- ***Changes in quantity demanded:*** movements along a given demand curve, in response to price changes of that good.
- ***Changes in demand:*** shifts of the demand curve due to changes in tastes, income, other goods, or expectations.

Tom's behavior in the Web-tutoring market will change if either the price of tutoring changes (a movement) or the underlying determinants of his demand are altered (a shift). Notice in Figure 3.3 that he ends up buying 12 hours of Web tutoring if either the price of tutoring falls or his income increases. Demand curves help us predict those market responses.

Whatever we say about demand for Web-design tutoring on the part of one wannabe Web master, we can also say about every student at Clearview College (or, for that matter, about all consumers). Some students have no interest in Web design and aren't willing to pay for related services: They don't participate in the Web-tutoring market. Other students want such services but don't have enough income to pay for them: They too are excluded from the Web-tutoring market. A large number of students, however, not only have a need (or desire) for Web tutoring but also are willing and able to purchase such services.

What we start with in product markets, then, is many individual demand curves. Fortunately, it's possible to combine all the individual demand curves into a single **market demand.** The aggregation process is no more difficult than simple arithmetic. Suppose you would be willing to buy one hour of tutoring per semester at a price of $80 per hour. George, who is also desperate to learn Web design, would buy two at that price; and I would buy none, since my publisher (McGraw-Hill) creates a Web page for me (try mhhe.com/economics/Schiller10). What would our combined (market) demand for hours of tutoring be at that price? Clearly, our individual inclinations indicate that we would be willing to buy a total of three hours of tutoring per semester if the price were $80 per hour. Our combined willingness to buy—our collective market demand—is nothing more than the sum of our individual demands. The same kind of aggregation can be performed for all consumers, leading to a summary of the total market demand for a specific good or service. This ***market demand is determined by the number of potential buyers and their respective tastes, incomes, other goods, and expectations.***

Figure 3.4 provides the basic market demand schedule for a situation in which only three consumers participate in the market. It illustrates the same market situation with demand curves. The three individuals who participate in the market demand for Web tutoring at Clearview College obviously differ greatly, as suggested by their respective demand schedules. Tom *has* to pass his Web-design classes or confront college and parental rejection. He also has a nice allowance (income), so can afford to buy a lot of tutorial help. His demand schedule is portrayed in the first column of the table (and is identical to the one we examined in Figure 3.2). George is also desperate to acquire some job skills and is willing to pay relatively high prices for Web-design tutoring. His demand is summarized in the second column under Quantity Demanded in the table.

The third consumer in this market is Lisa. Lisa already knows the nuts and bolts of Web design, so she isn't so desperate for tutorial services. She would like to upgrade

Movements vs. Shifts

WEBNOTE

Priceline.com is an online service for purchasing airline tickets, vacation packages, and car rentals. The site allows you to specify the *highest* price you're willing to pay for air travel between two cities. In effect, you reveal your demand curve to Priceline. If you use the price naming option and they find a ticket that costs no more than the price you're willing and able to pay, you must buy it. Priceline makes a profit by matching demand and supply. Try it at www.priceline.com.

Market Demand

market demand: The total quantities of a good or service people are willing and able to buy at alternative prices in a given time period; the sum of individual demands.

The Market Demand Curve

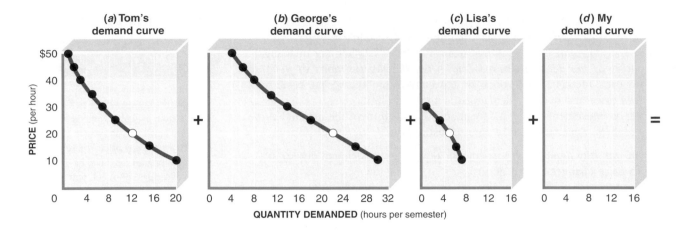

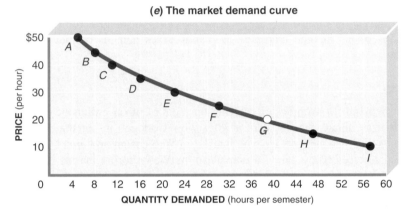

FIGURE 3.4

Construction of the Market Demand Curve

Market demand represents the combined demands of all market participants. To determine the total quantity of Web tutoring demanded at any given price, we add the separate demands of the individual consumers. Row G of this schedule indicates that a *total* quantity of 39 hours per semester will be demanded at a price of $20 per hour. This same conclusion is reached by adding the individual demand curves, leading to point G on the market demand curve (see above).

	Price (per hour)	Quantity of Tutoring Demanded (hours per semester)					Market Demand
		Tom +	George +	Lisa +	Me =		
A	$50	1	4	0	0		5
B	45	2	6	0	0		8
C	40	3	8	0	0		11
D	35	5	11	0	0		16
E	30	7	14	1	0		22
F	25	9	18	3	0		30
G	20	12	22	5	0		39
H	15	15	26	6	0		47
I	10	20	30	7	0		57

her skills, however, especially in animation and e-commerce applications. But her limited budget precludes paying a lot for help. She will buy some technical support only if the price falls to $30 per hour. Should tutors cost less, she'd even buy quite a few hours of design services. Finally, there is my demand schedule (column 4 under Quantity Demanded), which confirms that I really don't participate in the Web-tutoring market.

The differing personalities and consumption habits of Tom, George, Lisa, and me are expressed in our individual demand schedules and associated curves in Figure 3.4. To determine the *market* demand for tutoring from this information, we simply add these four separate demands. The end result of this aggregation is, first, a *market* demand schedule and, second, the resultant *market* demand curve. These market summaries describe the various quantities of tutoring that Clearview College students are *willing and able* to purchase each semester at various prices.

How much Web tutoring will be purchased each semester? Knowing how much help Tom, George, Lisa, and I are willing to buy at various prices doesn't tell you how much we're actually going to purchase. To determine the actual consumption of Web tutoring, we have to know something about prices and supplies. Which of the many different prices illustrated in Figures 3.3 and 3.4 will actually prevail? How will that price be determined?

SUPPLY

To understand how the price of Web tutoring is established, we must also look at the other side of the market: the supply side. We need to know how many hours of tutoring services people are willing and able to *sell* at various prices, that is, the **market supply.** As on the demand side, the *market supply* depends on the behavior of all the individuals willing and able to supply Web tutoring at some price.

Let's return to the Clearview campus for a moment. What we need to know now is how much tutorial Web service people are willing and able to provide. Generally speaking, Web-page design can be fun, but it can also be drudge work, especially when you're doing it for someone else. Software programs like PhotoShop, Flash, and Fireworks have made Web-page design easier and more creative. And Wi-Fi laptops have made Web tutoring more convenient. But teaching someone else to design Web pages is still work. So few people offer to supply tutoring services just for the fun of it. Web designers do it for money. Specifically, they do it to earn income that they, in turn, can spend on goods and services they desire.

How much income must be offered to induce Web designers to do a job depends on a variety of things. The *determinants of market supply include*

- *Technology*
- *Factor costs*
- *Other goods*
- *Taxes and subsidies*
- *Expectations*
- *Number of sellers*

The technology of Web design, for example, is always getting easier and more creative. With a program like PageOut, for example, it's very easy to create a bread-and-butter Web page. A continuous stream of new software programs (e.g., Fireworks, DreamWeaver) keeps stretching the possibilities for graphics, animation, interactivity, and content. These technological advances mean that Web-design services can be supplied more quickly and cheaply. They also make *teaching* Web design easier. As a result, they induce people to supply more tutoring services at every price.

How much Web-design service is offered at any given price also depends on the cost of factors of production. If the software programs needed to create Web pages are cheap (or, better yet, free), Web designers can afford to charge lower prices. If the required software inputs are expensive, however, they will have to charge more money per hour for their services.

market supply: The total quantities of a good that sellers are willing and able to sell at alternative prices in a given time period, *ceteris paribus.*

Determinants of Supply

WEBNOTE

Sellers of books and cars post asking prices for their products on the Internet. With the help of search engines such as autoweb.com and abcbooks.com, consumers can locate the seller who's offering the lowest price. By examining a lot of offers, you could also construct a supply curve showing how the quantity supplied increases at higher prices.

law of supply: The quantity of a good supplied in a given time period increases as its price increases, *ceteris paribus.*

Other goods can also affect the willingness to supply Web-design services. If you can make more income waiting tables than you can tutoring lazy students, why would you even boot up the computer? As the prices paid for other goods and services change, they will influence people's decision about whether to offer Web services.

In the real world, the decision to supply goods and services is also influenced by the long arm of Uncle Sam. Federal, state, and local governments impose taxes on income earned in the marketplace. When tax rates are high, people get to keep less of the income they earn. Once taxes start biting into paychecks, some people may conclude that tutoring is no longer worth the hassle and withdraw from the market.

Expectations are also important on the supply side of the market. If Web designers expect higher prices, lower costs, or reduced taxes, they may be more willing to learn new software programs. On the other hand, if they have poor expectations about the future, they may just sell their computers and find something else to do.

Finally, we note that the number of available tutors will affect the quantity of service offered for sale at various prices. If there are lots of willing tutors on campus, a large quantity of tutorial service will be available.

All these considerations—factor costs, technology, expectations—affect the decision to offer Web services and at what price. In general, we assume that Web architects will be willing to provide more tutoring if the per-hour price is high and less if the price is low. In other words, there is a **law of supply** that parallels the law of demand. On the supply side the law says that *larger quantities will be offered for sale at higher prices.* Here again, the laws rest on the *ceteris paribus* assumption: The quantity supplied increases at higher prices *if* the determinants of supply are constant. *Supply curves are upward-sloping to the right,* as in Figure 3.5. Note how the *quantity supplied* jumps from 39 hours (point *d*) to 130 hours (point *h*) when the price of Web service doubles (from $20 to $40 per hour).

Market Supply

Figure 3.5 also illustrates how market supply is constructed from the supply decisions of individual sellers. In this case, only three Web masters are available. Ann is willing to provide a lot of tutoring at low prices, whereas Bob requires at least $20 an hour. Cory won't talk to students for less than $40 an hour.

By adding the quantity each Webhead is willing to offer at every price, we can construct the market supply curve. Notice in Figure 3.5, for example, how the quantity supplied to the market at $45 (point *i*) comes from the individual efforts of Ann (93 hours), Bob (33 hours), and Cory (14 hours). *The market supply curve is just a summary of the supply intentions of all producers.*

None of the points on the market supply curve (Figure 3.5) tells us how much Web tutoring is actually being sold on the Clearview campus. *Market supply is an expression of sellers' intentions—an offer to sell—not a statement of actual sales.* My next door neighbor may be willing to sell his 1994 Honda Civic for $8,000, but most likely he'll never find a buyer at that price. Nevertheless, his *willingness* to sell his car at that price is part of the *market supply* of used cars.

Shifts of Supply

As with demand, there's nothing sacred about any given set of supply intentions. Supply curves *shift* when the underlying determinants of supply change. Thus, we again distinguish

- *Changes in quantity supplied:* movements along a given supply curve.
- *Changes in supply:* shifts of the supply curve.

Our Latin friend *ceteris paribus* is once again the decisive factor. If the price of a product is the only variable changing, then we can *track changes in quantity supplied along the supply curve.* But if *ceteris paribus* is violated—if technology,

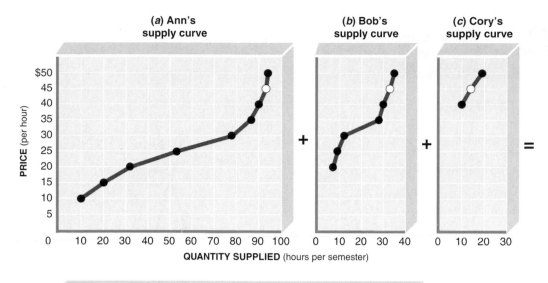

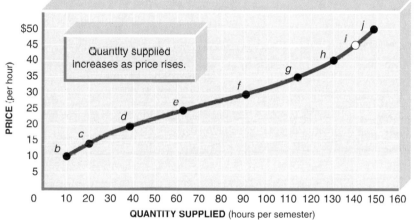

FIGURE 3.5
Market Supply

The market supply curve indicates the *combined* sales intentions of all market participants. If the price of tutoring were $45 per hour (point *i*), the *total* quantity of services supplied would be 140 hours per semester. This quantity is determined by adding the supply decisions of all individual producers. In this case, Ann supplies 93 hours, Bob supplies 33, and Cory supplies the rest.

	Price (per hour)	Quantity of Tutoring Supplied by				
		Ann	+	Bob	+ Cory	= Market
j	$50	94		35	19	148
i	45	93		33	14	140
h	40	90		30	10	130
g	35	86		28	0	114
f	30	78		12	0	90
e	25	53		9	0	62
d	20	32		7	0	39
c	15	20		0	0	20
b	10	10		0	0	10

factor costs, the profitability of producing other goods, tax rates, expectations, or the number of sellers change—then **changes in supply are illustrated by shifts of the supply curve.**

The News on the next page illustrates how a supply shift sent lettuce prices soaring in 2002. When a burst of cold weather reduced harvests, the lettuce supply curve shifted leftward and price doubled.

Prices Soar As Cold Snap Shreds Iceberg Lettuce Supply

In a classic collision of supply and demand, a cold snap in Arizona and California has chopped the iceberg lettuce harvest just as Americans are eating more of the salad and sandwich staple.

Grocery prices have soared to $3 a head, school cafeterias have pulled lettuce out of ham sandwiches, restaurants have substituted cheaper baby spinach in salads and consumers are suffering sticker shock.

Farm prices for lettuce doubled in March to a record $86.50 per hundred pounds, up 477% from March 2001, according to the Department of Agriculture. Much of that increase was in the iceberg category, the most popular lettuce in the USA.

Reasons for the increase in lettuce prices:

- *Higher demand.* Farmers say demand has surged over the past five years because of the rising popularity of prepackaged "bag lettuce."
- *Bad weather.* It was unusually cold in Yuma, Ariz, and in the Imperial Valley in California, the nation's "salad bowl" during winter. That led to a delayed harvest and smaller yields.

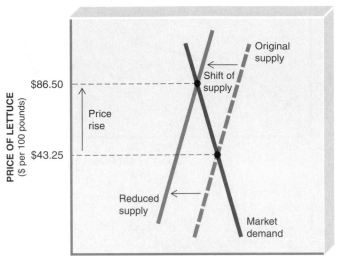

The weather isn't just making an impact on iceberg lettuce. Farm prices for cauliflower shot up 60% in March, while tomato prices rose 39%.

—Barbara Hagenbaugh

Source: *USA Today,* April 1, 2002. USA TODAY. Copyright 2002. Reprinted with permission.

Analysis: When factor costs or availability worsen, the supply curve shifts to the left. Such leftward supply-curve shifts push prices up the market demand curve.

EQUILIBRIUM

The abrupt spike in California lettuce prices offers some clues as to how the forces of supply and demand set, and change, market prices. To get a more detailed sense of how those forces work, we'll return to the mythical Clearview College Web tutoring market for a moment. How did supply and demand resolve the WHAT, HOW, and FOR WHOM questions in that market?

Figure 3.6 helps answer that question by bringing together the market supply and demand curves we've already examined (Figures 3.4 and 3.5). When we put the two curves together, we see that *only one price and quantity are compatible with the existing intentions of both buyers and sellers.* This equilibrium occurs at the intersection of the two curves in Figure 3.6. Once it's established, Web tutoring will cost $20 per hour. At that **equilibrium price,** campus Webheads will sell a total of 39 hours of tutoring per semester—the same amount that students wish to buy at that price. Those 39 hours of tutoring service will be part of WHAT is produced.

equilibrium price: The price at which the quantity of a good demanded in a given time period equals the quantity supplied.

Market Clearing

An equilibrium doesn't imply that everyone is happy with the prevailing price or quantity. Notice in Figure 3.6, for example, that some students who want to buy Web-design assistance services don't get any. These would-be buyers are arrayed along the demand curve *below* the equilibrium. Because the price they're *willing*

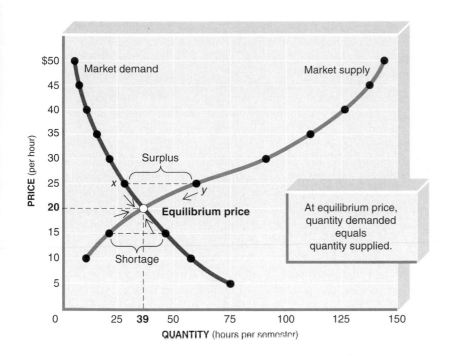

FIGURE 3.6
Equilibrium Price

Only at equilibrium is the quantity demanded equal to the quantity supplied. In this case, the equilibrium price is $20 per hour, and 39 hours is the equilibrium quantity. At higher prices, a market surplus exists—the quantity supplied exceeds the quantity demanded. At prices below equilibrium, a market shortage exists.

The intersection of the demand and supply curves in the graph represents equilibrium price and output in this market.

Price (per hour)	Quantity Supplied (hours per semester)		Quantity Demanded (hours per semester)
$50	148		5
45	140		8
40	130	market	11
35	114	surplus	16
30	90		22
25	62		30
20	39	equilibrium	39
15	20	market	47
10	10	shortage	57

to pay is less than the equilibrium price, they don't get any Web-design help. The market's FOR WHOM answer includes only those students willing and able to pay the equilibrium price.

Likewise, some would-be sellers in the market don't sell as much service as they might like. These people are arrayed along the supply curve *above* the equilibrium. Because they insist on being paid a price higher than the equilibrium price, they don't actually sell anything.

Although not everyone gets full satisfaction from the market equilibrium, that unique outcome is efficient. The equilibrium price and quantity reflect a compromise between buyers and sellers. No other compromise yields a quantity demanded that's exactly equal to the quantity supplied.

The Invisible Hand. The equilibrium price isn't determined by any single individual. Rather, it's determined by the collective behavior of many buyers and sellers, each acting out his or her own demand or supply schedule. It's this kind of impersonal price determination that gave rise to Adam Smith's characterization of the market mechanism as "the invisible hand." In attempting to explain how the **market mechanism** works, the famed eighteenth-century economist noted a certain feature of market

market mechanism: The use of market prices and sales to signal desired outputs (or resource allocations).

prices. The market behaves as if some unseen force (the invisible hand) were examining each individual's supply or demand schedule and then selecting a price that assured an equilibrium. In practice, the process of price determination isn't so mysterious: It's a simple process of trial and error.

Surplus and Shortage

price floor: Lower limit set for the price of a good.

To appreciate the power of the market mechanism, consider interference in its operation. Suppose, for example, that campus Webheads banded together and agreed to charge a minimum price of $25 per hour. By establishing a **price floor,** a minimum price for their services, the Webheads hope to increase their incomes. But they won't be fully satisfied. Figure 3.6 illustrates the consequences of this *dis*equilibrium pricing. At $25 per hour, campus Webheads would be offering more tutoring services (point *y*) than Tom, George, and Lisa were willing to buy (point *x*) at that price. A **market surplus** of Web services would exist in the sense that more tutoring was being offered for sale (supplied) than students cared to purchase at the available price.

market surplus: The amount by which the quantity supplied exceeds the quantity demanded at a given price; excess supply.

As Figure 3.6 indicates, at a price of $25 per hour, a market surplus of 32 hours per semester exists. Under these circumstances, campus Webheads would be spending many idle hours at their keyboards waiting for customers to appear. Their waiting will be in vain because the quantity of Web tutoring demanded will not increase until the price of tutoring falls. That is the clear message of the demand curve. As would-be tutors get this message, they'll reduce their prices. This is the response the market mechanism signals.

As sellers' asking prices decline, the quantity demanded will increase. This concept is illustrated in Figure 3.6 by the movement along the demand curve from point *x* to lower prices and greater quantity demanded. As we move down the market demand curve, the *desire* for Web-design help doesn't change, but the quantity people are *able and willing to buy* increases. When the price falls to $20 per hour, the quantity demanded will finally equal the quantity supplied. This is the *equilibrium* illustrated in Figure 3.6.

An Initial Shortage. A very different sequence of events would occur if a market shortage existed. Suppose someone were to spread the word that Web-tutoring services were available at only $15 per hour. Tom, George, and Lisa would be standing in line to get tutorial help, but campus Web designers wouldn't be willing to supply the quantity desired at that price. As Figure 3.6 confirms, at $15 per hour, the quantity demanded (47 hours per semester) would greatly exceed the quantity supplied (20 hours per semester). In this situation, we may speak of a **market shortage,** that is, an excess of quantity demanded over quantity supplied. At a price of $15 an hour, the shortage amounts to 27 hours of tutoring services.

market shortage: The amount by which the quantity demanded exceeds the quantity supplied at a given price; excess demand.

When a market shortage exists, not all consumer demands can be satisfied. Some people who are *willing* to buy Web help at the going price ($15) won't be able to do so. To assure themselves of sufficient help, Tom, George, Lisa, or some other consumer may offer to pay a *higher* price, thus initiating a move up the demand curve in Figure 3.6. The higher prices offered will in turn induce other enterprising Webheads to tutor more, thus ensuring an upward movement along the market supply curve. Thus, a higher price tends to evoke a greater quantity supplied, as reflected in the upward-sloping supply curve. Notice, again, that the *desire* to tutor Web design hasn't changed; only the quantity supplied has responded to a change in price.

Self-Adjusting Prices. What we observe, then, is that *whenever the market price is set above or below the equilibrium price, either a market surplus or a market shortage will emerge.* To overcome a surplus or shortage, buyers and sellers will change their behavior. Webheads will have to compete for customers by reducing prices when a market surplus exists. If a shortage exists, buyers will compete for service by offering to pay higher prices. Only at the *equilibrium* price will no further adjustments be required.

For Fans, What's 4 Nights for U2?

After an 80-hour ordeal—four nights stuffed in a car, three days breathing bus exhaust, scarfing Cokes and franks, running blocks for pit stops—the three University of Maryland seniors who camped out at RFK Stadium prevailed. They beat the scalpers to U2 concert tickets.

At 8 A.M. today they would be, if all went as planned, first in line at the RFK box office. By 9 A.M. the 52,000-seat stadium will sell out, predicted a Ticketmaster official.

"It's what you got to do to get good seats," said Crawford Conniff, 22, stretched out near the stadium among traffic island dandelions.

"We have unlimited time," said Mike Collins, 22. "If we had a job making 50 grand, we could pay $150 to scalpers."

Actually, $150 sounds cheap for the $28.50 face-value tickets. Today's ticket sale for the Aug. 15 concert, one of the summer's hottest, is likely to ignite an orgy of profiteering.

When the band played Los Angeles, scalpers scored up to $1,200 a ticket for prime seats. In Washington, as early as Tuesday, ticket brokers had stationed students, unemployed and even homeless people at ticket outlets to snap up hundreds of choice seats.

—Laura Blumenfeld

Source: *Washington Post*, April 25, 1992. © 1992 The Washington Post. Reprinted with permission. www.washingtonpost.com

Analysis: In equilibrium, everyone who is willing and able to pay the equilibrium price gets to see the show. If price is below equilibrium, the quantity demanded exceeds the quantity supplied, so only people willing and able to stand in line for tickets will get them initially.

Sometimes the market price is slow to adjust, and a disequilibrium persists. This is often the case with tickets to rock concerts, football games, and other one-time events. People initially adjust their behavior by standing in ticket lines for hours, hoping to buy a ticket at the below-equilibrium price (see News). The tickets are typically resold ("scalped"), however, at prices closer to equilibrium.

Business firms can discover equilibrium prices by trial and error. If they find that consumer purchases aren't keeping up with production, they may conclude that their price is above the equilibrium price. They'll have to get rid of their accumulated inventory. To do so they'll have to lower their price (by a Grand End-of-Year Sale, perhaps). In the happy situation where consumer purchases are outpacing production, a firm might conclude that its price was a trifle too low and give it a nudge upward. In any case, the equilibrium price can be established after a few trials in the marketplace.

No equilibrium price is permanent. The equilibrium price established in the Clearview College tutoring market, for example, was the unique outcome of specific demand and supply schedules. Those schedules themselves were based on our assumption of *ceteris paribus*. We assumed that the "taste" (desire) for Web-design assistance was given, as were consumers' incomes, the price and availability of other goods, and expectations. Any of these determinants of demand could change. When one does, the demand curve has to be redrawn. Such a shift of the demand curve will lead to a new equilibrium price and quantity. Indeed, ***the equilibrium price will change whenever the supply or demand curve shifts.***

Changes in Equilibrium

A Demand Shift. We can illustrate how equilibrium prices change by taking one last look at the Clearview College tutoring market. Our original supply and demand curves, together with the resulting equilibrium (point E_1), are depicted in Figure 3.7. Now suppose that all the professors at Clearview begin requiring class-specific Web pages from each student. The increased need (desire) for Web-design ability will affect market demand. Tom, George, and Lisa are suddenly willing to buy more Web tutoring

FIGURE 3.7
Changes in Equilibrium

If demand or supply change (shift), market equilibrium will change as well.

Demand shift. In (*a*), the rightward shift of the demand curve illustrates an increase in demand. When demand increases, the equilibrium price rises (from E_1 to E_2).

Supply shift. In (*b*), the leftward shift of the supply curve illustrates a decrease in supply. This raises the equilibrium price to E_3.

Demand and supply curves shift only when their underlying determinants change, that is, when *ceteris paribus* is violated.

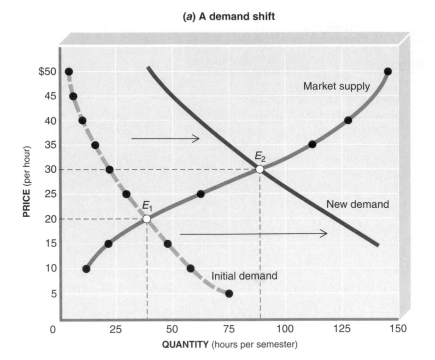

(a) A demand shift

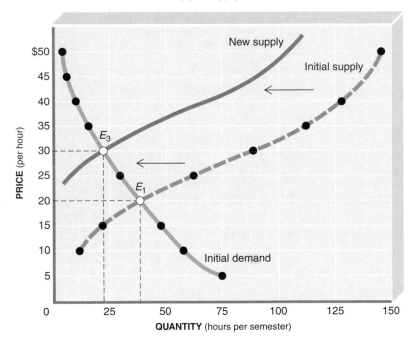

(b) A supply shift

at every price than they were before. That is, the *demand* for Web services has increased. We can represent this increased demand by a rightward *shift* of the market demand curve, as illustrated in Figure 3.7*a*.

Note that the new demand curve intersects the (unchanged) market supply curve at a new price (point E_2), the equilibrium price is now $30 per hour. This new equilibrium price will persist until either the demand curve or the supply curve shifts again.

A Supply Shift. Figure 3.7*b* illustrates a *supply* shift. The decrease (leftward shift) in supply might occur if some on-campus Webheads got sick. Or approaching exams might convince would-be tutors that they have no time to spare. ***Whenever supply decreases (shifts left), price tends to rise,*** as in Figure 3.7*b*.

The rock band U2 learned about changing equilibriums the hard way. As the NEWS on page 61 reported, ticket prices for the band's 1992 tour were below equilibrium, creating a *market shortage.* So U2 raised prices to as much as $52.50 a ticket for their 1997 tour—nearly double the 1992 price. By then, however, demand had shifted to the left, due to a lack of U2 hits and an increased number of competing concerts. By the time they got to their second city they were playing in stadiums with lots of empty seats. The apparent *market surplus* led critics to label the 1997 "Pop Mart" tour a disaster. For their 2001 "Elevation Tour," U2 offered "festival seating" for only $35.

Market outcomes shifted even more dramatically after the anthrax attacks on the U.S. mail in October 2001. Only one drug, Cipro, is approved to fight the deadly anthrax bacteria. When several people died from exposure to anthrax-laden mail, demand for Cipro soared (see NEWS below). This demand shift created an immediate market shortage.

The World View on the next page shows how rapid price adjustments can alleviate market shortages and surpluses. In this unusual case, a restaurant continuously adjusts its prices to ensure that everything on the menu is ordered.

MARKET OUTCOMES

Notice how the market mechanism resolves the basic economic questions of WHAT, HOW, and FOR WHOM.

The WHAT question refers to the amount of Web tutorial services to include in society's mix of output. The answer at Clearview College was 39 hours of tutoring per semester. This decision wasn't reached in a referendum, but instead in the market equilibrium (Figure 3.6). In the same way but on a larger scale, millions of consumers

WHAT

Demand for Cipro Rising

NYC Sees 62% Increase in Anti-Anthrax Prescriptions

Despite public health officials' admonitions against stockpiling drugs to protect against bioterrorism, new prescriptions for Cipro, the only drug approved to fight anthrax, in New York City have soared.

For the week ending Oct. 5, New York pharmacists filled 18,348 new prescriptions for the antibiotic, compared with just 11,313 for the same week in 2000, an increase of 62%, according to NDCHealth, a health-care information services company based in Atlanta.

Cipro, as well as a variety of other antibiotics, can prevent illness from anthrax exposure if taken before symptoms appear. Exposed individuals must take the drug for 60 days.

Still, Tommy Thompson, secretary of Health and Human Services, and other public health officials have urged Americans not to panic and hoard Cipro or other antibiotics. "You don't have to hoard antibiotics," Thompson said Friday at a briefing in which he announced a $643 million proposal to boost government stocks of antibiotics. "We're purchasing more."

Bayer, maker of Cipro, has said that it plans to reopen a German plant to meet increased demand for the drug.

—Rita Rubin

Source: *USA Today,* October 16, 2001. USA TODAY. Copyright 2001. Reprinted with permission.

Analysis: When a determinant of demand (e.g., tastes, expectations) changes, the demand curve shifts. When this happens, the equilibrium price will change.

Dining on the Downtick

Americans aren't the only consumers who fall for packaging. Since late January, Parisians (not to mention TV crews from around the world) have been drawn to 6 rue Feydeau to try La Connivence, a restaurant with a new gimmick. The name means "collusion," and yes, of course, La Connivence is a block away from the Bourse, the French stock exchange.

What's the gimmick? Just that the restaurant's prices fluctuate according to supply and demand. The more a dish is ordered, the higher its price. A dish that's ignored gets cheaper.

Customers tune in to the day's menu (couched in trading terms) on computer screens. Among a typical day's options: *forte baisse du haddock* ("precipitous drop in haddock"), *vif recul de la côte de boeuf* ("rapid decline in beef ribs"), *la brochette de lotte au plus bas* ("fish kabob hits bottom"). Then comes the major decision—whether to opt for the price that's listed when you order or to gamble that the price will have gone down by the time you finish your meal.

So far, only main dishes are open to speculation, but co-owners Pierre Guette, an ex-professor at a top French business school, and Jean-Paul Trastour, an ex-journalist at *Le Nouvel Observateur*, are adding wine to the risk list.

La Connivence is open for dinner, but the midday "session" (as the owners call it) is the one to catch. That's when the traders of Paris leave the floor to push their luck *à table.* But here, at least, the return on their $15 investment (the average price of a meal) is immediate—and usually good.

—Christina de Liagre

Source: *New York,* April 7, 1986. © 1986 K-III Magazine Corporation. All rights reserved. Reprinted with the permission of *New York* magazine. www.newyorkmag.com

Analysis: A market surplus signals that price is too high; a market shortage suggests that price is too low. This restaurant adjusts price until the quantity supplied equals the quantity demanded.

and a handful of auto producers decide to include 16 million or so cars and trucks in each year's mix of output. Auto prices and quantities adjust until consumers buy the same quantity that auto manufacturers produce.

HOW

The market mechanism also determines HOW goods are produced. Profit-seeking producers will strive to produce Web designs and automobiles in the most efficient way. They'll use market prices to decide not only WHAT to produce but also what resources to use in the production process. If new software simplifies Web design—and is priced low enough—Webheads will use it. Likewise, auto manufacturers will use robots rather than humans on the assembly line if robots reduce costs and increase profits.

FOR WHOM

Finally, the invisible hand of the market will determine who gets the goods produced. At Clearview College, who got Web tutoring? Only those students who were willing and able to pay $20 per hour for that service. FOR WHOM are all those automobiles produced each year? The answer is the same: those consumers who are willing and able to pay the market price for a new car.

Optimal, Not Perfect

Not everyone is happy with these answers, of course. Tom would like to pay only $10 an hour for a tutor. And some of the Clearview students don't have enough income to buy any tutoring. They think it's unfair that they have to design their own Web pages while richer students can have someone else do their design work for them. Students who can't afford cars are even less happy with the market's answer to the FOR WHOM question.

Although the outcomes of the marketplace aren't perfect, they're often optimal. Optimal outcomes are the best possible *given* our incomes and scarce resources. In other words, we expect the choices made in the marketplace to be the best possible choices for each participant. Why do we draw such a conclusion? Because Tom and George and everybody in our little Clearview College drama had (and continue to have) absolute freedom to make their own purchase and consumption decisions. And also because we assume that sooner or later they'll make the choices they find most satisfying. The results are *optimal* in the sense that everyone has done as well as she or he could, given their income and talents.

THE ECONOMY TOMORROW

Electric Shock: Energy-Price Spikes

The notion that markets generate optimal outcomes sounded absurd to Californians in 2000–01. As we noted earlier, wholesale energy prices jumped by over 1,000 percent in a single year. As Californians saw it, the only thing that protected them from these skyrocketing prices was government regulation. In 1996, the California legislature had set a ceiling on the *retail* price of electricity. The prices paid by consumers could *not* rise until at least 2002, no matter what happened to wholesale prices. As far as California's consumers were concerned, government intervention was their bulwark against the "price-gouging profiteers" that ruled the marketplace. Most of the state's residents welcomed Governor Gray Davis's January 2001 promises to keep cheap electricity flowing to the state's homes and businesses.

Equilibrium Pricing

As we've seen in this chapter, market prices aren't set by price-gouging profiteers. Sure, huge corporations, especially monopolies, can have a big influence on the market price of a good. But the equilibrium price must still reflect *both* sides of the market, that is, supply *and* demand. Furthermore, ***an increase in the equilibrium price can result from an increase (rightward shift) in demand or a decrease (leftward shift) of supply.*** Both shifts occurred in California.

Increased Demand

California's demand for electricity increases as its population grows and its economy expands. Abnormally cold winters or hot summers also increase the demand for electricity-driven heat and air conditioning. Between 1996 and 2001, the California economy grew by 29 percent. The winter of 2001 was colder than normal and the summer was a bit hotter than average. All these factors combined to shift the state's demand for electricity rightward as in Figure 3.8.

Decreased Supply

No new power plants or hydroelectric plants were built in California during the 1990s. The state managed to keep up with increased energy demand only by importing electricity from other states. With high-speed transmission lines, electricity can be shipped to California residents from power plants in Oregon, Idaho, and elsewhere. In 2001, however, several determinants of supply changed in adverse ways. Higher natural gas prices increased the cost of producing electricity in all states. Maintenance problems caused recurring shutdowns of California power plants. Low snowpacks reduced the power capacity of hydroelectric dams throughout the West. Market supply shifted to the left.

Disequilibrium Pricing

The consequences of a leftward supply shift and a rightward demand shift are evident in Figure 3.8; the equilibrium price of electricity skyrocketed. Residents of California didn't have to pay this higher price, however. Remember that the California legislature had put a **price ceiling** on retail electricity prices. By law, the retail price of electricity was stuck at 10 cents per kilowatt-hour, far below the new equilibrium price.

price ceiling: Upper limit imposed on the price of a good.

At first, Californians rejoiced at the low, government-set price. Then they learned the consequences of *dis*equilibrium pricing. At the ceiling price of 10 cents per kilowatt-hour, the quantity of electricity demanded (q_d in Figure 3.8) exceeded that quantity supplied (q_s). It was a classic case of *market shortage.* Because of the shortage, not everyone who was willing and able to pay the ceiling price (10 cents) could actually get the electricity they demanded. That's when the state had to resort to rolling blackouts. The blackouts left everyone with less electricity than they demanded. That experience helped convince Californians that price ceilings weren't as good as they appeared.

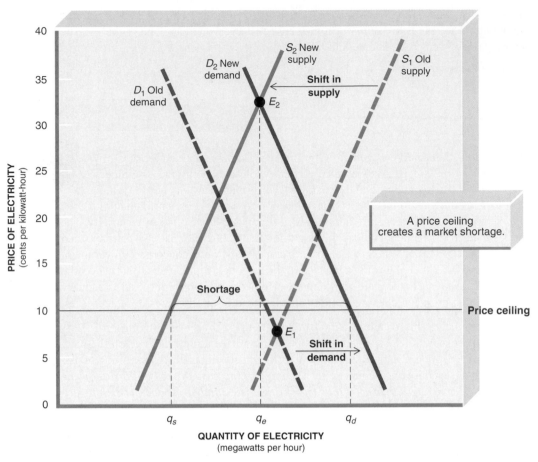

FIGURE 3.8
Price Ceilings Create Shortages

In 1996, the state of California set a price ceiling of 10 cents per kilowatt-hour. Initially, this price was above the market equilibrium (E_1) and had no impact. By 2001, however, demand had increased (to D_2) and supply had decreased (to S_2). At the ceiling price the quantity demanded (q_d) exceeded the quantity supplied (q_s), causing a market shortage and rolling blackouts. At the higher equilibrium (E_2) price there are no blackouts. Consumers reduce their energy consumption (to q_e from q_d) and power companies increase electricity deliveries (to q_e from q_s).

In fact, *price ceilings have three predictable effects; they*

- *Increase the quantity demanded.*
- *Decrease the quantity supplied.*
- *Create a market shortage.*

Given the choice between no electricity and high-priced electricity, state residents changed their view of market pricing. They didn't welcome higher prices but recognized that *higher prices*

- *Reduce quantity demanded.*
- *Increase quantity supplied.*
- *Alleviate market shortages.*

At the low, state-set price, consumers had no incentive to set air-conditioner thermostats higher, to set heater thermostats lower, or even turn off the lights and computer when they went out. At higher market prices, they'd think about those energy savings more often and reduce the quantity demanded. At the equilibrium price of E_2 in Figure 3.8, consumers are demanding (and using) less electricity than at q_d. On

Federal Price Limits Backfire

Some Generators Withhold Power Rather Than Abide by Rate Caps

Officials in California and Nevada, after months of lobbying for federal regulators to cap Western power prices, warned yesterday that the newly imposed limits have had the unintended consequence of increasing a threat of blackouts in the two states.

The warnings were issued as California came within minutes of rolling blackouts yesterday afternoon, and one day after the first-ever rolling blackouts in Las Vegas forced energy-hungry casinos to shut off fountains and reduce air conditioning. . . .

The crux of the problem is that price limits kick in during shortages, yet power companies say these caps force them to sell power at below-market rates during periods of high demand.

Some companies have responded by holding back power rather than face the expense of shipping electricity from state to state. Each mile that electricity must be transmitted adds to the overall cost.

"No one's going to pay for transmission if the cost is near the caps," said Gary Ackerman, executive director of the Western Power Trading Forum, an energy-industry association in Menlo Park.

Ackerman said several companies in his organization decided that there was no economic advantage to offering power in regional markets when price controls are in effect.

"This means individual regions like California or Las Vegas could end up not having enough," Ackerman said. "It increases the threat of blackouts."

—David Lazarus

Source: *San Francisco Chronicle*, July 4, 2001. Copyright 2001 by the San Francisco Chronicle. Reprinted with permission. www.sfgate.com/news

Analysis: Price ceilings diminish the profitability of producing a good and so reduce the quantity supplied to the market. This may worsen market shortages.

the supply side, higher market prices encourage both in-state and out-of-state power providers to increase power-generating capacity and even sell it to California utilities. Once California residents recognized the virtue of equilibrium pricing, they saw that government intervention (price ceilings) might have been as much to blame as "power-producing profiteers" for the state's blackouts. In April 2001, the 1996 price ceiling was raised closer to equilibrium pricing with a 26 percent increase in retail electricity prices.

Other states have been affected by California's electricity crisis. The continuing demand of California residents for out-of-state power (a substitute good) has increased demand and raised electricity prices in Oregon, Nevada, Idaho, and other states in the interconnected Western power grid. As their own electricity prices rise, consumers in those states asked the government to intervene. In 2001, they convinced the federal government (the Federal Energy Regulatory Commission) to impose price ceilings across the Western grid. As the accompanying News reports, however, those price ceilings backfired. Power providers decided it made less sense to supply electricity to the price-controlled states, much less to add to power capacity; the quantity of electricity supplied declined. Blackouts soon hit other Western states.

As battles over access to energy sources continue, the patience of the public will be tested. Consumers want cheap electricity and expect elected officials to supply it. But politicians don't produce energy; private companies do. Cheap prices imposed by government not only encourage more consumption but discourage production. Moreover, power plants can't be built overnight, and new energy sources won't appear instantly. It takes *time* for market supply and demand to adjust. The greatest risk for the economy tomorrow is that political impatience today may slow the market adjustments needed to bring energy markets into equilibrium.

Looming Battles of the Power Grid

For another view of energy policy visit Public Citizen at www.citizen.org.

SUMMARY

- Individual consumers, business firms, government agencies, and foreigners participate in the marketplace by offering to buy or sell goods and services, or factors of production. Participation is motivated by the desire to maximize utility (consumers), profits (business firms), or the general welfare (government agencies) from the limited resources each participant has.

- All market transactions involve the exchange of either factors of production or finished products. Although the actual exchanges can occur anywhere, they take place in product markets or factor markets, depending on what is being exchanged.

- People willing and able to buy a particular good at some price are part of the market demand for that product. All those willing and able to sell that good at some price are part of the market supply. Total market demand or supply is the sum of individual demands or supplies.

- Supply and demand curves illustrate how the quantity demanded or supplied changes in response to a change in the price of that good, if nothing else changes (*ceteris paribus*). Demand curves slope downward; supply curves slope upward.

- Determinants of market demand include the number of potential buyers and their respective tastes (desires), incomes, other goods, and expectations. If any of these determinants change, the demand curve shifts. Movements along a demand curve are induced only by a change in the price of that good.

- Determinants of market supply include factor costs, technology, profitability of other goods, expectations, tax rates, and number of sellers. Supply shifts when these underlying determinants change.

- The quantity of goods or resources actually exchanged in each market depends on the behavior of all buyers and sellers, as summarized in market supply and demand curves. At the point where the two curves intersect, an equilibrium price—the price at which the quantity demanded equals the quantity supplied—is established.

- A distinctive feature of the equilibrium price and quantity is that it's the only price-quantity combination acceptable to buyers and sellers alike. At higher prices, sellers supply more than buyers are willing to purchase (a market surplus); at lower prices, the amount demanded exceeds the quantity supplied (a market shortage). Only the equilibrium price clears the market.

- Price ceilings are disequilibrium prices imposed on the marketplace. Such price controls create an imbalance between quantities demanded and supplied, resulting in market shortages.

Key Terms

factor market	law of demand	law of supply
product market	substitute goods	equilibrium price
supply	complementary goods	market mechanism
demand	*ceteris paribus*	price floor
opportunity cost	shift in demand	market surplus
demand schedule	market demand	market shortage
demand curve	market supply	price ceiling

Questions for Discussion

1. In our story of Tom, the student confronted with a Web-design assignment, we emphasized the great urgency of his desire for Web tutoring. Many people would say that Tom had an "absolute need" for Web help and therefore was ready to "pay anything" to get it. If this were true, what shape would his demand curve have? Why isn't this realistic?

2. With respect to the demand for college enrollment, which of the following would cause (1) a movement along the demand curve or (2) a shift of the demand curve?
    a. An increase in incomes.
    b. Lower tuition.
    c. More student loans.
    d. An increase in textbook prices.

3. Illustrate the market situation for the U2 concert (see page 61). Why didn't the concert promoters set an equilibrium price?

4. Which determinants of pizza demand change when the White House is in crisis (page 52)?

5. Can you explain the practice of scalping tickets for major sporting events in terms of market shortages? How else might tickets be distributed?

6. How else besides higher prices could the 2001 market shortage in California's electricity market have been alleviated? Consider both demand- and supply-side options.

7. What would happen in the apple market if the government set a *minimum* price of $2.00 per apple? What might motivate such a policy?

8. The World View on page 64 describes the use of prices to achieve an equilibrium in the kitchen. What happens to the food at more traditional restaurants?

9. Is there a shortage of on-campus parking at your school? How might the shortage be resolved?

10. Do Internet price information services tend to raise or lower the price consumers pay for a product?

| PROBLEMS | The Student Problem Set at the back of this book contains numerical and graphing problems for this chapter. |
| WEB ACTIVITIES | to accompany this chapter can be found on the Online Learning Center: **http://www.mhhe.com/economics/schiller10** |

The Public Sector

The market has a keen ear for private wants, but a deaf ear for public needs.
—Robert Heilbroner

Markets do work: The interaction of supply and demand in product markets *does* generate goods and services. Likewise, the interaction of supply and demand in labor markets *does* yield jobs, wages, and a distribution of income. As we've observed, the market is capable of determining WHAT goods to produce, HOW, and FOR WHOM.
But are the market's answers good enough? Is the mix of output produced by unregulated markets the best possible mix? Will producers choose the production process that strikes a desirable balance between production and the environment? Will the market-generated distribution of income be fair enough? Will there be enough jobs for everyone who wants one?

In reality, markets don't always give us the best-possible outcomes. Markets dominated by a few powerful corporations may charge excessive prices, limit output, provide poor service, or even retard technological advance. In the quest for profits, producers may sacrifice the environment for cost savings. In unfettered markets, some people may not get life-saving health care, basic education, or even adequate nutrition. When markets generate such outcomes, government intervention may be needed to ensure better answers to the WHAT, HOW, and FOR WHOM questions.

This chapter identifies the circumstances under which government intervention is desirable. To this end, we answer the following questions:

- **Under what circumstances do markets fail?**
- **How can government intervention help?**
- **How much government intervention is desirable?**

As we'll see, there's substantial agreement about how and when markets fail to give us the best WHAT, HOW, and FOR WHOM answers. But there's much less agreement about whether government intervention improves the situation. Indeed, an overwhelming majority of Americans are ambivalent about government intervention. They want the government to "fix" the mix of output, protect the environment, and ensure an adequate level of income for everyone. But voters are equally quick to blame government meddling for many of our economic woes.

MARKET FAILURE

We can visualize the potential for government intervention by focusing on the WHAT question. Our goal here is to produce the best-possible mix of output with existing resources. We illustrated this goal earlier with production possibilities curves. Figure 4.1 assumes that of all the possible combinations of output we

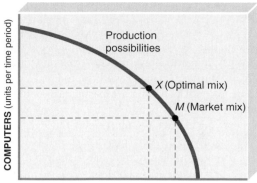

ALL OTHER GOODS (units per time period)

FIGURE 4.1
Market Failure

We can produce any mix of output on the production possibilities curve. Our goal is to produce the optimal (best-possible) mix of output, as represented by point *X*. Market forces, however, might produce another combination, like point *M*. In that case, the market fails—it produces a suboptimal mix of output.

could produce, the unique combination at point *X* represents the most desirable one. In other words, it's the **optimal mix of output,** the one that maximizes our collective social utility. We haven't yet figured out how to pinpoint that optimal mix; we're simply using the arbitrary point *X* in Figure 4.1 to represent that best-possible outcome.

Ideally, the **market mechanism** would lead us to point *X*. Price signals in the marketplace are supposed to move factors of production from one industry to another in response to consumer demands. If we demand more computers—offer to buy more at a given price—more resources (labor) will be allocated to computer manufacturing. Similarly, a fall in demand will encourage producers to stop making computers and offer their services in another industry. *Changes in market prices direct resources from one industry to another,* moving us along the perimeter of the production possibilities curve.

Where will the market mechanism take us? Will it move resources around until we end up at the optimal point *X*? Or will it leave us at another point on the production possibilities curve, with a *sub*optimal mix of output? (If point *X* is the *optimal,* or best-possible, mix, all other output mixes must be *sub*optimal.)

We use the term **market failure** to refer to situations where the market generates less than perfect (suboptimal) outcomes. If the invisible hand of the marketplace produces a mix of output that's different from the one society most desires, then it has failed. *Market failure implies that the forces of supply and demand haven't led us to the best point on the production possibilities curve.* Such a failure is illustrated by point *M* in Figure 4.1. Point *M* is assumed to be the mix of output generated by market forces. Notice that the market mix (*M*) doesn't represent the optimal mix, which is assumed to be at point *X*. The market in this case *fails;* we get the wrong answer to the WHAT question.

Market failure opens the door for government intervention. If the market can't do the job, we need some form of *nonmarket* force to get the right answers. In terms of Figure 4.1, we need something to change the mix of output—to move us from point *M* (the market mix of output) to point *X* (the optimal mix of output). Accordingly, *market failure establishes a basis for government intervention.* We look to the government to push market outcomes closer to the ideal.

Causes of Market Failure. Because market failure is the justification for government intervention, we need to know how and when market failure occurs. *The four specific sources of market failure are*

- *Public goods*
- *Externalities*
- *Market power*
- *Equity*

optimal mix of output: The most desirable combination of output attainable with existing resources, technology, and social values.

market mechanism: The use of market prices and sales to signal desired outputs (or resource allocations).

market failure: An imperfection in the market mechanism that prevents optimal outcomes.

We will first examine the nature of these problems, then see why government intervention is called for in each case.

Public Goods

The market mechanism has the unique capability to signal consumer demands for various goods and services. By offering to pay higher or lower prices for some goods, we express our preferences about WHAT to produce. However, this mode of communication works efficiently only if the benefits of consuming a particular good are available only to the individuals who purchase that product.

Consider doughnuts, for example. When you eat a doughnut, you alone get the satisfaction from its sweet, greasy taste—that is, you derive a private benefit. No one else benefits from your consumption of a doughnut: The doughnut you purchase in the market is yours alone to consume; it's a **private good.** Accordingly, your decision to purchase the doughnut will be determined only by your anticipated satisfaction, your income, and your opportunity costs.

No Exclusion. Most of the goods and services produced in the public sector are different from doughnuts—and not just because doughnuts look, taste, and smell different from "star wars" missile shields. When you buy a doughnut, you exclude others from consumption of that product. If Dunkin' Donuts sells you a particular pastry, it can't supply the same pastry to someone else. If you devour it, no one else can. In this sense, the transaction and product are completely private.

The same exclusiveness is not characteristic of national defense. If you buy a missile defense system to thwart enemy attacks, there's no way you can exclude your neighbors from the protection your system provides. Either the missile shield deters would-be attackers or it doesn't. In the former case, both you and your neighbors survive happily ever after; in the latter case, we're all blown away together. In that sense, you and your neighbors consume the benefits of a missile shield *jointly*. National defense isn't a divisible service. There's no such thing as exclusive consumption here. The consumption of nuclear defenses is a communal feat, no matter who pays for them. Accordingly, national defense is regarded as a **public good** in the sense that *consumption of a public good by one person doesn't preclude consumption of the same good by another person.* By contrast, a doughnut is a private good because if I eat it, no one else can consume it.

The Free-Rider Dilemma. The communal nature of public goods creates a dilemma. If you and I will *both* benefit from nuclear defenses, which one of us should buy the missile shield? I'd prefer that *you* buy it, thereby giving me protection at no direct cost. Hence, I may profess no desire for a missile shield, secretly hoping to take a **free ride** on your market purchase. Unfortunately, you too have an incentive to conceal your desire for national defenses. As a consequence, neither one of us may step forward to demand a missile shield in the marketplace. We'll both end up defenseless.

Flood control is also a public good. No one in the valley wants to be flooded out. But each landowner knows that a flood-control dam will protect *all* the landowners, regardless of who pays. Either the entire valley is protected or no one is. Accordingly, individual farmers and landowners may say they don't *want* a dam and aren't willing to *pay* for it. Everyone is waiting and hoping that someone else will pay for flood control. In other words, everyone wants a *free ride*. Thus, if we leave it to market forces, no one will *demand* flood control and all the property in the valley will be washed away.

The difference between public goods and private goods rests on *technical considerations* not political philosophy. The central question is whether we have the technical capability to exclude nonpayers. In the case of national defense or flood control, we simply don't have that capability. Even city streets have the characteristics of public goods. Although theoretically we could restrict the use of streets to those who paid to use them, a tollgate on every corner would be exceedingly expensive and impractical. Here again, joint or public consumption appears to be the only feasible alternative.

---

private good: A good or service whose consumption by one person excludes consumption by others.

public good: A good or service whose consumption by one person does not exclude consumption by others.

free rider: An individual who reaps direct benefits from someone else's purchase (consumption) of a public good.

IN THE NEWS

Napster Gets Napped

Shawn Fanning had a brilliant idea for getting more music: download it from friends' computers to the Internet. So he wrote software in 1999 that enabled online file-sharing of audio files. This peer-to-peer (P2P) online distribution system became an overnight sensation: in 2000–01 nearly 60 million consumers were using Napster's software to acquire recorded music.

At first blush, Napster's service looked like a classic "public good." The service was free, and one person's consumption did not impede another person from consuming the same service. Moreover, the distribution system was configured in such a way that nonpayers could not be excluded from the service.

The definition of "*public good*" relies, however, on whether nonpayers *can* be excluded, not whether they *are* excluded.

In other words, technology is critical in classifying goods as "public" or "private." In Napster's case, encryption technology that could exclude nonpayers was available, but the company had *chosen* not to use it. After being sued by major recording companies for copyright infringement, Napster changed its tune. In July 2001, it shut down its free download service. Two years later it re-opened with a *fee-based* service that could exclude nonpayers. Although free downloads are still available from offshore companies (e.g., Kazaa), fee-based services have sprung up all over (e.g., Apple's iTunes Music Store, Wal-Mart). For most consumers, music downloads are now a private good.

Source: "Napster is Back!" *NewsFlash*, October 2003.

Analysis: A product is a "public good" only if nonpayers *cannot* be excluded from its consumption. Napster had the technical ability to exclude nonpayers but initially chose not to do so. Fee-based music downloads are a private good.

As the accompanying News on Napster emphasizes, the technical capability to exclude nonpayers is the key factor in identifying "public goods."

To the list of public goods we could add snow removal, the administration of justice (including prisons), the regulation of commerce, the conduct of foreign relations, airport security, and even Fourth of July fireworks. These services—which cost tens of *billions* of dollars and employ thousands of workers—provide benefits to everyone, no matter who pays for them. In each instance it's technically impossible or prohibitively expensive to exclude nonpayers from the services provided.

Underproduction of Public Goods. The free riders associated with public goods upset the customary practice of paying for what you get. If I can get all the national defense, flood control, and laws I want without paying for them, I'm not about to complain. I'm perfectly happy to let you pay for the services while we all consume them. Of course, you may feel the same way. Why should you pay for these services if you can consume just as much of them when your neighbors foot the whole bill? It might seem selfish not to pay your share of the cost of providing public goods. But you'd be better off in a material sense if you spent your income on doughnuts, letting others pick up the tab for public services.

Because the familiar link between paying and consuming is broken, public goods can't be peddled in the supermarket. People are reluctant to buy what they can get free, a perfectly rational response for consumers who have limited incomes to spend. Hence, ***if public goods were marketed like private goods, everyone would wait for someone else to pay.*** The end result might be a total lack of public services. This is the kind of dilemma Robert Heilbroner had in mind when he spoke of the market's "deaf ear" (see quote at the beginning of this chapter).

The production possibilities curve in Figure 4.2 illustrates the dilemma created by public goods. Suppose that point *A* represents the optimal mix of private and public goods. It's the mix of goods and services we'd select if everyone's preferences were known and reflected in production decisions. The market mechanism won't lead us to point *A*, however, because the *demand* for public goods will be hidden. If we rely on

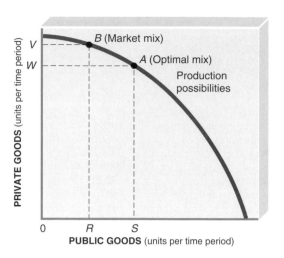

the market, nearly everyone will withhold demand for public goods, waiting for a free ride to point *A*. As a result, we'll get a smaller quantity of public goods than we really want. The market mechanism will leave us at a mix of output like that at point *B*, with few, if any, public goods. Since point *A* is assumed to be optimal, point *B* must be *suboptimal* (inferior to point *A*). The market fails: We can't rely on the market mechanism to allocate enough resources to the production of public goods, no matter how much they might be desired.

Note that we're using the term "public good" in a way different from how most people use it. To most people, "public good" refers to any good or service the government produces. In economics, however, the meaning is much more restrictive. The term "public good" refers only to those nonexcludable goods and services that must be consumed jointly, both by those who pay for them and by those who don't. Public goods can be produced by either the government or the private sector. Private goods can be produced in either sector as well. The problem is that ***the market tends to underproduce public goods and overproduce private goods.*** If we want more public goods, we need a *nonmarket* force—government intervention—to get them. The government will have to force people to pay taxes, then use the tax revenues to pay for the production of national defense, flood control, snow removal, and other public goods.

Externalities

The free-rider problem associated with public goods is one justification for government intervention. It's not the only justification, however. Further grounds for intervention arise from the tendency of costs or benefits of some market activities to "spill over" onto third parties.

Your demand for a good reflects the amount of satisfaction you expect from its consumption. The price you're willing to pay acts as a market signal to producers of your preferences. Often, however, your consumption may affect others. The purchase of cigarettes, for example, expresses a smoker's demand for that good. But others may suffer from that consumption. In this case, smoke literally spills over onto other consumers, causing them discomfort and possibly even ill health (see News on the next page). Yet their loss isn't reflected in the market: The harm caused to nonsmokers is *external* to the market price of cigarettes.

The term **externalities** refers to all costs or benefits of a market activity borne by a third party, that is, by someone other than the immediate producer or consumer. ***Whenever externalities are present, market prices aren't a valid measure of a good's value to society.*** As a consequence, the market will fail to produce the right mix of output. Specifically, ***the market will underproduce goods that yield external benefits and overproduce those which generate external costs.***

externalities: Costs (or benefits) of a market activity borne by a third party; the difference between the social and private costs (benefits) of a market activity.

Secondhand Smoke Poses Heart Attack Risk, CDC Warns

For the first time, the Centers for Disease Control and Prevention is warning people at risk of heart disease to avoid all buildings and gathering places that allow indoor smoking.

The CDC disclosed its new advisory in a commentary to a study published in the British Medical Journal yesterday, saying doctors need to warn people with heart problems that secondhand smoke can significantly increase their risk of a heart attack. The agency said that as little as 30 minutes' exposure can have a serious and even lethal effect.

The commentary accompanied a study showing that the number of heart attacks in Helena, Mont, decreased substantially after the city banned indoor smoking, then rose quickly to its former level after the law was struck down in court. . . .

Pechacek said the new study strengthens the growing body of research pointing to potentially fast and acute reactions to secondhand smoke, in addition to the long-term damage done to nonsmokers who live with smokers. The CDC has estimated that secondhand smoke causes 35,000 heart disease deaths a year in the United States, but Pechacek said that estimate is likely to be revised upward.

—Marc Kaufman

Source: *Washington Post,* April 23, 2004. © 2004 The Washington Post. Reprinted with permission.

Analysis: The health risks imposed on nonsmokers via "passive smoke" represent external costs. The market price of cigarettes doesn't reflect these costs borne by third parties.

External Costs. Figure 4.3 shows how external costs cause the market to overproduce cigarettes. The market demand curve includes only the wishes of smokers, that is, people who are willing and able to purchase cigarettes. The forces of market demand and supply result in a market equilibrium at E_M in which q_M cigarettes are produced and consumed. The market price P_M reflects the value of cigarettes to smokers.

The well-being of *non*smokers isn't reflected in the market equilibrium at E_M. To take the *nonsmoker's* interests into account, we must subtract the external costs

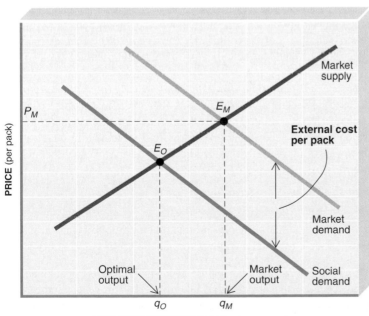

QUANTITY OF CIGARETTES (packs per year)

FIGURE 4.3
Externalities

The market responds to consumer demands, not externalities. Smokers demand q_M cigarettes. But external costs on nonsmokers imply that the *social* demand for cigarettes is less than (below) *market* demand. The socially optimal level of output is q_O, less than the market output q_M.

imposed on *them* from the value that *smokers* put on cigarettes. In general,

Social demand = market demand + externalities

In this case, the externality is a *cost,* so we must *subtract* the external cost from market demand to get a full accounting of social demand. The "social demand" curve in Figure 4.3 reflects this computation. To find this curve, we subtract the amount of external cost from every price on the market demand curve. What the *social* demand curve tells us is how much society would be willing and able to pay for cigarettes if the preferences of both smokers and nonsmokers were taken into account.

The social demand curve in Figure 4.3 creates a new equilibrium at q_O. This is the *optimal* quantity of cigarettes to produce (and consume). Yet the market alone would produce more than that (q_M). Government intervention may be needed to move the mix of output closer to society's optimal point.

The externalities associated with cigarette consumption have prompted many forms of government intervention, including mandatory health warnings on cigarette packaging, bans on advertising, and restrictions on locales where people may smoke. Courts have even determined that child custody decisions may be influenced by the smoking habits of the divorcing parents. All these interventions restrict the ability of individuals to maximize their personal utility in the marketplace. They're motivated by the recognition that the market mechanism responds only to the market demands of smokers and is unable to respond to nonmarketed externalities.

Externalities also exist in production. A power plant that burns high-sulfur coal damages the surrounding environment. Yet the damage inflicted on neighboring people, vegetation, and buildings is external to the cost calculations of the firm. Because the cost of such pollution is not reflected in the price of electricity, the firm will tend to produce more electricity (and pollution) than is socially desirable. To reduce this imbalance, the government has to step in and change market outcomes.

External Benefits. Externalities can also be beneficial. A product may generate external *benefits* rather than external *costs.* Your college is an example. The students who attend your school benefit directly from the education they receive. That's why they (and you) are willing to *pay* for tuition, books, and other services. The students in attendance aren't the only beneficiaries of this educational service, however. The research that a university conducts may yield benefits for a much broader community. The values and knowledge students acquire may also be shared with family, friends, and co-workers. These benefits would all be *external* to the market transaction between a paying student and the school. Positive externalities also arise from immunizations against infectious diseases.

If a product yields external benefits, the social demand is greater than the market demand. In this case, the social value of the good *exceeds* the market price (by the amount of external benefit). Accordingly, society wants *more* of the product than the market mechanism alone will produce at any given price. To get that additional output, the government may have to intervene with subsidies or other policies. We conclude then that **the market fails by**

- *Overproducing goods that have external costs.*
- *Underproducing goods that have external benefits.*

If externalities are present, the market won't produce the optimal mix of output. To get that optimal mix, we need government intervention.

Market Power

In the case of both public goods and externalities, the market fails to achieve the optimal mix of output because the price signal is flawed. The price consumers are willing and able to pay for a specific good doesn't reflect all the benefits or cost of producing that good.

Check out the pollution problems in your neighborhood at www.epa.gov/epahome/commsearch.htm.

The market may fail, however, even when the price signals are accurate. The *response* to price signals, rather than the signals themselves, may be flawed.

Restricted Supply. Market power is often the cause of a flawed response. Suppose there were only one airline company in the world. This single seller of airline travel would be a **monopoly**—that is, the only producer in that industry. As a monopolist, the airline could charge extremely high prices without worrying that travelers would flock to a competing airline. At the same time, the high prices paid by consumers would express the importance of that service to society. Ideally, such prices would act as a signal to producers to build and fly more planes—to change the mix of output. But a monopolist doesn't have to cater to every consumer's whim. It can limit airline travel and obstruct our efforts to achieve an optimal mix of output.

Monopoly is the most severe form of **market power.** More generally, market power refers to any situation in which a single producer or consumer has the ability to alter the market price of a specific product. If the publisher (McGraw-Hill) charges a high price for this book, you'll have to pay the tab. McGraw-Hill has market power because there are relatively few economics textbooks and your professor has required you to use this one. You don't have power in the textbook market because your decision to buy or not won't alter the market price of this text. You're only one of the million students who are taking an introductory economics course this year.

The market power McGraw-Hill possesses is derived from the copyright on this text. No matter how profitable textbook sales might be, no one else is permitted to produce or sell this particular book. Patents are another common source of market power because they also preclude others from making or selling a specific product. Market power may also result from control of resources, restrictive production agreements, or efficiencies of large-scale production.

Whatever the source of market power, the direct consequence is that one or more producers attain discretionary power over the market's response to price signals. They may use that discretion to enrich themselves rather than to move the economy toward the optimal mix of output. In this case, the market will again fail to deliver the most desired goods and services.

The mandate for government intervention in this case is to prevent or dismantle concentrations of market power. That's the basic purpose of **antitrust** policy. Another option is to *regulate* market behavior. This was one of the goals of the antitrust case against Microsoft. The government was less interested in breaking Microsoft's near monopoly on operating systems than in changing the way Microsoft behaved.

In some cases, it may be economically efficient to have one large firm supply an entire market. Such a situation arises in **natural monopoly,** where a single firm can achieve economies of scale over the entire range of market output. Utility companies, local telephone service, subway systems, and cable all exhibit such scale (size) efficiencies. In these cases, a monopoly *structure* may be economically desirable. The government may have to regulate the *behavior* of a natural monopoly, however, to ensure that consumers get the benefits of that greater efficiency.

Public goods, externalities, and market power all cause resource misallocations. Where these phenomena exist, the market mechanism will fail to produce the optimal mix of output in the best-possible way.

Beyond the questions of WHAT and HOW to produce, we're also concerned about FOR WHOM output is produced. The market answers this question by distributing a larger share of total output to those with the most income. Although this result may be efficient, it's not necessarily equitable. As we saw in Chapter 2, the market mechanism may enrich some people while leaving others to seek shelter in abandoned cars. If such outcomes violate our vision of equity, we may want the government to change the market-generated distribution of income.

monopoly: A firm that produces the entire market supply of a particular good or service.

market power: The ability to alter the market price of a good or a service.

antitrust: Government intervention to alter market structure or prevent abuse of market power.

natural monopoly: An industry in which one firm can achieve economies of scale over the entire range of market supply.

Inequity

Taxes and Transfers. The tax-and-transfer system is the principal mechanism for redistributing incomes. The idea here is to take some of the income away from those who have "too much" and give it to those whom the market has left with "too little." Taxes are levied to take back some of the income received from the market. Those tax revenues are then redistributed via transfer payments to those deemed needy, such as the poor, the aged, the unemployed. **Transfer payments** are income payments for which no goods or services are exchanged. They're used to bolster the incomes of those for whom the market itself provides too little.

> **transfer payments:** Payments to individuals for which no current goods or services are exchanged, like Social Security, welfare, and unemployment benefits.

Merit Goods. Often, our vision of what is "too little" is defined in terms of specific goods and services. There is a widespread consensus in the United States that everyone is entitled to some minimum levels of shelter, food, and health care. These are regarded as **merit goods,** in the same sense that everyone merits at least some minimum provision of such goods. When the market does not distribute that minimum provision, the government is called on to fill in the gaps. In this case, the income transfers take the form of *in-kind* transfers (e.g., Food Stamps, housing vouchers, Medicaid) rather than *cash* transfers (e.g., welfare checks, Social Security benefits).

> **merit good:** A food or service society deems everyone is entitled to some minimal quantity of.

Some people argue that we don't need the government to help the poor—that private charity alone will suffice. Unfortunately, private charity alone has never been adequate. One reason private charity doesn't suffice is the "free-rider" problem. If I contribute heavily to the poor, you benefit from safer streets (fewer muggers), a better environment (fewer slums and homeless people), and a clearer conscience (knowing fewer people are starving). In this sense, the relief of misery is a *public* good. Were I the only taxpayer to benefit substantially from the reduction of poverty, then charity would be a private affair. As long as income support substantially benefits the public at large, then income redistribution is a *public* good, for which public funding is appropriate. This is the *economic* rationale for public income-redistribution activities. To this rationale one can add such moral arguments as seem appropriate.

Macro Instability

The micro failures of the marketplace imply that we're at the wrong point on the production possibilities curve or inequitably distributing the output produced. There's another basic question we've swept under the rug, however. How do we get to the production possibilities curve in the first place? To reach the curve, we must utilize all available resources and technology. Can we be confident that the invisible hand of the marketplace will use all available resources? Or will some people face **unemployment**—that is, be willing to work but unable to find a job?

> **unemployment:** The inability of labor-force participants to find jobs.

And what about prices? Price signals are a critical feature of the market mechanism. But the validity of those signals depends on some stable measure of value. What good is a doubling of salary when the price of everything you buy doubles as well? Generally, rising prices will enrich people who own property and impoverish people who rent. That's why we strive to avoid **inflation**—a situation in which the *average* price level is increasing.

> **inflation:** An increase in the average level of prices of goods and services.

Historically, the marketplace has been wracked with bouts of both unemployment and inflation. These experiences have prompted calls for government intervention at the macro level. *The goal of macro intervention is to foster economic growth—to get us on the production possibilities curve (full employment), maintain a stable price level (price stability), and increase our capacity to produce (growth).*

GROWTH OF GOVERNMENT

The potential micro and macro failures of the marketplace provide specific justifications for government intervention. The question then turns to how well the activities of the public sector correspond to these implied mandates.

Until the 1930s the federal government's role was largely limited to national defense (a public good), enforcement of a common legal system (also a public good), and provision of postal service (equity). The Great Depression of the 1930s spawned a new range of government activities, including welfare and Social Security programs (equity), minimum wage laws and workplace standards (regulation), and massive public works (public goods and externalities). In the 1950s the federal government also assumed a greater role in maintaining macroeconomic stability (macro failure), protecting the environment (externalities), and safeguarding the public's health (externalities and equity).

These increasing responsibilities have greatly increased the size of the public sector. In 1902 the federal government employed fewer than 350,000 people and spent a mere $650 *million*. Today the federal government employs nearly 4 million people and spends roughly $2.5 *trillion* a year.

Direct Expenditure. Figure 4.4 summarizes the growth of the public sector since 1930. World War II caused a massive increase in the size of the federal government. Federal purchases of goods and services for the war accounted for over 40 percent of total output during the 1943–44 period. The federal share of total U.S. output fell abruptly after World War II, rose again during the Korean War (1950–53) and has declined slightly since then.

The decline in the federal share of total output is somewhat at odds with most people's perception of government growth. This discrepancy is explained by two phenomena. First, people see the *absolute* size of the government growing every year. But we're focusing here on the *relative* size of the public sector. Since the 1950s the public sector has grown a bit more slowly than the private sector, slightly reducing

FIGURE 4.4
Government Growth

During World War II the public sector purchased nearly half of total U.S. output. Since the early 1950s the public-sector share of total output has been closer to 20 percent. Within the public sector, however, there's been a major shift: State and local claims on resources have grown, while the federal share has declined significantly.

Source: *Economic Report of the President, 2004.*

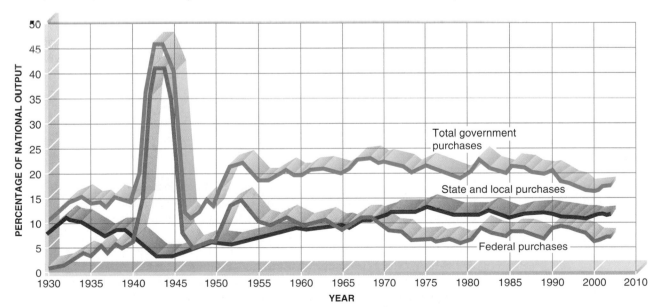

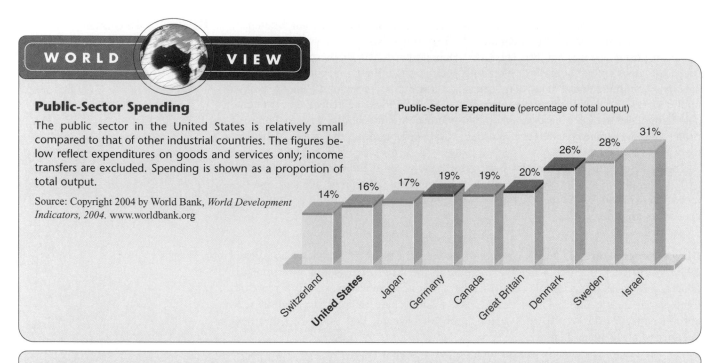

Public-Sector Spending

The public sector in the United States is relatively small compared to that of other industrial countries. The figures below reflect expenditures on goods and services only; income transfers are excluded. Spending is shown as a proportion of total output.

Source: Copyright 2004 by World Bank, *World Development Indicators, 2004.* www.worldbank.org

Public-Sector Expenditure (percentage of total output)

Switzerland 14% · United States 16% · Japan 17% · Germany 19% · Canada 19% · Great Britain 20% · Denmark 26% · Sweden 28% · Israel 31%

Analysis: The share of total output allocated to government services varies widely across nations. In the United States, the government share of output is relatively low.

its relative size. As the accompanying World View shows, other industrialized countries have significantly larger public sectors.

Income Transfers. Figure 4.4 depicts only government spending on goods and services, not *all* public spending. Not included in our depiction of government growth is spending on income transfers. Direct expenditure on goods and services absorbs real resources, but income transfers don't. Hence, income transfers don't directly alter the mix of output. Their effect is primarily *distributional* (the FOR WHOM question), not *allocative* (the WHAT question). Were income transfers included, the relative size and growth of the federal government would be larger than Figure 4.4 depicts. This is because ***most of the growth in federal spending has come from increased income transfers, not purchases of goods and services.***

State and Local Growth

State and local spending on goods and services has followed a very different path from federal expenditure. Prior to World War II, state and local governments dominated public-sector spending. During the war, however, the share of total output going to state and local governments fell, hitting a low of 3 percent in that period (Figure 4.4).

State and local spending caught up with federal spending in the mid-1960s and has exceeded it ever since. Today more than 80,000 state and local government entities buy much more output than Uncle Sam and employ five times as many people.

Figure 4.5 is an overview of state and local budgets. Education is a huge expenditure at both levels of government. Most direct state spending is on colleges; most local spending is for elementary and secondary education. The fastest-growing areas for state expenditure are prisons (public safety) and welfare. At the local level, sewage and trash services are claiming an increasing share of budgets.

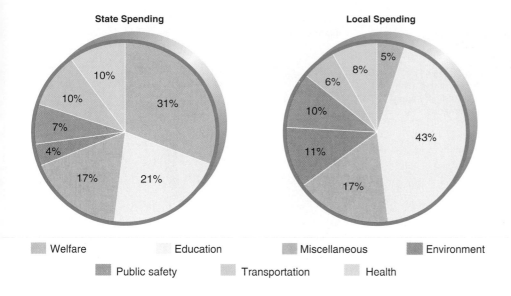

FIGURE 4.5
State and Local Spending

Spending on education and welfare accounts for half of all state and local expenditure. There are important differences, however, in the content of spending at each level of government.

Source: U.S. Bureau of the Census.

TAXATION

Whatever we may think of any specific government expenditure, we must recognize one basic fact of life: We pay for government spending. We pay not just in terms of tax *dollars* but in the more fundamental form of a changed mix of output. Government expenditures on goods and services absorb factors of production that could be used to produce consumer goods. The mix of output changes toward *more* public services and *less* private goods and services. Resources used to produce missile shields or elementary schools aren't available to produce cars, houses, or restaurant meals. In real terms, **the cost of government spending is measured by the private-sector output sacrificed when the government employs scarce factors of production.**

The **opportunity costs** of public spending aren't always apparent. We don't directly hand over factors of production to the government. Instead, we give the government part of our income in the form of taxes. Those dollars are then used to buy factors of production or goods and services in the marketplace. Thus, *the primary function of taxes is to transfer command over resources (purchasing power) from the private sector to the public sector.* Although the government sometimes also borrows dollars to finance its purchases, taxes are the primary source of government revenues.

opportunity costs: The most desired goods or services that are forgone in order to obtain something else.

As recently as 1902, much of the revenue the federal government collected came from taxes imposed on alcoholic beverages. The federal government didn't have authority to collect income taxes. As a consequence, *total* federal revenue in 1902 was only $653 million.

Federal Taxes

Income Taxes. All that has changed. The Sixteenth Amendment to the U.S. Constitution, enacted in 1915, granted the federal government authority to collect income taxes. The government now collects nearly $1 *trillion* in that form alone. Although the federal government still collects taxes on alcoholic beverages, the individual income tax has become the largest single source of government revenue (see Figure 4.6).

In theory, the federal income tax is designed to be **progressive**—that is, to take a larger *fraction* of high incomes than of low incomes. In 2004, for example, a single person with less than $7,800 of income paid no federal income tax. The next $7,000 of income was taxed at 10 percent, however. People with incomes of $50,000–$70,000 confronted a 25 percent tax rate on their additional income. The marginal tax rate got as high as 35 percent for people earning more than $300,000 in income. Thus people with high incomes not only pay more taxes but also pay a larger *fraction* of their income in taxes.

progressive tax: A tax system in which tax rates rise as incomes rise.

FIGURE 4.6
Federal Taxes

Taxes transfer purchasing power from the private sector to the public sector. The largest federal tax is the individual income tax. The second-largest source of federal revenue is the Social Security payroll tax.

Source: Office of Management and Budget, FY2005 data.

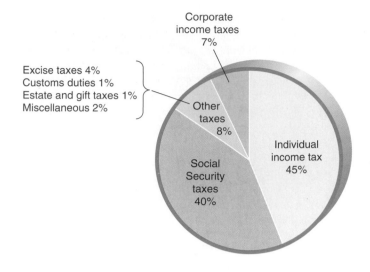

proportional tax: A tax that levies the same rate on every dollar of income.

regressive tax: A tax system in which tax rates fall as incomes rise.

WEBNOTE

The Office of Management and Budget's "A Citizen's Guide to the Federal Budget" provides convenient charts and data on federal revenues. See www.whitehouse.gov/omb/budget or www.access.gpo.gov.su_docs/budgetguide.html.

Social Security Taxes. The second major source of federal revenue is the Social Security payroll tax. People working now transfer part of their earnings to retired workers by making "contributions" to Social Security. There's nothing voluntary about these "contributions"; they take the form of mandatory payroll deductions. In 2004, each worker paid 7.65 percent of his or her wages to Social Security and employers contributed an equal amount. As a consequence, the government collected nearly $750 billion.

At first glance, the Social Security payroll tax looks like a **proportional tax,** that is, a tax that takes the *same* fraction of every taxpayer's income. But this isn't the case. The Social Security (FICA) tax isn't levied on every payroll dollar. Incomes above a certain ceiling (roughly $90,000 per year) aren't taxed. As a result, workers with really high salaries turn over a smaller fraction of their incomes to Social Security than do low-wage workers. This makes the Social Security payroll tax a **regressive tax.**

Corporate Taxes. The federal government taxes the profits of corporations as well as the incomes of consumers. But there are far fewer corporations (less than 4 million) than consumers (300 million), and their profits are small in comparison to total consumer income. In 2004, the federal government collected only $150 billion in corporate income taxes, despite the fact that it imposed a top tax rate of 38 percent on corporate profits.

"I can't find anything wrong here, Mr. Truffle . . . you just seem to have too much left after taxes."

Analysis: Taxes are a financing mechanism that enable the government to purchase scarce resources. Higher taxes imply less private-sector purchases.

Excise Taxes. The last major source of federal revenue is excise taxes. Like the early taxes on whiskey, excise taxes are sales taxes imposed on specific goods and services. The federal government taxes not only liquor ($13.50 per gallon) but also gasoline (18.4 cents per gallon), cigarettes (39 cents per pack), telephone service (3 percent), air fares, and a variety of other goods and services. Such taxes not only discourage production and consumption of these goods—by raising their price and thereby reducing the quantity demanded—they also raise a substantial amount of revenue.

Taxes. State and local governments also levy taxes on consumers and businesses. In general, cities depend heavily on property taxes, and state governments rely heavily on sales taxes (see Figure 4.7). Although nearly all states and many cities also impose income taxes, effective tax rates are so low (averaging less than 2 percent of personal income) that income tax revenues are much less than sales and property tax revenues.

Like the Social Security payroll tax, state and local taxes tend to be *regressive*—that is, they take a larger share of income from the poor than from the rich. Consider a 4 percent sales tax, for example. It might appear that a uniform tax rate like this would affect all consumers equally. But people with lower incomes tend to spend most of their income on goods and services. Thus, most of their income is subject to sales taxes. By contrast, a person with a high income can afford to save part of his or her income and thereby shelter it from sales taxes. A family that earns $40,000 and spends $30,000 of it on taxable goods and services, for example, pays $1,200 in sales taxes when the tax rate is 4 percent. In effect, then, they are handing over 3 percent of their *income* ($1,200 ÷ $40,000) to the state. By contrast, the family that makes only $12,000 and spends $11,500 of it for food, clothing, and shelter pays $460 in sales taxes in the same state. Their total tax is smaller, but it represents a much larger *share* (3.8 versus 3.0 percent) of their income.

Local property taxes are also regressive because poor people devote a larger portion of their incomes to housing costs. Hence, a larger share of a poor family's income is subject to property taxes. According to the Advisory Council on Intergovernmental Relations, a family earning $50,000 a year devotes only 2.5 percent of its income to property taxes, whereas a family earning $10,000 pays out 4.5 percent of its income in property taxes. State lotteries are also regressive, for the same reason (see News). Low-income players spend 1.4 percent of their incomes on lottery tickets while upper-income players devote only 0.1 percent of their income to lottery purchases.

WEBNOTE

Current excise tax rates are available from the U.S. Bureau of Alcohol, Tobacco, and Firearms. See www.atf.treas.gov.

State and Local Revenues

WEBNOTE

The U.S. Census Bureau compiles the most comprehensive data on state and local government finances. For details visit www.census.gov/ftp/pub.

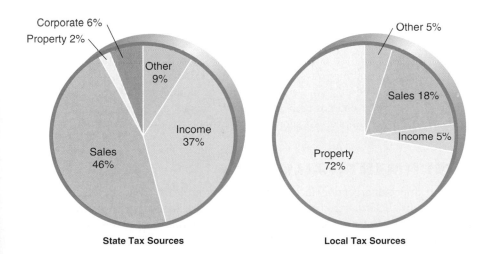

State Tax Sources (Corporate 6%, Property 2%, Other 9%, Income 37%, Sales 46%)

Local Tax Sources (Other 5%, Sales 18%, Income 5%, Property 72%)

FIGURE 4.7
State and Local Tax Sources

State governments get half their tax revenue from sales taxes. By contrast, local governments depend heavily on property taxes.

Source: U.S. Department of Commerce (2000–01 data).

IN THE NEWS

Soaking the Poor:

The Incidence of State-Sponsored Gambling

With many states suffering tax shortfalls and budget deficits, state-sponsored gambling again is offering a temptingly easy source of new revenue. Some argue that state-sponsored lotteries, slot machines, and other gambling opportunities simply give the local government the gambling profits that otherwise would have gone elsewhere, to other states or to the illegal gambling industry. Opponents of state-sponsored gambling respond that revenues derived from gambling take money that families otherwise would have spent on other kinds of consumption and that it affects the poor more than the rich;

these "voluntary taxes" are highly regressive, amounting to little more than the state picking the pocket of the poor and the ignorant.

A new study sheds light on this debate. Professor Melissa Kearney of Wellesley College reports that . . . the poor spend about the same number of dollars on lottery tickets (about $165 per adult per year) as those who are better off, so they spend a much larger share of their income on state lotteries.

—Bernard Wasow

Source: The Century Foundation, November 2002.

Analysis: Poor people spend a larger percentage of their income on lottery tickets than do rich people. This makes lotteries a regressive source of government revenue.

Federal Aid. Up until 1986, the federal government gave state and local governments some of its revenues for whatever purposes those entities desired. But such general *revenue sharing* was always small. Most federal aid to state and local governments is in the form of **categorical grants,** that is, grants that can be used only for specific activities. For example, the federal government spent $30 billion on natural resources and environment in 2004. But one-fifth of this amount was simply given to local communities for the construction of sewage treatment plants. The local governments actually purchased or built these plants; the federal government only provided the necessary revenue. Accordingly, the federal government maintained control over WHAT to produce, but local governments exercised some judgment on HOW to produce it.

> **categorical grants:** Federal grants to state and local governments for specific expenditure purposes.

In 2004, the federal government gave over $400 billion to state and local governments in the form of categorical grants (including those for employment programs, Medicaid, schools, and highways). These federal grants accounted for about one-fifth of all state and local revenues.

User Charges. The third major source of state and local revenues consists of **user charges.** The tuition that college students (or their parents) pay for attending a state university or community college is an all-too-familiar user charge. But tuition fees never cover the full costs of maintaining public colleges. Part of the costs of providing higher education are borne by all state taxpayers, whether or not they attend college. Public hospitals and highways are financed the same way, with users paying part of the costs directly and all taxpayers paying the remaining costs through state and local taxes. Hence, user charges aren't identical to market prices because they're not intended to cover the full costs of supplying a particular good.

> **user charge:** Fee paid for the use of a public-sector good or service.

GOVERNMENT FAILURE

Some government intervention in the marketplace is clearly desirable. The market mechanism can fail for a variety of reasons, leaving a laissez-faire economy short of its economic goals. But how much government intervention is desirable? Communist nations once thought that complete government control of production, consumption,

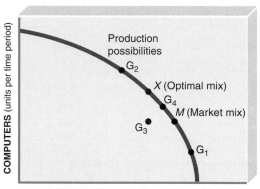

FIGURE 4.8
Government Failure

When the market produces a subop-timal mix of output (point M), the goal of government is to move output to the social optimum (point X). A move to G_4 would be an improvement in the mix of output. But government inter-vention *may* move the economy to points G_1, G_2, or G_3—all reflecting government failure.

and distribution decisions was the surest path to utopia. They learned the hard way that not only markets but governments as well can fail.

In this context, **government failure** means that government intervention fails to move us closer to our economic goals.

In Figure 4.8, the goal of government intervention is to move the mix of output from point M (failed market outcome) to point X (the social optimum). But gov-ernment intervention might unwittingly move us to point G_1, making matters worse. Or the government might overreact, sending us to point G_2. Red tape and onerous regulation might even force us to point G_3, *inside* the production possibilities curve (with less total output than at point M). All those possibilities (G_1, G_2, G_3) repre-sent government failure. Government intervention is desirable only to the extent that it *improves* market outcomes (e.g., G_4). Government intervention in the FOR WHOM question is desirable only if the distribution of income gets better, not worse, as a result of taxes and transfers. Even when outcomes improve, government failure may occur if the costs of government intervention exceeded the benefits of an improved output mix, cleaner production methods, or a fairer distribution of income.

> **government failure:** Government intervention that fails to improve economic outcomes.

Taxpayers seem to have strong opinions about government failure. When asked whether the government "wastes" their tax dollars or uses them well, the majority see waste in government (see News on "Persistent Doubts"). The average taxpayer now believes that state governments waste 29 cents out of each dollar, while the federal government wastes 42 cents out of each tax dollar!

Government "waste" implies that the public sector isn't producing as many serv-ices as it could with the sources at its disposal. Such inefficiency implies that we're producing somewhere *inside* our production possibilities curve rather than on it (e.g., point G_3 in Figure 4.8). If the government is wasting resources this way, we can't possibly be producing the optimal mix of output.

Perceptions of Waste

Even if the government weren't wasting resources, it might still be guilty of govern-ment failure. As important as efficiency in government may be, it begs the larger question of how many government services we really want. In reality, *the issue of government waste encompasses two distinct questions:*

Opportunity Cost

- *Efficiency:* Are we getting as much service as we could from the resources we allocate to government?
- *Opportunity cost:* Are we giving up too many private-sector goods in order to get those services?

If the government is producing goods inefficiently, we end up *inside* the produc-tion possibilities curve, with less output than attainable. Even if the government is efficient, however, the *mix* of output may not be optimal, as points G_1 and G_2 in

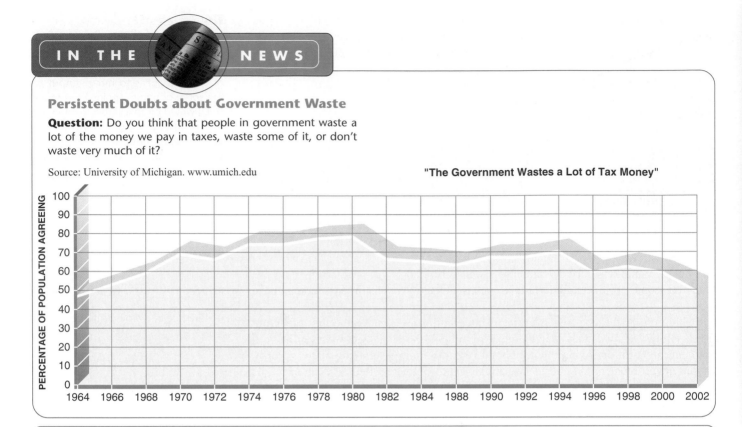

Persistent Doubts about Government Waste

Question: Do you think that people in government waste a lot of the money we pay in taxes, waste some of it, or don't waste very much of it?

Source: University of Michigan. www.umich.edu

"The Government Wastes a Lot of Tax Money"

Analysis: Market failure justifies government intervention. If the government wastes resources, however, it too may fail to satisfy our economic goals.

WEBNOTE

For more public opinion on the role of government, visit the University of Michigan's National Election Studies site at www.umich.edu/~nes/nesguide/gd-index.htm.

Figure 4.8 illustrate. *Everything the government does entails an opportunity cost.* The more police officers or schoolteachers employed by the public sector, the fewer workers available to private producers and consumers. Similarly, the more computers, pencils, and paper consumed by government agencies, the fewer accessible to individuals and private companies.

When assessing government's role in the economy, *we must consider not only what governments do but also what we give up to allow them to do it.* The theory of public goods tells us only what activities are appropriate for government, not the proper *level* of such activity. National defense is clearly a proper function of the public sector. Not so clear, however, is how much the government should spend on tanks, aircraft carriers, and missile shields. The same is true of environmental protection or law enforcement.

The concept of opportunity costs puts a new perspective on the whole question of government size. Before we can decide how big is "too big," we must decide what we're willing to give up to support the public sector. A military force of 1.4 million men and women is "too big" from an economic perspective only if we value the forgone private production and consumption more highly than we value the added strength of our defenses. The government has gone "too far" if the highway it builds is less desired than the park and homes it implicitly replaced. In these and all cases, the assessment of bigness must come back to a comparison of what is given up with what is received. The assessment of government failure thus comes back to points on the production possibilities curve. Has the government moved us closer to the optimal mix of output (e.g., point G_4 in Figure 4.8) or not?

This is a tough question to answer in the abstract. We can, however, use the concept of opportunity cost to assess the effectiveness of specific government interventions. From this perspective, ***additional public-sector activity is desirable only if the benefits from that activity exceed its opportunity costs.*** In other words, we compare the benefits of a public project to the value of the private goods given up to produce it. By performing this calculation repeatedly along the perimeter of the production possibilities curve, we could locate the optimal mix of output—the point at which no further increase in public-sector spending activity is desirable.

This same principle can be used to decide *which* goods to produce within the public sector. A public project is desirable only to the extent that it promises to yield some benefits (or utility). But all public projects involve opportunity costs. Hence, a project should be pursued only if its anticipated benefits exceeded the value of alternative resource uses. In this sense, the public sector confronts the same kind of dilemma we consumers have. There are hundreds of goods and services we'd *like* to have, but scarce resources require us to select only the best possible ones. That implies getting the highest possible ratio of benefits to costs.

Valuation Problems. Although the principles of cost-benefit analysis are simple enough, they're deceptive. How are we to measure the potential benefits of improved police services, for example? Should we estimate the number of robberies and murders prevented, calculate the worth of each, and add up the benefits? And how are we supposed to calculate the worth of a saved life? By a person's earnings? value of assets? number of friends? And what about the increased sense of security people have when they know the police are patrolling in their neighborhood? Should this be included in the benefit calculation? Some people will attach great value to this service; others will attach little. Whose values should be the standard?

When we're dealing with (private) market goods and services, we can gauge the benefits of a product by the amount of money consumers are willing to pay for it. This price signal isn't available for most public services, however, because of externalities and the nonexclusive nature of pure public goods (the free-rider problem). Hence, ***the value (benefits) of public services must be estimated because they don't have (reliable) market prices.*** This opens the door to endless political squabbles about how beneficial any particular government activity is.

The same problems arise in evaluating the government's efforts to redistribute incomes. Government transfer payments now go to retired workers, disabled people, veterans, farmers, sick people, students, pregnant women, unemployed people, poor people, and a long list of other recipients. To pay for all these transfers, the government must raise tax revenues. With so many people paying taxes and receiving transfer payments, the net effects on the distribution of income aren't easy to figure out. Yet we can't determine whether this government intervention is worth it until we know how the FOR WHOM answer was changed and what the tax-and-transfer effort cost us. Here again, there's at least a possibility of government failure.

In practice, we rely on political mechanisms, not cost-benefit calculations, to decide what to produce in the public sector and how to redistribute incomes. ***Voting mechanisms substitute for the market mechanism in allocating resources to the public sector and deciding how to use them.*** Some people have even suggested that the variety and volume of public goods are determined by the most votes, just as the variety and volume of private goods are determined by the most dollars. Thus, governments choose that level and mix of output (and related taxation) that seem to command the most votes.

Sometimes the link between the ballot box and output decisions is very clear and direct. State and local governments, for example, are often compelled to get voter approval before building another highway, school, housing project, or sewage plant. *Bond referenda* are direct requests by a government unit for the authority and

Cost-Benefit Analysis

Ballot Box Economics

The National Conference of State Legislatures tracks bond referenda and other ballot issues. Visit them at www.ncsl.org to review recent ballots.

purchasing power to expand the production of particular public goods. In 2002, for example, governments sought voter approval for $22 billion of new borrowing to finance public expenditure; over 60 percent of those requests were approved.

Although the direct link between bond referenda and spending decisions is important, it's more the exception than the rule. Bond referenda account for less than 1 percent of state and local expenditures (and none of federal expenditures). As a consequence, voter control of public spending is much less direct. Although federal agencies must receive authorization from Congress for all expenditures, consumers get a chance to elect new representatives only every two years. Much the same is true at state and local levels. Voters may be in a position to dictate the general level and pattern of public expenditures but have little direct influence on everyday output decisions. In this sense, the ballot box is a poor substitute for the market mechanism.

Even if the link between the ballot box and allocation decisions were stronger, the resulting mix of output might not be optimal. A democratic vote, for example, might yield a 51 percent majority for approval of new local highways. Should the highways then be built? The answer isn't obvious. After all, a large minority (49 percent) of the voters have stated that they don't want resources used this way. If we proceed to build the highways, we'll make those people worse off. Even the voters who voted for the highways may end up worse off, depending on how the benefits and costs of the highway are distributed and what other opportunities exist. The basic dilemma is really twofold. *We don't know what the real demand for public services is, and votes alone don't reflect the intensity of individual demands.* Moreover, real-world decision making involves so many choices that a stable consensus is impossible.

Public-Choice Theory

In the midst of all this complexity and uncertainty, another factor may be decisive—namely, self-interest. In principle, government officials are supposed to serve the people. It doesn't take long, however, before officials realize that the public is indecisive about what it wants and takes very little interest in government's day-to-day activities. With such latitude, government officials can set their own agendas. Those agendas may give higher priority to personal advancement than to the needs of the public. Agency directors may foster new programs that enlarge their mandate, enhance their visibility, and increase their prestige or income. Members of Congress may likewise pursue legislative favors like tax breaks for supporters more diligently than they pursue the general public interest. In such cases, the probability of attaining the optimal mix of output declines.

public choice: Theory of public-sector behavior emphasizing rational self-interest of decision makers and voters.

The theory of **public choice** emphasizes the role of self-interest in public decision making. Public-choice theory essentially extends the analysis of market behavior to political behavior. Public officials are assumed to have specific personal goals (for example, power, recognition, wealth) that they'll pursue in office. *A central tenet of public-choice theory is that bureaucrats are just as selfish (utility maximizing) as everyone else.*

Public-choice theory provides a neat and simple explanation for public-sector decision making. But critics argue that the theory provides a woefully narrow view of public servants. Some people do selflessly pursue larger, public goals, such critics argue, and ideas can overwhelm self-interest. Steven Kelman of Harvard, for example, argues that narrow self-interest can't explain the War on Poverty of the 1960s, the tax revolt of the 1970s, or the deregulation movement of the 1980s. These tidal changes in public policy reflect the power of ideas, not simple self-interest.

Although self-interest can't provide a complete explanation of public decision making, it adds important perspectives on the policy process. James Buchanan of George Mason University (Virginia) won the 1986 Nobel Prize in economics for helping develop this public-choice perspective. It adds a personal dimension to the faceless mechanics of ballot box economics, cost-benefit analysis, and other "objective" mechanisms of public-sector decision making.

Downsizing Government

The Great Depression of the 1930s devastated the world economy. For many people, it was compelling evidence that the market alone couldn't be trusted to answer the WHAT, HOW, and FOR WHOM questions. With unemployment, hunger, and homelessness at record levels, people everywhere turned to government for help. In the United States, Franklin Roosevelt's New Deal envisioned a more activist government, restoring full employment and assuring everyone some minimal level of economic security. In Eastern Europe, the Communist Party advanced the notion that outright government *control* of the economy was the only sure way to attain economic justice for all.

Confidence in the ability of government to resolve core economic issues continued to increase in the post–World War II era. Securing national defenses during the Cold War (1948–89) justified the maintenance of a large military establishment, both in the United States and elsewhere. The War on Poverty that began in the mid-1960s brought about a huge increase in government social programs and income transfers. As the U.S. population has aged, the government's health care and retirement programs (e.g., Social Security, military and civilian government pensions) have grown rapidly. In each case, there was a political consensus that expanded public services would enhance society's welfare. That consensus helped grow *total* federal spending (including purchases and income transfers) from 17 percent of GDP in 1965 to over 23 percent in 1982.

Deficit Financing. President Reagan railed against the relentless growth of the federal government. To reverse that growth, he pushed a massive tax cut through Congress, hoping thereby to cut off the major source of government finances. But he couldn't convince Congress to reduce social-program spending, and he wanted more military spending. So the federal government kept growing, using *borrowed* money to replace the lost tax revenue.

Military Cutbacks. The end of the Cold War sparked a significant cutback in military outlays. Between 1991 and 1998, annual military spending declined by $35 *billion* a year. The size of the armed forces shrank by nearly 500,000 personnel. All these "guns" weren't converted to civilian "butter," however. As military spending declined in the 1990s, federal social spending continued to increase. As a result, the federal share of total output declined very slowly.

Nonmilitary Downsizing. Public opinion has not kept pace with the continued growth of federal programs. As we noted earlier, most taxpayers think the government wastes a lot of money. More to the point, a 2003 CBS news survey revealed that Americans are highly skeptical about the federal government's ability to fix things. As the News on the next page shows, only 4 percent of the population "always" trusts the government to do what is right. A lot of people now suspect government intervention *creates* more problems than it solves.

The increasing skepticism about government intervention has prompted a worldwide downsizing of the public sector. The downsizing has been most dramatic in the former communist nations, like the Soviet Union, where the mechanisms of central planning have been removed. In Europe, Latin America, and Asia, the downsizing of government has taken the form of privatization of government-owned industries such as railroads, airlines, and telephone service. In the United States, every president since Reagan has made the downsizing of government a policy priority. To achieve that goal, however, requires chipping away at specific programs. That's always the hard part. The war against terrorism that began in September 2001 abruptly reversed the downtrend in defense spending, leaving social spending the only target for budget cuts. With baby boomers rapidly approaching retirement, spending on Social Security, Medicare, and

Little Confidence in Government

Public-opinion polls reveal that Americans have little confidence in government, as the following responses illustrate.

Question: How much of the time do you think you can trust the government in Washington to do what is right—just about always, most of the time, or only some of the time?

Source: Conducted by CBS News/New York Times, July 13–July 27, 2003.

Answers

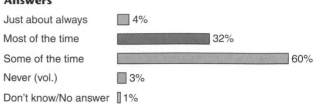

Just about always	4%
Most of the time	32%
Some of the time	60%
Never (vol.)	3%
Don't know/No answer	1%

Analysis: In principle, governments intervene to remedy market failure. But the public has little confidence in government performance.

Medicaid is also sure to rise substantially, however. That leaves little room for serious cutbacks in government spending. And even desirable cutbacks in other areas are sure to encounter stiff resistance from beneficiaries and bureaucrats. As a result, few seasoned observers expect the government sector to shrink any further in the economy tomorrow.

SUMMARY

- Government intervention in the marketplace is justified by market failure, that is, suboptimal market outcomes.
- The micro failures of the market originate in public goods, externalities, market power, and an inequitable distribution of income. These flaws deter the market from achieving the optimal mix of output or distribution of income.
- Public goods are those that can't be consumed exclusively; they're jointly consumed regardless of who pays. Because everyone seeks a free ride, no one demands public goods in the marketplace. Hence, the market underproduces public goods.
- Externalities are costs (or benefits) of a market transaction borne by a third party. Externalities create a divergence between social and private costs or benefits, causing suboptimal market outcomes. The market overproduces goods with external costs and underproduces goods with external benefits.
- Market power enables a producer to thwart market signals and maintain a suboptimal mix of output. Antitrust policy seeks to prevent or restrict market power. The government may also regulate the behavior of powerful firms.
- The market-generated distribution of income may be unfair. This inequity may prompt the government to intervene with taxes and transfer payments that redistribute incomes.

- The macro failures of the marketplace are reflected in unemployment and inflation. Government intervention is intended to achieve full employment and price stability.
- The federal government expanded greatly after 1930. More recent growth, however, has been in transfer payments, which now account for over half of federal expenditure.
- State and local governments purchase more output (12 percent of GDP) than the federal government (7 percent) and employ five times as many workers.
- Income and payroll taxes provide most federal revenues. States get most revenue from sales taxes; local governments rely on property taxes.
- Government failure occurs when intervention moves us away from rather than toward the optimal mix of output (or income). Failure may result from outright waste (operational inefficiency) or from a misallocation of resources.
- All government activity must be evaluated in terms of its opportunity cost, that is, the *private* goods and services forgone to make resources available to the public sector.
- Allocation decisions within the public sector may be based on cost-benefit analysis or votes. The self-interests of government agents may also affect decisions of when and how to intervene.

Key Terms

optimal mix of output	market power	progressive tax
market mechanism	antitrust	proportional tax
market failure	natural monopoly	regressive tax
private good	transfer payments	categorical grants
public good	merit good	user charge
free rider	unemployment	government failure
externalities	inflation	public choice
monopoly	opportunity cost	

Questions for Discussion

1. Why should taxpayers subsidize public colleges and universities? What external benefits are generated by higher education?
2. If everyone seeks a free ride, what mix of output will be produced in Figure 4.2? Why would anyone voluntarily contribute to the purchase of public goods like flood control or snow removal?
3. Could local fire departments be privately operated, with their services sold directly to customers? What problems would be involved in such a system?
4. Why might Fourth of July fireworks be considered a public good? Who should pay for them? What about airport security?
5. What is the specific market-failure justification for government spending on (*a*) public universities, (*b*) health care, (*c*) trash pickup, (*d*) highways, (*e*) police? Would a purely private economy produce any of these services?
6. Why should the well-being of nonsmokers affect the price and quantity of cigarettes produced?
7. The government now spends over $400 billion a year on Social Security benefits. Why don't we leave it to individuals to save for their own retirement?
8. What government actions might cause failures like points G_1, G_2, and G_3 in Figure 4.8? Can you give examples?
9. Are subway fares progressive or regressive? How about highway tolls?
10. Should the government be downsized? Which functions should be cut back?

PROBLEMS The Student Problem Set at the back of this book contains numerical and graphing problems for this chapter.

WEB ACTIVITIES to accompany this chapter can be found on the Online Learning Center: **http://www.mhhe.com/economics/schiller10**

PART 2

Product Markets:
The Basics

The prices and products we see every day emerge from decisions made by millions of individual consumers and firms. A primary objective of microeconomic theory is to explain how those decisions are made. How do consumers decide which products to buy and in what quantities? What does it cost business firms to produce the goods and services consumers demand? Chapters 5 and 6 address these issues.

The Demand for Goods

After the September 2001 terrorist attacks on the World Trade Center and the Pentagon, few Americans wanted to board an airplane. When U.S. airports reopened a week later, hardly any passengers showed up. Most planes departed with very light loads. Despite pleas from political and business leaders, consumers refused to fly. Then the airlines reduced airfares—to *really* low levels. Two weeks after the terrorist attacks, roundtrip cross-country fares got as low as $118, with no advance purchase or minimum-stay requirements. Suddenly, air travel regained popularity. Within days after the fare cuts, travelers started filling up the planes again.

The experience of the airlines underscores the importance of *prices* in determining consumer behavior. Consumers "want," "need," and "just have to have" a vast array of goods and services. When decision time comes, however, product *prices* often dictate what consumers will actually buy. As we observed in Chapter 3, the quantity of a product *demanded* depends on its price. When the airlines cut airfares in late September 2001, consumers purchased a *lot* more tickets.

This chapter takes a closer look at how product prices affect consumer decisions. We focus on three related questions:

- **How do we decide how much of any good to buy?**
- **How does a change in a product's price affect the quantity we purchase or the amount of money we spend on it?**
- **Why do we buy certain products but not others?**

The law of demand (first encountered in Chapter 3) gives us some clues for answering these questions. But we need to look beyond that law to fashion more complete answers. We need to know what forces give demand curves their downward-sloping shape. We also need to know more about how to *use* demand curves to predict consumer behavior.

DETERMINANTS OF DEMAND

In seeking explanations for consumer behavior, we have to recognize that the field of economics doesn't have all the answers. But it does offer a unique perspective that sets it apart from other fields of study.

Consider first the explanations of consumer behavior offered by other fields of study. Psychiatrists and psychologists have had a virtual field day formulating such explanations. Freud was among the first to describe us humans as bundles of subconscious (and unconscious) fears, complexes, and anxieties. From a Freudian perspective, we strive for ever higher levels of consumption to satisfy basic drives for security, sex, and ego gratifications. Like the most primitive of people, we clothe and adorn ourselves in ways that assert our identity and worth. We eat and smoke too much because we need the oral gratifications and security associated with

The Sociopsychiatric Explanation

mother's breast. Oversized homes and cars give us a source of warmth and security remembered from the womb. On the other hand, we often buy and consume some things we expressly don't desire, just to assert our rebellious feelings against our parents (or parent substitutes). In Freud's view, it's the constant interplay of these id, ego, and superego drives that motivates us to buy, buy, buy.

Sociologists offer additional explanations for our consumption behavior. Lloyd Warner and David Riesman, for example, noted our yearning to stand above the crowd, to receive recognition from the masses. For people with exceptional talents, such recognition may come easily. But for the ordinary person, recognition may depend on conspicuous consumption. A sleek car, a newer fashion, a more exotic vacation become expressions of identity that provoke recognition, even social acceptance. We strive for ever higher levels of consumption—not just to keep up with the Joneses but to surpass them.

Not *all* consumption is motivated by ego or status concerns, of course. Some food is consumed for the sake of self-preservation, some clothing worn for warmth, and some housing built for shelter. The typical U.S. consumer has more than enough income to satisfy these basic needs. In today's economy, most consumers also have *discretionary* income that can be used to satisfy psychological or sociological longings. Single women are able to spend a lot of money on clothes and pets, and men spend freely on entertainment, food, and drink (see News). Teenagers show off their affluence in purchases of electronic goods, cars, and clothes (see Figure 5.1).

Although psychiatrists and sociologists offer intriguing explanations for our consumption patterns, their explanations fall a bit short. Sociopsychiatric theories tell us why teenagers, men, and women *desire* certain goods and services. But they don't explain which goods will actually be *purchased*. Desire is only the first step in the consumption process. To acquire goods and services, one must be willing and able to *pay* for one's wants. Producers won't give you their goods just to satisfy your Freudian desires. They want money in exchange for their goods. Hence, ***prices and income are just as relevant to consumption decisions as are more basic desires and preferences.***

In explaining consumer behavior, economists focus on the *demand* for goods and services. As we observed in Chapter 3, **demand** entails the *willingness and ability to*

Each year the Bureau of Labor does another consumer expenditure survey. For the most recent data, visit www.bls.gov and first click on "Demographics" and then "Surveys and Programs."

The Economic Explanation

demand: The willingness and ability to buy specific quantities of a good at alternative prices in a given time period, *ceteris paribus*.

IN THE NEWS

Men vs. Women: How They Spend

Are men really different from women? If spending habits are any clue, males do differ from females. That's the conclusion one would draw from the latest Bureau of Labor Statistics (BLS) survey of consumer expenditure. Here's what BLS found out about the spending habits of young (under age 25) men and women who are living on their own:

Common Traits

- Young men have slightly more income to spend ($12,068 per year) than do young women ($11,253). Both sexes go deep into debt, however, by spending $4,000–$5,000 more than their incomes.
- Neither sex spends much on charity, reading, or health care.

Distinctive Traits

- Young men spend 25 percent more at fast-food outlets, restaurants, and carryouts.
- Men spend 60 percent more on alcoholic beverages and smoking.
- Men spend twice as much as women do on television and stereo equipment.
- Young women spend a lot more money on clothing, personal care items and their pets.

Source: U.S. Bureau of Labor Statistics, 2001–2002, Consumer Expenditure Survey. www.bls.gov

Analysis: Consumer patterns vary by gender, age, and other characteristics. Economists try to isolate the common influences on consumer behavior.

FIGURE 5.1
Affluent Teenagers

Teenagers spend over $200 billion a year. Much of this spending is for cars, stereos, and other durables. The percentage of U.S. teenagers owning certain items is shown here.

Source: Teenage Research Unlimited (2003 data).

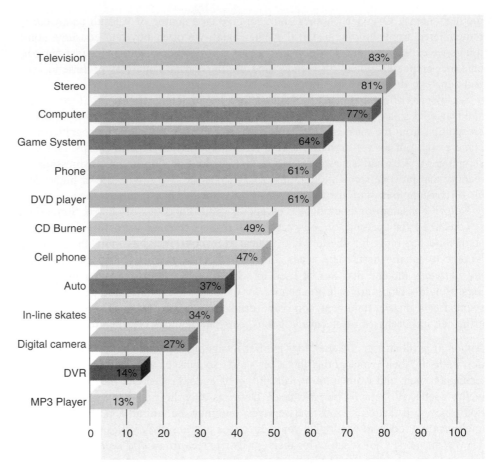

PERCENT OF TEENS OWNING PRODUCTS

pay for goods and services. To say that someone *demands* a particular good means that he or she will offer to *buy* it at some price(s). *An individual's demand for a specific product is determined by these four factors:*

- *Tastes* (desire for this and other goods).
- *Income* (of the consumer).
- *Expectations* (for income, prices, tastes).
- *Other goods* (their availability and prices).

Note again that desire (tastes) is only one determinant of demand. Other determinants of demand (income, expectations, and other goods) also influence whether a person will be willing and able to buy a certain good at a specific price.

The remainder of this chapter examines these determinants of demand. The objective is not only to explain consumer behavior but also to predict how consumption patterns change in response to *changes* in the price of a good or to *changes* in underlying tastes, income, prices or availability of other goods, or expectations.

THE DEMAND CURVE

Utility Theory

The starting point for an economic analysis of demand is quite simple. Economists accept consumer tastes as the outcome of sociopsychiatric and cultural influences. They don't look beneath the surface to see how those tastes originated. Economists simply note the existence of certain tastes (desires) and then look to see how those tastes affect consumption decisions. The first observation is that the more pleasure a product gives us, the higher the price we'd be willing to pay for it. If the oral sensation of buttered popcorn at the movies really turns you on, you're likely to be willing to pay dearly for it. If, on the other hand, you have no great taste or desire for popcorn, the theater might have to give it away before you'd eat it.

Total vs. Marginal Utility. Economists use the term **utility** to refer to the expected pleasure, or satisfaction, obtained from goods and services. We also make an important distinction between total utility and marginal utility. **Total utility** refers to the amount of satisfaction obtained from your *entire* consumption of a product. By contrast, **marginal utility** refers to the amount of satisfaction you get from consuming the *last* (i.e., "marginal") unit of a product. More generally, note that

$$\frac{\text{Marginal}}{\text{utility}} = \frac{\text{change in total utility}}{\text{change in quantity}}$$

utility: The pleasure or satisfaction obtained from a good or service.

total utility: The amount of satisfaction obtained from entire consumption of a product.

marginal utility: The change in total utility obtained by consuming one additional (marginal) unit of a good or service.

Diminishing Marginal Utility. The concepts of total and marginal utility explain not only why we buy popcorn at the movies but also why we stop eating it at some point. Even people who love popcorn (i.e., derive great *total* utility from it) don't eat endless quantities of it. Why not? Presumably because the thrill diminishes with each mouthful. The first box of popcorn may bring sensual gratification, but the second or third box is likely to bring a stomachache. We express this change in perceptions by noting that the *marginal* utility of the first box of popcorn is higher than the additional or *marginal* utility derived from the second box.

The behavior of popcorn connoisseurs isn't abnormal. As a rule, the amount of additional utility we obtain from a product declines as we continue to consume it. The third slice of pizza isn't as desirable as the first, the sixth beer not as satisfying as the fifth, and so forth. Indeed, this phenomenon of diminishing marginal utility is so nearly universal that economists have fashioned a law around it. This **law of diminishing marginal utility** states that each successive unit of a good consumed yields less *additional* utility.

The law of diminishing marginal utility does *not* say that we won't like the second box of popcorn, the third pizza slice, or the sixth beer; it just says we won't like them as much as the ones we've already consumed. Time is also important here: If the first box of popcorn was eaten last year, the second box may now taste just as good. The law of diminishing marginal utility applies to short time periods.

law of diminishing marginal utility: The marginal utility of a good declines as more of it is consumed in a given time period.

Figure 5.2 illustrates how utility changes with the level of consumption. Notice that total utility continues to rise as we consume the first five boxes (ugh!) of popcorn.

(*a*) Total utility	**(*b*) Marginal utility**
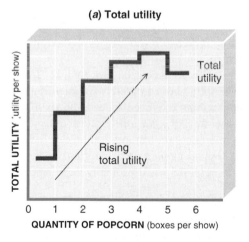	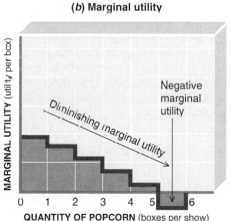

FIGURE 5.2
Total vs. Marginal Utility

The *total* utility derived from consuming a product comes from the *marginal* utilities of each successive unit. The total utility curve shows how each of the first five boxes of popcorn contributes to total utility. Note that each successive step is smaller. This reflects the law of diminishing marginal utility.

The sixth box of popcorn causes the total-utility steps to descend; the sixth box actually *reduces* total utility. This means that the sixth box has *negative* marginal utility.

The marginal utility curve (*b*) shows the change in total utility with each additional unit. It's derived from the total utility curve. Marginal utility here is positive but diminishing for the first five boxes.

From James Eggert, *Invitation to Economics*, 2nd ed. p. 160, © 1991 by Bristlecone Books. Reprinted with permission of The McGraw-Hill Companies, Inc.

Analysis: No matter how much we like a product, marginal utility is likely to diminish as we consume more of it. If marginal utility becomes *negative* (as here), total satisfaction will decrease.

WEBNOTE

Do Americans have a taste for Jumbo Jacks? Go to facts at www.jackinthebox.com.

But total utility increases by smaller and smaller increments. Each successive step of the total utility curve in Figure 5.2 is a little smaller.

The height of each step of the total utility curve in Figure 5.2 represents *marginal utility*—the increments to total utility. *Marginal* utility is clearly diminishing. Nevertheless, because marginal utility is still *positive,* total utility is increasing. **As long as marginal utility is positive, total utility must be increasing** (note that the total utility curve is still rising for the fifth box of popcorn).

The situation changes with the sixth box of popcorn. According to Figure 5.2, the good sensations associated with popcorn consumption are completely forgotten by the time the sixth box arrives. Nausea and stomach cramps take over. Indeed, the sixth box is absolutely *distasteful,* as reflected in the downturn of *total* utility and the *negative* value for marginal utility. We were happier—in possession of more total utility—with only five boxes of popcorn. The sixth box—yielding *negative* marginal utility—reduces total satisfaction. This is the kind of sensation you'd probably experience if you ate six hamburgers (see cartoon).

Not every good ultimately reaches negative marginal utility. Yet the more general principle of diminishing marginal utility is experienced daily. That is, **eventually additional quantities of a good yield increasingly smaller increments of satisfaction.**

Price and Quantity

Marginal utility is essentially a measure of how much we desire particular goods, our *taste*. But which ones will we buy? Clearly, we don't always buy the products we most desire. *Price* is often a problem. All too often we have to settle for goods that yield less marginal utility simply because they are available at a lower price. This explains why most people don't drive Porsches. Our desire ("taste") for a Porsche may be great, but its price is even greater. The challenge for most of us is to somehow reconcile our tastes with our bank balances.

In deciding whether to buy something, our immediate focus is typically on a single variable, namely *price*. Assume for the moment that a person's tastes, incomes, and expectations are set in stone, and that the prices of other goods are set as well. This is the **ceteris paribus** assumption we first encountered in Chapter 1. It doesn't mean that other influences on consumer behavior are unimportant. Rather, *ceteris paribus* simply allows us to focus on one variable at a time. In this case, we are focusing on price. What we want to know is how high a price a consumer is willing to pay for another unit of a product.

The concepts of marginal utility and *ceteris paribus* enable us to answer this question. The more marginal utility a product delivers, the more a consumer will be willing to pay for it. We also noted that marginal utility *diminishes* as increasing quantities of a product are consumed, suggesting that consumers are willing to pay progressively *less* for additional quantities of a product. The moviegoer willing to pay 50 cents for that first mouth-watering ounce of buttered popcorn may not be willing to pay so much for a second or third ounce. The same is true for a second pizza, the sixth beer, and so forth. **With given income, tastes, expectations, and prices of other goods and services, people are willing to buy additional quantities of a good only if its price falls.** In other words, as the marginal utility of a good diminishes, so does our willingness to pay. This **law of demand** is illustrated in Figure 5.3 with the downward-sloping **demand curve**.

The law of demand and the law of diminishing marginal utility tell us nothing about why we crave popcorn or why our cravings subside. Those explanations are reserved

ceteris paribus: The assumption of nothing else changing.

law of demand: The quantity of a good demanded in a given time period increases as its price falls, *ceteris paribus*.

demand curve: A curve describing the quantities of a good a consumer is willing and able to buy at alternative prices in a given period, *ceteris paribus*.

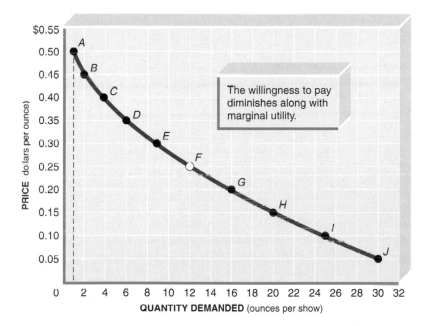

	Price (per ounce)	Quantity Demanded (ounces per show)
A	$0.50	1
B	0.45	2
C	0.40	4
D	0.35	6
E	0.30	9
F	0.25	12
G	0.20	16
H	0.15	20
I	0.10	25
J	0.05	30

FIGURE 5.3
An Individual's Demand Schedule and Curve

Consumers are generally willing to buy larger quantities of a good at lower prices. This demand schedule illustrates the specific quantities demanded at alternative prices. If popcorn sold for 25 cents per ounce, this consumer would buy 12 ounces per show (row *F*). At higher prices, less popcorn would be purchased.

A downward-sloping demand curve expresses the law of demand: The quantity of a good demanded increases as its price falls. Notice that points *A* through *J* on the curve correspond to the rows of the demand schedule.

for psychiatrists, sociologists, and physiologists. The laws of economics simply describe our market behavior.

PRICE ELASTICITY

The theory of demand helps explain consumer behavior. But it's not terribly helpful to the theater owner who's actually worried about popcorn sales. The general observation that popcorn sales decline when prices increase would be of little use. What the theater owner wants to know is *by how much* the quantity demanded would fall if the price were raised.

This is the same problem the airlines confronted after the September 2001 terrorist attacks. They knew more people would fly if airfares were reduced. But by *how much* did they have to cut fares to fill their planes again?

The central question in all these decisions is the response of quantity demanded to a change in price. ***The response of consumers to a change in price is measured by the price elasticity of demand.*** Specifically, the **price elasticity of demand** refers to the percentage change in quantity demanded divided by the percentage change in price—that is,

> **price elasticity of demand:** The percentage change in quantity demanded divided by the percentage change in price.

$$\text{Price elasticity } (E) = \frac{\% \text{ change in quantity demanded}}{\% \text{ change in price}}$$

What would the value of price elasticity be if air travel didn't change at all when price decreased by 5 percent? In that case the price elasticity of demand would be

$$E = \frac{\% \text{ change in quantity demanded}}{\% \text{ change in price}}$$

$$= \frac{0}{5} = 0$$

But is this realistic? According to the law of demand, the quantity demanded goes up when price goes down. So we'd expect *somebody* to buy more airline tickets if fares fell by 5 percent. In a large market like air travel, we don't expect *everybody* to jump on a plane when airfares are reduced. But if *some* consumers fly more, the percentage change in quantity demanded will be larger than zero. Indeed, ***the law of demand implies that the price elasticity of demand will always be greater than zero.*** Technically, the price elasticity of demand (E) would be a negative number since quantity demanded and price always move in opposite directions. For simplicity, however, E is typically expressed in absolute terms (without the minus sign). ***The key question, then, is how much greater than zero E actually is.***

Computing Price Elasticity

To get a feel for the dimensions of elasticity, let's return to the popcorn counter at the movies. We've already observed that at a price of 45 cents an ounce (point *B* in Figure 5.3), the average moviegoer demands 2 ounces of popcorn per show. At the lower price of 40 cents per ounce (point *C*), the quantity demanded jumps to 4 ounces per show.

We can summarize this response with the price elasticity of demand. To do so, we have to calculate the *percentage* changes in quantity and price. Consider the percentage change in quantity first. In this case, the change in quantity demanded is 4 ounces − 2 ounces = 2 ounces. The *percentage* change in quantity is therefore

$$\% \text{ change in quantity} = \frac{2}{q}$$

The problem is to transform the denominator q into a number. Should we use the quantity of popcorn purchased *before* the price reduction, that is, $q_1 = 2$? Or should we use the quantity purchased *after* the price reduction, that is, $q_2 = 4$? The choice of denominator will have a big impact on the computed percentage change. To ensure consistency, economists prefer to use the *average* quantity in the denominator.[1] The average quantity is simply

$$\text{Average quantity} = \frac{q_1 + q_2}{2} = \frac{2 + 4}{2} = 3 \text{ ounces}$$

We can now complete the calculation of the percentage change in quantity demanded. It is

$$\begin{array}{c} \% \text{ change in} \\ \text{quantity demanded} \end{array} = \frac{\begin{array}{c}\text{change in}\\ \text{quantity}\end{array}}{\begin{array}{c}\text{average}\\ \text{quantity}\end{array}} = \frac{q_2 - q_1}{\frac{q_1 + q_2}{2}} = \frac{2}{3} = 0.667$$

Popcorn sales increased by an average of 67 percent when the price of popcorn was reduced from 45 cents to 40 cents per ounce.

The computation of the percentage change in price is similar. We first note that the price of popcorn fell by 5 cents ($45¢ - 40¢$) when we move from point B to point C on the demand curve (Figure 5.3). We then compute the *average* price of popcorn in this range of the demand curve as

$$\begin{array}{c}\text{Average price}\\ \text{of popcorn}\end{array} = \frac{p_1 + p_2}{2} = \frac{45 + 40}{2} = 42.5 \text{ cents}$$

This average is our denominator in calculating the percentage price change. Using these numbers, we see that the absolute value of the percentage change is

$$\begin{array}{c}\% \text{ change}\\ \text{in price}\end{array} = \frac{\begin{array}{c}\text{change in}\\ \text{price}\end{array}}{\begin{array}{c}\text{average}\\ \text{price}\end{array}} = \frac{p_2 - p_1}{\frac{p_1 + p_2}{2}} = \frac{5}{42.5} = 0.118$$

The price of popcorn fell by 11.8 percent.

Now we have all the information required to compute the price elasticity of demand. In this case,

$$E = \frac{\begin{array}{c}\% \text{ change}\\ \text{in quantity}\\ \text{demanded}\end{array}}{\begin{array}{c}\% \text{ change}\\ \text{in price}\end{array}} = \frac{0.667}{0.118} = 5.65$$

What we get from all these calculations is a very useful number. It says that the consumer response to a price reduction will be extremely large. Specifically, the quantity of popcorn consumed will increase 5.65 times as fast as price falls. A 1 percent reduction in price brings about a 5.65 percent increase in purchases. The theater manager can therefore boost popcorn sales greatly by lowering price a little.

Elastic vs. Inelastic Demand. We characterize the demand for various goods in one of three ways: *elastic, inelastic,* or *unitary elastic.* If **E** *is larger than 1, demand is elastic.* Consumer response is large relative to the change in price.

---

[1]This procedure is referred to as the *arc* (midpoint) elasticity of demand. If a single quantity (price) is used in the denominator, we refer to the *point* elasticity of demand.

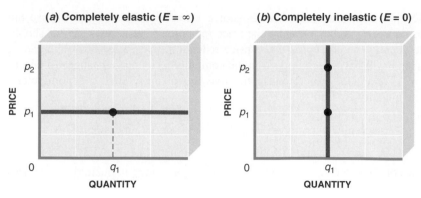

FIGURE 5.4
Extremes of Elasticity

If demand were perfectly elastic ($E = \infty$), the demand curve would be *horizontal*. In that case, any increase in price (e.g., p_1 to p_2) would cause quantity demanded to fall to zero.

A *vertical* demand curve implies that an increase in price won't affect the quantity demanded. In this situation of completely *in*elastic ($E = 0$) demand, consumers are willing to pay *any* price to get the quantity q_1.

In reality, elasticities of demand for goods and services lie between these two extremes (obeying the law of demand).

If E is less than 1, we say demand is inelastic. ***If demand is inelastic, consumers aren't very responsive to price changes.***

If E is equal to 1, demand is unitary elastic. In this case, the percentage change in quantity demanded is exactly equal to the percentage change in price.

Consider the case of smoking. Many smokers claim they'd "pay anything" for a cigarette after they've run out. But would they? Would they continue to smoke just as many cigarettes if prices doubled or tripled? If so, the demand curve would be vertical (as in Figure 5.4*b*) rather than downward-sloping. Research suggests this is not the case: Higher cigarette prices *do* curb smoking. There is at least *some* elasticity in the demand for cigarettes. But the elasticity of demand is low; Table 5.1 indicates that the elasticity of cigarette demand is only 0.4.

Although the average adult smoker is not very responsive to changes in cigarette prices, teen smokers apparently are. As the accompanying News indicates, teen smoking drops by almost 7 percent when cigarette prices increase by 10 percent. Thus, the price elasticity of *teen* demand for smoking is

$$E = \frac{\text{percent drop in quantity demanded}}{\text{percent increase in price}} = \frac{7\%}{10\%} = 0.7$$

Hence, higher cigarette prices can be an effective policy tool for curbing teen smoking. The drop in teen smoking after prices jumped in 1998 confirms this expectation.

According to Table 5.1, the demand for airline travel is even more price-elastic. Whenever a fare cut is announced, the airlines get swamped with telephone inquiries. If fares are discounted by 25 percent, the number of passengers may increase by as much as 60 percent. As Table 5.1 shows, the elasticity of airline demand is 2.4, meaning that the percentage change in quantity demanded (60 percent) will be 2.4 times larger than the price cut (25 percent).

Determinants of Elasticity

Why are consumers price-sensitive ($E > 1$) with some goods and not ($E < 1$) with others? To answer that, we must go back to the demand curve itself. The elasticity of demand is computed between points on a given demand curve. Hence, ***the price elasticity of demand is influenced by all the determinants of demand.*** Four factors are particularly worth noting.

TABLE 5.1
Elasticity Estimates

Price elasticities vary greatly. When the price of gasoline increases, consumers reduce their consumption only slightly. When the price of fish increases, however, consumers cut back their consumption substantially. These differences reflect the availability of immediate substitutes, the prices of the goods, and the amount of time available for changing behavior.

Product	Price Elasticity
Relatively elastic (E > 1)	
Airline travel, long run	2.4
Restaurant meals	2.3
Fresh fish	2.2
New cars, short run	1.2–1.5
Unitary elastic (E = 1)	
Private education	1.1
Radios and televisions	1.2
Shoes	0.9
Movies	0.9
Relatively inelastic (E < 1)	
Cigarettes	0.4
Coffee	0.3
Gasoline, short run	0.2
Electricity (in homes)	0.1
Long-distance phone calls	0.1

Source: Compiled from Hendrick S. Houthakker and Lester D. Taylor, *Consumer Demand in the United States, 1929–1970* (Cambridge: Harvard University Press, 1966); F. W. Bell, "The Pope and Price of Fish," *American Economic Review,* December 1968; Herbert Scarf and John Shoven, *Applied General Equilibrium Analysis* (New York: Cambridge University Press, 1984); and Michael Ward, "Product Substitutability and Competition in Long-Distance Telecommunications," *Economic Inquiry,* October 1999.

Necessities vs. Luxuries. Some goods are so critical to our everyday life that we regard them as "necessities". A hair brush, toothpaste, and perhaps textbooks might fall into this category. Our "taste" for such goods is so strong that we can't imagine getting along without them. As a result, we don't change our consumption of "necessities" very much when the price increases; ***demand for necessities is relatively inelastic.***

A "luxury" good, by contrast, is something we'd *like* to have but aren't likely to buy unless our income jumps or the price declines sharply, such as vacation travel,

IN THE NEWS

Dramatic Rise in Teenage Smoking

Smoking among youths in the United States rose precipitously starting in 1992 after declining for the previous 15 years. By 1997, the proportion of teenage smokers had risen by one-third from its 1991 trough.

A prominent explanation for the rise in youth smoking over the 1990s was a sharp decline in cigarette prices in the early 1990s, caused by a price war between the tobacco companies. Gruber and Zinman find that young people are very sensitive to the price of cigarettes in their smoking decisions. The authors estimate that for every 10 percent decline in the price, youth smoking rises by almost 7 percent, a much stronger price sensitivity than is typically found for adult smokers. As a

result, the price decline of the early 1990s can explain about a quarter of the smoking rise from 1992 through 1997. Similarly, the significant decline in youth smoking observed in 1998 is at least partially explainable by the first steep rise in cigarette prices since the early 1990s. The authors also find that black youths and those with less-educated parents are much more responsive to changes in cigarette prices than are white teens and those with more-educated parents.

However, price does not appear to be an important determinant of smoking by younger teens. This may be because they are more experimental smokers.

Source: National Bureau of Economic Research, *NBER Digest,* October 2000. www.nber.org/digest

Analysis: The effectiveness of higher cigarette prices in curbing teen smoking depends on the price elasticity of demand.

New York City's Costly Smokes

New York City has the nation's costliest smokes. NYC Mayor Michael Bloomberg raised the city's excise tax from 8 cents a pack to $1.50 effective July 2002. Together with state and federal taxes, that raised the retail price of smokes in NYC to nearly $8 a pack.

Mayor Bloomberg expected the city to reap a tax bonanza from the 350 million packs of cigarettes sold annually in NYC. What he got instead was a lesson in elasticity. NYC smokers can buy cigarettes for a lot less money outside the city limits.

Or they can stay home and buy cigarettes on the Internet from (untaxed) Indian reservations, delivered by UPS. They can also buy cigarettes smuggled in from low-tax states like Kentucky, Virginia, and North Carolina. What matters isn't the price elasticity of demand for cigarettes in general (around 0.4), but the elasticity of demand for *NYC-taxed* cigarettes. That turned out to be quite high. Unit sales of NYC cigarettes plummeted by 44 percent after the "Bloomberg tax" was imposed.

Source: *"NewsFlash," Economy Today,* October 2002.

Analysis: If demand is price-elastic, a price increase will lead to a disproportionate drop in unit sales. In this case, the ready availability of substitutes (cigarettes from other jurisdictions) made demand highly price-elastic.

new cars, and camera phones. We want them but can get by without them. That is, ***demand for luxury goods is relatively elastic.***

Availability of Substitutes. Our notion of which goods are necessities is also influenced by the availability of substitute goods. The high elasticity of demand for fish (Table 5.1) reflects the fact that consumers can always eat chicken, beef, or pork if fish prices rise. On the other hand, most coffee drinkers can't imagine any other product that could substitute for a cup of coffee. As a consequence, when coffee prices rise, consumers don't reduce their purchases very much at all. Likewise, the low elasticity of demand for gasoline reflects the fact that most cars can't run on alternative fuels. In general, ***the greater the availability of substitutes, the higher the price elasticity of demand.*** This is a principle that New York City learned when it raised the price of cigarettes in 2002. As the News explains, smugglers quickly supplied a substitute good and legal sales of cigarettes declined drastically in New York City.

Relative Price (to income). Another important determinant of elasticity is the price of the good in relation to a consumer's income. Airline travel and new cars are quite expensive, so even a small percentage change in their prices can have a big impact on a consumer's budget (and consumption decisions). The demand for such "big-ticket" items tends to be elastic. By contrast, coffee is so cheap for most people that even a large *percentage* change in price doesn't affect consumer behavior very much.

Because the relative price of a good affects price elasticity, the value of E_1 *changes* along a given demand curve. At current prices the elasticity of demand for coffee is low. How would consumers behave, however, if coffee cost $5 a cup? Some people would still consume coffee. At such higher prices, however, the quantity demanded would be much more sensitive to price changes. Accordingly, when we observe, as in Table 5.1, that the demand for coffee is price-inelastic, that observation applies only to the current range of prices. Were coffee prices dramatically higher, the price elasticity of demand would be higher as well. As a rule, ***the price elasticity of demand declines as price moves down the demand curve.***

Time. Finally, time affects the price elasticity of demand. Car owners can't switch to electric autos every time the price of gasoline goes up. In the short run, the elasticity

Professor Becker Corrects President's Math

President Clinton has seized upon the cigarette excise tax as an expedient and politically correct means of increasing federal revenue. In 1994, the federal government took in $12 billion from the present 24-cents-per-pack tax. If the tax were quadrupled to $1 a pack, Clinton figures tax revenues would increase by more than $50 billion over three years. Those added revenues would help finance the health-care reforms the President so dearly wants.

   Professor Gary Becker, a Nobel Prize–winning economist at the University of Chicago, says Clinton's math is wrong. The White House assumed that cigarette sales would drop by 4 percent for every 10 percent increase in price. Professor Becker says that reflects only the first-year response to higher prices, not the full adjustment of smokers' behavior. Over a three-year period, cigarette consumption is likely to decline by 8 percent for every 10 percent increase in price—twice as much as Clinton assumed. As a result, the $1-a-pack tax will bring in much less revenue than President Clinton projected.

Source: *BusinessWeek*, August 15, 1994. © 1994 The McGraw-Hill Companies, Inc. Reprinted with permission. www.businessweek.com

Analysis: It takes time for people to adjust their behavior to changed prices. Hence, the short-run price elasticity of demand is lower than the long-run elasticity.

of demand for gasoline is quite low. With more time to adjust, however, consumers can buy more fuel-efficient cars, relocate their homes or jobs, and even switch fuels. As a consequence, ***the long-run price elasticity of demand is higher than the short-run elasticity.*** Nobel Prize–winning economist Gary Becker used the distinction between long-run and short-run elasticities to explain why a proposed increase in cigarette excise taxes wouldn't generate nearly as much revenue as President Clinton expected (see News).

PRICE ELASTICITY AND TOTAL REVENUE

The concept of price elasticity refutes the popular misconception that producers charge the "highest price possible." Except in the very rare case of completely inelastic demand, this notion makes no sense. Indeed, higher prices may actually *lower* total sales revenue.

   The **total revenue** of a seller is the amount of money received from product sales and is determined by the quantity of the product sold and the price at which it is sold:

$$\text{Total revenue} = \text{price} \times \text{quantity sold}$$

total revenue: The price of a product multiplied by the quantity sold in a given time period.

In the movie theater example, if the price of popcorn is 40 cents per ounce and only 4 ounces are sold, total revenue equals $1.60 per show. This revenue is illustrated by the shaded rectangle in Figure 5.5. (The area of a rectangle is equal to its height [*p*] times its width [*q*].)

   Now consider what happens to total revenue when the price of popcorn is increased. From the law of demand, we know that an increase in price will lead to a decrease in quantity demanded. But what about total revenue? The change in total revenue depends on *how much* quantity demanded falls when price goes up.

   Suppose we raise popcorn prices again, from 40 cents back to 45 cents. What happens to total revenue? At 40 cents per box, 4 ounces are sold (see Figure 5.5) and total revenue equals $1.60. If we increase the price to 45 cents, only 2 ounces are sold and total revenue drops to 90 cents. In this case, an *increase* in price leads to a *decrease* in total revenue. This new and smaller total revenue is illustrated by the dashed rectangle in Figure 5.5.

FIGURE 5.5
Elasticity and Total Revenue

Total revenue is equal to the price of the product times the quantity sold. It is illustrated by the area of the rectangle formed by $p \times q$. The shaded rectangle illustrates total revenue ($1.60) at a price of 40 cents and a quantity demanded of 4 ounces. When price is increased to 45 cents, the rectangle and total revenue shrink (see dashed lines) because demand is relatively elastic in that price range. Price hikes increase total revenue only if demand is inelastic.

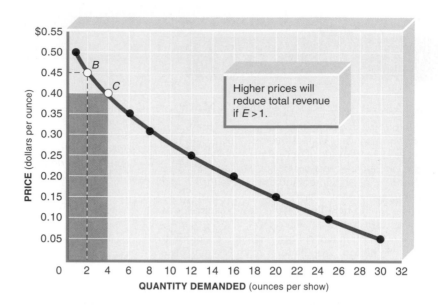

	Price	×	Quantity Demanded	=	Total Revenue
A	50¢		1		$0.50
B	45		2		0.90
C	40		4		1.60
D	35		6		2.10
E	30		8		2.40
F	25		12		3.00
G	20		16		3.20
H	15		20		3.00
I	10		25		2.50
J	5		30		1.50

Price increases don't always lower total revenue. If consumer demand was relatively *inelastic* ($E < 1$), a price increase would lead to *higher* total revenue. Thus, we conclude that

- *A price hike increases total revenue only if demand is inelastic ($E < 1$).*
- *A price hike reduces total revenue if demand is elastic ($E > 1$).*
- *A price hike does not change total revenue if demand is unitary-elastic $E = 1$.*

Table 5.2 summarizes these and other responses to price changes.

Changing Value of E. Once we know the price elasticity of demand, we can predict how consumers will respond to changing prices. We can also predict what will happen to the total revenue of the seller when price is raised or reduced. Figure 5.6

TABLE 5.2
Price Elasticity of Demand and Total Revenue

The impact of higher prices on total revenue depends on the price elasticity of demand. Higher prices result in higher total revenue only if demand is inelastic. If demand is elastic, *lower* prices result in *higher* revenues.

	Effect on Total Revenue of	
If Demand is	**Price Increase**	**Price Reduction**
Elastic ($E > 1$)	Decrease	Increase
Inelastic ($E < 1$)	Increase	Decrease
Unitary elastic ($E = 1$)	No change	No change

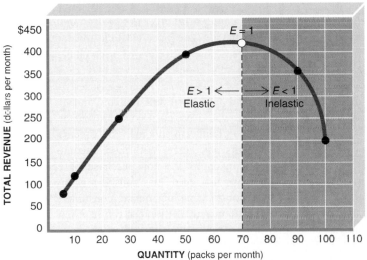

(a) The demand curve

PRICE (dollars per pack) vs *QUANTITY (packs per month)*

Elastic E > 1 · Unit elastic E = 1 · Inelastic E < 1

(b) Total revenue

TOTAL REVENUE (dollars per month) vs *QUANTITY (packs per month)*

E = 1 · E > 1 Elastic · E < 1 Inelastic

Price of Cigarettes	×	Quantity Demanded	=	Total Revenue	
$2		100		$200	Low elasticity
4		90		360	(total revenue rising
6		70		420	as price increases)
8		50		400	High elasticity
10		25		250	(total revenue falling
12		10		120	as price increases)
14		6		84	

FIGURE 5.6
Price Elasticity Changes along a Demand Curve

The concept of price elasticity can be used to determine whether people will spend more money on cigarettes when price rises. The answer to this question is yes and no, depending on how high the price goes.

Notice in the table and the graphs that total revenue rises when the price of cigarettes increases from $2 to $4 a pack and again to $6. At low prices, the demand for cigarettes appears relatively inelastic: Price and total revenue move in the same direction.

As the price of cigarettes continues to increase, however, total revenue starts to fall. As the price is increased from $6 to $8 a pack, total revenue drops. At higher prices, the demand for cigarettes is relatively elastic: Price and total revenue move in *opposite* directions. Hence, the price elasticity of demand depends on where one is on the demand curve.

shows how elasticity and total revenue change along a given demand curve. Demand for cigarettes is *elastic* (E > 1) at prices above $6 per pack but *inelastic* (E < 1) at lower prices.

The bottom half of Figure 5.6 shows how total revenue changes along the demand curve. At very high prices (e.g., $14 a pack), few cigarettes are sold and total revenue is low. As the price is reduced, however, the quantity demanded increases so much that total revenue *increases,* despite the lower price. With each price reduction from $14 down to $6 total revenue increases.

Price cuts below $6 a pack continue to increase the quantity demanded (the law of demand). The increase in unit sales is no longer large enough, however, to offset the price reductions. Total revenue starts falling after price drops below $6 per pack. The lesson to remember here is that *the impact of a price change on total revenue depends on the (changing) price elasticity of demand.*

OTHER ELASTICITIES

The price elasticity of demand tells us how consumers will respond to a change in the price of a good under the assumption of *ceteris paribus.* But other factors do change, and consumption behavior may respond to those changes as well.

Shifts vs. Movements

We recognized this problem in Chapter 3 when we first distinguished *movements* along a demand curve from *shifts* of the demand curve. A movement along an unchanged demand curve represents consumer response to a change in the *price* of that specific good. The magnitude of that movement is expressed in the price elasticity of demand.

When the underlying determinants of demand change, the entire demand curve shifts. These shifts also alter consumer behavior. The *price* elasticity of demand is of no use in gauging these behavioral responses, since it refers to price changes (movements along a constant demand curve) for that good only.

Income Elasticity

A change in any determinant of demand will shift the demand curve. Suppose consumer incomes were to increase. How would popcorn consumption be affected? Figure 5.7 provides an answer. Before the change in income, consumers demanded 12 ounces of popcorn at a price of 25 cents per ounce. With more income to spend, the new demand curve (D_2) suggests that consumers will now purchase a greater quantity of popcorn at every price. The increase in income has caused a rightward **shift in demand.** If popcorn continues to sell for 25 cents per ounce, consumers will now buy 16 ounces per show (point N) rather than only 12 ounces (point F).

It appears that changes in income have a substantial impact on consumer demand for popcorn. The graph in Figure 5.7 doesn't tell us, however, how large the change in income was. Will a *small* increase in income cause such a shift, or does popcorn demand increase only when moviegoers have a *lot* more money to spend?

shift in demand: A change in the quantity demanded at any (every) given price.

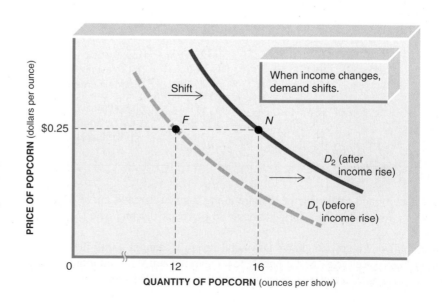

FIGURE 5.7
Income Elasticity

If income changes, the demand curve *shifts.* In this case, an increase in income enables consumers to buy more popcorn at every price. At a price of 25 cents, the quantity demanded increases from 12 ounces (point *F*) to 16 ounces (point *N*). The *income elasticity of demand* measures this response of demand to a change in income.

Figure 5.7 doesn't answer these questions. But a little math will. Specifically, the **income elasticity of demand** relates the *percentage* change in quantity demanded to the *percentage* change in income—that is,

$$\text{Income elasticity of demand} = \frac{\begin{array}{c}\text{\% change in}\\\text{quantity demanded}\\\text{(at given price)}\end{array}}{\begin{array}{c}\text{\% change in}\\\text{income}\end{array}}$$

income elasticity of demand: Percentage change in quantity demanded divided by percentage change in income.

The similarity to the price elasticity of demand is apparent. In this case, however, the denominator is *income* (a determinant of demand), not *price*.

Computing Income Elasticity. As was the case with price elasticity, we compute income elasticity with *average* values for the changes in quantity and income. Suppose that the shift in popcorn demand illustrated in Figure 5.7 occurred when income increased from $110 per week to $120 per week. We would then compute

$$\text{Income elasticity} = \frac{\dfrac{\text{change in quantity demanded}}{\text{average quantity}}}{\dfrac{\text{change in income}}{\text{average income}}}$$

$$= \frac{\dfrac{16 \text{ ounces} - 12 \text{ ounces}}{14 \text{ ounces}}}{\dfrac{\$120 - \$110}{\$115}}$$

$$= \frac{4}{14} \div \frac{10}{115}$$

$$= \frac{0.286}{0.087} = 3.29$$

Popcorn purchases are very sensitive to changes in income. When incomes rise by 8.7 percent, popcorn sales increase by a whopping 28.6 percent (that is, 8.7% × 3.29). The computed elasticity of 3.29 summarizes this relationship.

Normal vs. Inferior Goods. Demand and income don't always move in the same direction. Popcorn is a **normal good** because consumers buy more of it when their incomes rise. People actually buy *less* of some goods, however, when they have more income. With low incomes, people buy discount clothes, used textbooks, and cheap beer, and they eat at home. With more money to spend, they switch to designer clothes, new books, premium beers, and restaurant meals (see News on next page). The former items are called **inferior goods** because the quantity demanded falls when income rises. Similarly, when incomes *decline*, people demand *more* spaghetti and the services of credit agencies and pawnbrokers. ***For inferior goods, the income elasticity of demand is negative: for normal goods, it is positive.***

normal good: Good for which demand increases when income rises.

inferior good: Good for which demand decreases when income rises.

Changes in income are only one of the forces that shift demand curves. If popcorn were the only snack offered in movie theaters, people would undoubtedly eat more of it. In reality, people have other choices: candy, soda, ice cream, and more. Thus, the decision to buy popcorn depends not only on its price but also on the price and availability of other goods.

Suppose for the moment that the prices of these other goods were to fall. Imagine that candy bars were put on sale for a quarter, rather than the usual dollar. Would this price reduction on candy affect the consumption of popcorn?

Cross-Price Elasticity

IN THE NEWS

Stung by the Economy, Americans Lose Their Appetite for Dining Out

Restaurants' Sales Growth Slows as Consumers, Corporations Limit Nonessential Spending

Robin Gomes put her family on a budget last month, and that was bad news for restauranteurs.

Ms. Gomes, a 33-year-old home-loan coordinator in San Ramon, Calif., used to dine out with her husband and two children four times a week, dropping $50 to $60 a meal. Under the new budget, restaurant meals have been cut to once a week.

Far from being an isolated example, the Gomes family is part of a growing throng of stay-at-homes. As the shaky economy gives more consumers the jitters, the $258 billion restaurant and bar industry is grappling with its biggest slowdown in a decade. . . .

Growth in sales at restaurants and bars has declined steadily. For the 12 months ending this past Jan. 31, sales were 4.4 percent higher than the comparable year-earlier figure, according to figures from Technomic Inc., a Chicago food-consulting group, and the U.S. Census Bureau. But for the 12 months ending July 31, sales were only 2.4 percent above the prior 12-month period. Though sales are still above last year's, 2001 is shaping up to have the slowest growth since the 1991 recession, when sales dropped 1.2 percent. . . .

Upscale restaurants that thrived on corporate largesse are taking a big hit. Morton's Restaurant Group Inc., a chain of 61 steakhouses, saw same-store sales decline 9.6 percent in the second quarter.

—Shirley Leung

Source: *The Wall Street Journal,* August 22, 2001. Reprinted by permission of The Wall Street Journal. © 2001 Dow Jones & Company. All rights reserved worldwide. www.wsj.com

Analysis: Changes in income shift consumer demand curves. People buy fewer *normal* goods and more *inferior* goods when incomes decline.

According to Figure 5.8, the demand for popcorn might *decrease* if the price of candy fell. The leftward shift of the demand curve from D_1 to D_2 tells us that consumers now demand less popcorn at every price. At 25 cents per ounce, consumers now demand only 8 ounces of popcorn (point R) rather than the previous 12 ounces (point F). In other words, a decline in the price of *candy* has caused a reduction in the demand for *popcorn*. We conclude that candy and popcorn are **substitute goods**— when the price of one declines, demand for the other falls.

substitute goods: Goods that substitute for each other; when the price of good X rises, the demand for good Y increases, *ceteris paribus.*

FIGURE 5.8
Substitutes and Complements

The curve D_1 represents the initial demand for popcorn, given the prices of other goods. Other prices may change, however. If a reduction in the price of another good (candy) causes a *reduction* in the demand for this good (popcorn), the two goods are *substitutes.* Popcorn demand shifts to the left (to D_2) when the price of a substitute good falls.

If a reduction in the price of another good (e.g., Pepsi) leads to an *increase* in the demand for this good (popcorn), the two goods are *complements.* Popcorn demand shifts to the right (to D_3) when the price of a complementary good falls.

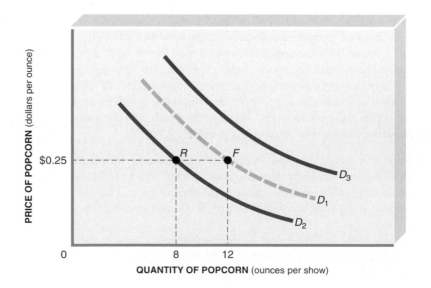

Music Sales Struggle

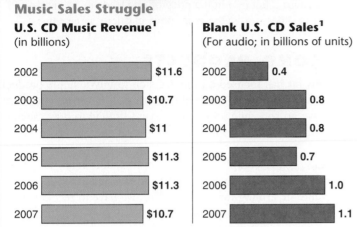

U.S. CD Music Revenue[1] (in billions)	
2002	$11.6
2003	$10.7
2004	$11
2005	$11.3
2006	$11.3
2007	$10.7

Blank U.S. CD Sales[1] (For audio; in billions of units)	
2002	0.4
2003	0.8
2004	0.8
2005	0.7
2006	1.0
2007	1.1

Sources: Forrester Research, Consumer Electronics Association
[1]Data based on estimates

Industry Tidbits

Downloading costs music industry:

- Percentage of U.S. households that download music: **14**
- Number of consumers who download: **23 million**
- Pre-recorded CDs bought by these consumers annually: **87 million**
- Additional CDs they would buy if not for downloading: **41 million**
- Average cost of CD: **$17**
- Revenue lost to music industry due to downloading: **$697 million**

—Marcy E. Mullins

Source: *USA Today*, October 27, 2003. USA TODAY Copyright 2003. Reprinted with permission.

Analysis: Music downloads and pre-recorded CDs are *substitute goods.* As the price of downloads falls, demand for music CDs declines. Music downloads and CD burners, on the other hand, are *complementary goods.*

Popcorn sales would follow a very different path if the price of soda fell. People like to wash down their popcorn with soda. When soda prices fall, moviegoers actually buy *more* popcorn. Here again, *a change in the price of one good affects the demand for another good.* In this case, however, we're dealing with **complementary goods,** since a decline in the price of one good causes an increase in the demand for the other good.

The distinction between substitute goods and complementary goods is illustrated in Figure 5.8. Note that *in the case of substitute goods the price of one good and the demand for the other move in the same direction.* (A *decrease* in candy prices causes a *decrease* in popcorn demand.) Likewise, as the price of music downloads *declined,* the demand for CD burners (a complementary good) *increased* but the demand for pre-recorded music CDs (substitute goods) *declined* (see News).

In the case of complementary goods (e.g., Pepsi and popcorn, cream and coffee), the price of one good and the demand for the other move in opposite directions. This helps explain why U.S. consumers bought more cars in 1998–99 when gasoline prices were falling and fewer SUVs in 2004 when gasoline prices were rising. The concept of complementary goods also explains why the demand for computer software increases when the price of computer hardware drops.

complementary goods: Goods frequently consumed in combination; when the price of good X rises, the demand for good Y falls, *ceteris paribus.*

Calculating Cross-Price Elasticity. The mathematical relationship between the price of one good and demand for another is summarized in yet another elasticity concept. The **cross-price elasticity of demand** is the *percentage* change in the quantity demanded on one good divided by the *percentage* change in the price of *another* good—that is,

cross-price elasticity of demand: Percentage change in the quantity demanded of X divided by percentage change in price of Y.

$$\text{Cross-price elasticity of demand} = \frac{\substack{\% \text{ change in quantity} \\ \text{demanded of good } X \\ \text{(at given price)}}}{\substack{\% \text{ change in price} \\ \text{of good } Y}}$$

What has changed here is the denominator again. Now the denominator refers to a change in the price of *another* good rather than the *same* good.

The cross-price elasticity of demand makes it easy to distinguish substitute and complementary goods. If the cross-price elasticity is positive, the two goods are *substitutes;* if the cross-price elasticity is negative, the two goods are *complements.* Pepsi and popcorn are complements because a fall (−) in the price of one leads to an increase (+) in the demand for the other; in other words, the cross-price elasticity is negative.

CHOOSING AMONG PRODUCTS

Our analysis of demand thus far has focused on the decision to buy a single product, at varying prices. Actual consumer behavior is multidimensional, however, and therefore more complex. When we go shopping, our concern isn't limited to how much of one good to buy. Rather, we must decide *which* of many available goods to buy at their respective prices.

The presence of so many goods complicates consumption decisions. Our basic objective remains the same, however: We want to get as much satisfaction as possible from our available income. In striving for that objective, we have to recognize that the purchase of any single good means giving up the opportunity to buy more of other goods. In other words, consuming popcorn (or any other good) entails distinct **opportunity costs.**

opportunity cost: The most desired goods or services that are forgone in order to obtain something else.

Marginal Utility vs. Price

The economic explanation for consumer choice builds on the theory of marginal utility and the law of demand. Suppose you have a choice between buying a Coke and playing a video game. The first proposition of consumer choice simply states that if you think a Coke will be more satisfying than playing a video game, you'll prefer to buy the Coke. Hardly a revolutionary proposition.

The second postulate of consumer-choice theory takes into account market prices. Although you may *prefer* to drink a Coke rather than play a video game, one play of a video game is cheaper than a Coke. Under these circumstances, your budget may win out over your desires. There's nothing irrational about playing a video game instead of buying a more desirable Coke when you have a limited amount of income to spend. On the contrary, *rational behavior requires one to compare the anticipated utility of each expenditure with its price.* The smart thing to do then is to choose those products which promise to provide the most pleasure for the amount of income available.

WEBNOTE

Find the current forecast for American teenage spending at www. demographics.com. Search for "teenagers."

Suppose your desire for a Coke is 1.5 times as great as your desire to play a video game. In economic terms, this means that the marginal utility of the first Coke is 1.5 times as high as the marginal utility of the first video game. Which one should you consume? Before reaching for the Coke, you'd better look at prices. What if a Coke costs 50 cents, whereas one play on a video game costs only 25 cents? In this case, you must pay *two* times as much for a Coke that gives only 1.5 times as much pleasure. This isn't a good deal. You could get more utility *per dollar* by playing video games.

The same kind of principle explains why some rich people drive a Ford rather than a shiny new Mercedes. The marginal utility (MU) of driving a Mercedes is substantially higher than the MU of driving a Ford. A nice Mercedes, however, costs about three times as much as a basic Ford. A rich person who drives a Ford must feel that driving a Mercedes is not three times as satisfying as driving a Ford. For such people, a Ford yields more *marginal utility per dollar spent.*

The key to utility maximization, then, isn't simply to buy the things you like best. Instead, you must compare goods on the basis of their marginal utility *and* price. *To maximize utility, the consumer should choose that good which delivers the most marginal utility per dollar.*

Utility Maximization

This basic principle of consumer choice is easily illustrated. Suppose you have $1.50 to spend on a combination of Cokes and video games, the only consumer goods available. Your objective, as always, is to get the greatest satisfaction possible from this

Quantity Consumed	Amount of Utility (in units of utility, or utils)			
	From Cokes		From Video Games	
	Total	Marginal	Total	Marginal
0	0		0	
		> 15		> 10
1	15		10	
		> 8		> 9
2	23		19	
		> 2		> 7
3	25		26	
		> 0		> 5
4	25		31	
		> −3		> 3
5	22		34	
		> −10		> 1
6	12		35	

TABLE 5.3
Maximizing Utility

Q: How can you get the most satisfaction (utility) from $1.50 if you must choose between buying Cokes that cost 50 cents each and video games that cost 25 cents each?

A: By drinking one Coke and playing four video games. See text for explanation.

limited income. That is, you want to maximize the *total* utility attainable from the expenditure of your income. The question is how to do it. What combination of Cokes and games will maximize the utility you get from $1.50?

We've already assumed that the marginal utility (MU) of the first Coke is 1.5 times as high as the MU of the first video game. This is reflected in the second row of Table 5.3. The MU of the first video game has been set arbitrarily at 10 utils (units of utility). We don't need to know whether 10 utils is a real thrill or just a bit of amusement. Indeed, the concept of "utils" has little meaning by itself; it's only a useful basis for comparison. In this case, we want to compare the MU of the first game with the MU of the first Coke. Hence, we set the MU of the first game at 10 utils and the MU of the first Coke at 15 utils. The first Coke is 1.5 times as satisfying as the first video game ($MU_{Coke} = 1.5\ MU_{game}$).

The remainder of Table 5.3 indicates how marginal utility diminishes with increasing consumption of a product. Look at what happens to the good taste of Coke. The marginal utility of the first Coke is 15; but the MU of the second Coke is only 8 utils. Once you've quenched your initial thirst, a second Coke still tastes good but isn't nearly so satisfying as the first one. A third Coke yields even less marginal utility, and a fourth one none at all ($MU = 0$). A fifth or sixth Coke would make your teeth rattle and cause other discomforts—its marginal utility is actually negative (−3 in Table 5.3).

Video games also conform to the law of diminishing marginal utility. However, marginal utility doesn't decline quite so rapidly in the consumption of video games. The second game is almost as much fun ($MU = 9$) as the first ($MU = 10$). Not until you've played several games do you begin to feel the tension and enjoy the game less. By the sixth game, marginal utility is fast approaching zero.

With these psychological insights to guide us, we can now determine how best to spend $1.50. What we're looking for is that combination of Cokes and video games which *maximizes* the total utility attainable from an expenditure of $1.50. We call this combination **optimal consumption**—that is, the mix of goods that yields the most utility for the available income.

We can start looking for the optimal mix of consumer purchases by assessing the utility of spending the entire $1.50 on video games. At 25 cents per play, we could buy 6 games. This would give us *total* utility of 35 utils (see Table 5.3).

Alternatively, you could also spend all your income on Cokes. With $1.50 to spend, you could buy 3 Cokes. However, this would generate only 25 utils of total utility. Hence, if you were forced to choose between *only* drinking Cokes or *only* playing video games, you'd pick the games.

Fortunately, we don't have to make such extreme choices. In reality, we can buy a *combination* of Cokes and video games. This complicates our decision making (with more choices) but permits us to attain higher levels of total satisfaction.

optimal consumption: The mix of consumer purchases that maximizes the utility attainable from available income.

To reach the peak of satisfaction, consider spending your $1.50 in three 50-cent increments. How should you spend the first 50 cents? If you spend it on 1 Coke, you'll get 15 utils of satisfaction. On the other hand, 50 cents will buy your first 2 video games. The first game has an MU of 10 and the second game adds another 9 utils to your happiness. Hence, by spending the first 50 cents on games, you reap 19 utils of total utility. This is superior to the pleasure of a first Coke and its therefore your first purchase.

Having played 2 video games, you now can spend the second 50 cents. How should it be spent? Your choice now is that first Coke or a third and fourth video game. That first unconsumed Coke still promises 15 utils of real pleasure. By contrast, the MU of a third video game is 7 utils and the MU of a fourth game only 5 utils. Together, then, the third and fourth games will increase your total utility by 12 utils, whereas a first Coke will give you 15 utils. You should spend the second 50 cents on a Coke.

The decision on how to spend the remaining half dollar is made the same way. The final choice is to purchase either a second Coke (MU = 8) or the third (MU = 7) and fourth (MU = 5) video games. The two games together offer more marginal utility and are thus the correct decision.

After working your way through these calculations, you'll end up drinking 1 Coke and playing 4 video games. Was it worth it? Do you end up with more total utility than you could have gotten from any other combination? The answer is yes. The *total* utility of 1 Coke (15 utils) and 4 games (31 utils) is 46 units of utility. This is significantly better than the alternatives of spending your $1.50 on Cokes alone (total utility = 25) or games alone (total utility = 35). In fact, the combination of 1 Coke and 4 games is the *best* one you can find. Because this combination maximizes the total utility of your income ($1.50), it represents *optimal consumption.*

Utility-Maximizing Rule

Optimal consumption refers to the mix of output that maximizes total utility for the limited amount of income you have to spend. The basic approach to utility maximization is to purchase that good next which delivers the most *marginal utility per dollar.* Marginal utility per dollar is simply the MU of the good divided by its price: MU ÷ P.

From Table 5.3 we know that a first Coke has an MU of 15 and a price of 50 cents. It thus delivers a marginal utility per dollar of

$$\frac{MU_{first\ Coke}}{P_{Coke}} = \frac{15}{0.50} = 30 \text{ utils per dollar}$$

On the other hand, the first video game has a marginal utility of 10 and a price of 25 cents. It offers a marginal utility per dollar of

$$\frac{MU_{first\ game}}{P_{game}} = \frac{10}{0.25} = 40 \text{ utils per dollar}$$

From this perspective, the first video game is a better deal than the first Coke and should be purchased.

Optimal consumption implies that the utility-maximizing combination of goods has been found. If this is true, you can't increase your total utility by trading one good for another. All goods included in the optimal consumption mix yield the *same* marginal utility per dollar. We know we've reached maximum utility when we've satisfied the following rule:

$$\text{Utility-maximizing rule: } \frac{MU_x}{P_x} = \frac{MU_y}{P_y}$$

where x and y represent any two goods included in our consumption.

Rational consumer choice thus depends on comparisons of marginal utilities and prices. If a dollar spent on product X yields more marginal utility than a dollar spent on product Y, we should buy product X. To use this principle, of course, we have to know the amounts of utility obtainable from various goods and be able to perform a little arithmetic. By doing so, however, we can get the greatest satisfaction from our limited income.

All these graphs and equations make consumer choice look dull and mechanical. Economic theory seems to suggest that consumers walk through shopping malls with marginal-utility tables and hand-held computers. In reality, no one does this—not even your economics instructor. Yet, economic theory is pretty successful in predicting consumer decisions. Consumers don't always buy the optimal mix of goods and services with their limited income. But after some trial and error, consumers adjust their behavior. What economic theory predicts is that the final choices—the *equilibrium* outcomes—will be the predicted optimal ones.

Equilibrium Outcomes

THE ECONOMY TOMORROW

Caveat Emptor

LeBron James is paid over $35 million a year to help convince us to drink Sprite and Powerade ("Flava 23"), wear Nike shoes, use Juice batteries, and chew Bubblicious gum (see News). Do his sponsors know something economic theory doesn't? Economists *assume* consumers know what they want and will act rationally to get the most satisfaction they can. The companies that sponsor basketball star LeBron James don't accept that assumption. They think your tastes will follow LeBron's lead.

Advertisers now spend over $200 *billion* per year to change our tastes. This spending works out to over $400 per consumer, one of the highest per capita advertising rates in the world (see World View on the next page). Some of this advertising (including product labeling) is intended to provide information about existing products or to bring new products to our attention. A great deal of advertising, however, is also designed to exploit our senses and lack of knowledge. Recognizing that we're guilt-ridden, insecure, and sex-hungry, advertisers promise exoneration, recognition, and love; all we have to do is buy the right product.

A favorite target of advertisers is our sense of insecurity. Thousands of products are marketed in ways that appeal to our need for identity. Thousands of brand images are designed to help the consumer answer the nagging question, Who am I? The answers, of course, vary. *Playboy* magazine says, I'm a virile man of the world; Marlboro

---

IN THE NEWS

James Still Blowin' Up With Bubblicious Deal

LeBron James has snapped up another big endorsement deal. The Cleveland Cavaliers' rookie star signed a four-year, $5 million contract with Bubblicious bubble gum, increasing his sponsorship deals to nearly $135 million.

Like his idol, Michael Jordan, the 19-year-old James chews gum during games and occasionally blows a bubble or two—making him a natural fit for London-based Cadbury Schweppes PLC.

Bubblicious will have a James-inspired flavor, according to his agent, Aaron Goodwin. Goodwin said he's talking with four or five companies, including McDonald's and Kraft, about future projects.

James has been racking up big-money endorsement contracts with sponsors since May, when he signed a seven-year, $90 million deal with Nike—the richest initial shoe contract ever offered an athlete.

He has deals with Coca Cola/Sprite ($16 million), Juice Batteries ($8 million) and Upper Deck ($5 million). James also signed a three-year, $13 million deal with the Cavaliers in July.

Source: *The Washington Post*, February 24, 2004. Reprinted with permission of the Associated Press.

Analysis: Companies pay huge amounts for celebrity endorsements, hoping to change consumer tastes (increase demand for a specific product).

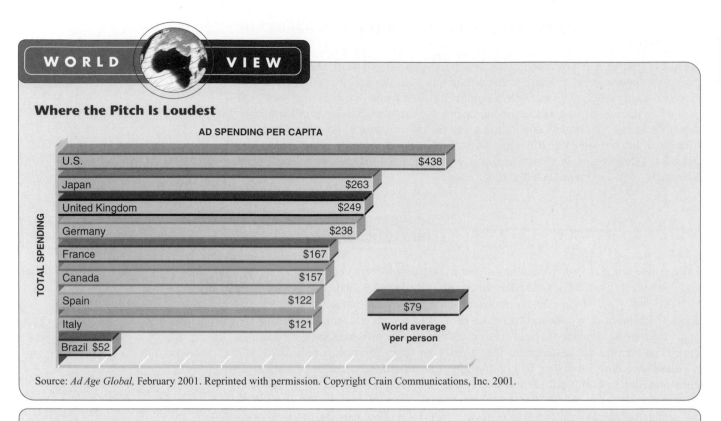

WORLD VIEW

Where the Pitch Is Loudest

AD SPENDING PER CAPITA

TOTAL SPENDING

U.S.	$438
Japan	$263
United Kingdom	$249
Germany	$238
France	$167
Canada	$157
Spain	$122
Italy	$121
Brazil	$52

$79
**World average
per person**

Source: *Ad Age Global,* February 2001. Reprinted with permission. Copyright Crain Communications, Inc. 2001.

Analysis: Producers advertise to change consumer tastes (preferences). At higher levels of income, advertising is likely to play a greater role in consumption decisions.

cigarettes say, I'm a rugged individualist who enjoys "man-sized flavor." Sprite says, I'll be a winner if I drink the same soda LeBron James does. And I'll be able to jump 8 feet high if I wear Air Zoom shoes.

Are Wants Created?

Advertising can't be blamed for all of our foolish consumption. Even members of the most primitive tribes, uncontaminated by the seductions of advertising, adorned themselves with rings, bracelets, and pendants. Furthermore, advertising has grown to massive proportions only in the past 50 years, but consumption spending has been increasing throughout recorded history. Finally, a lot of advertising simply fails to change buying decisions. Accordingly, it's a mistake to attribute the growth or content of consumption entirely to the persuasions of advertisers.

This isn't to say that advertising has necessarily made us happier. The objective of all advertising is to alter the choices we make. Just as product images are used to attract us to particular products, so are pictures of hungry, ill-clothed children used to persuade us to give money to charity. In the same way, public relations gimmicks are employed to sway our votes for public servants. In the case of consumer products, advertising seeks to increase tastes for particular goods and services and therewith our willingness to pay. *A successful advertising campaign is one that shifts the demand curve for a specific product to the right,* inducing consumers to increase their purchases of a product at every price (see Figure 5.9). Advertising may also increase brand loyalty, making the demand curve less elastic (reducing consumer responses to price increases). By influencing our choices in this way, advertising will affect the consumption choices we make in the economy tomorrow. Advertising alone is unlikely to affect the total *level* of consumption, however.

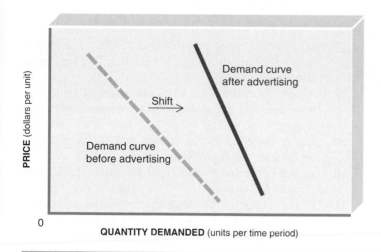

FIGURE 5.9
The Impact of Advertising on a Demand Curve

Advertising seeks to increase our taste for a particular product. If our taste (the product's perceived utility) increases, so will our willingness to buy. The resulting change in demand is reflected in a rightward shift of the demand curve, often accompanied by diminished elasticity.

SUMMARY

- Our desires for goods and services originate in the structure of personality and social dynamics and aren't explained by economic theory. Economic theory focuses on *demand*—that is, our ability and willingness to buy specific quantities of a good at various prices.
- Marginal utility measures the additional satisfaction obtained from consuming one more unit of a good. The law of diminishing marginal utility says that the more of a product we consume, the smaller the increments of pleasure we tend to derive from additional units of it. This is a basis for the law of demand.
- The price elasticity of demand is a numerical measure of consumer response to a change in price, *ceteris paribus*. It equals the percentage change in quantity demanded divided by the percentage change in price. Elasticity depends on the relative price of a good, the availability of substitutes, and time.
- The effect of a price change on total revenue depends on price elasticity. Total revenue and price move in the same direction only if demand is price-inelastic ($E < 1$).
- The shape and position of any particular demand curve depend on a consumer's income, tastes, expectations, and

the price and availability of other goods. Should any of these factors change, the assumption of *ceteris paribus* will no longer hold, and the demand curve will *shift*.
- The income elasticity of demand measures the response of demand to a change in income. If demand increases with income, the product is a normal good. If demand declines (shifts left) when income rises, it's an inferior good.
- Cross-price elasticity measures the response of demand for one good to a change in the price of another. The cross-price elasticity of demand is positive for substitute goods and negative for complementary goods.
- In choosing among alternative goods and services, a consumer compares the prices and anticipated satisfactions that they offer. To maximize utility with one's available income—to achieve an optimal mix of goods and services—one has to get the most utility for every dollar spent. To do so, one must compare the relative prices and pleasures and choose those goods which offer the most marginal utility per dollar.
- Advertising seeks to change consumer tastes and thus the willingness to buy. If tastes do change, the demand curve for that product, will shift.

Key Terms

demand	demand curve	substitute goods
utility	price elasticity of demand	complementary goods
total utility	total revenue	cross-price elasticity of demand
marginal utility	shift in demand	opportunity cost
law of diminishing marginal utility	income elasticity of demand	optimal consumption
ceteris paribus	normal good	
law of demand	inferior good	

Questions for Discussion

1. What does the demand for enrollments in your college look like? What is on the axes? Is the demand price-elastic? Income-elastic? How could you find out?
2. If the marginal utility of pizza never diminished, how many pizzas would you eat?
3. How does total and marginal utility change as you spend more time surfing the net?
4. If the price of gasoline doubled, how would consumption of (a) gasoline, (b) cars, (c) public transportation be affected? How quickly would these adjustments be made?
5. Identify two goods each whose demand exhibits (a) high income elasticity, (b) low income elasticity, (c) high price elasticity, (d) low price elasticity. What accounts for the differences in elasticity?
6. Why is the demand for New York City cigarettes so much more elastic than the overall market demand for cigarettes? (See News, page 104.)
7. Why are per capita advertising expenditures so high in the United States and so low in Brazil? (See World View, page 116.)
8. According to the News stories on pages 103 and 105, how does the price elasticity of demand differ for teenagers and adults? Why?
9. If you owned a movie theater, would you want the demand for movies to be elastic or inelastic?
10. How has the Internet affected the price elasticity of demand for air travel?
11. If the elasticity of demand for coffee is so low (Table 5.1), why doesn't Starbucks raise the price of coffee to $10 a cup?
12. What would happen to unit sales and total revenue for this textbook if the bookstore reduced its price?

| PROBLEMS | The Student Problem Set at the back of this book contains numerical and graphing problems for this chapter. |

| WEB ACTIVITIES | to accompany this chapter can be found on the Online Learning Center: **http://www.mhhe.com/economics/schiller10** |

A P P E N D I X

INDIFFERENCE CURVES

A consumer's demand for any specific product is an expression of many forces. As we've observed, the actual quantity of a product demanded by a consumer varies inversely with its price. The price-quantity relationship is determined by

- *Tastes* (desire for this and other goods).
- *Income* (of the consumer).
- *Expectations* (for income, prices, tastes).
- *Other goods* (their availability and price).

Economic theory attempts to show how each of these forces affects consumer demand. Thus far, we've used two-dimensional demand curves to illustrate the basic principles of demand. We saw that, in general, a change in the price of a good causes a movement along the demand curve, while a change in tastes, income, expectations, or other goods shifts the entire demand curve to a new position.

We haven't looked closely at the origins of demand curves, however. We assumed that a demand curve could be developed from observations of consumer behavior, such as the number of boxes of popcorn that were purchased at various prices (Figure 5.3). Likewise, we observed how the demand curve shifts in response to changes in tastes, income, expectations, or other goods (Figures 5.7 and 5.8).

It's possible, however, to derive a demand curve without actually observing consumer behavior. In theory we can identify consumer *preferences* (tastes), then use

Combination	Cokes	Video Games
A	1	8
B	2	5
C	3	4

TABLE 5A.1
Equally Satisfying Combinations

Different combinations of two goods may be equally satisfying. In this case we assume that the combinations A, B, and C all yield equal total utility. Hence, the consumer will be indifferent about which of the three combinations he or she receives.

those preferences to construct a demand curve. In this case, the demand curve is developed explicitly from known preferences rather than on the basis of market observations. The end result—the demand curve—is the same, at least so long as consumers' behavior in product markets is consistent with their preferences.

Indifference curves are a mechanism for illustrating consumer tastes. We examine their construction and use in this appendix. As suggested above, indifference curves provide an explicit basis for constructing a demand curve. In addition, they are another way of viewing how consumption is affected by price, tastes, and income. Indifference curves are also a useful tool for illustrating explicitly consumer *choice*—that is, the decision to purchase one good rather than another.

Constructing an Indifference Curve

Recall the dilemma that arises when you want Coke and video games but don't have enough money to buy enough of each. The income constraint compels you to make hard decisions. You have to consider the **marginal utility** each additional Coke or video game will provide, compare their respective prices, then make a selection. With careful introspection and good arithmetic you can select the optimal mix of Cokes and video games—that is, the combination that yields the most satisfaction (utility) for the income available. This process of identifying your **optimal consumption** was illustrated in Table 5.3.

Finding your optimal consumption is difficult because you must assess the marginal utility of each prospective purchase. In Table 5.3 we assumed that the marginal utility of the first Coke was 15 utils, while the first video game had a marginal utility of 10. Then we had to specify the marginal utility of every additional Coke and video game. Can we really be so specific about our tastes?

Indifference curves require a bit less arithmetic. *Instead of trying to measure the marginal utility of each prospective purchase, we now look for combinations of goods that yield equal satisfaction.* All we need do is determine that one particular combination of Cokes and video games is as satisfying as another. We don't have to say how many "units of pleasure" both combinations provide—it's sufficient that they're both equally satisfying.

The initial combination of 1 Coke and 8 video games is designated as a combination A in Table 5A.1. This combination of goods yields a certain, but unspecified, level of total utility. What we want to do now is to find another combination of Cokes and games that's just as satisfying as combination A. Finding other combinations of equal satisfaction isn't easy, but it's at least possible. After a lot of soul searching, we decide that 2 Cokes and 5 video games would be just as satisfying as 1 Coke and 8 games.[1] This combination is designated as B in Table 5A.1.

Table 5A.1 also depicts a third combination of Cokes and video games that's as satisfying as the first. Combination C includes 3 Cokes and 4 games, a mix of consumption assumed to yield the same total utility as 1 Coke and 8 games (combination A).

Notice that we haven't said anything about how much pleasure combinations A, B, and C provide. We're simply asserting that these three combinations are *equally* satisfying.

marginal utility: The change in total utility obtained by consuming one additional (marginal) unit of a good or service.

optimal consumption: The mix of consumer purchases that maximizes the utility attainable from available income.

[1]The utility computations used here aren't based on Table 5.3; a different set of tastes is assumed.

FIGURE 5A.1
An Indifference Curve

An indifference curve illustrates the various combinations of two goods that would provide equal satisfaction. The consumer is assumed to be indifferent to a choice between combinations *A, B,* and *C* (and all other points on the curve), as they all yield the same total utility.

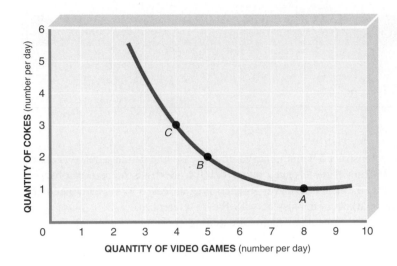

indifference curve: A curve depicting alternative combinations of goods that yield equal satisfaction.

Figure 5A.1 illustrates the information about tastes that we've assembled. Points *A, B,* and *C* represent the three equally satisfying combinations of Cokes and video games we've identified. By connecting these points we create an **indifference curve.** The indifference curve illustrates all combinations of two goods that are equally satisfying. A consumer would be just as happy with any combination represented on the curve, so a choice among them would be a matter of indifference.

An Indifference Map. Not all combinations of Cokes and video games are as satisfying as combination *A,* of course. Surely, 2 Cokes and 8 games would be preferred to only 1 Coke and 8 games. Indeed, *any combination that provided more of one good and no less of the other would be preferred.* Point *D* in Figure 5A.2 illustrates just one such combination. Combination *D* must yield more total utility than combination *A* because it includes one more Coke and no fewer games. A consumer wouldn't be indifferent to a choice between *A* and *D*; on the contrary, combination *D* would be preferred.

Combination *D* is also preferred to combinations *B* and *C*. How do we know? Recall that combinations *A, B,* and *C* are all equally satisfying. Hence, if combination *D* is better than *A,* it must also be better than *B* and *C*. Given a choice, a consumer would select combination *D* (2 Cokes, 8 games) in preference to *any* combination depicted on indifference curve I_1.

FIGURE 5A.2
An Indifference Map

All combinations of goods depicted on any given indifference curve (e.g., I_2) are equally satisfying. Other combinations are more or less satisfying, however, and thus lie on higher (I_2) or lower (I_3) indifference curves. An indifference map shows all possible levels of total utility (e.g., $I_1, I_2, I_3, \ldots, I_n$) and their respective consumption combinations.

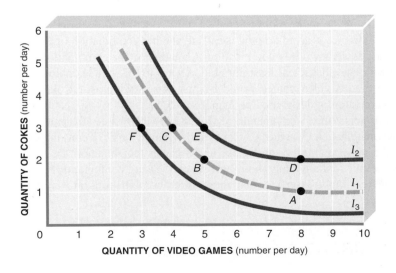

There are also combinations that are as satisfying as D, of course. These possibilities are illustrated on indifference curve I_2. All these combinations are equally satisfying and must therefore be preferred to any points on indifference curve I_1. In general, **the farther the indifference curve is from the origin, the more total utility it yields.**

The curve I_3 illustrates various combinations that are less satisfying. Combination F, for example, includes 3 Cokes and 3 games. This is 1 game less than the number available in combination C. Therefore, F yields less total utility than C and isn't preferred: A consumer would rather have combination C than F. By the same logic we used above, all points on indifference curve I_3 are less satisfying than combinations on curve I_2 or I_1.

Curves 1, 2, and 3 in Figure 5A.2 are the beginnings of an **indifference map.** An indifference map depicts all the combinations of goods that would yield various levels of satisfaction. A single indifference curve, in contrast, illustrates all combinations that provide a single (equal) level of total utility.

> **indifference map:** The set of indifference curves that depicts all possible levels of utility attainable from various combinations of goods.

Utility Maximization

We assume that all consumers strive to maximize their utility. They want as much satisfaction as they can get. In the terminology of indifference curves, this means getting to the indifference curve that's farthest from the origin. The farther one is from the origin, the greater the total utility.

Although the goal of consumers is evident, the means of achieving it isn't so clear. Higher indifference curves aren't only more satisfying, they're also more expensive. We're confronted again with the basic conflict between preferences and prices. With a limited amount of income to spend, we can't attain infinite satisfaction (the farthest indifference curve). We have to settle for less (an indifference curve closer to the origin). The question is: How do we maximize the utility attainable with our limited income?

The Budget Constraint. For starters, we have to determine how much we have to spend. Suppose for the moment that we can spend $2 per day and that Cokes and video games are still the only objects of our consumption desires. The price of a Coke is 50 cents; the price of a game is 25 cents. Accordingly, the maximum number of Cokes we could buy is 4 per day if we didn't play any video games. On the other hand, we could play as many as 8 games if we were to forsake Coke.

Figure 5A.3 depicts the limitations placed on our consumption possibilities by a finite income. The **budget constraint** illustrates all combinations of goods affordable with a given income. In this case, the outermost budget line illustrates the combinations of Cokes and video games that can be purchased with $2.

The budget line is easily drawn. The end points of the budget constraint are found by dividing one's income by the price of the good on the corresponding axis. Thus, the

> **budget constraint:** A line depicting all combinations of goods that are affordable with a given income and given prices.

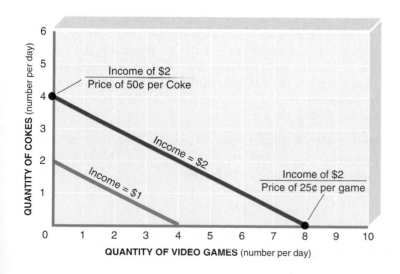

FIGURE 5A.3
The Budget Constraint

Consumption possibilities are limited by available income. The budget constraint illustrates this limitation. The end points of the budget constraint are equal to income divided by the price of each good. All points on the budget constraint represent affordable combinations of goods.

FIGURE 5A.4
Optimal Consumption

The optimal consumption combination—the one that maximizes the utility of spendable income—lies at the point where the budget line is tangent to (just touches) an indifference curve. In this case, point M represents the optimal mix of Cokes and video games, since no other affordable combination lies on a higher indifference curve than I_c.

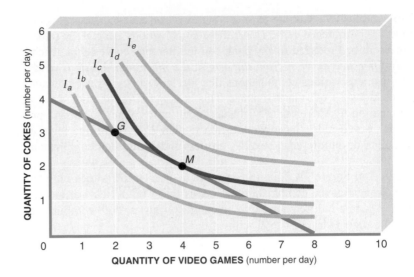

outermost curve begins at 4 Cokes ($2 ÷ 50 cents) and ends at 8 games ($2 ÷ 25 cents). All the other points on the budget constraint represent other combinations of Cokes and video games that could be purchased with $2.

A smaller income is also illustrated in Figure 5A.3. If we had only $1 to spend, we could afford fewer Cokes and fewer games. Hence, a smaller income is represented by a budget constraint that lies closer to the origin.

Optimal Consumption. With a budget constraint looming before us, the limitation on utility maximization is evident. We want to reach the highest indifference curve possible. Our limited income, however, restricts our grasp. We can go only as far as our budget constraint allows. In this context, ***the objective is to reach the highest indifference curve that is compatible with our budget constraint.***

Figure 5A.4 illustrates the process of achieving optimal consumption. We start with an indifference map depicting all utility levels and product combinations. Then we impose a budget line that reflects our income. In this case, we continue to assume that Coke costs 50 cents, video games cost 25 cents, and we have $2 to spend. Hence, ***we can afford only those consumption combinations that are on or inside the budget line.***

Which particular combination of Cokes and video games maximizes the utility of our $2? It must be 2 Cokes and 4 video games, as reflected in point M. Notice that point M isn't only on the budget line but also touches indifference curve I_c. No other point on the budget line touches I_c or any higher indifference curve. Accordingly, I_c represents the most utility we can get for $2 and is attainable only if we consume 2 Cokes and 4 video games. Any other affordable combination yields less total utility— that is, falls on a lower indifference curve. Point G, for example, which offers 3 Cokes and 2 video games for $2, lies on the indifference curve I_b. Because I_b lies closer to the origin than I_c, point G must be less satisfying than point M. We conclude, then, that ***the point of tangency between the budget constraint and an indifference curve represents optimal consumption.*** It's the combination we should buy if we want to maximize the utility of our limited income.

Marginal Utility and Price: A Digression. We earlier illustrated the utility-maximizing rule, which required a comparison of the ratios of marginal utilities to prices. Specifically, optimal consumption was represented as that combination of Cokes and video games that yielded

$$\frac{\text{MU Coke}}{P \text{ Coke}} = \frac{\text{MU games}}{P \text{ games}}$$

Does point M in Figure 5A.4 conform to this rule?

To answer this question, first rearrange the preceding equation as follows:

$$\frac{MU\ Coke}{MU\ games} = \frac{P\ Coke}{P\ games}$$

In this form, the equation says that the relative marginal utilities of Cokes and video games should equal their relative prices when consumption is optimal. In other words, if a Coke costs twice as much as a video game, then it must yield twice as much marginal utility if the consumer is to be in an optimal state. Otherwise, some substitution of Cokes for video games, or vice versa, would be desirable.

With this foundation, we can show that point M conforms to our earlier rule. Consider first the slope of the budget constraint, which is determined by the relative prices of Cokes and video games. In fact, **the (absolute) slope of the budget constraint equals the relative price of the two goods.** In Figure 5A.4 the slope equals the price of video games divided by the price of Cokes (25 cents $\div$ 50 cents = ½). It tells us the rate at which video games can be exchanged for Cokes in the market. In this case, one video game is "worth" half a Coke.

The relative marginal utilities of the two goods are reflected in the slope of the indifference curve. Recall that the curve tells at what rate a consumer is willing to substitute one good for another, with no change in total utility. In fact, the slope of the indifference curve is called the **marginal rate of substitution.** It's equal to the relative marginal utilities of the two goods. Presumably one would be indifferent to a choice between 2 Cokes + 5 games and 3 Cokes + 4 games—as suggested in Table 5A.1—only if the third Coke were as satisfying as the fifth video game.

At the point of optimal consumption (M) in Figure 5A.4 the budget constraint is tangent to the indifference curve I_c, which means that the two curves must have the same slope at the point. In other words,

> **marginal rate of substitution:** The rate at which a consumer is willing to exchange one good for another; the relative marginal utilities of two goods.

$$\frac{P\ games}{P\ Cokes} = \frac{MU\ games}{MU\ Cokes}$$

or alternatively,

$$\frac{Rate\ of}{market\ exchange} = \frac{marginal\ rate}{of\ substitution}$$

Both indifference curves and marginal utility comparisons lead us to the same optimal mix of consumption.

Deriving the Demand Curve

We noted at the beginning of this appendix that indifference curves not only give us an alternative path to optimal consumption but also can be used to derive a demand curve. To do this, we need to consider how the optimal consumption combination changes when the price of one good is altered. We can see what happens in Figure 5A.5.

Figure 5A.5 starts with the optimal consumption attained at point M, with income of $2 and prices of 50 cents for a Coke and 25 cents for a video game. Now we're going to change the price of video games and observe how consumption changes.

Suppose that the price of a video game doubles, from 25 cents to 50 cents. This change will shift the budget constraint inward: Our income of $2 now buys a maximum of 4 games rather than 8. Hence, the lower end point of the budget constraint moves from 8 games to 4 games. **Whenever the price of a good changes, the budget constraint shifts.**

Only one end of the budget constraint is changed in Figure 5A.5. The budget line still begins at 4 Cokes because the price of Coke is unchanged. If only one price is changed, then only one end of the budget constraint is shifted.

FIGURE 5A.5
Changing Prices

When the price of a good changes, the budget constraint shifts, and a new consumption combination must be sought. In this case, the price of video games is changing. When the price of games increases from 25 cents to 50 cents, the budget constraint shifts inward and optimal consumption moves from point *M* to point *N*.

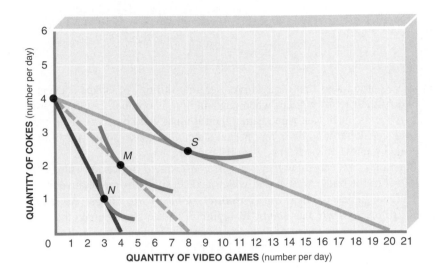

Because the budget constraint has shifted inward, the combination *M* is no longer attainable. Two Cokes (at 50 cents each) and 4 games (at 50 cents each) now cost more than $2. We're now forced to accept a lower level of total utility. According to Figure 5A.5, optimal consumption is now located at point *N*. This is the point of tangency between the new budget constraint and a lower indifference curve. At point *N* we consume 1 Coke and 3 video games.

Consider what has happened here. The price of video games has increased (from 25 cents to 50 cents), and the quantity of games demanded has decreased. This is the kind of relationship that demand curves describe. **Demand curves** indicate how the quantity demanded of a good changes in response to a change in its price, given a fixed income and all other things held constant. Not only does Figure 5A.5 provide

demand curve: A curve describing the quantities of a good a consumer is willing and able to buy at alternative prices in a given time period, *ceteris paribus.*

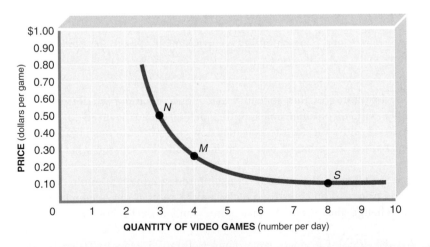

FIGURE 5A.6
The Demand for Video Games

Figure 5A.5 shows how optimal consumption is altered when the price of video games changes. From that figure we can determine the quantity of video games demanded at alternative prices, *ceteris paribus.* That information is summarized here in the demand schedule (below) and the demand curve (above).

Point	Price (per game)	Quantity Demanded (games per day)
N	50 cents	3
M	25	4
S	10	8

the same information, it also conforms to the **law of demand:** As the price of games increases, the quantity demanded falls.

Suppose the price of video games were to fall rather than increase. Specifically, assume that the price of a game fell to 10 cents. This price reduction would shift the budget constraint farther out on the horizontal axis, since as many as 20 games could then be purchased with $2. As a result of the price reduction, we can now buy more goods and thus attain a higher level of satisfaction.

Point *S* in Figure 5A.5 indicates the optimal combination of Cokes and video games at the new video game price. At these prices, we consume 8 video games and 2.4 Cokes (we may have to share with a friend). The law of demand is again evident: When the price of video games declines, the quantity demanded increases.

The Demand Schedule and Curve. Figure 5A.6 summarizes the information we've acquired about the demand for video games. The demand schedule depicts the price-quantity relationships prevailing at optimal consumption points *N*, *M*, and *S* (from Figure 5A.5). The demand curve generalizes these observations to encompass other prices. What we end up with is a demand curve explicitly derived from our (assumed) knowledge of consumer tastes.

law of demand: The quantity of a good demanded in a given time period increases as its price falls, *ceteris paribus.*

The Costs of Production

Last year U.S. consumers bought more than $1.5 *trillion* worth of imported goods, including Japanese cars, Italian shoes, and toys from China. As you might expect, this angers domestic producers, who frequently end up with unsold goods, half-empty factories, and unemployed workers. They rage against the "unfair" competition from abroad, asserting that producers in Korea, Brazil, and China can undersell U.S. producers because workers in these countries are paid dirt-poor wages.

But lower wages don't necessarily imply lower costs. You could pay me $2 per hour to type and still end up paying a lot for typing. Truth is, I type only about 10 words a minute, with lots of misteaks. The cost of producing goods depends not only on the price of inputs (e.g., labor) but also on how much they produce.

In this chapter we begin looking at the costs of producing the goods and services that market participants demand. We confront the following questions:

- **How much output *can* a firm produce?**
- **How do the *costs* of production vary with the rate of output?**
- **Do larger firms have a cost advantage over smaller firms?**

The answers to these questions are important not only to producers faced with foreign competition but to consumers as well. The costs of producing a good have a direct impact on the prices consumers pay.

THE PRODUCTION FUNCTION

No matter how large a business is or who owns it, all businesses confront one central fact: It costs something to produce goods. To produce corn, a farmer needs land, water, seed, equipment, and labor. To produce fillings, a dentist needs a chair, a drill, some space, and labor. Even the "production" of educational services such as this economics class requires the use of labor (your teacher), land (on which the school is built), and capital (the building, blackboard, computers). In short, unless you're producing unrefined, unpackaged air, you need **factors of production**—that is, resources that can be used to produce a good or service. The factors of production used in production provide the basic measure of economic cost. The costs of your economics class, for example, are measured by the amounts of land, labor, and capital it requires. These are *resource* costs of production.

To assess the costs of production, we must first determine how many resources are actually needed to produce a given product. You could use a lot of resources to produce a product or use just a few. What we really want to know is how *best* to produce. What's the *smallest* amount of resources needed to produce a specific product? Or we could ask the same question from a different perspective: What's the *maximum* amount of output attainable from a given quantity of resources.

factors of production: Resource inputs used to produce goods and services, such as land, labor, capital, entrepreneurship.

Capital Input (sewing machines per day)	Labor Input (workers per day)								
	0	1	2	3	4	5	6	7	8
	Jeans Output (pairs per day)								
0	0	0	0	0	0	0	0	0	0
1	0	15	34	44	48	50	51	51	47
2	0	20	46	64	72	78	81	82	80
3	0	21	50	73	83	92	99	103	103

TABLE 6.1
A Production Function

A production function tells us the maximum amount of output attainable from alternative combinations of factor inputs. This particular function tells us how many pairs of jeans we can produce in a day with a given factory and varying quantities of capital and labor. With one sewing machine, and one operator, we can produce a maximum of 15 pairs of jeans per day, as indicated in the second column of the second row. To produce more jeans, we need more labor or more capital.

The answers to these questions are reflected in the **production function,** which tells us the maximum amount of good *X* producible from various combinations of factor inputs. With one chair and one drill, a dentist can fill a *maximum* of 32 cavities per day. With two chairs, a drill, and an assistant, a dentist can fill up to 55 cavities per day.

A production function is a technological summary of our ability to produce a particular good.[1] Table 6.1 provides a partial glimpse of one such function. In this case, the output is designer jeans, as produced by Low-Rider Jeans Corporation. The essential inputs in the production of jeans are land, labor (garment workers), and capital (a factory and sewing machines). With these inputs, Low-Rider Jeans Corporation can produce and sell hip-hugging jeans to style-conscious consumers.

As in all production endeavors, we want to know how much output we can produce with available resources. To make things easy, we'll assume that the factory is already built, with fixed space dimensions. The only inputs we can vary are labor (the number of garment workers per day) and additional capital (the number of sewing machines we lease per day).

In these circumstances, the quantity of jeans we can produce depends on the amount of labor and capital we employ. *The purpose of a production function is to tell us just how much output we can produce with varying amounts of factor inputs.* Table 6.1 provides such information for jeans production.

Consider the simplest option, that of employing no labor or capital (the upper-left corner in Table 6.1). An empty factory can't produce any jeans; maximum output is zero per day. Even though land, capital (an empty factory), and even denim are available, some essential labor and capital inputs are missing, and jeans production is impossible.

Suppose now we employ some labor (a machine operator) but don't lease any sewing machines. Will output increase? Not according to the production function. The first row in Table 6.1 illustrates the consequences of employing labor without any capital equipment. Without sewing machines (or even needles, another form of capital), the operators can't make jeans. Maximum output remains at zero, no matter how much labor is employed in this case.

The dilemma of machine operators without sewing machines illustrates a general principle of production: *The* **productivity** *of any factor of production depends on*

production function: A technological relationship expressing the maximum quantity of a good attainable from different combinations of factor inputs.

Varying Input Levels

productivity: Output per unit of input, for example, output per labor-hour.

[1]By contrast, the production possibilities curve discussed in Chapter 1 expresses our ability to produce various *combinations* of goods, given the use of *all* our resources. The production possibilities curve summarizes the output capacity of the entire economy. A production function describes the capacity of a single firm.

the amount of other resources available to it. Industrious, hardworking machine operators can't make designer jeans without sewing machines.

We can increase the productivity of garment workers by providing them with machines. The production function again tells us by *how much* jeans output could increase. Suppose we leased just one machine per day. Now the second row in Table 6.1 is the relevant one. It says jeans output will remain at zero if we lease one machine but employ no labor. If we employ one machine *and* one worker, however, the jeans will start rolling out the front door. Maximum output under these circumstances (row 2, column 2) is 15 pairs of jeans per day. Now we're in business!

The remaining columns in row 2 tell us how many additional jeans we can produce if we hire more workers, still leasing only one sewing machine. With one machine and two workers, maximum output rises to 34 pairs per day. If a third worker is hired, output could increase to 44 pairs.

Table 6.1 also indicates how production would increase with additional sewing machines (capital). By reading down any column of the table, you can see how more machines increase potential jeans output.

Efficiency

The production function summarized in Table 6.1 underscores the essential relationship between resource *inputs* and product *outputs*. It's also a basic introduction to economic costs. To produce 15 pairs of jeans per day, we need one sewing machine, an operator, a factory, and some denim. All these inputs comprise the *resource cost* of producing jeans.

Another feature of Table 6.1 is that it conveys the *maximum* output of jeans producible from particular input combinations. The standard garment worker and sewing machine, when brought together at Low-Rider Jeans Corporation, can produce *at most* 15 pairs of jeans per day. They could also produce a lot less. Indeed, a careless cutter can waste a lot of denim. A lazy or inattentive one won't keep the sewing machines humming. As many a producer has learned, actual output can fall far short of the limits described in the production function. Indeed, jeans output will reach the levels in Table 6.1 only if the jeans factory operates with relative **efficiency.** This requires getting maximum output from the resources used in the production process. ***The production function represents maximum technical efficiency—that is, the most output attainable from any given level of factor inputs.***

efficiency (technical): Maximum output of a good from the resources used in production.

We can always be inefficient, of course. This merely means getting less output than possible for the inputs we use. But this isn't a desirable situation. To a factory manager, it means less output for a given amount of input (cost). To society as a whole, inefficiency implies a waste of resources. If Low-Rider Jeans isn't producing efficiently, we're being denied some potential output. It's not only a question of having fewer jeans. We could also use the labor and capital now employed by Low-Rider Jeans to produce something else. Specifically, the **opportunity cost** of a product is measured by the most desired goods and services that could have been produced with the same resources. Hence, if jeans production isn't up to par, society is either (1) getting fewer jeans than it should for the resources devoted to jeans production or (2) giving up too many other goods and services in order to get a desired quantity of jeans.

opportunity cost: The most desired goods or services that are forgone in order to obtain something else.

Although we can always do worse than the production function suggests, we can't do better, at least in the short run. The production function represents the *best* we can do with our current technological know-how. For the moment, at least, there's no better way to produce a specific good. As our technological and managerial capabilities increase, however, we'll attain higher levels of future productivity. These advances in our productive capability will be represented by new production functions.

Short-Run Constraints

Let's step back from the threshold of scientific advance for a moment and return to Low-Rider Jeans. Forget about possible technological breakthroughs in jeans production (e.g., electronic sewing machines or robot operators) and concentrate on the economic realities of our modest endeavor. For the present we're stuck with existing technology. In fact, all the output figures in Table 6.1 are based on the use of a specific factory. Once we've purchased or leased that factory, we've set a limit to current jeans production.

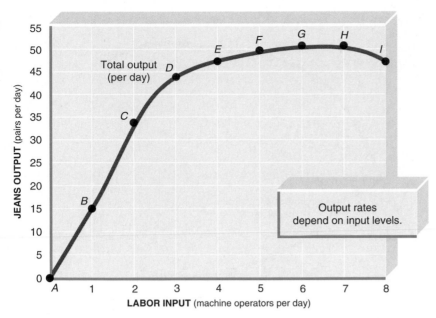

FIGURE 6.1
Short-Run Production Function

In the short run some inputs (e.g., land, capital) are fixed in quantity. Output then depends on how much of a variable input (e.g., labor) is used. The short-run production function shows how output changes when more labor is used. This figure and the table below are based on the second (one-machine) row in Table 6.1.

	A	B	C	D	E	F	G	H	I
Number of workers	0	1	2	3	4	5	6	7	8
Total output	0	15	34	44	48	50	51	51	47
Marginal physical product	—	15	19	10	4	2	1	0	−4

When such commitments to fixed inputs (e.g., the factory) exist, we're dealing with a **short-run** production problem. If no land or capital were in place—if we could build or lease any-sized factory—we'd be dealing with a *long-run* decision.

Our short-run objective is to make the best possible use of the factory we've acquired. This entails selecting the right combination of labor and capital inputs to produce jeans. To simplify the decision, we'll limit the number of sewing machines in use. If we lease only one sewing machine, then the second row in Table 6.1 is the only one we have to consider. In this case, the single sewing machine (capital) becomes another short-run constraint on the production of jeans. With a given factory and one sewing machine, the short-run rate of output depends entirely on how many workers are hired.

Figure 6.1 illustrates the short-run production function applicable to the factory with one sewing machine. As noted before, a factory with a sewing machine but no machine operators produces no jeans. This was observed in Table 6.1 (row 1, column 0) and is now illustrated by point *A* in Figure 6.1. To get any jeans output, we need to hire some labor. In this simplified example, ***labor is the variable input that determines how much output we get from our fixed inputs (land and capital).*** By placing one worker in the factory, we can produce 15 pairs of jeans per day. This possibility is represented by point *B*. The remainder of the production function shows how jeans output changes as we employ more workers in our single-machine factory.

short run: The period in which the quantity (and quality) of some inputs can't be changed.

MARGINAL PRODUCTIVITY

The short-run production function not only defines the *limit* to output but also shows how much each worker contributes to that limit. Notice again that jeans output increases from zero (point *A* in Figure 6.2) to 15 pairs (point *B*) when the first

FIGURE 6.2
Marginal Physical Product (MPP)

Marginal physical product is the *change* in total output that results from employing one more unit of input. The *third* unit of labor, for example, increases *total output* from 34 (point *C*) to 44 (point *D*). Hence the *marginal* output of the third worker is 10 pairs of jeans (point *d*). What's the MPP of the fourth worker? What happens to *total* output when this worker is hired?

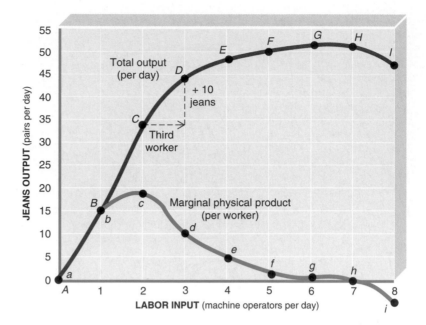

marginal physical product (MPP): The change in total output associated with one additional unit of input.

machine operator is hired. In other words, total output *increases* by 15 pairs when we employ the first worker. This increase is called the **marginal physical product (MPP)** of that first worker—that is, the *change* in total output that results from employment of one more unit of (labor) input, or

$$\text{Marginal physical} \atop \text{product (MPP)} = \frac{\text{change in total output}}{\text{change in input quantity}}$$

With zero workers, total output was zero. With the first worker, total output increases to 15 pairs of jeans per day. The MPP of the first worker is 15 pairs of jeans.

If we employ a second operator, jeans output more than doubles, to 34 pairs per day (point *C*). The 19-pair *increase* in output represents the marginal physical product of the *second* worker.

The higher MPP of the second worker raises a question about the first. Why was the first's MPP lower? Laziness? Is the second worker faster, less distracted, or harder working?

The second worker's higher MPP isn't explained by superior talents or effort. We assume, in fact, that all "units of labor" are equal—that is, one worker is just as good as another.[2] Their different marginal products are explained by the structure of the production process, not by their respective abilities. The first garment worker not only had to sew jeans but also to unfold bolts of denim, measure the jeans, sketch out the patterns, and cut them to approximate size. A lot of time was spent going from one task to another. Despite the worker's best efforts, this person simply couldn't to everything at once.

A second worker alleviates this situation. With two workers, less time is spent running from one task to another. While one worker is measuring and cutting, the other can continue sewing. This improved *ratio* of labor to other factors of production results in the large jump in total output. The second worker's superior MPP isn't unique to this person: It would have occurred even if we'd hired the workers in the reverse order.

Diminishing Marginal Returns

Unfortunately, total output won't keep rising so sharply if still more workers are hired. Look what happens when a third worker is hired. Total jeans production continues to increase. But the increase from point *C* to point *D* in Figure 6.2 is only 10 pairs per

---

[2]In reality, garment workers do differ greatly in energy, talent, and diligence. These differences can be eliminated by measuring units of labor in *constant-quality* units. A person who works twice as hard as everyone else would count as two *quality-adjusted* units of labor.

day. Hence, the third worker's MPP (10 pairs) is *less* than that of the second (19 pairs). Marginal physical product is *diminishing*. This concept is illustrated by point *d* in Figure 6.2.

What accounts for this decline in MPP? The answer lies in the ratio of labor to other factors of production. A third worker begins to crowd our facilities. We still have only one sewing machine. Two people can't sew at the same time. As a result, some time is wasted as the operators wait for their turns at the machine. Even if they split up the various jobs, there will still be some "downtime," since measuring and cutting aren't as time-consuming as sewing. Consequently, we can't make full use of a third worker. The relative scarcity of other inputs (capital and land) constrains the third worker's marginal physical product.

Resource constraints are even more evident when a fourth worker is hired. Total output increases again, but the increase this time is very small. With three workers, we got 44 pairs of jeans per day (point *D*); with four workers, we get a maximum of 48 pairs (point *E*). Thus the fourth worker's MPP is only 4 pairs of jeans. There simply aren't enough machines to make productive use of so much labor.

If a seventh worker is hired, the operators get in one another's way, argue, and waste denim. Notice in Figure 6.1 that total output doesn't increase at all when a seventh worker is hired (point *H*). The MPP of the seventh worker is zero (point *h*). Were an eighth worker hired, total output would actually *decline*, from 51 pairs (point *H*) to 47 pairs (point *I*). The eighth worker has a *negative* MPP (point *i* in Figure 6.2).

Law of Diminishing Returns. The problems of crowded facilities apply to most production processes. In the short run, a production process is characterized by a fixed amount of available land and capital. Typically, the only factor that can be varied in the short run is labor. Yet, *as more labor is hired, each unit of labor has less capital and land to work with.* This is simple division: The available facilities are being shared by more and more workers. At some point, this constraint begins to pinch. When it does, marginal physical product declines. This situation is so common that it's the basis for the **law of diminishing returns,** which says that the marginal physical product of any factor of production such as labor, will diminish at some point, as more of it is used in a given production setting. Notice in Figure 6.2 how diminishing returns set in when the third worker was hired.

law of diminishing returns: The marginal physical product of a variable input declines as more of it is employed with a given quantity of other (fixed) inputs.

RESOURCE COSTS

A production function tells us how much output a firm *can* produce with its existing plant and equipment. It doesn't tell us how much the firm will *want* to produce. A firm *might* want to produce at capacity if the profit picture were bright enough. On the other hand, a firm might not produce *any* output if costs always exceeded sales revenue. The most desirable rate of output is the one that maximizes total **profit**—the difference between total revenue and total costs.

The production function therefore is just a starting point for supply decisions. To decide how much output to produce with that function, a firm must next examine the costs of production. How fast do costs rise when output increases?

The law of diminishing returns provides a clue to how fast costs rise. *The economic cost of a product is measured by the value of the resources needed to produce it.* What we've seen here is that those resource requirements eventually increase. Each additional sewing machine operator produces fewer and fewer jeans. In effect, then, each additional pair of jeans produced uses more and more labor.

Suppose we employ one sewing machine and one operator again, for a total output of 15 pairs of jeans per day; see point *b* in Figure 6.3*a*. Now look at production from another perspective, that of *costs*. How much labor cost are we using at point *b* to produce one pair of jeans? The answer is simple. Since one worker is producing

profit: The difference between total revenue and total cost.

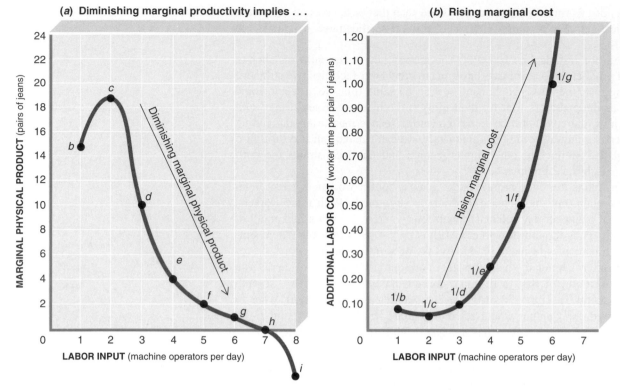

FIGURE 6.3
Falling MPP Implies Rising Marginal Cost

Marginal physical product (MPP) is the additional output obtained by employing one more unit of input. If MPP is falling, each additional unit of input is producing less additional output, which means that the input cost of each unit of output is rising.

The third worker's MPP is 10 pairs (point *d* in part *a*). Therefore, the labor cost of these additional jeans is approximately 1/10 unit of labor per pair (point 1/*d* in part *b*).

15 pairs of jeans, the labor input per pair of jeans must be one-fifteenth of a worker's day, that is, 0.067 unit of labor; see point 1/*b* in Figure 6.3*b*. All we're doing here is translating *output* data into related *input* (cost) data.

Marginal Resource Cost

The next question is, How do input costs change when output increases. As point *c* in Figure 6.3*a* reminds us, total output increases by 19 pairs when we hire a second worker. What's the implied labor cost of those *additional* 19 pairs? By dividing one worker by 19 pairs of jeans, we observe that the labor cost of that extra output is one-nineteenth, or 0.053 of a worker's day; see point 1/*c* in Figure 6.3*b*.

When we focus on the *additional* costs incurred from increasing production, we're talking about *marginal* costs. Specifically, **marginal cost (MC)** refers to the *increase* in total costs required to get one additional unit of output. More generally,

> **marginal cost (MC):** The increase in total cost associated with a one-unit increase in production.

$$\text{Marginal cost (MC)} = \frac{\text{change in total cost}}{\text{change in output}}$$

In our simple case where labor is the only variable input, the marginal cost of the added jeans is

$$\text{Marginal cost} = \frac{1 \text{ additional worker}}{19 \text{ additional pairs}}$$

$$= 0.053 \text{ workers per pair}$$

The amount 0.053 of labor represents the *change* in total resource cost when we produce one *additional* pair of jeans.

Notice in Figure 6.3b that the marginal labor cost of jeans production declines when the second worker is hired. Marginal cost falls from 0.067 unit of labor (plus denim) per pair (point 1/b in Figure 6.3b) to only 0.053 unit of labor per pair (point 1/c). It costs less labor *per pair* to use two workers rather than only one. This is a reflection of the second worker's increased MPP. *Whenever MPP is increasing, the marginal cost of producing a good must be falling.* This is illustrated in Figure 6.3 by the move from b to c in part a and the corresponding move from 1/b to 1/c in part b.

Unfortunately, marginal physical product typically declines at some point. As it does, the marginal costs of production rise. In this sense, each additional pair of jeans becomes more expensive—it uses more and more labor per pair. Figure 6.3 illustrates this inverse relationship between MPP and marginal cost. The third worker has an MPP of 10 pairs, as illustrated by point d. The marginal labor input of these extra 10 pairs is thus 1 ÷ 10, or 0.10 unit of labor. In other words, one-tenth of a third worker's daily effort goes into each pair of jeans. This additional labor cost *per unit* is illustrated by 1/d in part b of the figure.

Note in Figure 6.3 how marginal physical product declines after point c and how marginal costs rise after point 1/c. This is no accident. *If marginal physical product declines, marginal cost increases.* Thus, increasing marginal cost is as common as— and the direct result of—diminishing returns. These increasing marginal costs aren't the fault of any person or factor, simply a reflection of the resource constraints found in any established production setting (i.e., existing and limited plant and equipment). In the short run, the quantity and quality of land and capital are fixed, and we can vary only their intensity of use, such as with more or fewer workers. It's in this short-run context that we keep running into diminishing marginal returns and rising marginal costs.

DOLLAR COSTS

This entire discussion of diminishing returns and marginal costs may seem a bit alien. After all, we're interested in the costs of production, and costs are typically measured in *dollars,* not such technical notions as MPP. Jeans producers need to know how many dollars it costs to keep jeans flowing; they don't want a lecture on marginal physical product.

Jeans manufacturers don't have to study marginal physical products, or even the production function. They can confine their attention to dollar costs. The dollar costs observed, however, are directly related to the underlying production function. To understand *why* costs rise—and how they might be reduced—some understanding of the production function is necessary. In this section we translate production functions into dollar costs.

The **total cost** of producing a product includes the market value of all the resources used in its production. To determine this cost we simply identify all the resources used in production, determine their value, and then add up everything.

In the production of jeans, these resources included land, labor, and capital. Table 6.2 identifies these resources, their unit values, and the total dollar cost associated with their

Total Cost

total cost: The market value of all resources used to produce a good or service.

TABLE 6.2
The Total Costs of Production (total cost of producing 15 pairs of jeans per day)

The total cost of producing a good equals the market value of all the resources used in its production. In this case, the production of 15 pairs of jeans per day requires resources worth $245.

Resource Input	×	Unit Price	=	Total Cost
1 factory		$100 per day		$100
1 sewing machine		20 per day		20
1 operator		80 per day		80
1.5 bolts of denim		30 per bolt		45
Total cost				$245

use. This table is based on an assumed output of 15 pairs of jeans per day, with the use of one worker and one sewing machine (point *B* in Figure 6.2). The rent on the factory is $100 per day, a sewing machine rents for $20 per day, the wages of a garment worker are $80 per day. We'll assume Low-Rider Jeans Corporation can purchase bolts of denim for $30 apiece, with each bolt providing enough denim for 10 pairs of jeans. In other words, one-tenth of a bolt ($3 worth of material) is required for one pair of jeans. We'll ignore any other potential expenses. With these assumptions, the total cost of producing 15 pairs of jeans per day amounts to $245, as shown in Table 6.2.

Fixed Costs. Total costs will change of course as we alter the rate of production. But not all costs increase. In the short run, some costs don't increase at all when output is increased. These are **fixed costs,** in the sense that they don't vary with the rate of output. The factory lease is an example. Once you lease a factory, you're obligated to pay for it, whether or not you use it. The person who owns the factory wants $100 per day. Even if you produce no jeans, you still have to pay that rent. That's the essence of fixed costs.

> **fixed costs:** Costs of production that don't change when the rate of output is altered (e.g., the cost of basic plant and equipment).

The leased sewing machine is another fixed cost. When you rent a sewing machine, you must pay the rental charge. It doesn't matter whether you use it for a few minutes or all day long—the rental charge is fixed at $20 per day.

Variable Costs. Labor costs are another story altogether. The amount of labor employed in jeans production can be varied easily. If we decide not to open the factory tomorrow, we can just tell our only worker to take the day off without pay. We'll still have to pay rent, but we can cut back on wages. On the other hand, if we want to increase daily output, we can also get additional workers easily and quickly. Labor is regarded as a **variable cost** in this line of work—that is, a cost that *varies* with the rate of output.

> **variable costs:** Costs of production that change when the rate of output is altered (e.g., labor and material costs).

The denim itself is another variable cost. Denim not used today can be saved for tomorrow. Hence, how much we "spend" on denim today is directly related to how many jeans we produce. In this sense, the cost of denim input varies with the rate of jeans output.

Figure 6.4 illustrates how these various costs are affected by the rate of production. On the vertical axis are the costs of production, in dollars per day. Notice that the

FIGURE 6.4
The Cost of Jeans Production

Total cost includes both fixed and variable costs. Fixed costs must be paid even if no output is produced (point *A*). Variable costs start at zero and increase with the rate of output. The total cost of producing 15 pairs of jeans (point *B*) includes $120 in fixed costs (rent on the factory and sewing machines) and $125 in variable costs (denim and wages). Total cost rises as output increases, because additional variable costs must be incurred.

In this example, the short-run capacity is equal to 51 pairs (point *G*). If still more inputs are employed, costs will rise but not total output.

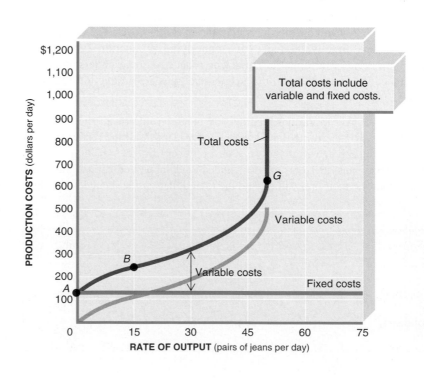

total cost of producing 15 pairs per day is still $245, as indicated by point *B*. This cost figure consists of

Dollar Cost of Producing 15 Pairs

Fixed costs:

Factory rent	$100	
Sewing machine rent	20	
Subtotal		$120

Variable costs:

Wages to labor	$80	
Denim	45	
Subtotal		$125
Total costs		$245

If we increase the rate of output, total costs will rise. ***How fast total costs rise depends on variable costs only,*** however, since fixed costs remain at $120 per day. (Notice the horizontal fixed-cost curve in Figure 6.4.)

With one sewing machine and one factory, there's an absolute limit to daily jeans production. According to the production function in Figure 6.1, the capacity of a factory with one machine is roughly 51 pairs of jeans per day. If we try to produce more jeans than this by hiring additional workers, our total costs will rise, but our output won't. Recall that the seventh worker had a *zero* marginal physical product (Figure 6.2). In fact, we could fill the factory with garment workers and drive total costs sky-high. But the limits of space and one sewing machine don't permit output in excess of 51 pairs per day. This limit to productive capacity is represented by point *G* on the total cost curve. Further expenditure on inputs will increase production *costs* but not *output*.

Although there's no upper limit to costs, there is a lower limit. If output is reduced to zero, total costs fall only to $120 per day, the level of fixed costs, as illustrated by point *A* in Figure 6.4. As before, ***there's no way to avoid fixed costs in the short run.*** Indeed, those fixed costs define the short run.

While Figure 6.4 illustrates *total* costs of production, other measures of cost are often desired. One of the most common measures of cost is average, or per-unit, cost. **Average total cost (ATC)** is simply total cost divided by the rate of output:

$$\text{Average total cost (ATC)} = \frac{\text{total cost}}{\text{total output}}$$

At an output of 15 pairs of jeans per day, total costs are $245. The average cost of production is thus $16.33 per pair (= 245 ÷ 15) at this rate of output.

Figure 6.5 shows how average costs change as the rate of output varies. Row *J* of the cost schedule, for example, again indicates the fixed, variable, and total costs of producing 15 pairs of jeans per day. Fixed costs are still $120; variable costs are $125. Thus the total cost of producing 15 pairs per day is $245, as we saw earlier.

The rest of row *J* shows the average costs of jeans production. These figures are obtained by dividing each dollar total (columns 2, 3, and 4) by the rate of physical output (column 1). At an output rate of 15 pairs per day, **average fixed cost (AFC)** is $8 per pair, **average variable cost (AVC)** is $8.33, and *average total cost (ATC)* is $16.33. ATC, then, is simply the sum of AFC and AVC:

$$\text{ATC} = \text{AFC} + \text{AVC}$$

Falling AFC. At this relatively low rate of output, fixed costs are a large portion of total costs. The rent paid for the factory and sewing machines works out to $8 per pair ($120 ÷ 15). This high average fixed cost accounts for nearly one-half of total average costs. This suggests that it's quite expensive to lease a factory and sewing

Average Costs

average total cost (ATC): Total cost divided by the quantity produced in a given time period.

average fixed cost (AFC): Total fixed cost divided by the quantity produced in a given time period.

average variable cost (AVC): Total variable cost divided by the quantity produced in a given time period.

FIGURE 6.5
Average Costs

Average total cost (ATC) in column 7 equals total cost (column 4) divided by the rate of output (column 1). Since total cost includes both fixed (column 2) and variable (column 3) costs, ATC also equals AFC (column 5) plus AVC (column 6). This relationship is illustrated in the graph. The ATC of producing 15 pairs per day (point *J*) equals $16.33; the sum of AFC ($8) and AVC ($8.33).

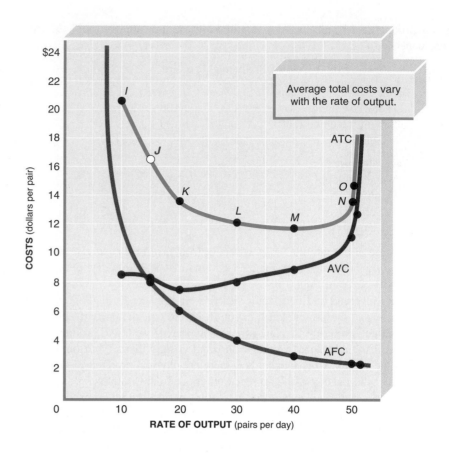

Average total costs vary with the rate of output.

	(1)	(2)		(3)		(4)	(5) Average Fixed Cost		(6) Average Variable Cost		(7) Average Total Cost
	Rate of Output	Fixed Costs	+	Variable Costs	=	Total Cost		+		=	
H	0	$120		$ 0		$120	—		—		—
I	10	120		85		205	$12.00		$ 8.50		$20.50
J	15	120		125		245	8.00		8.33		16.33
K	20	120		150		270	6.00		7.50		13.50
L	30	120		240		360	4.00		8.00		12.00
M	40	120		350		470	3.00		8.75		11.75
N	50	120		550		670	2.40		11.00		13.40
O	51	120		633		753	2.35		12.41		14.76

machine to produce only 15 pairs of jeans per day. To reduce average costs, we must make fuller use of our leased plant and equipment.

Notice what happens to average costs when the rate of output is increased to 20 pairs per day (row K in Figure 6.5). Average fixed costs go down, to only $6 per pair. This sharp decline in AFC results from the fact that total fixed costs ($120) are now spread over more output. Even though our rent hasn't dropped, the *average* fixed cost of producing jeans has.

If we produce more than 20 pairs of jeans per day, AFC will continue to fall. Recall that

$$\text{AFC} = \frac{\text{total fixed cost}}{\text{total output}}$$

The numerator is fixed (at $120 in this case). But the denominator increases as output expands. Hence, ***any increase in output will lower average fixed cost.*** This is reflected in Figure 6.5 by the constantly declining AFC curve.

As jeans output increases from 15 to 20 pairs per day, AVC falls as well. AVC includes the price of denim purchased and labor costs. The price of denim is unchanged, at $3 per pair ($30 per bolt). But per-unit *labor* costs have fallen, from $5.33 to $4.50 per pair. Thus, the reduction in AVC is completely due to the greater productivity of a second worker. To get 20 pairs of jeans, we had to employ a second worker part-time. In the process, the marginal physical product of labor rose and AVC fell.

With both AFC and AVC falling, ATC must decline as well. In this case, *average* total cost falls from $16.33 per pair to $13.50. This is reflected in row K in the table as well as in point *K* on the ATC curve in Figure 6.5.

Rising AVC. Although AFC continues to decline as output expands, AVC doesn't keep dropping. On the contrary, AVC tends to start rising quite early in the expansion process. Look at column 6 of the table in Figure 6.5. After an initial decline, AVC starts to increase. At an output of 20 pairs, AVC is $7.50. At 30 pairs, AVC is $8.00. By the time the rate of output reaches 51 pairs per day, AVC is $12.41.

Average variable cost rises because of diminishing returns in the production process. We discussed this concept before. As output expands, each unit of labor has less land and capital to work with. Marginal physical product falls. As it does, labor costs *per pair of jeans* rise, pushing up AVC.

U-Shaped ATC. The steady decline of AFC, when combined with the typical increase in AVC, results in a U-shaped pattern for average total costs. In the early stages of output expansion, the large declines in AFC outweigh any increases in AVC. As a result, ATC tends to fall. Notice that ATC declines from $20.50 to $11.75 as output increases from 10 to 40 pairs per day. This is also illustrated in Figure 6.5 with the downward move from point *I* to point *M*.

The battle between falling AFC and rising AVC takes an irreversible turn soon thereafter. When output is increased from 40 to 50 pairs of jeans per day, AFC continues to fall (row N in the table). But the decline in AFC (−60 cents) is overshadowed by the increase in AVC (+$2.25). Once rising AVC dominates, ATC starts to increase as well. ATC increases from $11.75 to $13.40 when jeans production expands from 40 to 50 pairs per day.

This and further increases in average total costs cause the ATC curve in Figure 6.5 to start rising. *The initial dominance of falling AFC, combined with the later resurgence of rising AVC, is what gives the ATC curve its characteristic U shape.*

Minimum Average Cost. It's easy to get lost in this thicket of intertwined graphs and jumble of equations. A couple of landmarks will help guide us out, however. One of those is located at the very bottom of the U-shaped average total cost curve. Point *M* in Figure 6.5 represents *minimum* average total costs. By producing exactly 40 pairs per day, we minimize the amount of land, labor, and capital used per pair of jeans. For Low-Rider Jeans Corporation, point *M* represents least-cost production—the lowest-cost jeans. For society as a whole, point *M* also represents the lowest possible opportunity cost: At point *M*, we're minimizing the amount of resources used to produce a pair of jeans and therefore maximizing the amount of resources left over for the production of other goods and services.

As attractive as point *M* is, you shouldn't conclude that it's everyone's dream. The primary objective of producers is to maximize *profits*. This is not necessarily the same thing as minimizing average *costs*.

One final cost concept is important. Indeed, this last concept is probably the most important one for production. It's *marginal cost*. We encountered this concept in our

Marginal Cost

Resources Used to Produce 16th Pair of Jeans	×	Market Value	=	Marginal Cost
0.053 unit of labor		0.053 × $80 per unit of labor		$4.24
0.1 bolt of denim		0.1 × $30 per bolt		3.00
				$7.24

TABLE 6.3
Resource Computation of Marginal Cost

Marginal cost refers to the value of the additional inputs needed to produce one more unit of output. To increase daily jeans output from 15 to 16 pairs, we need 0.053 unit of labor and one-tenth of a bolt of denim. These extra inputs cost $7.24.

discussion of resource costs, where we noted that marginal cost refers to the value of the resources needed to produce one more unit of a good. To produce *one* more pair of jeans, we need the denim itself and a very small amount of additional labor. These are the extra or added costs of increasing output by one pair of jeans per day. To compute the *dollar* value of these marginal costs, we could determine the market price of denim and labor and then add them up. Table 6.3 provides an example. In this case, we calculate that the additional or *marginal* cost of producing a sixteenth pair of jeans is $7.24. This is how much *total* costs will increase if we decide to expand jeans output by only one pair per day (from 15 to 16).

Table 6.3 emphasizes the link between resource costs and dollar costs. However, there's a much easier way to compute marginal cost. ***Marginal cost refers to the change in total costs associated with one more unit of output.*** Accordingly, we can simply observe *total* dollar costs before and after the rate of output is increased. The difference between the two totals equals the *marginal cost* of increasing the rate of output. This technique is much easier for jeans manufacturers who don't know much about marginal resource utilization but have a sharp eye for dollar costs. It's also a lot easier for economics students, of course. But they have an obligation to understand the resource origins of marginal costs and what causes marginal costs to rise or fall. As we noted before, ***diminishing returns in production cause marginal costs to increase as the rate of output is expanded.***

Figure 6.6 shows what the marginal costs of producing jeans looks like. At each output rate, marginal cost is computed as the *change* in total cost divided by the *change* in output. When output increases from 20 jeans to 30 jeans, total cost rises by $90. Dividing this change in costs by 10 (the change in output) gives us a marginal cost of $9, as illustrated by point *s*.

Notice in Figure 6.6 how the marginal cost curve slopes steeply up after 20 units of output have been produced. This rise in marginal costs reflects the law of diminishing returns. As increases in output become more difficult to achieve, they also become more expensive. Each additional pair of jeans beyond 20 requires a bit more labor than the preceding pair and thus entails rising marginal cost.

A Cost Summary

All these cost calculations can give you a real headache. They can also give you second thoughts about jumping into Low-Rider Jeans or any other business. There are tough choices to be made. A given firm can produce many different rates of output, each of which entails a distinct level of costs. ***The output decision has to be based not only on the* capacity *to produce (the production function) but also on the* costs *of production (the cost functions).*** Only those who make the right decisions will succeed in business.

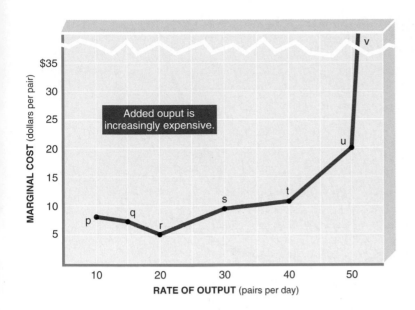

FIGURE 6.6
Marginal Costs

Marginal cost is the change in total cost that occurs when more output is produced. MC equals $\Delta TC/\Delta q$. When diminishing returns set in, MC begins rising, as it does here after the output rate of 20 pairs per day is exceeded.

	Rate of Output	Total Cost	$\dfrac{\Delta TC}{\Delta q} = MC$
	0	$120	
p	10	205	$85/10 = $8.5
q	15	245	$40/5 = $8.0
r	20	270	$25/5 = $5.0
s	30	360	$90/10 = $9.0
t	40	470	$110/10 = $11.0
u	50	670	$200/10 = $20.0
v	51	753	$83/1 = $83.0

The decision-making process is made a bit easier with the glossary in Table 6.4 and the generalized cost curves in Figure 6.7. As before, we're concentrating on a short-run production process, with fixed quantities of land and capital. In this case, however, we've abandoned the Low-Rider Jeans Corporation and provided hypothetical costs for an idealized production process. The purpose of these figures is to

---

Total costs of production are comprised of **fixed costs** and **variable costs**:

$$TC = FC + VC$$

Dividing total costs by the quantity of output yields the **average total cost**:

$$ATC = \frac{TC}{q}$$

which also equals the sum of **average fixed cost** and **average variable cost**:

$$ATC = AFC + AVC$$

The most important measure of changes in cost is **marginal cost**, which equals the increase in total costs when an additional unit of output is produced:

$$MC = \frac{\text{change in total cost}}{\text{change in output}}$$

TABLE 6.4
A Guide to Costs

A quick reference to key measures of cost.

FIGURE 6.7
Basic Cost Curves

With total cost and the rate of output, all other cost concepts can be computed. The resulting cost curves have several distinct features. The AFC curve always slopes downward. The MC curve typically rises, sometimes after a brief decline. The ATC curve has a U shape. And the MC curve will always intersect both the ATC and AVC curves at their lowest points (*m* and *n*, respectively).

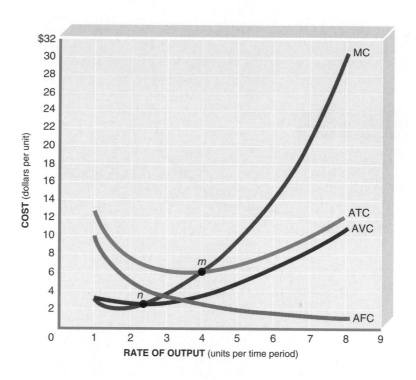

Rate of Output	TC	MC	ATC	AFC	AVC
0	$10.00	—	—	—	—
1	13.00	$ 3.00	$13.00	$10.00	$ 3.00
2	15.00	2.00	7.50	5.00	2.50
3	19.00	4.00	6.33	3.33	3.00
4	25.00	6.00	6.25	2.50	3.75
5	34.00	9.00	6.80	2.00	4.80
6	48.00	14.00	8.00	1.67	6.33
7	68.00	20.00	9.71	1.43	8.28
8	98.00	30.00	12.25	1.25	11.00

provide a more general view of how the various cost concepts relate to each other. Note that MC, ATC, AFC, and AVC can all be computed from total costs. All we need, then, are the first two columns of the table in Figure 6.7, and we can compute and graph all the rest of the cost figures.

The centerpiece of Figure 6.7 is the U-shaped ATC curve. Of special significance is its relationship to marginal costs. Notice that ***the MC curve intersects the ATC curve at its lowest point*** (point *m*). This will always be the case. So long as the marginal cost of producing one more unit is less than the previous average cost, average costs must fall. ***Thus, average total costs decline as long as the marginal cost curve lies below the average cost curve,*** as to the left of point *m* in Figure 6.7.

We already observed, however, that marginal costs rise as output expands, largely because additional workers reduce the amount of land and capital available to each worker (in the short run, the size of plant and equipment is fixed). Consequently, at some point (*m* in Figure 6.7) marginal costs will rise to the level of average costs.

As marginal costs continue to rise beyond point *m*, they begin to pull average costs up, giving the average cost curve its U shape. ***Average total costs increase whenever marginal costs exceed average costs.*** This is the case to the right of point *m*, since the marginal cost curve always lies above the average cost curve in that part of Figure 6.7.

To visualize the relationship between marginal cost and average cost, imagine computing the average height of people entering a room. If the first person who comes through the door is six feet tall, then the average height of people entering the room is six feet at that point. But what happens to average height if the second person entering the room is only three feet tall? *Average* height declines because the last (marginal) person entering the room is shorter than the previous average. Whenever the last entrant is shorter than the average, the average must fall.

The relationship between marginal costs and average costs is also similar to that between your grade in this course and your grade-point average. If your grade in economics is better (higher) than your other grades, then your overall grade-point average will rise. In other words, a high *marginal* grade will pull your *average* grade up. If you don't understand this, your grade-point average is likely to fall.

ECONOMIC VS. ACCOUNTING COSTS

The cost curves we observed here are based on *real* production relationships. The dollar costs we compute are a direct reflection of underlying resource costs: the land, labor, and capital used in the production process. Not everyone counts this way. On the contrary, accountants and businesspeople typically count dollar costs only and ignore any resource use that doesn't result in an explicit dollar cost.

Return to Low-Rider Jeans for a moment to see the difference. When we computed the dollar cost of producing 15 pairs of jeans per day, we noted the following resource inputs:

INPUTS	COST PER DAY
1 factory rent	$100
1 machine rent	20
1 machine operator	80
1.5 bolts of denim	45
Total cost	$245

The total value of the resources used in the production of 15 pairs of jeans was thus $245 per day. But this figure needn't conform to *actual* dollar costs. Suppose the owners of Low-Rider Jeans decided to sew jeans. Then they wouldn't have to hire a worker or pay $80 per day in wages. **Explicit costs**—the *dollar* payments—would drop to $165 per day. The producers and their accountant would consider this a remarkable achievement. They might assert that the cost of producing jeans had fallen.

An economist would draw no such conclusions. ***The essential economic question is how many resources are used in production.*** This hasn't changed. One unit of labor is still being employed at the factory; now it's simply the owner, not a hired worker. In either case, one unit of labor is not available for the production of other goods and services. Hence, society is still paying $245 for jeans, whether the owners of Low-Rider Jeans write checks in that amount or not. The only difference is that we now have an **implicit cost** rather than an explicit one. We really don't care who sews jeans—the essential point is that someone (i.e., a unit of labor) does.

The same would be true if Low-Rider Jeans owned its own factory rather than rented it. If the factory were owned rather than rented, the owners probably wouldn't write any rent checks. Hence, accounting costs would drop by $100 per day. But the factory would still be in use for jeans production and therefore unavailable for the production of other goods and services. The economic (resource) cost of producing 15 pairs of jeans would still be $245.

The distinction between an economic cost and an accounting cost is essentially one between resource and dollar costs. *Dollar cost* refers to the explicit dollar outlays

explicit cost: A payment made for the use of a resource.

Economic Cost

implicit cost: The value of resources used, even when no direct payment is made.

economic cost: The value of all resources used to produce a good or service; opportunity cost.

made by a producer; it's the lifeblood of accountants. **Economic cost,** in contrast, refers to the *value* of *all* resources used in the production process; it's the lifeblood of economists. In other words, economists count costs as

$$\text{Economic cost} = \text{explicit costs} + \text{implicit costs}$$

As this formula suggests, *economic and accounting costs will diverge whenever any factor of production is not paid an explicit wage (or rent, etc.).*

The Cost of Homework. These distinctions between economic and accounting costs apply also to the "production" of homework. You can pay people to write term papers for you or buy them off the Internet. At large schools you can often buy lecture notes as well. But most students do their own homework so they'll learn something and not just turn in required assignments.

Doing homework is expensive, however, even if you don't pay someone to do it. The time you spend reading this chapter is valuable. You could be doing something else if you weren't reading right now. What would you be doing? The forgone activity—the best alternative use of your time—represents the economic cost of doing homework. Even if you don't pay yourself for reading this chapter, you'll still incur that *economic* cost.

LONG-RUN COSTS

We've confined our discussion thus far to short-run production costs. *The short run is characterized by fixed costs*—a commitment to specific plant and equipment. A factory, an office building, or some other plant and equipment have been leased or purchased: We're stuck with *fixed costs*. In the short run, our objective is to make the best use of those fixed costs by choosing the appropriate rate of production.

long run: A period of time long enough for all inputs to be varied (no fixed costs).

The long run opens up a whole new range of options. In the **long run,** we have no lease or purchase commitments. We're free to start all over again, with whatever scale of plant and equipment we desire and whatever technology is available. Quite simply, *there are no fixed costs in the long run.* Nor are there any commitments to existing technology. In 2004, General Motors could have built an engine plant in China of any size. But they decided to build one with a capacity of 300,000 engines (see World View). In building the plant, the company incurred a fixed cost. Once the plant is

GM Plans to Invest $3 Billion In China to Boost Its Presence

BEIJING—General Motors Corp. said it plans to invest more than $3 billion in China in the next three years, underscoring its bid to become a leader in the world's fastest growing auto market. . . .

The new investments are mainly for expanding its production capacity for vehicles and engines, improving its research and development center, and a new auto-financing venture it is launching this year with its main partner in China, Shanghai Automotive Industry Corp. . . .

All in all, GM expects its vehicle-assembly capacity in China to reach 1.3 million units a year by 2007 from its current 530,000 units a year.

To support its expansion, GM also plans to build a new engine plant with a production capacity of 300,000 engines a year, and a new transmission plant.

—Jane Lanhee Lee

Source: *The Wall Street Journal,* June 7, 2004. Reprinted by permission of The Wall Street Journal, © 2004 Dow Jones & Company. All rights reserved worldwide.

Analysis: In the long run, a firm has no fixed costs and can select any desired plant size. Once a plant is built, leased, or purchased, a firm has fixed costs and focuses on short-run output decisions.

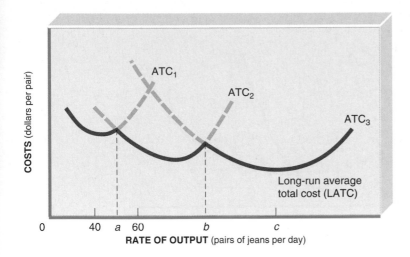

FIGURE 6.8
Long-Run Costs with Three Plant Size Options

Long-run cost possibilities are determined by all possible short-run options. In this case, there are three options of varying size (ATC$_1$, ATC$_2$, and ATC$_3$). In the long run, we'd choose that plant which yielded the lowest average cost for any desired rate of output. The solid portion of the curves (LATC) represents these choices. The smallest factory (ATC$_1$) is best for output levels below a; the largest (ATC$_3$), output rates in excess of b.

completed, GM will focus on the short-run production decision of how many engines to manufacture.

The opportunities available in the long run include building a plant of any desired size. Suppose we still wanted to go into the jeans business. In the long run, we could build or lease any size factory we wanted and could lease as many sewing machines as we desired. Figure 6.8 illustrates three choices: a small factory (ATC$_1$), a medium-sized factory (ATC$_2$) and a large factory (ATC$_3$). As we observed earlier, it's very expensive to produce lots of jeans with a small factory. The ATC curve for a small factory (ATC$_1$) starts to head straight up at relatively low rates of output. In the long run, we'd lease or build such a factory only if we anticipated a continuing low rate of output.

The ATC$_2$ curve illustrates how costs might fall if we leased or built a medium-sized factory. With a small-sized factory, ATC becomes prohibitive at an output of 50 to 60 pairs of jeans per day. A medium-sized factory can produce these quantities at lower cost. Moreover, ATC continues to drop as jeans production increases in the medium-sized factory—at least for a while. Even a medium-sized factory must contend with resource constraints and therefore rising average costs. Its ATC curve is U-shaped also.

If we expected to sell really large quantities of jeans, we'd want to build or lease a large factory. Beyond the rate of output b, the largest factory offers the lowest average total cost. There's a risk in leasing such a large factory, of course. If our sales don't live up to our high expectations, we'll end up with very high fixed costs and thus very expensive jeans. Look at the high average cost of producing only 60 pairs of jeans per day with the large factory (ATC$_3$).

In choosing an appropriate factory, then, we must decide how many jeans we expect to sell. Once we know our expected output, we can easily pick the right-sized factory. It will be the one that offers the lowest ATC for that rate of output. If we expect to sell fewer jeans than a, we'll choose the small factory in Figure 6.8. If we expect to sell jeans at a rate between a and b, we'll select a medium-sized factory. Beyond rate b, we'll want the largest factory. These choices are reflected in the solid part of the three ATC curves. The composite "curve" created by these three segments constitutes our long-run cost possibilities. ***The long-run cost curve is just a summary of our best short-run cost possibilities, using existing technology and facilities.***

We might confront more than three choices, of course. There's really no reason we couldn't build a factory to any desired size. In the long run, we face an infinite

Long-Run Average Costs

FIGURE 6.9
Long-Run Costs with Unlimited Options

If plants of all sizes can be built, short-run options are infinite. In this case, the LATC curve becomes a smooth U-shaped curve. Each point on the curve represents lowest-cost production for a plant size best suited to one rate of output. The long-run ATC curve has its own MC curve.

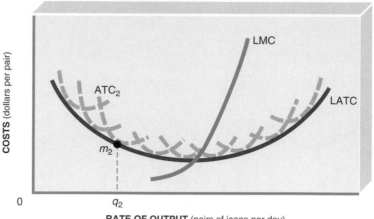

RATE OF OUTPUT (pairs of jeans per day)

number of scale choices, not just three. The effect of all these choices is to smooth out the long-run cost curve. Figure 6.9 depicts the long-run curve that results. Each rate of output is most efficiently produced by some size (scale) of plant. That sized plant indicates the minimum cost of producing a particular rate of output. Its corresponding short-run ATC curve provides one point on the long-run ATC curve.

Long-Run Marginal Costs

Like all average cost curves, the long-run (LATC) curve has its own marginal cost curve. The long-run marginal cost (LMC) curve isn't a composite of short-run marginal cost curves. Rather, it's computed on the basis of the costs reflected in the long-run ATC curve itself. We won't bother to compute those costs here. Note, however, that the long-run MC curve—like all MC curves—intersects its associated average cost curve at its lowest point.

ECONOMIES OF SCALE

Figure 6.8 seems to imply that a producer must choose either a small plant or a larger one. That isn't completely true. The choice is often between one large plant or *several* small ones. Suppose the desired level of output was relatively large, as at point *c* in Figure 6.8. A single small plant (ATC_1) is clearly not up to the task. But what about using several small plants rather than one large one (ATC_3)? How would costs be affected?

Notice what happens to *minimum ATC* in Figure 6.8 when the size (scale) of the factory changes. When a medium-sized factory (ATC_2) replaces a small factory (ATC_1), minimum average cost drops (the bottom of ATC_2 is below the bottom of ATC_1). This implies that a jeans producer who wants to minimize costs should build one medium-sized factory rather than try to produce the same quantity with two small ones. **Economies of scale** exist in this situation: Larger facilities reduce minimum average costs. Such economies of scale help explain why a single firm has come to dominate the funeral business (see News).

Larger production facilities don't always result in cost reductions. Suppose a firm has the choice of producing the quantity Q_m from several small factories or from one large, centralized facility. Centralization may have three different impacts on costs; these are illustrated in Figure 6.10. In each illustration, we see the average total cost (ATC) curve for a typical small firm or plant and the ATC curve for a much larger plant producing the same product.

Constant Returns. Figure 6.10*a* depicts a situation in which there's no economic advantage to centralization of manufacturing operations, because a large plant is no

economies of scale: Reductions in minimum average costs that come about through increases in the size (scale) of plant and equipment.

To learn more about the business of dying, go to www.sci-corp.com.

Funeral Giant Moves In on Small Rivals

Life's two certainties are death and taxes. Some day, it could be just as certain that Service Corp. International will handle your funeral.

The Houston-based company will handle one in 10 funeral services in the USA this year, or about 230,000. In just 32 years, the company has grown from a single funeral home into the world's biggest death-services provider with 2,631 funeral homes, 250 cemeteries and 137 crematoria in North America, Europe and Australia. . . .

SCI's sheer size provides big advantages over competitors. SCI is able to get cheaper prices on caskets and other products from suppliers.

Its funeral homes clustered in the same markets cut costs by sharing vehicles, personnel, services and supplies. That helps give SCI a profit of 31 cents on every dollar it takes in for a typical funeral, vs. 12 cents for the industry as a whole, SCI says.

Funeral directors "don't want to think of (death) as big business," says Betty Murray of the National Foundation of Funeral Directors. "But we're in the era of acquisitions and consolidations."

—Ron Trujillo

Source: *USA Today,* October 31, 1995. USA TODAY Copyright 1995. Reprinted with permission. www.usatoday.com

Analysis: As the size of a firm increases, it may be able to reduce the costs of doing business. Economies of scale give a large firm a competitive advantage over smaller firms.

more efficient than a lot of small plants. The critical focus here is on the *minimum average costs* attainable for a given rate of output. Note that the lowest point on the smaller plant's ATC curve (point *c*) is no higher or lower than the lowest point on the larger firm's ATC curve (point m_1). Hence, it would be just as cheap to produce the quantity Q_m from a multitude of small plants as it would be to produce Q_m from one large plant. Thus increasing the size (or *scale*) of individual plants won't reduce minimum average costs. This is a situation of **constant returns to scale.**

Economies of Scale. Figure 6.10*b* illustrates the situation in which a larger plant can attain a lower minimum average cost than a smaller plant. That is, economies of scale (or *increasing returns to scale*) exist. This is evident from the fact that the

> **constant returns to scale:** Increases in plant size do not affect minimum average cost: minimum per-unit costs are identical for small plants and large plants.

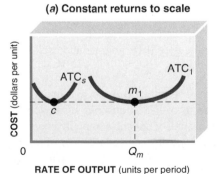

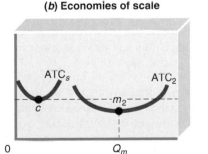

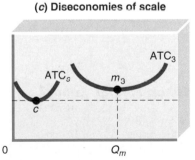

| (a) Constant returns to scale | (b) Economies of scale | (c) Diseconomies of scale |

FIGURE 6.10
Economies of Scale

A lot of output (Q_m) can be produced from one large plant or many small ones. Here we contrast the average total costs associated with one small plant (ATC$_s$) and three large plants (ATC$_1$, ATC$_2$, and ATC$_3$). If a large plant attains the same *minimum* average costs (point m_1 in part *a*) as a smaller plant (point *c*), there's no advantage to large size (scale). Many small plants can produce the same output just as cheaply. However, either economies (part *b*) or diseconomies (part *c*) of scale may exist.

larger firm's ATC curve falls *below* the dashed line in the graph (m_2 is less than c). The greater efficiency of the large factory might come from any of several sources. This is the situation of the funeral home depicted in the News feature. By centralizing core funeral services, Services Corp. International was able to reduce average costs per funeral. Larger organizations may also gain a cost advantage through specialization, by having each worker become expert in a particular skill. By contrast, a smaller establishment might have to use the same individual(s) to perform several functions, thereby reducing productivity at each task. Also, some kinds of machinery may be economical only if they're used to produce massive volumes,[3] an opportunity only very large factories have. Finally, a large plant might acquire a persistent cost advantage through the process of learning by doing. That is, its longer experience and greater volume of output may translate into improved organization and efficiency.

Diseconomies of Scale. Even though large plants may be able to achieve greater efficiencies than smaller plants, there's no assurance that they actually will. In fact, increasing the size (scale) of a plant may actually *reduce* operating efficiency, as depicted in Figure 6.10c. Workers may feel alienated in a plant of massive proportions and feel little commitment to productivity. Creativity may be stifled by rigid corporate structures and off-site management. A large plant may also foster a sense of anonymity that induces workers to underperform. When these things happen, *diseconomies of scale* result. Microsoft tries to avoid such diseconomies of scale by creating autonomous cells of no more than 35 employees ("small plants") within its larger corporate structure.

In evaluating long-run options, then, we must be careful to recognize that *efficiency and size don't necessarily go hand in hand.* Some firms and industries may be subject to economies of scale, but others may not. Bigger isn't always better.

THE ECONOMY TOMORROW

Global Competitiveness and B2B Cost Savings

From 1900 to 1970, the United States regularly exported more goods and services than it imported. Since then, America has had a trade deficit nearly every year. In 2003, U.S. imports exceeded exports by nearly $500 billion. To many people, such trade deficits are a symptom that the United States can no longer compete effectively in world markets.

Global competitiveness ultimately depends on the costs of production. If international competitors can produce goods more cheaply, they'll be able to undersell U.S. goods in global markets.

Cheap Foreign Labor?

Cheap labor keeps costs down in many countries. The average wage in Mexico, for example, ranges from $2 to $3 an hour, compared to over $14 an hour in the United States. Low wages are *not,* however, a reliable measure of global competitiveness. To compete in global markets, one must produce more *output* for a given quantity of *inputs*. In other words, labor is "cheap" only if it produces a lot of output in return for the wages paid.

A worker's contribution to output is measured by *marginal physical product (MPP)*. What we saw in this chapter was that *a worker's productivity (MPP) depends on the quantity and quality of other resources in the production process.* In this regard, U.S.

---

[3]In other words, the machinery itself may be subject to economies of scale.

workers have a tremendous advantage: They work with vast quantities of capital and state-of-the-art technology. They also come to the workplace with more education. Their high wages reflect this greater productivity.

A true measure of global competitiveness must take into account both factor costs (e.g., wages) and productivity. One such measure is **unit labor costs,** which indicates the labor cost of producing one unit of output. It's computed as

$$\text{Unit labor cost} = \frac{\text{wage rate}}{\text{MPP}}$$

Suppose the MPP of a U.S. worker is 6 units per hour and the wage is $12 an hour. The unit labor cost would be

$$\begin{array}{c}\text{Unit labor cost} \\ \text{(United States)}\end{array} = \frac{\$12/\text{hour}}{6 \text{ units/hour}} = \frac{\$2/\text{unit}}{\text{of output}}$$

By contrast, assume the average worker in Mexico has an MPP of 1 unit per hour and a wage of $3 an hour. In this case, the unit labor cost would be

$$\begin{array}{c}\text{Unit labor cost} \\ \text{(Mexico)}\end{array} = \frac{\$3}{1} = \frac{\$3/\text{unit}}{\text{of output}}$$

According to these hypothetical examples, "cheap" Mexican labor is no bargain. Mexican labor is actually *more* costly in production, despite the lower wage rate.

What these calculations illustrate is how important productivity is for global competitiveness. If we want the United States to stay competitive in global markets, U.S. productivity must increase as fast as that in other nations.

The production function introduced in this chapter helps illustrate the essence of global competitiveness in the economy tomorrow. Until now, we've regarded a firm's production function as a technological fact of life—the *best* we could do, given our state of technological and managerial knowledge. In the real world, however, the best is always getting better. Science and technology are continuously advancing. So is our knowledge of how to organize and manage our resources. These advances keep *shifting* production functions upward: More can be produced with any given quantity of inputs. In the process, the costs of production shift downward, as illustrated in Figure 6.11 by the downward shifts of the MC and ATC curves. These downward shifts imply that we can get more of the goods and services we desire with available resources. We can also compete more effectively in global markets.

Unit Labor Costs

> **unit labor cost:** Hourly wage rate divided by output per labor-hour.

Productivity Advance

For current data on unit labor costs and underlying wage and productivity trends, visit the U.S. Bureau of Labor Statistics at www.bls.gov.

(a) When the production function shifts up . . .

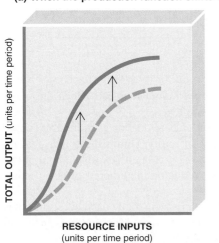

RESOURCE INPUTS
(units per time period)

(b) Cost curves shift down

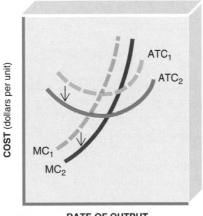

RATE OF OUTPUT
(units per time period)

FIGURE 6.11
Improvements in Productivity Reduce Costs

Advances in technological or managerial knowledge increase our productive capability. This is reflected in upward shifts of the production function (part *a*) and downward shifts of production cost curves (part *b*).

United States Gains Cost Advantage

In the 1970s, unit labor costs in the United States increased by 8 percent per year and by 2.6 percent in the 1980s. In the 1990s, however, productivity increased faster than wages; unit labor costs actually declined. This moderation of unit labor costs gave U.S. producers a cost advantage over most foreign producers, as the following figures reveal.

Country	Change in Unit Labor Costs, 1990–2002
Korea	37.1%
Germany	20.1
Denmark	9.2
Belgium	3.7
Canada	2.6
United States	−3.7
Japan	−8.2
Taiwan	−8.7
France	−10.0

Source: U.S. Bureau of Labor Statistics. www.bls.gov

Analysis: Global competitiveness depends on unit labor costs. U.S. unit labor costs have declined in the last decade or so, increasing America's competitiveness in world markets.

B2B Solutions

The Internet has been an important source of productivity gains in the last 10 years. Although the Internet originated over 30 years ago, its commercial potential emerged with the creation of the World Wide Web around 1990. As recently as 1995 there were only 10,000 Web sites. Now there are over 80 *million* sites. This vastly expanded spectrum of information has helped businesses cut costs in many ways. The cost of gathering information about markets and inputs has been reduced. With the reach of the Internet, firms can engage in greater specialization. Firms can also manage their inventories and supply chains much more efficiently. Transaction and communications costs are reduced as well. All of these productivity improvements are cutting U.S. production costs by $100–250 billion a year. These cost savings helped U.S. businesses *reduce* unit labor costs by 0.4 percent a year in the 1990s. As the accompanying World View confirms, those gains widened the United States' lead in the ongoing race for global competitiveness. To maintain that leading position in the economy tomorrow, U.S. productivity must continue to advance at a brisk pace.

SUMMARY

- A production function indicates the maximum amount of output that can be produced with different combinations of inputs. It's a technological relationship and changes (shifts) when new technology or management techniques are discovered.
- In the short run, some inputs (e.g., land and capital) are fixed in quantity. Increases in (short-run) output result from more use of variable inputs (e.g., labor).
- The contribution of a variable input to total output is measured by its marginal physical product (MPP). This is the amount by which *total* output increases when one more unit of the input is employed.
- The MPP of a factor tends to decline as more of it is used in a given production facility. Diminishing marginal returns result from crowding more of a variable input into a production process, reducing the amount of fixed inputs *per unit* of variable input.
- Marginal cost is the increase in total cost that results when output is increased by one unit. Marginal cost increases whenever marginal physical product diminishes.

- Not all costs go up when the rate of output is increased. Fixed costs such as space and equipment leases don't vary with the rate of output. Only variable costs such as labor and material go up when output is increased.
- Average total cost (ATC) equals total cost divided by the quantity of output produced. ATC declines whenever marginal cost (MC) is less than average cost and rises when MC exceeds it. The MC and ATC curves intersect at minimum ATC (the bottom of the U). That intersection represents least-cost production.
- The economic costs of production include the value of *all* resources used. Accounting costs typically include only those dollar costs actually paid (explicit costs).

- In the long run there are no fixed costs; the size (scale) of production can be varied. The long-run ATC curve indicates the lowest cost of producing output with facilities of appropriate size.
- Economies of scale refer to reductions in minimum average cost attained with larger plant size (scale). If minimum ATC rises with plant size, diseconomies of scale exist.
- Global competitiveness and domestic living standards depend on productivity advances. Improvements in productivity shift production functions up and push cost curves down.

Key Terms

factors of production
production function
productivity
efficiency
opportunity cost
short run
marginal physical product (MPP)
law of diminishing returns

profit
marginal cost (MC)
total cost
fixed costs
variable costs
average total cost (ATC)
average fixed cost (AFC)
average variable cost (AVC)

explicit cost
implicit cost
economic cost
long run
economies of scale
constant returns to scale
unit labor cost

Questions for Discussion

1. What are the production costs of your economics class? What are the fixed costs? The variable costs? What's the marginal cost of enrolling more students?
2. Suppose all your friends offered to help wash your car. Would marginal physical product decline as more friends helped? Why or why not?
3. How many cars *can* GM produce in China? (See World View, page 142.) How many cars will GM *want* to produce?
4. Owner/operators of small gas stations rarely pay themselves an hourly wage. How does this practice affect the economic cost of dispensing gasoline?
5. Corporate funeral giants have replaced small family-run funeral homes in many areas, in large part because of the

lower costs they achieve (see News, page 145.) What kind of economies of scale exist in the funeral business? Why doesn't someone build one colossal funeral home and drive costs down further?
6. Are colleges subject to economies of scale or diseconomies?
7. Why don't more U.S. firms move to Mexico to take advantage of low wages there? Would an *identical* plant in Mexico be as productive as its U.S. counterpart?
8. How would your productivity in completing course work be measured? Has your productivity changed since you began college? What caused the productivity changes? How could you increase productivity further?
9. What is the economic cost of doing this homework?

| PROBLEMS | The Student Problem Set at the back of this book contains numerical and graphing problems for this chapter. |
| WEB ACTIVITIES | to accompany this chapter can be found on the Online Learning Center: **http://www.mhhe.com/economics/schiller10** |

PART 3

Market Structure

A lthough market demand and production functions set limits to output choices, not all firms respond the same way to these limits. The number and size of the firms in a market—industry structure—also affect production and pricing decisions. Chapters 7 through 11 examine how different market structures affect the supply of goods and services—the quantity, quality, and prices of goods and services in specific product markets.

The Competitive Firm

America Online would love to raise the price of accessing its archive of information and Internet services. It isn't likely to do so, however, because too many other firms also offer online services and Net access. If America Online raises its prices, customers might sign up with another company.

Your campus bookstore may be in a better position to raise prices. On most college campuses there's only one bookstore. If the campus store increases the price of books or supplies, most of its customers (you) will have little choice but to pay the higher tab.

As we discover in this and the next few chapters, the degree of competition in product markets is a major determinant of product prices, quality, and availability. Although all firms are in business to make a profit, their profit opportunities are limited by the amount of competition they face.

This chapter begins an examination of how businesses make price and production decisions. We first explore the nature of profits and how they're computed. We then observe how one type of firm—a perfectly competitive one—can *maximize* its profits by selecting the right rate of output. The following questions are at the center of this discussion:

- **What are *profits?***
- **What are the unique characteristics of competitive firms?**
- **How much output will a competitive firm produce?**

The answers to these questions will shed more light on how the *supply* of goods and services is determined in a market economy.

THE PROFIT MOTIVE

The basic incentive for producing goods and services is the expectation of profit. Owning plant and equipment isn't enough. To generate a current flow of income, one must *use* that plant and equipment to produce and sell goods.

Profit is the difference between a firm's sales revenues and its total costs. It's the residual that the owners of a business receive. The recipient of the residual may be the sole owner of a corner grocery store, or it may be the group of stockholders who collectively own a large corporation. In either case, it's the quest for profit that motivates people to own and operate a business.

profit: The difference between total revenue and total cost.

Profit isn't the only thing that motivates producers. Like the rest of us, producers also worry about social status and crave recognition. People who need to feel important, to control others, or to demonstrate achievement are likely candidates for running a business. Many small businesses are maintained by people who gave up 40-hour weeks, $50,000 incomes, and a sense of alienation in exchange for 80-hour weeks, $45,000 incomes, and a sense of identity and control.

In large corporations, the profit motive may lie even deeper below the surface. Stockholders of large corporations rarely visit corporate headquarters. The people who

Other Motivations

"You know what I think, folks? Improving technology isn't important. Increased profits aren't important. What's important is to be warm, decent human beings."

Analysis: The principal motivation for producing goods and services is to earn a profit. Although other goals may seem desirable, businesses that fail to earn a profit won't survive.

manage the corporation's day-to-day business may have little or no stock in the company. Such nonowner-managers may be more interested in their own jobs, salaries, and self-preservation than in the profits that accrue to the stockholding owners. If profits suffer, however, the corporation may start looking for new managers. The accompanying cartoon notwithstanding, the "bottom line" for virtually all businesses is the level of profits.

If it weren't possible to make a profit, few people would choose to supply goods and services. Yet the general public remains suspicious of the profit motive. As the News indicates, one out of four people thinks the profit motive is bad. An even higher percentage believes the profit motive results in *inferior* products at inflated prices.

As we'll see, the profit motive *can* induce business firms to pollute the environment, restrict competition, or maintain unsafe working conditions. However, **the profit motive also encourages businesses to produce the goods and services consumers desire, at prices they're willing to pay.** The profit motive, in fact, moves the "invisible hand" that Adam Smith said orchestrates market outcomes.

Is the Profit Motive Bad?

ECONOMIC VS. ACCOUNTING PROFITS

Although profits might be a necessary inducement for producers, most consumers feel that profits are too high. And that may be so in many cases. But most consumers have no idea how much profit U.S. businesses actually make. Public *perceptions* of profit are seven or eight times higher than actual profits. The typical consumer believes that 35 cents of every sales dollar goes to profits. In reality, average profit per sales dollar is closer to 5 cents.

Faulty perceptions of profits aren't confined to the general public. As surprising as it might seem, most businesses also measure their profits incorrectly.

Everyone agrees that profit represents the difference between total revenues and total costs. Where people part ways is over the decision of what to include in total costs. Recall from Chapter 6 how economists compute costs. **Economic cost** refers to the value of *all* resources used in production, whether or not they receive an explicit payment. By contrast, most businesses count only **explicit costs**—that is, those they actually write checks for. They typically don't take into account the **implicit costs** of the labor or land and buildings they might own. As a result, they understate costs.

economic cost: The value of all resources used to produce a good or service; opportunity cost.

explicit costs: A payment made for the use of a resource.

Economic Profits

implicit cost: The value of resources used, even when no direct payment is made.

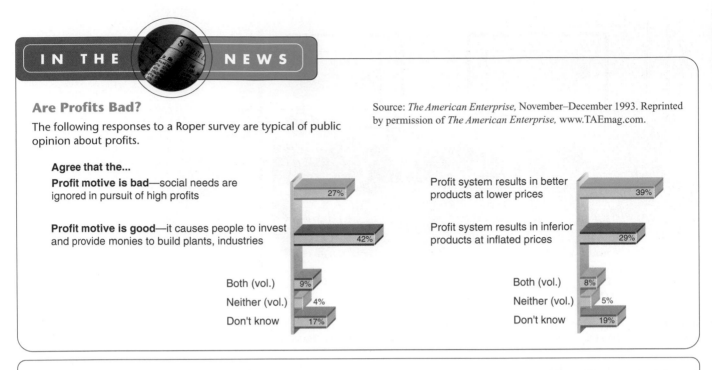

Source: *The American Enterprise*, November–December 1993. Reprinted by permission of *The American Enterprise*, www.TAEmag.com.

Are Profits Bad?

The following responses to a Roper survey are typical of public opinion about profits.

Agree that the...

Profit motive is bad—social needs are ignored in pursuit of high profits   27%

Profit motive is good—it causes people to invest and provide monies to build plants, industries   42%

Both (vol.)   9%
Neither (vol.)   4%
Don't know   17%

Profit system results in better products at lower prices   39%

Profit system results in inferior products at inflated prices   29%

Both (vol.)   8%
Neither (vol.)   5%
Don't know   19%

Analysis: The profit motive is the primary incentive for supplying goods and services. Many consumers are distrustful of that motive, however.

If businesses (and their accountants) understate true costs, they'll overstate true profits. Part of the accounting "profit" will really be compensation to unpaid land, labor, or capital used in the production process. ***Whenever economic costs exceed explicit costs, observed (accounting) profits will exceed true (economic) profits.*** Indeed, what appears to be an accounting profit may actually disguise an economic loss, as illustrated by Mr. Fujishige's strawberry farm once located right next to Disneyland (see News). To determine the **economic profit** of a business, we must subtract all implicit factor costs from observed accounting profits:

economic profit: The difference between total revenues and total economic costs.

$$\begin{aligned}\text{Economic profit} &= \text{total revenue} - \text{total economic cost} \\ &= \text{accounting profit} - \text{implicit costs}\end{aligned}$$

Suppose, for example, that Table 7.1 accurately summarizes the revenues and costs associated with a local drugstore. Monthly sales revenues amount to $27,000. Explicit costs paid by the owner-manager include the cost of merchandise bought from producers for resale to consumers ($17,000), wages to the employees of the drugstore, rent and utilities paid to the landlord, and local sales and business taxes. When all these explicit costs are subtracted from total revenue, we're left with an *accounting profit* of $6,000 per month.

The owner-manager of the drugstore may be quite pleased with an accounting profit of $6,000 per month. He's working hard for this income, however. To keep his store running, the owner-manager is working 10 hours per day, seven days a week. This adds up to 300 hours of labor per month. Were he to work this hard for someone else, his labor would be compensated explicitly—with a paycheck. Although he doesn't choose to pay himself this way, his labor still represents a real

IN THE NEWS

Strawberry Fields Forever?

ANAHEIM, CALIFORNIA—Hiroshi Fujishige is a successful strawberry farmer. For over 40 years he has been earning a profit growing and selling strawberries and other produce from his 58-acre farm. Mr. Fujishige could make even more money if he stopped growing strawberries. His 58-acre straw-berry patch is located across the street from Disneyland. The people from Disney have offered him $32 million just to *lease* the farm; developers have offered as much as $2 million per acre to *buy* the land. But Mr. Fujishige, who lives in a tiny house on the farm he bought 45 years ago (for $2500!) isn't selling. "I'm a farmer, and I've been farming since I got out of high school in 1941," he says. As long as he can make a profit from strawberries, he says, he'll keep growing them.

Source: *Washington Post,* March 9, 1994. © 1994, The Washington Post. Reprinted with permission. www.washingtonpost.com

Analysis: Accounting profits may overrate the profitability of an enterprise by failing to consider the opportunity cost of all resources used in production. If the opportunity cost of the land were deducted, this farm would show an economic loss. In 1998 Mr. Fujishige died and his family sold all but 3.5 acres of his farm to Disneyland for its new California Adventure theme park.

resource cost. To compute *economic* profit, we must subtract this implicit cost from the drugstore's accounting profits. Suppose the owner could earn $10 per hour in the best alternative job. Multiplying this wage rate ($10) by the number of hours he works in the drugstore (300), we see that the implicit cost of his labor is $3,000 per month.

The owner has also used his savings to purchase inventory for the store. He pur-chased the goods on his shelves for $120,000. If he had invested his savings in some other business, he could have earned a return of 10 percent per year. This forgone return represents a real cost. In this case, the implicit return (opportunity cost) on his capital investment amounts to $12,000 per year (10 percent × $120,000), or $1,000 per month.

To calculate the *economic* profit this drugstore generates, we count both explicit and implicit costs. Hence, we must subtract all implicit factor payments (costs) from reported profits. The residual in this case amounts to $2,000 per month. That's the drugstore's *economic* profit.

Total (gross) revenues per month	$27,000
less explicit costs:	
Cost of merchandise sold	$17,000
Wages to cashier, stock, and delivery help	2,500
Rent and utilities	800
Taxes	700
Total explicit costs	$21,000
Accounting profit (revenue minus explicit costs)	$ 6,000
less implicit costs:	
Wages of owner-manager, 300 hours @ $10 per hour	$ 3,000
Return on inventory investment, 10% per year on $120,000	1,000
Total implicit costs	$ 4,000
Economic profit (revenue minus *all* costs)	$ 2,000

TABLE 7.1
The Computation of Economic Profit

To calculate economic profit, we must take account of *all* costs of production. The economic costs of production in-clude the implicit (opportunity) costs of the labor and capital a producer contributes to the production process. The accounting profits of a business take into account only explicit costs paid by the owner. Reported (account-ing) profits will exceed economic prof-its whenever implicit costs are ignored.

normal profit: The opportunity cost of capital; zero economic profit.

Note that when we compute the drugstore's economic profit, we deduct the opportunity cost of the owner's capital. Specifically, we assumed that his funds would have reaped a 10 percent return somewhere else. In effect, we've assumed that a "normal" rate of return is 10 percent. This **normal profit** (the opportunity cost of capital) is an economic cost. Rather than investing in a drugstore, the owner could have earned a 10 percent return on his funds by investing in a fast-food franchise, a music store, a steel plant, or some other production activity. By choosing to invest in a drugstore instead, the owner was seeking a *higher* return on his funds—more than he could have obtained elsewhere. In other words, *economic profits represent something over and above "normal profits."*

Our treatment of "normal" returns as an economic cost leads to a startling conclusion: On average, economic profits are zero. Only firms that reap *above-average* returns can claim economic profits. This seemingly strange perspective on profits emphasizes the opportunity costs of all economic activities. *A productive activity reaps an economic profit only if it earns more than its opportunity cost.*

Entrepreneurship

Naturally, everyone in business wants to earn an economic profit. But relatively few people can stay ahead of the pack. To earn economic profits, a business must see opportunities that others have missed, discover new products, find new and better methods of production, or take above-average risks. In fact, economic profits are often regarded as a reward to entrepreneurship, the ability and willingness to take risks, to organize factors of production, and to produce something society desires.

Consider the local drugstore again. People in the neighborhood clearly want such a drugstore, as evidenced by its substantial sales revenue. But why should anyone go to the trouble and risk of starting and maintaining one? We noted that the owner-manager *could* earn $3,000 in wages by accepting a regular job plus $1,000 per month in returns on capital by investing in an "average" business. Why should he take on the added responsibilities and risk of owning and operating his own drugstore?

The inducement to take on the added responsibilities of owning and operating a business is the potential for economic profit, the extra income over and above normal factor payments. In the case of the drugstore owner, this extra income is the economic profit of $2,000 (Table 7.1). In the absence of such additional compensation, few people would want to make the extra effort required.

Risk

Don't forget, however, that the *potential* for profit is not a *guarantee* of profit. Quite the contrary. Substantial risks are attached to starting and operating a business. Tens of thousands of businesses fail every year, and still more suffer economic losses. From this perspective, profit also represents compensation for the risks incurred in owning or operating a business.

MARKET STRUCTURE

Not all businesses have an equal opportunity to earn an economic profit. The opportunity for profit may be limited by the *structure* of the industry in which the firm is engaged. One of the reasons Microsoft is such a profitable company is that it has long held a **monopoly** on computer operating systems. As the supplier of virtually all operating systems, Microsoft could raise software prices without losing many customers. T-shirt shops, by contrast, have to worry about all the other stores that sell similar products in the area (see News). Faced with so much competition, the owner of a T-shirt shop doesn't have the power to raise prices, or accumulate economic profits.

Figure 7.1 illustrates various **market structures.** At one extreme is the monopoly structure in which only one firm produces the entire supply of the good. At the other

monopoly: A firm that produces the entire market supply of a particular good or service.

market structure: The number and relative size of firms in an industry.

IN THE **NEWS**

T-Shirt Shop Owner's Lament: Too Many T-Shirt Shops

The small Texas beach resort of South Padre Island boasts white sand, blue skies (much of the time), the buoyant waters of the Gulf of Mexico and, at last count, more than 40 T-shirt shops.

And that's a problem for Shy Oogav, who owns one of those shops. "Every day you have to compete with other shops," he says. "And if you invent something new, they will copy you."

Padre Island illustrates a common condition in the T-shirt industry—unbridled, ill-advised growth. Many people believe T-shirts are the ticket to a permanent vacation—far too many people. "In the past years, everything that closed opened up again as a T-shirt shop," says Maria C. Hall, executive director of the South Padre Island Chamber of Commerce.

Mr. Oogav, a 29-year-old immigrant from Israel, came to South Padre Island on vacation six years ago, thought he had found paradise and stayed on. He subsequently got a job with one of the town's T-shirt shops, which then numbered fewer than a dozen. Now that he owns his own shop, and the competition has quadrupled, his paradise is lost. "I don't sleep at night," he says, morosely.

—Mark Pawlosky

Source: *The Wall Street Journal*, July 31, 1995. Reprinted by permission of The Wall Street Journal. © 1995 Dow Jones & Company, Inc. All rights reserved worldwide. www.wsj.com

Analysis: The ability to earn a profit depends on how many other firms offer similar products. A perfectly competitive firm, facing numerous rivals, has difficulty maintaining prices or profits.

extreme is **perfect competition.** In perfect competition a great many firms supply the same good.

There are relatively few monopolies or perfectly competitive firms in the real world. Most of the 20 million businesses in the United States fall between these extremes. They're more accurately characterized by gradations of *imperfect* competition—markets in which competition exists, but individual firms still retain some discretionary power over prices. In a *duopoly,* two firms supply the entire market. In an *oligopoly,* like credit-card services, a handful of firms (Visa, MasterCard, American Express) dominate. In *monopolistic competition,* like fast-food restaurants, there are enough firms to ensure some competition, but not so many as to preclude some limited monopoly-type power. We examine all these market structures in later chapters, after we establish the nature of perfect competition.

> **perfect competition:** A market in which no buyer or seller has market power.

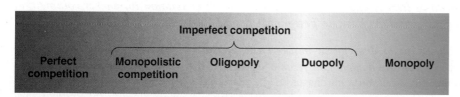

FIGURE 7.1
Market Structures

The number and relative size of firms producing a good vary across industries. Market structures range from perfect competition (a great many firms producing the same good) to monopoly (only one firm). Most real-world firms are along the continuum of *imperfect* competition. Included in that range are duopoly (two firms), oligopoly (a few firms), and monopolistic competition (many firms).

THE NATURE OF PERFECT COMPETITION

Structure

A perfectly competitive industry has several distinguishing characteristics, including

- *Many firms*—Lots of firms are competing for consumer purchases.
- *Identical products*—The products of the different firms are identical, or nearly so.
- *Low-entry barriers*—It's relatively easy to get into the business.

The T-shirt business has all these traits, which is why storeowners have a hard time maintaining profits (see previous News).

Price Takers

Because they always have to contend with a lot of competition, T-shirt shops can't increase profits by raising T-shirt prices. More than 1 billion T-shirts are sold in the United States each year, by tens of thousands of retail outlets. In such a competitive industry the many individual firms that make up the industry are all *price takers:* They take the price the market sets. A competitive firm can sell all its output at the prevailing market price. If it boosts its price above that level, consumers will shop elsewhere. In this sense, a perfectly competitive firm has no **market power**—no ability to control the market price for the good it sells.

> **market power:** The ability to alter the market price of a good or service.

At first glance, it might appear that all firms have market power. After all, who's to stop a T-shirt shop from raising prices? The important concept here, however, is *market* price, that is, the price at which goods are actually sold. If one shop raises its price to $15 and 40 other shops sell the same T-shirts for $10, it won't sell many shirts, and maybe none at all.

You may confront the same problem if you try to sell this book at the end of the semester. You might want to resell this textbook for $50. But you'll discover that the bookstore won't buy it at that price. With many other students offering to sell their books, the bookstore knows it doesn't have to pay the $50 you're asking. Because you don't have any market power, you have to accept the going price if you want to sell this book.

The same kind of powerlessness is characteristic of the small wheat farmer. Like any producer, the lone wheat farmer can increase or reduce his rate of output by making alternative production decisions. But his decision won't affect the market price of wheat.

WEBNOTE

To get a sense of how much competition exists in wheat farming, check out www.econ.ag.gov/briefing/wheat.

Even the largest U.S. wheat farmers can't change the market price of wheat. The largest wheat farm produces nearly 100,000 bushels of wheat per year. But *2 billion* bushels of wheat are brought to market every year, so another 100,000 bushels simply won't be noticed. In other words, *the output of the lone farmer is so small relative to the market supply that it has no significant effect on the total quantity or price in the market.*

> **competitive firm:** A firm without market power, with no ability to alter the market price of the goods it produces.

A distinguishing characteristic of *powerless* firms is that, individually, they can sell all the output they produce at the prevailing market price. We call all such producers **competitive firms;** they have no independent influence on market prices. *A perfectly competitive firm is one whose output is so small in relation to market volume that its output decisions have no perceptible impact on price.*

Market Demand Curves vs. Firm Demand Curves

It's important to distinguish between the market demand curve and the demand curve confronting a particular firm. T-shirt shops don't contradict the law of demand. The quantity of T-shirts purchased in the market still depends on T-shirt prices. That is, the *market* demand curve for T-shirts is still downward-sloping. A single T-shirt shop faces a horizontal demand curve only because its share of the market is so small that changes in its output don't disturb market equilibrium.

Collectively, though, individual firms do count. If all 40 of the T-shirt shops on South Padre Island (see previous News) were to increase shirt production at the same time, the market equilibrium would be disturbed. That is, a competitive market composed of individually powerless producers still sees a lot of action. The power here resides in the collective action of all the producers, however, not in the individual

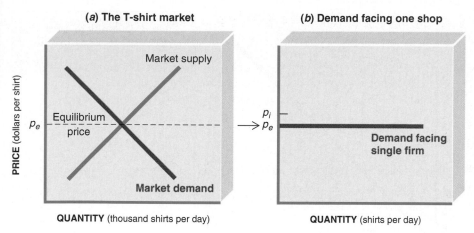

FIGURE 7.2
Market vs. Firm Demand

Consumer demand for any product is downward-sloping, as in the T-shirt market. The equilibrium price (p_e) of T-shirts is established by the intersection of *market* demand and *market* supply. This market-established price is the only one at which an individual shop can sell T-shirts. If the shop owner asks a higher price (e.g., p_i), no one will buy his shirts, since they can buy identical T-shirts from other shops at p_e. But he can sell all his shirts at the equilibrium price. The shop owner thus confronts a horizontal demand curve for his own output. (Notice the difference in market and individual shop quantities on the horizontal axes of the two graphs.)

action of any one. Were T-shirt production to increase so abruptly, the shirts could be sold only at lower prices, in accordance with the downward-sloping nature of the *market* demand curve. Figure 7.2 illustrates the distinction between the actions of a single producer and those of the market. Notice that

- *The market demand curve for a product is always downward-sloping (law of demand).*
- *The demand curve confronting a perfectly competitive firm is horizontal.*

THE PRODUCTION DECISION

Since a competitive firm can sell all its output at the market price, it has only one decision to make: how much to produce. Choosing a rate of output is a firm's **production decision.** Should it produce all the output it can? Or should it produce at less than capacity?

In searching for the most desirable rate of output, focus on the distinction between total *revenue* and total *profit*. **Total revenue** is simply the price of the good multiplied by the quantity sold:

Total revenue = price × quantity

Since a competitive firm can sell all its output at the market price (p_e), total revenue is a simple multiple of p_e. The total revenue of a T-shirt shop, for example, is the price of shirts (p_e) multiplied by the quantity sold. Figure 7.3 shows the total revenue curve that results from this multiplication. Note that *the total revenue curve of a perfectly competitive firm is an upward-sloping straight line, with a slope equal to* $\mathbf{p_e}$.

If a competitive firm wanted to maximize its total *revenue*, its production decision would be simple: It would always produce at capacity. Life isn't that simple, however; *the objective is to maximize profits, not revenues.*

> **production decision:** The selection of the short-run rate of output (with existing plant and equipment).

Output and Revenues

> **total revenue:** The price of a product multiplied by the quantity sold in a given time period: $p \times q$.

FIGURE 7.3
Total Revenue

Because a competitive firm can sell all its output at the prevailing price, its total revenue curve is linear. In this case, the market (equilibrium) price of T-shirts is assumed to be $8. Hence, a shop's total revenue is equal to $8 multiplied by quantity sold.

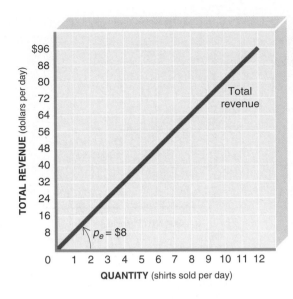

Price × (per shirt)	Quantity = (shirts per day)	Total revenue
$8	1	$ 8
8	2	16
8	3	24
8	4	32
8	5	40
8	6	48
8	7	56
8	8	64
8	9	72

Output and Costs

short run: The period in which the quantity (and quality) of some inputs can't be changed.

fixed costs: Costs of production that don't change when the rate of output is altered, e.g., the cost of basic plant and equipment.

variable costs: Costs of production that change when the rate of output is altered, e.g., labor and material costs.

marginal cost (MC): The increase in total costs associated with a one-unit increase in production.

To maximize profits, a firm must consider how increased production will affect *costs* as well as *revenues*. How do costs vary with the rate of output?

As we observed in Chapter 6, producers are saddled with certain costs in the **short run.** A T-shirt shop has to pay the rent every month no matter how few shirts it sells. The Low-Rider Jeans Corporation in Chapter 6 had to pay the rent on its factory and lease payments on its sewing machine. These **fixed costs** are incurred even if no output is produced. Once a firm starts producing output it incurs **variable costs** as well.

Since profits depend on the *difference* between revenues and costs, the costs of added output will determine how much profit a producer can make. Figure 7.4 illustrates a typical total cost curve. Total costs increase as output expands. But the rate of cost increase varies. At first total costs rise slowly (notice the gradually declining slope until point z), then they increase more quickly (the rising slope after point z). This S-shaped curve reflects the *law of diminishing returns.* As we first observed in Chapter 6, **marginal costs (MC)** often decline in the early stages of production and

FIGURE 7.4
Total Cost

Total cost increases with output. The rate of increase isn't steady, however. Typically, the rate of cost increase slows initially, then speeds up. After point z, diminishing returns (rising marginal costs) cause accelerating costs. These accelerating costs limit the profit potential of increased output.

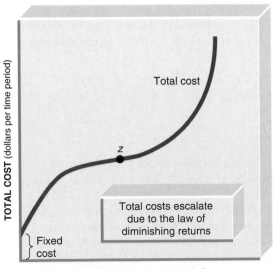

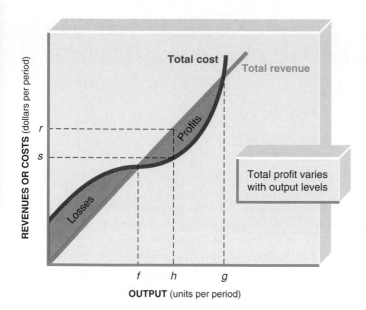

FIGURE 7.5
Total Profit

Profit is the *difference* between total revenue and total cost. It is represented as the vertical distance between the total revenue curve and the total cost curve. At output *h*, profit equals *r* minus *s*. The objective is to find that rate of output that *maximizes* profit.

then increase as the available plant and equipment are used more intensively. These changes in marginal cost cause *total* costs to rise slowly at first, then to pick up speed as output increases.

You may suspect by now that the road to profits is not an easy one. It entails comparing ever-changing revenues with ever-changing costs. Figure 7.5 helps simplify the problem by bringing together typical total revenue and total cost curves. Notice how total costs exceed total revenues at high rates of output (beyond point *g*). As production capacity is approached, costs tend to skyrocket, offsetting any gain in sales revenue.

Total profit in Figure 7.5 is represented by the vertical distance between the two curves. Total costs in this case exceed total revenue at low rates of output as well as at very high rates. The firm is profitable only at output rates between *f* and *g*.

Although all rates of output between *f* and *g* are profitable, they aren't *equally* profitable. A quick glance at Figure 7.5 confirms that the vertical distance between total revenue and total cost varies considerably within that range. ***The primary objective of the producer is to find that one particular rate of output that maximizes total profits.*** With a ruler, one could find it in Figure 7.5 by measuring the distance between the revenue and cost curves at all rates of output. In the real world, most producers need more practical guides to profit maximization.

PROFIT-MAXIMIZING RULE

The best single rule for maximizing profits in the short run is straightforward: Never produce a unit of output that costs more than it brings in. By following this simple rule, a producer is likely to make the right production decision. We see how this rule works by looking first at the revenue side of production ("what it brings in"), then at the cost side ("what it costs").

In searching for the most profitable rate of output, we need to know what an additional unit of output will bring in—that is, how much it adds to the total revenue of the firm. In general, the contribution to total revenue of an additional unit of output is called **marginal revenue (MR).** Marginal revenue is the *change* in total revenue that occurs when output is increased by one unit; that is,

$$\text{Marginal revenue} = \frac{\text{change in total revenue}}{\text{change in output}}$$

**Marginal
Revenue = Price**

marginal revenue (MR): The change in total revenue that results from a one-unit increase in the quantity sold.

TABLE 7.2
Total and Marginal Revenue

Marginal revenue (MR) is the *change* in total revenue associated with the sale of one more unit of output. A third bushel increases total revenue from $26 to $39; MR equals $13. If the price is constant (at $13 here), marginal revenue equals price.

Quantity Sold (bushels per day)	×	Price (per bushel)	=	Total Revenue (per day)	Marginal Revenue (per bushel)
0	×	$13	=	$ 0>	$13
1	×	13	=	13>	13
2	×	13	=	26>	13
3	×	13	=	39>	13
4	×	13	=	52>	13

To calculate marginal revenue, we compare the total revenues received before and after a one-unit increase in the rate of production; the *difference* between the two totals equals marginal revenue.

When the price of a product is constant, it's easy to compute marginal revenue. Suppose we're operating a catfish farm. Our product is catfish, sold at wholesale at the prevailing price of $13 per bushel. In this case, a one-unit increase in sales (one more bushel) increases total revenue by $13. As illustrated in Table 7.2, as long as the price of a product is constant, price and marginal revenue are one and the same thing. Hence, *for perfectly competitive firms, price equals marginal revenue.*

Marginal Cost   Keep in mind why we're breeding and selling catfish. It's not to maximize *revenues* but to maximize *profits*. To gauge profits, we need to know not only the price of fish but also how much each bushel costs to produce. As we saw in Chapter 6, the added cost of producing one more unit of a good is its *marginal cost*. Figure 7.6 summarizes the marginal costs associated with the production of catfish.

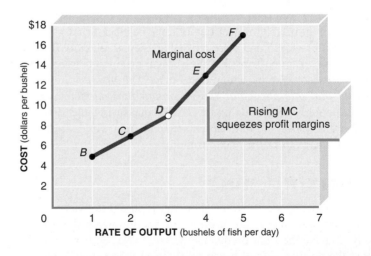

FIGURE 7.6
The Costs of Catfish Production

Marginal cost is the increase in total cost associated with a one-unit increase in production. When production expands from two to three units per day, total costs increase by $9 (from $22 to $31 per day). The marginal cost of the third bushel is therefore $9, as illustrated by point *D* in the graph.

	Rate of Output (bushels per day)	Total Cost (per day)	Marginal Cost (per unit)	Average Cost (per unit)
A	0	$10	—	—
B	1	15	$ 5	$15.00
C	2	22	7	11.00
D	3	31	9	10.33
E	4	44	13	11.00
F	5	61	17	12.20

The production process for catfish farming is wonderfully simple. The factory is a pond; the rate of production is the number of fish harvested from the pond per day. A farmer can alter the rate of production at will, up to the breeding capacity of the pond.

Assume that the *fixed* cost of the pond is $10 per day. The fixed costs include the rental value of the pond and the cost of electricity for keeping the pond oxygenated so the fish can breathe. These fixed costs must be paid no matter how many fish the farmer harvests.

To harvest catfish from the pond, the farmer must incur additional costs. Labor is needed to net and sort the fish. The cost of labor is *variable,* depending on how much output the farmer decides to produce. If no fish are harvested, no variable costs are incurred.

The *marginal costs* of harvesting are the additional costs incurred to harvest *one* more basket of fish. Generally, we expect marginal costs to rise as the rate of production increases. The law of diminishing returns we encountered in Chapter 6 applies to catfish farming as well. As more labor is hired, each worker has less space (pond area) and capital (access to nets, sorting trays) to work with. Accordingly, it takes a little more labor time (marginal cost) to harvest each additional fish.

Figure 7.6 illustrates these marginal costs. Notice how the MC rises as the rate of output increases. At the output rate of 4 bushels per day (point *E*), marginal cost is $13. Hence, the fourth bushel increases total costs by $13. The fifth bushel is even more expensive, with a marginal cost of $17.

We're now in a position to make a production decision. The rule about never producing anything that adds more to cost than it brings in can now be stated in more technical terms. Since price equals marginal revenue for competitive firms, we can base the production decision on a comparison of *price* and marginal cost.

MC > p. We don't want to produce an additional unit of output if its MC exceeds its price. If MC exceeds price, we're spending more to produce that extra unit than we're getting back: total profits will decline if we produce it.

p > MC. The opposite is true when price exceeds MC. If an extra unit brings in more revenue than it costs to produce, it is adding to total profit. Total profits must increase in this case. Hence, a competitive firm wants to expand the rate of production whenever price exceeds MC.

p = MC. Since we want to expand output when price exceeds MC and contract output if price is less than MC, the profit-maximizing rate of output is easily found. *For perfectly competitive firms, profits are maximized at the rate of output where price equals marginal cost.* The implications of this **profit-maximization rule** are summarized in Table 7.3.

Analysis: Fish farmers want to maximize profits.

Profit-Maximizing Rate of Output

> **profit-maximization rule:** Produce at that rate of output where marginal revenue equals marginal cost.

Price Level	Production Decision
price > MC	increase output
price = MC	maintain output (profits maximized)
price < MC	decrease output

TABLE 7.3
Short-Run Profit-Maximization Rules for Competitive Firm

The relationship between price and marginal cost dictates short-run production decisions. For competitive firms, profits are maximized at that rate of output where price = MC. (See Table 8.2 for long-run rules.)

FIGURE 7.7
Maximization of Profits for a Competitive Firm

A competitive firm maximizes total profit at the output rate where MC = p. If MC is less than price, the firm can increase profits by producing more. If MC exceeds price, the firm should reduce output. In this case, profit maximization occurs at an output of 4 bushels per day.

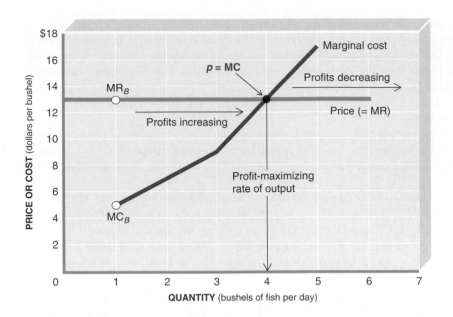

	(1) Number of Bushels (per day)	(2) Price	(3) Total Revenue		(4) Total Cost	=	(5) Total Profit	(6) Marginal Revenue	(7) Marginal Cost
A	0	—	—		$10		−$10	—	—
B	1	$13	$13		15		− 2	$13	$ 5
C	2	13	26		22		+ 4	13	7
D	3	13	39		31		+ 8	13	9
E	4	13	52		44		+ 8	13	13
F	5	13	65		61		+ 4	13	17

Figure 7.7 illustrates the application of our profit-maximization rule in catfish farming. The prevailing wholesale price of catfish is $13 a bushel. At this price we can sell all the catfish we can produce, up to our short-run capacity. The catfish can't be sold at a higher price because lots of farmers raise catfish and sell them for $13 (see News). If we try to charge a higher price, consumers will buy their fish from other vendors. Hence, we confront a horizontal demand curve at the price of $13.

The costs of producing catfish were examined in Figure 7.6. The key concept illustrated here is marginal cost. The MC curve slopes upward, in conventional fashion.

Figure 7.7 also depicts the total revenues, costs, and profits of alternative production rates. Study the table first. Notice that the firm loses $10 per day if it produces no fish (row A). At zero output, total revenue is zero ($p \times q = 0$). However, the firm must still contend with fixed costs of $10 per day. Total profit—total revenue minus total cost—is therefore *minus* $10; the firm incurs a loss.

Row B of the table shows how this loss is reduced when 1 bushel of fish is harvested per day. The production and sale of 1 bushel per day bring in $13 of total revenue (column 3). The total cost of producing 1 bushel per day is $15 (column 4). Hence, the total loss at an output rate of 1 bushel per day is $2 (column 5). This may not be what we hoped for, but it's certainly better than the $10 loss incurred at zero output.

The superiority of harvesting 1 bushel per day rather than none is also evident in columns 6 and 7 of row B. The first bushel produced has a *marginal revenue* of $13. Its *marginal cost* is only $5. Hence, it brings in more added revenue than it adds to costs. Under these circumstances—whenever price exceeds MC—output should definitely be expanded. That is one of the decision rules summarized in Table 7.3.

WEBNOTE

Check out the real world of catfish farming at www.aces.edu/pubs/docs/A/ANR-0273/.

Southern Farmers Hooked on New Cash Crop

Catfish are replacing crops and dairy farming as a cash industry in much of the South, particularly in Mississippi's Delta region, where 80 percent of farm-bred catfish are grown.

Production has skyrocketed in the USA from 16 million pounds in 1975 to an expected 340 million pounds this year.

The business is growing among farmers in Alabama, Arkansas and Louisiana.

Catfish farming is similar to other agriculture, experts say. One thing is the same: It takes money to get started.

"If you have a good row-crop farmer, you have a good catfish farmer," says James Hoffman of Farm Fresh Catfish Co. in Hollandale, Miss. "But you can't take a poor row-crop farmer and make him a good catfish farmer."

Greensboro, Ala., catfish farmer Steve Hollingsworth says he spends $18,000 a week on feed for the 1 million catfish in his ponds.

"Each of the ponds has about 100,000 fish," he says. "You get about 60 cents per fish, so that's about $60,000."

The investment can be lost very quickly "if something's wrong in that pond," like an inadequate oxygen level, Hollingsworth says.

"You can be 15 minutes too late getting here, and all your fish are gone," he says.

—Mark Mayfield

Source: *USA Today,* December 5, 1989. Copyright 1989 USA TODAY. Reprinted with permission. www.usatoday.com

Analysis: People go into a competitive business like catfish farming to earn a profit. Once in business, they try to maximize total profits by equating price and marginal cost.

The excess of price over MC for the first unit of output is also illustrated by the graph in Figure 7.7. Point MR_B ($13) lies above MC_B ($5); the *difference* between these two points measures the contribution that the first bushel makes to the total profits of the firm. In this case, that contribution equals $13 − $5 = $8, and production losses are reduced by that amount when the rate of output is increased from zero to 1 bushel per day.

As long as price exceeds MC, further increases in the rate of output increase total profit. Notice what happens to profits when the rate of output is increased from 1 to 2 bushels per day (row C). The price (MR) of the second bushel is $13, its MC is $7. Therefore it *adds* $6 to total profits. Instead of losing $2 per day, the firm is now making a profit of $4 per day.

The firm can make even more profits by expanding the rate of output further. The marginal revenue of the third bushel is $13; its marginal cost is $9 (row D of the table). Therefore, the third bushel makes a $4 contribution to profits.

This firm will never make huge profits. For the fourth unit of output price and MC both equal $13. It doesn't contribute to total profits, and it doesn't subtract from them. The fourth unit of output represents the highest rate of output the firm desires. *At the rate of output where price = MC, total profits of the firm are maximized.*[1]

Notice what happens if we expand output beyond 4 bushels per day. The price of the fifth bushel is still $13; its MC is $17. The fifth bushel adds more to costs than to revenue. If we produce that fifth bushel, total profit will decline by $4. In Figure 7.7 the MC curve lies above the price line at all output levels in excess of 4. The lesson here is clear: *Output should not be increased if MC exceeds price.*

The correct production decision—the profit-maximizing decision—is shown in Figure 7.7 by the intersection of the price and MC curves. At this intersection, price

---

[1] In this case, profits are the same at output levels of three and four. Given the choice between the two levels, most firms will choose the higher level. By producing the extra unit of output, the firm increases its customer base. This not only denies rival firms an additional sale but also provides some additional cushion when the economy slumps. Also, corporate size may connote both prestige and power. In any case, the higher output level defines the limit to maximum-profit production.

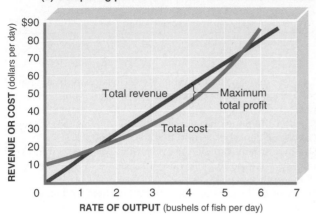

(a) Computing profits with total revenue and total cost

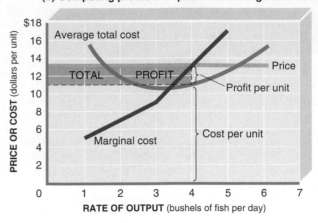

(b) Computing profits with price and average total cost

FIGURE 7.8
Alternative Views of Total Profit

Total profit can be computed as TR − TC, as in part *a*. Or it can be computed as profit *per unit* (*p* − ATC) multiplied by the quantity sold. This is illustrated in part *b* by the shaded rectangle. To find the profit-maximizing output, we could use either of these graphs or just the price and MC curves in Figure 7.7.

equals MC and profits are maximized. If we produced less, we'd be giving up potential profits. If we produced more, total profits would also fall (review Table 7.3).

Adding Up Profits

To reach the right production decision, we've relied on *marginal* revenues and costs. Having found the desired rate of output, however, we may want to take a closer look at the profits we are accumulating. Figure 7.8 provides pictures of our success.

Total profits are represented in Figure 7.8*a* by the vertical distance between the total revenue and total cost curves. This is a straightforward interpretation of our definition of total profits—that is,

$$\text{Total profits} = \text{TR} - \text{TC}$$

The vertical distance between the TR and TC curves is maximized at the output of 4 bushels per day.

Our success in catfish farming can also be illustrated by *average* revenue and costs. Total profit is equal to *average* profit per unit multiplied by the number of units produced. Profit *per unit,* in turn, is equal to price *minus* average total cost—that is,

$$\text{Profit per unit} = p - \text{ATC}$$

The price of catfish is illustrated in Figure 7.8*b* by the horizontal price line at $13. The average total cost of producing catfish is shown by the ATC curve. Like the ATC curve we encountered in Chapter 6, this one has a U shape. The *difference* between price and average cost—profit per unit—is illustrated by the vertical distance between the price and ATC curves. At 4 bushels per day, for example, profit per unit equals $13 − $11 = $2.

To compute *total* profits, we note that

$$\text{Total profits} = \text{profit per unit} \times \text{quantity}$$
$$= (p - \text{ATC}) \times q$$

In this case, the 4 bushels generate a profit of $2 each, for a *total* profit of $8 per day. *Total* profits are illustrated in Figure 7.8*b* by the shaded rectangle. (Recall that the area of a rectangle is equal to its height, the profit per unit, multiplied by its width, the quantity sold.)

Profit per unit is not only used to compute total profits but is often also of interest in its own right. Businesspeople like to cite statistics on "markups," which are a crude index to per-unit profits. However, *the profit-maximizing producer never seeks to maximize per-unit profits. What counts is* total *profits, not the amount of profit per unit.* This is the old $5 ice cream problem again. You might be able to maximize profit per unit if you could sell 1 cone for $5, but you would make a lot more money if you sold 100 cones at a per-unit profit of only 50 cents each.

Similarly, *the profit-maximizing producer has no desire to produce at that rate of output where ATC is at a minimum.* Minimum ATC does represent least-cost production. But additional units of output, even though they raise average costs, will increase total profits. This is evident in Figure 7.8; price exceeds MC for some output to the right of minimum ATC (the bottom of the U). Therefore, total profits are increasing as we increase the rate of output beyond the point of minimum average costs.

THE SHUTDOWN DECISION

The rule established for short-run profit maximization doesn't guarantee any profits. By equating price and marginal cost, the competitive producer is only assured of achieving the *optimal* output. This is the best possible rate of output for the firm, given the existing market price and the (short-run) costs of production.

But what if the best possible rate of output generates a loss? What should the producer do in this case? Keep producing output? Or shut down the factory and find something else to do?

The first instinct may be to shut down the factory to stop the flow of red ink. But this isn't necessarily the wisest course of action. It may be smarter to keep operating a money-losing operation than to shut it down.

The rationale for this seemingly ill-advised course of action resides in the fixed costs of production. *Fixed costs must be paid even if all output ceases.* The firm must still pay rent on the factory and equipment even if it doesn't use these inputs. That's why we call such costs "fixed."

The persistence of fixed costs casts an entirely different light on the shutdown decision. Since fixed costs will have to be paid in any case, the question becomes: Which option creates greater losses? Does the firm lose more money by continuing to operate (and incurring a loss) or by shutting down (and incurring a loss equal to fixed costs)? In these terms, the answer becomes clear. *A firm should shut down only if the losses from continuing production exceed fixed costs.* This happens when total revenue is less than total *variable* cost.

The shutdown decision can be made without explicit reference to fixed costs. Figure 7.9 shows how. The relationship to focus on is between the price of a good and its average *variable* cost.

Price vs. AVC

The curves in Figure 7.9 represent the short-run costs and potential demand curves for catfish. As long as the price of catfish is $13 per bushel, the typical firm will produce 4 a day, as determined by the intersection of the MC and MR (= price) curves (point *X*, in part *a*). In this case, price ($13) exceeds average *total* cost ($11) and catfish farming is profitable.

The situation wouldn't look so good, however, if the market price of catfish fell to $9. Following the rule for profit maximization, the firm would be led to point *Y* in part *b*, where MC intersects the new demand (price) curve. At this intersection, the firm would produce three bushels per day. But total revenues would no longer cover total costs, as can be seen from the fact that the ATC curve now lies *above* the price line. The ATC of producing 3 bushels is $10.33 (Figure 7.6); price is $9. Hence, the firm is incurring a loss of $4 per day (3 bushels at a loss of $1.33 each).

Should the firm stay in business under the circumstances? The answer is yes. Recall that the catfish farmer has already dug the pond and installed equipment at a (fixed) cost of $10 per day. The producer will have to pay these fixed costs whether or not the machinery is used. Stopping production would result in a loss amounting to $10 per day. Staying in business, even when catfish prices fall to $9 each, generates a loss

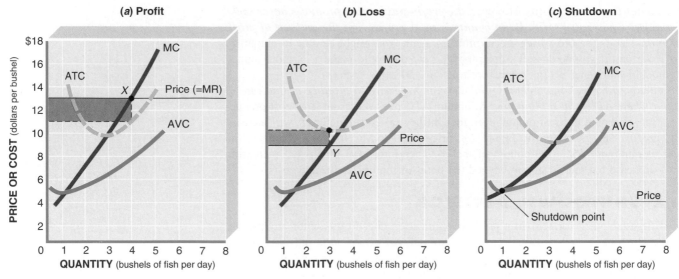

FIGURE 7.9
The Firm's Shutdown Point

A firm should cease production only if total revenue is lower than total *variable* cost. The shutdown decision may be based on a comparison of price and AVC. If the price of catfish per bushel was $13, a firm would earn a profit at point X in part a. At a price of $9, (point Y in part b), the firm is losing money (p is less than ATC) but is more than covering all variable costs (p is greater than AVC). If the price falls to $4 per bushel, as in part c, output should cease (p is less than AVC).

The Shutdown Point

> **shutdown point:** That rate of output where price equals minimum AVC.

of only $4 a day. In this case, *where price exceeds average variable cost but not average total cost, the profit-maximization rule minimizes losses.*

If the price of catfish falls far enough, the producer may be better off ceasing production altogether. Suppose the price of catfish fell to $4 per bushel (Figure 7.9c). A price this low doesn't even cover the variable cost of producing 1 bushel per day ($5). Continued production of even 1 bushel per day would imply a total loss of $11 per day ($10 of fixed costs plus $1 of variable costs). Higher rates of output would lead to still greater losses. Hence, the firm should shut down production, even though that action implies a loss of $10 per day. In all cases *where price doesn't cover average variable costs at any rate of output, production should cease.* Thus, the **shutdown point** occurs where price is equal to minimum average *variable* cost. Any lower price will result in losses larger than fixed costs. In Figure 7.9, the shutdown point occurs at a price of $5, where the MC and AVC curves intersect.

THE INVESTMENT DECISION

When a firm shuts down, it doesn't necessarily leave (exit) the industry. General Motors still produces Cadillacs, for example, even though it idled one of its plants in 2001 (see News). *The shutdown decision is a **short-run** response.* It's based on the fixed costs of an established plant and the variable costs of operating it.

> **investment decision:** The decision to build, buy, or lease plant and equipment; to enter or exit an industry.

Ideally, a producer would never get into a money-losing business in the first place. Entry was based on an **investment decision** that the producer now regrets. *Investment decisions are **long-run** decisions,* however, and the firm now must pay for its bad luck or poor judgment. The investment decision entails the assumption of fixed costs (e.g., the lease of the factory); once the investment is made, the short-run production decision is designed to make the best possible use of those fixed inputs. The short-run profit-maximizing rule we've discussed applies only to this second decision; it assumes that a production unit exists. The accompanying News shows the contrast between production and investment decisions.

> **long run:** A period of time long enough for all inputs to be varied (no fixed costs).

GM to Idle Cadillac Plant for Four Weeks

General Motors said Wednesday that it will idle the Lansing, Mich., Craft Center vehicle-assembly plant for four weeks beginning May 21 to cut inventories of unsold Cadillac Eldorado coupes. That will result in the temporary layoff of 300 workers, who will continue to receive 95 percent of their take-home pay.

Source: *Associated Press*, February 22, 2001. Reprinted with permission of The Associated Press.

Kmart Cuts 37,000 Jobs

Chain Plans to Close 326 Stores

NEW YORK—Kmart will close nearly one out of five stores and eliminate up to 37,000 jobs in its painful bid to emerge from bankruptcy protection by early spring, CEO Jim Adamson said Tuesday.

The struggling discount merchant will shed 326 of about 1,830 stores, which employ about 220,000. . . .

As it restructures, closing underperforming stores enables the discount chain to save money because it can exit lease obligations on the properties.

—Lorrie Grant

Source: *USA Today*, January 15, 2003. USA TODAY Copyright 2003. Reprinted with permission.

Analysis: GM's decision to idle a plant was a short-run *shutdown* decision; they are still in business. Kmart, by contrast, made a long-run decision to cease operations and *exit* the industry in specific markets.

The investment decision is of enormous importance to producers. The fixed costs that we've ignored in the production decision represent the producers' (or the stockholders') investment in the business. If they're going to avoid an economic loss, they have to generate at least enough revenue to recoup their investment—that is, the cost of (fixed) plant and equipment. Failure to do so will result in a net loss, despite allegiance to our profit-maximizing rule.

Whether fixed costs count, then, depends on the decision being made. For producers trying to decide how best to utilize the resources they've purchased or leased, fixed costs no longer enter the decision-making process. For producers deciding whether to enter business, sign a lease, or replace existing machinery and plant, fixed costs count very much. Businesspeople will proceed with an investment only if the *anticipated* profits are large enough to compensate for the effort and risk undertaken.

Long-Run Costs

When businesspeople make an investment decision, they confront not one set of cost figures but many. A plant not yet built can be designed for various rates of production and alternative technologies. In making long-run decisions, a producer isn't bound to one size of plant or to a particular mix of tools and machinery. In the long run, one can be flexible. In general, *a producer will want to build, buy, or lease a plant that's the most efficient for the anticipated rate of output.* This is the (dis)economy of scale phenomenon we discussed in the previous chapter. Once the right plant size is selected, the producer may proceed with the problem of short-run profit maximization. Once production is started, he can only hope that the investment decision was a good one and that a shutdown can be avoided.

DETERMINANTS OF SUPPLY

Whether the time frame is the short run or the long run, the one central force in production decisions is the quest for profits. Producers will go into production—incur fixed costs—only if they see the potential for economic profits. Once in business, they'll expand the rate of output so long as profits are increasing. They'll shut down—cease production—when revenues don't at least cover variable costs (loss exceeds fixed costs).

Nearly anyone could make money with these principles if given complete information on costs and revenues. What renders the road to fortune less congested is the general absence of such complete information. In the real world, production decisions involve considerably more risk. People often don't know how much profit or loss they'll incur until it's too late to alter production decisions. Consequently, businesspeople are compelled to make a reasoned guess about prices and costs, then proceed. By way of summary, we can identify the major influences that will shape their short- and long-run decisions on how much output to supply to the market.

Short-Run Determinants

A competitive firm's short-run production decisions are dominated by marginal costs. Hence, the quantity of a good supplied will be affected by all forces that alter MC. Specifically, *the determinants of a firm's supply include*

- *The price of factor inputs.*
- *Technology* (the available production function).
- *Expectations* (for costs, sales, technology).
- *Taxes and subsidies.*

Each determinant affects a producer's ability and willingness to supply output at any particular price.

The price of factor inputs determines how much the producer must pay for resources used in production. Technology determines how much output the producer will get from each unit of input. Expectations are critical because they express producers' perceptions of what future costs, prices, sales, and profits are likely to be. And finally, taxes and subsidies may alter costs or the amount of profit a firm gets to keep.

The Short-Run Supply Curve. By using the familiar *ceteris paribus* assumption, we can isolate the effect of price on supply decisions. In other words, we can draw a short-run **supply curve** the same way we earlier constructed consumer demand curves. In this case, the forces we assume constant are input prices, technology, expectations, and taxes. The only variable we allow to change is the price of the product itself.

Figure 7.10 illustrates the response of quantity supplied to a change in price. Notice the critical role of marginal costs: *The marginal cost curve is the short-run supply curve for a competitive firm.* Recall our basic profit-maximization rule. A

> **supply curve:** A curve describing the quantities of a good a producer is willing and able to sell (produce) at alternative prices in a given time period, *ceteris paribus*.

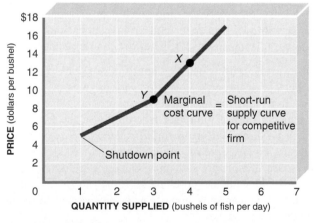

FIGURE 7.10

A Competitive Firm's Short-Run Supply Curve

For competitive firms, marginal cost defines the lowest price a firm will accept for a given quantity of output. In this sense, the marginal cost curve is the supply curve; it tells us how quantity supplied will respond to price. At $p = \$13$, the quantity supplied is 4; at $p = \$9$, the quantity supplied is 3.

Recall, however, that the firm will shut down if price falls below minimum average variable cost. The supply curve does not exist below minimum AVC ($5 in this case).

competitive producer wants to supply a good only if its price exceeds its marginal cost. Hence, marginal cost defines the lower limit for an "acceptable" price. A catfish farmer is willing and able to produce 4 bushels per day only if the price of a bushel is $13 (point X). If the price of catfish dropped to $9, the *quantity* supplied would fall to 3 (point Y). The marginal cost curve tells us what the quantity supplied would be at all other prices as well. As long as price exceeds minimum AVC (the shutdown point), the MC curve summarizes the response of a producer to price changes: It *is* the short-run supply curve of a perfectly competitive firm.

The shape of the marginal cost curve provides a basic foundation for the *law of supply.* Because marginal costs tend to rise as output expands, an increase in output makes sense only if the price of that output rises. If the price does rise, it's profitable to increase the quantity supplied.

Supply Shifts

All the forces that shape the short-run supply curve are subject to change. Factor prices change; technology changes; expectations change; and tax laws get revised. *If any determinant of supply changes, the supply curve shifts.*

A reduction in wage rates, for example, would reduce the marginal cost of producing catfish. This would shift the supply curve downward, making it possible for producers to supply larger quantities at any given price.

An improvement in technology would have the same effect. By increasing productivity, new technology would lower the marginal cost of producing a good. The supply curve would shift downward.

Tax Effects

Changes in taxes will also alter supply behavior. But not all taxes have the same effect; some alter short-run supply behavior, others affect only long-run supply decisions.

Property Taxes. Property taxes are levied by local governments on land and buildings. The tax rate is typically some small fraction (e.g., 1 percent) of total value. Hence, the owner of a $10 million factory might have to pay $100,000 per year in property taxes.

Property taxes have to be paid regardless of whether the factory is used. Hence, *property taxes are a fixed cost* for the firm. These additional fixed costs increase total costs and thus shift the average total cost (ATC) upward, as in Figure 7.11a.

Notice that the MC curve doesn't move when property taxes are imposed. Property taxes aren't based on the quantity of output produced. Accordingly, the production decision of the firm isn't affected by property taxes. The quantity q_1 in Figure 7.11a remains the optimal rate of output even after a property tax is introduced.

Although the optimal output remains at q_1, the profitability of the firm is reduced by the property tax. Profit per unit has been reduced by the upward shift of the ATC curve. If property taxes reduce profits too much, firms may move to a low-tax jurisdiction or another industry (investment decisions).

Payroll Taxes. Payroll taxes have very different effects on business decisions. Payroll taxes are levied on the wages paid by the firm. Employers must pay, for example, a 7.65 percent Social Security tax on the wages they pay (employees pay an identical amount). This tax is used to finance Social Security retirement benefits. Other payroll taxes are levied by federal and state governments to finance unemployment and disability benefits.

All payroll taxes add to the cost of hiring labor. In the absence of a tax, a worker might cost the firm $8 per hour. Once Social Security and other taxes are levied, the cost of labor increases to $8 plus the amount of tax. Hence, $8-per-hour labor might end up costing the firm $9 or more. In other words, *payroll taxes increase marginal costs.* This is illustrated in Figure 7.11b by the upward shift of the MC curve.

Notice how payroll taxes change the production decision. The new MC curve (MC_b) intersects the price line at a lower rate of output (q_b). Thus payroll taxes tend to reduce output and employment.

(a) Property taxes affect fixed costs

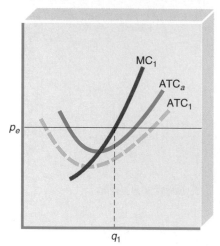

(b) Payroll taxes alter marginal costs

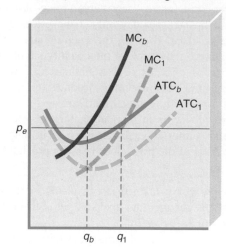

(c) Profits taxes don't change costs

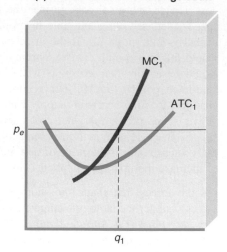

FIGURE 7.11
Impact of Taxes on Business Decisions

(a) Property taxes are a fixed cost for the firm. Since they don't affect marginal costs, they leave the optimal rate of output (q_1) unchanged. Property taxes raise average costs, however, and so reduce profits. Lower profits may alter investment decisions.

(b) Payroll taxes add directly to marginal costs and so reduce the optimal rate of output (to q_b). Payroll taxes also increase average costs and lower total and per-unit profits.

(c) Taxes on profits are neither a fixed cost nor a variable cost since they depend on the existence of profits. They don't affect marginal costs or price and so leave the optimal rate of output (q_1) unchanged. By reducing after-tax profits, however, such taxes lessen incentives to invest.

Profit Taxes. Taxes are also levied on the profits of a business. Such taxes are very different from either property or payroll taxes since profit taxes are paid only when profits are made. Thus they are neither a fixed cost nor a variable cost! As Figure 7.11c indicates, neither the MC nor the ATC curve moves when a profits tax is imposed. The only difference is that the firm now gets to keep less of its profits, instead "sharing" its profits with the government.

Although a profits tax has no direct effect on marginal or average costs, it does reduce the take-home (after-tax) profits of a business. This may reduce investments in new businesses. For this reason, many people urge the government to *reduce* corporate tax rates and so encourage increased investment. This was the objective of President Bush's 2002–3 tax cuts.

THE ECONOMY TOMORROW

E-Commerce Increasing Competition

Ten years ago the T-shirt shop owners on South Padre Island (see News, page 157) had to worry only about the other 40 shops at that beach resort. They worried that other shops might offer T-shirts at lower prices, forcing all the shops to cut prices. Now the level of competition is much higher. Beachgoers can now buy T-shirts at virtual shops on the Internet. Indeed, consumers can click on the Internet to find out the price of almost anything. There are even electronic shopping services that will find the lowest price for a product. Want a better deal on a car? You don't have to visit a dozen dealerships. With a few clicks, you can find the lowest price for the car you want and get directions to the appropriate dealer. In fact, you don't have to go anywhere: More and more producers will sell you their products directly over the Internet.

E-commerce intensifies competition in many ways. By allowing a consumer to shop worldwide, the Net vastly increases the number of firms in a virtual market. Even your campus bookstore now has to worry about textbook prices available at Amazon.com, Barnes and Noble, and other online booksellers.

Electronic commerce also reduces transaction costs. Retailers don't need stores or catalogs to display their products, and they can greatly reduce inventories by producing to order. This is how Dell computer supplies the $20 million of computers it sells per day online.

Electronic retailers also get a tax break. Transactions on the Net aren't subject to sales taxes. Hence, electronic retailers can offer products at lower prices without cutting profit margins, especially in high-tax states.

The evident advantages of e-commerce have made it the virtual mall of choice for many consumers. In 2004, consumers spent over $100 billion on electronic purchases. That was less than 1 percent of total consumer spending. But the trend is what counts. With Net sales more than doubling every year, e-commerce is sure to intensify competition in the economy tomorrow.

WEBNOTE

If you want to shop for T-shirts at a cybermall, check out www.tshirtmall.com.

SUMMARY

- Economic profit is the difference between total revenue and total cost. Total economic cost includes the value (opportunity cost) of *all* inputs used in the production, not just those inputs for which an explicit payment is made.

- Because it must contend with many competitors, a competitive firm has no control over the price of its output. It effectively confronts a horizontal demand for its output (even though the *market* demand for the product is downward-sloping).

- The short-run objective of a firm is to maximize profits from the operation of its existing facilities (fixed costs). For a competitive firm, the profit-maximizing output occurs at the point where marginal cost equals price (marginal revenue).

- A firm may incur a loss even at the optimal rate of output. It shouldn't shut down, however, so long as price exceeds average *variable* cost. If revenues at least cover variable costs, the firm's loss from production is less than fixed cost.

- In the long run a producer can be flexible. There are no fixed costs and the firm may choose any-sized plant it wants. The decision to incur fixed costs (i.e., build, buy, or lease a plant) or to enter or exit an industry is an investment decision.

- A competitive firm's supply curve is identical to its marginal cost curve (above the shutdown point at minimum average variable cost). In the short run, the quantity supplied will rise or fall with price.

- The determinants of supply include the price of inputs, technology, taxes, and expectations. Should any of these determinants change, the firm's supply curve will shift.

- Business taxes alter business behavior. Property taxes raise fixed costs; payroll taxes increase marginal costs. Profit taxes raise neither fixed costs nor marginal costs but diminish the take-home (after-tax) profits of a business.

- The Internet has created virtual stores that intensify price competition.

Key Terms

profit
economic cost
explicit cost
implicit cost
economic profit
normal profit
monopoly
market structure

perfect competition
market power
competitive firm
production decision
total revenue
short run
fixed costs
variable costs

marginal cost (MC)
marginal revenue (MR)
profit-maximization rule
shutdown point
investment decision
long run
supply curve

Questions for Discussion

1. What economic costs will a large corporation likely overlook when computing its "profits"? How about the owner of a family-run business or farm?

2. How can the demand curve facing a firm be horizontal if the market demand curve is downward-sloping?

3. How many fish should a commercial fisherman try to catch in a day? Should he catch as many as possible or return to dock before filling the boat with fish? Under what economic circumstances should he not even take the boat out?

4. If a firm is incurring an economic loss, would society be better off if the firm shut down? Would the firm want to shut down? Explain.

5. Why wouldn't a profit-maximizing firm want to produce at the rate of output that minimizes average total cost?

6. What rate of output is appropriate for a "nonprofit" corporation (such as a hospital)?

7. Why did GM only temporarily shut down its production facilities while Kmart permanently got out of its business in several markets (see News, p. 169)? Explain in terms of fixed and variable costs.

8. What was the opportunity cost of Mr. Fujishige's farm? (See News, page 155.) Is society better off with another Disney theme park? Explain.

9. Is America Online a perfectly competitive firm? Explain your answer.

10. If a perfectly competitive firm raises its price above the prevailing market rate, how much of its sales might it lose? Why? Can a competitive firm ever raise its prices? If so, when?

PROBLEMS The accompanying Student Problem Set contains numerical and graphing problems for this chapter.

WEB ACTIVITIES to accompany this chapter can be found on the Online Learning Center:
http://www.mhhe.com/economics/schiller10

8 Competitive Markets

Catfish farmers in the South are very upset. During the past two decades they've invested millions of dollars in converting cotton farms into breeding ponds for catfish. They now have over 150,000 acres of ponds and supply 80 percent of the nation's catfish. But unfortunately, catfish prices have been dropping. In 2003 alone catfish prices fell 15 percent, to a low of 55 cents per pound. With production costs averaging 65 cents a pound, most catfish farmers are now losing money. Indeed, many farmers in Arkansas, Mississippi, and Louisiana have simply stopped feeding their fish. A lot of farmers are expected to refill their ponds with dirt and start planting cotton again.

It wasn't supposed to happen this way. Ten years ago, catfish looked like a sure thing. But so many Southern farmers got into the business that catfish prices started falling. Then Vietnam started exporting catfish to the United States, putting still further pressure on prices (see World View on next page).

The dilemma catfish farmers find themselves in is a familiar occurrence in competitive markets. When profits look good, everybody wants to get in on the act. As more and more firms start producing the good, prices and profits tumble. This helps explain why over 200,000 new firms are formed each year and why over 50,000 others fail.

This chapter focuses on the behavior of competitive markets. We have three principal questions:

- **How are prices determined in competitive markets?**
- **How does competition affect the profits of a firm or industry?**
- **What does society gain from market competition?**

The answers to these questions will reveal how markets work when all producers are relatively small and lack market power. In subsequent chapters we emphasize how market outcomes change when markets are less competitive.

THE MARKET SUPPLY CURVE

In the previous chapter we examined the supply behavior of a perfectly competitive firm. The perfectly competitive firm is a price taker. It *responds* to the market price by producing that rate of output where marginal cost equals price.

But what about the *market* supply of catfish? We need a market supply curve to determine the **equilibrium price** the individual farmer will confront. In the previous chapter we simply drew a market supply curve arbitrarily, in order to establish a market price. Now, our objective is to find out where that **market supply** curve comes from.

Like the market supply curves we first encountered in Chapter 3, we can calculate the market supply of catfish by simple addition. All we have to do is add

equilibrium price: The price at which the quantity of a good demanded in a given time period equals the quantity supplied.

market supply: The total quantities of a good that sellers are willing and able to sell at alternative prices in a given time period, *ceteris paribus*.

Whiskered Catfish Stir a New Trade Controversy

LAKE VILLAGE, ARK.—Alleamer Tyler works in quality control at Farm Fresh Catfish, a processing plant in this small Delta town on the edge of the Mississippi River. Her days are sometimes slower than in the past, because she doesn't test as many fish as she once did.

"The imports have made a huge impact," says Ms. Tyler, one of Farm Fresh's 100 employees.

Because of Vietnamese fish imports, the US catfish production has plunged in the past year. At Farm Fresh, 95,000 pounds a day were processed last year. This year, it's down to 65,000.

Mississippi leads the nation in catfish production, followed by Arkansas and Louisiana. Most US catfish are raised in the Delta, one of the most poverty-stricken areas in the country. It's a place where the loss of even a few jobs that pay $8 an hour leaves a void in the local economy.

Catfish producers say imports from Vietnam have soared from 575,000 pounds in 1998 to as much as 20 million pounds this year.

—Suzi Parker

Source: *Suzi Parker,* October 3, 2001. © 2001 Suzi Parker. www.csmonitor.com

Analysis: When economic profits exist in an industry, more producers try to enter. As they do, prices and economic profits decline. When losses are incurred, firms begin to exit the industry.

---

marginal cost (MC): The increase in total cost associated with a one-unit increase in production.

up the quantities each of America's 2,000 catfish farmers stands ready to supply at each price. Then we'll know the total quantity of fish to be supplied to the market at that price. Figure 8.1 illustrates this summation. Notice that *the market supply curve is the sum of* the marginal cost *curves of all the firms.* Hence, whatever determines the marginal cost of a typical firm will also affect industry supply. Specifically, *the market supply of a competitive industry is determined by*

- *The price of factor inputs.*
- *Technology.*
- *Expectations.*
- *Taxes and subsidies.*
- *The number of firms in the industry.*

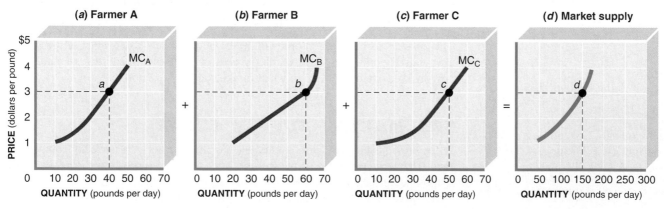

FIGURE 8.1
Competitive Market Supply

The portion of the MC curve that lies above AVC is a competitive firm's short-run supply curve. The curve MC_A tells us that Farmer A will produce 40 pounds of catfish per day if the market price is $3 per pound.

To determine the *market* supply, we add up the quantities supplied at each price by every farmer. The total quantity supplied to the market at the price of $3 is 150 pounds per day ($a + b + c$). Market supply depends on the number of firms and their respective marginal costs.

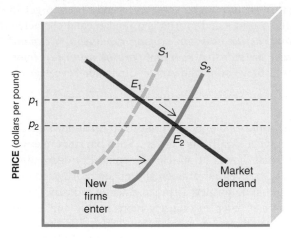

(a) Market entry pushes price down and . . .

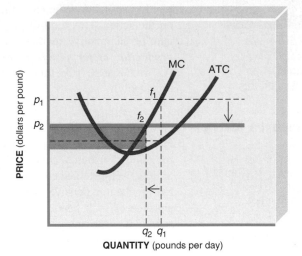

(b) Reduces profits of competitive firm

FIGURE 8.2
Market Entry

If economic profits exist in an industry, more firms will want to enter it. As they do, the market supply curve will shift to the right and cause the market price to drop from p_1 to p_2 (part a). The lower market price, in turn, will reduce the output and profits of the typical firm. In part b, the firm's output falls from q_1 to q_2.

If more firms enter an industry, the market supply curve will shift to the right. This is the problem confronting the catfish farmers in Mississippi (see World View). It's fairly inexpensive to get into the catfish business: You can start with a pond, some breeding stock, and relatively little capital equipment. These **investment decisions** shift the market supply curve to the right and drive down catfish prices. This process is illustrated in Figure 8.2.

If prices fall too far, entry will cease and some catfish farmers will drain their ponds and plant cotton again. As they leave (exit) the industry, the market supply curve will shift to the left.

The profit motive drives these entry and exit decisions. Ten years ago catfish farming looked a whole lot more profitable than cotton farming. Farmers responded by flooding their cotton fields to create fish ponds.

The resulting shift of market supply caused the **economic profits** in catfish farming to disappear. Eventually the returns in catfish farming were no better than those in cotton farming. When that happened, cotton farmers stopped building fish ponds and resumed planting cotton. ***When economic profits disappear, entry ceases, and the market stabilizes.*** At that new equilibrium, catfish farmers earn only a normal (average) rate of return.

Catfish farmers would be happier, of course, if the price of catfish didn't decline to the point where economic profits disappear. But how are they going to prevent it? Alleamer Tyler evidently knows all about the laws of supply and demand (see the previous World View). She would dearly like to keep all those Vietnamese catfish out of this country. She also wishes those farmers in Maine would keep cranberries in their ponds rather than catfish. She would also like to get other farmers in the South to slow production a little before all the profits disappear. But Ms. Tyler is powerless to stop the forces of a **competitive market.** She can't even afford to reduce her *own* catfish production. Even though she has 200 acres of ponds, nobody would notice the resulting drop in market supplies, and catfish prices would continue to slide. The only one affected would be Ms. Tyler, who'd be denying herself the opportunity to share in the (dwindling) fortunes of the catfish market while they lasted.

Entry and Exit

investment decision: The decision to build, buy, or lease plant and equipment; to enter or exit an industry.

Tendency toward Zero Profits

economic profit: The difference between total revenues and total economic costs.

competitive market: A market in which no buyer or seller has market power.

You can track catfish output and prices and even get recipes at the Catfish Institute's Web site: www.catfishinstitute.com.

Low Barriers to Entry

barriers to entry: Obstacles, such as patents, that make it difficult or impossible for would-be producers to enter a particular market.

Market Characteristics of Perfect Competition

Ms. Tyler's dilemma goes a long way toward explaining why catfish farming isn't highly profitable. Whenever the profit picture looks good, everybody tries to get in on the action. This kind of pressure on prices and profits is a fundamental characteristic of competitive markets. *As long as it's easy for existing producers to expand production or for new firms to enter an industry, economic profits won't last long.* As we'll see shortly, this is a lesson Steve Jobs and Apple Computer have learned repeatedly.

New producers will be able to enter a profitable industry and help drive down prices and profits as long as they don't encounter significant barriers. Such **barriers to entry** may include patents, control of essential factors of production, control of distribution outlets, well-established brand loyalty, or even governmental regulation. All such barriers make it expensive, risky, or impossible for new firms to enter an industry. In the absence of such barriers, new firms can enter an industry more readily and at less risk. Not surprisingly, firms already entrenched in a profitable industry do their best to keep out newcomers by erecting barriers to entry. Unfortunately for Ms. Tyler, there are few barriers to entering the catfish business; all you need to get started is a pond and a few fish.

This brief review of catfish economics illustrates a few general observations about the structure, behavior, and outcomes of a competitive market:

- *Many firms.* A competitive market includes a great many firms, none of which has a significant share of total output.
- *Perfect information.* All buyers and sellers have complete information on available supply, demand, and prices.
- *Identical products.* Products are homogeneous. One firm's product is the same as any other firm's product.
- *MC = p.* All competitive firms will seek to expand output until marginal cost equals price, in as much as price and marginal revenue are identical for such firms.
- *Low barriers.* Barriers to enter the industry are low. If economic profits are available, more firms will enter the industry.
- *Zero economic profit.* The tendency of production and market supplies to expand when profit is high puts heavy pressures on prices and profits in competitive industries. Economic profit will approach zero in the long run as prices are driven down to the level of average production costs.

COMPETITION AT WORK: MICROCOMPUTERS

Few markets have all the characteristics listed above. That is, *few, if any, product markets are perfectly competitive.* However, many industries function much like the competitive model we sketched out. In addition to catfish farming, most other agricultural product markets are characterized by highly competitive market structures, with hundreds or even thousands of producers supplying the market. Other highly competitive, and hence not very profitable, businesses are T-shirt shops, retail food, printing, clothing manufacturing and retailing, dry-cleaning establishments, beauty salons, and furniture. Online stockbroker services have also become highly competitive. In these markets, prices and profits are always under the threat of expanded supplies brought to market by existing or new producers.

The electronics industry offers numerous examples of how competition reduces prices and profits. Between 1972 and 1983, the price of small, hand-held calculators fell from $200 to under $10. The price of digital watches fell even more dramatically, from roughly $2,000 in 1975 to under $7 in 1990. Videocassette recorders (VCRs)

Competition Helps Drop Laptop Prices

Worldwide Sales Jump 40%

Laptop bargains abound this holiday season, partly because of stiff competition between tech heavy-weights Dell and Hewlett-Packard.

Laptops likely will sell for an average $1,300 this month—a new low, says researcher NPD Group. In 2003's first 10 months, 15% of laptops sold for less than $1,000 vs. 6% last year.

Entry-level laptops have seen the steepest drops. This is the first year it's easy to find quality ones for less than $1,000, says NPD computer analyst Stephen Baker.

Savvy shoppers find even better deals. Best Buy recently sold an entry-level Toshiba laptop with Windows XP and a DVD player for $499, after rebates.

Makers and retailers are dropping prices to compete in the fast-growing laptop market

—Michelle Kessler

Source: *USA Today,* December 8, 2003. USA TODAY Copyright 2003. Reprinted with permission.

Analysis: Competitive pressures compel laptop producers to keep improving the product and reducing prices. The lure of profits encourages firms to enter this expanding market even as prices drop.

that sold for $2,000 in 1979 now sell for less than $70. DVD players that cost $1,500 in 1997 now sell for under $80. Cell phones that sold for $1,000 ten years ago are now given away. The same kind of competitive pressures have reduced the price of laptop computers. New entrants keep bringing better laptops to market, while driving prices down (see News).

The driving force behind all these price reductions and quality improvements is *competition.* Do you really believe the price of accessing the Net would be falling if only one firm controlled access to the Internet? Do you think thousands of software writers would be toiling away right now if popular programs didn't generate enormous profits? Would America Online and Dell Computer keep rolling out new products and services if other companies weren't always snapping at their heels?

Market Evolution

To appreciate how the process of competition works, we will examine the development of the personal computer industry. *As in other industries, the market structure of the computer industry has evolved over time. It was never a monopoly, nor was it ever perfect competition.* In its first couple of years it was dominated by only a few companies (like Apple) that were enormously successful. The high profits the early microcomputer producers obtained attracted swarms of imitators. Over 250 firms entered the microcomputer industry between 1976 and 1983 in search of high profits. The entry of so many firms transformed the industry's market structure: The industry became *more* competitive, even though not *perfectly* competitive. The increased competition pushed prices downward and improved the product. When prices and profits tumbled, scores of companies went bankrupt. They left a legacy, however, of a vastly larger market, much improved computers, and sharply lower prices.

We'll use the early experiences of the microcomputer industry to illustrate the key behavioral features of a competitive market. As we'll see, many of these competitive features are still at work in the PC market and even more visible in the markets for Internet services, content software, and digital music players.

Initial Conditions: The Apple I

The microcomputer industry really got started in 1977. Prior to that time, microcomputers were essentially a hobby item for engineers and programmers, who bought circuits, keyboards, monitors, and tape recorders and then assembled their own basic computers. Steve Jobs, then working at Atari, and Steven Wozniak, then working at

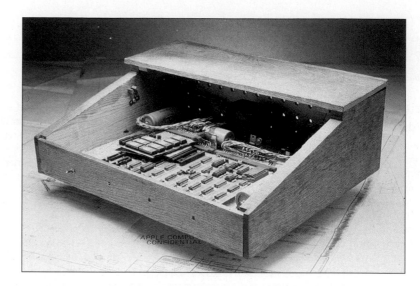

Analysis: The Apple I launched the personal computer industry in 1976. Hundreds of firms entered the industry to improve on this first preassembled microcomputer.

Hewlett-Packard, were among these early computer enthusiasts. They spent their days working on large systems and their nights and weekends trying to put together small computers from mail-order parts.

Eventually, Jobs and Wozniak decided they had the capability to build commercially attractive small computers. They ordered the parts necessary for building 100 computers and set up shop in the garage of Jobs's parents. Their finished product—the Apple I (see photo)—was nothing more than a circuit board with a simple, built-in operating system. This first microcomputer was packaged in a wooden box. Despite primitive characteristics, the first 100 Apple I computers sold out immediately. This quick success convinced Jobs and Wozniak to package their computers more fully—which they did by enclosing them in plastic housing—and to offer more of them for sale. Shortly thereafter, in January 1977, Apple Computer, Inc. was established.

Apple revolutionized the market by offering a preassembled desktop computer with attractive features and an accessible price. The impact on the marketplace was much like that of Henry Ford's early Model T: Suddenly a newfangled piece of technology came into reach of the average U.S. household, and everybody, it seemed, wanted one. The first mass-produced Apple computer—called the Apple II—was just a basic keyboard with an operating system that permitted users to write their own programs. The computer had no disk drive, no monitor, and only 4K of random access memory (RAM). Consumers had to use their TV sets as screens and audiocassettes for data storage. This primitive Apple II was priced at just under $1,300 when it debuted in June 1977. Apple was producing computers at the rate of 500 per month.

Apple didn't engineer or manufacture chips or semiconductor components. Instead, it simply packaged existing components purchased from outside suppliers. Hence, it was easy for other companies to follow Apple's lead. Within a very brief time, other firms, such as Tandy (Radio Shack), also started to assemble computers. By the middle of 1978, the basic small computer was selling for $1,000, and industry sales were about 20,000 a month. Figure 8.3 depicts the initial (1978) equilibrium in the computer market and the approximate costs of production for the typical computer manufacturer at that time.

The Production Decision

The short-run goal of every producer is to find the rate of output that maximizes profits. Finding this rate entails making the best possible **production decision.** In this short-run context, *each competitive firm seeks the rate of output at which marginal cost equals price.*

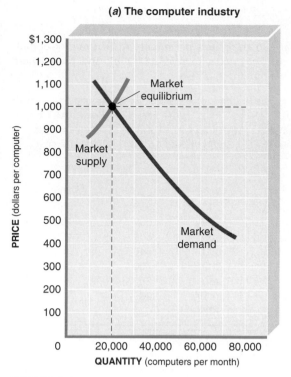

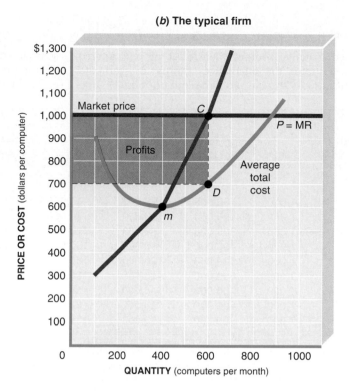

FIGURE 8.3
Initial Equilibrium in the Computer Market

(*a*) **The Industry**   In 1978, the market price of microcomputers was $1,000. This price was established by the intersection of the market supply and demand curves.

(*b*) **A Firm**   Each competitive producer in the market sought to produce computers at that rate (600 per month) where marginal cost equaled price (point *C*). Profit per computer was equal to price (point *C*) minus average total cost (point *D*). Total profits for the typical firm are indicated by the shaded rectangle.

Figure 8.3*b* illustrates the cost and price curves the typical computer producer confronted in 1978. As in most lines of production, the marginal costs of computer production increased with the rate of output. Marginal costs rose in part because output could be increased in the short-run (with existing plant and equipment) only by crowding additional workers onto the assembly line. In 1978, Apple had only 10,000 square feet of manufacturing space. As more workers were hired, each worker had less capital and land to work with, and marginal physical product fell. The law of diminishing returns pushed marginal costs up.

The upward-sloping marginal cost curve intersected the price line at an output level of 600 computers per month (point *C* in Figure 8.3*b*).[1] That was the profit-maximizing rate of output (MC = *p*) for the typical manufacturer. To manufacture any more than 600 computers per month would raise marginal costs over price and reduce total profits. To manufacture any less would be to pass up an opportunity to make another buck.

production decision: The selection of the short-run rate of output (with existing plant and equipment).

Table 8.1 shows how much *profit* a typical computer manufacturer was making in 1978. As the profit column indicates, the typical computer manufacturer could make a real killing in the computer market, reaping a monthly profit of $180,000 by producing and selling 600 microcomputers.

Profit Calculations

[1]The marginal cost curves depicted here rise more steeply than they did in reality, but the general shape of the curves is our primary concern at this point.

TABLE 8.1
Computer Revenues, Costs, and Profits

Producers seek that rate of output where total profit is maximized. This table illustrates the alternatives the typical computer producer faced in 1978. The profit-maximizing rate of output occurred at 600 computers per month. At that rate of output, marginal cost was equal to price ($1,000), and profits were $180,000 per month.

Output per Month	Price	Total Revenue	Total Cost	Total Profit	Marginal Revenue*	Marginal Cost*	Average Total Cost	Profit per Unit (price minus average cost)
0	—	—	$ 60,000	−$60,000	—	—	—	—
100	$1,000	$100,000	90,000	10,000	$1,000	$ 300	$ 900	$100
200	1,000	200,000	130,000	70,000	1,000	400	650	350
300	1,000	300,000	180,000	120,000	1,000	500	600	400
400	1,000	400,000	240,000	160,000	1,000	600	600	400
500	1,000	500,000	320,000	180,000	1,000	800	640	360
600	1,000	600,000	420,000	180,000	1,000	1,000	700	300
700	1,000	700,000	546,000	154,000	1,000	1,260	780	220
800	1,000	800,000	720,000	80,000	1,000	1,740	900	100
900	1,000	900,000	919,800	−19,800	1,000	1,998	1,022	−22

*Note that output levels are calibrated in hundreds in this example; that's why we must have divided the *change* in total costs and revenues from one output level to another by 100 to calculate marginal revenue and marginal cost. Very few manufacturers deal in units of 1.

We could also calculate the computer manufacturers' profits by asking how much the manufacturers make on *each* computer and then multiplying that figure by total output since

Total profit = profit per unit × quantity sold

We can compute these profits by studying the first and last columns in Table 8.1 or by using a little geometry in Figure 8.3*b*. In the figure, average costs (total costs divided by the rate of output) are portrayed by the **average total cost (ATC)** curve. At the output rate of 600 (the row in white in Table 8.1), the distance between the price line ($1,000 at point *C*) and the ATC curve ($700 at point *D*) is $300, which represents the average **profit per unit.** Multiplying this figure by the number of units sold (600 per month) will give us *total* profit per month. Total profits are represented by the shaded rectangle in Figure 8.3*b* and are equal to our earlier profit figure of $180,000 per month.

average total cost (ATC): Total cost divided by the quantity produced in a given time period.

profit per unit: Total profit divided by the quantity produced in a given time period; price minus average total cost.

The Lure of Profits

While gaping at the computer manufacturer's enormous profits, we should remind ourselves that those profits might not last long. Indeed, the more quick-witted among us already will have seen and heard enough to know they've discovered a good thing. And in fact, the kind of profits the early microcomputer manufacturers attained attracted a lot of entrepreneurial interest. *In competitive markets, economic profits attract new entrants.* This is what happened in the catfish industry and also in the computer industry. Within a very short time, a whole crowd of profit maximizers entered the microcomputer industry in hot pursuit of its fabulous profits. By the end of 1980, Apple had a lot of competition, including new entrants from IBM, Xerox, Digital Equipment, Casio, Sharp, and others.

Low Entry Barriers

A critical feature of the microcomputer market was its lack of entry barriers. A microcomputer is little more than a box containing a microprocessor "brain," which connects to a keyboard (to enter data), a memory (to store data), and a screen (to display data). Although the microprocessors that guide the computer are extremely sophisticated, they can be purchased on the open market. Thus, to enter the computer industry, all one needs is some space, some money to buy components, and some dexterity in putting parts together. Such *low entry barriers permit new firms to enter competitive markets.* According to Table 8.1, the typical producer needed only $60,000 of plant and equipment (fixed costs) to get started in the microcomputer market. Jobs and Wozniak had even less when they started making Apples in their garage.

Figure 8.4 shows what happened to the computer market and the profits of the typical firm once the word got out. As more and more entrepreneurs heard how profitable computer manufacturing could be, they quickly got hold of a book on electronic circuitry, rushed to the bank, got a little financing, and set up shop. Before many months had passed, scores of new firms had started producing small computers. *The entry of new firms shifts the market supply curve to the right.* In Figure 8.4a, the supply curve shifted from S_1 to S_2. Almost as fast as a computer can calculate a profit (loss) statement, the willingness to supply increased abruptly.

But the new computer companies were in for a bit of disappointment. With so many new firms hawking microcomputers, it became increasingly difficult to make a fast buck. The downward-sloping market demand curve confirms that a greater quantity of microcomputers could be sold only if the price of computers dropped. And drop it did. The price slide began as computer manufacturers found their inventories growing and so offered price discounts to maintain sales volume. The price fell rapidly, from $1,000 in mid-1978 to $800 in early 1980.

The sliding market price squeezed the profits of each firm, causing the profit rectangle to shrink (compare Figure 8.3b to Figure 8.4b). The lower price also changed the production decision of the typical firm. The new price ($800) intersected the unchanged MC curve at the output rate of 500 computers per month (point G in Figure 8.4b). With average production costs of $640 (Table 8.1), the firm's total prof-

A Shift of Market Supply

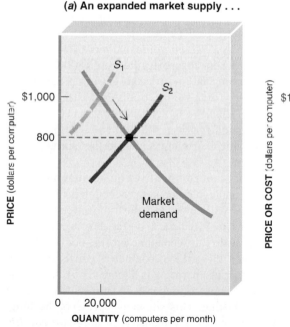

(a) An expanded market supply . . .

(b) Lowers price and profits for the typical firm

FIGURE 8.4
The Competitive Price and Profit Squeeze

(*a*) **The Industry** The economic profits in the computer industry encouraged new firms to enter the industry. As they did, the market supply curve shifted from S_1 to S_2. This rightward shift of the supply curve lowered the equilibrium price of computers.

(*b*) **A Firm** The lower market price, in turn, forced the typical producer to reduce output to the point where MC and price were equal again (point G). At this reduced rate of output, the typical firm earned less total profit than it had earned before.

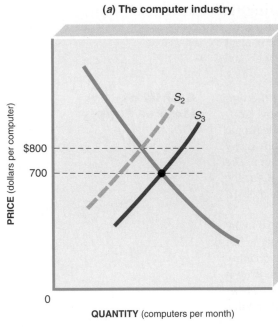

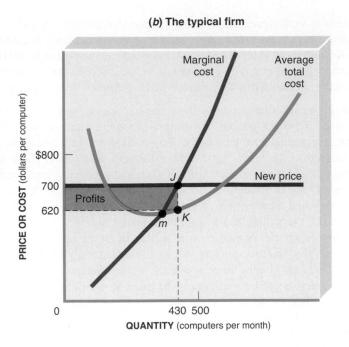

FIGURE 8.5

The Competitive Squeeze Approaching Its Limit

(a) **The Industry** Even at a price of $800 per computer, economic profits attracted still more entrepreneurs, shifting the market supply curve further (S_3). The next short-term equilibrium occurred at a price of $700 per computer.

(b) **A Firm** At this reduced market price, the typical manufacturer wanted to supply only 430 computers per month (point *J*). Total profits were much lower than they had been earlier, with fewer producers and higher prices.

its in 1980 were only $80,000 per month [$(P - \text{ATC}) \times 500$]. Not a paltry sum, to be sure, but nothing like the fantastic fortunes pocketed earlier.

As long as an economic profit is available, it will continue to attract new entrants. Those entrepreneurs who were a little slow in absorbing the implications of Figure 8.3 eventually woke up to what was going on and tried to get in on the action, too. Even though they were a little late, they didn't want to miss the chance to cash in on the $80,000 in monthly profits still available to the typical firm. Hence, the market supply curve continued to shift, and computer prices slid further, as in Figure 8.5. This process squeezed the profits of the typical firm still more, further shrinking the profit rectangle.

As long as economic profits exist in **short-run competitive equilibrium,** that equilibrium won't last. If the rate of profit obtainable in computer production is higher than that available in other industries, new firms will enter the industry. Conversely, if the short-run equilibrium is unprofitable, firms will exit the industry. Profit-maximizing entrepreneurs have a special place in their hearts for economic profits, not computers.

Price and profit declines will cease when the price of computers equals the minimum average cost of production. At that price (point *m* in Figure 8.5*b*), there's no more economic profit to be squeezed out. Firms no longer have an incentive to enter the industry, and the supply curve stops shifting. This situation represents the **long-run competitive equilibrium** for the firm and for the industry. *In long-run equilibrium, entry and exit cease, and zero economic profit (that is, normal profit) prevails* (see Figure 8.6). Table 8.2 summarizes the profit-maximizing rules that bring about this long-run equilibrium.

Once a long-run equilibrium is established, it will continue until market demand shifts or technological progress reduces the cost of computer production. In fact, that's just what happened in the computer market.

short-run competitive equilibrium: $p = \text{MC}$.

long-run competitive equilibrium: $p = \text{MC} = \text{minimum ATC}$.

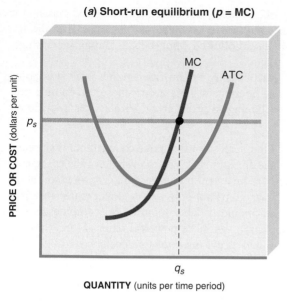

(a) Short-run equilibrium (p = MC)

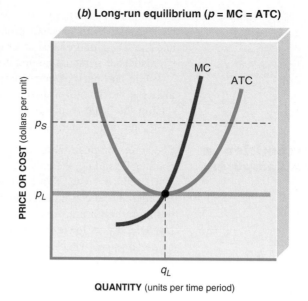

(b) Long-run equilibrium (p = MC = ATC)

FIGURE 8.6

Short- vs. Long-run Equilibrium for the Competitive Firm

(a) Short-Run Competitive firms strive for the rate of output at which marginal cost (MC) equals price. When they achieve that rate of output, they are in *short-run equilibrium*. They have no incentive to alter the rate of output produced with existing (fixed) plant and equipment.

(b) Long-Run If the short-run equilibrium (q_S) is profitable ($p >$ ATC), other firms will want to enter the industry. As they do, market price will fall until it reaches the level of minimum ATC. In this *long-run equilibrium* (q_L), economic profits are zero and nobody wants to enter or exit the industry.

As profit margins narrowed to the levels shown in Figure 8.5, quick-thinking entrepreneurs realized that future profits would have to come from product improvements or cost reductions. By adding features to the basic microcomputer, firms could expect to increase the demand for microcomputers and fetch higher prices. On the other hand, cost reductions would permit firms to widen their profit margins at existing prices or to reduce prices and increase sales. This second strategy wouldn't require assembling more complex computers or risking consumer rejection of an upgraded product.

In late 1979 and early 1980, both product-development strategies were pursued. In the process, two distinct markets were created. Microcomputers upgraded with new features came to be known as *personal* computers, or PCs. The basic unadorned computer first introduced by Apple came to be known as a *home* computer. The limited capabilities of that basic home computer greatly restricted its usefulness to simple household record keeping, games, and elementary programming.

Apple chose the personal computer route. It started enlarging the memory of the Apple II in late 1978 (from 4K to as much as 48K). It offered a monitor (produced

Home Computers vs. Personal Computers

Price Level	Result for a Typical Firm	Market Response
$p >$ ATC	Profits	Enter industry (or expand capacity)
$p <$ ATC	Loss	Exit industry (or reduce capacity)
$p =$ ATC	Break even	Maintain existing capacity (no entry or exit)

TABLE 8.2

Long-Run Rules for Entry and Exit

Firms will enter an industry if economic profits exist ($p >$ ATC). They will exit if economic losses prevail ($p <$ ATC). Entry and exit cease in long-run equilibrium ($p =$ ATC). (See Table 7.4 for short-run profit-maximization rules.)

by Sanyo) for the first time in May 1979. Shortly thereafter, Apple ceased making the basic Apple II and instead produced only upgraded versions (the Apple IIe, the IIc, and the III). Hundreds of other companies followed Apple's lead, touting increasingly sophisticated personal computers.

While one pack of entrepreneurs was chasing PC profits, another pack was going after the profits still available in home computers. This group chose to continue producing the basic Apple II look-alike, hoping to profit from greater efficiency, lower costs, and increasing sales.

Price Competition in Home Computers

The home computer market confronted the fiercest form of price competition. With prices continually sliding, the only way to make an extra buck was to push down the cost curve.

To reduce costs, firms sought to reduce the number of microprocessor chips installed in the computer's "brain." Fewer chips not only reduce direct materials costs, but more important, they decrease the amount of labor required for computer assembly. The key to lower manufacturing costs was more powerful chips. More powerful chips appeared when Intel, Motorola, and Texas Instruments developed 16-bit chips, doubling the computer's "brain" capabilities.

Further Supply Shifts

The impact of the improved chips on computer production costs and profits is illustrated in Figure 8.7, which takes over where Figure 8.5 left off. Recall that the market price of computers had been driven down to $700 by the beginning of 1980. At this price the typical firm maximized profits by producing 430 computers per month, as determined by the intersection of the prevailing price and MC curves (point *J* in Figure 8.7).

The only way for the firm to improve profitability at this point was to reduce costs. The new chips made such cost reductions easy. Such ***technological improvements are illustrated by a downward shift of the ATC and MC curves.*** Notice, for example, that the new technology permits 430 home computers to be produced for a lower marginal cost (about $500) than previously (point *J*).

The lower cost structure increases the profitability of computer production and stimulates a further increase in production. Note in particular that the "new MC" curve intersects the price ($700) line at an output of 600 computers per month (point *N*). By contrast, the old, higher MC curve dictated a production rate of only 430 computers

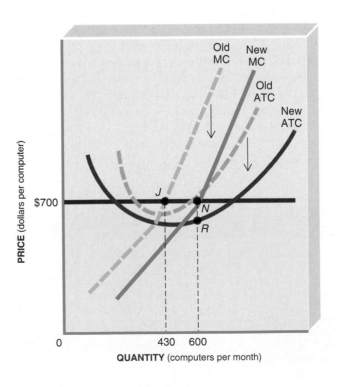

FIGURE 8.7
A Downward Shift of Costs Improves Profits and Stimulates Output

The quest for profits encouraged producers to discover cheaper ways to manufacture computers. The resulting improvements lowered costs and encouraged further increases in the rate of output. The typical computer producer increased output from point J (where *p* = old MC) to point N (where *p* = new MC).

Date		Price of Texas Instruments Model 99/4A
December	1979	$950
February	1980	700
June	1980	650
April	1981	525
December	1981	400
April	1982	249
September	1982	199
January	1983	149
September	1983	99
November	1983	49

TABLE 8.3
Plummeting Prices

Improved technology and fierce competition forced home computer prices down. In the span of only a few years, the price of a basic home computer fell from just under $1,000 to only $49. In the process, price fell below average variable cost, and many firms were forced to shut down.

per month for the typical firm (point *J*) at that price. Thus, existing producers suddenly had an incentive to *expand* production, and new firms had a greater incentive to *enter* the industry. The great rush into computer production was on again.

The market implications of another entrepreneurial stampede should now be obvious. As more and more firms tried to get in on the action, the market supply curve again shifted to the right. As output increased, computer prices slid further down the market demand curve.

Table 8.3 illustrates how steeply home computer prices fell after 1980. Texas Instruments (TI) was one of the largest firms producing home computers in 1980. The lower costs made possible by improved microprocessors enabled TI to sell its basic home computer for $650 in 1980. Despite modest improvements in the TI machine, TI had to reduce its price to $525 in early 1981 in order to maintain unit sales. Shortly thereafter, the additional output of new entrants and existing companies pushed market prices down still further, to around $400.

Even at $400, TI and other home computer manufacturers were making handsome profits. In the fourth quarter of 1981, total industry sales were in excess of 200,000 per month—10 times the volume sold just three years earlier. Profits were good, too. A single company, Atari, recorded total profits of $137 million in the fourth quarter of 1981, far more profit than Apple Computer, Inc. had made during its first five *years* of production. The profits of the home computer market appeared boundless.

The remainder of Table 8.3 shows the consequences of the continued competition for those "boundless" profits. Between December 1981 and January 1983, the retail price of home computers fell from $400 to $149. Profit margins became razor-thin. Fourth-quarter profits at Atari, for example, fell from $137 million in 1981 to only $1.2 million in 1983.

Shutdowns

That didn't stop the competitive process, however. At Texas Instruments, minimum *variable* costs were roughly $100 per computer, so TI and other manufacturers could afford to keep producing even at lower prices. And they had little choice but to do so, since if they didn't, other companies would quickly take up the slack. Industry output kept increasing, despite shrinking profit margins. The increased quantity supplied pushed computer prices ever lower.

By the time computer prices reached $99, TI was losing $300 million per year. In September 1983, the company recognized that the price would no longer even cover average variable costs. ***Once a firm is no longer able to cover variable costs, it should shut down production.*** When the price of home computers dipped below minimum average variable costs, TI had reached the **shutdown point,** and the company ceased production. At the time TI made the shutdown decision, the company had an inventory of nearly 500,000 unsold computers. To unload them, TI reduced its price to $49, forcing lower prices and losses on other computer firms.

shutdown point: The rate of output where price equals minimum AVC.

IBM to Halt PCjr Output Next Month

Computer's Sales Dried Up After Steep Price Cuts Ended Earlier This Year

NEW YORK—International Business Machines Corp. ended its up-and-down struggle to revive its PCjr home computer by announcing it would stop making the product next month.

The surprise move marks IBM's most visible product failure since its enormously successful entry into the personal-computer business four years ago. IBM announced the PCjr in late 1983 and began selling it early last year with an advertising campaign believed to exceed $40 million. IBM's efforts to make junior a hit ranged from technical changes to steep price

cuts. But while aggressive IBM price cuts before Christmas increased PCjr sales substantially, sales dried up after the promotions ended in January. . . .

At the time of its introduction, the PCjr had a list of $699 or $1,269, depending on the model. The prices later were cut to $599 and $999, and the more powerful model's price dropped below the $800 level during the Christmas promotion.

—Dennis Kneale

Source: *The Wall Street Journal,* March 20, 1985. Reprinted by permission of The Wall Street Journal. © 1985 Dow Jones & Company, Inc. All rights reserved worldwide. www.wsj.com

Analysis: Competition forces firms to improve products and reduce prices. Those firms that can't keep up are forced to shut down and perhaps exit the industry.

Exits

Shortly after Texas Instruments shut down its production, it got out of the home computer business altogether. Mattel, Atari, and scores of smaller companies also withdrew from the home computer market. The exit rate between 1983 and 1985 matched the entry rate of the period 1979 to 1982.

The Personal Computer Market

The same kind of price competition that characterized the home computer market eventually hit the personal computer market too. As noted earlier, the microcomputer industry split into two segments around 1980, with most firms pursuing the upgraded personal computer market.

At first, competition in the PC market was largely confined to product improvements. Firms added more memory, faster microprocessors, better monitors, expanded operating systems, new applications software, and other features. New entrants into the market—Compaq in 1982; then Dell, AST, Gateway, and more—were the source of most product innovations.

The stampede of new firms and products into the PC market soon led to outright price competition too. As firms discovered that they couldn't sell all the PCs they were producing at prevailing prices, they were forced to offer price discounts. These discounts soon spread, and the slide down the demand curve accelerated.

Firms that couldn't keep up with the dual pace of improving technology and falling prices soon fell by the wayside. Scores of firms ceased production and withdrew from the industry once prices fell below minimum average variable cost. Even Apple, which had taken the "high road" to avoid price competition in home computers, was slowed by price competition. And IBM, which had entered the industry late, was forced to shut down its PC division after realizing that steep price cuts would be required to sell its small PCs (the "PCjr") to household users (News).

THE COMPETITIVE PROCESS

It is now evident that consumers reaped substantial benefits from competition in the computer market. Over 400 million home and personal computers have been sold. Along the way, technology has made personal computers 200 times faster than the first Apple IIs, with 300 times more memory. The iMac computer introduced by Apple in 1998 makes the Apple I of 1976 look prehistoric (see Table 8.4). A lot of

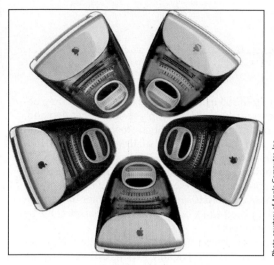

Photo courtesy of Apple Computer, Inc.

Analysis: The 1998 iMac evolved from the Apple I because of intense competition.

Basic Features	Apple I (1976)	iMac (1998)
Microprocessor	MOS Technology 6502, 1.023 MHz	Power PC G3, 233 MHz
Internal RAM (random access memory)	4K (expandable to 8K)	32 MB (expandable to 128 MB)
Interfaces	Keyboard; cassette board connector; 44 pin edge connector	Two 12-Mbps universal serial bus port connectors; infrared technology port; 10/100 BASE-T Ethernet port; Internal 56-Kbps modem
Video	No monitor; interfaces with TV or other video monitor	Supports millions of colors at 800 × 600 resolutions
Multimedia capabilities	None	Accelerated 2- and 3-dimension graphics chip; built-in stereo speakers with SRS surround sound; built-in microphone; two front headphone jacks; 16-bit stereo in/output jacks; 44.1-kHz sampling rate
Data storage	Via cassette interface (sold separately)	Internal 4GB hard disk drive; internal 24x-speed CD ROM
Price	$666.66 ($1,943 in 1998 dollars)	$1,299.00

Source: The Computer Museum History Center, Boston, www.computerhistory.org.

Analysis: Competition in the computer industry spurred product innovations and new technology that revolutionized computers. Today's iMac bears little resemblance to the Apple I. Despite its far superior capabilities, the iMac's inflation-adjusted price is much less than that of the Apple I (page 500).

TABLE 8.4
Apple I vs. iMac

Price War Squeezes PC Makers

Cuts Make Companies Bleed As Profits, Sales Decline; Some Predict a Shakeout

It's getting ugly in the personal-computer market.

Just last summer computer makers were boosting already-strong sales by hawking sleek new hardware designs and faster processors. Today, the PC business is showing all the signs of a brutal price war: rapid price cuts, rebates and lots of freebies. Dell Computer Corp., which launched the current price battle at the end of last year, now is tossing in free delivery, a free printer and free Internet access to customers who buy a PC through its website.

That's a good thing for customers. But computer makers are reeling as the stiffening competition slices into profits. Compaq Computer Corp., the world's largest PC maker, said earlier this month it will consolidate operations and cut more than 7,000 workers to help compensate for new price reductions. Other major players also are axing jobs and warning investors of lower sales.

In the past, computer prices have fallen steadily as they became cheaper to make, yet that simply fueled higher demand. But recent price cuts have been much steeper than anything seen before, and, combined with a slowdown in demand, could result in a first-ever decline in PC revenue in the U.S.

If prices continue to fall at the current pace, the resulting squeeze also could trigger a wave of consolidation among the biggest PC makers, analysts say, as the companies try to cope either by selling businesses or seeking more market clout by acquiring competitors.

"The earnings risk from price pressure on all these PC hardware companies is increasing rapidly," warns UBS Warburg analyst Don Young. "At some point, either this industry says enough is enough, or . . . everybody loses."

—Gary McWilliams

Source: *The Wall Street Journal,* March 26, 2001, p. B1. Reprinted by permission of The Wall Street Journal. © 2001 Dow Jones & Company, Inc. All rights reserved worldwide. www.wsj.com

Analysis: Competitive pressures force companies to continually improve products and cut prices.

---

consumers have found that computers are great for doing accounting chores, keeping records, writing papers, playing games, and accessing the Internet. Perhaps it's true that an abundance of inexpensive computers would have been produced in other market (or nonmarket) situations as well. But we can't ignore the fact that *competitive market pressures were a driving force in the spectacular growth of the computer industry.* And they still are, as the accompanying News confirms.

Allocative Efficiency: The Right Output Mix

market mechanism: The use of market prices and sales to signal desired outputs (or resource allocations).

The squeeze on prices and profits that we've observed in the computer market is a fundamental characteristic of the competitive process. Indeed, the **market mechanism** works best under such circumstances. The existence of economic profits is an indication that consumers place a high value on a particular product and are willing to pay a comparatively high price to get it. The high price and profits signal this information to profit-hungry entrepreneurs, who come forward to satisfy consumer demands. Thus, *high profits in a particular industry indicate that consumers want a different mix of output* (more of that industry's goods). The competitive squeeze on those same profits indicates that resources are being reallocated to produce that desired mix. In a competitive market, consumers get more of the goods they desire—and at a lower price.

opportunity cost: The most desired goods or services that are forgone in order to obtain something else.

The ability of competitive markets to allocate resources efficiently across industries originates in the way competitive prices are set. To attain the optimal mix of output, we must know the **opportunity cost** of producing different goods. A competitive market gives us the information necessary for making such choices. Why? Because competitive firms always strive to produce at the rate of output at which price equals marginal cost. Hence, *the price signal the consumer gets in a competitive market is an accurate reflection of opportunity cost.* As such, it offers a reliable basis for making choices about the mix of output and attendant allocation of resources. In this sense, the **marginal cost pricing** characteristic of competitive markets permits society to answer the WHAT-to-produce question efficiently. The amount consumers are willing to pay for a good (its price) equals its opportunity cost (marginal cost).

marginal cost pricing: The offer (supply) of goods at prices equal to their marginal cost.

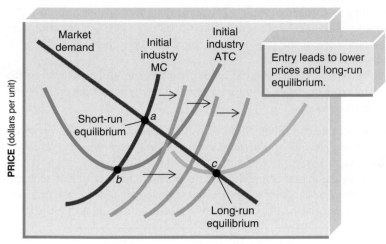

PRICE (dollars per unit)

QUANTITY (units per time period)

FIGURE 8.8
Summary of Competitive Process

All competitive firms seek to produce at that output where MC = *p*. Hence, a competitive *industry* will produce at that rate of output where *industry* MC (the sum of all firms' MC curves) intersects market demand (point *a*).

If economic profits exist in the industry (as they do here), more firms will enter the industry. As they do, the *industry* MC (supply) curve will shift to the right. The shifting MC curve will pull the *industry* ATC curve along with it. As the *industry* MC curve continues to shift rightward, the intersection of MC and ATC (point *b*) eventually will reach the demand curve at point *c*. At point *c*, MC still equals price, but no economic profits exist and entry (shifts) will cease. Point *c* will be the *long-term* equilibrium of the industry.

If competitive pressures reduce costs (i.e., improve technology), the supply (MC) curve will shift further to the right and *down,* reducing long-term prices even more.

Note that MC = *p* in both short- and long-run equilibrium. Notice also that equilibrium must occur on the market demand curve.

When the competitive pressure on prices is carried to the limit, we also get the right answer to the HOW to produce question. Competition drives costs down to their bare minimum—the hallmark of economic **efficiency.** This was illustrated by the tendency of computer prices to be driven down to the level of *minimum* average costs. Figure 8.8 summarizes this competitive process, showing how the industry moves from short-run to long-run equilibrium. Once the long-run equilibrium has been established, society is getting the most it can from its available (scarce) resources.

Competitive pressures also affect the FOR WHOM question. At the limit of long-run equilibrium, all economic profit is eliminated. This doesn't mean that producers are left empty-handed, however. First, the zero-profit limit is rarely, if ever, reached, because new products are continually being introduced, consumer demands change, and more efficient production processes are discovered. In fact, the competitive process creates strong pressures to pursue product and technological innovation. In a competitive market, the adage about the early bird getting the worm is particularly apt. As we observed in the computer market, the first ones to perceive and respond to the potential profitability of computer production were the ones who made the greatest profits.

The sequence of events common to competitive markets evolves as follows:

- High prices and profits signal consumers' demand for more output.
- Economic profit attracts new suppliers.
- The market supply curve shifts to the right.
- Prices slide down the market demand curve.

Production Efficiency: Minimum Average Cost

efficiency: Maximum output of a good from the resources used in production.

Zero Economic Profit

Relentless Profit Squeeze

- A new equilibrium is reached at which increased quantities of the desired product are produced and its price is lower. Average costs of production are at or near a minimum, much more of the product is supplied and consumed, and economic profit approaches zero.
- Throughout the process, producers experience great pressure to keep ahead of the profit squeeze by reducing costs, a pressure that frequently results in product and technological innovation.

What is essential to remember about the competitive process is that the *potential threat of other firms expanding production or of new firms entering the industry keeps existing firms on their toes.* Even the most successful firm can't rest on its laurels for long. To stay in the game, competitive firms must continually update technology, improve their product, and reduce costs. It is the same lesson a lot of entrepreneurs learned in the unusually fast rise and quick death of "dot.com" companies (1998–2001).

THE ECONOMY TOMORROW

$49 iPods

Competition didn't end with computers or dot.com companies. Just ask Steve Jobs, the guy who started the personal computer business back in 1977. He introduced another hot consumer product in November 2001—the iPod. The iPod was the first mass-produced portable digital music player. It allowed consumers to download, store, and retrieve up to 1,000 songs. Its compact size, sleek design, and simple functionality made it an instant success: Apple was selling iPods as fast as they could be produced, piling up huge profits in the process.

So what happened? Other entrepreneurs quickly got the scent of iPod's profits. Within a matter of months, competitors were designing their own digital music players. By 2003, the "attack of the iPod clones" (see News) was in full force. Major players like Sony (MusicBox), Dell (JukeBox), Samsung (Yepp), and Creative Technology (Muvo Slim) were all bringing MP3 players to the market. Competitors were adding new features, shrinking the size, and reducing prices.

IN THE NEWS

Attack of the iPod Clones

New Players Give Apple a Run For Its Money in Portable Music; Recording Songs From the Radio

APPLE COMPUTER'S iPod portable music player is one of the best digital products of any kind ever invented. Its design is simply brilliant, and, since its debut two years ago next month, it has become an icon. Nearly 1.5 million iPods have been sold, and the slender white gadget has become the best-selling portable music player on the market, even though it is also the most expensive.

There have been other high-capacity digital music players, both before and since the iPod appeared. Most have been cheaper, but all have been inferior to the iPod, mainly because they were too big, and too clumsy to use. Meanwhile, Apple has kept improving the iPod, making it smaller and more capable.

Now, however, a new generation of would-be iPod killers is hitting the market. And, after two years of studying Apple's work, the makers of these new players are finally giving the iPod a run for its money. These products are nearly as small as the iPod, and have aped its widely admired user interface. Some have more features, and are less expensive.

—Walter S. Mossberg

Analysis: Economic profits attract entrepreneurs. As competition intensifies, products improve and prices fall.

Under these circumstances, Apple could not afford to sit back and admire its profits. Steve Jobs knew he'd have to keep running to stay ahead of the MP3-player pack. He kept improving the iPod. Within two years, Apple had three generations of iPods, each substantially better than the last. Memory capacity increased tenfold (to 10,000 songs), features were added, and the size shrank further. In January 2004, Apple brought out the iPodMini, a credit card–sized MP3 player that is 40 percent smaller than the original iPod but has the same 1,000-song capacity. Its initial price was $249, 40 percent less than the original iPod. Hence, in less than two and a half years, the price fell by 40 percent even while quality improved dramatically.

Is that the end of the story? No way. By mid 2004 there were at least 60 iPod clones in the market, with more entrants in sight. Rivals were using flash memory chips rather than hard disks to cut costs (even though this reduces memory capacity) and prices. Microsoft was working on a new MP3 player to interface with its Media Player software and huge music library. Sony was promising to bring a $60 digital music player to the market.

With this kind of unrelenting pressure, Apple will have to keep improving the iPod and reducing its price. By the time you graduate, iPods will surely be selling for $49 or less. If that sounds preposterous, look back at the price/quality history of personal computers. The unrelenting pressure of competition is what forces producers to keep delivering better products at lower prices. Competition is not *perfect* in the MP3-player market (as we'll see), but it is still a *powerful* force.

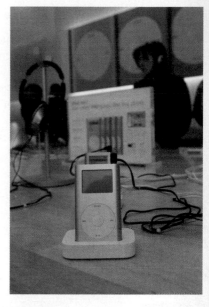

Analysis: Competition forces Apple to make better and cheaper iPods.

SUMMARY

- A perfectly competitive firm has no power to alter the market price of the product it sells. The perfectly competitive firm confronts a horizontal demand curve for its own output even though the relevant *market* demand curve is negatively sloped.
- Profit maximization induces the competitive firm to produce at that rate of output where marginal costs equal price. This represents the short-run equilibrium of the firm.
- If short-run profits exist in a competitive industry, new firms will enter the market. The resulting shift of supply will drive market prices down the market demand curve. As prices fall, the profit of the industry and its constituent firms will be squeezed.
- The limit to the competitive price and profit squeeze is reached when price is driven down to the level of minimum average total cost. At this point (long-run equilibrium) additional output and profit will be attained only if technology is improved (lowering costs) or if market demand increases.
- Firms will shut down production if price falls below average variable cost. Firms will exit the industry if they foresee continued economic losses.
- The most distinctive thing about competitive markets is the persistent pressure they exert on prices and profits. The threat of competition is a tremendous incentive for producers to respond quickly to consumer demands and to seek more efficient means of production. In this sense, competitive markets do best what markets are supposed to do—efficiently allocate resources.

Key Terms

equilibrium price
market supply
marginal cost (MC)
investment decision
economic profit
competitive market

barriers to entry
production decision
average total cost (ATC)
profit per unit
short-run competitive equilibrium
long-run competitive equilibrium

shutdown point
market mechanism
opportunity cost
marginal cost pricing
efficiency

Questions for Discussion

1. Why would anyone want to enter a profitable industry knowing that profits would eventually be eliminated by competition?

2. Why wouldn't producers necessarily want to produce output at the lowest average cost? Under what conditions would they end up doing so?

3. What industries do you regard as being highly competitive? Can you identify any barriers to entry in those industries?

4. At what point will the "enough is enough" statement in the News on the PC price war (page 190) be located?

5. What might cause catfish prices to rise far enough to eliminate losses in the industry? (See News, page 176.)

6. As the price of computers fell, what happened to their quality? How is this possible?

7. Why is the price of "laptop computers" declining? (See News, page 179.)

8. Is "long-run" equilibrium permanent? What forces might dislodge it?

9. What would happen to iPod sales and profits if Apple kept price and profit margins high?

10. Identify two products that have either (*a*) fallen sharply in price or (*b*) gotten significantly better without price increases. How did these changes come about?

PROBLEMS	The Student Problem Set at the back of this book contains numerical and graphing problems for this chapter.
WEB ACTIVITIES	to accompany this chapter can be found on the Online Learning Center: **http://www.mhhe.com/economics/schiller10**

9 Monopoly

n 1908 Ford produced the Model T, the car "designed for the common man." It was cheap, reliable, and as easy to drive as the horse and buggy it was replacing. Ford sold 10,000 Model Ts in its first full year of production (1909). After that, sales more than doubled every year. In 1913, nearly 200,000 Model Ts were sold; and Ford was fast changing U.S. patterns of consumption, travel, and living standards.

During this early development of the U.S. auto industry, Henry Ford dominated the field. There were other producers, but the Ford Motor Company was the only producer of an inexpensive "motorcar for the multitudes." In this situation, Henry Ford could dictate the price and the features of his cars. When he opened his new assembly line factory at Highland Park, he abruptly raised the Model T's price by $100—an increase of 12 percent—to help pay for the new plant. Then he decided to paint all Model Ts black. When told of consumer complaints about the lack of colors, Ford advised one of his executives in 1913: "Give them any color they want so long as it's black."[1]

Henry Ford had **market power.** He could dictate what color car Americans would buy. And he could raise the price of Model Ts without fear of losing all his customers. Such power is alien to competitive firms. Competitive firms are always under pressure to reduce costs, improve quality, and cater to consumer preferences.

In this chapter we examine how market structure influences market outcomes. Specifically, we examine how a market controlled by a single producer—a monopoly—behaves. We're particularly interested in the following questions:

- **What price will a monopolist charge?**
- **How much output will the monopolist produce?**
- **Are consumers better or worse off when only one firm controls an entire market?**

> **market power:** The ability to alter the market price of a good or service.

MARKET POWER

The essence of market power is the ability to alter the price of a product. The catfish farmers in Chapter 8 had no such power. Because 2,000 farms were producing and selling the same good, each catfish producer had to act as a *price taker*. Each producer could sell all it wanted at the prevailing price but would lose all its customers if it tried to charge a higher price.

Firms that have market power *can* alter the price of their output without losing all their customers. Sales volume may drop when price is increased, but the quantity demanded won't drop to zero. In other words, *firms with market power confront downward-sloping demand curves for their own output.*

The Downward-Sloping Demand Curve

[1]Charles E. Sorensen, *My Forty Years with Ford* (New York: W. W. Norton & Co., 1956), p. 127.

FIGURE 9.1
Firm vs. Industry Demand

A competitive firm can sell its entire output at the prevailing market price. In this sense, the firm confronts a horizontal demand curve, as in part *a*. Nevertheless, market demand for the product still slopes downward. The demand curve confronting the industry is illustrated in part *b*. Note the difference in the units of measurement (single bushels vs. thousands).

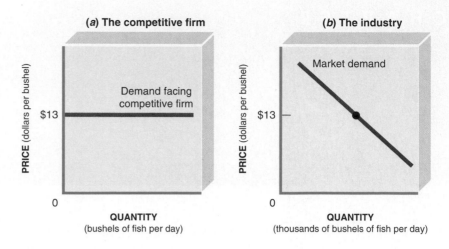

(a) The competitive firm

PRICE (dollars per bushel)

$13   Demand facing competitive firm

0   QUANTITY
(bushels of fish per day)

(b) The industry

PRICE (dollars per bushel)

Market demand

$13

0   QUANTITY
(thousands of bushels of fish per day)

The distinction between perfectly competitive (powerless) and imperfectly competitive (powerful) firms is illustrated again in Figure 9.1. Figure 9.1*a* re-creates the market situation that confronts a single catfish farmer. In Chapter 7, we assumed that the prevailing price of catfish was $13 a bushel and that a small, competitive firm could sell its entire output at this price. Hence, each individual firm effectively confronted a horizontal demand curve.

We also noted earlier that catfish don't violate the law of demand. As good as catfish taste, people aren't willing to buy unlimited quantities of them at $13 a bushel. To induce consumers to buy more catfish, the market price of catfish must be reduced.

This seeming contradiction between the law of demand and the situation of the competitive firm is resolved in Figure 9.1. There are *two* relevant demand curves. The one on the left, which appears to contradict the law of demand, refers to a single competitive producer. The one on the right refers to the entire *industry,* of which the competitive producer is one very tiny part. The industry or market demand curve *does* slope downward, even though individual competitive firms are able to sell their own output at the going price.

Monopoly

monopoly: A firm that produces the entire market supply of a particular good or service.

An industry needn't be composed of many small firms. The entire output of catfish could be produced by a single large producer. Such a firm would be a **monopoly**—a single firm that produces the entire market supply of a good.

The emergence of a monopoly obliterates the distinction between industry demand and the demand curve facing the firm. A monopolistic firm *is* the industry. Hence, there's only *one* demand curve to worry about, and that's the market (industry) demand curve, as illustrated in Figure 9.1*b*. This simplifies things: ***In monopoly situations, the demand curve facing the firm is identical to the market demand curve for the product.***

Price and Marginal Revenue

profit-maximization rule: Produce at that rate of output where marginal revenue equals marginal cost.

Although monopolies simplify the geometry, they complicate the arithmetic of **profit maximization.** The basic rule for maximizing profits is unchanged—that is, produce the rate of output where marginal revenue equals marginal cost. This rule applies to *all* firms. In a competitive industry, however, this general rule was simplified. For competitive firms, marginal revenue is equal to price. Hence, a competitive firm can maximize profits by producing at that rate of output where marginal cost equals *price.*

This special adaptation of the profit-maximizing rule doesn't work for a monopolist. The demand curve facing a monopolist is downward-sloping. Because of this, ***marginal revenue isn't equal to price for a monopolist.*** On the contrary, marginal revenue is always *less* than price in a monopoly, which makes it just a bit more difficult to find the profit-maximizing rate of output.

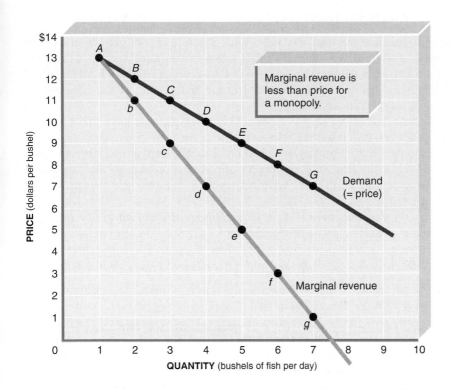

FIGURE 9.2
Price Exceeds Marginal Revenue in Monopoly

If a firm must lower its price to sell additional output, marginal revenue is less than price. If this firm wants to increase its sales from 1 to 2 bushels per day, for example, price must be reduced from $13 to $12. The marginal revenue of the second bushel is therefore only $11. This is indicated in row B of the table and by point *b* on the graph.

	(1)		(2)		(3)	(4)
	Quantity	×	Price	=	Total Revenue	Marginal Revenue ($= \Delta TR \div \Delta q$)
A	1		$13		$13	
						$11
B	2		12		24	
						9
C	3		11		33	
						7
D	4		10		40	
						5
E	5		9		45	

Figure 9.2 is a simple illustration of the relationship between price and marginal revenue. The monopolist can sell 1 bushel of fish per day at a price of $13. If he wants to sell a larger quantity of fish, however, he has to reduce his price. According to the demand curve shown here, the price must be lowered to $12 to sell 2 bushels per day. This reduction in price is shown by a movement along the demand curve from point *A* to point *B*.

How much additional revenue does the second bushel bring in? It's tempting to say that it brings in $12, since that's its price. **Marginal revenue (MR),** however, refers to the *change* in *total* revenue that results from a one-unit increase in output. More generally, we use the formula

$$\frac{\text{Marginal}}{\text{revenue}} = \frac{\text{change in total revenue}}{\text{change in quantity sold}} = \frac{\Delta TR}{\Delta q}$$

where the delta symbol Δ denotes "change in." According to this formula, the marginal revenue of the second bushel is only $11, not the $12 price for which it was sold.

marginal revenue (MR): The change in total revenue that results from a one-unit increase in the quantity sold.

Figure 9.2 summarizes the calculations necessary for computing MR. Row A of the table indicates that the total revenue resulting from one sale per day is $13. To increase sales, price must be reduced. Row B indicates that total revenue rises to $24 per day when fish sales double. The *increase* in total revenue resulting from the added sales is thus $11. This concept is illustrated in the last column of the table and by point *b* on the marginal revenue curve.

Notice that the MR of the second bushel ($11) is *less* than its price ($12) because both bushels are being sold for $12 apiece. In effect, the firm is giving up the opportunity to sell only 1 bushel per day at $13 in order to sell a larger quantity at a lower price. In this sense, the firm is sacrificing $1 of potential revenue on the first bushel in order to increase *total* revenue. Marginal revenue measures the change in total revenue that results.

So long as the demand curve is downward-sloping, MR will always be less than price. Compare columns 2 and 4 of the table in Figure 9.2. At each rate of output in excess of 1 bushel, marginal revenue is less than price. This is also evident in the graph: ***The MR curve lies below the demand (price) curve at every point but the first.***

Profit Maximization

Although the presence of market power adds a new wrinkle, the rules of profit maximization remain the same. Now instead of looking for an intersection of marginal cost and price, we look for the intersection of marginal cost and marginal revenue. This is illustrated in Figure 9.3 by the intersection of the MR and MC curves (point *d*). Looking down from that intersection, we see that the associated rate of output is 4 bushels per day. Thus 4 bushels is the profit-maximizing rate of output.

How much should the monopolist charge for these 4 bushels? Naturally, the monopolist would like to charge a very high price. But the ability to charge a high price is limited by the demand curve. If the monopolist charges $13, consumers will buy only 1 bushel, leaving 3 unsold bushels of dead fish. Not a pretty picture. As the monopolist will soon learn, ***only one price is compatible with the profit-maximizing rate of output.*** In this case, the price is $10. This price is found in Figure 9.3 by moving up from the quantity 4 until reaching the demand curve at point *D*. Point *D* tells us that consumers are able and willing to buy 4 bushels of fish per day only at the price of $10 each. A monopolist who tries to charge more than $10 won't be able to sell all 4 bushels.

FIGURE 9.3
Profit Maximization

The most profitable rate of output is indicated by the intersection of marginal revenue and marginal cost (point *d*). This intersection (MC = MR) establishes 4 bushels as the profit maximizing rate of output. Point *D* indicates that consumers will pay $10 per bushel for this much output. Total profits equal price ($10) minus average total cost ($8), multiplied by the quantity sold (4).

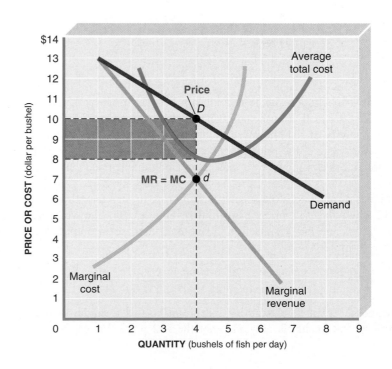

Figure 9.3 also illustrates the total profits of the catfish monopoly. To compute total profits we can first calculate profit per unit, that is, price minus *average* total cost. In this case, profit per unit is $2. Multiplying profit per unit by the quantity sold (4) gives us total profits of $8 per day, as illustrated by the shaded rectangle.

MARKET POWER AT WORK:
THE COMPUTER MARKET REVISITED

To develop a keener appreciation for the nature of market power, we can return to the computer market of Chapter 8. This time we make some different assumptions about market structure. In particular, assume that a single firm, Universal Electronics, acquires an exclusive patent on the production of the microprocessors that function as the computer's "brain." This one firm is now in a position to deny potential competitors access to the basic ingredient of computers. The patent thus functions as a **barrier to entry,** to be erected or set aside at the will of Universal Electronics.

Universal's management is familiar enough with the principles of economics (including W. C. Fields's advice about never giving a sucker an even break) to know when it's onto a good thing. It's not about to let every would-be Horatio Alger have a slice of the profit pie. Even the Russians understood this strategy during the heyday of communism. They made sure no one else could produce sable furs that could compete with their monopoly (see World View). Let's assume that Universal Electronics is equally protective of its turf and will refuse to sell or give away any rights to its patent or the chips it produces. That is, Universal Electronics sets itself up as a computer monopoly.

Let's also assume that Universal has a multitude of manufacturing plants, each of which is identical to the typical competitive firm in Chapter 8. This is an unlikely situation because a monopolist would probably achieve **economies of scale** by closing at least a few plants and consolidating production in larger plants. Universal would maintain a multitude of small plants only if constant returns to scale or actual diseconomies of scale were rampant. Nevertheless, by assuming that multiple plants are

> **barriers to entry:** Obstacles, such as patents, that make it difficult or impossible for would-be producers to enter a particular market.

> **economies of scale:** Reductions in minimum average costs that come about through increases in the size (scale) of plant and equipment.

WORLD VIEW

Foxy Soviets Pelt the West

Sable Monopoly Traps Hard Currency, Coats, Capitalists

LENINGRAD—Crown sable from the eastern Siberian region of Barguzin, star of the Soviet fur collection, went on sale just as a deep freeze gripped this former imperial city. . . .

Fur is one of the Soviet Union's best known consumer goods exports. It is also bait for a country eager to trap hard currency: last year, the Soviet Union earned $100 million in fur sales.

In the case of sable, the Soviet Union has something no one else has—in capitalist lingo, a monopoly.

Ivan the Terrible is said to have made the sale of live sables abroad a crime punishable by death. Peter the Great on his travels in the West is said to have carried along trunks of sable skins to use as currency.

In the best-selling novel *Gorky Park,* popular among fur traders, it was the Soviet sable monopoly that was the key to the tangled tale of murderous intrigue.

There is another story, origin and veracity unknown, that an American once traded a rare North American species to the Soviets in exchange for two live Russian sables—only to find when he got home that they had been sterilized.

—Celestine Bohlen

Source: *The Washington Post,* February 5, 1985. © 1985 The Washington Post. Reprinted with permission. www.washingtonpost.com

Analysis: To ward off potential competition, a monopoly must erect barriers to entry. By not letting live sables leave the country, Russia maintained a monopoly on sable furs.

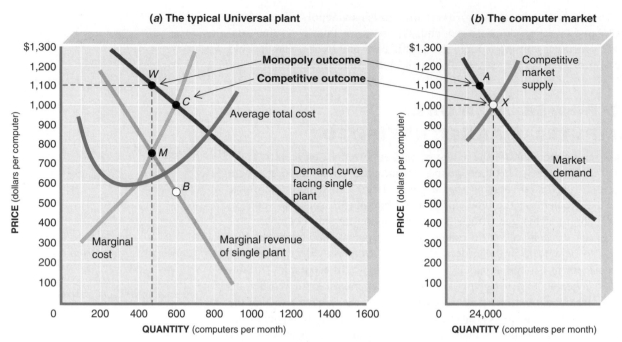

FIGURE 9.4
Initial Conditions in the Monopolized Computer Market

We assume that a monopoly firm (Universal Electronics) would confront the same costs (MC and ATC) and demand as would the competitive industry in Chapter 8. In the initial short-run equilibrium, the competitive price was $1,000 (point C). However, the monopolist isn't bound by the competitive market price. Instead, the monopolist must contend with downward-sloping demand and marginal revenue curves. If each monopoly plant produced where MC = $1,000 (point C in part a), marginal cost (point C) would exceed marginal revenue (point B). To maximize profits, the monopolist must find that rate of output where MC = MR (point M in part a). That rate of output can be sold at the monopoly price of $1,100 (point W in part a). Part b illustrates the market implications of the monopolist's production decision: A reduced quantity is sold at a higher price (point A).

maintained, we can compare monopoly behavior with competitive behavior on the basis of identical cost structures. In particular, if Universal continues to operate the many plants that once comprised the competitive home computer industry, it will confront the same short-run marginal and average cost curves already encountered in Chapter 8. Later in this chapter we relax this assumption of multiplant operations to determine whether, in the long run, a monopolist may actually lower production costs below those of a competitive industry.

Figure 9.4a re-creates the marginal costs the typical competitive firm faced in the early stages of the microcomputer boom (from Figure 8.3 and Table 8.1). We now assume that this MC curve also expresses the costs of operating one of Universal's many (identical) plants. Thus, the extension of monopoly control is assumed to have no immediate effect on production costs.

The market demand for computers is also assumed to be unchanged. There's no reason why people should be less willing to buy computers now than they were when the market was competitive. Most consumers have no notion of how many firms produce a product. Even if they knew, there's no reason why their demand for the product would change. Thus, Figure 9.4b expresses an unchanged demand for computers.

Our immediate concern is to determine how Universal Electronics, as a monopolist, will respond to these unchanged demand and cost curves. Will it produce exactly as many computers as the competitive industry did? Will it sell the computers at the same price that the competitive industry did? Will it improve the product as much or as fast?

The Production Decision   Like any producer, Universal Electronics will strive to produce its output at the rate that maximizes total profits. But unlike competitive firms, Universal will explicitly take account of the fact that an increase in output will put downward pressure on computer prices. This may threaten corporate profits.

The implications of Universal's market position for the **production decision** of its many plants can be seen in the new price and marginal revenue curves imposed on each of its manufacturing plants. Universal can't afford to let each of its plants compete with the others, expanding output and driving down prices; that's the kind of folly reserved for truly competitive firms. Instead, Universal will seek to *coordinate* the production decisions of its plants, instructing all plant managers to expand or contract output simultaneously, to achieve the corporate goal of profit maximization.

A simultaneous reduction of output by each Universal plant will lead to a significant reduction in the quantity of computers supplied to the market. This reduced supply will cause a move up the market demand curve to higher prices. By the same token, an expansion of output by all Universal plants will lead to an increase in the quantity supplied to the market and a slide down the market demand curve. As a consequence, each of the monopolist's plants effectively confronts a downward-sloping demand curve. These downward-sloping demand curves are illustrated in Figure 9.4a.[2]

Notice that in Figure 9.4b the *market* demand for computers is unchanged; only the demand curve confronting each plant (firm) has changed. A competitive *industry*, like a monopoly, must obey the law of demand. But the individual firms that comprise a competitive industry all act independently, *as if* they could sell unlimited quantities at the prevailing price. That is, they all act as if they confronted a horizontal demand curve at the market price of $1,000. A competitive firm that doesn't behave in this fashion will simply lose sales to other firms. In contrast, *a monopolist not only foresees the impact of increased production on market price but can also prevent such production increases by its separate plants.*

Marginal Revenue. The downward-sloping demand curve now confronting each Universal plant implies that marginal revenue no longer equals price. Notice that the marginal revenue curve in Figure 9.4a lies *below* the demand curve at every rate of output. Because marginal revenue is less than price for a monopoly, Universal's plants would no longer wish to produce up to the point where marginal cost equals price. *Only firms that confront a horizontal demand curve (perfect competitors) equate marginal cost and price.* Universal's plants must stick to the generic profit-maximizing rule about equating marginal revenue and marginal cost. Should the individual plant managers forget this rule, Universal's central management will fire them.

The output and price implications of Universal's monopoly position become apparent as we examine the new revenue and cost relationships. Recall that the equilibrium price of computers in the early stages of the home computer boom was $1,000. This equilibrium price is indicated in Figure 9.4b by the intersection of the competitive market supply curve with the market demand curve (point X). Each competitive *firm* produced up to the point where marginal cost (MC) equaled that price (point C in Figure 9.4a). At that point, each competitive firm was producing 600 computers a month.

Reduced Output. The emergence of Universal as a monopolist alters these production decisions. Now each Universal plant *does* have an impact on market price because its behavior is imitated simultaneously by all Universal plants. In fact, the marginal revenue associated with the 600th computer is only $575, as indicated by point B in Figure 9.4a. At this rate of output, the typical Universal plant would be operating with marginal costs ($1,000) far in excess of marginal revenues ($575). Such behavior is inconsistent with profit maximization.

production decision: The selection of the short-run rate of output (with existing plant and equipment).

---

[2]The demand and marginal revenue curves in Figure 9.4a are illustrative; they're not derived from earlier tables. As discussed above, we're assuming that the central management of Universal determines the profit-maximizing rate of output and then instructs all individual plants to produce equal shares of that output.

The enlightened Universal plant manager will soon discover that the profit-maximizing rate of output is less than 600 computers per month. In Figure 9.4a we see that the marginal revenue and marginal cost curves intersect at point *M*. This MR = MC intersection occurs at an output level of only 475 computers per month. Accordingly, the typical Universal plant will want to produce *fewer* computers than were produced by the typical competitive firm in the early stages of the home computer boom. Recall that individual competitive firms had no incentive to engage in such production cutbacks. They couldn't alter the market supply curve or price on their own and weren't coordinated by a central management. Thus, the first consequence of Universal's monopoly position is a reduction in the rate of industry output.

The Monopoly Price

The reduction in output at each Universal plant translates automatically into a decrease in the *quantity supplied* to the market. As consumers compete for this reduced market supply, they'll bid computer prices up. We can observe the increased prices in Figure 9.4 by looking at either the typical Universal plant or the computer market. Notice that in Figure 9.4a the price is determined by moving directly up from point *M* to the demand curve confronting the typical Universal plant. The demand curve always tells how much consumers are willing to pay for any given quantity. Hence, once we've determined the quantity that's going to be supplied (475 computers per month), we can look at the demand curve to determine the price ($1,100 at point *W*) that consumers will pay for these computers. That is,

- *The intersection of the marginal revenue and marginal cost curves establishes the profit-maximizing rate of output.*
- *The demand curve tells us how much consumers are willing to pay for that specific quantity of output.*

Figure 9.4a shows how Universal's monopoly position results in both reduced output and increased prices. This result is also evident in Figure 9.4b, where we see that a smaller quantity supplied to the market will force a move up the demand curve to the higher price of $1,100 per computer (point *A*).

Monopoly Profits

Universal's objective was and remains the maximization of profits. That it has succeeded in its effort can be confirmed by scrutinizing Figure 9.5. As you can see, the

FIGURE 9.5
Monopoly Profits: The Typical Universal Plant

The profit-maximizing rate of output occurs where the marginal cost and marginal revenue curves intersect (point *M*). The demand curve indicates the price (point *W*) that consumers will pay for this output. Total profit equals price (*W*) minus average total cost (*K*) multiplied by the quantity sold (475). Total profits are represented by the shaded rectangle.

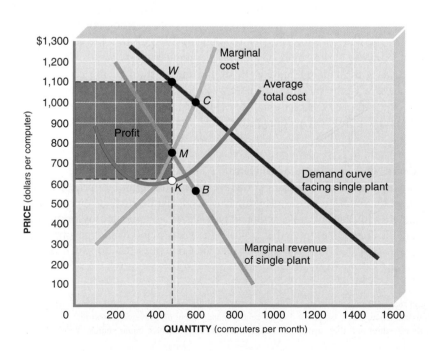

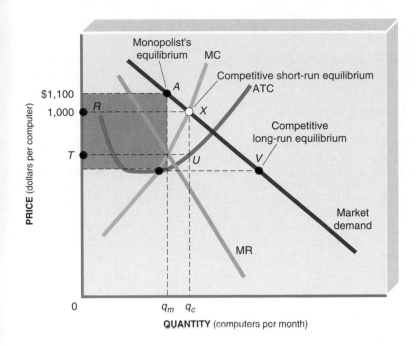

FIGURE 9.6
Monopoly Profit: The Entire Company

Total profits of the monopolist (including all plants) are illustrated by the shaded rectangle. The monopolist's total output q_m is determined by the intersection of the (industry) MR and MC curves. The price of this output is determined by the market demand curve (point *A*). In contrast, a competitive industry would produce q_c computers in the short run and sell them at a lower price (*X*) and profit per unit (*X* − *U*). Those profits would attract new entrants until long-run equilibrium (point *V*) was reached. (See Figure 8.8 for a summary of competitive market equilibrium.)

typical Universal plant ends up selling 475 computers a month at a price of $1,100 each (point *W*). The **average total cost (ATC)** of production at this rate of output is only $630 (point *K*), as was detailed in Table 8.1.

As always, we can compute total profit as

$$\text{Total profit} = \text{profit per unit} \times \text{quantity sold}$$

In this case, we see that

$$\text{Total profit} = (\$1,100 - \$630) \times 475$$

$$= \$223,250$$

This figure may be compared with the monthly profit of $180,000 earned by the typical competitive firm in the early stages of the computer boom (see Table 8.1).

It's apparent from these profit figures that Universal management has learned its economic principles well. By reducing the output of each plant and raising prices a little, it has managed to enlarge the size of the profit pie while keeping it all to itself, of course. This can be seen again in Figure 9.6, which is an enlarged illustration of the *market* situation for the home computer industry. The figure translates the economics of our single-plant and competitive-firm comparison into the dimensions of the whole industry.

Figure 9.6 reaffirms that the competitive industry in Chapter 8 initially produces the quantity q_c and sells it at a price of $1,000 each. Its profits are denoted by the rectangle formed by the points *R*, *X*, *U*, *T*. The monopolist, on the other hand, produces the smaller q_m and charges a higher price, $1,100. The monopoly firm's profits are indicated by the larger profit rectangle shaded in the figure. We see that *a monopoly receives larger profits than a comparable competitive industry by reducing the quantity supplied and pushing prices up.* The larger profits make Universal very happy and make consumers a little sadder and wiser. Consumers are now paying more and getting less.

The higher profits Universal Electronics attained as a result of its monopoly position aren't the end of the story. The existence of economic profit tends to bring profit-hungry entrepreneurs swarming like locusts. In the competitive home computer industry in Chapter 8, the lure of high profits brought about an enormous expansion of

average total cost (ATC): Total cost divided by the quantity produced in a given time period.

Barriers to Entry

Concerts Becoming a Pricier Affair; Music Industry Consolidation Has Brought Higher Ticket Fees. Some Cry Foul.

Members of the popular heavy-rock band Godsmack say they want to make tickets affordable for their current U.S. tour. But the economics of the concert industry may jar fans harder than the mosh pit at the band's show.

The face value of a general admission ticket to Godsmack's concert Wednesday at Verizon Wireless Amphitheater is $20. But no one attending the band's performance gets to pay that amount.

Instead, fans who purchase tickets on the phone or online are socked with a series of surcharges that boost the price to $35.60. These added costs, tacked on by distribution giant Ticketmaster and concert promotion conglomerate Clear Channel Entertainment, include a convenience fee, a facility fee and a handling charge.

Moreover, a hidden $3.50 parking fee is buried in the price of each ticket by Clear Channel, owner of the Verizon

Amphitheater in Irvine. All told, the fees add a 116% markup to the cost of a $16.50 ticket. . . .

In recent years, Clear Channel has emerged as the dominant force in the $1.6-billion concert industry. . . .

"They can pretty much dictate the costs, ad rates and ticket prices," said Jon Stoll, president of Fantasma Productions, a competing promoter in West Palm Beach, Fla. "If one company controls the live-music industry, there's nobody that can really bring ticket prices down."

—Jeff Leeds

Source: *Los Angeles Times*, July 17, 2001. © 2001 Tribune Media Services, Inc. All rights reserved. Reprinted with permission.

Analysis: Control of concert sites and ticket distribution allow Clear Channel and Ticketmaster to charge monopoly prices for live concerts.

home computer output and a steep decline in home computer prices. In Figure 9.6 the long-run equilibrium of a competitive industry is indicated by point *V.* What then can we expect to happen in the home computer market now that Universal has a monopoly position and is enjoying huge profits?

Remember that Universal is now assumed to have an exclusive patent on microprocessor chips and can use this patent as an impassable barrier to entry. Consequently, would-be competitors can swarm around Universal's profits until their wings drop off; Universal isn't about to let them in on the spoils. By locking out the potential competition, Universal can prevent the surge in computer output that pushed prices down the market demand curve. As long as Universal is able to keep out the competition, only the more affluent consumers will be able to use computers. The same phenomenom explains why ticket prices for live concerts are so high. Because Clear Channel controls most concert venues and Ticketmaster is the exclusive ticket distributor, fans have to pay monopoly prices to see Godsmack, Bare Naked Ladies, Pearl Jam, or other live concerts (see News). A monopoly has no incentive to move from point *A* in Figure 9.6, and there's no competitive pressure to force such a move. Universal may discover ways to reduce the costs of production and thus lower prices, but there's no *pressure* on it to do so, as there was in the competitive situation.

A COMPARATIVE PERSPECTIVE OF MARKET POWER

The different outcomes of the computer industry under competitive and monopoly conditions illustrate basic features of market structures. We may summarize the sequence of events that occurs in each type of market structure as follows:

COMPETITIVE INDUSTRY	MONOPOLY INDUSTRY
• High prices and profits signal consumers' demand for more output.	• High prices and profits signal consumers' demand for more output.
• The high profits attract new suppliers.	• Barriers to entry are erected to exclude potential competition.
• Production and supplies expand.	• Production and supplies are constrained.
• Prices slide down the market demand curve.	• Prices don't move down the market demand curve.
• A new equilibrium is established wherein more of the desired product is produced, its price falls, average costs of production approach their minimum, and economic profits approach zero.	• No new equilibrium is established; average costs aren't necessarily at or near a minimum, and economic profits are at a maximum.
• Price equals marginal cost throughout the process.	• Price exceeds marginal cost at all times.
• Throughout the process, there's great pressure to keep ahead of the profit squeeze by reducing costs or improving product quality.	• There's no squeeze on profits and thus no pressure to reduce costs or improve product quality.

In our discussion, we assumed that the competitive industry and the monopoly both started from the same position—an initial equilibrium in which the price of computers is $1,000. In reality, an industry may manifest concentrations of market power *before* such an equilibrium is established. That is, the sequence of events we've depicted may be altered (with step 3 occurring first, for example). Nevertheless, the basic distinctions between competitive and monopolistic behavior are evident.

Productivity Advances. To the extent that monopolies behave as we've discussed, they affect not just the price and output of a specific product but broader economic outcomes as well. Remember that competitive industries tend, in the long run, to produce at minimum average costs. Competitive industries also pursue cost reductions and product improvements relentlessly. These pressures tend to expand our production possibilities. No such forces are at work in the monopoly we've discussed here. Hence, there's a basic tendency for monopolies to inhibit productivity advances and economic growth.

The Mix of Output. Another important feature of competitive markets is their observed tendency toward **marginal cost pricing**. Marginal cost pricing is important to consumers because it permits rational choices among alternative goods and services. In particular, it informs consumers of the true opportunity costs of various goods, thereby allowing them to choose the mix of output that delivers the most utility with available resources. In our monopoly example, however, consumers end up getting fewer computers than they'd like, while the economy continues to produce other, less desired goods. Thus, the mix of output shifted away from computers when Universal took over the industry.

marginal cost pricing: The offer (supply) of goods at prices equal to their marginal cost.

The power to influence prices and product flows may have far-reaching consequences for our economic welfare. Changes in prices and product flows directly influence the level and composition of output, employment and resource allocation, the level and distribution of income, and, of course, the level and structure of prices. Hence, firms that wield significant market power affect all dimensions of economic welfare.

Political Power. Market power isn't the only kind of power wielded in society, of course. Political power, for example, is a different kind of power and important in its own right. Indeed, the power to influence an election or to sway a Senate committee vote may ultimately be more important than the power to increase the price of laundry soap. Nevertheless, market power is a force that influences the way we live, the incomes we earn, and our relationships with other countries. Moreover, market power may be the basis for political power: The individual or firm with considerable market power is likely to have the necessary resources to influence an election or sway a vote on a congressional committee.

The Limits to Power

Even though market power enables a producer to manipulate market outcomes, there's a clear limit to the exercise of power. Even a monopolist can't get everything it wants. Universal, for example, would really like to sell q_m computers at a price of $1,500 each because that kind of price would bring it even greater profits. Yet, despite its monopoly position, Universal is constrained to sell that quantity of computers at the lower price of $1,100 each. Even monopolists have their little disappointments.

The ultimate limit to a monopolist's power is evident in Figure 9.6. Universal's attainment of a monopoly position allows it only one prerogative: the ability to alter the quantity of output *supplied* to the market. This is no small prerogative, but it's far from absolute power. Universal, and every other monopolist, must still contend with the market *demand* curve. Note again that the new equilibrium in Figure 9.6 occurs at a point on the *unchanged* demand curve. In effect, ***a monopolist has the opportunity to pick any point on the market demand curve and designate it as the new market equilibrium.*** The point it selects will depend on its own perceptions of effort, profit, and risk (in this case point *A*, determined by the intersection of marginal revenue and marginal cost).

The ultimate constraint on the exercise of market power, then, resides in the market demand curve. How great a constraint the demand curve imposes depends largely on the **price elasticity of demand.** The greater the price elasticity of demand, the more a monopolist will be frustrated in attempts to establish both high prices and high volume. Consumers will simply reduce their purchases if price is increased. If, however, consumer demand is highly inelastic—if consumers need or want that product badly and few viable substitutes are available—the monopolist can reap tremendous profits from market power.

price elasticity of demand: The percentage change in quantity demanded divided by the percentage change in price.

Price Discrimination

Even in situations where the *market* demand is relatively elastic, a monopolist may be able to extract high prices. A monopolist has the power not only to raise the market price of a good (by reducing the quantity supplied) but also to charge various prices for the same good. Recall that the market demand curve reflects the combined willingness of many individuals to buy. Some of those individuals are willing to buy the good at prices higher than the market price, just as other individuals will buy only at lower prices. A monopolist may be able to increase total profits by selling each unit of the good separately, at a price each *individual* consumer is willing to pay. This practice is called **price discrimination.**

price discrimination: The sale of an identical good at different prices to different consumers by a single seller.

The airline industry has practiced price discrimination for many years. Basically, there are two distinct groups of travelers: business and nonbusiness travelers. Business executives must fly from one city to another on a certain day and at a particular time. They typically make flight arrangements on short notice and may have no other way to get to their destination. Nonbusiness travelers, such as people on vacation and students going home during semester break, usually have more flexible schedules. They may plan their trips weeks or months in advance and often have the option of traveling by car, bus, or train.

The different travel needs of business and vacation travelers are reflected in their respective demand curves. Business demand for air travel tends to be less price-elastic than the demand of nonbusiness travelers. Few business executives would stop flying if airfares increased. Higher airfares would, however, discourage air travel by nonbusiness travelers.

What should airlines do in this case? Should they *raise* airfares to take advantage of the relative price inelasticity of business demand, or should they *lower* airfares to attract more nonbusiness travelers?

They should do both. In fact, they *have* done both. The airlines offer a full-fare ride, available at any time, and a discount-fare ride, available only by purchasing a ticket in advance and agreeing to some restrictions on time of departure. The advance purchase and other restrictions on discount fares effectively exclude most business travelers, who end up paying full fare. The higher full fare doesn't, however, discourage most nonbusiness travelers, who can fly at a discount. Consequently, the airlines are able to sell essentially identical units of the same good (an airplane ride) at substantially different prices to different customers. Indeed, by experimenting with various discount fares and travel restrictions, airlines can discriminate even more thoroughly among passengers, thereby reaping the highest possible *average* price for the quantity supplied. Doctors, lawyers, and car dealers commonly practice the same type of price discrimination. In all these cases, the seller may "adjust" the price to the income and taste of each individual consumer. In effect, the seller is able to "divide and conquer" the individual consumers who are positioned along the length of the market demand curve. A monopolist is best positioned to engage in price discrimination, since consumers have no competitive alternatives.

It's the lack of competitors that gives monopolists such pricing power. Accordingly, *the preservation of monopoly power depends on keeping potential competitors out of the market.* A monopolist doesn't want anyone else to produce an *identical* product or even a *close substitute*. To do that, a monopoly must erect and maintain barriers to market entry. It was the absence of significant entry barriers that permitted iPod clones to attack Apple's profits (News, p. 192). Some of the entry barriers used to repel such attacks include:

Entry Barriers

Patents. This was the critical barrier in the mythical Universal Electronics case. A government-awarded patent gives a producer 20 years of exclusive rights to produce a particular product. The Polaroid Corporation used its patents to keep Eastman Kodak and other potential rivals out of the market for instant development cameras.

Monopoly Franchises. The government also creates and maintains monopolies by giving a single firm the exclusive right to supply a particular good or service, even though other firms can produce it. Local cable TV stations and telephone companies are examples. Congress also bestows monopoly privileges to baseball teams and the U.S. Postal Service. Your campus bookstore may have exclusive rights to sell textbooks on campus.

Control of Key Inputs. A company may lock out competition by securing exclusive access to key inputs. Airlines need landing rights and terminal gates in order to compete. Oil and gas producers need pipelines to supply their product. Utility companies need transmission networks to supply consumers with electricity. Pepsi says it needs access to Coke-dominated restaurants (see News on the next page). Software vendors need to know the features of computer operating systems. If a single company controls these critical inputs, it can lock out potential competition. That's alleged to be a prime source of Microsoft's monopoly power (see The Economy Tomorrow).

Lawsuits. In the event that competitors actually surmount other entry barriers, a monopoly may sue it out of existence. Typically, start-up firms are rich in ideas but cash poor. They need to get their products to the market quickly to generate some cash. A timely lawsuit alleging patent or copyright infringement can derail such a company by absorbing critical management, cash, and time. Long before the merits of the lawsuit are adjudicated, the company may be forced to withdraw from the market.

Pepsi Takes Coke to Court

Rival Presses for Monopoly of Fountain Sales, Suit Says

NEW YORK, May 7—Pepsi accused Coke today of monopolizing the sales of fountain soft drinks at restaurant chains and movie theaters by threatening to take away Coke from distributors that carried Pepsi as well.

The lawsuit filed in U.S. District Court did not pertain to sales of bottles or cans of the soft drinks, only to fountain-dispensed drinks handled by large food service distributors who control deliveries to chains of restaurants and theaters.

The lawsuit, filed by Pepsi-Cola's parent, PepsiCo Inc., asked the court to restrain Coca-Cola from entering into agreements with its distributors to exclude Pepsi and to award Pepsi undetermined damages.

"Coca-Cola's message to food service distributors is clear: If a distributor carries Pepsi at a customer's request, the distributor will be terminated by Coke," the lawsuit said.

Source: *The Washington Post*, May 8, 1998. © 1998 The Washington Post. Reprinted with permission. www.washingtonpost.com

Analysis: A firm can acquire a monopoly by attaining exclusive access to key inputs or distribution systems.

Acquisition. When all else fails, a monopolist may simply purchase a potential competitor. As the accompanying cartoon suggests, mergers tend to raise consumer prices.

Economies of Scale. Last but far from least, a monopoly may persist because of economies of scale. If large firms have a substantial cost advantage over smaller firms, the smaller firms may not be able to compete. We look at this entry barrier again in a moment.

PROS AND CONS OF MARKET POWER

Despite the strong case against market power, it's conceivable that monopolies could also benefit society. One argument made for concentrations of market power is that monopolies have greater ability to pursue research and development. Another argument is that the lure of market power creates a tremendous incentive for invention and innovation. A third argument in defense of monopoly is that large companies can

Analysis: Mergers and acquisitions reduce competition in an industry. The increased industry concentration may lead to higher prices.

IN THE NEWS

Jury Rules Magnetek Unit Is Liable for Keeping Technology off Market

SAN FRANCISCO—Is a company liable if it deliberately keeps a technology off the market? Apparently so, judging from an unusual ruling by a California jury.

A county superior court jury in Oakland ordered a unit of Magnetek Inc. to pay $25.8 million to two California entrepreneurs and their companies. They charged that the unit had failed to bring the pair's energy-saving fluorescent-light technology to market in a profitable manner, suppressing it in favor of an outmoded technology.

The lawsuit reads like familiar legends of big business quashing inventions that threaten its interests. . . .

In 1984, the two entrepreneurs, C. R. Stevens and William R. Alling, charged that Universal Manufacturing Corp., now a unit of Los Angeles–based Magnetek, buried a technology

through which fluorescent lights use 70 percent less energy. The two said they sold Universal the technology, called a solid-state ballast, in 1981 after the company promised to market it aggressively.

Instead, they charged, Universal suppressed the technology to protect its less-efficient existing ballast models. "They told us they were going to be first on the market with our tech, yet they planned otherwise," said Mr. Alling.

—Stephen Kreider Yoder

Source: *The Wall Street Journal*, January 10, 1990. Reprinted by permission of The Wall Street Journal. © 1990 Dow Jones & Company, Inc. All rights reserved worldwide. www.wsj.com

Analysis: A monopoly has little incentive (no competitive pressure) to pursue R&D. In fact, R&D that threatens established products or processes may be suppressed.

produce goods more efficiently than smaller firms. Finally, it's argued that even monopolies have to worry about *potential* competition and will behave accordingly.

Research and Development

In principle, monopolies are well positioned to undertake valuable research and development. First, such firms are sheltered from the constant pressure of competition. Second, they have the resources (monopoly profits) with which to carry out expensive R&D functions. The manager of a perfectly competitive firm, by contrast, has to worry about day-to-day production decisions and profit margins. As a result, she is unable to take the longer view necessary for significant research and development and couldn't afford to purchase such a view even if she could see it.

The basic problem with the R&D argument is that it says nothing about *incentives*. Although monopolists have a clear financial advantage in pursuing research and development activities, they have no clear incentive to do so. Research and development aren't necessarily required for profitable survival. In fact, research and development that make existing plant and equipment technologically obsolete run counter to a monopolist's vested interest and so may actually be suppressed (see News). In contrast, a perfectly competitive firm can't continue to make significant profits unless it stays ahead of the competition. This pressure constitutes a significant incentive to discover new products or new and cheaper ways of producing existing products.

Entrepreneurial Incentives

The second defense of market power uses a novel incentive argument. Every business is out to make a buck, and it's the quest for profits that keeps industries running. Thus, it's argued, even greater profit prizes will stimulate more entrepreneurial activity. Little Horatio Algers will work harder and longer if they can dream of one day possessing a whole monopoly.

The incentive argument for market power is enticing but not entirely convincing. After all, an innovator can make substantial profits in a competitive market before the competition catches up. Recall that the early birds did get the worm in the competitive computer industry (see Chapter 8), even though profit margins were later squeezed. It's not evident that the profit incentives available in a competitive industry are at all inadequate.

We must also recall the arguments about research and development efforts. A monopolist has little incentive to pursue R&D. Furthermore, entrepreneurs who might pursue product innovation or technological improvements may be dissuaded by their inability to penetrate a monopolized market. The barriers to entry that surround market power may not only keep out potential competitors but also lock out promising ideas.

Economies of Scale

A third defense of market power is the most convincing. A large firm, it's argued, can produce goods at a lower unit (average) cost than a small firm. If such *economies of scale* exist, we could attain greater efficiency (higher productivity) by permitting firms to grow to market-dominating size.

We sidestepped this argument in our story about the Universal Electronics monopoly. We explicitly assumed that Universal confronted the same production costs as the competitive industry. We simply converted each typical competitive firm into a separate plant owned and operated by Universal. Universal wasn't able to produce computers any more cheaply than the competitive counterpart, and we concerned ourselves only with the different production decisions made by competitive and monopolistic firms.

A monopoly *could,* however, attain greater cost savings. By centralizing various functions it might be able to eliminate some duplicative efforts. It might also shut down some plants and concentrate production in fewer facilities. If these kinds of efficiencies are attained, a monopoly would offer attractive resource savings.

There's no guarantee, however, of such economies of scale. As we observed in Chapter 6, increasing the size (scale) of a plant may actually *reduce* operating efficiency (see Figure 6.10). In evaluating the economies-of-scale argument for market power, then, we must recognize that **efficiency and size don't necessarily go hand in hand. Some firms and industries may be subject to economies of scale, but others won't.**

Even when economies of scale are present there is no guarantee that consumers will benefit. This is why the Pentagon opposed the merger of the nation's only two nuclear-ship builders (see News). Even though there were substantial short-run economies of scale in eliminating duplicate facilities, the Navy concluded that even a little competition (two firms) was better than none (a monopoly) in the long run.

IN THE NEWS

Pentagon Opposes Ship Monopoly

The Pentagon yesterday approved Northrop Grumman Corp.'s bid to purchase Newport News Shipbuilding Inc., and antitrust regulators sued to block a competing offer from General Dynamics, citing concern about consolidating the nation's construction of nuclear ships into one company.

Allowing General Dynamics to buy Newport News would have united the only two U.S. builders of nuclear submarines, creating a "merger-to-monopoly" that "would reduce innovation and, ultimately, the quality of the products supplied to the military, while raising prices to the U.S. military and to U.S. taxpayers," Justice Department antitrust chief Charles A. James said in a news release. . . .

Navy officials hoped that Falls Church-based General Dynamics, which builds nuclear submarines at its Electric Boat shipyard in Connecticut, could cut costs at Newport News by eliminating overlap between the two similar businesses.

But Northrop Grumman argued that allowing General Dynamics to make the purchase would have increased costs over time by eliminating competition for nuclear-ship contracts.

"In the end you could argue that the competition angle outweighed the cost savings. That's a message that will resonate throughout the rest of the defense industry," said Byron Callan, an industry analyst with Merrill Lynch in New York.

—Greg Schneider

Source: *The Washington Post*, October 24, 2001. © 2001 The Washington Post. Reprinted with permission. www.washingtonpost.com

Analysis: Monopolies may enjoy economies of scale. In the long run, however, consumers may benefit more from competitive pressures to reduce costs, improve product quality, and lower prices.

Natural Monopolies. Industries that exhibit economies of scale over the entire range of market output are called **natural monopolies.** In these cases, one single firm can produce the entire market supply more efficiently than any large number of (smaller) firms. As the size (scale) of the one firm increases, its minimum average costs continue to fall. These economies of scale give the one large producer a decided advantage over would-be rivals. Hence, *economies of scale act as a "natural" barrier to entry.*

Local telephone and utility services are classic examples of natural monopoly. A single telephone or utility company can supply the market more efficiently than a large number of competing firms.

Although natural monopolies are economically desirable, they may be abused. We must ask whether and to what extent consumers are reaping some benefit from the efficiency a natural monopoly makes possible. Do consumers end up with lower prices, expanded output, and better service? Or does the monopoly keep most of the benefits for itself, in the form of higher prices and profits? Multiplex movie theaters, for example, achieve economies of scale by sharing operating and concession facilities among as many as 30 screens. But do moviegoers get lower prices for movies or popcorn? Not often. Because megamultiplex theaters tend to drive out competition, they don't have to reduce prices when costs drop. Under such circumstances, we may need government "trustbusters" to ensure that the benefits of increased efficiency are shared with consumers. (The potential and pitfalls of government regulation are examined in Chapter 12.)

Governmental regulators aren't necessarily the only force keeping monopolists in line. Even though a firm may produce the entire supply of a particular product at present, it may face *potential* competition from other firms. Potential rivals may be sitting on the sidelines, watching how well the monopoly fares. If it does too well, these rivals may enter the industry, undermining the monopoly structure and profits. In such **contestable markets,** monopoly behavior may be restrained by potential competition.

How "contestable" a market is depends not so much on its structure as on entry barriers. If entry barriers are insurmountable, would-be competitors are locked out of the market. But if entry barriers are modest, they'll be surmounted when the lure of monopoly profits is irresistible. When CNN's profits reached irresistible proportions, both domestic and foreign companies decided to invade CNN's monopoly market (see World View on next page). Since then, CNN hasn't been nearly as profitable.

Structure vs. Behavior. From the perspective of contestable markets, the whole case against monopoly is misconceived. Market *structure* per se isn't a problem; what counts is market *behavior.* If potential rivals force a monopolist to behave like a competitive firm, then monopoly imposes no cost on consumers or on society at large.

The experience with the Model T Ford illustrates the basic notion of contestable markets. At the time Henry Ford decided to increase the price of the Model T and paint them all black, the Ford Motor Company enjoyed a virtual monopoly on mass-produced cars. But potential rivals saw the profitability of offering additional colors and features such as a self-starter and left-hand drive. When rivals began producing cars in volume, Ford's market power was greatly reduced. In 1926, the Ford Motor Company tried to regain its dominant position by again supplying cars in colors other than black. By that time, however, consumers had more choices. Ford ceased production of the Model T in May 1927.

The experience with the Model T suggests that potential competition can force a monopoly to change its ways. Critics point out, however, that even contestable markets don't force a monopolist to act *exactly* like a competitive firm. There will always be a gap between competitive outcomes and those monopoly outcomes likely to entice

natural monopoly: An industry in which one firm can achieve economies of scale over the entire range of market supply.

Contestable Markets

contestable market: An imperfectly competitive industry subject to potential entry if prices or profits increase.

New Competition May Mean Bad News for CNN

A growing crowd of media giants wants to make sure that most people don't get their news from Cable News Network. They're all gunning for the lucrative, Turner Broadcasting System unit with a host of rival 24-hour news networks, spurred by new technologies for delivering TV programs and shifting alliances in the cable business. . . .

Last year, with the market to itself, CNN and its related news businesses, including a Headline News channel, generated about $227 million in operating profit for Turner Broadcasting System Inc.

But CNN may not keep its monopoly for long. If the proposed services can overcome huge distribution hurdles caused by lack of space on crowded cable systems, their strong brand names and well-known correspondents and anchors may be enough to lure viewers away from CNN.

Capital Cities/ABC Inc., for example, said yesterday that it will launch a 24-hour news service in the U.S. in 1997, using ABC News's star talent and rerunning some of its popular shows. . . .

Other companies have similar ideas. General Electric Co.'s NBC for the past year has been putting together a detailed plan for launching its own national news network with a strong local component. . . .

Meanwhile, Britain's BBC is also trying to start a global news channel. And News Corp. Chairman Rupert Murdoch, whose British BSkyB service already offers a 24-hour news channel, said last week that he wants to launch a U.S. competitor to CNN. . . .

Behind all the expansion plans is a straightforward economic calculation: Companies already in the news business think they can squeeze out more profits with relatively little new cost by expanding to 24 hours of TV news.

—Elizabeth Jensen and John Lippman

Analysis: As a monopolist's profits grow, would-be competitors will try to overcome barriers to entry. If entry is possible, a monopolized market may be contestable.

---

new entry. That gap can cost consumers a lot. The absence of *existing* rivals is also likely to inhibit product and productivity improvements. From 1913 to 1926, all Model Ts were black, and consumers had few alternatives. Ford changed its behavior only after *potential* competition became *actual* competition. Even after 1927, when the Ford Motor Company could no longer act like a monopolist, it still didn't price its cars at marginal cost.

THE ECONOMY TOMORROW

Microsoft: Bully or Genius?

Ford Motor Company's experience is a useful reminder that monopolies rarely last forever. Potential competitors will always look for ways to enter a profitable market. Eventually they'll surmount entry barriers or develop substitute goods that supplant a monopolist's products.

Consumer advocates assert that we shouldn't have to wait for the invisible hand to dismantle a monopoly. They say the government should intervene to dismantle a monopoly or at least force it to change its behavior. Then consumers would get lower prices and better products a whole lot sooner.

Microsoft's dominant position in the computer industry highlights this issue. Microsoft produces the operating system (Windows) that powers 9 out of 10 personal computers. It also produces a huge share of applications software, including Internet browsers. Critics fear that this kind of monopoly power is a threat to consumers. They say Microsoft charges too much for its systems software, suppresses substitute

Judge Says Microsoft Broke Antitrust Law

A federal judge yesterday found Microsoft Corp. guilty of violating antitrust law by waging a campaign to crush threats to its Windows monopoly, a severe verdict that opens the door for the government to seek a breakup of one of the most successful companies in history.

Saying that Microsoft put an "oppressive thumb on the scale of competitive fortune," U.S. District Judge Thomas Penfield Jackson gave the Justice Department and 19 states near-total victory in their lawsuit. His ruling puts a black mark on the reputation of a software giant that has been the starter engine of the "new economy."

"Microsoft mounted a deliberate assault upon entrepreneurial efforts that, left to rise or fall on their own merits, could well have enabled the introduction of competition into the market for Intelcompatible PC operating systems," Jackson said.

The sweeping guilty verdict—coming two days after out-of-court settlement talks collapsed—harkens back to the monumental monopolization cases against Standard Oil and AT&T and validates the government's power to enforce antitrust law in the information age. It comes at a time when Microsoft faces substantial business obstacles to expanding its software dominance from the desktop to the Internet.

In blunt language, Jackson depicted a powerful and predatory company that employed a wide array of tactics to destroy any innovation that posed a danger to the dominance of Windows. Among the victims were corporate stars of the multibillion-dollar computer industry: Intel Corp., Apple Computer Inc., International Business Machines Corp. and RealNetworks Inc.

To crush the competitive threat posed by the Internet browser, Jackson ruled, Microsoft integrated its own Internet browser into its Windows operating system "to quell incipient competition," bullied computer makers into carrying Microsoft's browser by threatening to withhold price discounts and demanded that computer makers not feature rival Netscape's browser in the PC desktop as a condition of licensing the Windows operating system.

Only when the separate categories of conduct are viewed, as they should be, as a single, well-coordinated course of action does the full extent of the violence that Microsoft has done to the competitive process reveal itself," Jackson wrote in the 43-page ruling.

—James V. Grimaldi

Source: *The Washington Post*, April 4, 2000. © 2000 The Washington Post. Reprinted with permission. www.washingtonpost.com

Analysis: A federal court concluded that Microsoft followed the textbook script of monopoly: erecting entry barriers, suppressing innovation, and charging high prices.

---

technologies, and pushes potential competitors around. In short, Microsoft is a bully. In April 2000, a federal court accepted this argument (see News). To weaken Microsoft's grip on the computer market, the court considered forcing changes in both Microsoft's behavior and structure.

The federal government's authority to mend Microsoft's ways originates in the Sherman, the Clayton, and the Federal Trade Commission Acts. As noted in Table 9.1, these acts give the government broad **antitrust** authority to break up monopolies or compel them to change their behavior. The government used this authority in 1984 to dismantle American Telephone and Telegraph's (AT&T's) phone monopoly. AT&T then supplied 96 percent of all long-distance service and over 80 percent of local telephone service. AT&T kept long-distance charges high and compelled consumers to purchase hardware from its own subsidiary (Western Electric). Potential competitors claimed they could supply better and cheaper services if the government ended the AT&T monopoly. After four years of antitrust litigation, AT&T agreed to (1) separate its long-distance and local services and (2) turn over the local transmission networks to new "Baby Bell" companies. Since then there has been a competitive revolution in telephone hardware, services, and pricing.

The U.S. Department of Justice filed a similar antitrust action against Microsoft. The first accusation leveled against Microsoft was that it thwarted competitors in operating systems by erecting entry barriers such as exclusive purchase agreements with

The AT&T Case

antitrust: Government intervention to alter market structure or prevent abuse of market power.

The Microsoft Case

TABLE 9.1
Antitrust Laws

The legal foundations for antitrust intervention are contained in three landmark antitrust laws.

- ***The Sherman Act (1890).*** The Sherman Act prohibits "conspiracies in restraint of trade," including mergers, contracts, or acquisitions that threaten to monopolize an industry. Firms that violate the Sherman Act are subject to fines of up to $1 million, and their executives may be subject to imprisonment. In addition, consumers who are damaged—for example, via high prices—by a "conspiracy in restraint of trade" may recover treble damages. With this act as its principal "trustbusting" weapon, the U.S. Department of Justice has blocked attempted mergers and acquisitions, forced changes in price or output behavior, required large companies to sell some of their assets, and even sent corporate executives to jail for "conspiracies in restraint of trade."
- The Clayton Act (1914). The Clayton Act of 1914 was passed to outlaw specific antitrust behavior not covered by the Sherman Act. The principal aim of the act was to prevent the development of monopolies. To this end, the Clayton Act prohibited price discrimination, exclusive dealing agreements, certain types of mergers, and interlocking boards of directors among competing firms.

- ***The Federal Trade Commission Act (1914).*** The increased antitrust responsibilities of the federal government created the need for an agency that could study industry structures and behavior so as to identify anticompetitive practices. The Federal Trade Commission was created for this purpose in 1914.

Although the Sherman, Clayton, and FTC Acts create a legal basis for government antitrust activity, they leave some basic implementation issues unanswered. What, for example, constitutes a "monopoly" in the real world? Must a company produce 100 percent of a particular good to be a threat to consumer welfare? How about 99 percent? Or even 75 percent?

And what specific monopolistic practices should be prohibited? Should we be looking for specific evidence of price gouging? Or should we focus on barriers to entry and unfair market practices?

These kinds of questions determine how and when antitrust laws will be enforced. The first question relates to the *structure* of markets, the second to their *behavior*.

computer manufacturers. These agreements either forbade manufacturers from installing a rival operating system or made it prohibitively expensive. The second accusation against Microsoft was that it used its monopoly position in *operating* systems to gain an unfair advantage in the *applications* market. It did this by not disclosing operating features that make applications run more efficiently or by bundling software, thereby forcing consumers to accept Microsoft applications along with the operating system. When the latter occurs, consumers have little incentive to buy a competing product. Microsoft also prohibited computer manufacturers from displaying rival product icons on the Windows desktop. Finally, Microsoft was accused of thwarting competition by simply buying out promising rivals.

Microsoft's Defense   Bill Gates, Microsoft's chairman, scoffed at the government's charges. He contends that Microsoft dominates the computer industry only because it continues to produce the best products at attractive prices. Microsoft doesn't need to lock out potential competitors, he argues, because it can and does beat the competition with superior products. Furthermore, Gates argues, the software industry is a highly *contestable* market even if not a perfectly competitive one. So Microsoft has to behave like a competitive firm even though it supplies most of the industry's output. In short, Microsoft is a genius, not a bully. Therefore, the government should leave Microsoft alone and let the market decide who best serves consumers.

The Verdict   After nine years of litigation, a federal court determined that Microsoft was more of a bully than a genius. The court concluded that Microsoft not only held a monopoly position in operating systems but that it had abused that position in a variety of anticompetitive ways. As a result, consumers were harmed. **The real economic issue, the court asserted, was not whether Microsoft was improving its products (it was) or reducing prices (it was) but instead how much *faster* products would have improved and prices fallen in a more competitive market.** By limiting consumer

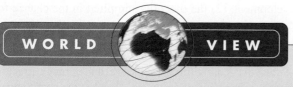

Europeans Come Down Hard on Microsoft

BERLIN, March 24—Microsoft Corp. is abusing a "near monopoly" in crucial computer software to squeeze out competitors, the European Union ruled Wednesday after a contentious five-year investigation. It ordered the company to pay a fine of more than $600 million, and to offer two versions of its Windows operating system in Europe, one without software for playing digital music and videos.

The order effectively puts Microsoft on notice that future attempts to add features to Windows could be challenged in Europe if the additions put rival products at a competitive disadvantage. The ruling is intended to ensure that "anyone who develops new software has a fair opportunity to compete in the marketplace," EU competition commissioner Mario Monti said in Brussels. . . .

EU officials, in defense of their action, said they sought to establish what has eluded Microsoft competitors in the United States: legal precedent to limit the company's 20-year-old practice of constantly incorporating new applications such as the Windows Media Player into the operating system, then capitalizing on Windows' nearly universal distribution to overwhelm rival products.

—John Burgess

Source: *The Washington Post*, March 24, 2004. © 2004 The Washington Post. Reprinted with permission.

Analysis: EU regulators are seeking to lower entry barriers for firms that want to compete for software applications.

choices and stifling competition, Microsoft had denied consumers better and cheaper information technology.

The trial judge suggested that Microsoft might have to be broken into two companies—an operating software company and an applications software company—to ensure enough competition. Such a *structural* remedy would have resembled the court-ordered breakup of AT&T. In November 2001, however, the U.S. Department of Justice decided to seek *behavioral* remedies only. With Windows XP about to be launched, the Justice Department only required Microsoft to lower entry barriers for competing software applications (e.g., disclose middleware specifications, refrain from exclusive contracts, open desktops to competition). Although Microsoft reluctantly agreed to change its conduct in many ways, rivals complained that they still didn't have a fair chance of competing against the Microsoft monopoly. European regulators agreed, imposing still greater restrictions on Microsoft's business practices in 2004 (see World View). Critics contend, however, that market *structure* is still the critical factor in determining market outcomes.

The Remedy

WEBNOTE

You can track the antitrust case against Microsoft on several Web sites. See www.antitrust.org, a source for news and research, and www.nsdoj.gov/atr/pubdocs.html for DOJ documents.

SUMMARY

- Market power is the ability to influence the market price of goods and services. The extreme case of market power is monopoly, a situation in which only one firm produces the entire supply of a particular product.
- The distinguishing feature of any firm with market power is the fact that the demand curve it faces is downward-sloping. In the case of monopoly, the demand curve facing the firm and the market demand curve are identical.

- The downward-sloping demand curve facing a monopolist creates a divergence between marginal revenue and price. To sell larger quantities of output, the monopolist must lower product prices. A firm without market power has no such problem.
- Like other producers, a monopolist will produce at the rate of output at which marginal revenue equals marginal cost. Because marginal revenue is always less than price

in monopoly, the monopolist will produce less output than a competitive industry confronting the same market demand and costs. That reduced rate of output will be sold at higher prices, in accordance with the (downward-sloping) market demand curve.

- A monopoly will attain a higher level of profit than a competitive industry because of its ability to equate industry (that is, its own) marginal revenues and costs. By contrast, a competitive industry ends up equating marginal costs and price, because its individual firms have no control over market supply.
- Because the higher profits attained by a monopoly will attract envious entrepreneurs, barriers to entry are needed to prohibit other firms from expanding market supplies. Patents are one such barrier to entry.
- The defense of market power rests on (1) the alleged ability of large firms to pursue long-term research and development, (2) the incentives implicit in the chance to attain market power, (3) the efficiency that larger firms may attain, and (4) the contestability of even monopolized markets. The first two arguments are weakened by the fact that competitive firms are under much greater pressure to innovate and can stay ahead of the profit game only if they do so. The contestability defense at best concedes some amount of monopoly exploitation.
- A natural monopoly exists when one firm can produce the output of the entire industry more efficiently than can a number of small firms. This advantage is attained from economies of scale. Large firms aren't necessarily more efficient, however, because either constant returns to scale or diseconomies of scale may prevail.
- Antitrust laws restrain the acquisition and abuse of monopoly power. Where barriers to entry aren't insurmountable, market forces may ultimately overcome a monopoly as well.

Key Terms

market power	economies of scale	price discrimination
monopoly	production decision	natural monopoly
profit maximization rule	average total cost (ATC)	contestable market
marginal revenue (MR)	marginal cost pricing	antitrust
barriers to entry	price elasticity of demand	

Questions for Discussion

1. The objective in the game of Monopoly is to get all the property and then raise the rents. Can this power be explained with market supply and demand curves?
2. Is single ownership of a whole industry necessary to exercise monopoly power? How might an industry with many firms achieve the same result? Can you think of any examples?
3. Why don't monopolists try to establish "the highest price possible," as many people allege? What would happen to sales? To profits?
4. In 1990, a federal court decided that Eastman Kodak had infringed on Polaroid's patent when it produced similar instant-photo cameras. The court then had to award Polaroid compensation for damages. What was the nature of the damages to Polaroid? How could you compute them? (The court awarded Polaroid a record $900 million!)
5. What would have happened to iPod prices and features if Apple had not faced competition from iPod clones (Chapter 8)?
6. What entry barriers helped protect the following?
   (a) The Russian sable monopoly (see World View, page 199).
   (b) The Ticketmaster monopoly (see News, page 204).
   (c) The CNN monopoly (see World View, page 212).
7. What similarities exist between the AT&T and Microsoft antitrust cases? What should the government do?
8. Why wouldn't the Pentagon favor a shipyard merger (News, p. 210) that would reduce shipbuilding costs?
9. Do price reductions and quality enhancements on Microsoft products prove that Microsoft is a perfectly competitive firm? What should be the test of competitiveness?

PROBLEMS The Student Problem Set at the back of this book contains numerical and graphing problems for this chapter.

WEB ACTIVITIES to accompany this chapter can be found on the Online Learning Center:
http://www.mhhe.com/economics/schiller10

10 Oligopoly

People of the same trade seldom meet together, but the conversation ends in a conspiracy against the public, or in some diversion to raise prices.

—Adam Smith, *The Wealth of Nations*, 1776

Although it's convenient to think of the economy as composed of the powerful and the powerless, market realities don't always provide such clear distinctions. There are very few perfectly competitive markets in the world, and few monopolies. Market power is an important phenomenon nonetheless; it's just that it's typically shared by several firms rather than monopolized by one. In the soft drink industry, for example, Coca-Cola and Pepsi share tremendous market power, even though neither company qualifies as a pure monopoly. The same kind of power is shared by Kellogg, General Mills, and General Foods in the breakfast cereals market, and by Sony, Nintendo, and Microsoft in the video game console market. Apple Computer, Inc., too, now has power in the digital music player market, which it shares with Sony, Dell, and other firms.

These market structures fall between the extremes of perfect competition and pure monopoly; they represent *imperfect competition.* They contain some elements of competitive rivalry but also exhibit traces of monopoly. In many cases, imperfect competitors behave much like a monopoly, restricting output, charging higher prices, and reaping greater profits than firms in a competitive market. But behavior in imperfectly competitive markets is more complicated than in a monopoly because it involves a number of decision makers (firms) rather than only one.

This chapter focuses on one form of imperfect competition: *oligopoly.* We examine the nature of decision making in this market structure and the likely impacts on prices, production, and profits. What we want to know is:

- **What determines how much market power a firm has?**
- **How do firms in an oligopoly set prices and output?**
- **What problems does an oligopoly have in maintaining price and profit?**

MARKET STRUCTURE

As we saw in Chapter 9, Microsoft is virtually the sole supplier of computer operating systems; as a monopoly, it has tremendous market power. The corner grocery store, on the other hand, must compete with other stores and has less control over prices. But even the corner grocery isn't completely powerless. If it's the only grocery within walking distance, or the only one open on Sunday—it too exerts *some* influence on prices and product flows. The amount of power it possesses depends on the availability of *substitute goods,* that is, the proximity and convenience of alternative retail outlets.

TABLE 10.1
Characteristics of Market Structures

Market structure varies, depending on the number of producers, their size, barriers to entry, and the availability of substitute goods. An oligopoly is an imperfectly competitive structure in which a few firms dominate the market.

Characteristic	Market Structure				
	Perfect Competition	Monopolistic Competition	Oligopoly	Duopoly	Monopoly
Number of firms	Very large number	Many	Few	Two	One
Barriers to entry	None	Low	High	High	High
Market power (control over price)	None	Some	Substantial	Substantial	Substantial
Type of product	Standardized	Differentiated	Standardized or differentiated	Standardized or differentiated	Unique

Degrees of Power

market structure: The number and relative size of firms in an industry.

oligopoly: A market in which a few firms produce all or most of the market supply of a particular good or service.

Determinants of Market Power

contestable market: An imperfectly competitive industry subject to potential entry if prices or profits increase.

Between the extremes of monopoly and perfect competition are many gradations of market power (see Figure 7.1). To sort them out, we classify firms into five specific **market structures,** based on the number and relative size of firms in an industry.

Table 10.1 summarizes the characteristics of the five major market structures. At one extreme is the structure of *perfect competition,* the subject of Chapters 7 and 8. At the other extreme of the power spectrum is perfect *monopoly.* A perfect monopoly exists when only one firm is the exclusive supplier of a particular product. Our illustration of Universal Electronics (the imaginary computer monopolist in Chapter 9) exemplifies such a firm.

Between the two extremes of perfect competition and perfect monopoly lies most of the real world, which we call *imperfectly competitive.* **In imperfect competition, individual firms have some power in a particular product market.** *Oligopoly* refers to one of these imperfectly competitive market structures. **Oligopoly** is a situation in which only a *few* firms have a great deal of power in a product market. An oligopoly may exist because only a few firms produce a particular product or because a few firms account for most, although not all, of a product's output.

The number of firms in an industry is a key characteristic of market structure. The amount of market power the firms possess, however, depends on several factors. *The determinants of market power include*

- *Number of producers.*
- *Size of each firm.*
- *Barriers to entry.*
- *Availability of substitute goods.*

When only one or a few producers or suppliers exist, market power is automatically conferred. In addition to the number of producers, however, the size of each firm is also important. Over 800 firms supply long-distance telephone service in the United States. But just three of those firms (ATT, Verizon, MCI) account for 74 percent of all calls. Hence, it wouldn't make sense to categorize that industry on the basis of only the number of firms; relative size is also important.

A third and critical determinant of market power is the extent of barriers to entry. A highly successful monopoly or oligopoly arouses the envy of other profit maximizers. If it's a **contestable market,** potential rivals will seek to enter the market and share in the spoils. Should they succeed, the power of the former monopolist or oligopolists would be reduced. Accordingly, ease of entry into an industry limits the ability of a powerful firm to dictate prices and product flows. In Chapter 9 we saw how monopolies erect barriers to entry (e.g., patents) to maintain their power.

A fourth determinant of market power is the availability of substitute goods. If a monopolist or other power baron sets the price of a product too high, consumers may decide to switch to close substitutes. Thus, the price of Coors is kept in check by the price of Coke, and the price of sirloin steak is restrained by the price of chicken and pork. By the same token, a lack of available substitute products keeps the prices of insulin and AZT high.

Although there are many determinants of market power, most observers use just one yardstick to measure the extent of power in an industry.

Concentration Ratio. The standard measure of market power is the **concentration ratio.** This ratio tells the share of output (or combined market share) accounted for by the largest firms in an industry. Using this ratio one can readily distinguish between an industry composed of hundreds of small, relatively powerless firms and another industry also composed of hundreds of firms but dominated by a few that are large and powerful. Thus, *the concentration ratio is a measure of market power that relates the size of firms to the size of the product market.*

Table 10.2 gives the concentration ratios for selected products in the United States. The standard measure used here depicts the proportion of domestic production accounted for by the largest firms, usually the four largest. As is apparent from the table, the supply side of these product markets can be described as *oligopolies,* since most of the industry's output is produced by just three or four firms. Indeed, in some markets, one single firm is so large that an outright monopoly is nearly attained. For example, 70 percent of all canned soup is produced by Campbell. Eastman Kodak supplies two-thirds of all still cameras and film. Procter & Gamble makes 62 percent of this country's disposable diapers. All firms that have a market share of at least 40 percent are denoted by **boldface** type in Table 10.2.

Firm Size. We noted before that market power isn't necessarily associated with firm size—in other words, a small firm could possess a lot of power in a relatively small market. Table 10.2, however, should be convincing testimony that we're not talking about small product markets here. Every one of the products listed enjoys a broad-based market. Even the chewing gum market (94 percent concentration ratio) rings up annual sales of $2 billion. The three oligopolists that produce video game consoles (Sony, Nintendo, Microsoft) have 100 percent of a $10 billion market. Accordingly, for most of the firms listed in the table, market power and firm size go hand in hand. Indeed, the largest firms enjoy sales volumes that exceed the entire output of most of the *countries* in the world (see World View).

A high concentration ratio or large firm size isn't the only way to achieve market power. The supply and price of a product can be altered by many firms acting in unison. Even 1,000 small producers can band together to change the quantity supplied to the market, thus exercising market power. Recall how our mythical Universal Electronics (Chapter 9) exercised market power by coordinating the production decisions of its many separate plants. Those plants could have attempted such coordination on their own even if they hadn't all been owned by the same corporation. Lawyers and doctors exercise this kind of power by maintaining uniform fee schedules for members of the American Bar Association (ABA) and the American Medical Association (AMA).[1] Similarly, dairy farmers act jointly through three large cooperatives (the American Milk Producers, Mid-America Dairies, and Dairymen, Inc.), which together control 50 percent of all milk production.

---

[1]The courts have ruled that uniform fee schedules are illegal and that individual lawyers and doctors have the right to advertise their prices (fees). Nevertheless, a combination of inertia and self-interest has effectively maintained high fee schedules and inhibited advertising.

Measuring Market Power

> **concentration ratio:** The proportion of total industry output produced by the largest firms (usually the four largest).

WEBNOTE

The Federal Trade Commission publishes data on *industry*, not product concentration; check www.ftc.gov.

Measurement Problems

TABLE 10.2
Power in U.S. Product Markets

The domestic production of many familiar products is concentrated among a few firms. These firms have substantial control over the quantity supplied to the market and thus over market price. The concentration ratio measures the share of total output produced by the largest producers in a given market.

Product	Largest Firms	Concentration Ratio (%)
Video game consoles	**Sony,** Nintendo, Microsoft	100%
Baby food	**Gerber Products,** Heinz, Beech-Nut	100
Instant breakfast	**Carnation,** Pillsbury, Dean Foods	100
Laser eye surgery	**VISX,** Summit Technology	100
Tennis balls	**Gen Corp (Penn),** PepsiCo **(Wilson),** Dunlop, Spalding	100
Credit cards	**Visa,** MasterCard, American Express, Discover	99
Disposable diapers	**Procter & Gamble,** Kimberly-Clark, Curity, Romar Tissue Mills	99
Razor blades	**Gillette,** Warner-Lambert (Schick; Wilkinson), Bic, American Safety Razor	98
Sports drinks	**PepsiCo** (Gatorade), Coca-Cola (PowerAde), Monarch (All Sport)	98
Baseball cards	Topps, Upper Deck, Fleer, Leaf Inc. (Donruss)	96
Electric razors	**Norelco,** Remington, Warner-Lambert, Sunbeam	96
Sanitary napkins	**Johnson & Johnson,** Kimberly-Clark, Procter & Gamble	96
Batteries	**Duracell,** Eveready, Ray-O-Vac, Kodak	94
Camera, film	**Eastman Kodak,** Fuji, Polaroid	94
Chewing gum	**Wm. Wrigley,** Pfizer, Hershey	94
Soft drinks	**Coca-Cola,** Pepsico, Cadbury Schweppes (7-Up, Dr. Pepper, A&W), Royal Crown	93
Net search engines	Google, Yahoo, AOL, MSN	92
Breakfast cereals	General Mills, Kelloggs, Philip Morris (Kraft Foods), PepsiCo (Quaker Oats).	92
Toothpaste	Colgate-Palmolive, Procter & Gamble, Lever Bros., Beecham	91
Local phone service	Verizon, SBC, Bellsouth, Qwest	90
Detergents	**Procter & Gamble,** Lever Bros., Dial, Colgate-Palmolive	90
Art auctions	**Sotheby's, Christie's**	90
Cigarettes	**Philip Morris,** Reynolds American, Lorillard	89
Soap	Lever Bros., Procter & Gamble, Dial, Colgate-Palmolive	89
Greeting cards	**Hallmark,** American Greetings, Gibson	88
Coffee	General Foods, Procter & Gamble, Nestlé, Philip Morris	86
Contact lens care	Bausch & Lomb, Allergan Optical, Alcon, Coopervision	86
Beer	**Anheuser-Busch,** Philip Morris (Miller), Coors, Pabst	85
Canned soup	**Campbell,** Progresso	85
Chocolate candy	Hershey, Mars, Nestlé, Brach	85
Tires and tubes	Goodyear, Firestone, Uniroyal, B.F. Goodrich	85
Cable TV (for-pay)	TimeWarner (HBO), Viacom (Showtime), Cinemax, Movie Channel	83
Canned tuna	**Heinz** (Starkist), Unicord (Bumble Bee), Van Camp (Chicken of the Sea)	82
Wireless phone service	AT&T, Cingular, Verizon, Nextel	82
Spaghetti sauce	Unilever (Ragu), Campbell Soup (Prego), Hunt-Wesson (Healthy Choice)	80

Sources: Data from Federal Trade Commission, *The Wall Street Journal, Advertising Age, Financial World, Standard & Poor's, Fortune,* and industry sources.

Note: Individual corporations with a market share of at least 40 percent are designated in **boldface type.** Market shares based on selected years, 2000–2004.

Finally, all the figures and corporations cited here refer to *national* markets. They don't convey the extent to which market power may be concentrated in a *local* market. In fact, many industries with low concentration ratios nationally are represented by just one or a few firms locally. Prime examples include milk, newspapers, and transportation (both public and private). For example, fewer than 60 cities in the United States have two or more independently owned daily newspapers, and nearly all those newspapers rely on only two news services (Associated Press and United

Putting Size in Global Perspective

The largest firms in the United States are also the dominant forces in global markets. They export products to foreign markets and produce goods abroad for sale there or to import back into the United States. In terms of size alone, these business giants rival most of the world's nations. GM's gross sales, for example, would make it the twenty-fifth largest "country" in terms of national GDP.

American corporations aren't the only giants in the global markets. Toyota (Japan) and Royal Dutch Shell (Netherlands) are among the foreign giants that contest global markets.

Rank	Country or Corporation	Sales or GDP	Rank	Country or Corporation	Sales or GDP
1	United States	$10,383	21	**British Petroleum**	$233
2	Japan	3,993	22	**ExxonMobil**	223
3	Germany	1,984	23	Austria	204
4	United Kingdom	1,566	24	**Royal Dutch/Shell**	202
5	France	1,431	25	**General Motors**	195
6	China	1,266	26	Norway	190
7	Italy	1,184	27	Poland	189
8	Canada	714	28	Saudi Arabia	188
9	Spain	653	29	Turkey	183
10	Mexico	637	30	Denmark	173
11	India	510	31	Indonesia	173
12	South Korea	477	32	**Ford Motor**	164
13	Brazil	452	33	Hong Kong	162
14	The Netherlands	418	34	**Daimler/Chrysler**	158
15	Australia	409	35	**Toyota**	153
16	Russia	347	36	**General Electric**	134
17	Switzerland	267	37	Greece	133
18	**Wal-Mart Stores**	263	38	Finland	131
19	Belgium	245	39	Thailand	127
20	Sweden	240	40	**Total**	118

Sources: World Bank and *Fortune* magazine (2002–2003 data in billions).

Analysis: Firm size is a determinant of market power. The size of the largest firms, as measured by total revenue, exceeds the value of total output in most of the world's 200-plus countries.

Press International). Perhaps you've also noticed that most college campuses have only one bookstore. It may not be a *national* powerhouse, but it does have the power to influence what goods are available on campus and how much they cost.

OLIGOPOLY BEHAVIOR

With so much market power concentrated in so few hands, it's unrealistic to expect market outcomes to resemble those of perfect competition. As we observed in Chapter 9, *market structure affects market behavior and outcomes.* In that chapter we focused on the contrast between monopoly and perfect competition. Now we focus on the behavior of a more common market structure: oligopoly.

To isolate the unique character of oligopoly, we'll return to the computer market. In Chapter 8 we observed that the computer market was highly competitive in its early stages, when entry barriers were low and hundreds of firms were producing similar

FIGURE 10.1
Initial Conditions in the Computer Market

As in Chapters 8 and 9, we assume that the initial equilibrium in the home computer market occurs at a price of $1,000 and a quantity of 20,000 per month. How will an oligopoly alter these outcomes?

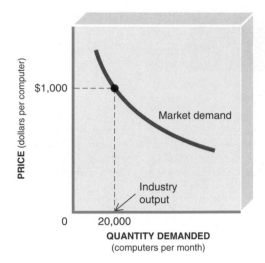

oligopolist: One of the dominant firms in an oligopoly.

The Initial Equilibrium

market share: The percentage of total market output produced by a single firm.

The Battle for Market Shares

products. In Chapter 9 we created an impassable barrier to entry (a patent on the electronic brain of the computer) that transformed the computer industry into a monopoly of Universal Electronics. Now we'll transform the industry again. This time we'll create an oligopoly by assuming that three separate firms (Universal, World, and International) all possess patent rights. The patent rights permit each firm to produce and sell all the computers it wants and to exclude all other would-be producers from the market. With these assumptions, we create three **oligopolists,** the firms that share an *oligopoly.* Our objective is to see how market outcomes would change in such a market structure.

As before, we'll assume that the initial conditions in the computer market are represented by a market price of $1,000 and market sales of 20,000 computers per month, as illustrated in Figure 10.1.

We'll also assume that the **market share** of each producer is accurately depicted in Table 10.3. Thus, Universal Electronics is assumed to be producing 8,000 computers per month, or 40 percent of total market supply. World Computers has a market share of 32.5 percent, while International Semiconductor has only a 27.5 percent share.

The first thing to note about the computer oligopoly is that it's likely to exhibit great internal tension. Neither World Computers nor International Semiconductor is really happy playing second or third fiddle to Universal Electronics. Each company would like to be number one in this market. On the other hand, Universal too would like a larger market share, particularly in view of the huge profits being made on computers. As we observed in Chapter 8, the initial equilibrium in the computer industry yielded an *average* profit of $300 per computer, and total *industry* profits of $6 million per month (20,000 × $300). Universal would love to acquire the market shares of its rivals, thereby grabbing all this industry profit for itself.

But how does an oligopolist acquire a larger market share? In a truly competitive market, a single producer could expand production at will, with no discernible impact on market supply. But *in an oligopoly, increased sales on the part of one firm will be noticed immediately by the other firms.*

TABLE 10.3
Initial Market Shares of Microcomputer Producers

The market share of a firm is the percentage of total market output it produces. These are hypothetical market shares of three fictional oligopolists.

Producer	Output (computers per month)	Market Share (%)
Universal Electronics	8,000	40.0%
World Computers	6,500	32.5
International Semiconductor	5,500	27.5
Total industry output	20,000	100.0%

How do we know that increased sales will be noticed so quickly? Because increased sales by one firm will have to take place either at the existing market price ($1,000) or at a lower price. Either of these two events will ring an alarm at the corporate headquarters of the other two firms.

Increased Sales at the Prevailing Market Price. Consider first the possibility of Universal Electronics increasing its sales at the going price of $1,000 per computer. We know from the demand curve in Figure 10.1 that consumers are willing to buy *only* 20,000 microcomputers per month at that price. Hence, any increase in computer sales by Universal must be immediately reflected in *lower* sales by World or International. That is, ***increases in the market share of one oligopolist necessarily reduce the shares of the remaining oligopolists.*** If Universal were to increase its sales from 8,000 to 9,000 computers per month, the combined monthly sales of World and International would have to fall from 12,000 to 11,000 (see Table 10.3). The *quantity demanded* at $1,000 remains 20,000 computers per month (see Figure 10.1). Thus, any increased sales at that price by Universal must be offset by reduced sales by its rivals.

This interaction among the market shares of the three oligopolists ensures that Universal's sales success will be noticed. It won't be necessary for World Computers or International Semiconductor to engage in industrial espionage. These firms can quickly figure out what Universal is doing simply by looking at their own (declining) sales figures.

Increased Sales at Reduced Prices. Universal could pursue a different strategy. Specifically, Universal could attempt to increase its sales by lowering the price of its computers. Reduced prices would expand total market sales, possibly enabling Universal to increase its sales without directly reducing the sales of either World or International.

But this outcome is most unlikely. If Universal lowered its price from $1,000 to, say, $900, consumers would flock to Universal Computers, and the sales of World and International would plummet. After all, we've always assumed that consumers are rational enough to want to pay the lowest possible price for any particular good. It's unlikely that consumers would continue to pay $1,000 for a World or International machine when they could get basically the same computer from Universal for only $900. If there were no difference, either perceived or real, among the computers of the three firms, a *pure* oligopoly would exist. In that case, Universal would capture the *entire* market if it lowered its price below that of its rivals.

More often, consumers perceive differences in the products of rival oligopolists, even when the products are essentially identical. These perceptions (or any real differences that may exist) create a *differentiated* oligopoly. In this case, Universal would gain many but not all customers if it reduced the price of its computers. That's the outcome we'll assume here. In either case, there simply isn't any way that Universal can increase its sales at reduced prices without causing all the alarms to go off at World and International.

So what if all the alarms do go off at World Computers and International Semiconductor? As long as Universal Electronics is able to enlarge its share of the market and grab more profits, why should it care if World and International find out? Indeed, Universal might even get some added satisfaction knowing that World and International are upset by its marketing success.

Universal *does* have something to worry about, though. World and International may not be content to stand by and watch their market shares and profits diminish. On the contrary, World and International are likely to take some action of their own once they discover what's going on.

There are two things World and International can do once they decide to act. In the first case, where Universal is expanding its market share at prevailing prices ($1,000), World and International can retaliate by

- Stepping up their own marketing efforts.
- Cutting prices on their computers.

Retaliation

Pop Culture: RC Goes for the Youth Market

RC Cola, like the Brady Bunch and push-up bras, is attempting a '90s comeback. . . .

To that end, the company is spending $15 million on a new advertising campaign—the largest in RC's history—designed to cast the blue-collar drink of the Midwest and South as the hip alternative to "corporate colas," as it refers to market leaders Coke and Pepsi. Accompanying the ad blitz are new products, including a sour-tasting, Windex-colored Nehi and a long-neck brew called RC Draft, formulated specifically for younger palates.

"This company spent no money on advertising during the 1980s, and we lost an entire generation of cola drinkers who grew up in that decade," said John Carson, Royal Crown's chief executive. . . .

"Anybody in the soft drink business trying to compete with Pepsi and Coke has an uphill battle—they have huge amounts of marketing muscle, financial resources, experience and bottling agreements," said John Sicher, co-editor of Beverage Digest, an industry publication. "But RC's new tactics are smart. They are tossing out a bunch of beverages targeted toward younger drinkers. Against Coke and Pepsi, guerrilla warfare is the only thing that might work."

—Anthony Faiola

The U.S. Soda Market

Market share of soft drink makers, 2001.

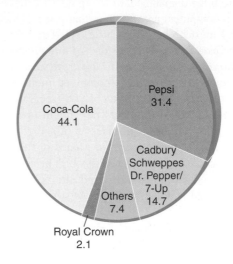

Source: *The Washington Post*, February 17, 1995. © 1995 The Washington Post. Reprinted with permission. www.washingtonpost.com

Analysis: Because price competition is typically self-defeating in an oligopoly, rival firms in an oligopoly rely on advertising and product differentiation (nonprice competition) to gain market share.

---

product differentiation: Features that make one product appear different from competing products in the same market.

To step up their marketing efforts, World and International might increase their advertising expenditures, repackage their computers, put more sales representatives on the street, or sponsor a college homecoming week. This is the kind of behavior RC Cola used to gain market share from Coke and Pepsi (see News). Such attempts at **product differentiation** are designed to make one firm's products appear different and superior to those produced by other firms. If successful, such marketing efforts will increase RC Cola sales and market share or at least stop its rivals from grabbing larger shares.

An even quicker way to stop Universal from enlarging its market share is for World and International to lower the price of *their* computers. Such price reductions will destroy Universal's hopes of increasing its market share at the old price. In fact, this is the other side of a story we've already told. If the price of World and International computers drops to, say, $900, it's preposterous to assume that Universal will be able to expand its market share at a price of $1,000. Universal's market share will shrink if it maintains a price of $1,000 per computer after World and International drop their prices to $900. Hence, the threat to Universal's market share grab is that the other two oligopolists will retaliate by reducing *their* prices. Should they carry out this threat, Universal would be forced to cut computer prices too, or accept a greatly reduced market share.

The same kind of threat exists in the second case, where we assumed that Universal Electronics expands its sales by initiating a price reduction. World and International aren't going to just sit by and applaud Universal's marketing success. They'll

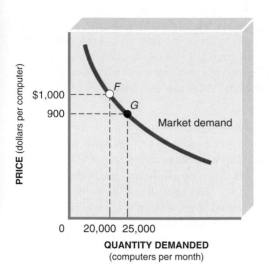

FIGURE 10.2
Rivalry for Market Shares Threatens an Oligopoly

If oligopolists start cutting prices to capture larger market shares, they'll be behaving much like truly competitive firms. The result will be a slide down the market demand curve to lower prices, increased output, and smaller profits. In this case, the market price and quantity would move from point *F* to point *G* if rival oligopolists cut prices to gain market shares.

have to respond with price cuts of their own. Universal would then have the highest price on the market, and computer buyers would flock to cheaper substitutes. Accordingly, it's safe to conclude that *an attempt by one oligopolist to increase its market share by cutting prices will lead to a general reduction in the market price.* The three oligopolists will end up using price reductions as weapons in the battle for market shares, the kind of behavior normally associated with competitive firms. Should this behavior continue, not only will oligopoly become less fun, but it will also become less profitable as prices slide down the market demand curve (Figure 10.2). This is why *oligopolists avoid price competition and instead pursue nonprice competition* (e.g., advertising, production differentiation).

THE KINKED DEMAND CURVE

The close interdependence of oligopolists—and the limitations it imposes on individual price and output decisions—is the principal moral of this story about Universal Electronics, World Computers, and International Semiconductor. We can summarize this story with the aid of the kinked demand curve in Figure 10.3.

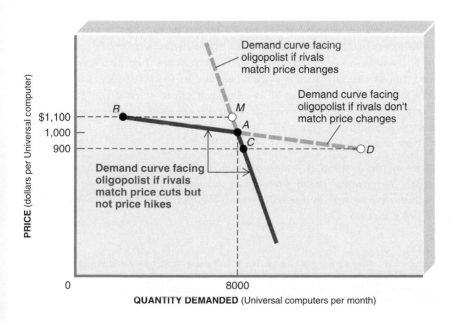

FIGURE 10.3
The Kinked Demand Curve Confronting an Oligopolist

The shape of the demand curve facing an oligopolist depends on the responses of its rivals to its price and output decisions. If rival oligopolists match price reductions but not price increases, the demand curve will be kinked.

Initially, the oligopolist is at point *A*. If it raises its price to $1,100 and its rivals don't raise their prices, it will be driven to point *B*. If its rivals match a price reduction (to $900), the oligopolist will end up at point *C*.

Recall that at the beginning of this oligopoly story Universal Electronics had a market share of 40 percent and was selling 8,000 computers per month at a price of $1,000 each. This output is represented by point *A* in Figure 10.3. The rest of the demand curve illustrates what would happen to Universal's unit sales if it changed its selling price. What we have to figure out is why this particular demand curve has such a strange "kinked" shape.

Rivals' Response to Price Reductions

Consider first what would happen to Universal's sales if it lowered the price of its computers to $900. In general, we expect a price reduction to increase sales. However, *the degree to which an oligopolist's sales increase when its price is reduced depends on the response of rival oligopolists.* Suppose World and International didn't match Universal's price reduction. In this case, Universal would have the only low-priced computer in the market. Consumers would flock to Universal, and sales would increase dramatically, to point *D*. But point *D* is little more than a dream, as we've observed. World and International are sure to cut their prices to $900 too, in order to maintain their market shares. As a consequence, Universal's sales will expand only slightly, to point *C* rather than to point *D*. Universal's increased sales at point *C* reflect the fact that the total quantity demanded in the market has risen as the market price has fallen to $900 (see Figure 10.2). Thus, although Universal's *market share* may not have increased, its monthly sales have.

The section of the demand curve that runs from point *A* to point *D* is unlikely to exist in an oligopolistic market. Instead, *we expect rival oligopolists to match any price reductions* that Universal initiates, forcing Universal to accept the demand curve that runs from point *A* through point *C*. The News illustrates such behavior in the airline industry, where rivals were forced to match price cuts introduced by Delta.

Rivals' Response to Price Increases

What about price increases? How will World and International respond if Universal raises the price of its computers to $1,100?

Recall that the demand for computers is assumed to be price-elastic in the neighborhood of $1,000 and that all computers are basically similar. Accordingly, if Universal raises its price and neither World nor International follows suit, Universal will be out there alone with a higher price and reduced sales. *Rival oligopolists may choose not to match price increases.* In terms of Figure 10.3, a price increase that isn't matched by rival oligopolists will drive Universal from point *A* to point *B*. At point *B*, Universal is selling very few computers at its price of $1,100 each.[2]

Is this a likely outcome? Suffice it to say that World Computers and International Semiconductor wouldn't be unhappy about enlarging their own market shares. Unless they see the desirability of an industrywide price increase, they're not likely to come to Universal's rescue with price increases of their own. This is why Northwest Airlines decided not to match the fare hikes announced by its rivals (see News).

Anything is possible, however, and World and International might match Universal's price increase. In this case, the *market price* would rise to $1,100 and the total quantity of computers demanded would diminish. Under such circumstances Universal's sales would diminish, too, in accordance with its (constant) share of a smaller market. This would lead us to point *M* in Figure 10.3.

We may draw two conclusions from Figure 10.3:

- *The shape of the demand curve an oligopolist faces depends on the responses of its rivals to a change in the price of its own output.*
- *That demand curve will be kinked if rival oligopolists match price reductions but not price increases.*

---

[2]Notice again that we're assuming that Universal is able to sell some computers at a higher price (point *B*) than its rivals. The kinked demand curve applies primarily to differentiated oligopolies. As we'll discuss later, such differentiation may result from slight product variations, advertising, customer habits, location, friendly service, or any number of other factors. Most oligopolies exhibit some differentiation.

Airlines Drop Fare Hikes

Major airlines abandoned fare increases of as much as $20 on one-way tickets after all carriers failed to match the increases. . . .

Continental Airlines and AMR Corp.'s American Airlines yesterday became the last of the major airlines to roll back increases that were put in place last Tuesday and were matched initially by most airlines except Northwest Airlines.

—Gary McWilliams

Source: *The Wall Street Journal,* May 25, 2004. Reprinted by permission of The Wall Street Journal, © 2004 Dow Jones & Company. All rights reserved worldwide.

Delta Cuts Fares 25 Percent; Rival Lines Follow Suit

Major airlines slashed fares about 25 percent yesterday in the hope that leisure summer passengers will make up for the sharp decline in business travel that has pushed airline revenue down dramatically.

Delta Air Lines cut fares in the United States, Latin America and Asia. Other airlines such as United, American, Continental, Northwest and US Airways immediately said they would match Delta's 25 percent fare reductions in markets where they compete.

—Keith L. Alexander

Source: *The Washington Post,* June 26, 2001. © 2001 The Washington Post. Reprinted with permission. www.washingtonpost.com

Analysis: If rivals match price cuts but not price increases, the demand curve confronting an oligopolist will be kinked. Prices will increase only when all firms agree to raise them at the same time.

GAME THEORY

One implication of the kinked demand curve is that oligopolists can't make truly independent price or output decisions. Because only a few producers participate in the market, **each oligopolist has to consider the potential responses of rivals when formulating price or output strategies.** This *strategic interaction* is the inevitable consequence of their oligopolistic position.

What makes oligopoly particularly interesting is the *uncertainty* of rivals' behavior. For example, Universal *would* want to lower its prices *if* it thought its rivals wouldn't retaliate with similar price cuts. But it can't be sure of that response. Universal must instead consider the odds of its rivals not matching a price cut. If the odds are low, Universal might decide *not* to initiate a price cut. Or maybe Universal might offer price discounts to just a few select customers, hoping World and International might not notice or react to small changes in market share.

The Payoff Matrix. Table 10.4 summarizes the strategic options each oligopolist confronts. In this case, let's assume that Universal is contemplating a price cut. The "payoff matrix" in the table summarizes the various profit consequences of such a move. One thing should be immediately clear: **The payoff to an oligopolist's price cut depends on how its rivals respond.** Indeed, the only scenario that increases Universal's profit is one in which Universal reduces its price and its rivals don't. We visualized this outcome earlier as a move from point *A* to point *D* in Figure 10.3. Note again that this scenario implies losses for Universal's two rival oligopolists.

The remaining cells in the payoff matrix show how profits change with other action/response scenarios. One thing is evident: If Universal *doesn't* reduce prices, it can't increase profits. In fact, it might end up as the Big Loser if its rivals reduce *their* prices while Universal stands pat.

The option of reducing price doesn't guarantee a profit, but at least it won't decimate Universal's market share or profits. If rivals match a Universal price cut, all three oligopolists will suffer small losses.

TABLE 10.4
Oligopoly Payoff Matrix

The payoff to an oligopolist's price cut depends on its rivals' responses. Each oligopolist must assess the risks and rewards of each scenario before initiating a price change. Which option would you choose?

Universal's Options	Rivals' Actions	
	Reduce Price	Don't Reduce Price
Reduce price	Small loss for everyone	Huge gain for Universal; rivals lose
Don't reduce price	Huge loss for Universal; rivals gain	No change

WEBNOTE

The "Prisoner's Dilemma" (who should confess) is a classic game theory problem. Try solving this and other games at www.cmu.edu/comlabgames.

So what should Universal do? The *collective* interests of the oligopoly are protected if no one cuts the market price. But an individual oligopolist could lose big time if it holds the line on price when rivals reduce price. Hence each oligopolist might decide to play it safe by *initiating* a price cut.

Expected Gain (Loss). The decision to initiate a price cut boils down to an assessment of *risk*. If you thought the risk of a "first strike" was high, you'd be more inclined to reduce price. This kind of risk assessment is the foundation of game theory. You could in fact make that decision by *quantifying* the risks involved. Consider again the option of reducing price. As the first row of Table 10.4 shows, rivals can respond in one of only two ways. If they follow suit, a small loss is incurred by Universal. If they don't, there's a huge gain for Universal. To quantify the risk assessment, we need two pieces of information: (1) the size of each "payoff" and (2) the probability of its occurrence.

Suppose the "huge gain" is $1 million and the "small loss" is $20,000. What should Universal do? The huge gain looks enticing, but we now know it's not likely to happen. But *how* unlikely is it? What if there's only a 1 percent chance of rivals not matching a price reduction? In that case, the *expected* payoff to a Universal price cut is

$$\text{Expected value} = \left[\begin{array}{c} \text{Probability of} \\ \text{rivals matching} \end{array} \times \begin{array}{c} \text{Size of} \\ \text{loss from} \\ \text{price cuts} \end{array} \right] + \left[\begin{array}{c} \text{Probability} \\ \text{of rivals} \\ \text{not matching} \end{array} \times \begin{array}{c} \text{Gain} \\ \text{from lone} \\ \text{price cut} \end{array} \right]$$

$$= [(0.99) \times (-\$20,000)] + [(0.01) \times (\$1 \text{ million})]$$

$$= -\$19,800 + \$10,000$$

$$= -\$9,800$$

Hence, it's not a good idea. Once potential payoffs and probabilities are taken into account, a unilateral price cut doesn't look promising.

These kinds of computations underlay the Cold War games that the world's one-time super powers played. Neither side was certain of the enemy's next move but knew it could bring total destruction. As a consequence, the United States and the former Soviet Union continually probed each other's responses but were quick to retreat from the brink whenever all-out retaliation was threatened. Oligopolists play the same kind of game on a much smaller scale, using price discounts and advertising rather than nuclear warheads as their principal weapons. The reward they receive for coexistence is the oligopoly profits that they continue to share. This reward, together with the

Coke and Pepsi May Call Off Pricing Battle

ATLANTA—A brief but bitter pricing war within the soft-drink industry might be drawing to a close—all because no one wants to be blamed for having fired the first shot.

Coca-Cola Enterprises Inc., Coca-Cola Co.'s biggest bottler, said in a recent memorandum to executives that it will "attempt to increase prices" after July 4 amid concern that heavy price discounting in most of the industry is squeezing profit margins.

The memo is a response to statements made to analysts last week by top PepsiCo Inc. executives. Pepsi, of Purchase, N.Y., said "irrational" pricing in much of the soft-drink industry might temporarily squeeze domestic profits, and it laid the blame for the price cuts at Coke's door.

That clearly incensed executives at Coca-Cola and Coca-Cola Enterprises, which had no desire to be criticized for

threatening profit margins for the entire industry. Indeed, industry analysts in the wake of Pepsi's statements expressed concern that profit margins for Pepsi and Coke bottlers may erode as a result of cutthroat pricing. . . .

In the June 5 memo, Summerfield K. Johnston Jr. and Henry A. Schimberg, the chief executive and the president of Coca-Cola Enterprises, respectively, said the bottler's plan is to "succeed based on superior marketing programs and execution rather than the short-term approach of buying share through price discounting. . . . We have absolutely no motivation to decrease prices except in response to a competitive initiative."

—Nikhil Deogun

Analysis: Price discounting can destroy oligopoly profits. When it occurs, rival oligopolists seek to end it as quickly as possible.

---

threat of mutual destruction, leads oligopolists to limit their price rivalry. This explains why Coke and Pepsi quickly ended their brief 1997 price war (see News). After finger-pointing about who started the war, the companies pulled back from the brink of mutual profit destruction.

This isn't to say oligopolists won't ever cut prices or use other means to gain market share. They might, given the right circumstances and certain expectations of how rivals will behave. Indeed, there are a host of different price, output, and marketing strategies an oligopolist might want to pursue. The field of **game theory** is dedicated to the study of how decisions are made when such strategic interaction exists, for example, when the outcome of a business strategy depends on the decisions rival firms make. Just as there are dozens of different moves and countermoves in a chess game, so too are there numerous strategies oligopolists might use to gain market share.

> game theory: The study of decision making in situations where strategic interaction (moves and counter-moves) between rivals occurs.

OLIGOPOLY VS. COMPETITION

While contemplating alternative strategies for maximizing their *individual* profits, oligopolists are also mindful of their common interest in maximizing *joint* (industry) profits. They want to avoid behavior that destroys the very profits that they're vying for. Indeed, they might want to coordinate their behavior in a way that maximizes *industry* profits. If they do, how will market outcomes be affected?

Thus far we've focused on a single oligopolist's decision about whether to *change* the price of its output. But how was the initial (market) price determined? In this example, we assumed that the initial price was $1,000 per computer, the price that prevailed initially in a *competitive* market. But the market is no longer competitive. As we saw in the previous chapter, a change in industry structure will affect market outcomes. A monopolist, for example, would try to maximize *industry* profits, all of which it would keep. To do this, it would select that one rate of output where

Price and Output

FIGURE 10.4
Maximizing Oligopoly Profits

An oligopoly strives to behave like a monopoly. Industry profits are maximized at the rate of output at which the industry's marginal cost equals the marginal revenue (point *J*). In a monopoly, this profit all goes to one firm; in an oligopoly, it must be shared among a few firms.

In an oligopoly, the MC and ATC curves represent the combined production capabilities of several firms, rather than only one. The industry MC curve is derived by horizontally summing the MC curves of the individual firms.

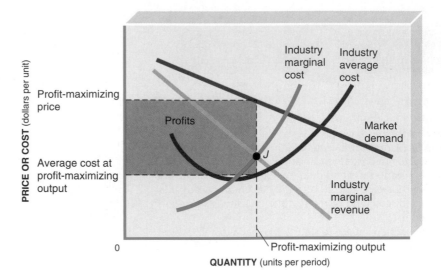

marginal revenue equals marginal cost, and it would charge whatever price consumers were willing and able to pay for that rate of output (see Figure 10.4).

An oligopoly would seek similar profits. An oligopoly is really just a *shared* monopoly. Hence, ***an oligopoly will want to behave like a monopoly, choosing a rate of industry output that maximizes total industry profit.***

The challenge for an oligopoly is to replicate monopoly outcomes. To do so, the firms in an oligopoly must find the monopoly price and maintain it. This is what the members of OPEC are trying to do when they meet to establish a common price for the oil they sell (see World View). To reach agreement requires a common view of the industry demand curve, satisfaction with respective market shares, and precise coordination.

Competitive industries would also like to reap monopoly-like profits. But competitive industries experience relentless pressure on profits, as individual firms expand output, reduce costs, and lower prices. To maximize industry profits, competitive firms

WEBNOTE

To assess the effects of OPEC's 2004 agreement, check the trend of oil prices at www.eia.doe.gov.

WORLD VIEW

OPEC Plans Cut In Output to Keep Oil Prices High

The world's cartel of major oil-producing countries pledged to cut its production by about 9%, a move that could keep oil prices high and contribute to spikes in U.S. gasoline prices.

Already, a confluence of relatively strong crude-oil prices, low gasoline inventories and more complicated blends of gasoline had set the stage for volatile gasoline prices across the country. In past years, this combination of factors has led prices to soar above $2 a gallon in some areas, analysts say.

Higher prices became much more likely yesterday when the 11-nation Organization of Petroleum Exporting Countries,

meeting in Algiers, agreed to reduce its official production by one million barrels a day beginning April 1, compared with the current 24.5 million barrels a day. . . .

After OPEC's move, benchmark crude prices yesterday rose $1.04 to $33.87 in New York Mercantile Exchange trading.

—Alexei Barrionuevo and Chip Cummins

Source: *The Wall Street Journal*, February 11, 2004. Reprinted by permission of The Wall Street Journal, © 2004 Dow Jones & Company. All rights reserved worldwide.

Analysis: An oligopoly tries to act like a shared monopoly. To maximize industry profit, the firms in an oligopoly must concur on what the monopoly price is and agree to maintain it by limiting output and allocating market shares.

would have to band together and agree to restrict output and raise prices. If they did, though, the industry would no longer be competitive. The potential for maximizing industry profits is clearly greater in an oligopoly because fewer firms are involved and each is aware of its dependence on the behavior of the others.

An oligopoly may not be coordinated enough to set the price that maximizes industry profits. Whatever price is established, however, will tend to be stable. This price stability is partly a reflection of the strategic interdependence that characterizes oligopoly. As the kinked demand curve illustrates, unilateral price changes can be self-destructive. So price competition is generally avoided.

Price stability is also facilitated by the "cost cushion" that surrounds an oligopolist's production decision. Like all producers, an oligopolist wants to produce where MR = MC. This **profit-maximization rule** implies that a *change* in marginal cost will alter the production decision. This isn't necessarily the case for an oligopolist, however. An oligopolist has a gap in its MR curve that serves as a cushion against small changes in MC. This cushion results from the kink in the oligopolist's demand curve.

The kinked demand curve is really a composite of two separate demand curves (Figure 10.5). One curve is predicated on the assumption that rival oligopolists don't respond to price increases (d_1). The other curve is predicated on the assumption that rivals do respond to price cuts (d_2). Each demand curve has its own marginal revenue curve, as shown in Figure 10.5. The demand curve d_1 has **marginal revenue (MR)** curve mr_1, for example, while demand curve d_2 has marginal revenue curve mr_2.

If the kinked demand curve dictates an oligopolist's behavior, each firm confronts the possibility of starting down the demand curve d_1 and switching to d_2 at point A. Hence, from point S to point A the curve mr_1 depicts the relevant marginal revenues. At point A (the quantity of 8,000 computers per month), however, we suddenly switch demand curves (to d_2). Hence, we must seek out a new marginal revenue curve corresponding to d_2. To the right of point A, the marginal revenue curve mr_2 is operational.

The oligopolist's marginal revenue curve thus contains two distinct segments. In Figure 10.5, the first segment runs from point S to point F. The second segment runs from point G down to point H (below the horizontal axis MR is negative and so of no interest here).

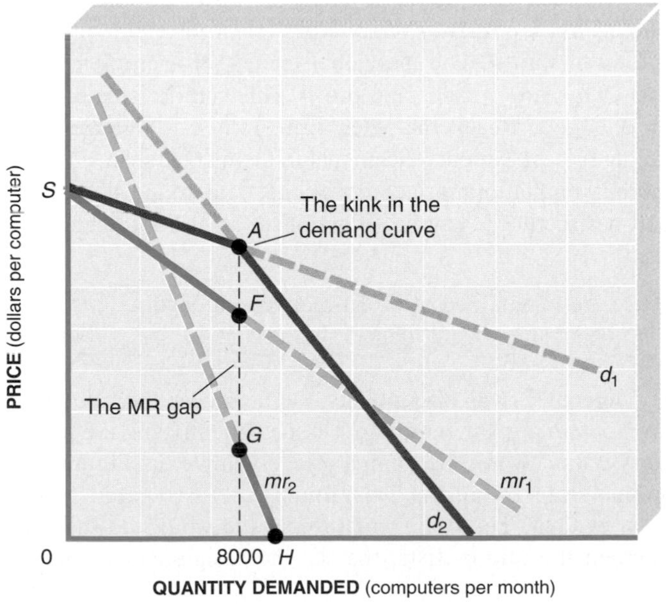

Sticky Prices

profit-maximization rule: Produce at that rate of output where marginal revenue equals marginal cost.

marginal revenue (MR): The change in total revenue that results from a one-unit increase in the quantity sold.

FIGURE 10.5
An Oligopolist's Marginal Revenue Curve

A kinked demand curve incorporates portions of two different demand curves (d_1 and d_2). Hence a kinked demand curve also has portions of two distinct marginal revenue curves (mr_1 and mr_2). Below the kink in the demand curve (point A), a gap exists between the two marginal revenue curves. The segment SF comes from marginal revenue curve mr_1; the segment GH comes from mr_2.

FIGURE 10.6
The Cost Cushion

The gap in an oligopolist's marginal revenue curve creates a "cost cushion." If marginal cost rises (MC$_2$) or falls (MC$_3$) within that gap ($F - G$), the profit-maximizing rate of output (MC = MR) is unchanged.

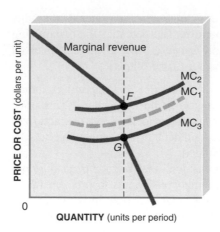

Between points F and G *there's a gap in the oligopolist's marginal revenue curve.* Notice that *this gap occurs just below the kink in the demand curve.* This gap creates a cost cushion. Look at the marginal cost curves in Figure 10.6. If the marginal cost curve passes through the gap in the marginal revenue curve, ***modest shifts of the marginal cost curve will have no impact on the production decision of an oligopolist.*** That is, an oligopolist need not reduce its rate of output when marginal costs rise somewhat or increase its rate of output when marginal costs fall. As a consequence, an oligopolist's output doesn't fluctuate as much as either a competitive firm's or a profit-maximizing monopolist's. The cost cushion implied by the gap in its MR curve allows the oligopolist to maintain a given price for longer periods and to incur higher marketing costs (such as advertising) if the need arises. In other words, the kinked demand curve results in "sticky" prices. Given the uncertain consequences of any unilateral price change, this cost cushion reinforces the aversion of oligopolists to price competition.

COORDINATION PROBLEMS

A successful oligopoly will achieve monopoly-level profits by restricting industry output. As we've observed, however, this outcome depends on mutual agreement and coordination among the oligopolists. This may not come easy. ***There's an inherent conflict in the joint and individual interests of oligopolists.*** Their joint, or collective, interest is in maximizing industry profit. The individual interest of each oligopolist, however, is to maximize its own share of sales and profit. This conflict creates great internal tension within an oligopoly. Recall that each firm wants as large a market share as possible, at prevailing prices. But encroachments in the market shares of rival oligopolists threaten to bring retaliation, price reductions, and reduced industry profits. To avoid such self-destructive behavior, oligopolists must coordinate their production decisions so that

- *Industry* output and price are maintained at profit-maximizing levels.
- Each oligopolistic *firm* is content with its market share.

Price-Fixing

To bring about this happy outcome, rival oligopolists could discuss their common interests and attempt to iron out an agreement on both issues. Identifying the profit-maximizing rate of industry output would be comparatively simple, as Figure 10.4 illustrated. Once the optimal rate of output was found, the associated profit-maximizing price would be evident. The only remaining issue would be the division of industry output among the oligopolists, that is, the assignment of market shares.

IN THE NEWS

Charitable Conspiracy

A Judge Finds M.I.T. and the Ivy League Guilty of Price-Fixing

For more than 30 years the eight Ivy League colleges and M.I.T., as well as dozens of other private institutions, mostly in the Northeast, agreed that they would not try to outbid one another for talented students who needed financial assistance. Each spring this so-called Overlap Group, led by M.I.T. and the Ivies (Brown, Columbia, Cornell, Dartmouth, Harvard, Pennsylvania, Princeton, and Yale), would share information about needy students accepted by more than one of the member schools, working out a standard financial-aid package. Last year the Justice Department charged that this practice violated U.S. antitrust laws by suppressing competition among the schools.

Said Charles James, the Justice Department's lawyer: "Students and their families are entitled to the full benefits of price competition when they pick a college." But M.I.T. President Charles Vest warned that the decision would make it harder for colleges to admit students without regard to financial need and "effectively erode the freedom of opportunity to get a college education, regardless of income."

Source: *Time*, September 14, 1992. © 1992 Time Inc. Reprinted by permission. www.time.com

Analysis: Agreements to limit scholarship assistance effectively fix the price of college tuition. Ivy League schools routinely engaged in such price-fixing practices until the U.S. Justice Department intervened.

The most explicit form of coordination among oligopolists is called **price-fixing.** In this case, the firms in an oligopoly explicitly agree to charge a uniform (monopoly) price. This is what OPEC members do when they get together to set oil prices (World View, p. 230). This is also what Ivy League schools did when they met to establish uniform scholarship and tuition rates (see News). Some other examples of price-fixing include the following:

> **price-fixing:** Explicit agreements among producers regarding the price(s) at which a good is to be sold.

Electric Generators. In 1961, General Electric and Westinghouse were convicted of fixing prices on $2 billion worth of electrical generators that they'd been selling to the Tennessee Valley Authority and commercial customers. Among the corporate executives, 7 went to prison and 23 others were put on probation. In addition, the companies were fined a total of $1.8 million and compelled to pay triple damages in excess of $500 million to their victimized customers. Nevertheless, another suit was filed against General Electric and Westinghouse in 1972, charging these same companies—still the only two U.S. manufacturers of turbine generators—with continued price-fixing.

School Milk. Between 1988 and 1991, the U.S. Justice Department filed charges against 50 companies for fixing the price of milk sold to public schools in 16 states. Dairy companies paid over $20 million in fines. In 1993, Borden Inc. paid $8 million in fines for fixing bids on milk sold to Texas Tech University, public schools, and hospitals.

Vitamins. Seven firms from four nations were accused of fixing global prices on bulk vitamins from 1990 to 1998. They also allocated market shares for vitamins A, B2, C, and E. In 1999, the companies paid a record $1.05 billion fine.

Baby Formula. Two makers of baby formula (Bristol-Myers Squibb and American Home Products) agreed to pay $5 million in 1992 to settle Florida charges that they had fixed prices on baby formula. Three companies control 95 percent of this $1.3 billion national market.

Cola. The Coca-Cola Bottling Co. of North Carolina agreed to pay a fine and give consumers discount coupons to settle charges of conspiring to fix soft drink prices from 1982 to 1985. Similar charges in Virginia led to fines and prison sentences for local executives of Coca-Cola and PepsiCo.

Auction Commissions. Sotheby's and Christie's, who together control 90 percent of the world's art auction business, admitted in 2000 to fixing commission rates throughout the 1990s. They paid a $512 million fine when they got caught.

Music CDs. In 2001, the Federal Trade Commission charged AOL–TimeWarner and Universal Music with fixing prices on the best-selling "Three Tenors" CD. The FTC also forced TimeWarner, Sony, Bertelsman, and EMI to end prohibitions on the advertising of discounted CD prices. The companies paid a $67 million fine and gave away $76 million in free CDs in 2002 to settle the case.

Laser Eye Surgery. The FTC charged the two companies that sell the lasers used for corrective eye surgery (VISX and Summit Technology) with price-fixing that inflated the retail price of surgery by $500 per eye.

Memory Chips. In 2004, prosecutors claimed that the world's largest memory-chip (DRAM) manufacturers (Samsung, Micron, Infineon) fixed prices in the $16 billion-a-year DRAM market.

Price Leadership

> **price leadership:** An oligopolistic pricing pattern that allows one firm to establish the (market) price for all firms in the industry.

Although price-fixing agreements are still a reality in many product markets, oligopolies have discovered that they don't need *explicit* agreements to arrive at uniform prices; they can achieve the same outcome in more subtle ways. **Price leadership** rather than price-fixing will suffice. If all oligopolists in a particular product market follow the lead of one firm in raising prices, the result is the same as if they had all agreed to raise prices simultaneously. Instead of conspiring in motel rooms (as in the electrical products and soft drink cases), the firms can achieve their objective simply by reading *The Wall Street Journal* or industry publications and responding appropriately. This is apparently how Coke and Pepsi communicated their desire to end their 1997 price war (see News on page 229).

According to the U.S. Department of Justice, the major airlines developed a highly sophisticated form of price leadership. They used their shared computer reservation systems to signal *intended* price hikes (see the following News). Rival oligopolists then responded with their own *intended* price changes. Only after it was clear that all the airlines would match a planned price increase was the price hike announced. The Justice Department argued that this "electronic dialogue" was equivalent to a price-fixing conspiracy that cost consumers $1.9 billion in excessive fares. In response, the major airlines agreed to stop using the reservations system to communicate *planned* fare hikes.

Allocation of Market Shares

> **cartel:** A group of firms with an explicit, formal agreement to fix prices and output shares in a particular market.

Whenever oligopolists successfully raise the price of a product, the law of demand tells us that unit sales will decline. Even in markets with highly inelastic demand (such as those for school milk and generic drugs), *some* decrease in sales always accompanies an increase in price. When this happens in a monopolistic industry, the monopolist simply cuts back his rate of output. In an oligopoly, however, no single firm will wish to incur the whole weight of that cutback. Some form of accommodation is required by all the oligopolists.

The adjustment to the reduced sales volume can take many forms. Members of OPEC, for example, assign explicit quotas for the oil output of each member country (see World View on page 230). Such open and explicit production-sharing agreements transform an oligopoly into a **cartel.**

IN THE NEWS

Behind the Screens

The Justice Department says airlines can illegally fix fares by electronically posting future fare changes or restrictions, watching rivals' responses and adjusting the fares until all airlines agree. Here's a hypothetical example:

MONDAY	TUESDAY	WEDNESDAY	THURSDAY	FRIDAY
D.C. to Orlando: $200 Jan. 15 – Feb. 15	D.C. to Orlando: $250 Feb. 1 – Feb. 15 D.C. to Denver: $300 Jan. 15 – March 1	D.C. to Orlando: $250 Feb. 1 – Feb. 15 D.C. to Denver: $350 Jan. 15 – March 1	D.C. to Orlando: $250 Feb. 1 – Feb. 15 D.C. to Denver: $350 Jan. 15 – March 1	D.C. to Orlando: $250 Feb. 1 – Feb. 15 D.C. to Denver: $350 Jan. 15 – March 1

Airline A: Posts $200 fare to Orlando, a cut from $300.

Airline B: Posts a smaller, later fare cut to Orlando, a profitable route, and posts a $300 fare, down from $400, to Denver, a big route for Airline A.

Airline A: Changes its Orlando fare to match Airline B's, but posts a smaller fare cut on Denver route.

Airline B: Matches the higher Denver fare because Airline A matched its higher Orlando fare. At this point the fares take effect.

Travel agents and consumers learn of the fare cuts, but never know of the even deeper cuts initially proposed by both airlines.

Source: *The Washington Post*, December 23, 1992. © 1992 The Washington Post. Reprinted with permission. www.washingtonpost.com

Analysis: Before changing prices, an oligopolist must know how its rivals will respond. The U.S. Department of Justice has accused major airlines of using their common computer reservation systems to test rivals' responses and set common prices.

Because cartels openly violate U.S. antitrust laws, American oligopolies have to be more circumspect in divvying up shared markets. A particularly novel method of allocating market shares occurred in the price-fixing case involving General Electric and Westinghouse. Agreeing to establish high prices on electric generators wasn't particularly difficult. But how would the companies decide who was to get the restricted sales? Their solution was to designate one firm as the "low" bidder for a particular phase of the moon. The "low" bidder would charge the previously agreed-upon (high) price, with the other firms offering their products at even higher prices. The "low" bidder would naturally get the sale. Each time the moon entered a new phase, the order of "low" and "high" bidders changed. Each firm got a share of the business, and the price-fixing scheme hid behind a facade of "competitive" bidding.

Such intricate systems for allocating market shares are more the exception than the rule. More often the oligopolists let the sales and output reduction be divided up according to consumer demands, intervening only when market shares are thrown markedly out of balance. At such times an oligopolist may take drastic action, such as **predatory pricing.** Predatory price cuts are temporary price reductions intended to drive out new competition or reestablish market shares. The sophisticated use of price cutting can also function as a significant barrier to entry, inhibiting potential competitors from trying to gain a foothold in the price cutter's market. The following

predatory pricing: Temporary price reductions designed to alter market shares or drive out competition.

News feature describes how three major airlines were accused in 1999 of using this technique to reduce competition on their routes.

BARRIERS TO ENTRY

barriers to entry: Obstacles, such as patents, that make it difficult or impossible for would-be producers to enter a particular market.

If oligopolies succeed in establishing monopoly prices and profits, they'll attract the envy of would-be entrants. To keep potential competitors out of their industry, oligopolists must maintain **barriers to entry.** *Above-normal profits can't be maintained over the long run unless barriers to entry exist.* The entry barriers erected include those monopolists use (Chapter 9).

Patents

Patents are a very effective barrier to entry. Potential competitors can't set up shop until they either develop an alternative method for producing a product or receive permission from the patent holder to use the patented process. Such permission, when given, costs something, of course.

Distribution Control

Another way of controlling the supply of a product is to take control of distribution outlets. If a firm can persuade retail outlets not to peddle anyone else's competitive wares, it will increase its market power. This control of distribution outlets can be accomplished through selective discounts, long-term supply contracts, or expensive gifts at Christmas. Recall from Chapter 9 (see News, page 204) how Clear Channel and Ticketmaster locked up concert arenas. According to the U.S. Justice Department, Visa and MasterCard prevent banks that issue their credit cards from offering rival cards. Frito-Lay elbows out competing snack companies by paying high fees to "rent" shelf space in grocery stores (see the News on next page). Such up-front costs create an entry barrier for potential rivals. Even if a potential rival can come up with the up-front money, the owner of an arena or grocery store chain may not wish to anger the firm that dominates the market.

New car warranties also serve as an entry barrier. The warranties typically require regular maintenance at authorized dealerships and the exclusive use of authorized parts. These provisions limit the ability of would-be competitors to provide cheaper auto parts and service. Frequent-flier programs have similar effects in the airline industry.

IN THE NEWS

New Airline Accuses Rivals of Predatory Pricing Tactics

AccessAir, the nation's newest airline, accused three major competitors of using artificially low fares in an effort to drive it out of business just as airline competition and passenger rights have begun to emerge as part of the national political debate.

The Des Moines–based airline asked Transportation Secretary Rodney E. Slater to investigate charges that Trans World Airlines, Delta Air Lines and Northwest Airlines are offering fares so far below their costs that it amounts to illegal predatory pricing.

"Unfortunately, the expected bear hug by the major airlines has begun," AccessAir President D. Roger Ferguson wrote to Slater on Monday. "Three of the [major airlines] are now offering fares in AccessAir markets that are one-third below our fares—and far below both their normal fares and their costs. If continued, these fares will force us out of business."

—Frank Swoboda

Source: *The Washington Post,* March 17, 1999. © 1999 The Washington Post. Reprinted with permission. www.washingtonpost.com

Analysis: Predatory pricing entails the use of temporary price cuts to weaken the financial condition of rival companies. It can be used to enforce higher prices or otherwise reduce competition.

IN THE NEWS

Frito-Lay Devours Snack-Food Business

Once again, Frito-Lay is chewing up the competition.

The announcement Wednesday that Anheuser-Busch Cos. is selling off its Eagle Snacks business highlights the danger of trying to compete against Frito-Lay in the salty-snacks game. The company owns half of the $15 billion salty-snacks market.

"Frito's a fortress," says Michael Branca, an analyst at NatWest Securities. "And it continues to expand its realm. I'd tell anyone else trying to get into the business, don't try to expand, don't try to impinge on Frito's territory or you'll get crushed."

In fact, competitors say that it is Frito-Lay's tactics with retailers that make it an invincible foe. Because many retailers are charging more and more for shelf space—$40,000 a foot annually in some instances—many regional companies say Frito-Lay is paying retailers to squeeze out competing brands.

"Frito can afford it," says a regional snack company executive. "But we can't. It's become a real-estate business."

Frito-Lay can also afford to out-promote its competitors. In 1993, the company spent more than $60 million on advertising, while Eagle spent less than $2 million.

—Robert Frank

Snack-Food Giant

Frito-Lay's market share in various snack-food categories.

	Salty Snacks		Potato Chips		Tortilla Chips	
	1990	1995	1990	1995	1990	1995
Market share	43%	52%	45%	52%	63%	72%

Source: *The Wall Street Journal*, October 27, 1995. Reprinted by permission of The Wall Street Journal. © 1995 Dow Jones & Company. All rights reserved worldwide. www.wsj.com

Analysis: Barriers to entry such as self-space rental and advertising enable a firm to maintain market dominance. Acquisitions also reduce competition.

Mergers and Acquisition

Large and powerful firms can also limit competition by outright *acquisition*. A *merger* between two firms amounts to the same thing, although mergers often entail the creation of new corporate identities.

Perhaps the single most dramatic case of acquisition for this purpose occurred in the breakfast cereals industry. In 1946, General Foods acquired the cereal manufacturing facilities of Campbell Cereal Company, a substantial competitor. Following this acquisition, General Foods dismantled the production facilities of Campbell Cereal and shipped them off to South Africa!

Although the General Foods acquisition was more dramatic than most, acquisitions have been the most popular route to increased market power. General Motors attained a dominant share of the auto market largely by its success in merging with and acquiring two dozen independent manufacturers. In the cigarette industry, the American Tobacco Company attained monopoly powers by absorbing 250 independent companies. Later antitrust action (1911) split up the resultant tobacco monopoly into an oligopoly consisting of four companies, which continued to dominate the cigarette market until 2004, when R. J. Reynolds bought Brown & Williamson, leaving only three firms to dominate the cigarette industry. Other companies that came to dominate their product markets through mergers and acquisitions include U.S. Steel, U.S. Rubber, General Electric, United Fruit, National Biscuit Company, International Salt, and Ticketmaster. Frito-Lay's 1995 acquisitions of Eagle Snacks (see News) extended its already dominant control of the chip, pretzel, and nuts markets.

WEBNOTE

Vanderbilt University has an Antitrust Policy site that tracks news on mergers, price-fixing, and related issues. Visit www.Antitrust.org.

Government Regulation

The government often helps companies acquire and maintain control of market supply. Patents are issued by and enforced by the federal government and so represent one form of supply-restricting regulation. Barriers to international trade are another government-imposed barrier to entry. By limiting imports of everything from Chinese mushrooms to Japanese cars (see Chapter 20), the federal government reduces potential competition in U.S. product markets. Government regulation also limits *domestic* competition in many industries. From 1984 to 1990, the Federal Communications Commission (FCC) allowed only one company (GTE Corporation) to provide telephone service on airlines. When the FCC ended the monopoly in 1990, phone charges declined sharply.

New York City also limits competition—in this case, the number of taxicabs on the streets. The maximum number of cabs was set at 11,787 in 1937 and stayed at that ceiling until 1996. The city's Taxi and Limousine Commission raised the ceiling by a scant 400 cabs in 1996. That didn't do much to eliminate New York's perennial taxi shortage, much less reduce fares. As a result, license holders continue to reap monopoly-like profits. A good measure of those profits is the price of the medallions that the city sells as taxi licenses. The market price of a New York City taxi medallion—and thus the price of entry into the industry—was $205,000 in 2004. By contrast, a Washington, D.C., taxi license costs only $35, and fares are about half those in New York.

Nonprice Competition

Producers who control market supply can enhance their power even further by establishing some influence over market demand. The primary mechanism of control is *advertising.* To the extent that a firm can convince you that its product is essential to your well-being and happiness, it has effectively shifted your demand curve. ***Advertising not only strengthens brand loyalty but also makes it expensive for new producers to enter the market.*** A new entrant must buy both production facilities and advertising outlets.

The cigarette industry is a classic case of high concentration and product differentiation. As Table 10.2 shows, the top three cigarette companies produce 89 percent of all domestic output; small, generic firms produce the rest. Yet you would never guess that such high concentration exists in the industry if you glanced at the cigarette shelves at the local supermarket. Together, the three cigarette companies produce well over 100 brands. To solidify brand loyalties, the cigarette industry spent over $10 billion on advertising and promotions in 2004.

Another highly concentrated industry that advertises heavily is the $10 billion per year breakfast cereals industry. Although the Federal Trade Commission has suggested that "a corn flake is a corn flake no matter who makes it," the four firms (Kellogg, General Mills, Philip Morris, and Quaker Oats) that supply more than 90 percent of all ready-to-eat breakfast cereals spend over $400 million a year—about $1 per box!— to convince consumers otherwise. During the last 20 years, more than 200 brands of cereal have been marketed by these companies. As the FTC has documented, the four companies "produce basically similar RTE [ready-to-eat] cereals, and then emphasize and exaggerate trivial variations such as color and shape. . . . [They] employ trademarks to conceal such basic similarities and to differentiate cereal brands."[3]

Training

In today's technology-driven markets, early market entry can create an important barrier to later competition. Customers of computer hardware and software, for example, often become familiar with a particular system or computer package. To switch to a new product may entail significant cost, including the retraining of user staff. As a consequence, would-be competitors will find it difficult to sell their products even if they offer better quality and lower prices.

The popular Lotus 1-2-3 spreadsheet program illustrates this market barrier. Lotus Development Corporation introduced Lotus 1-2-3 in 1982 as one of the first spreadsheets for the IBM personal computer. By 1988, Lotus had 3.5 million copies of its program in use—82 percent of all spreadsheet sales. Although other software firms offered comparable (and even better) products at much lower prices, users were

[3]Complaint, *Kellogg Company et al.,* FTC Dkt. 8883 (1972).

reluctant to try new software that would require retraining. (IBM bought Lotus in 1995, further raising the entry barrier.) Microsoft gained a similar advantage by bundling Net-access and applications software with Windows. Once consumers become accustomed to Microsoft features, they're less inclined to purchase potential substitutes.

The widespread use of a particular product may also heighten its value to consumers, thereby making potential substitutes less viable. The utility of instant messaging—or even a telephone—depends on how many of your friends have computers or telephones. If no one else had a phone or computer, there'd be no reason to own one. In other words, the larger the network of users, the greater the value of the product. Such network economies help explain why software developers prefer to write Windows-based programs than programs for rival operating systems. Network economics also explains why Microsoft doesn't want computer manufacturers to display icons for rival instant-messaging services on the Windows XP desktop. Whichever instant-messaging service expands the quickest may achieve a network entry barrier.

Network Economies

THE ECONOMY TOMORROW

Examples of market power at work in product markets could be extended to the closing pages of this book. The few cases cited here, however, are testimony enough to the fact that market power has some influence on our lives. Market power *does* exist; market power *is* used. Although market power may result in economies of scale, the potential for abuse is evident. Market power contributes to **market failure** when it leads to resource misallocation (restricted output) or greater inequity (monopoly profits; higher prices).

What should we do about these abuses? Should we leave it to market forces to find ways of changing industry structure and behavior? Or should the government step in to curb noncompetitive practices?

Our primary concern is the *behavior* of market participants. What ultimately counts is the quantity of goods supplied to the market, their quality, and their price. Few consumers care about the underlying *structure* of markets; what we seek are good market *outcomes*.

In principle, the government could change industry behavior without changing industry structure. We could, for example, explicitly outlaw collusive agreements and cast a wary eye on industries that regularly exhibit price leadership. We could also dismantle barriers to entry and thereby promote contestable markets. We might also prohibit oligopolists from extending their market power via such mechanisms as acquisitions, excessive or deceptive advertising, and, alas, the financing of political campaigns. In fact, the existing **antitrust** laws—the Sherman Act, the Clayton Act, and the Federal Trade Commission Act (see Table 9.1)—explicitly forbid most of these practices.

There are several problems with this behavioral approach. The first limitation is scarce resources. Policing markets and penalizing noncompetitive conduct require more resources than the public sector can muster. Indeed, the firms being investigated often have more resources than the public watchdogs. The advertising expenditures of just one oligopolist, Procter & Gamble, are more than 10 times as large as the *combined* budgets of both the Justice Department's Antitrust Division and the Federal Trade Commission. As Ralph Nader has suggested, "The posture of two agencies with a combined budget of $20 million and 550 lawyers and economists trying to deal with

Antitrust Enforcement

market failure: An imperfection in the market mechanism that prevents optimal outcomes.

Industry Behavior

antitrust: Government intervention to alter market structure or prevent abuse of market power.

anticompetitive abuses in a trillion-dollar economy, not to mention an economy where the 200 largest corporations control two-thirds of all manufacturing assets, is truly a charade."[4]

The paucity of antitrust resources is partly a reflection of public apathy. Consumers generally are unaware of the relationship between market structure and their own economic welfare. They (and you) rarely think about the connection between market power and the price of the goods they buy, the wages they receive, or the way they live. As Ralph Nader discovered, "Antitrust violations are part of a phenomenon which, to the public is too complex, too abstract, and supremely dull."[5] As a result, there's little political pressure to regulate market behavior.

The behavioral approach also suffers from the "burden-of-proof" requirement. How often will "trustbusters" catch colluding executives in the act? More often than not, the case for collusion rests on such circumstantial evidence as simultaneous price hikes, identical bids, or other market outcomes. The charge of explicit collusion is hard to prove. Even in the absence of explicit collusion, however, consumers suffer. If an oligopoly price is higher than what a competitive industry would charge, consumers get stuck with the bill whether or not the price was "rigged" by explicit collusions. The U.S. Supreme Court recognized that consumers may suffer from *tacit* collusion, even where no *explicit* collusion occurs.

Industry Structure

The concept of tacit collusion directs attention to the *structure* of an industry. It essentially says that oligopolists and monopolists will act in their own best interest. As former Supreme Court Chief Justice Earl Warren observed, "An industry which does not have a competitive structure will not have competitive behavior."[6] To expect an oligopolist to disavow profit opportunities or to ignore its interdependence with fellow oligopolists is naive. It also violates the basic motivations imputed to a market economy. As long as markets are highly concentrated, we must expect to observe oligopolistic behavior.

Judge Learned Hand used these arguments to dismantle the Aluminum Company of America (Alcoa) in 1945. Alcoa wasn't charged with any illegal *behavior*. Nevertheless, the company controlled over 90 percent of the aluminum supplied to the market. This monopoly structure, the Supreme Court concluded, was itself a threat to the public interest.

Public efforts to alter market structure have been less frequent than efforts to alter market behavior. With the exception of the AT&T case (Chapter 9) and Alcoa, the few really concerted efforts to break up market concentration occurred at the beginning of the century, when Standard Oil and the Tobacco Trust were partially dismantled. In 2001, the Justice Department withdrew a proposal to break up Microsoft into separate systems and applications companies. The prevalent feeling today, even among antitrust practitioners, is that the powerful firms are too big and too entrenched to make deconcentration a viable policy alternative.

Objections to Antitrust

Some people think *less* antitrust activity is actually a wise policy. The companies challenged by the public "trustbusters" protest that they're being penalized for their success. Alcoa, for example, attained a monopoly by investing heavily in a new product before anyone else recognized its value. Other firms too have captured dominant market shares by being first, best, or most efficient. Having "won" the game fairly, why should they have to give up their prize? They contend that noncompetitive *behavior,* not industry *structure,* should be the only concern of antitrust.

---

[4]Mark J. Green et al., *The Closed Enterprise System: The Report on Antitrust Enforcement* (New York: Grossman, 1972), p. x.
[5]Ibid, p. ix.
[6]Ibid., p. 7.

Essentially the same argument is made for proposed mergers and acquisitions. The firms involved claim that the increased concentration will enhance productive efficiency (e.g., via economies of scale). They also argue that big firms are needed to maintain America's competitive position in international markets (which are themselves often dominated by foreign monopolies and oligopolies). Those same global markets, they contend, ensure that even highly concentrated domestic markets will be contested by international rivals.

Finally, critics of antitrust suggest that market forces themselves will ensure competitive behavior. Foreign firms and domestic entrepreneurs will stalk a monopolist's preserve. People will always be looking for ways to enter a profitable market. Monopoly or oligopoly power may slow entry but is unlikely to stop it forever. Eventually, competitive forces will prevail.

There are no easy answers. In theory, competition is valuable, but some mergers and acquisitions undoubtedly increase efficiency. Moreover, some international markets may require a minimum firm size not consistent with perfect competition. Finally, our regulatory resources are limited; not every acquisition or merger is worthy of public scrutiny.

Where would we draw the line? Can a firm hold a 22 percent market share, but not 30 percent? Are five firms too few, but six firms in an industry enough? Someone has to make those decisions. That is, ***the broad mandates of the antitrust laws must be transformed into specific guidelines for government intervention.***

In 1982, the Antitrust Division of the U.S. Department of Justice adopted specific guidelines for intervention based on industry *structure* alone. They're based on an index that takes into account the market share of *each* firm rather than just the *combined* market share of the top four firms. Specifically, the **Herfindahl-Hirshman Index (HHI)** of market concentration is calculated as

$$HHI = \sum_{i=1}^{n} = \left(\frac{\text{share of}}{\text{firm 1}}\right)^2 + \left(\frac{\text{share of}}{\text{firm 2}}\right)^2 + \cdots + \left(\frac{\text{share of}}{\text{firm } n}\right)^2$$

Thus, a three-firm oligopoly like that described in Table 10.3 would have an HHI value of

$$HHI = (10.0)^2 + (32.5)^2 + (27.5)^2 = 3,412.5$$

where the numbers in parentheses indicate the market shares of the three fictional computer companies. The calculation yields an HHI value of 3,412.5.

For policy purposes, the Justice Department decided it would draw the line at 1,800. Any merger that creates an HHI value over 1,800 will be challenged by the Justice Department. If an industry has an HHI value between 1,000 and 1,800, the Justice Department will challenge any merger that *increases* the HHI by 100 points or more. Mergers and acquisitions in industries with an HHI value of less than 1,000 won't be challenged.

The HHI is an arbitrary but workable tool for deciding when the government should intervene to challenge mergers and acquisitions. The Justice Department reviews about 2,500 mergers a year but challenges less than 50.

Even when intervention is signaled, however, there are still decisions to make. Should a challenged merger be allowed? The same old questions arise. Will the proposed merger enhance efficiency in domestic and global markets? Or will it tend to constrain competitive forces, keeping consumer prices high?

In 1992, the Justice Department broadened its antitrust focus. Rather than just look at the *existing* market structure, the department decided to examine entry barriers as well. If entry barriers were low enough, even a highly concentrated industry might be compelled to behave more competitively. In other words, *contestability* as well as *structure* now motivates antitrust decisions.

Structural Guidelines: The Herfindahl-Hirshman Index

Herfindahl-Hirshman Index (HHI): Measure of industry concentration that accounts for number of firms and size of each.

For concentration ratios and HHIs in U.S. industries, go to www.census.gov/epcd/concentration.html.

Contestability

Behavioral Guidelines: Cost Savings

In 1996, the Federal Trade Commission (FTC) moved even further away from strict *structural* (market share) criteria by deciding to take potential cost savings into account. Previously, the FTC and Justice Department had declined to consider greater efficiencies that might result from a merger. The focus was strictly on the structural threat to competition. Since 1996, the focus has shifted from the concept of "unfair competition" to an emphasis on consumer welfare. If companies can show how a merger or acquisition will result in greater efficiency and lower costs, they will get the green light from the trustbusters in the economy tomorrow.

SUMMARY

- Imperfect competition refers to markets in which individual suppliers (firms) have some independent influence on the price at which their output is sold. Examples of imperfectly competitive market structures are duopoly, oligopoly, and monopolistic competition.
- The extent of market power (control over price) depends on the number of firms in an industry, their size, barriers to entry, and the availability of substitutes.
- The concentration ratio is a measure of market power in a particular product market. It equals the share of total industry output accounted for by the largest firms, usually the top four.
- An oligopoly is a market structure in which a few firms produce all or most of a particular good or service; it's essentially a shared monopoly.
- Because oligopolies involve several firms rather than only one, each firm must consider the effect of its price and output decisions on the behavior of rivals. Such firms are highly interdependent.
- Game theory attempts to identify different strategies a firm might use, taking into account the consequences of rivals' moves and countermoves.
- The kinked demand curve illustrates a pattern of strategic interaction in which rivals match a price cut but not a price hike. Such behavior reinforces the oligopolistic aversion to price competition.
- A basic conflict exists between the desire of each individual oligopolist to expand its market share and the *mutual* interest of all the oligopolists in restricting total output so as to maximize industry profits. This conflict must be resolved in some way, via either collusion or some less explicit form of agreement (such as price leadership).
- Oligopolists may use price-fixing agreements or price leadership to establish the market price. To maintain that price, the oligopolists must also agree on their respective market shares.
- To maintain economic profits, an oligopoly must erect barriers to entry. Patents are one form of barrier. Other barriers include predatory price cutting (price wars), control of distribution outlets, government regulations, advertising (product differentiation), training, and network economies. Outright acquisition and merger may also eliminate competition.
- Market power may cause market failure. The symptoms of that failure include increased prices, reduced output, and a transfer of income from the consuming public to a relatively few powerful corporations and the people who own them.
- Government intervention may focus on either market structure or market behavior. In either case, difficult decisions must be made about when and how to intervene.
- The Herfindahl-Hirshman Index is a measure of industry concentration that takes into account the number of firms and the size of each. It is used as a structural guideline to identify cases worthy of antitrust concern.

Key Terms

market structure
oligopoly
contestable market
concentration ratio
oligopolist
market share
product differentiation

game theory
profit-maximization rule
marginal revenue (MR)
price-fixing
price leadership
cartel
predatory pricing

barriers to entry
market failure
antitrust
Herfindahl-Hirshman
    Index (HHI)

Questions for Discussion

1. How many bookstores are on or near your campus? If there were more bookstores, how would the price of new and used books be affected?
2. What entry barriers exist in (*a*) the fast-food industry, (*b*) cable television, (*c*) the auto industry, (*d*) illegal drug trade, (*e*) beauty parlors?
3. Why does RC Cola depend on advertising to gain market share? (See News, page 224.) Why not offer cheaper sodas than Coke or Pepsi?
4. Why would OPEC members have a difficult time setting and maintaining a monopoly price? (See World View, page 230.)
5. If an oligopolist knows rivals will match a price cut, would he ever reduce his price?
6. How might the high concentration ratio in the credit card industry (Table 10.2) affect the annual fees and interest charges on credit card services?
7. Identify three products you purchase that aren't listed in Table 10.2. What's the structure of those three markets?
8. What reasons might Northwest Airlines have for *not* matching its rivals' fare increases? (See News, page 227.)
9. The Ivy League schools defended their price-fixing arrangement (see News, page 233) by arguing that their coordination assured a fair distribution of scholarship aid. Who was hurt or helped by this arrangement?
10. Using the payoff matrix in Table 10.4, decide whether Universal should cut its price. What factors will influence the decision?
11. Dominos and Pizza Hut hold 66 percent of the delivered-pizza market. Should antitrust action be taken?

ALERT!

PROBLEMS   The Student Problem Set at the back of this book contains numerical and graphing problems for this chapter.

WEB ACTIVITIES   to accompany this chapter can be found on the Online Learning Center: **http://www.mhhe.com/economics/schiller10**

Monopolistic Competition

Starbucks is already the biggest coffee bar chain in the country, with roughly 8,000 locations on four continents. And the company is determined to keep growing by setting up coffee bars in airports, department stores, and just about anywhere consumers congregate. Even if Starbucks achieves such meteoric growth, however, it will never have great market power. There are more than 9,000 other coffee bars in the United States, not to mention a million or so other places you can buy a cup of coffee (e.g., Dunkin' Donuts). With so many other close substitutes, the best Starbucks can hope for is a little brand loyalty. If enough consumers think of Starbucks when they get the caffeine urge, Starbucks will at least be able to charge more for coffee than a perfectly competitive firm. It won't enjoy *monopoly* profits, or even share the kind of monopoly profits *oligopolies* sometimes achieve. It may, however, be able to maintain an economic profit for many years.

Starbucks is an example of yet another market structure—*monopolistic competition*. In this chapter we focus on how such firms make price and output decisions and the market outcomes that result. Our objective is to determine

- **The unique features of monopolistic competition.**
- **How market outcomes are affected by this market structure.**
- **The long-run consequences of different market structures.**

In this chapter we'll also see why we can't escape the relentless advertising that bombards us from every angle.

STRUCTURE

As we first noted in Table 10.1, the distinguishing structural characteristic of **monopolistic competition** is that there are *many* firms in an industry. "Many" isn't an exact specification, of course. It's best understood as lying somewhere between the few that characterize oligopoly and the hordes that characterize perfect competition.

A more precise way to distinguish monopolistic competition is to examine **concentration ratios.** Oligopolies have very high four-firm concentration ratios. As we saw in Chapter 10 (Table 10.2), concentration ratios of 70 to 100 percent are common in oligopolies. By contrast, there's much less concentration in monopolistic competition. A few firms may stand above the rest, but the combined market share of the top four firms will typically be in the range of 20 to 40 percent. Hence, *low concentration ratios are common in monopolistic competition.*

Starbucks has less than 15 percent of the coffee bar business and a mere 7 percent of all coffee sales. The top four coffee bar outlets (Starbucks, Second Cup, The Coffee Beanery, and Barnie's) have a concentration ratio of only 28 percent

monopolistic competition: A market in which many firms produce similar goods or services but each maintains some independent control of its own price.

Low Concentration

concentration ratio: The proportion of total industry output produced by the largest firms (usually the four largest).

TABLE 11.1
Monopolistic Competition

Monopolistically competitive industries are characterized by modest concentration ratios and low entry barriers. Contrast these four-firm concentration ratios with those of oligopoly (see Table 10.2).

Product	Largest Firms (market share)	Concentration Ratio (%)
Movie studios	Paramount (15.8%), Disney (15.7%), 20th Century Fox (10.8%), Sony (10.6%)	53%
Personal computers	Dell (15%), Hewlett-Packard (14%), IBM (6%), NEC (3%)	38
Auto tires (replacement)	Goodyear (16%), Michelin (8%), Firestone (7.5%), General (5%)	36
Bottled water	PepsiCo (Aquafina 15.8%), Coca-Cola (Dasani 8.7%), Perrier (Poland Spring, 6.4%), Dannon (5.3%)	36
Toys	Hasbro (15%), Mattel (11%), Tyco (5%), Fisher-Price (4%)	35
Coffee bars	Starbucks (15%), Second Cup (9%), Coffee Beanery (3%), Barnie's (1.5%)	28
Drugs	Glaxo-Wellcome (5.8%), Hoechst-Marion Merrell Dow (4.4%), Merck (4.4%), American Home Products (3.8%)	18

Source: Industry sources and business publications (2000–2004 data).

(see Table 11.1). Other examples of monopolistic competition include banks, radio stations, health spas, apparel stores, convenience stores, and law firms. Notice in Table 11.1 that the personal computer market now has a monopolistically competitive structure as well. Even as large a firm as McDonald's might be regarded as a monopolistic competitor. Although "Mickey D's" has a huge share (40 percent) of the quickie *hamburger* market, its share of the much larger *fast-food* market is significantly smaller. The 12,000+ McDonald's outlets in the United States compete with over 200,000 fast-food outlets. If consumers regard pizzas, Chinese carry-outs, and delis as close substitutes for hamburgers, then the broader fast-food market is the appropriate basis for measuring market power and concentration.

Although concentration rates are low in monopolistic competition, the individual firms aren't powerless. There is a *monopoly* aspect to monopolistic competition. Each producer in monopolistic competition is large enough to have some **market power.** If a perfectly competitive firm increases the price of its product, it will lose all its customers. Recall that a perfectly competitive firm confronts a horizontal demand curve for its output. Competition is less intense in monopolistic competition. *A monopolistically competitive firm confronts a downward-sloping demand curve for its output.* When Starbucks increases the price of coffee, it loses some customers, but nowhere close to all of them (see News, next page). Starbucks, like other monopolistically competitive firms, has some control over the price of its output. This is the *monopoly* dimension of monopolistic competition.

In an oligopoly, a firm that increased its price would have to worry about how rivals might respond. In monopolistic competition, however, there are many more firms. As a result, *modest changes in the output or price of any single firm will have no perceptible influence on the sales of any other firm.* This relative independence results

Market Power

market power: The ability to alter the market price of a good or service.

Independent Production Decisions

Analysis: A monopolistically-competitive firm has the power to increase price unilaterally. The greater the brand loyalty, the less unit sales will decline in response.

from the fact that the effects of any one firm's behavior will be spread over many other firms (rather than only two or three other firms, as in an oligopoly).

The relative independence of monopolistic competitors means that they don't have to worry about retaliatory responses to every price or output change. As a result, they confront more traditional demand curves, with no kinks. The kink in the oligopolist's curve results from the likelihood that rival oligopolists would match any price reduction (to preserve market shares) but not necessarily any price increase (to increase their shares). In monopolistic competition, the market shares of rival firms aren't perceptibly altered by one firm's price changes.

Low Entry Barriers

barriers to entry: Obstacles, such as patents, that make it difficult or impossible for would-be producers to enter a particular market.

Another characteristic of monopolistic competition is the presence of *low* **barriers to entry**—it's relatively easy to get in and out of the industry. To become a coffee vendor, all you need is boiling water, some fresh beans, and cups. You can save on rent by using a pushcart to dispense the brew. These unusually low entry barriers keep Starbucks and other coffee bars on their toes. Low entry barriers also tend to push economic profits toward zero. This is the *competitive* dimension of monopolistic competition.

BEHAVIOR

Given the unique structural characteristics of monopolistic competition we should anticipate some distinctive behavior.

Product Differentiation

product differentiation: Features that make one product appear different from competing products in the same market.

One of the most notable features of monopolistically competitive behavior is **product differentiation.** A monopolistically competitive firm is distinguished from a purely competitive firm by its downward-sloping demand curve. Individual firms in a perfectly competitive market confront horizontal demand curves because consumers view their respective products as interchangeable (homogeneous). As a result, an attempt by one firm to raise its price will drive its customers to other firms.

Brand Image. In monopolistic competition, each firm has a distinct identity—a *brand image*. Its output is perceived by consumers as being somewhat different from the output of all other firms in the industry. Nowhere is this more evident than in the

Analysis: By differentiating their products, monopolistic competitors establish brand loyalty. Brand loyalty gives producers greater control over the price of their products.

fast-growing bottled water industry. Pepsi and Coke have become the leaders in the bottled water market as a result of effective marketing (see News above). Although Aquafina (Pepsi) and Dasani (Coke) are just filtered municipal water, clever advertising campaigns have convinced consumers that these branded waters are different— and better—than hundreds of other bottled waters. As a result of such product differentiation, Pepsi and Coke can raise the price of their bottled waters without losing all their customers to rival firms.

At first blush, the demand curve facing a monopolistically competitive firm looks like the demand curve confronting a monopolist. There's a profound difference, however. In a monopoly, there are no other firms. In monopolistic competition, *each firm has a monopoly only on its brand image; it still competes with other firms offering close substitutes.* This implies that the extent of power a monopolistically competitive firm has depends on how successfully it can differentiate its product from that of other firms. The more brand loyalty a firm can establish, the less likely consumers are to switch brands when price is increased. In other words, *brand loyalty makes the demand curve facing the firm less price-elastic.*

Brand Loyalty

Brand loyalty exists even when products are virtually identical. Gasoline of a given octane rating is a very standardized product. Nevertheless, most consumers regularly buy one particular brand. Because of that brand loyalty, Texaco can raise the price of its gasoline by a penny or two a gallon without losing its customers to competing companies. According to the accompanying News feature, brand loyalty is particularly high for cigarettes, toothpaste, and even laxatives. Brand loyalty is less strong for paper towels and virtually nonexistent for tomatoes.

In the computer industry, product differentiation has been used to establish brand loyalty. Although virtually all computers use identical microprocessor "brains" and operating platforms, the particular mix of functions performed on any computer can be varied, as can its appearance (packaging). Effective advertising can convince consumers that one computer is "smarter," more efficient, or more versatile than another. Also, a single firm may differentiate itself by providing faster or more courteous customer

Who Can Be Loyal to a Trash Bag?

When generic products were coming on strong a few years ago, J. Walter Thompson, the New York–based ad agency, gauged consumers' loyalty to brands in 80 product categories. It found that the leader in market share was not necessarily the brand-loyalty leader. At that time, Bayer aspirin was the market share leader among headache remedies, but Tylenol had the most loyal following.

Thompson measured the degree of loyalty by asking people whether they'd switch for a 50 percent discount. Cigarette smokers most often said no, making them the most brand-loyal of consumers (see table). Film is the only one of the top five products that the user doesn't put in his mouth—so why such loyalty? According to Edith Gilson, Thompson's senior vice president of research, 35-mm film is used by photography buffs, who are not your average snapshooter: "It's for long-lasting emotionally valued pictures, taken by someone who has invested a lot of money in his camera." Plenty of shoppers will try a different cola for 50 percent off, and most consumers think one plastic garbage bag or facial tissue is much like another.

—Anne B. Fisher

High-Loyalty Products	Medium-Loyalty Products	Low-Loyalty Products
Cigarettes	Cola drinks	Paper towels
Laxatives	Margarine	Crackers
Cold remedies	Shampoo	Scouring powder
35-mm film	Hand lotion	Plastic trash bags
Toothpaste	Furniture polish	Facial tissue

Brand names matter more in some products than in others, researchers find.

Analysis: Brand loyalty implies that consumers shun substitute goods even when they are cheaper. This renders the demand curve less price-elastic.

service. If successful in any of these efforts, ***each monopolistically competitive firm will establish some consumer loyalty.*** With such loyalty a firm can alter its own price somewhat, without fear of great changes in unit sales (quantity demanded). In other words, the demand curve facing each firm will slope downward, as in Figure 11.1a.

One symptom of brand loyalty is consumers' tendency to repurchase the same brand. Nearly 9 out of 10 Apple Macintosh users stick with Apple products when they upgrade or replace computer components. Repurchase rates are 74 percent for Dell, 72 percent for Hewlett-Packard, and 66 percent for Gateway.

Another symptom of brand loyalty is the price differences between computer brands. Consumers are willing to pay more for an HP- or Dell-branded computer than a no-name computer with identical features. For the same reason, consumers are willing to pay more for Starbuck's coffee or ice cream, even when identical products are available at lower prices.

Short-Run Price and Output

production decision: The selection of the short-run rate of output (with existing plant and equipment).

The monopolistically competitive firm's **production decision** is similar to that of a monopolist. Both types of firms confront downward-sloping demand and marginal revenue curves. To maximize profits, both seek the rate of output at which marginal revenue equals marginal cost. This short-run profit-maximizing outcome is illustrated by point K in Figure 11.1a. That MC = MR intersection establishes q_a as the profit-maximizing rate of output. The demand curve indicates (point F) that q_a of output can be sold at the price of p_a. Hence q_a, p_a illustrates the short-run equilibrium of the monopolistically competitive firm.

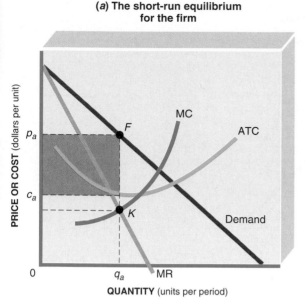

(a) The short-run equilibrium for the firm

(b) The long-run equilibrium for the firm

FIGURE 11.1

Equilibrium in Monopolistic Competition

(a) Short run   In the short run, a monopolistically competitive firm equates marginal revenue and marginal cost (point K). In this case, the firm sells the resulting output at a price (point F) above marginal cost. Total profits are represented by the shaded rectangle.

(b) Long run   In the long run, more firms enter the industry. As they do so, the demand curve facing each firm *shifts* to the left, as all market shares decline. Firms still equate MR and MC. Ultimately, however, the demand curve will be tangent to the ATC curve (point G), at which point price equals average total cost and no economic profits exist.

Figure 11.1*a* indicates that this monopolistically competitive firm is earning an **economic profit:** Price (p_a) exceeds average total cost (c_a) at the short-run rate of output. These profits are of course a welcome discovery for the firm. They also portend increased competition, however.

If firms in monopolistic competition are earning an economic profit, other firms will flock to the industry. Remember that *entry barriers are low in monopolistic competition so new entrants can't be kept out of the market.* If they get wind of the short-run profits depicted in Figure 11.1*a*, they'll come running.

As new firms enter the industry, supply increases and prices will be pushed down the market demand curve, just as in competitive markets. Figure 11.2*a* illustrates these market changes. The initial price p_1 is set by the intersection of *industry* MC and MR. Because that price generates a profit, more firms enter. This entry shifts the *industry* cost structure to the right, creating a new equilibrium price, p_2.

The impact of this entry on the firms already in the market will be different from that in competitive markets, however. As new firms enter a monopolistically competitive industry, existing firms will lose customers. This is illustrated by the leftward shift of the demand curve facing each firm, as in Figure 11.2*b*. Accordingly, we conclude that *when firms enter a monopolistically competitive industry,*

- *The industry cost curves shift to the right, pushing down price* (Figure 11.2*a*).
- *The demand curves facing individual firms shift to the left* (Figure 11.2*b*).

As the demand curve it faces shifts leftward, the monopolistically competitive firm will have to make a new production decision. It need not charge the same price as its rivals, however, or coordinate its output with theirs. Each monopolistically competitive firm has some independent power over its (shrinking numbers of) captive customers.

Entry and Exit

economic profit: The difference between total revenues and total economic costs.

(a) Effect of entry on the industry

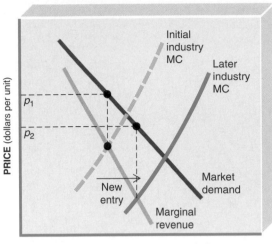

(b) Effect of entry on the monopolistically competitive firm

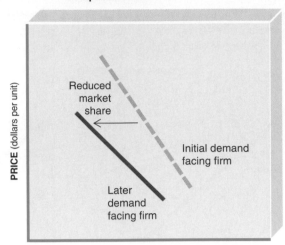

FIGURE 11.2
Market vs. Firm Effects of Entry

Barriers to entry are low in monopolistic competition. Hence, new firms will enter if economic profits are available.

(*a*) **The Market**   The entry of new firms will shift the *market* cost curves to the right, as in part *a*. This pushes the average price down the *market* demand curve.

(*b*) **The Firm**   The entry of new firms also affects the demand curve facing the typical firm. The *firm's* demand curve shifts to the left and becomes more elastic because more close substitutes (other firms) are available.

No Long-Run Profits

Although each firm has some control over its own pricing decisions, continued leftward shifts of its demand curve will ultimately eliminate economic profits.

Long-run Equilibrium. Notice in Figure 11.1*b* where the firm eventually ends up. In long-run equilibrium, marginal cost is again equal to marginal revenue. At that rate of output (q_g), however, there are no economic profits. At that output, price (p_g) is exactly equal to average total cost. The profit-maximizing equilibrium (point *G*) occurs where the demand curve is tangent to the ATC curve. If the demand curve shifted any farther left, price would always be less than ATC and the firm would incur losses. If the demand curve were positioned farther to the right, price would exceed ATC at some rates of output. When the demand curve is *tangent* to the ATC curve, the firm's best possible outcome is to break even. At point *G* in Figure 11.1*b*, price equals ATC and economic profit is zero.

Will a monopolistically competitive firm end up at point *G*? As long as other firms can enter the industry, the disappearance of economic profits is inevitable. Firms will enter as long as the demand (price) line lies above ATC at some point. Firms will exit when the demand facing the firm lies to the left and below the ATC curve. Entry and exit cease when the firm's demand curve is *tangent* to the ATC curve. Once entry and exit cease, the long-run equilibrium has been established. *In the long run, there are no economic profits in monopolistic competition.*

Inefficiency

The zero-profit equilibrium of firms in monopolistic competition, as illustrated in Figure 11.1*b*, differs from the perfectly competitive equilibrium. In the long run, a competitive industry produces at the *lowest* point on the ATC curve and thus maximizes efficiency. In monopolistic competition, however, the demand curve facing each firm slopes downward. Hence, it can't be tangent to the ATC curve at its lowest point (the bottom of the U), as in perfect competition. Instead, the demand curve of a monopolistically competitive firm must touch the ATC curve on the *left* side of the U. Note in

Figure 11.1*b* how point *G* lies above and to the left of the bottom of the ATC curve. This long-run equilibrium occurs at an output rate that is less than the minimum-cost rate of production. In long-run equilibrium, the monopolistically competitive industry isn't producing at minimum average cost. As a consequence, *monopolistic competition tends to be less efficient in the long run than a perfectly competitive industry.*

Excess Capacity. One symptom of the inefficiencies associated with monopolistic competition is industrywide excess capacity. Each firm tries to gain market share by building more outlets and advertising heavily. In equilibrium, however, the typical firm is producing at a rate of output that's less than its minimum-ATC output rate. This implies that the *same* level of *industry* output could be produced at lower cost with fewer firms. If that happened, the resources used to develop that excess capacity could be used for more desired purposes.

Flawed Price Signals. The misallocation of resources that occurs in monopolistic competition is a by-product of the flawed price signal that is transmitted in imperfectly competitive markets. Because the demand curve facing a firm in monopolistic competition slopes downward, such a firm will violate the principle of **marginal cost pricing.** Specifically, it will always price its output above the level of marginal costs, just like firms in an oligopoly or monopoly. Notice in Figure 11.1 that price lies above marginal cost in both the short- and long-run equilibrium. As a consequence, price always exceeds the opportunity cost. Consumers respond to these flawed signals by demanding fewer goods from monopolistically competitive industries than they would otherwise. We end up with the wrong (suboptimal) mix of output and misallocated resources.

Thus, *monopolistic competition results in both production inefficiency (above-minimum average cost) and allocative inefficiency (wrong mix of output).* This contrasts with the model of perfect competition, which delivers both minimum average total cost and efficient (MC-based) price signals.

> **marginal cost pricing:** The offer (supply) of goods at prices equal to their marginal cost.

No Cease-Fire in Advertising Wars

Models of oligopoly and monopolistic competition show how industry structure affects market behavior. Of particular interest is the way different kinds of firms "compete" for sales and profits. *In truly (perfectly) competitive industries, firms compete on the basis of price.* Competitive firms win by achieving greater efficiency and offering their products at the lowest possible price.

Firms in imperfectly competitive markets don't "compete" in the same way. In oligopolies, the kink commonly found in the demand curve facing each firm inhibits price reductions. In monopolistic competition, there's also a reluctance to engage in price competition. Because each firm has its own captive market—consumers who prefer its particular brand over competing brands—price reductions by one firm won't induce many consumers to switch brands. Thus, price reductions aren't a very effective way to increase sales or market share in monopolistic competition.

If imperfectly competitive firms don't compete on the basis of price, do they really compete at all? The answer is evident to anyone who listens to the radio, watches television, reads magazines or newspapers, or drives on the highway: *Imperfectly competitive firms engage in nonprice competition.*

The most prominent form of *nonprice competition* is advertising. An imperfectly competitive firm typically uses advertising to enhance its own product's image, thereby increasing the size of its captive market (consumers who identify with a particular brand). The Coca-Cola Company hires rock stars to create the image that Coke is superior to other soft drinks (see News), thereby creating brand loyalty. In 2003, oligopolies and monopolistic competitive firms spent over $300 *billion* on advertising for such purposes. Procter & Gamble alone spent $3.3 billion (see Table 11.2). P&G

The Cola Wars: It's Not All Taste

American consumers gulp nearly 40 million soft drinks per day. The Coca-Cola Company produces about 40 percent of those soft drinks, while Pepsi-Cola produces about 30 percent of the market supply. With nearly 70 percent of the market between them, Pepsi and Coke wage fierce battles for market share.

The major weapon in these "cola wars" is advertising. Coke spends over $900 million a year to convince consumers that its products are superior. Pepsi spends almost as much to win the hearts and taste buds of American consumers. The advertisements not only tout the superior taste of their respective products but also try to create a particular image for each cola.

The advertising apparently works. Half of all soft drink consumers profess loyalty to either Coke or Pepsi. In their view, there's only one "real" cola, and that's the one they'll buy every time. Few of these loyalists can be persuaded to switch cola brands, even when offered lower prices for the "other" cola.

Ironically, few people can identify their favorite cola in blind taste tests. Seventy percent of the people who swore loyalty to either Coke or Pepsi picked the wrong cola in a taste test.

The moral of the story? That in imperfectly competitive markets, product *image* and *perceptions* may be as important as product quality and price in winning market shares.

Analysis: Advertising is intended to create brand loyalty. Loyal consumers are likely to buy the same brand all the time, even if competitors offer nearly identical products.

---

hopes that these expenditures shift the demand for its products (e.g., Ivory Soap, Pampers, Jif peanut butter, Crest, Tide) to the right, while perhaps making it less price-elastic as well. America Online, Yahoo!, and Amazon.com spent hundreds of millions of dollars in the 1990s to establish brand loyalty in crowded dot.com markets. By contrast, perfectly competitive firms have no incentive to advertise because they can individually sell their entire output at the current market price.

A company that runs a successful advertising campaign can create enormous *goodwill* value. That value is reflected in stronger brand loyalty—as expressed in greater demand and smaller price elasticity. Often a successful brand image can be used to sell related products as well. According to the World View, the most valuable brand name in the world is Coca-Cola, whose worldwide name recognition is worth nearly $70 *billion*.

Advertising isn't the only form of nonprice competition. Before the airline industry was deregulated (1978), individual airlines were compelled to charge the same price for any given trip; hence, price competition was prohibited. But airlines did compete—not only by advertising, but also by offering "special" meals, movies, more frequent or convenient departures, and faster ticketing and baggage services.

WEBNOTE

Forecasts of advertising spending can be found at www.myersreport.com.

TABLE 11.2
Top 10 Advertisers

Firms with market power attempt to preserve and extend that power through advertising. A successful advertising campaign alters the demand curve facing the firm, thus increasing potential profits. Shown here are the advertising outlays of the biggest advertisers in 2003.

Company	Ad Spending in 2003 ($billion)
General Motors	$3.4 billion
Procter & Gamble	3.3
TimeWarner	3.1
Pfizer	2.8
DaimlerChrysler	2.3
Ford Motor	2.2
Walt Disney Company	2.2
Johnson & Johnson	2.0
Sony Corporation	1.8
Toyota Motor Corp.	1.7

Source: *Ad Age*, June 28, 2004. Reprinted by permission. www.adage.com

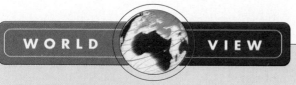

WORLD VIEW

The Best Global Brands

A belief in the power of brands and brand management has spread far beyond the traditional consumer-goods marketers who invented the discipline. For companies in almost every industry, brands are important in a way they never were before. Why? For one thing, customers for everything from soda pop to software now have a staggering number of choices. And the Net can bring the full array to any computer screen with a click of the mouse. Without trusted brand names as touchstones, shopping for almost anything would be overwhelming. Meanwhile, in a global economy, corporations must reach customers in markets far from their home base. A strong brand acts as an ambassador when companies enter new markets or offer new products.

That's why companies that once measured their worth strictly in terms of tangibles such as factories, inventory, and cash have realized that a vibrant brand, with its implicit promise of quality, is an equally important asset. A brand has the power to command a premium price among customers and a premium stock price among investors. It can boost earnings and cushion cyclical downturns—and now, a brand's value can be measured.

The World's 10 Most Valuable Brands

Rank	Brand	2003 Brand Value ($billions)
1	Coca-Cola	67.4
2	Microsoft	61.4
3	IBM	53.8
4	GE	44.1
5	Intel	33.5
6	Disney	27.1
7	McDonald's	25.0
8	Nokia	24.0
9	Toyota	22.3
10	Marlboro	22.1

Data: Interbrand, Citigroup.

Source: *BusinessWeek*, August 6, 2001 and August 2, 2004. © 2004 The McGraw Hill Companies, Inc. Reprinted with permission www.businessweek.com

Analysis: Brand names are valuable economic assets and assist a firm in maintaining a base of loyal customers. These brands have worldwide recognition as a result of heavy advertising.

Is there anything wrong with nonprice competition? Surely airline passengers enjoyed their "special" meals, "extra" services, and "more convenient" departure times. But these services weren't free. As always, there were opportunity costs. From an air traveler's perspective, the "special" services stimulated by nonprice competition substituted for cheaper fares. With more price competition, customers could have chosen travel more cheaply *or* in greater comfort. From society's perspective, the resources used in advertising and other forms of nonprice competition could be used instead to produce larger quantities of desired goods and services (including airplane trips). Unless consumers are given the chance to *choose* between "more" service and lower prices, there's a presumption that nonprice competition leads to an undesirable use of our scarce resources. For example, marketing costs absorb over a third of the price of breakfast cereal. As a result of such behavior, consumers end up with more advertising but less cereal than they would otherwise. They could, of course, save money by buying store brand or generic cereals. But they've never seen athletes or cartoon characters endorse such products. So consumers pay the higher price for branded cereals.

Models of imperfect competition imply that advertising wars between powerful corporations won't end anytime soon. As long as markets have the *structure* of oligopoly or monopolistic competition, we expect the *behavior* of nonprice competition. Advertising jingles will be as pervasive in the economy tomorrow as they are today.

SUMMARY

- There are many (rather than few) firms in monopolistic competition. The concentration ratio in such industries tends to be low (20–40 percent).
- Each monopolistically competitive firm enjoys some brand loyalty. This brand loyalty, together with its relatively small market share, gives each firm a high degree of independence in price and output decisions.
- The amount of market share and power a monopolistically competitive firm possesses depends on how successfully it differentiates its product from similar products. Accordingly, monopolistically competitive firms tend to devote more resources to advertising.
- Low entry barriers permit new firms to enter a monopolistically competitive industry whenever economic profits

exist. Such entry eliminates long-run economic profit and reduces (shifts leftward) the demand for the output of existing firms.
- Monopolistic competition results in resource misallocations (due to flawed price signals) and inefficiency (above-minimum average cost).
- Monopolistic competition encourages nonprice competition instead of price competition. Because the resources used in nonprice competition (advertising, packaging, service, etc.) may have more desirable uses, these industry structures lead to resource misallocation.

Key Terms

monopolistic competition
concentration ratio
market power

barriers to entry
product differentiation
production decision

economic profit
marginal cost pricing

Questions for Discussion

1. Why does Starbucks worry less about a potential "fall off" than does Maxwell House (News, p. 246)?
2. What are the entry barriers to the pizza business? Are they relatively high or low?
3. If auto firms eliminated their advertising, could they reduce car prices? What would happen to unit sales?
4. If one gas station reduces its prices, must other gas stations match the price reduction? Why or why not?
5. The News article on page 252 suggests that most consumers can't identify their favorite cola in blind taste tests. Why then do people stick with one brand? What accounts for brand loyalty in bottled water (News, p. 247)?
6. What kinds of resources are used in a TV advertising campaign? How else might those resources be used?
7. Why is the mix of output produced in competitive markets more desirable than that in monopolistically competitive markets?
8. How would our consumption of cereal change if cereal manufacturers stopped advertising? Would we be better or worse off?
9. Why are people willing to pay more for Dreyer's ice cream when it has a Starbucks brand on it?
10. According to the World View on page 253, what gives brand names their value?

ALERT!

PROBLEMS The Student Problem Set at the back of this book contains numerical and graphing problems for this chapter.

WEB ACTIVITIES to accompany this chapter can be found on the Online Learning Center:
http://www.mhhe.com/economics/schiller10

PART 4

Regulatory Issues

Microeconomic theory provides insights into how prices and product flows are determined in unregulated markets. Sometimes those market outcomes are not optimal and the government intervenes to improve them. In this section we examine government regulation of natural monopolies (Chapter 12), environmental protection (Chapter 13), and farm output and prices (Chapter 14). The goal is to determine whether and how government regulation might improve market outcomes or worsen them.

(De)Regulation of Business

The lights went out in California in 2001—not just once but repeatedly. Offices went dark, air conditioners shut down, assembly lines stopped, and TV screens went blank. The state governor blamed power-company "profiteers" for the rolling blackouts. He charged the companies with curtailing power supplies and hiking prices. He wanted *more* regulation of the power industry. Industry representatives responded that government regulation was itself responsible for throwing California into a new Dark Age. *Less* regulation, not more, would keep the lights on, they claimed.

The battle over government regulation of the power industry quickly spread to other states. Some states that were deregulating power companies suspended the process. Other states also put (de)regulation plans on hold until they could better assess what went wrong in California.

Everyone agrees that markets sometime fail—that unregulated markets may produce the wrong mix of output, undesirable methods of production, or an unfair distribution of income. But government intervention can fail as well. Hence, we need to ask,

- **When is government regulation necessary?**
- **What form should that regulation take?**
- **When is it appropriate to deregulate an industry?**

In answering these questions we draw on economic principles as well as recent experience. This will permit us to contrast the theory of (de)regulation with reality.

ANTITRUST VS. REGULATION

A perfectly competitive market provides a model for economic efficiency. As we first observed in Chapter 3, the market mechanism can answer the basic economic questions of WHAT to produce, HOW to produce it, and FOR WHOM. Under ideal conditions, the market's answers may also be optimal—that is, they may represent the best possible mix of output. To achieve this **laissez-faire** ideal, all producers must be perfect competitors; people must have full information about tastes, costs and prices; all costs and benefits must be reflected in market prices; and pervasive economies of scale must be absent.

In reality, these conditions are rarely if ever fully attained. Markets may be dominated by large and powerful producers. In wielding their power, these producers may restrict output, raise prices, stifle competition, and inhibit innovation. In other words, market power may cause **market failure,** leaving us with suboptimal market outcomes.

As we observed in Chapter 10, the government has two options for intervention where market power prevails. It may focus on the *structure* of an industry or on its

laissez faire: The doctrine of "leave it alone," or nonintervention by government in the market mechanism.

market failure: An imperfection in the market mechanism that prevents optimal outcomes.

Behavioral Focus

behavior. **Antitrust** laws cover both options: They prohibit mergers and acquisitions that reduce potential competition (structures) and forbid market practices (behavior) that are anticompetitive.

Government **regulation** has a different focus. Instead of worrying about industry structure, regulation focuses almost exclusively on *behavior.* In general, regulation seeks to change market outcomes directly, by imposing specific limitations on price, output, or investment decisions.

NATURAL MONOPOLY

When a natural monopoly exists, the choice between structural remedies and behavioral remedies is simplified. A **natural monopoly** is a *desirable* market structure, because it generates pervasive economies of scale. Because of these scale economies, a natural monopoly can produce the products consumers want at the lowest possible price. A single cable company is more efficient than a horde of cable firms developing a maze of cable networks. The same is true of local telephone service and many utilities. In all of these cases, a single company can deliver products at lower cost than a bunch of smaller firms. Dismantling such a natural monopoly would destroy that cost advantage. Hence, *regulation,* not antitrust, is the more sensible intervention.

Do we need to regulate natural monopolies? Even though a natural monopoly might enjoy economies of scale, it might not pass those savings along to consumers. In that case, the economies of scale don't do consumers any good, and the government might have to regulate the firm's behavior.

To determine whether regulation is desirable, we first have to determine how an *unregulated* natural monopoly will behave.

Figure 12.1 illustrates the unique characteristics of a natural monopoly. *The distinctive characteristic of a natural monopoly is its downward-sloping average total cost (ATC) curve.* Because unit costs keep falling as the rate of production increases, a single large firm can underprice any smaller firm. Ultimately, it can produce all the

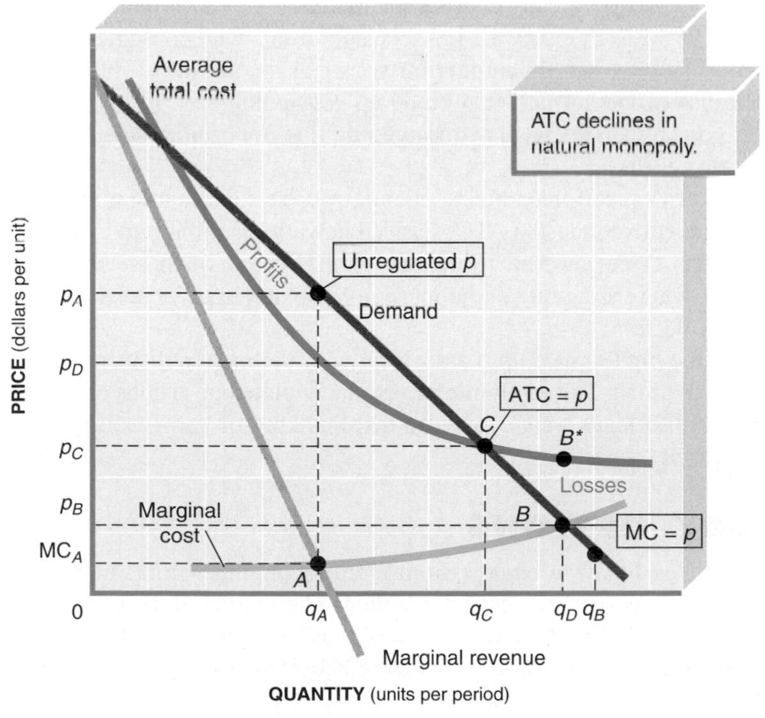

antitrust: Government intervention to alter market structure or prevent abuse of market power.

regulation: Government intervention to alter the behavior of firms, for example, in pricing, output, or advertising.

natural monopoly: An industry in which one firm can achieve economies of scale over the entire range of market supply.

Declining ATC Curve

FIGURE 12.1
Natural Monopoly: Price Regulation

A natural monopoly confronts a downward-sloping ATC curve; MC is always less than ATC. If unregulated, a natural monopoly will produce q_A and charge p_A, as determined by the intersection of the marginal cost and marginal revenue curves (point *A*).

Regulation designed to achieve efficient prices will seek point *B*, where p = MC. Still lower average costs (production efficiency) are attainable at higher rates of output, however. On the other hand, a zero-profit, zero-subsidy outcome exists only at point *C*.

Which price-output combination should be sought?

market supply at the lowest attainable cost. In an unregulated market, such a firm will "naturally" come to dominate the industry.

The force that pulls down the ATC curve in a natural monopoly is low marginal cost. Notice in Figure 12.1 that *the marginal cost (MC) curve lies below the ATC curve at all rates of output for a natural monopoly.* The ATC curve never rises into its conventional U shape because marginal costs never exceed average costs.

Subway systems, local telephone and utility companies, and cable TV operators are examples of natural monopoly. In all these cases, huge fixed costs are required to establish production facilities (such as subway tunnels and transmission cables). The marginal cost of producing another rider, call, or program is negligible, however. As a result, average total costs start high but continuously decline until capacity is reached.

The declining costs of a natural monopoly are of potential benefit to society. The **economies of scale** offered by a natural monopoly imply that no other market structure can supply the good as cheaply. Hence, *natural monopoly is a desirable market structure.* A competitive market structure—with many smaller firms—would have higher average cost.

> **economies of scale:** Reductions in minimum average costs that come about through increases in the size (scale) of plant and equipment.

Unregulated Behavior

Although the structure *of a natural monopoly may be beneficial, its* behavior *may leave something to be desired.* Natural monopolists have the same profit-maximizing motivations as other producers. Moreover, they have the monopoly power to achieve and maintain economic profits. Hence, there's no guarantee that consumers will reap the benefits of a natural monopoly. Critics charge that the monopolist tends to keep most of the benefits. This has been a recurrent criticism of cable TV operators: Consumers have complained about high prices, poor service, and a lack of programming choices from local cable monopolies.

Figure 12.1 illustrates the unregulated behavior of a natural monopolist. Like all other producers, the natural monopolist will maximize profits by producing at that rate of output where marginal revenue equals marginal cost. Point A in Figure 12.1 indicates that an unregulated monopoly will end up producing the quantity q_A and charging the price p_A.

The natural monopolist's preferred outcome isn't the most desirable one for society. This price-output combination violates the competitive principle of **marginal cost pricing.** The monopoly price p_A greatly exceeds the marginal cost of producing q_A of output, as represented by MC_A in Figure 12.1. As a result of this gap, consumers aren't getting accurate information about the **opportunity cost** of this product. This flawed price signal is the cause of market failure. We end up consuming less of this product (and more of other goods) than we would if charged its true opportunity cost. A suboptimal mix of output results.

> **marginal cost pricing:** The offer (supply) of goods at prices equal to their marginal cost.

> **opportunity cost:** The most desired goods or services that are forgone in order to obtain something else.

The natural monopolist's profit-maximizing output (q_A) also fails to minimize average total cost. In a competitive industry, ATC is driven down to its minimum by relentless competition. In this case, however, reductions in ATC cease when the monopolist achieves the profit-maximizing rate of output (q_A). Were output to increase further, average total costs would fall.

Finally, notice that the higher price (p_A) associated with the monopolist's preferred output (q_A) ensures a fat profit. The **economic profit** may violate our visions of equity. In 2001, millions of Californians were convinced that this kind of "profiteering" was the root of their electricity woes.

> **economic profit:** The difference between total revenues and total economic costs.

REGULATORY OPTIONS

The suboptimal outcomes likely to emerge from a free-swinging natural monopoly prompt consumers to demand government intervention. The market alone can't overcome the natural advantage of pervasive economies of scale. But the government could compel different outcomes. The question is, Which outcomes do we want? And how will we get them?

For starters, we might consider price regulation. The natural monopolist's preferred price (p_A) is, after all, a basic cause of market failure. By regulating the firm, the government can compel a lower price. The California legislature did this in 1996 when it set a maximum retail price for electricity.

As is apparent from Figure 12.1 there are lots of choices in setting a regulated price. We start with the conviction that the unregulated price p_A is too high. But where on the demand curve below p_A do we want to be?

Price Efficiency. One possibility is to set the price at a level consistent with opportunity costs. As we saw earlier, a monopolist's unregulated price sends out a flawed price signal. By charging a price in excess of marginal cost, the monopolist causes a suboptimal allocation of resources. We could improve market outcomes, therefore, by compelling the monopolist to set the price equal to marginal cost. Such an efficient price would lead us to point B in Figure 12.1, where the demand curve and the marginal cost curve intersect. At that price (p_B), consumers would get optimal use of the good or service produced.

Subsidy. Although the price p_B will ensure allocative efficiency, it will also bankrupt the producer. In a natural monopoly, MC is always less than ATC. Hence, *marginal cost pricing by a natural monopolist implies a loss on every unit of output produced.* In this case, the loss per unit is equal to $B^* - B$. If confronted with the regulated price p_B, the firm will ultimately shut down and exit from the market. This was one of the many problems that plagued California. Unable to charge a price high enough to cover their costs, some of the state's utility companies were forced into bankruptcy.

If we want to require efficient pricing (p = MC), we must provide a subsidy to the natural monopoly. In Figure 12.1 the amount of the subsidy would have to equal the anticipated loss at q_B, that is, the quantity q_B multiplied by the per-unit loss ($B^* - B$). Such subsidies are provided to subway systems. With subsidies, local subway systems can charge fees below *average* cost and closer to *marginal* cost. These subsidized fares increase ridership, thus ensuring greater use of very expensive transportation systems.

Despite the advantages of this subsidized pricing strategy, taxpayers always complain about the cost of such subsidies. Taxpayers are particularly loath to provide them for private companies. Hence, political considerations typically preclude efficient (marginal cost) pricing, despite the economic benefits of this regulatory strategy.

Production Efficiency. Even if it were possible to impose marginal cost pricing, we still wouldn't achieve maximum production efficiency. Production efficiency is attained at the lowest possible average total cost. At q_B we're producing a lot of output but still have some unused capacity. Since ATC falls continuously, we could achieve still lower average costs if we increased output beyond q_B. *In a natural monopoly, production efficiency is achieved at capacity production, where ATC is at a minimum.*

Increasing output beyond q_B raises the same problems we encountered at that rate of output. At production rates in excess of q_B, ATC is always higher than price. Even MC is higher than price to the right of point B. Thus, *no regulated price can induce the monopolist to achieve minimum average cost. A subsidy would be required to offset the market losses.*

Instead of price regulation, we could try profit regulation. If we choose not to subsidize a natural monopolist, we must permit it to charge a price high enough to cover all its costs, including a normal profit. We can achieve the result by mandating a price equal to average total cost. In Figure 12.1 this regulatory objective is achieved at point C. In this case, the rate of output is q_C and the regulated price is p_C.

Profit regulation looks appealing for two reasons. First, it eliminates the need to subsidize the monopolist. Second, it allows us to focus on profits only, thus removing the need to develop demand and cost curves. In theory, all we have to do is check the firm's annual profit-and-loss statement to confirm that it's earning a normal (average) profit. If its profits are too high, we can force the firm to reduce its price; if profits are too low, we may permit a price increase.

Bloated Costs. While beautiful in principle, profit regulation can turn out ugly in practice. In particular, profit regulation can lead to bloated costs and dynamic inefficiency. ***If a firm is permitted a specific profit rate (or rate of return), it has no incentive to limit costs.*** On the contrary, higher costs imply higher profits. If permitted to charge 10 percent over unit costs, a monopolist may be better off with average costs of $6 rather than only $5. The higher costs translate into 60 cents of profit per unit rather than only 50 cents. Hence, there's an incentive to "pad costs." If those costs actually represent improvements in wages and salaries, fringe benefits, or the work environment, then cost increases are doubly attractive to the firm and its employees. Cost efficiency is as welcome as the plague under such circumstances.

Profit regulation can also motivate a firm to inflate its costs by paying above-market prices for products purchased from an unregulated subsidiary. This was the strategy AT&T used to increase its *regulated* cost base while ringing up high profits at Western Electric, its *unregulated* subsidiary (see Chapter 9). The FCC accused Nynex (the "Baby Bell" that provided phone service in New York and New England in the 1970s) of using the same strategy to pad its profits (see News).

Output Regulation

Given the difficulties in regulating prices and profits, regulators may choose to regulate output instead. The natural monopolist's preferred output rate is q_A, as illustrated again in Figure 12.2. We could compel this monopolist to provide a minimum level of service in excess of q_A. This regulated minimum is designated q_D in Figure 12.2. At q_D consumers get the benefit not only of more output but also of a lower price (p_D). At q_D total monopoly profit must also be less than at q_A, since q_A was the profit-maximizing rate of output.

It appears, then, that compelling any rate of output in excess of q_A can only benefit consumers. Moreover, output regulation is an easy rule to enforce.

Quality Deterioration. Unfortunately, minimum-service regulation can also cause problems. If forced to produce at the rate of q_D, the monopolist may seek to increase profits by cutting cost corners. This can be accomplished by deferring plant and equipment maintenance, reducing quality control, or otherwise lowering the quality of service. ***Regulation of the quantity produced may induce a decline in quality.*** Since a monopolist has no direct competition, consumers pretty much have to accept whatever quality the monopolist offers. This structural reality may explain why consumers complain so much about the services of local cable monopolies.

In addition to encouraging quality deterioration, output regulation at q_D also violates the principle of marginal cost pricing. Because an economic profit exists at q_D, equity goals may be jeopardized as well. Hence, minimum service (output) regulation isn't a panacea for the regulatory dilemma. In fact, there is no panacea: ***Goal conflicts are inescapable, and any regulatory rule may induce undesired producer responses.***

Imperfect Answers

The call for public regulation of natural monopolies is based on the recognition that the profit motive doesn't generate optimal outcomes in any monopoly environment. If unregulated, a natural monopolist will charge too much and produce too little. The regulatory remedy for these market failures isn't evident, however. Regulators can compel efficient prices or least-cost production only by offering a subsidy. Profit regulation is likely to induce cost-inflating responses. Output regulation is an incentive for quality deterioration. No matter which way we turn, regulatory problems result.

IN THE NEWS

FCC: Nynex Padded Millions in Profits

Commission Urges Refunds, $1.4 Million Fine

Regional phone company Nynex Corp. overcharged its customers by tens of millions of dollars over a four-year period so that the company could pad its profits illegally, the Federal Communications Commission said yesterday.

The commission proposed refunds as well as a $1.4 million fine that would be the largest it has ever imposed.

Nynex, which provides phone service in New York and New England, denied wrongdoing, saying that the commission was applying newly passed rules retroactively. "There was no intent to overcharge," said Nynex Chairman William C. Ferguson. Under FCC rules, Nynex has 30 days in which to respond to the charges and seek dismissal of them.

The commission found that Nynex violated complex rules of accounting that are designed to keep telephone companies from subsidizing unregulated subsidiaries with money that they collect from customers of their monopoly phone service. This resulted, the FCC said, in a transfer of profits to a subsidiary whose bottom line is not regulated, boosting the overall profits of Nynex.

—John Burgess

Source: *The Washington Post*, February 8, 1990. © 1990 The Washington Post. Reprinted with permission. www.washingtonpost.com

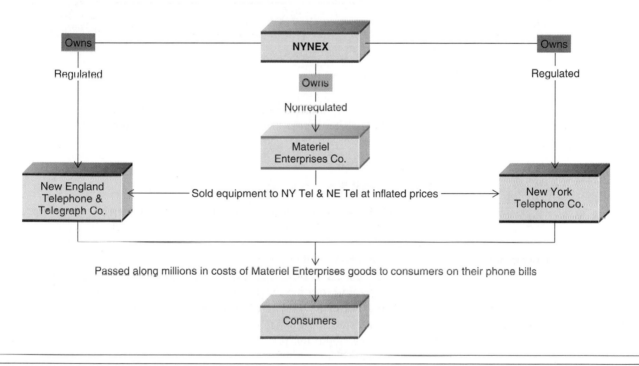

Analysis: Profit regulation creates incentives for a regulated firm to inflate ("pad") its costs. One way to accomplish that is to pay high prices for products purchased from unregulated subsidiaries.

There's not much hope for transforming unregulated market failure into perfect regulated outcomes. In reality, regulators must choose a strategy that balances competing objectives (e.g., price efficiency and equity). A realistic goal for regulation is to *improve* market outcomes, not to *perfect* them. In the real world, ***the choice isn't between imperfect markets and flawless government intervention but rather between imperfect markets and imperfect intervention.***

The argument for *deregulation* rests on the observation that government regulation sometimes worsens market outcomes. In some cases, **government failure** may be

government failure: Government intervention that fails to improve economic outcomes.

FIGURE 12.2
Minimum Service Regulation

Regulation may seek to ensure some minimal level of service. In this case, the required rate of output is arbitrarily set at q_D. Consumers are willing to pay p_D per unit for that output.

Regulated output q_D is preferable to the unregulated outcome (q_A, p_A) but may induce a decline in quality. Cost cutting is the only way to increase profits when the rate of output is fixed and price is on the demand curve.

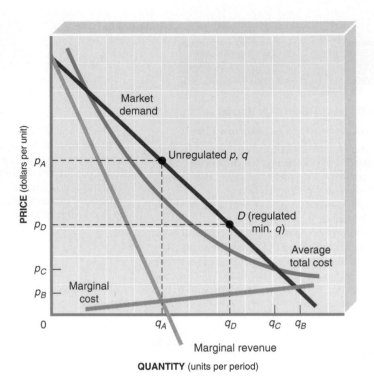

worse than market failure. Specifically, regulation may lead to price, cost, or production outcomes that are inferior to those of an unregulated market.

THE COSTS OF REGULATION

Improving outcomes in a particular market isn't adequate proof of regulatory success. We also have to consider the *costs* incurred to change market outcomes.

Administrative Costs

As we've observed, industry regulation entails various options and a host of trade-offs. Someone must sit down and assess these trade-offs. To make a sound decision, a regulatory administration must have access to lots of information. At a minimum, the regulator must have some clue as to the actual shape and position of the demand and cost curves depicted in Figures 12.1 and 12.2. Crude illustrations won't suffice when decisions about the prices, output, or costs of a multibillion-dollar industry are being made. The regulatory commission needs volumes of details about actual costs and demand and a platoon of experts to collect and analyze the needed data. When Congress passed the 1992 Cable Act, for example, the Federal Communications Commission (FCC) had to develop and enforce new regulations of cable TV operators. To do this, the FCC asked Congress for $16 million to hire 240 more lawyers, accountants, engineers, and other staff (see News). All this labor represents a real cost to society, since the commission's lawyers, accountants, and economists could be employed elsewhere. The staff of the FCC is only the tip of a much larger bureaucratic iceberg. As Table 12.1 illustrates, nearly 200,000 people are employed in regulatory agencies of the federal government. Thousands more have regulatory responsibilities in smaller agencies and the major executive departments. In addition to these federal workers, tens of thousands more people are employed by state and local regulatory agencies. All of these regulators are part of our limited labor resources. By using them to regulate private industry, we are forgoing their use in the production of desired goods and services. This is a significant economic cost.

FCC Seeking More Money to Enforce New Cable Rules

In an effort to bring down cable TV prices, the Federal Communications Commission is proposing to raise them.

With a tidal wave of rate hearings, consumer complaints and other bureaucratic duties looming, the FCC wants to charge the nation's cable TV operators $16 million to carry out provisions of the new cable price law. Without the money, interim FCC Chairman James C. Quello warned yesterday, the agency won't have enough staff to enforce regulations projected to save cable subscribers as much as $1.5 billion a year.

"Either we get the people or we won't be able to implement" it, Quello said in an interview. "This is essential." . . .

Even if he gets the additional funds, Quello said he would be pressed to find work space for new employees. The FCC's downtown headquarters are already at capacity.

—Paul Farhi

Source: *The Washington Post*, May 14, 1993. © 1993 The Washington Post. Reprinted with permission. www.washingtonpost.com

Analysis: Regulation entails the use of scarce resources to write and enforce industry rules. Regulated firms also incur real costs in complying with regulatory rules.

TABLE 12.1

Employment in Federal Regulatory Agencies

The human and capital resources the bureaucracy employs represent a real opportunity cost. The 192,210 people employed in 63 federal agencies—and tens of thousands more employed in state and local bureaucracies—could be producing other goods and services. These and other costs must be compared to the benefits of regulation.

Agency	Number of Employees	Agency	Number of Employees
Social Regulation		**Economic Regulation**	
Consumer Safety and Health		*General Business*	
Consumer Product Safety Commission	471	Patent and Trademark Office	7,666
Animal and Plant Health Inspection	5,407	Dept. of Justice Antitrust Division	851
Food Safety and Inspection Service	9,834	Federal Trade Commission	1,080
Food and Drug Administration	10,111	Library of Congress: Copyright Office	530
Coast Guard	19,493	Securities and Exchange Commission	3,731
Federal Aviation Administration	5,636	Subtotal—General Business	15,448
Federal Highway Administration	128	*Finance and Banking*	
Bureau of Alcohol, Tobacco, Firearms	4,772	Comptroller of the Currency	2,813
Transportation Security Administration	55,156	Federal Deposit Insurance Corporation	4,498
Subtotal—Consumer Safety and Health	116,432	Federal Reserve Banks	3,726
Job Safety and Working Conditions		Subtotal—Finance and Banking	13,252
Employment Standards Administration	2,147	*Industry-Specific Regulation*	
Mine Safety and Health Administration	2,334	Commodity Futures Trading Commission	489
Occupational Safety and Health Adm.	2,236	Federal Communications Commission	2,007
Equal Employment Opportunity Com.	2,765	Federal Energy Regulatory Commission	1,250
National Labor Relations Board	1,952	Federal Maritime Commission	137
Subtotal—Job Safety and Working Conditions	12,465	Subtotal—Industry-Specific Regulation	6,569
Environment and Energy			
Army Corps of Engineers	1,450	**Totals**	
Fish and Wildlife Service	1,791	*Social regulation*	156,941
Environmental Protection Agency	17,500	*Economic regulation*	35,269
Nuclear Regulatory Commission	2,907		
Subtotal—Environment and Energy	28,044	**Grand Total**	192,210

Source: Melinda Warren, Weidenbaum Center on the Economy, Government, and Public Policy, Washington University, 2004.

Costs of Trucking Seen Rising Under New Safety Rules

The first major changes in truck-driver work hours since 1939 are expected to reduce highway fatalities, but also contribute to the biggest increase in trucking rates in two decades. . . .

The new rules increase the time that truck drivers must set aside to rest in each 24-hour period to 10 hours from eight hours, and the total time a driver can be on duty will fall to 14 hours from 15 hours. . . .

The government estimates the new rules could cost trucking companies about $1.3 billion a year. . . .

Because trucks haul so much commerce, accounting for more than 81% of the nation's $571 billion freight-transportation bill last year, the effects could be far-reaching. Some users of truck transportation say higher trucking rates could lead to a broad-based increase in prices of goods from paper to chemicals, diapers to trash cans. . . .

Still, "there are about 410 fatalities a year attributed to fatigue-related truck crashes, and that's 410 very good reasons for changing the rule," says Annette Sandberg, administrator of the Transportation Department's Federal Motor Carrier Safety Administration. The agency expects the new rules to save up to 75 lives a year and prevent as many as 1,326 fatigue-related crashes a year.

—Daniel Machalaba

Source: *The Wall Street Journal,* November 12, 2003. Reprinted by permission of The Wall Street Journal, © 2003 Dow Jones & Company. All rights reserved worldwide.

Analysis: Regulations designed to improve market outcomes typically impose higher costs. The challenge is to balance benefits and costs.

Compliance Costs

The administrative costs of regulation focus on resources used in the public sector. By its very nature, however, regulation also changes resource use in the private sector. Regulated industries must expend resources to educate themselves about the regulations, to change their production behavior, and often to file reports with the regulatory authorities. The human and capital resources used for these purposes represent the *compliance* cost of regulation.

New rules on trucking illustrate how regulation can increase production costs. In 2003, the U.S. Department of Transportation reduced the amount of permitted driving time for interstate truckers (see News). This rule requires freight companies to use more trucks and more labor to transport goods, thereby raising economic costs. Although the resultant gain in safety is desired, the cost of achieving that gain is not inconsequential.

Efficiency Costs

Finally, we have to consider the potential costs of changes in output. Most regulation alters the mix of output, either directly or indirectly. Ideally, regulation will always improve the mix of output. But it's possible that bad decisions, incomplete information, or faulty implementation may actually *worsen* the mix of output. If this occurs, then the loss of utility associated with an inferior mix of output imposes a further cost on society, over and above administrative and compliance costs.

Efficiency costs may increase significantly over time. Consumer tastes change, demand and marginal revenue curves shift, costs change, and new technologies emerge. Can regulatory commissions respond to these changes as fast as the market mechanism does? If not, even optimal regulations may soon become obsolete and counterproductive. Worse still, the regulatory process itself may impede new technology, new marketing approaches, or improved production processes. These losses may be the most important. As Robert Hahn of the American Enterprise Institute observed:

> The measurable costs of regulation pale against the distortions that sap the economy's dynamism. The public never sees the factories that weren't built, the new products that didn't appear, or the entrepreneurial idea that drowned in a cumbersome regulatory process.[1]

[1]Cited in *Fortune,* October 19, 1992, p. 94.

These kinds of dynamic efficiency losses are a drag on economic growth, limiting outward shifts of the production possibilities curve while perpetuating an increasingly undesired mix of output.

The economic costs of regulation are a reminder of the "no free lunch" maxim. Although regulatory intervention may improve market outcomes, that intervention isn't without cost. The real resources used in the regulatory process could be used for other purposes. Hence, even if we could achieve perfect outcomes with enough regulation, the cost of achieving perfection might outweigh the benefits. ***Regulatory intervention must balance the anticipated improvements in market outcomes against the economic cost of regulation.*** In principle, the marginal benefit of regulation must exceed its marginal cost. If this isn't the case, then additional regulation isn't desirable, even if it would improve short-run market outcomes.

Balancing Benefits and Costs

DEREGULATION IN PRACTICE

The push to *de*regulate was prompted by two concerns. The first concern focused on the dynamic inefficiencies that regulation imposes. It appeared that these inefficiencies had accumulated over time, rendering regulated industries less productive than desired. The other push for deregulation came from advancing technology, which destroyed the basis for natural monopoly in some industries. A brief review of the resulting deregulation illustrates the impact of these forces.

The railroad industry was the federal government's first broad regulatory target. Railroads are an example of natural monopoly, with high fixed costs and negligible marginal costs. Furthermore, there were no airports or interstate highways to compete with the railroads in 1887, when Congress created the Interstate Commerce Commission (ICC). The ICC was established to limit monopolistic exploitation of this situation while assuring a fair profit to railroad owners. The ICC established rates and routes for the railroads while limiting both entry to and exit from the industry.

Railroads

With the advent of buses, trucks, subways, airplanes, and pipelines as alternative modes of transportation, railroad regulation became increasingly obsolete. Regulated cargoes, routes, and prices prevented railroads from adapting their prices or services to meet changing consumer demands. With regulation-protected routes, they also had little incentive to invest in new technologies or equipment. As a result, railroad traffic and profits declined while other transportation industries flourished.

The Railroad Revitalization and Regulatory Reform Act of 1976 was a response to this crisis. Its major goal was to reduce the scope of government regulation. Reinforced by the Staggers Rail Act of 1980, railroads were granted much greater freedom to adapt their prices and service to market demands.

Railroad companies used that flexibility to increase their share of total freight traffic. Fresh fruits and vegetables, for example, were exempted from ICC rate regulation in 1979. Railroads responded by *reducing* their rates and improving service. In the first year of deregulated rates, fruits and vegetable shipments increased over 30 percent. As Figure 12.3 shows, this was a dramatic reversal of earlier trends. Deregulation of coal traffic (in 1980) and piggyback (trucks on railroad flatcars) traffic (in 1982) prompted similar turnarounds. The railroads prospered by reconfiguring routes and services, cutting operating costs, and offering lower rates. Between 1986 and 1993, the average cost of moving freight by rail dropped by 69 percent.

Not all rates have fallen. Indeed, one worrisome effect of deregulation is the increased concentration in the rail industry. After a series of mergers and acquisitions, the top four railroads moved nearly 90 percent of all rail freight (ton-miles) during 1998 and 1999. Moreover, these same firms held monopoly positions on specific routes. Shippers in these captive markets were paying rates 20 to 30 percent higher than in nonmonopoly routes.

FIGURE 12.3
Railroad Traffic, before and after Deregulation

Deregulation enabled railroads to offer more competitive prices and services. When fruit and vegetable freight rates were deregulated in 1979, railroads reduced their prices and reversed a serious decline in traffic.

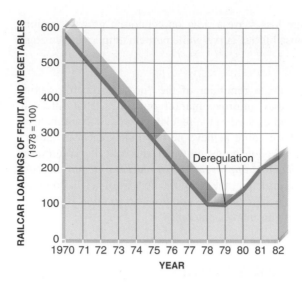

Telephone Service

The telephone industry has long been the classic example of a natural monopoly. Although enormous fixed costs are necessary to establish a telephone network, the marginal cost of an additional telephone call approaches zero. Hence, it made economic sense to have a single network of telephone lines and switches rather than a maze of competing ones. Recognizing these economies of scale, Congress permitted AT&T to maintain a monopoly on both long-distance and most local telephone service. To assure that consumers would benefit from this natural monopoly, the Federal Communications Commission (FCC) regulated phone services and prices.

Once again, technology outpaced regulation. Communications satellites made it much easier and less costly for new firms to provide long-distance telephone service. Moreover, the rate structure that AT&T and the Federal Communications Commission had established made long-distance service highly profitable. Accordingly, start-up firms clamored to get into the industry, and consumers petitioned for lower rates.

Long Distance. In 1982, the courts put an end to AT&T's monopoly, transforming long-distance telecommunications into a more competitive industry with more firms and less regulation. Since then, over 800 firms have entered the industry, and long-distance telephone rates have dropped sharply. Between 1983 and 1990, long-distance telephone rates fell more than 40 percent. The quality of service also improved with fiber-optic cable, advanced switching systems, cell phones, and myriad new phone-line services such as fax transmissions, remote access, and Internet access. All these changes have contributed to a tripling of long-distance telephone use in the United States. The same kinds of changes have occurred around the world as other telephone monopolies have crumbled (see World View).

Local Service. The deregulation of long-distance services was so spectacularly successful that observers wondered whether local telephone service might be deregulated as well. As competition in *long-distance* services increased, the monopoly nature of *local* rates became painfully apparent: Local rates kept increasing after 1983 while long-distance rates were tumbling.

The Baby Bells that held monopolies on local service defended their high rates based on the high costs of building and maintaining transmission networks. But new technologies permitted wireless companies to offer local service if they could gain access to the monopoly networks. Congress responded in 1996. The Telecommunications Act of 1996 required the Baby Bells to grant rivals access to their transmission networks. Rivals are supposed to be able to lease excess capacity from the Baby Bells, then resell services directly to consumers. Potential rivals accuse the Baby Bells of foot dragging,

WEBNOTE

Find out what has happened to the Telecommunications Act of 1996 at www.fcc.gov/telecom.html.

Demise of Telephone Monopolies

The breakup of AT&T was spurred by new technology that undercut the basis for natural monopoly. The same technological advances have transformed the telecommunications industry around the world:

- **Canada:** In 1994, the 10 regional phone companies were required to provide equal access to their transmission networks. Over 200 new companies entered the industry, and telephone rates fell by 40 percent.
- **Japan:** In 1984, the Japanese government ended the monopoly long held by Nippon Telegraph & Telephone (NTT). More than 500 companies have now entered the industry, chipping away at NTT's market share.
- **Great Britain:** The British government has privatized British Telecommunications and licensed another company to build a second, competing network.
- **France:** The French government has retained a single, state-owned network but opened the door to competition in equipment and services.

- **Germany:** The former state-owned monopoly was privatized in 1996. Competitive entry began in 1998.
- **Chile:** The long-established monopoly (Entel) was deregulated in 1994, and entry barriers dropped. Rates plunged and volume doubled. Within two years Entel's market share fell from 100 to 40 percent.
- **Brazil:** The state-owned monopoly (Telebras) was opened to competition in 1998.
- **Mexico:** In 1997, Mexico opened its telecommunications market to competition. New domestic and international fiber-optic networks have been built, and phone rates have dropped dramatically.
- **European Union:** At the beginning of 1998, all local and long-distance markets were opened to competition.
- **China:** At the end of 2001, China split its fixed-line monopoly into two regional companies.

Analysis: The deregulation of telephone industries has spurred price competition and innovation, while greatly increasing the volume of telephone service.

however. They say the Baby Bells charge excessive access fees, impose overly complex access codes, require unnecessary capital equipment, and raise other entry barriers. Five years after the mandate for "open access," the Baby Bells still held near monopoly positions in local phone service, and local phone charges were still rising.

The Federal Communications Commission (FCC) and state regulatory commissions lowered entry barriers in 2001–2 by forcing local Bell monopolies to sell rivals access to local networks at wholesale prices. Within three years, rivals tripled their market share, to roughly 12 percent, and phone prices started to decline (see News on next page). In 2004, however, the courts ruled that such forced network-leasing was illegal. Within days, rivals started exiting local markets, and phone prices stopped falling.

Airlines

The Civil Aeronautics Board (CAB) was created in 1938 to regulate airline routes and fares. From its inception, the primary concern of the CAB was to ensure a viable system of air transportation for both large and small communities. Such a system would be ensured, the CAB believed, only if a fair level of profits was maintained by entry and price regulations. Thus, the focus of the CAB was on *profit* regulation.

Price Regulation. Initially, the CAB set airline fares at roughly the levels of Pullman rates for train travel. This implied that airfares would be proportional to distance, as they were for train travel. In the late 1930s, this fare structure wasn't unreasonable, as most flights were relatively short and planes were small.

As the airline industry grew, the CAB abandoned fare comparisons with trains but maintained the basic distance-based fare structure. To ensure fair profits, the CAB set fares in accordance with airline costs. This required the CAB to undertake intensive cost studies, based on accounting data provided by the airlines. Once the average cost

IN THE NEWS

Bell Monopolies Push to Disconnect Competition

Seven years ago, Congress set out to break up the local Bell telephone monopolies and bring competition to consumers' homes. But just as states are finally figuring out how to make that promise a reality, and some communities are seeing phone bills drop, federal regulators may unplug the competitors at the behest of the four Bell monopolies.

The Bells want to gut rules spurring competition that were enacted in the wake of the 1996 Telecommunications Act. They require the Bells to rent their networks at reasonable prices to potential rivals that may want to offer local phone service but can't afford to set up their own phone networks.

For years, the law wasn't an issue because states let the Bells charge exorbitant fees that kept competitors out of their markets. Now that several states are ordering them to cut their network fees, competition is emerging, and phone rates are decreasing. On Monday, AT&T announced plans to compete in Washington, D.C., after the local government cut the charges for tapping into the network operated by Verizon. Nationwide, 11% of local phone lines were serviced by competitors through last June, nearly double their share two years earlier.

Faced with the first real threat to their grip on local service, Verizon and the other Bells are crying to the Federal Communications Commission (FCC) that they're forced to rent their networks at a loss. They want to go back to the way it was: higher fees for rivals and less choice for consumers.

—Marcy E. Mullins

Source: *USA Today,* January 14, 2003. USA TODAY. Copyright 2003. Reprinted with permission.

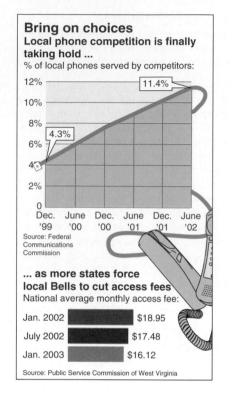

Bring on choices
Local phone competition is finally taking hold ...
% of local phones served by competitors:

(Graph showing increase from 4.3% at Dec. '99 to 11.4% at June '02)

Source: Federal Communications Commission

... as more states force local Bells to cut access fees
National average monthly access fee:

Jan. 2002	$18.95
July 2002	$17.48
Jan. 2003	$16.12

Source: Public Service Commission of West Virginia

Analysis: To enter local phone markets, would-be rivals must pay an access fee to the local phone monopoly. High fees are a substantial entry barrier.

---

of service and capital equipment was established, the CAB then set an average price that would ensure a fair rate of return (profit) (see point *C* in Figure 12.1).

A secondary objective of the CAB was to ensure air service to smaller, less traveled communities. Short hauls entail higher average costs and therefore justify higher fares. To avoid high fares on such routes, the CAB permitted airlines to charge prices well in excess of average costs on longer, more efficient routes as long as they maintained service on shorter, unprofitable routes. This **cross-subsidization** was similar to that of the telephone industry, in which long-distance profits helped keep local telephone charges low.

To maintain this price and profit structure, the CAB had to regulate routes and limit entry into the airline industry. Otherwise, established carriers would abandon short, unprofitable routes, and new carriers would offer service only on more profitable routes. Unregulated entry thus threatened both cross-subsidization and the CAB's vision of a fair profit.

No Entry. The CAB was extremely effective in restricting entry into the industry. Would-be entrants had to demonstrate to the CAB that their proposed service was required by

> **cross-subsidization:** Use of high prices and profits on one product to subsidize low prices on another product.

"public convenience and necessity" and was superior to that of established carriers. Established carriers could oppose a new application by demonstrating sufficient service, offering to expand their service, or claiming superior service. In view of the fact that new applicants had no airline experience, established carriers easily won the argument. From 1938 until 1977, the CAB *never* awarded a major route to a new entrant.

No Price Competition. The CAB also eliminated price competition between established carriers. The CAB fixed airfares on all routes. Airlines could reduce fares no more than 5 percent and couldn't increase them more than 10 percent without CAB approval.

Bloated Costs. Ironically, the established airlines failed to reap much profit from these high fares. Unable to compete on the basis of price, the established carriers had to engage in nonprice competition. The most costly form of nonprice competition was frequency of service. Once the CAB authorized service between any two cities, a regulated carrier could provide as many flights as desired. This enticed the regulated carriers to purchase huge fleets of planes and provide frequent departures. In the process, load factors (the percentage of seats filled with passengers) fell and average costs rose.

The regulated carriers also pursued **product differentiation** by offering special meals, first-run movies, free drinks, better service, and wider seats. This nonprice competition further inflated average costs and reduced profits.

Profit regulation ultimately came to be regarded as a failure. The regulated airline industry was not as profitable as anticipated. And consumers weren't being offered very many price-service combinations.

New Entrants. The Airline Deregulation Act of 1978 changed the structure and behavior of the airline industry. Entry regulation was effectively abandoned. With the elimination of this **barrier to entry,** the number of carriers increased greatly. Between 1978 and 1985, the number of airline companies increased from 37 to 174! The new entrants intensified competition on nearly all routes. The share of domestic markets with four or more carriers grew from 13 percent in May 1978 to 73 percent in May 1981.

The new entrants into the airline industry brought not only more service possibilities but also sharply lower costs. In the era of regulation, airlines had little incentive to control costs. Wages and salaries had increased continually, while productivity had declined. By contrast, new entrants were able to offer lower wages and experiment with new management systems, greatly reducing the average cost of providing service. In 1995, for example, Southwest Airlines had average costs of 6.3 cents per available seat-mile, while United Airlines had an average cost of 10.6 cents and Delta had 9.1 cents. This cost advantage enabled the new entrants to offer significantly lower fares. The resulting price competition reduced average fares as much as 40 percent below regulated levels (see Table 12.2).

The CAB's authority over airfares ended January 1, 1983. Since then, airlines have been able to adapt their fares to market supply and demand. The CAB itself was eliminated at the end of 1984. Its remaining responsibilities—for foreign travel, mail

product differentiation: Features that make one product appear different from competing products in the same market.

barriers to entry: Obstacles that make it difficult or impossible for would-be producers to enter a particular market, such as patents.

Market Distance	Percentage Change in Airfare by Market Density (passengers per day)			
	10–50	51–200	201–500	500+
1–400 miles	+14	+12	−5	−29
401–1,500 miles	+10	−3	−13	−20
1,501+ miles	N/A	−25	−35	−40

Source: Civil Aeronautics Board, *Implementation of the Provisions of the Airline Deregulation Act of 1978,* January 1984.

TABLE 12.2
Airfare Reductions after Deregulation (deregulated fares as percentage of regulated levels)

Five years after being deregulated, fares on heavily used long-distance routes were 40 percent lower than those dictated by the CAB's pricing formula. Rates on previously subsidized short hauls were higher, however, as cross-subsidies disappeared.

service, mergers, and operating authority—were transferred to the U.S. Department of Transportation.

Deregulation of the airline industry greatly increased market entry and price competition. According to a 1988 study by the Federal Trade Commission, deregulation saved consumers $100 billion in airfares and enabled millions of Americans who otherwise couldn't afford it to fly. The massive increase in airline use even had an unforseen externality. As air traffic increased from 250 million to 455 million trips per year, highways became less congested. According to Richard McKenzie, airline deregulation resulted in 600,000 fewer *auto* accidents a year and reduced traffic fatalities by nearly 1,700 per year. At the same time, *air* traffic safety also improved, as evidenced by a decline in the rate of air accidents and fatalities.

Increasing Concentration. Although airline deregulation is hailed as one of the greatest policy achievements of the 1980s, airline industry structure and behavior remain imperfect. Of particular concern has been the sharp increase in the industry's concentration ratio in the last 10 years. In the competitive fray spawned by deregulation, lots of new entrants and even some established airlines went broke. Unable to match lower fares and increased service, scores of airline companies exited the industry in the period 1985–95. In the process, a handful of major carriers increased their market share. The combined market share of the three largest carriers (American, United, Delta) increased from 35 percent in 1985 to 60 percent in 2001. In many cases, firms gained near-monopoly power in specific hub airports; for example, USAir provides 70 percent of the flights departing Pittsburgh; and 85 percent of the traffic in Charlotte, Northwest has 60 percent of the Minneapolis market and 54 percent of Detroit's. Southwest services 86 percent of the flights from Love Field in Dallas; Delta has 92 percent of Cincinnati; American has 58 percent of St. Louis, and United, 50 percent of Denver. Not surprisingly, a study by the U.S. General Accounting Office found that ticket prices are 45 to 85 percent higher on monopolized routes than on routes where at least two airlines compete. In 2004, USAir charged $206 to fly its monopoly route between Pittsburgh and Washington, D.C. Yet the fare for Las Vegas to Los Angeles trips—approximately the same distance but with several carriers—was as low as $61.

Entry Barriers. To exploit their hub dominance, major carriers must keep out rivals. One of the most effective entry barriers is their ownership of landing slots. Air traffic is limited by the number of these slots, or authorized landing permits. In 1998, United Airlines controlled 82 percent of the slots at Chicago's O'Hare, up from 66 percent in 1986. Delta controls 83 percent of the slots at New York's Kennedy Airport. Smaller airlines complain that they can't get access to these slots, even when the slots aren't being used.

Defenders of deregulation are quick to point out that despite increasing *industry* concentration, there's more competition in most airline markets. In 1979, about 22 percent of all traffic was in monopoly markets, where a single carrier supplied at least 90 percent of all traffic. By 1989, only 11 percent of all traffic was in such monopoly markets. Furthermore, entry is still easier today than it was before deregulation, as a flock of new entrants attests. Hence, the airline industry is more of a **contestable market,** even if not a perfectly competitive one. When entry barriers (including slot access) are lowered, consumers continue to enjoy the low fares deregulation has made possible (see News on the "JetBlue effect").

Airline Security. Since the September 11, 2001, terrorist attacks that used commercial airliners as weapons, consumers have worried more about airline security than lower airfares. Individual airlines, of course, want safe flights as well. However, security at airports is a **public good;** all travelers benefit from increased security regardless of who pays for it. Moreover, firms or travelers who don't pay for increased airport security can't easily be excluded from its benefits. This creates a classic "free-rider" problem, wherein everyone waits for someone else to pay for tighter security. Hence, unregulated airlines are likely to minimize expenditures on airport security.

WEBNOTE

For a sense of how competition affects airfares, check the number of carriers serving each of the following routes and the cheapest available fare *per mile:* (a) Detroit–Boston, (b) Pittsburgh–Washington, (c) Minneapolis–Milwaukee, (d) Denver–Colorado Springs, (e) Charlotte–Atlanta, (f) Las Vegas–Los Angeles. For information on carriers and fares, check expedia.com or visit www.travelocity.com and set up a free user's account.

contestable market: An imperfectly competitive industry subject to potential entry if prices or profits increase.

public good: A good or service whose consumption by one person does not exclude consumption by others.

The JetBlue Effect

When the carrier comes to town, fares go down, traffic goes up, and the airline ends up with a big chunk of the business.

Source: *BusinessWeek*, February 16, 2004. Reprinted by permission. Copyright 2004 by The McGraw-Hill Companies.

	Change in Daily Passengers	Change in Average Fare	JetBlue Local Traffic Share
New York to Miami/Fort Lauderdale	+14%	−17% to $121.50	23.1%
New York to Los Angeles Basin	+2%	−26% to $219.31	18%
New York to Buffalo	+94%	−40% to $86.09	61.2%

Figures as of second quarter, 2003.
Data: Back Aviation Solutions (www.backaviation.com).

Analysis: If entry barriers are low enough, new entrants will contest a market, keeping pressure on prices and service.

Government intervention is required to assure that enough of the public good is produced, even in an otherwise unregulated industry.

Cable TV

The cable TV industry offers examples of both deregulation and *re*regulation. Up until 1986, city and county governments had the authority to franchise (approve) local cable TV operators and regulate their rates. In almost all cases, local governments franchised only one operator, thus establishing local monopolies. The monopoly structure was justified by pervasive economies of scale and the desire to avoid the cost and disruption of laying multiple cable systems. The rationale behind local regulation of cable prices (rates) was to ensure that consumers shared in the benefits of natural monopoly.

Deregulation. By 1984, Congress was convinced that broadcast TV and emerging technologies (such as microwave transmissions and direct satellite broadcasts) offered sufficient competition to ensure consumers fair prices and quality service. The Cable Communications Policy Act of 1984 *de*regulated cable TV by stripping local governments of the authority to regulate prices. From 1986 to 1992, cable TV was essentially unregulated.

Soon after price regulation ended, cable companies began increasing their rates sharply. As Figure 12.4 shows, the rate of price acceleration nearly doubled after the cable industry was deregulated. Consumers also complained that local cable companies offered poor service. They demanded that Congress *re*regulate the industry.

Reregulation. In 1992, Congress responded with the Cable Television Consumer Protection and Competition Act. That act gave the Federal Communications Commission authority to reregulate cable TV rates. The FCC required cable operators to *reduce* prices by nearly 17 percent in 1993–94. It then issued 450 pages of new rules that would limit future price increases. As Figure 12.4 illustrates, these interventions had a dramatic effect on cable prices.

While consumers applauded the new price rules, cable operators warned of unwelcome long-term effects. The rate cuts reduced cable-industry revenues by nearly $4 billion between 1993 and 1995. The cable companies say they would have used

FIGURE 12.4
Annual Increase in Price of Basic Cable Service

After cable TV prices were deregulated in 1986, monthly charges moved up sharply. In 1992 Congress *re*regulated cable TV and prices stabilized. The Telecommunications Act of 1996 again deregulated prices and they surged.

Source: Industry publications.

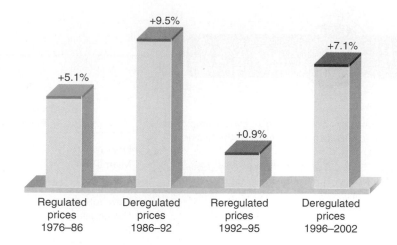

that revenue to invest in improved networks and services. The cable companies also argued that increased competition from satellite transmissions and the Internet made government regulation of (wired) cable TV increasingly unnecessary.

Deregulation. Congress responded to these industry complaints by *de*regulating the cable industry again. The Telecommunications Act of 1996 mandated that rate regulation be phased out and ended completely by March 1999. Almost immediately, cable prices soared again, as Figure 12.4 shows. Critics asserted that alternative technologies were still not viable competitors to local cable monopolies.

Electricity

The electric utility industry is the latest target for deregulation. Here again, the industry has long been regarded as a natural monopoly. The enormous fixed costs of a power plant and transmission network, combined with negligible marginal costs for delivering another kilowatt of electricity, gave electric utilities a downward-sloping average total cost curve. The focus of government intervention was therefore on rate regulation (behavior) rather than promoting competition (structure).

Bloated Costs, High Prices. Critics of local utility monopolies complained that local rate regulation wasn't working well enough. In order to get higher (retail) prices, the utility companies allowed costs to rise. They also had no incentive to pursue new technologies that would reduce the costs of power generation or distribution. Big power users like steel companies complained that high electricity prices were crippling their competitive position. The only viable option for consumers was to move from a state with a high-cost power monopoly to a state with low-cost power monopoly.

Demise of Power Plant Monopolies. Advances in transmission technology gave consumers a new choice. High-voltage transmission lines can carry power thousands of miles with negligible power loss. Utility companies used these lines to link their power grids, thereby creating backup power sources in the event of regional blackouts. In doing so, however, they created a new entry point for potential competition. Now a Kentucky power plant with surplus capacity can supply electricity to consumers in California. There's no longer any need to rely on a regional utility monopoly. At the wholesale level, utility companies have been trading electricity across state lines since 1992.

Local Distribution Monopolies. Although technology destroyed the basis for natural monopolies in power *production,* local monopolies in power *distribution* remain. Electricity reaches consumers through the wires attached to every house and business. As with TV cables, there is a natural monopoly in electricity distribution; competing wire grids would be costly and inefficient.

To deliver the benefits of competition in power *production,* rival producers must be able to access these local distribution grids. This is the same problem that has plagued competition in local telephone service. The local power companies that own the local distribution grids aren't anxious to open the wires to new competition. The central problem for electricity deregulation has been to assure wider access to local distribution grids.

California's Mistakes. The California legislature decided to resolve this problem by stripping local utility monopolies of their production capacity. By forcing utility companies to sell their power plants, California transformed its utilities into pure power *distributors*. This seemed to resolve the conflict between ownership and access to the distribution system. However, it also made California's utility companies totally dependent on third-party power producers, many of which were then out of state.

California also put a ceiling on the *retail* price its utilities could charge. But the state had no power to control the *wholesale* price of electricity in interstate markets. When wholesale prices rose sharply in 2000 (see News), California's utilities were trapped between rising costs and a fixed price ceiling. Fearful of a political backlash, the governor refused to raise the retail price ceiling. As a result, some of the utility companies were forced into bankruptcy and power supplies were interrupted. The state itself entered the utility business by buying power plants and more out-of-state power supplies. In the end, Californians ended up with very expensive electricity.

Better Strategies. Other states and countries have demonstrated how deregulation can generate much better results. Norway deregulated its electric industry in 1991, and prices soon declined by 20 percent. After the European Union started deregulating its electric industries in 1999, prices fell as well. In the United States, the 50 states are at various stages of deregulation, amassing lots of evidence on how best to use competition to reduce electricity costs and prices.

WEBNOTE

Visit the Center for the Advancement of Energy Markets at www.caem.org to see how states differ in the extent of electricity deregulation and price changes.

IN THE NEWS

Financial Woes Heating Up

Pacific Gas and Electric is in financial trouble because the cost of power it purchases on the wholesale market is soaring higher than the fixed rate it charges its customers:

—Suzy Parker

Source: *USA Today,* January 10, 2001. Copyright 2001 USA TODAY. Reprinted with permission. www.usatoday.com

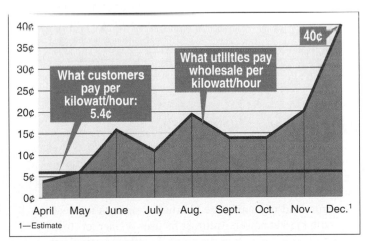

Source: Pacific Gas and Electric, (www.pge.com).

Analysis: When wholesale prices for electricity rose above the retail price ceiling established by the California legislature, the state's utility companies lost money on every kilowatt supplied. It was a recipe for financial disaster.

Deregulate Everything?

Deregulation of the railroad, telephone, airline, and electricity industries has yielded substantial benefits: more competition, lower prices, and improved services. Such experiences bolster the case for laissez faire. Nevertheless, we shouldn't jump to the conclusion that all regulation of business should be dismantled. All we know from experience is that the regulation of certain industries has become outmoded. Changing consumer demands, new technologies, and substitute goods had simply made existing regulations obsolete, even counterproductive. A combination of economic and political forces doomed them to extinction.

But were these regulations ever necessary? In the 1880s there were no viable alternatives to railroads for overland transportation. The forces of natural monopoly could easily have exploited consumers and retarded economic growth. The same was largely true for long-distance telephone service prior to the launching of communications satellites. Even the limitations on competition in trucking and banking made some sense in the depths of the Great Depression. One shouldn't conclude that regulatory intervention never made sense just because the regulations themselves later became obsolete.

Even today, most people recognize the need for regulation of many industries. The transmission networks for local telephone service and electricity delivery are still natural monopolies. The government can force owners to permit greater access. But an unregulated network owner could still extract monopoly profits through excessive prices. Hence, even a deregulated industry may still require some regulation at critical entry or supply junctures. Existing regulations may not be optimal, but they probably generate better outcomes than totally unregulated monopolies.

Likewise, few people seriously propose relying on competition and the good judgment of consumers to determine the variety or quality of drugs on the market. Regulations imposed by the Food and Drug Administration restrain competition in the drug industry, raise production costs, and inhibit new technology. But they also make drugs safer. Here, as in other industries, there's a trade-off between the virtues of competition and those of regulation. The basic policy issue, as always, is whether the benefits of regulation exceed their administrative, compliance, and efficiency costs. The challenge for public policy in the economy tomorrow is to adapt regulations—or to discard them (that is, deregulate)—as market conditions, consumer demands, or technology changes.

WEBNOTE

The Brookings Institution and the American Enterprise Institute have a joint project to analyze regulatory programs at www.aei.brookings.org.

SUMMARY

- Government intervention is justified when the market fails to generate the optimal (best possible) mix of output or distribution of income.
- Antitrust and regulation are alternative options for dealing with market power. Antitrust focuses on market structure and anticompetitive practices. Regulation stipulates specific market behavior.
- Natural monopolies offer pervasive economies of scale. Because of this potential efficiency, a more competitive market *structure* may be inappropriate.

- Regulation of natural monopoly can focus on price, profit, or output *behavior*. Price regulation may require subsidies; profit regulation may induce cost escalation; and output regulation may lead to quality deterioration. These problems compel compromises and acceptance of second-best solutions.
- The demand for deregulation rests on the argument that the costs of regulation exceed the benefits. These costs include the opportunity costs associated with regulatory administration and compliance as well as the (dynamic)

efficiency losses that result from inflexible pricing and production rules.

- Deregulation of the railroad, telephone, and airline industries has been a success. In all these industries, regulation has been outmoded by changing consumer demands, products, and technology. As regulation was relaxed, these industries became more competitive, output increased, and prices fell.

- Recent experiences with deregulation don't imply that all regulation should end. Regulation is appropriate if market failure exists *and* if the benefits of regulation exceed the costs. As benefits and costs change, decisions about what and how to regulate must be reevaluated.

Key Terms

laissez faire
market failure
antitrust
regulation
natural monopoly

economies of scale
marginal cost pricing
opportunity cost
economic profit
government failure

cross-subsidization
product differentiation
barriers to entry
contestable market
public good

Questions for Discussion

1. Given the inevitable limit on airplane landings, how should available airport slots be allocated? How would market outcomes be altered?
2. Should the airline industry be reregulated?
3. Prior to 1982, AT&T kept local phone rates low by subsidizing them from long-distance profits. Was such cross-subsidization in the public interest? Explain.
4. In most cities local taxi fares are regulated. Should such regulation end? Who would gain or lose?
5. The News story on page 261 describes how Nynex inflated its regulated costs. What advantage did Nynex gain from this practice? How else might a regulated company pad its costs?
6. How could a local phone or cable company reduce service quality if forced to accept price ceilings?
7. If cable TV were completely deregulated, would local monopolies ever confront effective competition? Does profit regulation inhibit or accelerate would-be competition?
8. Why is there resistance to (*a*) local phone companies providing video and data services and (*b*) mergers of local cable and telephone companies?
9. Will reregulation of cable TV prices slow or hasten competition from alternative technologies?
10. What should California have done to get better results from electricity deregulation?

ALERT!

PROBLEMS The Student Problem Set at the back of this book contains numerical and graphing problems for this chapter.

WEB ACTIVITIES to accompany this chapter can be found on the Online Learning Center:
http://www.mhhe.com/economics/schiller10

Environmental Protection

Progress in environmental problems is impossible without a clear understanding
of how the economic system works in the environment and what alternatives are
available to take away the many roadblocks to environmental quality.
—Council on Environmental Quality, First Annual Report

What good is a clean river if you've got no jobs?
—Steelworkers Union Official in Youngstown, Ohio

A hole in the ozone layer is allowing increased ultraviolet radiation to
reach the earth's surface. The hole is the result of excessive release of
chlorine gases (chlorofluorocarbons, or CFCs) from air conditioners,
plastic-foam manufacture, industrial solvents, and aerosol spray cans
such as deodorants and insecticides. The resulting damage to the
stratosphere is causing skin cancer, cataracts, and immune-system disorders.

Skin cancer may turn out to be one of our less serious problems. As carbon
dioxide is building up in the atmosphere, it is creating a gaseous blanket around
the earth that is trapping radiation and heating the atmosphere. Scientists predict
that this greenhouse effect will melt the polar ice caps, raise sea levels, flood
coastal areas, and turn rich croplands into deserts within 60 years.

Everyone wants a cleaner and safer environment. So why don't we stop polluting the environment with CFCs, carbon dioxide, toxic chemicals, and other
waste? If we don't do it ourselves, why doesn't the government force people to
stop polluting?

Economics is part of the answer. To reduce pollution, we have to change our patterns of production and consumption. This entails economic costs, in terms of
restricted consumption choices, more expensive ways of producing goods, and
higher prices. Thus, we have to weigh the benefits of a cleaner, safer environment
against the costs of environmental protection.

Instinctively, most people don't like the idea of measuring the value of a cleaner
environment in dollars and cents. But most people might also agree that spending
$2 trillion to avoid a few cataracts is awfully expensive. There has to be *some* bal-
ance between the benefits of a cleaner environment and the cost of cleaning it up.

This chapter assesses our environmental problems from this economic perspective, considering three primary concerns:

- **How do (unregulated) markets encourage pollution?**
- **What are the costs of greater environmental protection?**
- **How can government policy best ensure an *optimal* environment?**

To answer these questions, we first survey the major types and sources of pollution.
Then we examine the benefits and costs of environmental protection, highlighting
the economic incentives that shape market behavior.

THE ENVIRONMENTAL THREAT

The hole in the ozone layer and the earth's rising temperature are at the top of the list of environmental concerns. The list is much longer, however, and very old as well. As early as A.D. 61, the statesman and philosopher Seneca was complaining about the smoky air emitted from household chimneys in Rome. Lead emissions from ancient Greek and Roman silver refineries poisoned the air in Europe and the remote Arctic. And historians are quick to remind us that open sewers running down the street were once the principal mode of urban waste disposal. Typhoid epidemics were a recurrent penalty for water pollution. So we can't say that environmental damage is a new phenomenon or that it's now worse than ever before.

But we do know more about the sources of environmental damage than our ancestors did, and we can better afford to do something about it. Our understanding of the economics of pollution has increased as well. We've come to recognize that pollution impairs health, reduces life expectancy, and thus reduces labor-force activity and output. Pollution also destroys capital (such as the effects of air pollution on steel structures) and diverts resources to undesired activities (like car washes, laundry, and cleaning). Not least of all, pollution directly reduces our social welfare by denying us access to clean air, water, and beaches.

Air pollution is as familiar as a smoggy horizon. But smog is only one form of air pollution.

Air Pollution

Acid Rain. Sulfur dioxide (SO_2) is an acrid, corrosive, and poisonous gas that's created by burning high-sulfur fuels such as coal. As a contributor to acid rain, it destroys vegetation and forests. Electric utilities and industrial plants that burn high-sulfur coal or fuel oil are the prime sources of SO_2. Coal burning alone accounts for about 60 percent of all emissions of sulfur oxides. As the World View on the next page illustrates, SO_2 pollution is a serious problem not only in U.S. cities but all over the world.

Smog. Nitrogen oxides (NO_x), another ingredient in the formation of acid rain, are also a principal ingredient in the formation of smog. Smog not only irritates the eyes and spoils the view, but it also damages plants, trees, and human lungs. Automobile emissions account for 40 percent of urban smog. Bakeries, dry cleaners, and production of other consumer goods account for an equal amount of smog. The rest comes from electric power plants and industrial boilers.

The Greenhouse Effect. The prime villain in the greenhouse effect is the otherwise harmless carbon dioxide (CO_2) that we exhale. Unfortunately, we and nature now release so much CO_2 that the earth's oceans and vegetation can no longer absorb it all. The excess CO_2 is creating a gaseous blanket around the earth that may warm the earth to disastrous levels. The burning of fossil fuels is a significant source of CO_2 buildup. The destruction of rain forests, which absorb CO_2, also contributes to the greenhouse effect.

Water pollution is another environmental threat. Its effects are apparent in the contamination of drinking water, restrictions on swimming and boating, foul-smelling waterways, swarms of dead fish, and floating debris.

Water Pollution

Organic Pollution. The most common form of water pollution occurs in the disposal of organic wastes from toilets and garbage disposals. The wastes that originate there are collected in sewer systems and ultimately discharged into the nearest waterway. The key question is whether the wastes are treated (separated and decomposed) before ultimate discharge. Sophisticated waste-treatment plants can reduce organic pollution up to 99 percent. Unfortunately, only 70 percent of the U.S. population is served by a system of sewers and adequate (secondary) treatment

WORLD VIEW

Polluted Cities

The air in New York City may be unhealthy, but it's not nearly as polluted with sulfur dioxide (SO_2) as that in some other major cities.

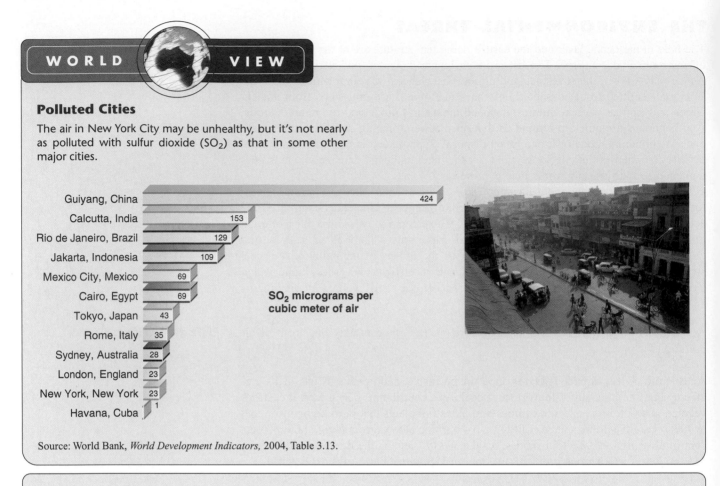

City	SO_2 micrograms per cubic meter of air
Guiyang, China	424
Calcutta, India	153
Rio de Janeiro, Brazil	129
Jakarta, Indonesia	109
Mexico City, Mexico	69
Cairo, Egypt	69
Tokyo, Japan	43
Rome, Italy	35
Sydney, Australia	28
London, England	23
New York, New York	23
Havana, Cuba	1

Source: World Bank, *World Development Indicators,* 2004, Table 3.13.

Analysis: Pollution is a worldwide phenomenon, with common origins and potential remedies.

WEBNOTE

Find out about pollution in your zip code area from the Environmental Defense Fund's Chemical Scoreboard at www.scorecard.org.

plants. Inadequate treatment systems often result in the closure of waterways and beaches (see News).

In addition to household wastes, our waterways must also contend with industrial wastes. Over half the volume of industrial discharge comes from just a few industries—principally paper, organic chemicals, petroleum, and steel. Finally, there are all those farm animals: The 7.5 billion chickens and 161 million cows and hogs raised each year generate 1.4 billion tons of manure (whew!). If improperly managed, that organic waste will contaminate water supplies and trigger algae blooms that can choke waterways and kill fish. Animal wastes don't cause too great a problem in Boston or New York City, but they can wreak havoc on the water supplies of towns in California, Texas, Kansas, and Iowa.

Thermal Pollution. Thermal pollution is an increase in the temperature of waterways brought about by the discharge of steam or heated water. Heat discharges can kill fish, upset marine reproductive cycles, and accelerate biological and chemical processes in water, thereby reducing its ability to retain oxygen. Electric power plants account for over 80 percent of all thermal discharges, with primary metal, chemical, and petroleum-refining plants accounting for nearly all the rest.

Solid-Waste Pollution

Solid waste is yet another environmental threat. Solid-waste pollution is apparent everywhere, from the garbage can to litter on the streets and beaches, to debris in the water, to open dumps. According to EPA estimates, we generate over 5 billion tons

Beach Closings Linked to Pollution on Rise

Beach closings and advisories caused by high bacteria levels are increasing nationwide, according to a report released Thursday. The report awards high praise for pollution control to only five beach areas. The nationwide survey by the Natural Resources Defense Council singles out four states—Louisiana, Oregon, Texas and Washington—as "beach burns" for failing to regularly monitor their coastlines. There were 6,160 beach closings and advisories nationwide in 1999, up

almost 50 percent from 1997. About 70 percent were due to bacteria associated with sewage or polluted runoff, according to the council's 10th annual report. The "beach buddies" were East Haven Town Beach in Connecticut; North Beach and Oceanside at the Assateague Island National Seashore in Maryland; and Revere Beach and Short Beach in Massachusetts.

Source: *USA Today*, August 4, 2000. Copyright 2000 USA TODAY. Reprinted with permission. www.usatoday.com

Analysis: The pollution that closes beaches can be avoided with better sewage treatment facilities. Who should bear that cost?

---

of solid waste each year. This figure includes more than 30 billion bottles, 60 billion cans, 100 million tires, and millions of discarded automobiles and major appliances. Where do you think all this refuse goes?

Most solid wastes originate in agriculture (slaughter wastes, orchard prunings, harvest residues) and mining (slag heaps, mill tailings). The much smaller amount of solid waste originating in residential and commercial use is considered more dangerous, however, simply because it accumulates where people live. New York City alone generates 24,000 tons of trash a day. Because it has neither the land area nor the incinerators needed for disposal, it must ship its garbage to other states. Seattle ships its trash to Oregon; Los Angeles transports its trash to the Mojave Desert; New York City sludge is dumped in west Texas; and Philadelphia ships its garbage all the way to Panama.

POLLUTION DAMAGES

Shipping garbage to Panama is an expensive answer to our waste disposal problem. But even those costs are a small fraction of the total cost of environmental damage. Much greater costs are associated with the damage to our health (labor), buildings (capital), and land. Even the little things count, like being able to enjoy a clear sunset or take a deep breath.

Although many people don't like to put a price on the environment, some monetary measure of environmental damage is important in decision making. Unless we value the environment above everything else, we have to establish some method of ranking the importance of environmental damage. Although it's tempting to say that clean air is priceless, *we won't get clean air unless we spend resources to get it.* This economic reality suggests that we begin by determining how much cleaner air is worth to us.

In some cases, it's fairly easy to put a price on environmental damage. Scientists can measure the increase in cancer, heart attacks, and other disorders attributable to air pollution, as the EPA does for air toxins (see News on next page). Engineers can also measure the rate at which buildings decay or forests and lakes die. Economists can then estimate the dollar value of this damage by assessing the economic value of lives, forests, lakes, and other resources. For example, if people are willing to pay $5,000 for a cataract operation, then the avoidance of such eye damage is worth at least $5,000. Saving a tree is worth whatever the marketplace is willing to pay for the products of that tree. Using such computations, the EPA estimates that air pollution alone inflicts health, property, and vegetation damage in excess of $50 billion a year.

Assigning Prices

The Earth Policy Institute offers data on the costs of pollution at www.earth-policy.org.

IN THE NEWS

Dirty Air Can Shorten Your Life

The largest study ever conducted on the health effects of airborne particles from traffic and smokestacks has found that people in the nation's most polluted cities are 15 to 17 percent more likely to die prematurely than those in cities with the cleanest air.

This form of pollution is killing citizens even in areas that meet Environmental Protection Agency air quality standards, said study coauthor Douglas Dockery of the Harvard School of Public Health, who said "the impact on life and health is more pervasive than previously thought."

In Washington, where levels of airborne particles fall in the low middle range for U.S. cities, the average long-term resident loses approximately one year of life expectancy compared to the average for such relatively pristine places as Topeka, Kan., or Madison, Wis., Dockery said. In highly polluted places like Los Angeles or Salt Lake City, the toll is much greater: Compared to people in the cleanest metropolitan areas, those exposed to the highest concentrations of particles run a risk of premature death about one-sixth as great as if they had been smoking for 25 years.

—Curt Suplee

Source: *The Washington Post*, March 10, 1995. © 1995 The Washington Post. Reprinted with permission. www.washingtonpost.com

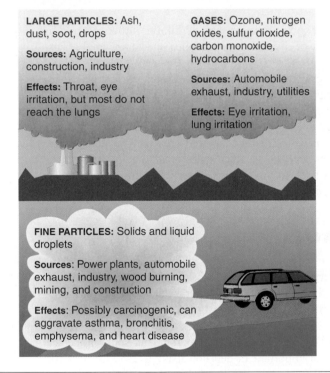

LARGE PARTICLES: Ash, dust, soot, drops

Sources: Agriculture, construction, industry

Effects: Throat, eye irritation, but most do not reach the lungs

GASES: Ozone, nitrogen oxides, sulfur dioxide, carbon monoxide, hydrocarbons

Sources: Automobile exhaust, industry, utilities

Effects: Eye irritation, lung irritation

FINE PARTICLES: Solids and liquid droplets

Sources: Power plants, automobile exhaust, industry, wood burning, mining, and construction

Effects: Possibly carcinogenic, can aggravate asthma, bronchitis, emphysema, and heart disease

Analysis: Pollution entails real costs, as measured by impaired health, reduced life spans, and other damages.

The job of pricing environmental damage is much more difficult with intangible losses like sunsets. Nevertheless, when governmental agencies and courts are asked to assess the damages of oil spills and other accidents, they must try to inventory *all* costs, including polluted sunsets, reduced wildlife, and lost recreation opportunities. The science of computing such environmental damage is very inexact. Nevertheless, crude but reasonable procedures generate damage estimates measured in hundreds of billions of dollars per year.

One of the most frustrating things about all this environmental damage is that it can be avoided. The EPA estimates that *95 percent of current air and water pollution could be eliminated by known and available technology.* Nothing very exotic is needed: just simple things like auto-emission controls, smokestack cleaners, improved sewage and waste treatment facilities, and cooling towers for electric power plants. Even solid-waste pollution could be reduced by comparable proportions if we used less packaging, recycled more materials, or transformed our garbage into a useful (relatively low-polluting) energy source. The critical question here is, Why don't we do these things? Why do we continue to pollute so much?

Cleanup Possibilities

MARKET INCENTIVES

Previous chapters emphasized how market incentives influence the behavior of individual consumers, firms, and government agencies. Incentives in the form of price reductions can be used to change consumer buying habits. Incentives in the form of high profit margins encourage production of desired goods and services. And market incentives in the form of cost differentials help allocate resources efficiently. Accordingly, we shouldn't be too surprised to learn that **market incentives play a major role in pollution behavior.**

Imagine that you're the majority stockholder and manager of an electric power plant. Such plants are responsible for a significant amount of air pollution (especially sulfur dioxide and particulates) and nearly all thermal water pollution. Hence, your position immediately puts you on the most-wanted list of pollution offenders. But suppose you bear society no grudges and would truly like to help eliminate pollution. Let's consider the alternatives.

As the owner-manager of an electric power plant, you'll strive to make a profit-maximizing **production decision.** That is, you'll seek the rate of output at which marginal revenue equals marginal cost. Let's assume that the electric power industry is still regulated by the state power commission so that the price of electricity is fixed, at least in the short run. The effect of this assumption is to render marginal revenue equal to price, thus giving us a horizontal price line, as in Figure 13.1*a*.

The Production Decision

> **production decision:** The selection of the short-run rate of output (with existing plant and equipment).

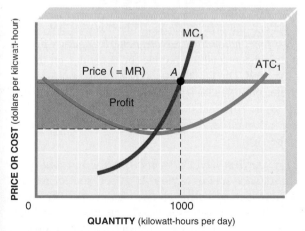

(a) Maximizing profits by using cheap but polluting process

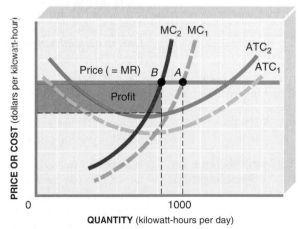

(b) Protecting the environment by using more expensive but less polluting process

FIGURE 13.1
Profit Maximization in Electric Power Production

Production processes that control pollution may be more expensive than those that don't. If they are, the MC and ATC curves will shift upward (to MC_2 and ATC_2). At the new profit-maximizing rate of output (point *B*), output and total profit shrink. Hence, a producer has an incentive to continue polluting, using cheaper technology.

The Efficiency Decision

efficiency decision: The choice of a production process for any given rate of output.

Figure 13.1*a* also depicts the marginal and average total costs (MC and ATC) associated with the production of electricity. By equating marginal cost (MC) to price (marginal revenue, MR), we observe (point *A*) that profit maximization occurs at an output of 1,000 kilowatt-hours per day. Total profits are illustrated by the shaded rectangle between the price line and the average total cost (ATC) curve.

The profits illustrated in Figure 13.1*a* are achieved in part by use of the cheapest available fuel under the boilers (which create the steam that rotates the generators). Recall that the construction of a marginal cost curve presumes some knowledge of alternative production processes. Recall too that the **efficiency decision** requires a producer to choose that production process (and its associated cost curve) that minimizes costs for any particular rate of output.

Costs of Pollution Abatement. Unfortunately, the efficiency decision in this case leads to the use of high-sulfur coal, the prime villain in SO_2 and particulate pollution. Other fuels, such as low-sulfur coal, fuel oil, and nuclear energy, cost considerably more. Were you to switch to one of them, the ATC and MC curves would both shift upward, as in Figure 13.1*b*. Under these conditions, the most profitable rate of output would be lower than before (point *B*), and total profits would decline (note the smaller profit rectangle in Figure 13.1*b*). Thus, ***pollution abatement can be achieved, but only at significant cost to the plant.***

The same kind of cost considerations lead the plant to engage in thermal pollution. Cool water must be run through an electric utility plant to keep the turbines from overheating. Once the water has run through the plant, it's too hot to recirculate. It must be either dumped back into the adjacent river or cooled off by being circulated through cooling towers. As you might expect, it's cheaper to simply dump the hot water in the river. The fish don't like it, but they don't have to pay the construction costs associated with cooling towers.

The big question here is whether you and your fellow stockholders would be willing to incur higher costs in order to cut down on pollution. Eliminating either the air pollution or the water pollution emanating from the electric plant will cost a lot of money. And to whose benefit? To the people who live downstream and downwind? We don't expect profit-maximizing producers to take such concerns into account. ***The behavior of profit maximizers is guided by comparisons of revenues and costs, not by philanthropy, aesthetic concerns, or the welfare of fish.***

MARKET FAILURE: EXTERNAL COSTS

The moral of this story—and the critical factor in pollution behavior—is that ***people tend to maximize their personal welfare, balancing private benefits against private costs.*** For the electric power plant, this means making production decisions on the basis of revenues received and costs incurred. The fact that the power plant imposes costs on others, in the form of air and water pollution, is irrelevant to its profit-maximizing decisions. Those costs are *external* to the firm and don't appear on its profit-and-loss statement. Those **external costs**—or *externalities*—are no less real, but they're incurred by society at large rather than by the firm.

external cost: Cost of a market activity borne by a third party; the difference between the social and private costs of a market activity.

Externalities in Production

Whenever external costs exist, a private firm won't allocate its resources and operate its plant in such a way as to maximize social welfare. In effect, society permits the power plant the free use of valued resources—clean air and clean water. The power plant has a tremendous incentive to substitute those resources for others (such as high-priced fuel or cooling towers) in the production process. The inefficiency of such an arrangement is obvious when we recall that the function of markets is to allocate scarce resources in accordance with the consumer's expressed demands. Yet here we are, proclaiming a high value for clean air and clean water and encouraging the power plant to use up both resources by offering them at zero cost to the firm.

social costs: The full resource costs of an economic activity, including externalities.

The inefficiency of this market arrangement can be expressed in terms of a distinction between social costs and private costs. **Social costs** are the total costs of all

"*Where there's smoke, there's money.*"

Analysis: If a firm can substitute external costs for private (internal) costs, its profits may increase.

the resources used in a particular production activity. On the other hand, **private costs** are the resource costs incurred by the specific producer.

Ideally, a producer's private costs will encompass all the attendant social costs, and production decision will be consistent with our social welfare. Unfortunately, this happy identity doesn't always exist, as our experience with the power plant illustrates. *When social costs differ from private costs, external costs exist. In fact, external costs are equal to the difference between the social and private costs*—that is,

$$\text{External costs} = \text{social costs} - \text{private costs}$$

When external costs are present, the market mechanism won't allocate resources efficiently. This is a case of **market failure.** The price signal confronting producers is flawed. By not conveying the full (social) cost of scarce resources, the market encourages excessive pollution. We end up with a suboptimal mix of output (too much electricity, too little clean air) and the wrong production processes.

The consequences of this market failure are illustrated in Figure 13.2, which again depicts the cost situation confronting the electric power plant. Notice that we use two

> **private costs:** The costs of an economic activity directly borne by the immediate producer or consumer (excluding externalities).

> **market failure:** An imperfection in the market mechanism that prevents optimal outcomes.

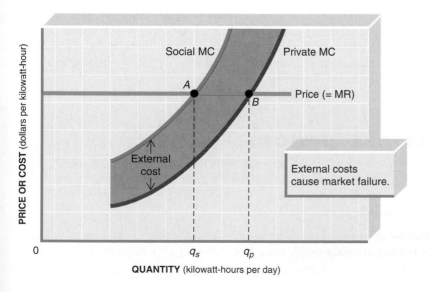

FIGURE 13.2
Market Failure

Social costs exceed private costs by the amount of external costs. Production decisions based on private costs alone will lead us to point *B*, where private MC = MR. At point *B*, the rate of output is q_p.

To maximize social welfare, we equate *social* MC and MR, as at point *A*. Only q_s of output is socially desirable. The failure of the market to convey the full costs of production keeps us from attaining this outcome.

different marginal cost curves this time. The lower one, the *private* MC curve, reflects the private costs incurred by the power plant when it operates on a profit-maximization basis, using high-sulfur coal and no cooling towers. It's identical to the MC curve in Figure 13.1*a*. We now know, however, that such operations impose external costs on others in the form of air and water pollution. These external costs must be added on to private marginal costs. When this is done, we get a *social* marginal cost curve that lies above the private MC curve.

To maximize profits, private firms seek the rate of output that equates private MC to MR (price). ***To maximize social welfare, we need to equate social marginal cost to marginal revenue (price).*** This social optimum occurs at point *A* in Figure 13.2 and results in output of q_s. By contrast, the firm's private profit maximization occurs at point *B*, where q_p is produced. Hence, the private firm ends up producing more output than socially desired, while earning more profit and causing more pollution. As a general rule, ***if pollution costs are external, firms will produce too much of a polluting good.***

Externalities in Consumption

A divergence between private and social costs can also be observed in consumption. A consumer, like a producer, tends to maximize personal welfare. We buy and use more of those goods and services that yield the highest satisfaction (marginal utility) per dollar expended. By implication (and the law of demand), we tend to use more of a product if we can get it at a discount—that is, pay less than the full price. Unfortunately, the "discount" often takes the form of an external cost imposed on neighbors and friends.

Automobile driving illustrates the problem. The amount of driving one does is influenced by the price of a car and the marginal costs of driving it. People buy smaller cars and drive less when the attendant marginal costs (for instance, gasoline prices) increase substantially. But automobile use involves not only *private costs* but *external costs* as well. Auto emissions (carbon monoxide, hydrocarbons, and nitrogen oxides) are a principal cause of air pollution. In effect, automobile drivers have been able to use a valued resource, clean air, at no cost to themselves. Few motorists see any personal benefit in installing exhaust control devices because the quality of the air they breathe would be little affected by their efforts. Hence, low private costs lead to excessive pollution when high social costs are dictating cleaner air.

A divergence between social and private costs can be observed even in the simplest of consumer activities, such as throwing an empty soda can out the window of your car. To hang on to the can and later dispose of it in a trash barrel involves personal effort and thus private marginal costs. To throw it out the window not only is more exciting but also effectively transfers the burden of disposal costs to someone else. The resulting externality ends up as roadside litter.

The same kind of divergence between private and social costs helps explain why people abandon old cars in the street rather than haul them to scrapyards. It also explains why people use vacant lots as open dumps. In all these cases, ***the polluter benefits by substituting external costs for private costs.*** In other words, market incentives encourage environmental damage.

REGULATORY OPTIONS

The failure of the market to include external costs in production and consumption decisions creates a basis for government intervention. As always, however, we confront a variety of policy options. We may define these options in terms of ***two general strategies for environmental protection:***

- *Alter market incentives* in such a way that they discourage pollution.
- *Bypass market incentives* with some form of regulatory intervention.

Insofar as market incentives are concerned, the key to environmental protection is to eliminate the divergence between private costs and social costs. The opportunity to shift some costs onto others lies at the heart of the pollution problem. If we could somehow compel producers to *internalize* all costs—pay for both private and previously external costs—the divergence would disappear, along with the incentive to pollute.

Emission Charges. One possibility is to establish a system of **emission charges,** direct costs attached to the act of polluting. Suppose that we let you keep your power plant and permit you to operate it according to profit-maximizing principles. The only difference is that we no longer agree to supply you with clean air and cool water at zero cost. From now on, we'll charge you for these scarce resources. We might, say, charge you 2 cents for every gram of noxious emission you discharge into the air. In addition we might charge you 3 cents for every gallon of water you use, heat, and discharge back into the river.

Confronted with such emission charges, you'd have to alter your production decision. ***An emission charge increases private marginal cost and encourages lower output and cleaner technology.*** Figure 13.3 illustrates this effect. Notice how the fee raises private marginal costs and induces a lower rate of (polluting) production (q_1 rather than q_0).

Once an emission fee is in place, a producer may also reevaluate the efficiency decision. Consider again the choice of fuels to be used in our fictional power plant. We earlier chose high-sulfur coal, for the very good reason that it was the cheapest fuel available. Now, however, there's an additional cost attached to burning such fuel, in the form of an emission charge. This added cost may encourage the firm to switch to cleaner sources of energy, which would increase private marginal costs but reduce emission fees.

An emission charge might also persuade a firm to incur higher fixed costs. Rather than pay emission charges, it might be more economical to install scrubbers and other smokestack controls that reduce the volume of emissions from the burning of high-sulfur coal. This would entail additional capital outlays for the necessary abatement equipment but might not alter marginal costs. In this case, the fee-induced change in fixed costs might reduce pollution without any reduction in output.

The actual response of producers will depend on the relative costs involved. If emission charges are too low, it may be more profitable to continue burning and polluting with high-sulfur coal and simply pay a nominal fee. This is a simple pricing problem. We could set the emission price higher, prompting the behavioral responses we desire.

The same kind of relative cost considerations would apply to the thermal pollution associated with the power plant. The choice heretofore has been between building

Market-Based Options

emission charge: A fee imposed on polluters, based on the quantity of pollution.

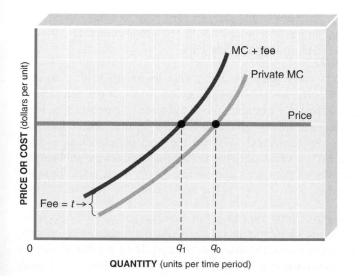

FIGURE 13.3
Emission Fees

Emission charges can be used to close the gap between marginal social costs and marginal private costs. Faced with an emission charge of *t*, a private producer will reduce output from q_0 to q_1. Emission charges may also induce different investment and efficiency decisions.

expensive cooling towers (and not polluting) or not incurring such capital costs (and simply discharging the heated water into the river). The profit-maximizing choice was fairly obvious. Now, however, the choice is between building cooling towers or paying out a steady flow of emission charges. The profit-maximizing decision is no longer evident. The decisive factor will be how high we set the emission charges. If the emission charges are set high enough, the producer will find it unprofitable to pollute.

Economic incentives can also change consumer behavior. At one time, beverage producers imposed deposits to encourage consumers to bring the bottle back so it could be used again. But producers discovered that such deposits discouraged sales and yielded very little cost savings. Today, returnable bottles are rarely used. One result is the inclusion of over 30 billion bottles and 60 billion cans in our solid-waste disposal problem. We could reverse this trend by imposing a deposit on all beverage containers. Many states do this, at least for certain cans and bottles. Such deposits internalize pollution costs for the consumer and render the throwing of a soda can out the window equivalent to throwing away money.

Some communities have also tried to reduce solid-waste processing by charging a fee for each container of garbage collected. In Charlotte, Virginia, a fee of 80 cents per 32-gallon bag of garbage had a noticeable impact on consumer behavior. Economists Don Fullerton and Thomas Kinnaman observed that households reduced the weight of their garbage by 14 percent and the volume by 37 percent. As they noted, "Households somehow stomped their garbage to get more in a container and trim their garbage bill."

Trends in recycling are posted by the U.S. Environmental Protection Agency (EPA) at www.epa.gov/epaoswer/non-hw/recycle.htm.

Recycling Materials. An important bonus that emission charges offer is an increased incentive for the recycling of materials. The glass and metal in used bottles and cans can be recycled to produce new bottles and cans. Such recycling not only eliminates a lot of unsightly litter but also diminishes the need to mine new resources from the earth, a process that often involves its own environmental problems. The critical issues are once again relative costs and market incentives. *A container producer has no incentive to use recycled materials unless they offer superior cost efficiency and thus greater profits.* The largest component in the costs of recycled materials is usually the associated costs of collection and transportation. In this regard, an emission charge such as the 5-cent container deposit lowers collection costs because it motivates consumers to return all their bottles and cans to a central location.

Higher User Fees. Another market alternative is to raise the price consumers pay for scarce resources. If people used less water, we wouldn't have to build so many sewage treatment plants. In most communities, however, the price of water is so low that people use it indiscriminately. Higher water fees would encourage water conservation.

A similar logic applies to auto pollution. The cheapest way to cut down on auto pollution is to drive less. Higher gasoline prices would encourage people to use alternative transportation and drive more fuel-efficient cars.

"Green" Taxes. Automakers don't want gasoline prices to go up; neither do consumers. So the government may have to impose *green taxes* to get the desired response. A green tax on gasoline, for example, raises the price of gasoline. The taxes not only curb auto emissions (less driving) but also create a revenue source for other pollution-abatement efforts. As the World View on the next page indicates, other nations impose far more green taxes than does the United States. Because public opinion polls show that a plurality of American consumers oppose such taxes, this disparity isn't likely to disappear.

Pollution Fines. Not far removed from the concept of emission and user charges is the imposition of fines or liability for cleanup costs. In some situations, such as an oil spill, the pollution is so sudden and concentrated that society has little choice but to clean it up quickly. The costs for such cleanup can be imposed on the polluter, however, through

WORLD VIEW

Guess Who Taxes Pollution Least?
Making a Mess Costs Less in the U.S.

Economists have long argued that an efficient way to control pollution is to make those who cause it bear some of the costs via environmentally related or "green" taxes. These can run the gamut from retail taxes on gasoline to landfill charges on waste disposal.

By dint of its economic heft, the U.S. is commonly regarded as the world's biggest polluter. Yet the Organization for Economic Cooperation & Development reports that it imposes the lowest green taxes as a percent of gross domestic product of any industrial nation. While the average for OECD countries in 1998 was 2.7 percent of GDP, for example, the U.S. level was estimated at less than 1 percent.

Between 1994 and 1998, a majority of OECD members boosted their green-tax ratios, with Denmark's and Turkey's both rising by a full percentage point to 5 percent and 3 percent respectively. By contrast, the U.S., Germany, and France actually reduced their green-tax levels over the four-year period.

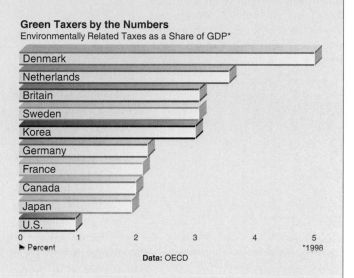

Green Taxers by the Numbers
Environmentally Related Taxes as a Share of GDP*

Denmark · Netherlands · Britain · Sweden · Korea · Germany · France · Canada · Japan · U.S.

► Percent   Data: OECD   *1998

Source: *BusinessWeek*, September 17, 2001. © 2001 The McGraw-Hill Companies, Inc. Reprinted with permission. www.businessweek.com

Analysis: "Green" taxes can be used to reduce the level of polluting consumption or production activities. They are not popular in the United States, however.

appropriate fines. Such fines place the cost burden where it belongs. In addition, they serve as an incentive for greater safety, for such things as double-hulled oil tankers and more efficient safety mechanisms on offshore oil wells. When Royal Caribbean Cruises was fined $9 million in 1998 for dumping garbage and oil from its cruise ships, the firm decided to monitor waste disposal practices more closely. In the absence of such fines, firms have little incentive to invest in environmental protection.

The EPA acquired still greater authority to control oil and chemical spills with passage of the Comprehensive Environmental Response, Compensation, and Liability Act of 1980. The act established a tax on crude oil and an assortment of chemical products. The resulting revenues created a superfund used to monitor and clean up hazardous oil and chemical spills. The act also allows the EPA to recoup *treble* damages from a firm that causes a spill but fails to help clean it up.

Another environmental policy option makes even greater use of market incentives. Rather than penalize firms that have already polluted, let firms *purchase* the right to continue polluting. As crazy as this policy might sound, it can be highly effective in limiting environmental damage.

The key to the success of pollution permits is that they're bought and sold among private firms. The system starts with a government-set standard for pollution reduction. Firms that reduce pollution by more than the standard earn pollution credits. They may then sell these credits to other firms, who are thereby relieved of cleanup chores. ***The principal advantage of pollution permits is their incentive to minimize the cost of pollution control.***

To see how the permits work, suppose the policy objective is to reduce sulfur dioxide emissions by 2 tons. There are only two major polluters in the community:

Tradable Pollution Permits

TABLE 13.1
Pricing Pollution Permits

If both firms reduce emissions by 1 ton each, the cost is $300. If the utility instead reduces emissions by 2 tons, the cost is only $250. A permit system allows the smelter to pay the utility for assuming the added abatement responsibility.

Reduction in Emissions (in tons)	Marginal Cost of Pollution Abatement	
	Copper Smelter	Electric Utility
1	$200	$100
2	250	150
3	300	200

a copper smelter and an electric utility. Should each company be required to reduce its SO_2 emissions by 1 ton? Or can the same SO_2 reduction be achieved more cheaply with marketable pollution rights?

Table 13.1 depicts the assumed cost of pollution abatement at each plant. The copper smelter would have to spend $200 to achieve a 1-ton reduction in SO_2 emissions. The utility can do it for only $100. Table 13.1 also indicates that the utility can attain a *second* ton of SO_2 abatement for $150. Even though its marginal cost of pollution control is increasing, the utility still has lower abatement costs than the smelter. This cost advantage creates an interesting economic opportunity.

Recall that the policy goal is to reduce emissions by 2 tons. The copper smelter would have to spend $200 to achieve its share. But the utility can abate that second ton for $150. Accordingly, the smelter would save money by *paying* the utility for additional pollution abatement.

How much would the smelter have to pay? The utility would want at least $150 to cover its own costs. The smelter would benefit at any price below $200. Accordingly, the price of this transaction would be somewhere between $150 (the utility's cost) and $200 (the smelter's cost). The smelter would continue to pollute, but total SO_2 emissions would still drop by 2 tons. Both firms and society would be better off.

At the first real auction of pollution credits the average price paid was $156 (see News). For this price a firm could pay someone else to reduce SO_2 emissions by 1 ton rather than curb its own emissions. The Carolina Power and Light Company spent $11.5 *million* buying such permits.

IN THE NEWS

Auction: $156 to Emit a Ton of Pollutants

CHICAGO—The right to spew a ton of sulfur dioxide into the air in 1995 costs about $156. That was the average sale price Tuesday at the first auction of pollution credits.

Total sold: 150,010 permits for $21.4 million. Permits sold for the year 2000 were cheaper, an average $136.

Price range: $122 to $450.

The auction of credits, at the Chicago Board of Trade, is key to the Environmental Protection Agency's efforts to halve acid rain pollutants by 2010. . . .

Who sells credits? Utilities that have less pollution than al-

lowed under EPA rules. Who buys? Utilities with pollution problems, or speculators.

Top buyer: Carolina Power & Light Co. spent $11.5 million. . . .

Consumers could gain: The program could halve the cost of anti-pollution rules for utilities, which could lower bills.

—Kevin Johnson

Source: *USA Today*, March 31, 1993. Copyright 1993, USA TODAY. Reprinted with permission. www.usatoday.com. For current price on pollution credits see www.epa.gov/airmarkets/trading/SO2 market.

Analysis: Marketable pollution permits encourage firms with more efficient pollution control technologies to overachieve, thereby earning pollution permits that can be sold to firms with more expensive pollution control technologies. Such trades reduce the *average* cost of pollution control.

Since they first became available in 1992, tradable pollution permits ("allowances") have become a popular mechanism for pollution control. Millions of allowances are now traded in the open market every year. Moreover, the permit market has gotten increasingly efficient, with visible bid and ask prices, broker specialists, and low transaction costs. In 2000, 12.7 *million* sulfur dioxide allowances were traded, each covering one ton of emission reduction. The price of a permit has also steadily declined, indicating that companies are discovering cheaper methods of pollution control. Entrepreneurs now have an incentive to discover cheaper methods for pollution abatement. They don't have to own a smelter or utility; they can now *sell* their pollution control expertise to the highest bidder. As the market for permits has expanded, the profit opportunities for environmental engineering firms have increased. This has accelerated productivity and reduced the cost of pollution abatement by 25 to 34 percent. In view of these results, EPA extended the pollution-permit trading system to *water* pollution in 2003.

Command-and-Control Options

Public policy needn't rely on tradable permits or other market incentives to achieve desired pollution abatement. The government could instead simply *require* firms to reduce pollutants by specific amounts and even specify which abatement technology must be used. This approach is often referred to as the "command-and-control" option. The government *commands* firms to reduce pollution and then *controls* the process for doing so.

The potential inefficiency of the command-and-control strategy was outlined earlier in Table 13.1. Had the government required *each* firm to reduce pollution by 1 ton, the total cost would have been $300. By allowing firms to use tradable permits, the cost of obtaining the same level of pollution abatement was only $250. The cost saving of $50 represents valuable resources that could be used to produce other desired goods and services.

Despite the superior efficiency of market-based environmental policies, the government often relies on the command-and-control approach. The Clean Air Acts of 1970 and 1990, for example, mandated not only fewer auto emissions but also specific processes such as catalytic converters and lead-free gasoline for attaining them. Specific processes and technologies are also required for toxic waste disposal and water treatment. Laws requiring the sorting and recycling of trash are other examples of process regulation.

Although such command-and-control regulation can be effective, this policy option also entails risks. By requiring all market participants to follow specific rules, the regulations may impose excessive costs on some activities and too low a constraint on others. Some communities may not need the level of sewage treatment the federal government prescribes. Individual households may not generate enough trash to make sorting and separate pickups economically sound. Some producers may have better or cheaper ways of attaining environmental standards. *Excessive process regulation may raise the costs of environmental protection* and discourage cost-saving innovation. There's also the risk of regulated processes becoming entrenched long after they are obsolete. When that happens we may end up with worse outcomes than a less regulated market would have generated—that is, **government failure.**

government failure: Government intervention that fails to improve economic outcomes.

Central Planning

Some of the worst government failure occurs in the most regulated economies. Prior to 1990, Eastern Europe relied on central planning to make production and investment decisions. There was no *market* incentive to pollute since there was no opportunity for private profit. On the other hand, the central planners had to set priorities. Their choice was to maximize production. Environmental concerns had lower priority. This set of priorities created an environmental catastrophe: polluted air and water, dying forests, poisoned food, and deteriorating human health. Poland, for example, produced six times more air pollution per unit of output than did Western Europe. Europe's largest coal-burning power plant, located in Belchatow, burns soft brown coal, covering the countryside with sulfur and soot. The world's largest single source of air pollution is the complex of ore smelters in Norilsk (central Siberia), which emits 2 *million* tons of sulfur a day. Cars made in Russia and Eastern Europe still burn leaded gas. The Volga River has been crippled by factory waste, untreated sewage, and hydroelectric dams, while the Black Sea has virtually been destroyed. The polluted environments of Eastern Europe and the former Soviet republics amply document that government-directed production isn't necessarily more environment-friendly than market-directed production.

BALANCING BENEFITS AND COSTS

Protecting the environment entails costs as well as benefits. Installing smokestack scrubbers on factory chimneys and catalytic converters on cars requires the use of scarce resources. Taking the lead out of gasoline wears out engines faster and requires expensive changes in technology. Switching to clean fuels requires enormous investments in technology, plant, and equipment. The EPA estimates that a 10-year program to achieve national air and water standards would cost more than $1 trillion. Restoring the ozone layer, removing hazardous wastes, and cleaning up the rest of the environment would cost trillions more.

Opportunity Costs

Whatever the exact costs of environmental protection, it's apparent that we're talking about an enormous reallocation of productive resources. Although cleaning up the environment is a universally acknowledged goal, we must remind ourselves that those resources could be used to fulfill other goals as well. The multitrillion-dollar tab would buy a lot of subways and parks or build decent homes for the poor. If we choose to devote those resources instead to pollution-abatement efforts, we'll have to forgo some other goods and services. This isn't to say that environmental goals don't deserve that kind of priority but simply to remind us that any use of our scarce resources involves an **opportunity cost.**

opportunity cost: The most desired goods or services that are forgone in order to obtain something else.

Fortunately, the amount of additional resources required to clean up the environment is relatively modest in comparison to our productive capacity. Over a 10-year period we'll produce well over $100 trillion of goods and services (GDP). On this basis, the environmental expenditures contemplated by present environmental policies and goals represent only 1 to 3 percent of total output.

The Optimal Rate of Pollution

optimal rate of pollution: The rate of pollution that occurs when the marginal social benefit of pollution control equals its marginal social cost.

Whether a small percentage of GDP is too much or too little to spend on environmental protection depends on the value we assign to other goods and services and to a cleaner environment. That is, the **optimal rate of pollution** occurs at the point at which the opportunity costs of further pollution control equal the benefits of further reductions in pollution. To determine the optimal rate of pollution, we need to compare the marginal social benefits of additional pollution abatement with the marginal social costs of additional pollution control expenditure. The optimal rate of pollution is achieved when we've satisfied the following equality:

$$\begin{matrix} \text{Optimal} \\ \text{rate of} \\ \text{pollution} \end{matrix} : \begin{matrix} \text{marginal benefit} \\ \text{of pollution} \\ \text{abatement} \end{matrix} = \begin{matrix} \text{marginal cost} \\ \text{of pollution} \\ \text{abatement} \end{matrix}$$

This formulation is analogous to the utility-maximizing rule in consumption. If another dollar spent on pollution control yields less than a dollar of social benefits, then additional pollution control expenditure isn't desirable. In such a situation, the goods and services that would be forsaken for additional pollution control are more valued than the environmental improvements that would result. The News on the top of the next page suggests that we may already have crossed that threshold in combating air pollution.

A 2003 White House study concluded that past efforts to clean up the air have yielded far more benefits than costs. As the accompanying News reports, the benefits of a 10-year (1992–2002) air pollution abatement program exceeded costs by 5–8 times.

IN THE NEWS

Two Economists Question Benefit of Cleaning Up a Major Air Pollutant

The health benefits of cleaning up a widespread urban air pollutant, ground-level ozone, may not be worth the price, two economists argue in a new study.

The economists at Resources for the Future, a respected non-advocacy research institute in Washington, compared the costs of plans for Los Angeles and the nation as a whole to meet national air quality standards for ground-level ozone with their potential health benefits. In both cases, the most optimistic estimate of the costs fell far short of the most optimistic measure of the health benefits.

They chose to look at ground-level ozone because it is one of the most difficult air pollution problems to solve. They also said they believed they could effectively apply cost-benefit analysis to it.

According to cost estimates based on 1989 government data, they found the cost for the nation to meet the standards would be $8.8 billion to $12.8 billion through 2004 while health benefits would be $250 million to $1 billion. They

estimated that the cost of a more ambitious 1989 Los Angeles plan would be $13 billion through 2010 but that it would yield only $3 billion in health benefits.

Basis of Conclusions

The economists, Alan J. Krupnick and Paul R. Portney, concluded that air should be cleaned up in the most polluted areas but that investing billions of dollars to get people to quit smoking, control radon gas and provide better prenatal and neonatal care might contribute much more. . . .

"I don't expect people to like the conclusion," Mr. Portney said, "But this is not a justification for not cleaning up the air. It just says maybe we could get more health benefits for our money if we spent it someplace else."

The New York Times

Source: *The New York Times*, April 30, 1991. © 1991 The New York Times Company. Reprinted by permission. www.nytimes.com

Analysis: The costs of environmental protection are substantial and must be compared to the benefits. The *optimal* amount of pollution balances marginal benefits and costs.

Although pollution abatement has been an economic success, that doesn't mean *all* pollution controls are desirable. The focus must still be on *marginal* benefits and costs. As the above News reports, the cost of cleaning up ground-level ozone exceeds resultant benefits by as much as 50-1. More generally, the formula for the optimal rate of pollution implies that *a totally clean environment isn't economically desirable.* The

WEBNOTE

OMB's annual cost-benefit analysis of pollution control is at www.omb.gov.

IN THE NEWS

Study Finds Net Gain From Pollution Rules

A new White House study concludes that environmental regulations are well worth the costs they impose on industry and consumers, resulting in significant public health improvements and other benefits to society. . . .

The report, issued this month by the Office of Management and Budget, concludes that the health and social benefits of enforcing tough new clean-air regulations during the past decade were five to seven times greater in economic terms than were the costs of complying with the rules. The value of reductions in hospitalization and emergency room visits,

premature deaths and lost workdays resulting from improved air quality were estimated between $120 billion and $193 billion from October 1992 to September 2002.

By comparison, industry, states and municipalities spent an estimated $23 billion to $26 billion to retrofit plants and facilities and make other changes to comply with new clean-air standards, which are designed to sharply reduce sulfur dioxide, fine-particle emissions and other health-threatening pollutants.

—Eric Pianin

Source: *The Washington Post*, September 27, 2003. © 2003 The Washington Post. Reprinted with permission.

Analysis: The benefits of pollution abatement have generally exceeded its costs. However, *marginal* benefits and costs are critical in setting policy goals.

marginal benefit of achieving zero pollution is infinitesimally small. But the marginal cost of eliminating that last particle of pollution will be very high. As we weigh the marginal benefits and costs, we'll conclude that *some* pollution is cost-effective.

Cost-Benefit Analysis

Although marginal analysis tells us that a zero-pollution goal isn't economically desirable, it doesn't really pinpoint the optimal level of pollution. To apply those guidelines we need to identify and evaluate the marginal benefits of any intervention and its marginal costs. Sometimes such calculations yield extraordinarily high cost-benefit ratios. According to researchers at the Harvard Center for Risk Analysis, the *median* cost per life-year saved by EPA regulations is $7.6 million. One of the highest cost-benefit ratios is attached to chloroform emission controls at pulp mills: The cost per life-year saved exceeds $99 billion. A human life may in fact be too precious to value in dollars and cents. But in a world of limited resources, the opportunity costs of every intervention need to be assessed. How many lives would be saved if we spent $99 billion on cancer or AIDS research?

Mayor Bloomberg performed the same kind of analysis for New York City's recycling program. Sure, everyone thinks recycling is a good idea. But Mayor Bloomberg started looking at the cost of the recycling program and decided it didn't make economic sense (see News). He figured the city could use the $57 million for higher-priority programs, yielding greater (marginal) benefits to NYC residents.

Who Will Pay?

The costs of pollution control aren't distributed equally. In New York City, the cost of the recycling program is borne by those who end up with fewer city services and amenities (opportunity costs). A national pollution-abatement program would

IN THE NEWS

Forced Recycling Is a Waste

As New York City faces the possibility of painful cuts to its police and fire department budgets, environmentalists are belly-aching over garbage. Mayor Michael Bloomberg's proposed budget for 2003 would temporarily suspend the city's recycling of metal, glass and plastic, saving New Yorkers $57 million.

The city's recycling program—like many others around the country—has long hemorrhaged tax dollars. . . .

The city spends about $240 per ton to "recycle" plastic, glass, and metal, while the cost of simply sending waste to landfills is about $130 per ton.

You don't need a degree is economics to see that something is wrong here. Isn't recycling supposed to save money and resources? Some recycling does—when driven by market forces. Private parties don't voluntarily recycle unless they know it will save money, and, hence, resources. But forced recycling can be a waste of both because recycling itself entails using energy, water and labor to collect, sort, clean and process the materials. There are also air emissions, traffic and wear on streets from the second set of trucks prowling for recyclables. The bottom line is that most mandated recycling hurts, not helps the environment. . . .

M.E. Cohen

"You could do a lot better things in the world with $57 million," says Mayor Bloomberg.

—Angela Logomasini

Source: *The Wall Street Journal,* March 19, 2002. Reprinted by permission of The Wall Street Journal and Angela Logomasini, © 2002 Dow Jones & Company. All rights reserved worldwide.

Analysis: Recycling uses scarce resources that could be employed elsewhere. The benefits of recycling may not exceed its (opportunity) costs.

target the relatively small number of economic activities that account for the bulk of emissions and effluents. These activities will have to bear a disproportionate share of the cleanup burden.

To ascertain how the burden of environmental protection will be distributed, consider first the electric power plant discussed earlier. As we observed (Figure 13.2), the plant's output will decrease if production decisions are based on social rather than private marginal costs—that is, if environmental consequences are considered. If the plant itself is compelled to pay full social costs, in the form of either compulsory investment or emission charges, its profits will be reduced. Were no other changes to take place, the burden of environmental improvements would be borne primarily by the producer.

Such a scenario is unlikely, however. Rather than absorb all the costs of pollution controls themselves, producers will seek to pass on some of this burden to their customers in the form of higher prices. Their ability to do so will depend on the extent of competition in their industry, their relative cost position in it, and the price elasticity of consumer demand. In reality, the electric power industry isn't very competitive as yet, and its prices are still subject to government regulation. In addition, consumer demand is relatively price-inelastic. Accordingly, the profit-maximizing producer will appeal to the state or local power commission for an increase in electricity prices based on the costs of pollution control. Electric power consumers are likely to end up footing part or all of the environmental bill. The increased prices will more fully reflect the social costs associated with electricity use.

In addition to the electric power industry, the automobile, paper, steel, and chemical industries will be adversely affected by pollution controls. In all of these cases, the prices of the related products will increase, in some instances by significant percentages. These price increases will help reduce pollution in two ways. First, they'll help pay for pollution control equipment. Second, they'll encourage consumers to change their expenditure patterns in the direction of less polluting goods.

WEBNOTE

Find out how economists measure the costs and benefits of environmental programs at www.epa.gov. Click on "Programs," then "Research," then "Office of Research and Development."

THE ECONOMY TOMORROW

Forget about littered beaches, smelly landfills, eye-stinging smog, and contaminated water. The really scary problem for the economy tomorrow is much more serious: Some scientists say that the carbon emissions we're now spewing into the air are warming the earth's atmosphere. If the earth's temperature rises only a few degrees, they contend, polar caps will melt, continents will flood, and weather patterns will go haywire (see World View on the next page). If things get bad enough, there may not be any economy tomorrow.

The Greenhouse Threat

The earth's climate is driven by solar radiation. The energy the sun absorbs must be balanced by outgoing radiation from the earth and the atmosphere. Scientists fear that a flow imbalance is developing. Of particular concern is a buildup of carbon dioxide (CO_2) that might trap heat in the earth's atmosphere, warming the planet.

The natural release of CO_2 dwarfs the emissions from human activities. But there's a concern that the steady increase in man-made CO_2 emissions—principally from burning fossil fuels like gasoline and coal—is tipping the balance.

The Greenhouse Effect

Other scientists are skeptical about both the temperature change and its causes. A 1988 National Oceanic and Atmospheric Administration study concluded that there's been no ocean warming in this past century. Furthermore, they say, the amount of CO_2 emitted into the atmosphere by human activity (about 7 billion tons per year) is only a tiny fraction of natural emissions from volcanoes, fires, and lightning (200 billion tons per year). Skeptics also point out that the same computer models predicting global warming in the next generation predicted a much larger increase in temperature for the previous century than actually occurred.

The Skeptics

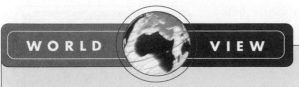

WORLD **VIEW**

Scientists Issue Dire Prediction on Warming
Faster Climate Shift Portends Global Calamity This Century

BEIJING, Jan. 22—In the most forceful warning yet on the threat of global warming, an international panel of hundreds of scientists issued a report today predicting brutal droughts, floods and violent storms across the planet over the next century because air pollution is causing surface temperatures to rise faster than anticipated.

The report, approved unanimously at a U.N. conference in Shanghai and described as the most comprehensive study on the subject to date, says that Earth's average temperature could rise by as much as 10.4 degrees over the next 100 years—the most rapid change in 10 millennia and more than 60 percent higher than the same group predicted less than six years ago.

If new scientific models are accurate, rising temperatures will melt polar ice caps and raise sea levels by as much as 34 inches, causing floods that could displace tens of millions of people in low-lying areas—such as China's Pearl River Delta, much of Bangladesh and the most densely populated area of Egypt. Droughts will parch farmlands and aggravate world hunger. Storms triggered by such climatic extremes as El Niño will become more frequent. Diseases such as malaria and dengue fever will spread. . . .

The report cited "new and stronger evidence that most of the observed warming of the last 50 years is attributable to human activities," primarily the burning of oil, gasoline and coal, which produces carbon dioxide and other gases that trap heat in Earth's atmosphere. . . .

The global warming issue has proved highly contentious among environmental scientists, with many respected figures arguing that Earth undergoes periodic climatic changes with or without contributions from mankind.

—Philip P. Pan

Source: *The Washington Post*, January 23, 2001. © 2001 The Washington Post. Reprinted with permission. www.washingtonpost.com

Analysis: The external costs of consumption and production activities contribute to global environmental problems. What should be done to curb these global external costs?

The 2004 White House report to Congress on climate change is at www.climatescience.gov.

Global Externalities

In mid-2001, the National Academy of Sciences resolved one of those issues. The Academy confirmed that the earth is warming, largely due to the increased buildup of greenhouse gas concentrations. A 2004 analysis by the National Center for Atmospheric Research concluded that natural climate changes were responsible for the earth's warming from 1900 to 1950, but could not explain the continuing rise in the earth's temperature since then. Human activity seemed to be the only possible culprit.

Despite accumulating evidence, lingering uncertainty about the causes of the greenhouse effect has made policy decisions difficult. One thing is certain, however: ***CO_2 emissions are a global externality*** of industrial production and fuel consumption. Without some form of government intervention, there's little likelihood that market participants will voluntarily reduce CO_2 emissions.

Kyoto Treaty. In December 1997, most of the world's industrialized nations pledged to reduce CO_2 emissions. The Kyoto treaty they initialed in 1997 expressed an international commitment to reduce greenhouse emissions during the period 2008–12. The world's industrialized nations promised to cut their emissions by 5.2 percent below 1990 levels. That would require some industries (e.g., autos, steel, paper, electric power) to substantially alter production methods and, possibly, output. For their part, the developing nations of the world promised to curb their *growth* of emissions.

After four years of design and debate, 178 nations signed the Kyoto treaty at a June 2001 United Nations convention. The United States, however, refused to sign. The Bush administration argued that the implied costs of pollution abatement were far too high, especially in view of the uncertain payoff. President Bush also argued that the treaty put the United States and other industrialized nations at a competitive disadvantage, since only they (not developing nations) had to absorb the higher pollution-abatement costs.

The United Nations provides information on climate change and emissions data for individual nations at www.unfccc.de.

With neither universal support nor enforcement mechanisms, the Kyoto treaty will not achieve the target levels of pollution abatement. However, the treaty has increased public awareness of global environmental externalities and encouraged more efforts to control them. As with domestic policy, the challenge for the economy tomorrow is to find a policy mix that will generate the optimal level of global pollution.

SUMMARY

- Air, water, and solid-waste pollution impose social and economic costs. The costs of pollution include the direct damages inflicted on our health and resources, the expense of cleaning up, and the general aesthetic deterioration of the environment.

- Pollution is an external cost, a cost of a market activity imposed on someone (a third party) other than the immediate producer or consumer.

- Producers and consumers generally operate on the basis of private benefits and costs. Accordingly, a private producer or consumer has an incentive to minimize his own costs by transforming private costs into external costs. One way of making such a substitution is to pollute—to use "free" air and water rather than install pollution control equipment, or to leave the job of waste disposal to others.

- Social costs are the total amount of resources used in a production or consumption process. When social costs are greater than private costs, the market's price signals are flawed. This market failure will induce people to harm the environment by using suboptimal processes and products.

- One way to correct the market inefficiency created by externalities is to compel producers and consumers to internalize all (social) costs. This can be done by imposing emission charges and higher user fees. Such charges create an incentive to invest in pollution abatement

equipment, recycle reusable materials, and conserve scarce elements of the environment.

- Tradable pollution permits help minimize the cost of pollution control by (a) promoting low-cost controls to substitute for high-cost controls and (b) encouraging innovation in pollution control technology.

- An alternative approach to cleaning up the environment is to require specific pollution controls or to prohibit specific kinds of activities. Direct regulation runs the risk of higher cost and discouraging innovations in environmental protection.

- The opportunity costs of pollution abatement are the most desired goods and services given up when factors of production are used to control pollution. The optimal rate of pollution is reached when the marginal social benefits of further pollution control equal associated marginal social costs.

- In addition to diverting resources, pollution control efforts alter relative prices, change the mix of output, and redistribute incomes. These outcomes cause losses for particular groups and may thus require special economic or political attention.

- The greenhouse effect represents a global externality. Reducing global emissions requires consensus on optimal pollution levels (i.e., the optimal balance of pollution-abatement costs and benefits).

Key Terms

production decision
efficiency decision
external cost
social costs

private costs
market failure
emission charge
government failure

opportunity cost
optimal rate of pollution

Questions for Discussion

1. What are the *economic* costs of the externalities caused by air toxins? Or beach closings? (See News, page 279.) How would you measure their value?

2. Should we try to eliminate *all* pollution? What economic considerations might favor permitting some pollution?

3. Why would auto manufacturers resist exhaust control devices? How would their costs, sales, and profits be affected?

4. Does anyone have an incentive to maintain auto-exhaust control devices in good working order? How can we ensure that they will be maintained?

5. Suppose we established a $10,000 fine for water pollution. Would some companies still find that polluting was economical? Under what conditions?

6. What economic costs are imposed by mandatory sorting of trash?

7. The issuance of a pollution permit is just a license to destroy the environment. Do you agree? Explain.

8. What opportunity costs of combating ozone pollution are identified in the News article on page 291?

9. If a high per-bag fee were charged for garbage collection, would illegal dumping increase?

10. Should the United States have signed the Kyoto treaty? What are the arguments for and against U.S. participation?

PROBLEMS The Student Problem Set at the back of this book contains numerical and graphing problems for this chapter.

WEB ACTIVITIES to accompany this chapter can be found on the Online Learning Center:
http://www.mhhe.com/economics/schiller10

The Farm Problem

I n 1996, the U.S. Congress charted a new future for U.S. farmers. No longer would they look to Washington, D.C., for decisions on what crops to plant or how much farmland to leave fallow. The Freedom to Farm Act would get the government out of the farm business and let "laissez faire" dictate farm outcomes. Farmers would lose their federal subsidies but could earn as much as they wanted in the marketplace. Taxpayers loved the idea. So did most farmers, who were enjoying high prices and bumper profits in 1996.

The Asian crisis that began in mid-1997 dealt farmers a severe blow. U.S. farms export 25–50 percent of all the wheat, corn, soybeans, and cotton they grow. When Asia's economies plunged into recession, those export sales plummeted. With sales, prices, and profits all declining, farmers lost their enthusiasm for the "freedom to farm"; they wanted Uncle Sam to jump back into the farm business with price and income guarantees. The U.S. Congress obliged by passing the Farm Security Act of 2001. That act not only increased farm subsidies, but also extended them to peanut farmers, hog farmers, and horse breeders. Between 2002 and 2012, these subsidies will cost taxpayers $15–20 billion per year.

This chapter examines the rationale for continuing farm subsidies and their effects on farm production, prices, and exports. In particular, we confront these questions:

- Why do farmers need any subsidies?
- How do government subsidies affect farm production, prices, and incomes?
- Who pays for farm subsidies?

DESTABILIZING FORCES

Competition in Agriculture

The agriculture industry is one of the most competitive of all U.S. industries. First, there are 2 million farms in the United States. Although some of these farms are immense—with tens of thousands of acres—no single farm has the power to affect the market supply or price of farm products. That is, individual farmers have no **market power.**

market power: The ability to alter the market price of a good or service.

Competition in agriculture is maintained by low **barriers to entry.** Although farmers need large acreages, expensive farm equipment, substantial credit, hard work, and hired labor, all these resources become affordable when farming is generating **economic profits.** When farming is profitable, existing farmers expand their farms and farmers' children are able to start new farms. It would be much harder to enter the automobile industry, the airline business, or even the farm machinery market than it would be to enter farming. Because of these low barriers to entry, economic profits don't last long in agriculture.

barriers to entry: Obstacles, such as patents, that make it difficult or impossible for would-be producers to enter a particular market.

Given the competitive structure of U.S. agriculture, *individual farmers tend to behave like perfect competitors.* Individual farmers seek to expand their rate of

economic profit: The difference between total revenues and total economic costs.

output until marginal cost equals price. By following this rule, each farmer makes as much profit as possible from existing resources, prices, and technology.

Like other competitive firms, U.S. farmers can maintain economic profits only if they achieve continuing cost reductions. Above-normal profits obtained from current production techniques and prices aren't likely to last. Such economic profits will entice more people into agriculture and will stimulate greater output from existing farmers. That is exactly the kind of dilemma that confronted the early producers of microcomputers. To stay ahead, individual firms (farms) must continue to improve their productivity.

Technological Advance

The rate of technological advance in agriculture has, in fact, been spectacular. Since 1929, the farm labor force has shrunk by two-thirds, yet farm output has increased by 70 percent. Between the early 1950s and today,

* Annual egg production has jumped from 183 to 259 eggs per laying chicken.
* Milk output has increased from 5,400 to 18,749 pounds per cow annually.
* Wheat output has increased from 17.3 to 42 bushels per acre.
* Corn output has jumped from 39.4 to 148 bushels per acre.

Farm output per labor hour has grown even faster, having increased 10 times over in the same period. Such spectacular rates of productivity advance rival those of our most high-tech industries. These technological advances resulted from the development of higher-yielding seeds (the "green revolution"), advanced machinery (mechanical feeders and milkers), improved animal breeding (crossbreeding), improved plants (rust-resistant wheat), better land-use practices (crop rotation and fertilizers), and computer-based management systems.

Inelastic Demand

In most industries, continuous increases in technology and output would be most welcome. The agricultural industry, however, confronts a long-term problem. Simply put, there's a limit to the amount of food people want to eat.

This constraint on the demand for agricultural output is reflected in the relatively inelastic demand for food. Consumers don't increase their food purchases very much when farm prices fall. The **price elasticity** of food demand is low. As a consequence, when harvests are good, farmers must reduce prices a lot to induce a substantial increase in the quantity of food demanded. Even if the price elasticity of demand were as high as 0.2, the percentage change in price would have to be five times as large as the percentage change in quantity produced. Hence, prices would have to fall 25 percent in order to sell a bumper crop that was 5 percent larger than normal, that is,

price elasticity of demand: The percentage change in quantity demanded divided by the percentage change in price.

$$\text{Required percentage change in price} = \frac{\text{percentage change in quantity (harvest)}}{\text{price elasticity of demand}}$$

so,

$$\% \, \Delta p = \frac{0.05}{0.20} = 0.25$$

In 1998, the *corn* crop was 6 percent larger than the year before. In 1999, the corn crop *decreased* by 3.5 percent. As Figure 14.1 illustrates, ***with low price elasticity of demand, abrupt changes in farm output have a magnified effect on market prices.***

The **income elasticity** of food demand is also low. The income elasticity of demand for food refers to the responsiveness of food demand to changes in income. Specifically,

income elasticity of demand: Percentage change in quantity demanded divided by percentage change in income.

$$\text{Income elasticity of demand} = \frac{\% \text{ change in quantity demanded (at constant price)}}{\% \text{ change in income}}$$

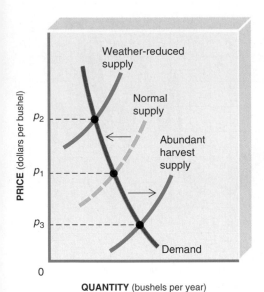

FIGURE 14.1
Short-Term Instability

Changes in weather cause abrupt shifts of the food supply curve. When combined with the relatively inelastic demand for food, these supply shifts result in wide price swings. Notice how the price of grain jumps from p_1 to p_2 when bad weather reduces the harvest. If good weather follows, prices may fall to p_3.

Since 1929, per capita income has tripled. But per capita food consumption has increased only 85 percent. Hence, neither lower prices nor higher incomes significantly increase the quantity of food demanded.

In the long run, then, the increasing ability of U.S. agriculture to produce food must be reconciled with very slow growth of U.S. demand for food. Over time, this implies that farm prices will fall, relative to nonfarm prices. And they have. Between the years 1910–14 and 2004, the ratio of farm prices to nonfarm prices fell 60 percent. In the absence of government price-support programs and foreign demand for U.S. farm products, farm prices would have fallen still further.

Abrupt Shifts of Supply

The long-term downtrend in (relative) farm prices is only one of the major problems confronting U.S. agriculture. The second major problem is short run in nature. Prices of farm products are subject to abrupt short-term swings. If the weather is good, harvests are abundant. As we saw in Figure 14.1, abundant harvests imply a severe drop in prices, however, particularly when food demand is relatively price-inelastic. On the other hand, a late or early freeze, a drought, or an infestation by disease or insect pests can reduce harvests and push prices sharply higher.

Response Lags. Natural forces aren't the only cause of short-term price instability. Time lags between the production decision and the resultant harvest also contribute to price instability. If prices are high one year, farmers have an incentive to increase their rate of output. In this sense, prices serve the same signaling function in agriculture as they do in nonfarm industries. What distinguishes the farmers' response is the lack of inventories and the fixed duration of the production process. In the computer industry, a larger quantity of output can be supplied to the market fairly quickly by drawing down inventories or stepping up the rate of production. In farming, supply can't respond so quickly. In the short run, the farmer can only till more land, plant additional seed, or breed more livestock. No additional food supplies will be available until a new crop or herd grows. Hence, the agricultural supply response to a change in prices is always one harvest (or breeding period) later.

The natural lag in responses of agricultural supplies intensifies short-term price swings. Suppose corn prices are exceptionally high at the end of a year, because of a

FIGURE 14.2
Unstable Corn Prices

Most agricultural prices are subject to abrupt short-term changes. Notice how corn prices rose dramatically during World Wars I and II, then fell sharply. Poor harvests in the rest of the world increased demand for U.S. food in 1973–74. Since then prices have moved sharply in both directions.

Source: U.S. Department of Agriculture.

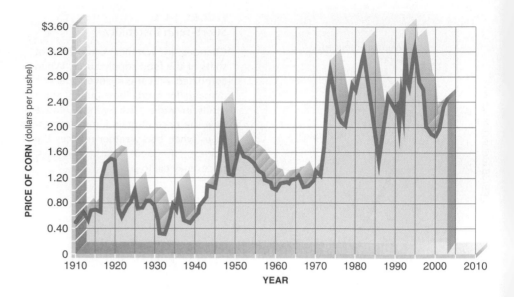

reduced harvest. High prices will make corn farming appear unusually profitable. Farmers will want to expand their rate of output—plant more corn acreage—to share in these high profits. But the corn won't appear on the market until the following year. By that time, there's likely to be an abundance of corn on the market, as a result of both better weather and increased corn acreage. Hence, corn prices are likely to plummet (look again at Figure 14.1).

No single farmer can avoid the boom-or-bust movement of prices. Even a corn farmer who has mastered the principles of economics has little choice but to plant more corn when prices are high. If he doesn't plant additional corn, prices will fall anyway, because his own production decisions don't affect market prices. By not planting additional corn, he only denies himself a share of corn market sales. ***In a highly competitive market, each producer acts independently.***

Figure 14.2 demonstrates the historical instability of corn prices. Notice how corn prices repeatedly rise, then abruptly fall. This kind of price swing is particularly evident in 1915–20, 1935–37, 1946–48, 1973–76, 1980–84, and 1997–2000.

THE FIRST FARM DEPRESSION, 1920-1940

The U.S. agricultural industry operated without substantial government intervention until the 1930s. In earlier decades, an expanding population, recurrent wars, and less advanced technology had helped maintain a favorable supply-demand relationship for farm products. There were frequent short-term swings in farm prices, but these were absorbed by a generally healthy farm sector. The period 1910–19 was particularly prosperous for farmers, largely because of the expanded foreign demand for U.S. farm products by countries engaged in World War I.

The two basic problems of U.S. agriculture grew to crisis proportions after 1920. In 1919, most farm prices were at historical highs (see Figures 14.2 and 14.3). After World War I ended, however, European countries no longer demanded as much American food. U.S. exports of farm products fell from nearly $4 billion in 1919 to $1.9 billion in 1921. Farm exports were further reduced in the following years by

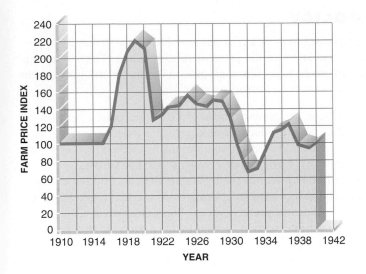

FIGURE 14.3
Farm Prices, 1910–1940
(1910–1914 = 100)

Farm prices are less stable than non-farm prices. During the 1930s, relative farm prices fell 50 percent. This experience was the catalyst for government price supports and other agricultural assistance programs.

increasing restrictions on international trade. At home, the end of the war implied an increased availability of factors of production and continuing improvement in farm technology.

The impact of reduced demand and increasing supply is evident in Figure 14.3. In 1919 farm prices were more than double their levels of the period 1910–14. Prices then fell abruptly. In 1921 alone, farm prices fell nearly 40 percent.

Farm prices stabilized in the mid-1920s but resumed a steep decline in 1930. In 1932 average farm prices were 75 percent lower than they had been in 1919. At the same time, the average income per farmer from farming fell from $2,651 in 1919 to $855 in 1932.

The Great Depression hit small farmers particularly hard. They had fewer resources to withstand consecutive years of declining prices and income. Even in good times, small farmers must continually expand output and reduce costs just to maintain their incomes. Hence, the Great Depression accelerated an exodus of small farmers from agriculture, a trend that continues today.

Table 14.1 shows that the number of small farms has declined dramatically. In 1910, there were 3.7 million farmers under 100 acres in size. Today, there are fewer than 1 million small farms. During the same period, the number of huge farms (1000 acres or more) has more than tripled. This loss of small farmers, together with the increased mechanization of larger farms, has reduced the farm population by 23 million people since 1910.

Size of Farm	Number, 1910	Percent	Number, 2002	Percent
Under 100 acres	3,691,611	58.0	943,118	44.3
100–499 acres	2,494,461	39.2	847,322	39.8
500–999 acres	125,295	2.0	161,552	7.6
1000 acres and over	50,135	0.8	176,990	8.3
Total	6,361,502	100.0	2,128,982	100.0

Source: U.S. Department of Agriculture.

TABLE 14.1
Size Distribution of U.S. Farms, 1910 and 2002

Inelastic food demand, combined with increasing agricultural productivity, implies a declining number of farmers. Small farmers are particularly vulnerable because they don't have the resources to maintain a high rate of technological improvement. As a result, the number of small farms has declined dramatically, while the number of large farms has grown.

U.S. FARM POLICY

The U.S. Congress has responded to these agricultural problems with a variety of programs. Most seek to raise and stabilize the price of farm products. Other programs seek to reduce the costs of production. When all else fails, the federal government also provides direct income support to farmers.

Price Supports

market surplus: The amount by which the quantity supplied exceeds the quantity demanded at a given price; excess supply.

parity: The relative price of farm products in the period 1910–14.

Supply Restrictions

acreage set-aside: Land withdrawn from production as part of policy to increase crop prices.

Price supports have always been the primary focus of U.S. farm policy. As early as 1926, Congress decreed that farm products should sell at a fair price. By "fair," Congress meant a price higher than the market equilibrium. The consequences of this policy are evident in Figure 14.4: *A price floor creates a **market surplus**.*

Once it set an above-equilibrium price for food, Congress had to find some way of disposing of the resultant food surplus. Initially, Congress proposed to get rid of this surplus by selling it abroad at world market prices. President Calvin Coolidge, a staunch opponent of government intervention, vetoed this legislation both times Congress passed it.

The notion of fair prices resurfaced in the Agricultural Adjustment Act of 1933. During the Great Depression farmers were going bankrupt in droves. To help them, Congress sought to restore the purchasing power of farm products to the 1909–14 level. The farm-nonfarm price relationships of 1909–14 were regarded by Congress as fair and came to be known as **parity** prices. If parity prices could be restored, Congress reasoned, farm incomes would improve.

The goal of parity pricing couldn't be attained without altering market supply and demand in some way.

Set-Asides. The easiest way to increase farm prices without creating a surplus is to reduce the production of food. Congress does this by paying farmers for voluntary reductions in crop acreage. These **acreage set-asides** shift the food supply curve to the left. In 1995, roughly 50 *million* acres of farmland—nearly one-fifth of the nation's wheat, corn, sorghum, rice, and cotton acreage—was idled by government set-asides. If farmers didn't agree to these set-asides, they couldn't participate in the price support programs.

Dairy Termination Program. To prop up dairy prices, the federal government also started a Dairy Termination Program in 1985. This is analogous to a set-aside program. In this case, however, the government pays dairy farmers to slaughter or export

FIGURE 14.4
Fair Prices and Market Surplus

The interaction of market supply and demand establishes an equilibrium price (p_e) for any product, including food. If a higher price (p_f) is set, the quantity of food supplied (q_s) will be larger than the quantity demanded (q_d). Hence, attempts to establish a "fair" (higher) price for farm products must cope with resultant market surpluses.

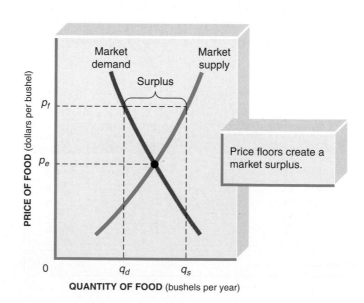

dairy cattle. Between 1995 and 1987, the government paid dairy farmers over $1 billion to "terminate" 1.6 million cows. The reduction in dairy herds boosted prices for milk and other dairy products.

Marketing Orders. The federal government also permits industry groups to limit the quantity of output brought to market. By themselves, individual farmers can't raise the market price by withholding output. If they act collectively, however, they can. If a quantity greater than authorized is actually grown, the "surplus" is disposed of by individual farmers. In the 1980s, these *marketing orders* forced farmers to waste each year roughly 500 million lemons, 1 billion(!) oranges, 70 million pounds of raisins, 70 million pounds of almonds, and millions of plums, nectarines, and other fruits. This wholesale destruction of crops gave growers market power and kept farm prices artificially high.

Import Quotas. The market supply of farm products is also limited by import restrictions. Imports of sugar, dairy products, cotton, and peanuts are severely limited by import quotas. Imports of beef are limited by "voluntary" export limits in foreign countries. Import taxes (duties) limit the foreign supply of other farm products.

While trying to limit the *supply* of farm products, the government also inflates the *demand* for selected farm products.

Government Stockpiles. An executive order signed by President Franklin Roosevelt in 1933 altered the demand for farm products. The Commodity Credit Corporation (CCC) created at that time is effectively a buyer of last resort for selected farm products.

The CCC becomes a buyer of last resort through its loan programs. Farmers can borrow money from the CCC at **loan rates** set by Congress (see Table 14.2). In 2004, for example, a wheat farmer could borrow $2.75 in cash for every bushel of wheat he relinquished to the CCC. If the market price of wheat went above $2.75, the farmer could sell the wheat, repay the CCC, and pocket the difference. If, instead, the price fell below the loan rate, the farmer could simply let the CCC keep the wheat and repay nothing. Hence, *whenever market prices are below CCC loan rates, the government ends up buying surplus crops.*

Figure 14.5 illustrates the effect of CCC price supports on individual farmers and the agricultural market. In the absence of price supports, competitive farmers would confront a horizontal demand curve at price p_e, itself determined by the intersection of market supply and demand (in part *b*). The CCC's offer to buy ("loan") unlimited quantities at a higher price shifts the demand curve facing each farmer upward, to the guaranteed price p_2. This higher price induces individual farmers to increase their rate of output, from q_1 to q_2.

Demand Distortions

loan rate: The implicit price paid by the government for surplus crops taken as collateral for loans to farmers.

Commodity	Loan Rate
Corn	$1.95 per bushel
Sorghum	1.95
Barley	1.85
Oats	1.33
Wheat	2.75
Soybeans	5.00
Cotton (upland)	0.52 per pound
Rice	6.50 per hundredweight

Source: U.S. Department of Agriculture.

TABLE 14.2
2004 Loan Rates

The Commodity Credit Corporation lends money to farmers at fixed "loan rates" that are implicit price floors. If the market price falls below the CCC loan rate, the government keeps the crop as full payment of the loan or *pays* farmers a "loan deficiency payment."

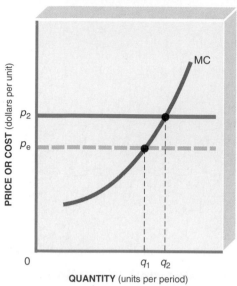

(a) Impact of price supports on the individual farmer

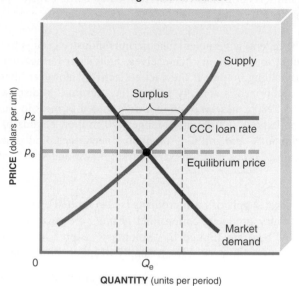

(b) Impact of price supports on the agricultural market

FIGURE 14.5

The Impact of Price Supports

In the absence of price supports, the price of farm products would be determined by the intersection of market supply and demand. In this case, the equilibrium price would be p_e, as shown in part *b*. All individual farmers would confront this price and produce up to the point where MC = p_e, as in part *a*.

Government price supports raise the price to p_2. By offering to buy (or "loan") unlimited quantities at this price, the government shifts the demand curve facing each farmer upward. Individual farmers respond by increasing their output from q_1 to q_2. As farmers increase their output, a market surplus develops (part *b*).

As farmers respond to price supports, the agriculture market is pushed out of equilibrium. At the support level p_2, more output is supplied than demanded. The market surplus created by government price supports creates an additional policy dilemma. ***The market surplus induced by price supports must be eliminated in one of three ways:***

- ***Government purchases*** and stockpiling of surplus food.
- ***Export sales.***
- ***Restrictions on supply.***

Government purchases of surplus crops have led to massive stockpiles of wheat, cotton, corn, and dairy products. At one time, the excess wheat was stored in old ammunition bunkers in Nebraska and scrubbed-out oil tanks in Texas. More than 130 *million* pounds of surplus nonfat dry milk is now stored in limestone caverns under Kansas City, and surplus cotton fills warehouses in the South. Even today about one fourth of U.S. farm output is destroyed or stored.

To keep these stockpiles from growing further, Congress amended the CCC loan program in 2001. When market prices fall below CCC loan rates (Table 14.2), farmers don't have to turn over their crops to the government. Instead, the government pays them a *loan deficiency payment* equal to the *difference* between the loan rate and the market price. The farmer can then sell his crop on the open market. By dumping excess supply on the market rather than stockpiling it, this policy tends to aggravate downward price swings.

Because farm prices are artificially high in the United States, export sales are sometimes difficult. As a result, the federal government must give away lots of food to poor nations and even subsidize exports to developed nations. The United States isn't alone in this regard: The European Union maintains even higher prices and subsidies (see World View).

For more on the EU, see europa.eu.int/index-en.htm.

WORLD VIEW

EU Farm Subsidies

In Europe, believe it or not, the subsidy for every cow is greater than the personal income of half the people in the world.

—Former British Prime Minister Margaret Thatcher

United States farm policy isn't unique. Most industrialized countries go to even greater lengths to protect domestic agriculture. For example, France, Germany, and Switzerland all shield their farmers from international competition while subsidizing their exports. Japan protects its inefficient rice producers, while the Netherlands subsidizes greenhouse vegetable farmers.

The motivations for farm subsidies are pretty much the same in every country in the world. Every country wants a secure source of food in the event of war. Most nations also want to maintain a viable farm sector, which is viewed as a source of social stability. Finally, politicians in every country must be responsive to a well-established and vocal political constituency.

The European Union (EU) imposes high tariffs on imported food, keeping domestic prices high. The member governments also agree to purchase any surplus production. To get rid of the surplus, the governments then subsidize exports. In 2000, direct EU farm subsidies exceeded $45 billion, triple the size of U.S. farm subsidies. All this protection costs the average EU consumer over $200 a year.

Analysis: Farm subsidies are common around the world. Such subsidies alter not only domestic output decisions but international trade patterns as well.

Cost Subsidies

The market surplus induced by price supports is exacerbated by cost subsidies. Irrigation water, for example, is delivered to many farmers by federally funded reclamation projects. The price farmers pay for the water is substantially below the cost of delivering it; the difference amounts to a subsidy. In 1986, this water subsidy cost taxpayers over $500 million. The Department of Agriculture has distributed an additional $150 million to $200 million a year to farmers to help defray the costs of fertilizer, drainage, and other production costs.

The federal government has also provided basic research, insurance, marketing, grading, and inspection services to farmers at subsidized prices. All these subsidies serve to lower fixed or variable costs. Their net impact is to stimulate additional output, as illustrated in Figure 14.6.

Direct Income Support

Price supports, cost subsidies, and supply restrictions are designed to stabilize agricultural markets and assure farmers an adequate income. As we've seen, however, they entail significant distortions of market outcomes. The Congressional Budget Office estimates that the milk price supports alone have increased retail dairy prices 3 to 6 percent, reduced consumption 1 to 5 percent, and encouraged excessive dairy production. Because of such distortions, direct income supports were authorized by the Agriculture and Consumer

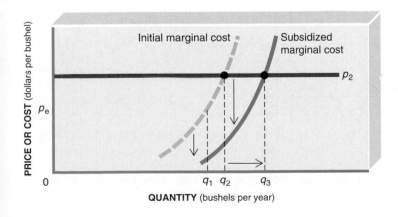

FIGURE 14.6
The Impact of Cost Subsidies

Cost subsidies lower the marginal cost of producing at any given rate of output, thereby shifting the marginal cost curve downward. The lower marginal costs make higher rates of output more profitable and thus increase output. At price p_2, lower marginal costs increase the farmer's profit-maximizing rate of output from q_2 to q_3.

TABLE 14.3
2004 Target Prices

Congress sets target prices for selected commodities. If the market price falls below the target price, a *deficiency payment* is made directly to the farmer.

Commodity	Target Price
Corn	$ 2.63 per bushel
Sorghum	2.57
Barley	2.24
Oats	1.44
Wheat	3.92
Soybeans	5.80
Cotton (upland)	0.7240 per pound
Rice	10.50 per hundredweight

Source: U.S. Department of Agriculture.

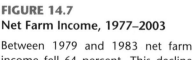

counter-cyclical payment: Income transfer paid to farmers for difference between target and market prices.

Protection Act of 1973. ***The advantage of direct income supports is that they achieve the goal of income security without distortions of market prices and output.***

The principal form of direct income support is so-called **counter-cyclical payments.** Congress identifies specific "target prices" for selected crops. In 2004, the target price for wheat was $3.92 a bushel (see Table 14.3). If market prices fall below these targets, the government makes up the difference. Target prices are another form of price floor. Unlike the case of CCC loan rates, however, target prices don't trigger government purchases of surplus crops. The target price is only used to compute the amount of the "counter-cyclical" payment paid directly to farmers.

In principle, direct income payments are a more efficient mechanism for subsidizing farm incomes. But farmers don't like them. Five thousand angry farmers drove their tractors to Washington, D.C., in February 1979 to protest this policy approach. Their rallying cry was "parity, not charity." They wanted higher price supports (an indirect subsidy) rather than more direct payments (a direct subsidy).

THE SECOND FARM DEPRESSION, 1980–1986

With so many price supports, supply restrictions, cost subsidies, and income transfers, one would think that farming is a riskless and profitable business. But this hasn't been the case. Incomes remain low and unstable, especially for small farmers. In fact, the entire agricultural sector experienced another setback in the 1980s. In 1980, the net income of U.S. farmers fell 42 percent. As Figure 14.7 shows, farm incomes recovered somewhat in 1981 but then resumed their steep decline in 1982. In 1983, farmers'

FIGURE 14.7
Net Farm Income, 1977–2003

Between 1979 and 1983 net farm income fell 64 percent. This decline was steeper than the income slide that occurred during the Great Depression (when net farm income fell 45 percent between 1929 and 1933). Farm incomes rose sharply from 1983 to 1989 but were unstable throughout the 1990s.

Source: *Economic Report of the President, 2004.*

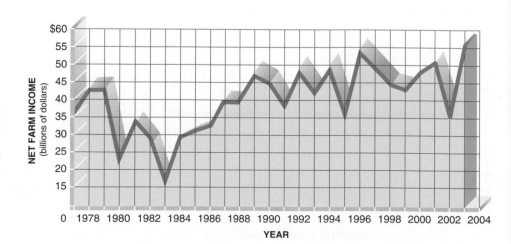

net income was only one-third the level of 1979. This income loss was steeper than that of the Great Depression. Real farm income was actually lower in 1983 than in 1933. This second depression of farm incomes accelerated the exodus of small farmers from agriculture, severely weakened rural economies, and bankrupted many farm banks and manufacturers of farm equipment and supplies.

This second depression of farm incomes was not caused by abrupt price declines. Prices for farm products increased slightly between 1979 and 1983, but production costs rose much faster. Average farm production costs rose 30 percent between 1979 and 1983 while the average price of farm products increased only 1.5 percent. As a result, the **profit** (net income) of farmers fell abruptly.

Fuel Costs. The cost squeeze on farm incomes started with an abrupt increase in fuel prices. In 1979, the OPEC nations raised crude oil prices 50 percent. This action pushed up the price of gasoline and related fuels 37 percent in 1980 alone, making it more expensive to operate farm equipment.

Fertilizer Costs. The increase in crude oil prices also pushed up the price of fertilizer. Most fertilizers are manufactured from a petroleum base. As a consequence, fertilizer prices rose in tandem with fuel prices, increasing 24 percent in 1980 and another 7 percent in 1981.

Interest Rates. The third, and perhaps most devastating, source of the farmers' cost squeeze was an increase in interest rates. Farming is extremely land- and capital-intensive. The value of U.S. farmers' assets is roughly $1.4 trillion. Many of these assets (such as land and machinery) are purchased with borrowed funds, often at variable interest rates. Farmers also borrow money for planting and harvesting. All this debt renders farmers vulnerable to abrupt changes in interest rates. When interest rates skyrocketed—the prime rate rose from 9 percent in 1978 to over 20 percent in 1980—the debt burden of farmers mounted.

Declining Land Values. High interest rates and declining incomes also reduced the value of farmers' most important asset—their land. The value of land reflects its present and future income-generating potential. The cost squeeze reduced potential income, and high interest rates made future income less valuable. These twin forces sent land values into a tailspin, which made it more difficult and more expensive for farmers to get needed credit.

Declining Exports. The farmers' plight was worsened still further by declining export sales. In 1980, in response to the Soviet invasion of Afghanistan, President Jimmy Carter imposed an embargo on grain sales to the Soviet Union. This directly reduced wheat sales by 15,000 to 20,000 tons per year and indirectly encouraged foreign competition.

Export sales were reduced even further by the strong value of the U.S. dollar. Between 1980 and 1984, the international value of the dollar rose a staggering 50 percent. This made it much more expensive for global consumers to buy U.S. farm output. As a result, the quantity of exports declined.

The Cost Squeeze

> **profit:** The difference between total revenue and total cost.

THE ECONOMY TOMORROW

Farmers on the Dole

To a large extent, the farm crisis of the 1980s had nothing to do with federal farm policy. The increase in oil prices was initiated by OPEC. Higher interest rates were a reflection of macroeconomic conditions. Likewise, the high value of the dollar was a response to U.S. interest rates and the economic recovery, and its effects weren't confined to the farm sector. All these adverse forces were reversed in the mid-1980s, and farm incomes rose sharply from their 1983 lows (see Figure 14.7).

Steps toward Deregulation

The post-1983 recovery of the farm sector created an opportunity to redesign farm policy. With production, prices, exports, and incomes all rising, the timing was perfect for the deregulation of the farm sector.

1985 Farm Act. The Farm Security Act of 1985 took a few steps in that direction. The core feature of the act was a gradual reduction in government support prices. For example, the support price ("loan rate") for wheat was reduced from $3.30 per bushel in 1986 to $1.95 in 1990. By reducing the support price, the government hoped to discourage overproduction and recurrent market surpluses.

Another feature of the 1985 act was to limit the government purchase of market surpluses. Rather than buying surpluses at the guaranteed loan rate, the government encouraged farmers to sell their surpluses at market prices. The government then reimbursed the farmers for the difference between the guaranteed (support) price and the market price.

The 1985 act also capped deficiency payments at $50,000 per farm. The intent of this cap was to reduce subsidy payments to huge corporate farms and to lessen their incentive for overproduction. In practice, however, large farms were subdivided into many smaller farms, allowing individual farmers to collect multiple deficiency payments.

The 1990 Act. By the time the authority of the 1985 act expired (in 1990), crop prices, farm incomes, and the price of farmland had all risen significantly. These improvements had little to do with government farm policy, however. Rather they reflected the continued expansion of the U.S. economy, declining oil and fertilizer costs, and strong foreign demand for U.S. farm products.

Despite the increased prosperity of farming during the 1985–90 period, the basic structure of farm subsidies was continued in the 1990 Farm Act. Indeed, loan rates were *increased,* effectively raising the price floor for farm products. At the same time, however, Congress reduced the amount of set-aside acreage by 15 percent. It also gave farmers more discretion to farm on unsubsidized acreage. Target prices were reduced and frozen for five years.

The net effect of the 1990 legislation was to move farming another small step closer to market realities. A bit more acreage was freed from government regulation, target prices were set closer to market prices, and more market surpluses were sold rather than stored in government warehouses.

The 1996 Freedom to Farm Act. In 1996, Congress moved farmers considerably further down the road toward deregulation with two radical changes in farm policy. The first change was the phaseout of deficiency payments. Target prices (Table 14.3) and their associated deficiency payments were terminated. In their place, farmers were offered "market transition payments." The size of the transition payments wasn't dependent on commodity prices but instead was fixed by Congress for a period of seven years. In this way, Congress focused on stabilizing farm *incomes* rather than farm *prices.* In 2002, all such income support was scheduled to end, leaving farmers the "freedom to farm" (off the dole).

The 1996 act also eliminated many restrictions on acreage set-asides. Up to 36.4 million acres were still eligible for "production flexibility contract payments" (set-asides). But farmers no longer had to keep set-aside acreage completely idle or to grow only specific commodities. Markets, not politicians, would decide what to grow.

At first, farmers loved the 1996 policy reforms. In the 1996–97 crop year, commodity prices were up and farm incomes were at an all-time high (Figure 14.7). Yet farmers were still getting billions of dollars in taxpayer subsidies. What a great deal!

The Asian Crisis. Then the farm economy turned sour again. The Asian crisis that began in July 1997 was the principal cause. When the currencies of Thailand, Korea, Indonesia, Malaysia, and other Asian nations tumbled, the foreign price of U.S. farm output soared. When the economies of these Asian nations stumbled into recession, their ability to buy American farm products was further diminished. As a result, U.S. farm exports fell sharply during 1997 and 1998.

The decline in export demand weakened farm prices. Abundant harvests in the United States, China, Europe, and elsewhere also depressed farm prices. Between October 1997 and October 1998, grain prices tumbled 40 to 60 percent. These price declines rivaled those of 1929–32 and 1980–85.

Renewed Subsidies. When farm prices and incomes plunged, farmers again demanded federal aid. Just prior to the November 1998 elections, Congress increased market transition payments by 50 percent. Congress also authorized the early payment of $5 billion in farm aid not due until 1999. Finally, Congress approved $500 million in "disaster payments"—a new form of aid—to offset falling prices and exports. Congress continued "emergency" funding of the farm sector for several years.

The 2001 Farm Act. The intent of the 1996 Farm Act ostensibly was to wean farmers off the dole, making them more reliant on market forces. "Freedom to farm" implied a deregulation of farm prices and production decisions. That isn't how it worked out, however. Farmers only *promised* to forsake price supports in exchange for temporary (seven-year) income support. By 1998, however, it was clear that *farmers were prepared to rely only on* good *markets, not* bad *ones.* When the market for farm products went bad, they expected more federal aid, not more freedom to farm.

Farmers got more permanent aid in 2001. Even before the 1996 Freedom to Farm Act had expired, farm lobbyists petitioned Congress not only to continue deficiency payments (based on target prices) but also to increase loan rates. With the U.S. and global economies sliding into recession, the farmers' appeal was well timed. The September 11, 2001, terrorist attacks also enhanced the chances of congressional approval. In explaining the October 5, 2001, House of Representatives vote to approve the Farm Security Act of 2001, a congressional aide noted that "you can't be going to war and beating up on farmers at the same time." Congress responded by increasing farm subsidies and creating new ones for sugar growers, peanut farmers, hog operators, and even horse breeders.

Moral Hazard. The Farm Act of 2001 assures that U.S. farmers will remain on the government dole in the economy tomorrow. Even while on the dole, however, farmers could do more to manage the inevitable risks of the weather, price changes, and global competition. Farmers can buy crop insurance to mitigate the effects of the weather. They can also use forward contracts to eliminate the risks of price swings. At present, however, few farmers engage in such risk management. Why? Because they've come to expect the government to bail them out if the weather or prices turn out badly. So they've no incentive to pay insurance premiums or sign forward contracts that limit their profit potential. This is the kind of **moral hazard** that government assistance often creates. The very offer of government aid encourages farmers to behave in ways that worsen market outcomes. The challenge for farm policy in the economy tomorrow is to maximize market incentives and minimize moral hazards, even for farmers on the dole.

Back from the Brink

WEBNOTE

The U.S. Department of Agriculture makes available a broad array of statistics on the U.S. farm sector at www.usda.gov.

WEBNOTE

See the latest U.S. House of Representatives Agriculture Committee at www.house.gov/agriculture.

moral hazard: An incentive to engage in undesirable behavior.

SUMMARY

- The agricultural sector has a highly competitive structure, with approximately 2 million farms. Many crops are regulated, however, by government restrictions and subsidies.
- Most farm output is produced by the small percentage of large farms that enjoy economies of scale. Most small farmers rely on nonfarm employment for their income.
- In a free market, farm prices tend to decline over time because of increasing productivity and low income elasticity of demand. Variations in harvests, combined with a low price elasticity of demand, make farm prices unstable.
- Most of today's farm policies originated during the Great Depression, in response to low farm prices and incomes.
- The government uses price supports and cost subsidies to raise farm prices and profits. These policies cause resource misallocations and create market surpluses of specific commodities.

- Direct income support in the form of counter-cyclical payments also generates excess supply, but can be targeted more to income needs.
- Farm incomes declined sharply between 1979 and 1983, causing a second depression in the farm sector. The drop was caused by sharp increases in fuel, fertilizer, and interest costs. The Asian crisis that began in 1997 caused another farm crisis.
- The 1996 Farm Act called for a phaseout of farm subsidies. Falling prices and incomes during 1997–2001 stalled and eventually reversed that process.
- Government regulation not only risks design flaws but creates moral hazards that may reduce efficiency.

Key Terms

market power	income elasticity of demand	loan rate
barriers to entry	market surplus	counter-cyclical payment
economic profit	parity	profit
price elasticity of demand	acreage set-aside	moral hazard

Questions for Discussion

1. Would the U.S. economy be better off without government intervention in agriculture? Who would benefit? Who would lose?
2. Are large price movements inevitable in agricultural markets? What other mechanisms might be used to limit such movement?
3. Why doesn't the United States just give its crop surpluses to poor countries? What problems might such an approach create?
4. Farmers can eliminate the uncertainties of fluctuating crop prices by selling their crops in futures markets (agreeing to a fixed price for crops to be delivered in the future). Who gains or loses from this practice?
5. Why do farmers prefer price supports to direct payments?
6. If two-thirds of all U.S. farms fail to earn a profit, why do they stay in business?
7. You need a government permit (allotment) to grow tobacco. Who gains or loses from such regulation?

PROBLEMS — The Student Problem Set at the back of this book contains numerical and graphing problems for this chapter.

WEB ACTIVITIES — to accompany this chapter can be found on the Online Learning Center:
http://www.mhhe.com/economics/schiller10

PART 5

Factor Markets: Basic Theory

Factor markets operate like product markets, with supply and demand interacting to determine prices and quantities. In factor markets, however, resource inputs rather than products are exchanged. Those exchanges determine the wages paid to workers and the rent, interest, and profits paid to other inputs. The micro theories presented in Chapters 15 through 17 explain how those factor payments are determined.

The Labor Market

I n 2004, the CEO of Walt Disney Company was ending a 10-year contract that could have paid him as much as $771 million for his services. LeBron James was in the second year of a Nike endorsement contract worth at least $90 million. Yet the president of the United States was paid only $400,000. And the secretary who typed the manuscript of this book was paid just $19,000. What accounts for these tremendous disparities in earnings?

Why does the average college graduate earn over $50,000 while the average high school graduate earns just $27,000? Are such disparities simply a reward for enduring four years of college, or do they reflect real differences in talent?

Surely we can't hope to explain these earnings disparities on the basis of the willingness to work. After all, my secretary would be more than willing to work day and night for $77 million per year. For that matter, so would I. Accordingly, the earnings disparities can't be attributed to differences in the quantity of labor supplied. If we're going to explain why some people earn a great deal of income while others earn very little, we must consider both the *supply* and the *demand* for labor. In this regard, the following questions arise:

- **How do people decide how much time to spend working?**
- **What determines the wage rate an employer is willing to pay?**
- **Why are some workers paid so much and others so little?**

To answer these questions, we must examine the behavior of labor *markets*.

LABOR SUPPLY

The following two ads recently appeared in the campus newspaper of a well-known university:

Will do ANYTHING for money: able-bodied liberal-minded male needs money, will work to get it. Have car. Call Tom 765-3210.

Web architect. Experienced website designer. Looking for part-time or consulting position on or off campus. Please call Margaret, ext. 0872, 9–5.

Although placed by individuals of very different talents, the ads clearly expressed Tom's and Margaret's willingness to work. Although we don't know how much money they were asking for their respective talents, or whether they ever found jobs, we can be sure that they were prepared to take a job at some wage rate. Otherwise, they wouldn't have paid for the ads in the "Jobs Wanted" column of their campus newspaper.

The advertised willingness to work expressed by both Tom and Margaret represents a **supply of labor.** They're offering to sell their time and talents to anyone who's willing to pay the right price. Their explicit offers are similar to those of anyone who looks for a job. Job seekers who check the current job openings at the

labor supply: The willingness and ability to work specific amounts of time at alternative wage rates in a given time period, *ceteris paribus.*

WORLD VIEW

In Moscow, 25,000 Apply for 630 Jobs at McDonald's

More than 25,000 Muscovites have dreams of flipping burgers beneath the golden arches as a member of the worldwide Big Mac and French fry brigade, eager to share in the West's most greasy right of passage.

The flood of job seekers started almost immediately after a Moscow newspaper advertisement was published last month. More than 1,000 applications for the 630 available crew spots came the first day, said George Cohon, deputy chairman of Moscow McDonald's. More than 3,100 interviews have been conducted, seven days a week. . . .

Many job seekers are housewives and students from the prestigious Moscow University, and more than 20 percent speak two languages. . . .

The Pushkin Square outlet, the biggest McDonald's in the world, will serve 15,000 diners a day, with 700 seats inside and 200 outside. . . .

Part-time Soviet workers make about 1½ rubles per hour, said Cohon, which is $2.50 at the commercial rate. But workers will also be rewarded every few months for productivity.

—Kara Swisher

Source: *The Washington Post*, December 14, 1989. © 1989 The Washington Post. Reprinted with permission. www.washingtonpost.com

Analysis: The quantity of labor supplied at any given wage rate depends on the value of leisure and the desire for income. Even a seemingly low wage offer attracted a huge quantity of labor in Moscow.

student employment office or e-mail résumés to potential employers are demonstrating a willingness to accept employment—that is, to *supply* labor. The 25,000 Muscovites who applied for jobs at Russia's first McDonald's were also offering to supply labor (see World View).

Our first concern in this chapter is to explain these labor supply decisions. How do people decide how many hours to supply at any given wage rate? Do people try to maximize their total wages? If they did, we'd all be holding three jobs and sleeping on the commuter bus. Since most of us don't behave this way, other motives must be present. What are these other motivations, and how do they affect the quantity of labor supplied at various wage rates?

Income vs. Leisure

The reward for working comes in two forms: (1) the intrinsic satisfaction of working and (2) a paycheck. MBA grads say they care more about the intrinsic satisfaction than the pay (see News on the next page). They also get huge paychecks, however. Those big paychecks are explained in part by the quantity of labor supplied: MBA grads often end up working 60 or more hours a week. The reason people are willing to work so many hours is that they want more income.

Not working obviously has some value, too. In part, we need some nonwork time just to recuperate from working. We also want some time to watch television, go to a soccer game, or enjoy other goods and services we've purchased.

Our conflicting desires for income and leisure create a dilemma: The more time we spend working, the more income we have but also less time to enjoy it. Working, like all activities, involves an opportunity cost. Generally, we say that *the opportunity cost of working is the amount of leisure time that must be given up in the process.*

The inevitable trade-off between labor and leisure explains the shape of individual labor supply curves. As we work more hours, our leisure time becomes more scarce—and thus more valuable. Hence, *higher wage rates are required to compensate for the increasing opportunity cost of labor.* We'll supply a larger quantity of labor only if offered a higher wage rate. This is reflected in the labor supply curve in Figure 15.1.

The upward slope of the labor supply curve may be reinforced with the changing value of income. Those first few dollars earned on the job are really precious, especially if you have bills to pay. As you work and earn more, however, your most urgent

WEBNOTE

Cornell University tracks the salaries of its MBA graduates at www.johnson.cornell.edu/carrier/statistics.html.

MBA Grads Seek Challenge at Work, Not Just Big Bucks

Cynics might argue, but money apparently isn't what drives most graduate business students, *Inc.* magazine says. . . .

Inc. talked to 907 graduating MBA students at 10 schools this spring. Just 12 percent of those questioned said they went into graduate school primarily because of big salaries down the road. Only 24 percent rated a high salary as one of the most important considerations in choosing their next job.

Those answers don't surprise Teresa Miles, 23, who just earned her MBA at Duke University's Fuqua School of Business. "There are definitely some students who fit that greedy mold," says Miles, a native of Greenwich, Conn. "But it's such a stereotype I have to laugh at it."

Miles, who starts work June 15 at the Bank of New York's commercial lending department, will earn about $60,000 annually. But it was "a challenging experience and something that will do something for me" that led her to accept the bank's offer.

Most students think along those lines, says Associate Dean Dennis Weidenear at Purdue University's Krannert School of Management. "I don't think you should discount the pay they'll be getting because it is important," he says. "But they're not willing to walk over their grandmothers just to get a better salary."

Other poll results:

Challenging work was rated a "most important" job characteristic by 75 percent of the students; 44 percent ranked atmosphere first; 40 percent, location. . . .

—Mark Memmott

What MBAs at Some Top Schools Earn

School	Starting Salaries in 2003
Stanford	$107,320
Harvard	105,896
MIT	99,539
Northwestern	98,358
Chicago	97,872
Michigan	97,039
Dartmouth	96,714
Virginia	92,855

Source: *U.S. News & World Report,* April 12, 2004. Copyright 2004 U.S. News & World Report, L.P. Reprinted with permission. www.usnews.com

Source: *USA Today,* May 28, 1987. USA TODAY. Copyright 1987. Reprinted with permission (updated in 2001 by author). www.usatoday.com

Analysis: The quantity of labor supplied depends on the intrinsic satisfaction of working and the wages paid. MBA grads apparently work long hours for both high wages and job satisfaction.

needs will be satisfied. You may still want more things, but the urgency of your consumption desires is likely to be diminished. In other words, ***the marginal utility of income may decline as you earn more.*** If this happens, the wages offered for more work lose some of their allure. You may not be willing to work more hours unless offered a higher wage rate.

FIGURE 15.1
The Supply of Labor

The quantity of any good or service offered for sale typically increases as its price rises. Labor supply responds in the same way. At the wage rate w_1, the quantity of labor supplied is q_1 (point A). At the higher wage w_2, workers are willing to work more hours per week, that is, to supply a larger quantity of labor (q_2).

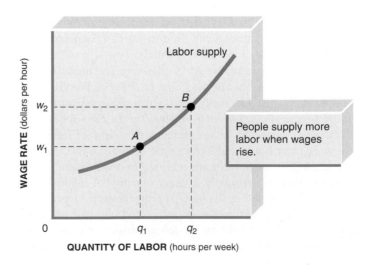

The upward slope of an individual's labor supply curve is thus a reflection of two potential phenomena:

- The increasing opportunity cost of labor as leisure time declines.
- The decreasing marginal utility of income as a person works more hours.

Money isn't necessarily the only thing that motivates people to work. People *do* turn down higher-paying jobs in favor of lower-wage jobs that they like. Many parents forgo high-wage "career" jobs in order to have more flexible hours and time at home. Volunteers offer their services just for the sense of contributing to their communities; they don't need a paycheck. Even MBA graduates say they're motivated more by the challenge of high-paying jobs than the money (see News). But money almost always makes a difference: People *do* supply more labor when offered higher wages.

The force that drives people up the labor supply curve is the lust for more income. Higher wages enable people to buy more goods and services. The quest for higher levels of consumption induces people to *substitute* labor for leisure.

At some point, however, additional goods and services will lose their allure. Individuals with extremely high incomes already have lots of toys. If they are offered a higher wage rate, the **substitution effect of wages** may not be persuasive. Rather than supplying *more* labor, they might even *reduce* the number of hours they work, thereby maintaining a high income *and* increasing their leisure. While you might do cartwheels for $50 an hour, Bill Gates or Brad Pitt might not lift a finger for such a paltry sum. Muhammad Ali once announced that he wouldn't spend an hour in the ring for less than $1 million and would box *less,* not more, as the pay for his fights exceeded $3 million. For him, the added income from one championship fight was so great that he felt he didn't have to fight more to satisfy his income and consumption desires.

A low-wage worker might also respond to higher wage rates by working *less,* not more. People receiving very low wages (such as migrant workers, household help, and babysitters) have to work long hours just to pay the rent. The increased income made possible by higher wage rates might permit them to work *fewer* hours. These *negative* labor supply responses to increased wage rates are referred to as the **income effect** of a wage increase.

A utility-maximizing individual will respond to these income and substitution effects by offering different quantities of labor at alternative wage rates. The *substitution effect* of high wages encourages people to work more hours. The *income effect,* on the other hand, allows them to reduce work hours without losing income. If substitution effects dominate, the labor supply curve will be upward-sloping. ***If income effects outweigh substitution effects, an individual will supply less labor at higher wages.*** This kind of reaction is illustrated by the backward-bending portion of the supply curve in Figure 15.2.

A Backward Bend?

substitution effect of wages: An increased wage rate encourages people to work more hours (to substitute labor for leisure).

income effect of wages: An increased wage rate allows a person to reduce hours worked without losing income.

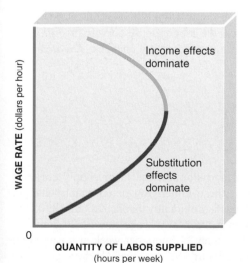

FIGURE 15.2
The Backward-Bending Supply Curve

Increases in wage rates make additional hours of work more valuable, but also less necessary. Higher wage rates increase the quantity of labor supplied as long as substitution effects outweigh income effects. At the point where income effects begin to outweigh substitution effects, the labor supply curve starts to bend backward.

WORLD VIEW

Your Money or Your Life

Would you rather have more time or more money? Here's how people in six countries answered.

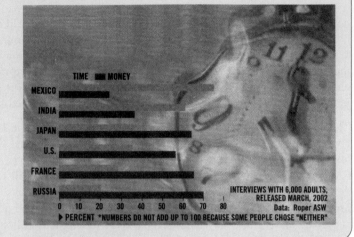

Source: Reprinted from the May 26, 2003 issue of *BusinessWeek* by permission. Copyright 2003 by The McGraw-Hill Companies.

Analysis: Despite already high incomes, Americans are still willing to sacrifice leisure for more income; *substitution effects* outweigh *income effects*.

Backward-bending labor supply curves are more the exception than the rule. Most Americans do want more leisure. But given the choice between more leisure or more income, Americans are more likely to choose added income (see World View). In other words, substitution effects outweigh income effects in the U.S. labor force. This explains why Americans work such long hours despite their comparatively high incomes.

MARKET SUPPLY

market supply of labor: The total quantity of labor that workers are willing and able to supply at alternative wage rates in a given time period, *ceteris paribus*.

The **market supply of labor** represents the sum of all individual labor supply decisions. Although it's true that some individuals have backward-bending supply curves, these negative responses to higher wages are swamped by positive responses from the 150 million individuals who participate in the U.S. labor market. As a result, the *market* supply curve is upward-sloping.

The upward slope of the labor supply curve doesn't imply that we'll all be working longer hours in the future. As time passes, the labor supply curve can *shift*. And it will whenever one of the underlying determinants of supply changes. ***The determinants of labor supply include***

- *Tastes* (for leisure, income, and work).
- *Income and wealth.*
- *Expectations* (for income or consumption).
- *Prices* of consumer goods.
- *Taxes.*

These shift factors determine the position and slope of the labor supply curve at any point in time. As time passes, however, these underlying determinants change, causing the labor supply curve to shift. This has evidently happened. In 1890, the average U.S. worker was employed 60 hours a week at a wage rate of 20 cents an hour. In 2004, the average worker worked less than 34 hours per week at a wage rate of $16 an hour. Contributing to this long-run leftward shift has been (1) the spectacular rise in living standards (a change in income and wealth), (2) the growth of income transfer programs that provide economic security when one isn't working (a change in income and expectations), and (3) the increased diversity and attractiveness of leisure activities (a change in tastes and other goods).

Despite the evident long-run shifts of the labor supply curve, workers still respond positively to higher wage rates in the short run. To measure the resulting movements along the labor supply curve, we use the concept of elasticity. Specifically, **elasticity of labor supply** is the percentage change in the quantity of labor supplied divided by the percentage change in the wage rate—that is,

$$\text{Elasticity of labor supply} = \frac{\%\text{ change in quantity of labor supplied}}{\%\text{ change in wage rate}}$$

Elasticity of Labor Supply

elasticity of labor supply: The percentage change in the quantity of labor supplied divided by the percentage change in wage rate.

The elasticity of labor tells us how much more labor will be available if a higher wage is offered. If the elasticity of labor is 0.2, a 10 percent increase in wage rates will induce a 2 percent increase in the quantity of labor supplied.

The actual responsiveness of workers to a change in wage rates depends on the determinants of labor supply. Time is also important for labor supply elasticity, as individuals can't adjust their schedules or change jobs instantaneously.

The labor supply curve and its related elasticities tell us how much time people would like to allocate to work. We must recognize, however, that people seldom have the opportunity to adjust their hours of employment at will. True, a Bill Gates or a Britney Spears can easily choose to work more or fewer hours. Most workers, however, face more rigid choices. They must usually choose to work at a regular job for eight hours a day, five days a week, or not to work at all. Very few firms are flexible enough to accommodate a desire to work only between the hours of 11 A.M. and 3 P.M. on alternate Thursdays. Adjustments in work hours are more commonly confined to choices about overtime work or secondary jobs (moonlighting) and vacation and retirement. Families may also alter the labor supply by varying the number of family members sent into the labor force at any given time. Students, too, can often adjust their work hours. The flow of immigrants into the U.S. labor market also increases when U.S. wages rise.

Institutional Constraints

LABOR DEMAND

Regardless of how many people are *willing* to work, it's up to employers to decide how many people will *actually* work. That is, there must be a **demand for labor.** What determines the number of workers employers are willing to hire at various wage rates?

In earlier chapters we emphasized that employers are profit maximizers. In their quest for maximum profits, firms seek the rate of output at which marginal revenue equals marginal cost. Once they've identified the profit-maximizing rate of output, firms enter factor markets to purchase the required amounts of labor, equipment, and other resources. Thus, *the quantity of resources purchased by a business depends on the firm's expected sales and output.* In this sense, the demand for factors of production, including labor, is a **derived demand;** it's derived from the demand for goods and services.

Consider the plight of strawberry pickers. Strawberry pickers are paid very low wages and are employed only part of the year. But their plight can't be blamed on the

demand for labor: The quantities of labor employers are willing and able to hire at alternative wage rates in a given time period, *ceteris paribus.*

Derived Demand

derived demand: The demand for labor and other factors of production results from (depends on) the demand for final goods and services produced by these factors.

IN THE NEWS

Majoring in Money

Unfortunately, wisdom apparently is its only reward, as the job market for professional philosophers—or at least philosophy majors—continues to be weak, according to the latest Monthly Labor Review.

Daniel Hecker, an economist for the federal Bureau of Labor Statistics, computed the annual earnings of everyone who had graduated from college before 1991 and had a full-time job in 1993.

The least lucrative majors for both men and women: philosophy, religion and theology, probably because many of the paying gigs for these students are in church, where the rewards presumably come in the next lifetime and not in the pay envelope.

Among mid-career men between the ages of 35 and 44, Hecker found that those who had majored in engineering and math as undergraduates earned the most. For similarly aged women, an economics degree was golden.

—Richard Morin

Source: *The Washington Post*, March 24, 1996. © 1996 The Washington Post. Reprinted with permission. www.washingtonpost.com

Annual Earnings by College Undergraduate Major Men and Women Ages 35–44

Men		Women	
Top Five Majors		**Top Five Majors**	
1. Engineering	$53,286	1. Economics	$49,170
2. Mathematics	51,584	2. Engineering	49,070
3. Computer science	50,509	3. Pharmacy	48,427
4. Pharmacy	50,480	4. Architecture	46,353
5. Physics	50,128	5. Computer science	43,757
Bottom Five Majors		**Bottom Five Majors**	
1. Philosophy/religion	$31,848	1. Philosophy/religion	$25,788
2. Social work	32,171	2. Education	27,988
3. Visual and performing arts	32,972	3. Home economics	28,275
4. Foreign language/linguistics	33,780	4. Social work	28,594
5. Education	34,470	5. Agriculture	28,751

Source: Bureau of Labor Statistics.

Analysis: The earnings of college graduates depend in part on what major they chose. Graduates who can produce goods and services in great demand get the highest pay.

WEBNOTE

Average earnings by occupation can be obtained from the U.S. Bureau of Labor Statistics at stats.bls.gov. Under "Wages, Earnings, and Benefits" choose "Wages by Area and Occupation."

greed of the strawberry growers. Strawberry growers, like most producers, would love to sell more strawberries at higher prices. If they did, the growers would hire more pickers and might even pay them higher wages. But the growers must contend with the market demand for strawberries: Consumers aren't willing to buy more strawberries at higher prices. As a consequence, the growers can't afford to hire more pickers or pay them higher wages. In contrast, information-technology (IT) firms are always looking for more workers and offer very high wages to get them. This helps explain why college students who major in engineering, math, or computer science get paid a lot more than philosophy majors (see News). IT specialists benefit from the growing demand for Internet services, while philosophy majors suffer because the search for the meaning of life is not a growth industry.

The principle of derived demand suggests that if consumers really want to improve the lot of strawberry pickers, they should eat more strawberries. An increase in the demand for strawberries will motivate growers to plant more berries and hire more labor to pick them. Until then, the plight of the pickers isn't likely to improve.

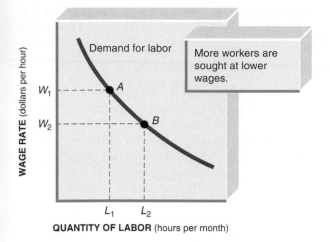

FIGURE 15.3
The Demand for Labor

The higher the wage rate, the smaller the quantity of labor demanded (*ceteris paribus*). At the wage rate W_1, only L_1 of labor is demanded. If the wage rate falls to W_2, a larger quantity of labor (L_2) will be demanded. The labor demand curve obeys the law of demand.

The number of strawberry pickers hired by the growers isn't completely determined by the demand for strawberries. The number of pickers hired will also depend on the wage rate. That is, ***the quantity of labor demanded depends on its price (the wage rate).*** In general, we expect that strawberry growers will be *willing to hire* more pickers at low wages than at higher wages. Hence, the demand for labor looks very much like the demand for any good or service (see Figure 15.3).

The fact that the demand curve for labor slopes downward doesn't tell us what quantity of labor will be hired. Nor does it tell us what wage rate will be paid. To answer such questions, we need to know what determines the particular shape and position of the labor demand curve.

A strawberry grower will be willing to hire another picker only if that picker contributes more to output than he or she costs. Growers, as rational businesspeople, recognize that *every* sale, *every* expenditure has some impact on total profits. Hence, the truly profit-maximizing grower will evaluate each picker's job application in terms of the applicant's potential contribution to profits.

Fortunately, a strawberry picker's contribution to output is easy to measure; it's the number of boxes of strawberries he or she picks. Suppose for the moment that Marvin, a college dropout with three summers of experience as a canoe instructor, is able to pick 5 boxes per hour. These 5 boxes represent Marvin's **marginal physical product (MPP)**. In other words, Marvin's MPP is the *addition* to total output that occurs when the grower hires him for an hour:

$$\text{Marginal physical product} = \frac{\text{change in total output}}{\text{change in quantity of labor}}$$

Marginal physical product establishes an *upper* limit to the grower's willingness to pay. Clearly the grower can't afford to pay Marvin more than 5 boxes of strawberries for an hour's work; the grower won't pay Marvin more than he produces.

Most strawberry pickers don't want to be paid in strawberries. At the end of a day in the fields, the last thing a picker wants to see is another strawberry. Marvin, like the rest of the pickers, wants to be paid in cash. To find out how much cash he might be paid, we need to know what a box of strawberries is worth. This is easy to determine. The market value of a box of strawberries is simply the price at which the grower can sell it. Thus, Marvin's contribution to output can be measured in either marginal physical product (5 boxes per hour) or the dollar value of that product.

The Labor Demand Curve

Marginal Physical Product

marginal physical product (MPP): The change in total output associated with one additional unit of input.

Marginal Revenue Product

marginal revenue product (MRP): The change in total revenue associated with one additional unit of input.

The dollar value of a worker's contribution to output is called **marginal revenue product (MRP).** Marginal revenue product is the change in total revenue that occurs when more labor is hired—that is,

$$\frac{\text{Marginal}}{\text{revenue product}} = \frac{\text{change in total revenue}}{\text{change in quantity of labor}}$$

In Marvin's case, the "change in quantity of labor" is one extra hour of picking strawberries. The "change in total revenue" is the *value* of the extra 5 boxes of berries Marvin picks in that hour. If the grower can sell strawberries for $2 a box, Marvin's marginal revenue product is simply 5 boxes per hour × $2 per box, or $10 per hour. We could have come to the same conclusion by multiplying marginal *physical* product times *price,* that is

$$MRP = MPP \times p$$

or

$$\$10 \text{ per hour} = 5 \text{ boxes per hour} \times \$2 \text{ per box}$$

We calculate MRP to determine how much Marvin should be paid. In compliance with the rule about not paying anybody more than he or she contributes, the profit-maximizing grower should be willing to pay Marvin up to $10 an hour. Thus, *marginal revenue product sets an upper limit to the wage rate an employer will pay.*

But what about a lower limit? Suppose the pickers aren't organized and that Marvin is desperate for money. Under such circumstances, he might be willing to work—to supply labor—for only $4 an hour.

Should the grower hire Marvin for such a low wage? The profit-maximizing answer is obvious. If Marvin's marginal revenue product is $10 an hour and his wages are only $4 an hour, the grower will be eager to hire him. The difference between Marvin's marginal revenue product ($10) and his wage ($4) implies additional profits of $6 an hour. In fact, the grower will be so elated by the economics of this situation that he'll want to hire everybody he can find who's willing to work for $4 an hour. After all, if the grower can make $6 an hour by hiring Marvin, why not hire 1,000 pickers and accumulate profits at an even faster rate?

The Law of Diminishing Returns

The exploitive possibilities suggested by Marvin's picking are too good to be true. It isn't at all clear, for example, how the grower could squeeze 1,000 workers onto one acre of land and have any room left over for strawberry plants. There must be some limit to the profit-making potential of this situation.

A few moments' reflection on the absurdity of trying to employ 1,000 people to pick one acre of strawberries should be ample warning of the limits to profits here.

IN THE NEWS

Merit Pay for Priests

The Episcopal Diocese of Newark, N.J., next year starts paying priests according to performance. Under the merit-pay plan, priests can qualify for salary raises based on goals that could include parish growth, education and choir programs, and quality of sermons.

Analysis: A profit-maximizing employer will pay wages that reflect a worker's contribution to output. That contribution is measured by marginal physical product (MPP) and marginal revenue product (MRP).

You don't need two years of business school to recognize this. But some grasp of economics may help explain exactly why the grower's eagerness to hire additional pickers will begin to fade long before 1,000 are hired. The operative concept here is *marginal productivity.*

Diminishing MPP. The decision to hire Marvin originated in his marginal physical product—that is, the 5 boxes of strawberries he can pick in an hour's time. To assess the wisdom of hiring still more pickers, we have to consider how total output will change if additional labor is employed. To do so, we need to keep track of marginal physical product.

Figure 15.4 shows how strawberry output changes as additional pickers are hired. Marvin picks 5 boxes of strawberries per hour. Total output and his marginal physical product are identical, because he's initially the only picker employed. When the grower hires George, Marvin's old college roommate, we observe the total output increases

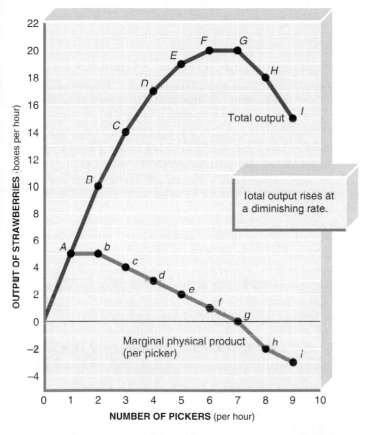

FIGURE 15.4
Diminishing Marginal Physical Product

The marginal physical product of labor is the increase in total production that results when one additional worker is hired. Marginal physical product tends to fall as additional workers are hired in any given production process. This decline occurs because each worker has increasingly less of other factors (e.g., land) with which to work.

When the second worker (George) is hired, total output increases from 5 to 10 boxes per hour. Hence, the second worker's MPP equals 5 boxes per hour. Thereafter, capital and land constraints diminish marginal physical product.

	Number of Pickers (per hour)	Total Strawberry Output (boxes per hour)	Marginal Physical Product (boxes per hour)
A	1 (Marvin)	5	5
B	2 (George)	10	5
C	3	14	4
D	4	17	3
E	5	19	2
F	6	20	1
G	7	20	0
H	8	18	−2
I	9	15	−3

to 10 boxes per hour (point *B* in Figure 15.4). This figure represents another increase of 5 boxes per hour. Accordingly, we may conclude that George's *marginal physical product* is 5 boxes per hour, the same as Marvin's. Given such productivity, the grower will want to hire George and continue looking for more pickers.

As more workers are hired, total strawberry output continues to increase but not nearly as fast. Although the later hires work just as hard, the limited availability of land and capital constrain their marginal physical product. One problem is the number of boxes. There are only a dozen boxes, and the additional pickers often have to wait for an empty box. The time spent waiting depresses marginal physical product. The worst problem is space: As additional workers are crowded onto the one-acre patch, they begin to get in one another's way. The picking process is slowed, and marginal physical product is further depressed. Note that the MPP of the fifth picker is 2 boxes per hour, while the MPP of the sixth picker is only 1 box per hour. By the time we get to the seventh picker, marginal physical product actually falls to zero, as no further increases in total strawberry output take place.

Things get even worse if the grower hires still more pickers. If 8 pickers are employed, total output actually *declines*. The pickers can no longer work efficiently under such crowded conditions. The MPP of the eighth worker is *negative,* no matter how ambitious or hardworking this person may be. Figure 15.4 illustrates this decline in marginal physical product.

Our observations on strawberry production are similar to those made in most industries. In the short run, the availability of land and capital is limited by prior investment decisions. Hence, additional workers must share existing facilities. As a result, ***the marginal physical product of labor eventually declines as the quantity of labor employed increases.*** This is the **law of diminishing returns** we first encountered in Chapter 6. It's based on the simple observation that an increasing number of workers leaves each worker with less land and capital to work with. At some point, this "crowding" causes MPP to decline.

law of diminishing returns: The marginal physical product of a variable factor declines as more of it is employed with a given quantity of other (fixed) inputs.

Diminishing MRP. As marginal *physical* product diminishes, so does marginal *revenue* product (MRP). As noted earlier, marginal revenue product is the increase in the *value* of total output associated with an added unit of labor (or other input). In our example, it refers to the increase in strawberry revenues associated with one additional picker and is calculated as MPP $\times$ *p*.

The decline in marginal revenue product mirrors the drop in marginal physical product. Recall that a box of strawberries sells for \$2. With this price and the output statistics in Figure 15.4, we can readily calculate marginal revenue product, as summarized in Table 15.1. As the growth of output diminishes, so does marginal revenue

TABLE 15.1
Diminishing Marginal Revenue Product

Marginal revenue product (MRP) measures the change in total revenue that occurs when one additional worker is hired. At constant product prices, MRP equals MPP $\times$ price. Hence, MRP declines along with MPP.

Number of Pickers (per hour)	Total Strawberry Output (in boxes per hour)	$\times$	Price of Strawberries (per box)	=	Total Strawberry Revenue (per hour)	Marginal Revenue Product
0	0		$2		0	—
1 (Marvin)	5		2		$10	$10
2 (George)	10		2		20	10
3	14		2		28	8
4	17		2		34	6
5	19		2		38	4
6	20		2		40	2
7	20		2		40	0
8	18		2		36	−4
9	15		2		30	−6

product. Marvin's marginal revenue product of $10 an hour has fallen to $6 by the time 4 pickers are employed and reaches zero when 7 pickers are employed.[1]

A FIRM'S HIRING DECISION

The tendency of marginal revenue product to diminish will cool the strawberry grower's eagerness to hire 1,000 pickers. We still don't know, however, how many pickers will be hired.

Our earlier discussion of labor supply indicated that more workers are available only at higher wage rates. But that's true only for the *market* supply. A single producer may be able to hire an unlimited number of workers at the prevailing wage rate—if the firm is perfectly competitive in the labor market. In other words, *a firm that's a perfect competitor in the labor market can hire all the labor it wants at the prevailing market wage.*

Let's assume that the strawberry grower is so small that his hiring decisions have no effect on local wages. As far as he's concerned, there's an unlimited supply of strawberry pickers willing to work for $4 an hour. His only decision is how many of these willing pickers to hire at that wage rate.

Figure 15.5 provides the answer. We already know that the grower is eager to hire pickers whose marginal revenue product exceeds their wage. He'll therefore hire at least 1 worker at that wage, because the MRP of the first picker is $10 an hour (point *A* in Figure 15.5). A second worker will be hired as well, because that picker's MRP (point *B* in Figure 15.5) also exceeds the going wage rate. In fact, *the grower will continue hiring pickers until the MRP has declined to the level of the market wage rate.* Figure 15.5 indicates that this intersection (point *C*) occurs when 5 pickers are employed. We can conclude that the grower will be willing to hire—will *demand*—5 pickers if wages are $4 an hour.

The folly of hiring more than 5 pickers is also apparent in Figure 15.5. The marginal revenue product of the sixth worker is only $2 an hour (point *D*). Hiring a sixth picker will cost more in wages than the picker brings in as revenue. The *maximum* number of pickers the grower will employ at prevailing wages is 5 (point *C*).

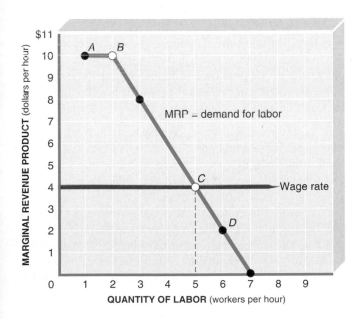

FIGURE 15.5
The Marginal Revenue Product Curve Is the Labor Demand Curve

The MRP curve tells us how many workers an employer would want to hire at various wage rates. An employer is willing to pay a worker no more than the marginal revenue product. In this case, a grower would gladly hire a second worker, because that worker's MRP (point *B*) exceeds the wage rate ($4). The sixth worker won't be hired at that wage rate, however, since the MRP (at point *D*) is less than $4. The MRP curve is the labor demand curve.

[1] Marginal revenue product would fall even faster if the price of strawberries declined as increasing quantities were supplied. We're assuming that the grower's output doesn't influence the market price of strawberries and hence that the grower is a *competitive* producer.

Analysis: Marginal revenue product measures what a worker is worth to an employer. The New York Yankees are expecting a high MRP from A-Rod.

The law of diminishing returns also implies that all 5 pickers will be paid the same wage. Once 5 pickers are employed, we can't say that any single picker is responsible for the observed decline in marginal revenue product. Marginal revenue product of labor diminishes because each worker has less capital and land to work with, not because the last worker hired is less able than the others. Accordingly, the "fifth" picker can't be identified as any particular individual. Once 5 pickers are hired, Marvin's MRP is no higher than any other picker's. ***Each (identical) worker is worth no more than the marginal revenue product of the last worker hired, and all workers are paid the same wage rate.***

The principles of marginal revenue product apply to baseball players as well as strawberry pickers. The New York Yankees are paying Alex Rodriguez $112 million to play baseball. As the News reports, the Yankees expect "A-Rod" to generate at least that much added revenue in extra ticket sales, merchandise sales, and ad revenue. The Yankees think A-Rod's MRP justifies his extraordinarily high salary.

Whatever the explanation for the disparity between the incomes of baseball players and strawberry pickers, the enormous gap between them seems awfully unfair. An obvious question then arises: Can't the number of pickers or their wages be increased?

Changes in Wage Rates

Suppose the government were to set a minimum wage for strawberry pickers at $6 an hour. At first glance this action would appear to boost the wages of pickers, who have been earning only $4 an hour. This isn't all good news for the strawberry pickers, however. ***There's a trade-off between wage rates and the number of workers demanded.*** If wage rates go up, growers will hire fewer pickers.

Figure 15.6 illustrates this trade-off. The grower's earlier decision to hire 5 pickers was based on a wage of $4 an hour (point *C*). If the wage jumps to $6 an hour, it no longer makes economic sense to keep 5 pickers employed. The MRP of the fifth worker is only $4 an hour. The grower will respond to higher wage rates by moving up the labor demand curve to point *G*. At point *G*, only 4 pickers are hired and MRP again equals the wage rate. If more workers are to be hired, the wage rate must drop.

Changes in Productivity

The downward slope of the labor demand curve doesn't doom strawberry pickers to low wages. It does emphasize, however, the inevitable link between workers' productivity and wages. ***To get higher wages without sacrificing jobs, productivity (MRP) must increase.***

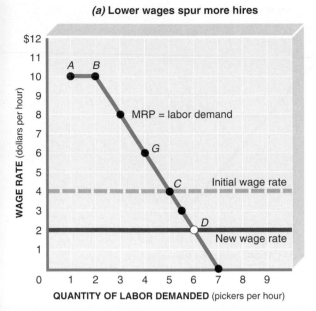

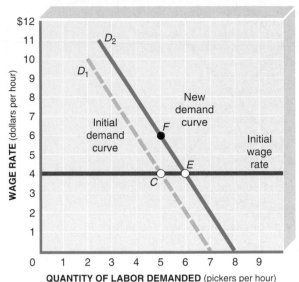

FIGURE 15.6
Incentives to Hire

(*a*) **Lower wage** If the wage rate drops, an employer will be willing to hire more workers, *ceteris paribus*. At $4 an hour, only 5 pickers per hour would be demanded (point *C*). If the wage rate dropped to $2 an hour, 6 pickers per hour would be demanded (point *D*).

(*b*) **Higher productivity** If the marginal revenue product of labor improves, the employer will hire a greater quantity of labor at any given wage rate. The labor demand curve will shift up (from D_1 to D_2). In this case, an increase in MRP leads the employer to hire 6 workers (point *E*) rather than only 5 workers (point *C*) at $4 per hour.

Suppose Marvin and his friends all enroll in a local agricultural extension course and learn new methods of strawberry picking. With these new methods, the marginal physical product of each picker increases by 1 box per hour. With the price of strawberries still at $2 a box, this productivity improvement implies an increase in marginal *revenue* product of $2 per worker. This change causes an upward *shift* of the labor demand (MRP) curve, as in Figure 15.6*b*.

Notice how the improvement in productivity has altered the value of strawberry pickers. The MRP of the fifth picker is now $6 an hour (point *F*) rather than $4 (point *C*). Hence, the grower can now afford to pay higher wages. Or the grower could employ more pickers than before, moving from point *C* to point *E*. ***Increased productivity implies that workers can get higher wages without sacrificing jobs or more employment without lowering wages.*** Historically, increased productivity has been the most important source of rising wages and living standards.

An increase in the price of strawberries would also help the pickers. Marginal revenue product reflects the interaction of productivity and product prices. If strawberry prices were to double, strawberry pickers would become twice as valuable, even without an increase in physical productivity. Such a change in product prices depends, however, on changes in the market supply and demand for strawberries.

Changes in Price

MARKET EQUILIBRIUM

The principles that guide the hiring decisions of a single strawberry grower can be extended to the entire labor market. This suggests that ***the market demand for labor depends on***

- ***The number of employers.***
- ***The marginal revenue product of labor in each firm and industry.***

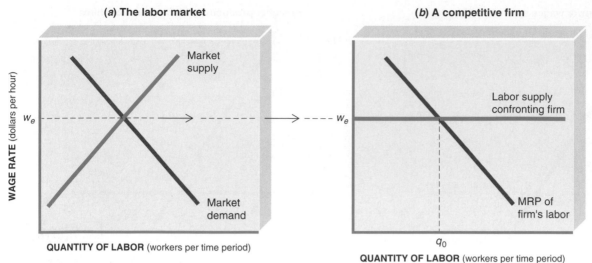

FIGURE 15.7
Equilibrium Wage

The intersection of *market* supply and demand determines the equilibrium wage in a competitive labor market. All the firms in the industry can then hire as much labor as they want at that

equilibrium wage. In this case, the firm can hire all the workers it wants at the equilibrium wage, w_e. It chooses to hire q_0 workers, as determined by their marginal revenue product within the firm.

Increases in either the demand for final products or the productivity of labor will tend to increase the demand for labor.

On the supply side of the labor market we have already observed that *the market supply of labor depends on*

- *The number of available workers.*
- *Each worker's willingness to work at alternative wage rates.*

The supply decisions of each worker are in turn a reflection of tastes, income, wealth, expectations, other prices, and taxes.

Equilibrium Wage

equilibrium wage: The wage rate at which the quantity of labor supplied in a given time period equals the quantity of labor demanded.

Figure 15.7 brings these market forces together. *The intersection of the market supply and demand curves establishes the* **equilibrium wage.** This is the only wage rate at which the quantity of labor supplied equals the quantity of labor demanded. Everyone who's willing and able to work for this wage will find a job.

If the labor market is perfectly competitive, all employers will be able to hire as many workers as they want at the equilibrium wage. Like our strawberry grower, every competitive firm is assumed to have no discernible effect on market wages. *Competitive employers act like price takers with respect to wages as well as prices.* This phenomenon is also portrayed in Figure 15.7.

Minimum Wages

Some people will be unhappy with the equilibrium wage. Employers may grumble that wages are too high. Workers may complain that wages are too low. They may seek government intervention to change market outcomes. This is the goal of Congress when it seeks to increase the federal minimum wage (see Table 15.2).

Figure 15.8 illustrates the effects of such government intervention. The equilibrium wage is W_e, and q_e workers are employed. A minimum wage of W_M is then set, above the market equilibrium. The wage W_M encourages more low-skilled workers to seek employment; the quantity supplied increases from q_e to q_s. At the same time, however, the number of available jobs declines from q_e to q_d. This leaves a market surplus at the wage W_M. As a result of the increased wage, some workers have lost

Oct. '38	$0.25	Jan. '75	$2.10
Oct. '39	0.30	Jan. '76	2.30
Oct. '45	0.40	Jan. '78	2.65
Jan. '50	0.75	Jan. '79	2.90
Mar. '56	1.00	Jan. '80	3.10
Sept. '61	1.15	Jan. '81	3.35
Sept. '63	1.25	Apr. '90	3.80
Feb. '67	1.40	Apr. '91	4.25
Feb. '68	1.60	Oct. '96	4.75
May '74	2.00	Sept. '97	5.15

TABLE 15.2
Minimum Wage History

The federal minimum wage has been increased periodically since first set in 1938. In 2004 Congress was considering another increase, to $7 by 2006.

jobs ($q_e - q_d$) and some new entrants fail to find employment ($q_s - q_e$). Only those workers who remain employed (q_d) benefit from the higher wage.

Government-imposed wage floors thus have two distinct effects: *A minimum wage*

- *Reduces the quantity of labor demanded.*
- *Increases the quantity of labor supplied.*
- *Creates a market surplus.*

The extent of job loss resulting from a minimum wage hike is hotly debated. How many jobs are lost obviously depends on how far the minimum wage is raised. The elasticity of labor demand is also important. Democrats argue that labor demand is inelastic, so few jobs will be lost. Republicans assert that labor demand is elastic, so more jobs will be lost. In the early 1980s, the elasticity of labor demand was found to be 0.10. Hence, a 10 percent increase in the minimum wage would cause a 1 percent reduction in employment. Between 1981 and 1990, however, the minimum was stuck at $3.35 an hour while average wages increased 30 percent. By 1989, the federal minimum may have actually been below the equilibrium wage for low-skilled labor. When the minimum wage is below the equilibrium wage, an increase in the minimum may have little or no adverse employment effects. This appeared to be the case again in 1996. Because the federal minimum hadn't been raised for five years (see Table 15.2), the 50 cents per hour hike in October 1996 caused few job losses. According to Federal Reserve estimates, the 1997 wage hike may have reduced employment growth by only 100,000 to 200,000 jobs. However, *the further the minimum wage rises above the market's equilibrium wage, the greater the job loss.* That is why small-business owners objected to Senator John Kerry's proposal to raise the federal minimum to $7 an hour by 2007 (see News on next page).

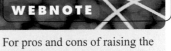

WEBNOTE

For pros and cons of raising the minimum wage, see the Electronic Policy Network (pro) at www.movingideas.org/issuesindepth/ and Employment Policies Institute (con) at www.epionline.org/index_mw.cfm.

WEBNOTE

For historical data on the federal minimum wage, in real and nominal terms, visit the U.S. Department of Labor at www.dol.gov/esa/whd/flsa.

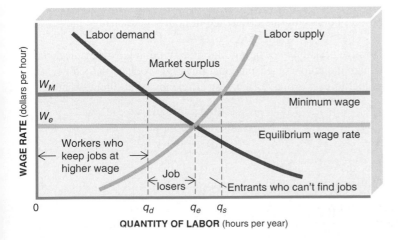

FIGURE 15.8
Minimum Wage Effects

If the minimum wage exceeds the equilibrium wage, a labor surplus will result: More workers will be willing to work at that wage rate than employers will be willing to hire. Some workers will end up with higher wages, but others will end up unemployed.

IN THE NEWS

Kerry Backs $7-an-Hour Minimum Wage

Sen. John F. Kerry called yesterday for a 36 percent hike in the federal minimum wage over the next three years, contending that such an increase would help 7 million working people escape poverty.

The current federal minimum, established eight years ago, is $5.15 an hour. Kerry supports legislation introduced in April by fellow Massachusetts Sen. Edward M. Kennedy (D) that would raise the rate in steps to $7 an hour by 2007. . .

Democrats have typically advocated increasing the minimum, which plays well with less-affluent voters. Republicans tend to oppose such proposals, saying that increases hurt the least skilled workers by forcing employers to cut back when labor costs rise. . .

"It is absurd to propose a minimum wage hike which will negatively impact small businesses employing people in entry-level jobs," Rob Green, vice president of the National Restaurant Association, said in a statement. He added that it would "impede job creation and will ultimately hurt the people it is designed to help. It is baffling that Sen. Kerry would suggest such a dramatic and punitive increase during a time of economic recovery."

—Paul Farhi
Washington Post
Saturday, June 19, 2004; Page A02

Source: *The Washington Post,* June 19, 2004. © 2004 The Washington Post. Reprinted with permission. www.washingtonpost.com.

Analysis: A higher minimum wage encourages firms to hire fewer workers. How many jobs are lost depends on the size of the wage hike and the price elasticity of labor demand.

CHOOSING AMONG INPUTS

One of the options employers have when wage rates rise is to utilize more machinery in place of labor. In most production processes there are possibilities for substituting capital inputs for labor inputs. In the long run, there are still more possibilities for redesigning the whole production process. Given these options, how should the choice of inputs be made?

Suppose a mechanical strawberry picker can pick berries twice as fast as Marvin. Who will the grower hire, Marvin or the mechanical picker? At first it would seem that the grower would choose the mechanical picker. But the choice isn't so obvious. So far, all we know is that the mechanical picker's MPP is twice as large as Marvin's. But we haven't said anything about the *cost* of the mechanical picker.

Cost Efficiency

Suppose that a mechanical picker can be rented for $10 an hour, while Marvin is still willing to work for $4 an hour. Will this difference in hourly cost change the grower's input choice?

To determine the relative desirability of hiring Marvin or renting the mechanical picker, the grower must compare the ratio of their marginal physical products to their cost. This ratio of marginal product to cost expresses the **cost efficiency** of an input—that is,

cost efficiency: The amount of output associated with an additional dollar spent on input; the MPP of an input divided by its price (cost).

$$\text{Cost efficiency} = \frac{\text{marginal physical product of an input}}{\text{cost of an input}}$$

Marvin's MPP is 5 boxes of strawberries per hour and his cost (wage) is $4. Thus, the return on each dollar of wages paid to Marvin is

$$\text{Cost efficiency of labor} = \frac{\text{MPP}_{\text{labor}}}{\text{cost}_{\text{labor}}} = \frac{5 \text{ boxes}}{\$4} = 1.25 \text{ boxes per } \$1 \text{ of cost}$$

By contrast, the mechanical picker has an MPP of 10 boxes per hour and costs $10 per hour; thus

$$\begin{array}{c}\text{Cost}\\\text{efficiency of}\\\text{mechanical}\\\text{picker}\end{array} = \dfrac{\begin{array}{c}\text{MPP of}\\\text{mechanical}\\\text{picker}\end{array}}{\begin{array}{c}\text{cost of}\\\text{mechanical}\\\text{picker}\end{array}} = \dfrac{10\text{ boxes}}{\$10} = 1\text{ box per }\$1\text{ of cost}$$

These calculations indicate that Marvin is more cost-effective than the mechanical picker. From this perspective, the grower is better off hiring Marvin than renting a mechanical picker.

From the perspective of cost efficiency, the cheapness of a productive input is measured not by its price but by the amount of output it delivers for that price. Thus, *the most cost-efficient factor of production is the one that produces the most output per dollar.*

The concept of cost efficiency helps explain why American firms don't move en masse to Haiti, where peasants are willing to work for as little as 80 cents an hour. Although this wage rate is far below the minimum wage in the United States, the marginal physical product of Haitian peasants is even further below American standards. American workers remain more cost-efficient than the "cheap" labor available in Haiti, making it unprofitable to **outsource** U.S. jobs. So long as U.S. workers deliver more output per dollar of wages, they will remain cost-effective in global markets.

Typically a producer doesn't choose between individual inputs but rather between alternative production processes. General Motors, for example, can't afford to compare the cost efficiency of each job applicant with the cost efficiency of mechanical tire mounters. Instead, GM compares the relative desirability of a **production process** that is labor-intensive (uses a lot of labor) with others that are less labor-intensive. GM ignores individual differences in marginal revenue product. Nevertheless, the same principles of cost efficiency guide the decision.

Let's return to the strawberry patch to see how the choice of an entire production process is made. We again assume that strawberries can be picked by either human or mechanical hands. Now, however, we assume that one ton of strawberries can be produced by only one of the three production processes described in Table 15.3. Process A is most *labor-intensive,* it uses the most labor and thus keeps more human pickers employed. By contrast, process C is *capital-intensive;* it uses the most mechanical pickers and provides the least employment to human pickers. Process B falls between these two extremes.

Which of these three production processes should the grower use? If he used labor-intensive process A, he'd be doing the pickers a real favor. But his goal is to maximize profits, so we assume he'll choose the production process that best serves this objective. That is, he'll choose the *least-cost* process to produce one ton of strawberries.

outsourcing: The relocation of production to foreign countries.

Alternative Production Processes

production process: A specific combination of resources used to produce a good or service.

The Efficiency Decision

Input	Alternative Processes for Producing One Ton of Strawberries		
	Process A	Process B	Process C
Labor (hours)	400	270	220
Machinery (hours)	13	15	18
Land (acres)	1	1	1

TABLE 15.3
Alternative Production Processes

One ton of strawberries can be produced with varying input combinations. Which process is most efficient? What information is missing?

TABLE 15.4
The Least-Cost Combination

A producer wants to produce a given rate of output for the least cost. Choosing the least expensive production process is the efficiency decision. In this case, process C represents the most cost-efficient production process for producing one ton of strawberries.

Input	Cost Calculation
Process A	
Labor	400 hours at $4 per hour = $1,600
Machinery	13 hours at $10 per hour = 130
Land	1 acre at $500 = 500
	Total cost $2,230
Process B	
Labor	270 hours at $4 per hour = $1,080
Machinery	15 hours at $10 per hour = 150
Land	1 acre at $500 = 500
	Total cost $1,730
Process C	
Labor	220 hours at $4 per hour = $ 880
Machinery	18 hours at $10 per hour = 180
Land	1 acre at $500 = 500
	Total cost $1,560

But which of the production processes in Table 15.3 is least expensive? We really can't tell on the basis of the information provided. To determine the relative cost of each process—and thus to understand the producer's choice—we must know something more about input costs. In particular, we have to know how much an hour of mechanical picking costs and how much an hour of human picking (labor) costs. Then we can determine which combination of inputs is least expensive in producing one ton of strawberries—that is, which is most *cost-efficient.* Note that we don't have to know how much the land costs, because the same amount of land is used in all three production processes. Thus, land costs won't affect our efficiency decision.

Suppose that strawberry pickers are still paid $4 an hour and that mechanical pickers can be rented for $10 an hour. The acre of land rents for $500 per year. With this information we can now calculate the total dollar cost of each production process and quickly determine the most cost-efficient. Table 15.4 summarizes the required calculations.

The calculations performed in Table 15.4 clearly identify process C as the least expensive way of producing one ton of strawberries. Process A entails a total cost of $2,230, whereas the capital-intensive process C costs only $1,560 to produce the same quantity of output. As a profit maximizer, the grower will choose process C, even though it implies less employment for strawberry pickers.

The choice of an appropriate production process—the decision about *how* to produce—is called the **efficiency decision.** As we've seen, a producer seeks to use the combination of resources that produces a given rate of output for the least cost. The efficiency decision requires the producer to find that particular least-cost combination.

efficiency decision: The choice of a production process for any given rate of output.

THE ECONOMY TOMORROW

Capping CEO Pay

At the beginning of this chapter we noted that Michael Eisner, the CEO of Walt Disney Company, signed a 10-year contract that could have paid him an astronomical $771 million. When challenged to defend his pay, Disney's CEO asserted he had earned every penny of it by enhancing the value of the company's stock.

*"O.K. guys, now lets go and _earn_ that four
hundred times our workers' salaries."*

Analysis: The wages of top corporate officers may not
be fully justified by their marginal revenue product.

Critics of CEO pay don't accept this explanation. They make three points. First, the
rise in the price of Disney's *stock* is not a measure of marginal revenue product. Only
part of the increase in share prices was due to the company's performance; the rest
was caused by a general upswing in the stock market. Second, the revenues of the
Walt Disney Company probably wouldn't be $771 million lower in the absence of Eis-
ner. Hence, his marginal revenue product is less than $771 million. Finally, Eisner
probably would have worked just as hard for, say, just $400 million or so. Therefore,
his actual pay was more than required to elicit the desired supply response.

Critics conclude that many CEO paychecks are out of line with realities of supply
and demand (see cartoon). They want corporations to reduce CEO pay and revise the
process used for setting CEO pay levels.

WEBNOTE

Motivated by money? Check
out the highest-paying occupations at www.acinet.org/acinet.

Unmeasured MRP

One of the difficulties in determining the appropriate level of CEO pay is the
elusiveness of marginal revenue product. It's easy to measure the MRP of a strawberry
picker or even a salesclerk who sells Disney toys. But a corporate CEO's contributions
are less well defined. A CEO is supposed to provide strategic leadership and a sense
of mission. These are critical to a corporation's success but hard to quantify.

Congress confronts the same problem in setting the president's pay. We noted earlier that the president of the United States is paid $400,000 a year. Can we argue that
this salary represents the president's marginal revenue product? The News on the next
page suggests that the president's pay would be in the range of $38–58 million if he
was paid on performance (MRP). The wage we actually pay a president is less a reflection of contribution to total output than a matter of custom. The salary also reflects
the price voters believe is required to induce competent individuals to forsake private-
sector jobs and assume the responsibilities of the presidency. In this sense, the wage
paid to the president and other public officials is set by their **opportunity wage**—
that is, the wage they could earn in private industry.

The same kinds of considerations influence the wages of college professors. The
marginal revenue product of a college professor isn't easy to measure. Is it the number of students she teaches, the amount of knowledge conveyed, or something else?
Confronted with such problems, most universities tend to pay college professors
according to their opportunity wage—that is, the amount the professors could earn
elsewhere.

Opportunity wages also help explain the difference between the wage of the CEO
of Disney and the workers who peddle its products. The lower wage of salesclerks

opportunity wage: The highest
wage an individual would earn in
his or her best alternative job.

IN THE NEWS

What's a President Worth?

So what if the president were paid like a CEO? Based on performance, a president would be worth up to $58 million a year—if he meets certain goals, compensation experts say. What those goals might be are shown below.

If the nation's president and chief executive were running a major corporation, he probably would find a proposed pay raise to $400,000 laughable.

Compared with what Jack Welch makes at General Electric and Lou Gerstner makes at IBM, that's pocket change.

In the private sector, a CEO running a huge corporation would earn $34 million to $58 million a year, much of it from incentive bonuses and stock options, says compensation expert Graef Crystal of the on-line newsletter *crystal-report.com*.

At $200,000 a year, the president makes more than 99 percent of all workers. But he oversees a budget of $1.8 trillion, 11 times the annual revenue of the nation's largest company,

General Motors. He's boss of 4.2 million employees, both civilian and military, six times as many as the largest private employer, Wal-Mart.

Yet he would have to work 2,878 years to bring home the $576 million that Walt Disney CEO Michael Eisner made last year, largely from exercising stock options he was granted as incentives.

In 1980, *Fortune* 500 CEOs averaged $625,000 a year, a little more than three times what President Carter was making. By 1990, the average CEO was making 10 times more than President Bush. And last year, in the wake of generous stock options awarded in a booming market, the CEO-to-president ratio swelled to 53-to-1.

—Del Jones and Gary Strauss

Source: *USA Today*, May 27, 1999. USA TODAY. Copyright 1999. Reprinted with permission. www.usatoday.com

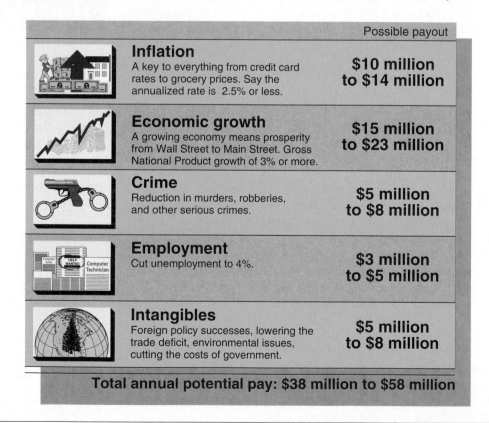

		Possible payout
Inflation	A key to everything from credit card rates to grocery prices. Say the annualized rate is 2.5% or less.	**$10 million to $14 million**
Economic growth	A growing economy means prosperity from Wall Street to Main Street. Gross National Product growth of 3% or more.	**$15 million to $23 million**
Crime	Reduction in murders, robberies, and other serious crimes.	**$5 million to $8 million**
Employment	Cut unemployment to 4%.	**$3 million to $5 million**
Intangibles	Foreign policy successes, lowering the trade deficit, environmental issues, cutting the costs of government.	**$5 million to $8 million**

Total annual potential pay: $38 million to $58 million

Analysis: If the nation's president were paid on the basis of his marginal revenue product, his salary would be a lot higher than $400,000.

DiscoverEcon*
with Paul Solman Videos
<u>NEW</u>
with this edition of
Schiller

DISCOVERECON

Welcome to the DiscoverEcon campus. You can explore the campus by clicking on one of our buildings.

Name: Lee Jones
Course: ECON 101, Section A
Instructor: Bill Entwistle

EDIT USER PROFILE

LOG OUT

VIDEO LAB
Enter here to view course-related movies.

CLASSROOM
Enter here for an interactive text, complete with exercises.

INSTRUCTORS' OFFICES
Enter here to view syllabus, homework results, and email instructor.

LIBRARY
Enter here for additional information and resources.

developed by Gerald C. Nelson, University of Illinois–Urbana/Cham

The **McGraw·Hill** Companies

To use DiscoverEcon with Paul Solman Videos

1. Visit www.mhhe.com/economics/schiller10/discoverecon

2. Click Register to create a login username and password
   with this code:

   uryev-gxny8-76cp7   (Do only once)

3. Click the cover of the text you are using (The Economy Today,
   The Macro Economy Today, The Micro Economy Today)

   Login with the username and password you created in Step 3.

   Click the Classroom to use DiscoverEcon tutorials, exercises, and/or
   eos. Click the Video Lab for immediate access to the videos.

   e having problems accessing the software, please
   technical support website: www.mhhe.com/support
   -331-5094.

   UIREMENTS

   th Pentium® 200 MHz or higher processor / Microsoft®
   dows 2000 Professional™, Windows ME™ or Windows XP™
   ternet Explorer 6.0™ with Java VM™ and valid Internet
   Cookies and Active X™ enabled) / 32 MB of RAM for
   for Windows 2000 Professional™ or Windows XP™ /
   osoft ® IntelliMouse™, or compatible pointing device /
   r monitor supporting 800x600 screen resolution / Local
   e of video memory / 16-bit sound card with speakers or

   paign

ISBN: 0-07-304211-0

reflects not only their marginal revenue product at Disney stores but also the fact that they're not trained for many other jobs. That is, their opportunity wages are low. By contrast, Disney's CEO has impressive managerial skills that are in demand by many corporations; his opportunity wages are high.

Opportunity wages help explain CEO pay but don't fully justify such high pay levels. If Disney's CEO pay is justified by opportunity wages, that means that another company would be willing to pay him that much. But what would justify such high pay at another company? Would his MRP be any easier to measure? Maybe *all* CEO paychecks have been inflated.

Critics of CEO pay conclude that the process of setting CEO pay levels should be changed. All too often, executive pay scales are set by self-serving committees composed of executives of the same or similar corporations. Critics want a more independent assessment of pay scales, with nonaffiliated experts and stockholder representatives. Some critics want to go a step further and set mandatory "caps" on CEO pay. President Clinton rejected legislated caps but convinced Congress to limit the tax deductibility of CEO pay. Any "unjustified" CEO pay in excess of $1 million a year can't be treated as a business expense but instead must be paid out of after-tax profits. This change puts more pressure on corporations to examine the rationale for multimillion-dollar paychecks.

If markets work efficiently, such government intervention shouldn't be necessary. Corporations that pay their CEOs excessively will end up with smaller profits than companies who pay market-based wages. Over time, "lean" companies will be more competitive than "fat" companies, and excessive pay packages will be eliminated. Legislated CEO pay caps imply that CEO labor markets aren't efficient or that the adjustment process is too slow. To forestall more government intervention in pay decisions, companies may tie executive pay more explicitly to performance (marginal revenue product) in the economy tomorrow.

WEBNOTE

Read more about top CEO salaries and check CEO/worker pay ratios at www.aflcio.org/paywatch.

SUMMARY

- The motivation to work arises from social, psychological, and economic forces. People need income to pay their bills, but they also need a sense of achievement. As a consequence, people are willing to work—to supply labor.

- There's an opportunity cost involved in working— namely, the amount of leisure time one sacrifices. By the same token, the opportunity cost of not working (leisure) is the income and related consumption possibilities thereby forgone. Thus each person confronts a trade-off between leisure and income.

- Increases in wage rates induce people to work more—that is, to substitute labor for leisure. But this substitution effect may be offset by an income effect. Higher wages also enable a person to work fewer hours with no loss of income. When income effects outweigh substitution effects, the labor supply curve bends backward.

- A firm's demand for labor reflects labor's marginal revenue product. A profit-maximizing employer won't pay a worker more than the worker produces.

- The marginal revenue product of labor diminishes as additional workers are employed on a particular job (the law of diminishing returns). This decline occurs because additional workers have to share existing land and capital, leaving each worker with less land and capital to work with.

- A producer seeks to get the most output for every dollar spent on inputs. This means getting the highest ratio of marginal product to input price. A profit-maximizing producer will choose the most cost-efficient input (not necessarily the one with the cheapest price).

- The efficiency decision involves the choice of the least-cost productive process and is also made on the basis of cost efficiency. A producer seeks the least expensive process to produce a given rate of output.

- Differences in marginal revenue product are an important explanation of wage inequalities. But the difficulty of measuring MRP in some jobs leaves many wage rates to be determined by opportunity wages or other mechanisms.

Key Terms

labor supply
substitution effect of wages
income effect of wages
market supply of labor
elasticity of labor supply
demand for labor

derived demand
marginal physical product (MPP)
marginal revenue product (MRP)
law of diminishing returns
equilibrium wage

cost efficiency
outsourcing
production process
efficiency decision
opportunity wage

Questions for Discussion

1. Why are you doing this homework? What are you giving up? What utility do you expect to gain?

2. Would you continue to work after winning a lottery prize of $50,000 a year for life? Would you change schools, jobs, or career objectives? What factors besides income influence work decisions?

3. The News on page 318 implies that students sacrifice a lot of potential income when they major in philosophy, education, or other social work. Is such behavior rational?

4. What's the justification for the merit pay plan discussed in the News on page 320? How could you compute marginal revenue product for priests?

5. Is this course increasing your marginal productivity? If so, in what way?

6. How might you measure the marginal revenue product of (*a*) a quarterback and (*b*) the team's coach?

7. Who is hurt and who is helped by an increase in the legal minimum wage? Under what circumstances might a higher minimum *not* reduce employment?

8. Explain why marginal physical product would diminish as
   (*a*) More secretaries are hired in an office.
   (*b*) More professors are hired in the economics department.
   (*c*) More construction workers are hired to build a school.

9. Is it possible that the president of the United States is overpaid? How should his MRP be measured?

10. The minimum wage in Mexico is less than $1 an hour. Does this make Mexican workers more cost-effective than U.S. workers? Explain.

PROBLEMS   The Student Problem Set at the back of this book contains numerical and graphing problems for this chapter.

WEB ACTIVITIES   to accompany this chapter can be found on the Online Learning Center:
http://www.mhhe.com/economics/schiller10

Labor Unions

The United Auto Workers Union (UAW) launched a strike against Caterpillar, Inc. in November 1991. The union wanted the manufacturer of construction machinery to increase pay, benefits, and job security. *Four years* later, Caterpillar hadn't budged; it continued to operate with replacement workers, management crews, and union members who crossed the picket line. The union finally capitulated in December 1995, sending its 8,700 members back to work with neither higher pay nor even a new contract. The union struck again in 1996 but relented after 17 months. Seven years after their first strike, the Caterpillar workers still had no contract.

To many observers, the failed UAW strike at Caterpillar climaxed a steady decline in the power of labor unions. But, the union movement is far from dead. Labor unions are even expanding in some sectors (especially government employment). Many unions still have **market power**—the ability to alter market outcomes. This chapter focuses on how power in the labor market affects wages, employment, and other economic outcomes. We address the following questions:

> **market power:** The ability to alter the market price of a good or service.

- **How do large and powerful employers affect market wages?**
- **How do labor unions alter wages and employment?**
- **What outcomes are possible from collective bargaining between management and unions?**

In the process of answering these questions, we look at the nation's most powerful unions and their actual behavior.

THE LABOR MARKET

To gauge the impact of labor market power, we must first observe how a competitive labor market sets wages and employment. On the supply side, we have all those individuals who are willing to work—to supply labor—at various wage rates. By counting the number of individuals willing to work at each and every wage rate, we can construct a *market* **labor supply** curve, as in Figure 16.1.

> **labor supply:** The willingness and ability to work specific amounts of time at alternative wage rates in a given time period, *ceteris paribus.*

The willingness of producers (firms) to hire labor is reflected in the market labor demand curve. The curve itself is constructed by counting the number of workers each firm says it is willing and able to hire at each and every wage rate. The curve illustrates the market **demand for labor**.

> **demand for labor:** The quantities of labor employers are willing and able to hire at alternative wages in a given time period, *ceteris paribus.*

The intersection of the labor supply and labor demand curves (point C in Figure 16.1) reveals the **equilibrium wage** rate (w_e): the wage rate at which the quantity of labor supplied equals the quantity demanded. At this wage rate, every job seeker who's willing and able to work for the wage w_e is employed. In addition, firms are able to acquire all the labor they're willing and able to hire at that wage.

> **Competitive Equilibrium**

FIGURE 16.1
Competitive Equilibrium in the Labor Market

The market labor supply curve includes all persons willing to work at various wage rates. The labor demand curve tells us how many workers employers are willing to hire. In a competitive market, the intersection of the labor supply and labor demand curves (point *C*) determines the equilibrium wage (w_e) and employment (q_e) levels.

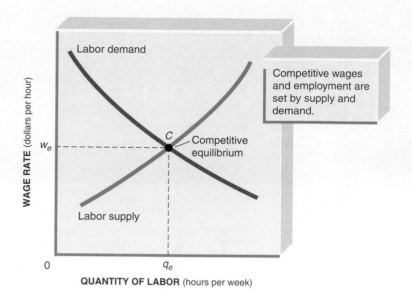

Competitive wages and employment are set by supply and demand.

equilibrium wage: The wage rate at which the quantity of labor supplied in a given time period equals the quantity of labor demanded.

Not everyone is employed in equilibrium. Workers who demand wages in excess of w_e are unable to find jobs. By the same token, employers who refuse to pay a wage as high as w_e are unable to attract workers.

Local Labor Markets

Figure 16.1 appears to suggest that there's only *one* labor market and thus only one equilibrium wage. This is a gross oversimplification. If you were looking for a job in Tulsa, you'd have little interest in employment prospects or power configurations in New York City. You'd be more concerned about the available jobs and wages in Tulsa—that is, the condition of the *local* labor market.

Even within a particular geographical area, interest usually focuses on particular occupations and workers rather than on all the people supplying or demanding labor. If you were looking for work as a dancer, you'd have little interest in the employment situation for carpenters or dentists. Rather, you'd want to know how many nightclubs or dance troupes had job vacancies, and what wages and working conditions they offered.

The distinction among various geographical, occupational, and industrial labor markets provides a more meaningful basis for analyzing labor market power. The tremendous size of the national labor market, with over 150 million workers, precludes anyone from acquiring control of the entire market. The largest employer in the United States (Wal-Mart) employs less than 0.8 percent of the labor force. General Motors employs fewer than that, and the top 500 industrial corporations employ less than 20 percent of all workers. The situation on the supply side is similar. The largest labor union (the Teamsters) represents less than 1 percent of all workers in the country. All unions together represent only one-eighth of the labor force. This doesn't mean that particular employers or unions have no influence on our economic welfare. It does suggest, however, that ***power in labor markets is likely to be more effective in specific areas, occupations, and industries.***

LABOR UNIONS

Types of Unions

The immediate objective of labor unions is to alter the equilibrium wage and employment conditions in specific labor markets. ***To be successful, unions must be able to exert control over the market supply curve.*** That's why workers have organized themselves along either industry or occupational craft lines. *Industrial unions* include workers in a particular industry (the United Auto Workers, for example). *Craft unions* represent workers with a particular skill (like the International Brotherhood of Electrical Workers), regardless of the industry in which they work.

The purpose of both types of labor unions is to coordinate the actions of thousands of individual workers, thereby achieving control of market supply. If a union is able to control the supply of workers in a particular industry or occupation, the union acquires a *monopoly* in that market. Like most monopolies, unions attempt to use their market power to increase their incomes.

Union Objectives

A primary objective of unions is to raise the wages of union members. In the 1998 dispute between pro basketball team owners and players, money was the sole issue. The players, who were already getting an average paycheck of $2.6 million per season, were resisting a salary cap that would restrain wages. The team owners wanted to limit total player salaries to 51.8 percent of league revenues.

An exclusive focus on wages is somewhat unusual. Union objectives also include improved working conditions, job security, and other nonwage forms of compensation, such as retirement (pension) benefits, vacation time, and health insurance. The Players Association and the National Football League have bargained about the use of artificial turf, early retirement, player fines, television revenues, game rules, and the use of team doctors, drug tests, pensions, and the number of players permitted on a team. In 1998, the foremost concern of the United Auto Workers was job security. Cutbacks and plant closings had eliminated more than 400,000 auto industry jobs in the 1980s. When General Motors announced plans to buy more parts from outside suppliers, the UAW feared still more job losses. To protest proposed new work rules and more threatened job losses, the union struck GM's Flint, Michigan, parts plant in June 1998. The resulting parts shortage shut down virtually all GM operations within a matter of weeks.

Although union objectives tend to be as broad as the concerns of union members, we focus here on just one objective, wage rates. This isn't too great a simplification, because most nonwage issues can be translated into their effective impact on wage rates. In 2003, for example, the UAW and GM agreed to nearly two dozen different job provisions, ranging from job security to child care (see News below). It was possible, however, to figure out the cost of these many provisions ($4,625 per worker per year). Hence, the "bottom line" of the compensation package could be expressed in

For an overview and update on UAW activity, visit the organization's Web site at www.uaw.org.

IN THE NEWS

What Autoworkers Won

After two months of negotiations, the UAW and GM signed a new four-year contract in October 2003. The contract included these provisions.

- **Wages** $3,000 lump-sum payments in 2003 and 2004 plus 2 percent increase in 2005 and 3% in 2006.
- **Holidays** Increased to 67 days with addition of a National Election Day in November 2005.
- **Pensions** Increased by $4.20 per month for each year of service.
- **Tool Allowance** Increased by 30 cents per hour.
- **Eye care** Coverage extended to LASIK.
- **Vehicle vouchers** $1,000 each in first and third years.

- **Contraceptives** Newly covered.
- **Job security** Requires new employees to be hired as attrition replacements.
- **Tuition assistance** Increased from $4,200 to $4,600 per year.
- **Dental services** Benefit increased from $1,600 to $1,700 per year.
- **Supplemental unemployment benefits** Increased from $175 to $190 per week.
- **Relocation allowance** Increased from $23,500 to $25,000.
- **Life insurance** Survivor benefit increased by $50 per month.

Analysis: Labor unions bargain with management over a variety of employment conditions. Most issues, however, can be expressed in terms of their impact on wage costs.

terms of wage costs. What we seek to determine is whether and how unions can raise effective wage rates in a specific labor market by altering the competitive equilibrium depicted in Figure 16.1.

THE POTENTIAL USE OF POWER

In a competitive labor market, each worker makes a labor supply decision on the basis of his or her own perceptions of the relative values of labor and leisure (Chapter 15). Whatever decision is made won't alter the market wage. One worker simply isn't that significant in a market composed of thousands. Once a market is unionized, however, these conditions no longer hold. A **union evaluates job offers on the basis of the collective interests of its members.** In particular, it must be concerned with the effects of increased employment on the wage rate paid to its members.

The Marginal Wage

Like all monopolists, unions have to worry about the downward slope of the demand curve. In the case of labor markets, a larger quantity of labor can be "sold" only at lower wage rates. Suppose the workers in a particular labor market confront the market labor demand schedule depicted in Figure 16.2. This schedule tells us that employers aren't willing to hire any workers at a wage rate of $6 per hour (row S) but will hire 1 worker per hour if the wage rate is $5 (row T). At still lower rates, the quantity of labor demanded increases; 5 workers per hour are demanded at a wage of $1 per hour.

An individual worker offered a wage of $1 an hour would have to decide whether such wages merited the sacrifice of an hour's leisure. But a union would evaluate the offer differently. A union must consider how the hiring of one more worker will affect the wages of all the workers.

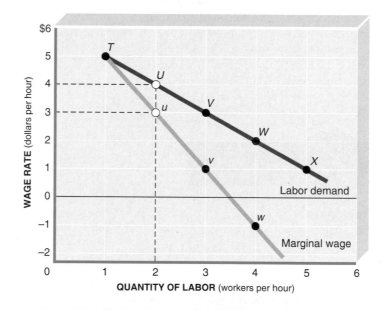

FIGURE 16.2
The Marginal Wage

The *marginal wage* is the change in *total wages* (paid to all workers) associated with the employment of an additional worker. If the wage rate is $4 per hour, only 2 workers will be hired (point *U*). The wage rate must fall to $3 per hour if 3 workers are to be hired (point *V*). In the process, *total* wages paid rise from $8 ($4 × 2 workers) to $9 ($3 × 3 workers). The *marginal* wage of the third worker is only $1 (point *v*).

The graph illustrates the relationship of the marginal wage to labor demand. The marginal wage curve lies below the labor demand curve, because the marginal wage is less than the nominal wage. Compare the marginal wage (point *v*) and the nominal wage (point *V*) of the third worker.

	Wage Rate (per hour)	×	Number of Workers Demanded (per hour)	=	Total Wages Paid (per hour)		Marginal Wage (per labor hour)
S	$6		0		$0		
T	5		1		5	>	$5
U	4		2		8	>	3
V	3		3		9	>	1
W	2		4		8	>	−1
X	1		5		5	>	−3

Total Wages Paid. Notice that when 4 workers are hired at a wage rate of $2 an hour (row W), total wages are $8 per hour. In order for a fifth worker to be employed, the wage rate must drop to $1 an hour (row X). At wages of $1 per hour, the *total* wages paid to the 5 workers amount to only $5 per hour. Thus, total wages paid to the workers actually *fall* when a fifth worker is employed. Collectively the workers would be better off sending only 4 people to work at the higher wage of $2 an hour and paying the fifth worker $1 an hour to stay home!

The basic mandate of a labor union is to evaluate wage and employment offers from this *collective* perspective. To do so, **a union must distinguish the marginal wage from the market wage.** The market wage is simply the current wage rate paid by the employer; it's the wage received by individual workers. The **marginal wage,** on the other hand, is the change in *total* wages paid (to all workers) when an additional worker is hired—that is,

$$\frac{\text{Marginal}}{\text{wage}} = \frac{\text{change in total wages paid}}{\text{change in quantity of labor employed}}$$

> **marginal wage:** The change in total wages paid associated with a one-unit increase in the quantity of labor employed.

The distinction between marginal wages and market wages arises from the downward slope of the labor demand curve. It's analogous to the distinction we made between marginal revenue and price for monopolists in product markets. The distinction simply reflects the law of demand: As wages fall, the number of workers hired increases.

The impact of increased employment on marginal wages is also illustrated in Figure 16.2. According to the labor demand curve, 1 worker will be hired at a wage rate of $5 an hour (point *T*); 2 workers will be hired only if the market wage falls to $4 an hour (point *U*), at which point the first and second workers will each be getting $4 an hour. Thus, the increased wages of the second worker (from zero to $4) will be partially offset by the reduction in the wage rate paid to the first worker (from $5 to $4). *Total* wages paid will increase by only $3; this is the *marginal* wage (point *u*). The marginal wage actually becomes negative at some point, when the implied wage loss to workers already on the job begins to exceed the wage of a new hired worker.

The Union Wage Goal

A union never wants to accept a negative marginal wage, of course. At such a point, union members would be better off paying someone to stay home. The question, then, is what level of (positive) marginal wage the union should accept.

We can answer this question by looking at the labor supply curve. The labor supply curve tells us how much labor workers are *willing to supply* at various wage rates. Hence, the labor supply curve defines the lowest wage *individual* union members would accept. If the union adopts a *collective* perspective on the welfare of its members, however, it will view the wage offer differently. From their collective perspective, the wage that union members are getting for additional labor is the *marginal* wage, not the nominal (market) wage. Hence, the marginal wage curve, not the labor demand curve, is decisive in the union's assessment of wage offers.

If the union wants to maximize the *total* welfare of its members, it will seek that level of employment which equates the marginal wage with the supply preferences of union members. In Figure 16.3, **the intersection of the marginal wage curve with the labor supply curve identifies the desired level of employment for the union.** This intersection occurs at point *u*, yielding total employment of 2 workers per hour.

The marginal wage at point *u* is $3. However, the union members will get a higher actual wage than that. Look up from point *u* on the marginal wage curve to point *U* on the employer's labor demand curve. Point *U* tells us that the employer is *willing to pay* a wage rate of $4 an hour to employ two workers. The union knows it can demand and get $4 an hour if it supplies only two workers to the firm.

What the union is doing here is choosing a point on the labor demand curve that the union regards as the optimal combination of wages and employment. In a

FIGURE 16.3

The Union Wage Objective

The intersection of the marginal wage and labor supply curves (point *u*) determines the union's desired employment. Employers are willing to pay a wage rate of $4 per hour for that many workers, as revealed by point *U* on the labor demand curve.

More workers (*N*) are willing to work at $4 per hour than employers demand (*U*). To maintain that wage rate, the union must exclude some workers from the market. In the absence of such power, wages would fall to the competitive equilibrium (point *C*).

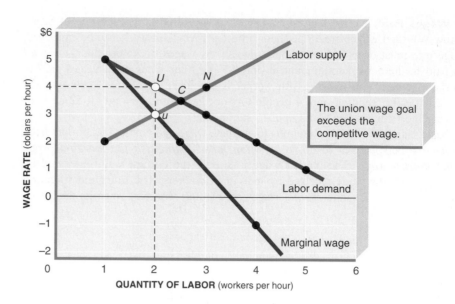

The union wage goal exceeds the competitve wage.

competitive market, point *C* would represent the equilibrium combination of wages and employment. But the union forces employers to point *U*, thereby attaining a higher wage rate and reducing employment.

Exclusion

The union's ability to maintain a wage rate of $4 an hour depends on its ability to exclude some workers from the market. Figure 16.3 suggests that three workers are willing and able to work at the union wage of $4 an hour (point *N*), whereas only two are hired (point *U*). If the additional worker were to offer his services, the wage rate would be pushed down the labor demand curve (to $3 per hour). Hence, ***to maintain a noncompetitive wage, the union must be able to exercise some control over the labor supply decisions of individual workers.*** The essential force here is union solidarity. Once unionized, the individual workers in an industry or occupation must agree not to compete among themselves by offering their labor at nonunion wage rates. Instead, the workers must agree to withhold labor—to strike, if necessary—if wage rates are too low, and to supply labor only if a specified wage rate is offered.

Unions can solidify their control of the labor supply by establishing **union shops,** workplaces where workers must join the union within 30 days after being employed. In this way, the unions gain control of all the workers employed in a particular company or industry, thereby reducing the number of replacement workers available for employment during a strike. Stiff penalties (such as loss of seniority or pension rights) and general union solidarity ensure that only nonunion workers will "fink" or "scab"—take the job of a worker on strike.

union shop: An employment setting in which all workers must join the union within 30 days after being employed.

Replacement Workers. Even union shops, however, are subject to potential competition from substitute labor. When the UAW struck Caterpillar in 1991, the company advertised nationally for replacement workers and set up a toll-free phone line for applicants. In the midst of a recession the company got a huge response. The resulting flow of replacement workers crippled the UAW strike. Professional baseball players faced the same problem in 1995. When the continued strike threatened a second consecutive season, the team owners started hiring new players to replace the regulars. The huge supply of aspiring ball players forced the strikers to reconsider.

Replacement workers are even more abundant in agriculture. The United Farm Workers has been trying for decades to organize California's 20,000 strawberry pickers. But the workers know that thousands of additional workers will flock to California from Mexico if they protest wages and working conditions.

THE EXTENT OF UNION POWER

The first labor unions in America were organized in the 1780s, and the first worker protests as early as 1636. Union power wasn't a significant force in labor markets, however, until the 1900s, when heavily populated commercial centers and large-scale manufacturing became common. Only then did large numbers of workers begin to view their employment situations from a common perspective.

Early Growth

The period 1916–20 was one of particularly fast growth for labor unions, largely because of the high demand for labor resulting from World War I. All these membership gains were lost, however, when the Great Depression threw millions of people out of work. By 1933, union membership had dwindled to the levels of 1915.

As the depression lingered on, public attitudes and government policy changed. Too many people had learned the meaning of layoffs, wage cuts, and prolonged unemployment. In 1933, the National Industrial Recovery Act (NIRA) established the right of employees to bargain collectively with their employers. When the NIRA was declared unconstitutional by the Supreme Court in 1935, its labor provisions were incorporated into a new law, the Wagner Act. With this legislative encouragement, union membership doubled between 1933 and 1937. Unions continued to gain in strength as the production needs of World War II increased the demand for labor. Figure 16.4 reflects the tremendous spurt of union activity between the depths of the depression and the height of World War II.

Union membership stopped increasing in the 1950s, even though the labor force kept growing. As a result, the unionized percentage of the labor force—the **unionization rate**—has been in steady decline for more than 40 years. The current unionization rate of 12.9 percent is less than half of its post–World War II peak and far below unionization rates in other industrialized nations (see World View on the next page).

Union Power Today

> **unionization ratio:** The percentage of the labor force belonging to a union.

Private vs. Public-Sector Trends. The decline in the *national* unionization rate conceals two very different trends. Union representation of *private*-sector workers has plunged even more sharply than Figure 16.4 suggests. In the last 10 years, the unionization rate in the private sector has fallen from 11.5 percent to only 8.2 percent. At the same time, union membership has increased sharply among teachers, government workers, and nonprofit employees. As of 2004, over 37 percent of workers on government payrolls were union members. ***The old industrial unions are being supplanted by unions of service workers, especially those employed in the public sector.***

Although industrial unions have been in general decline, they still possess significant pockets of market power. The Teamsters, the UAW, the United Mine Workers, the Union of Needletrades and Textile Employees, and the Food Workers all have substantial representation in their respective markets. Their strength in those specific markets, not national averages, determines their ability to alter market outcomes.

The AFL-CIO. One labor organization with a decidedly national focus is the AFL-CIO (the American Federation of Labor–Congress of Industrial Organizations). The AFL-CIO is not a separate union but a representational body of 120 national unions. It doesn't

WEBNOTE

The AFL-CIO's Web site offers a brief mission statement and a map of affiliated unions; visit www.aflcio.org.

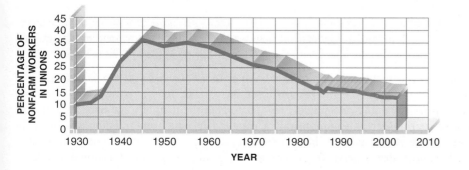

FIGURE 16.4
Changing Unionization Rates

Unions grew most rapidly during the decade 1935–1945. Since that time, the growth of unions hasn't kept pace with the growth of the U.S. labor force. Most employment growth has occurred in service industries that have traditionally been nonunion.

Source: U.S. Department of Labor.

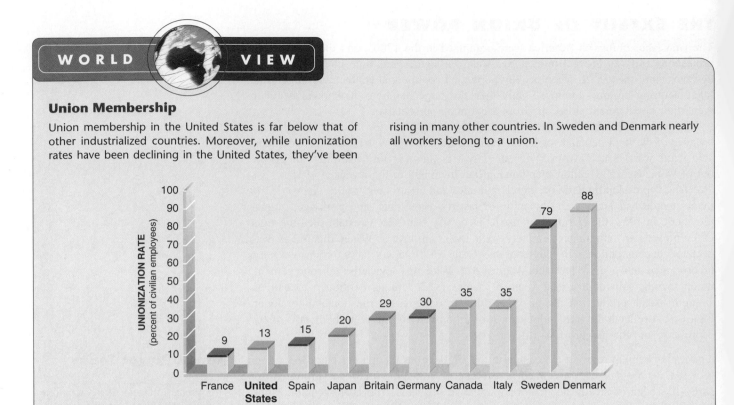

Union Membership

Union membership in the United States is far below that of other industrialized countries. Moreover, while unionization rates have been declining in the United States, they've been rising in many other countries. In Sweden and Denmark nearly all workers belong to a union.

UNIONIZATION RATE (percent of civilian employees)

	France	United States	Spain	Japan	Britain	Germany	Canada	Italy	Sweden	Denmark
	9	13	15	20	29	30	35	35	79	88

Source: European Foundation (2002 data).

Analysis: Unionization rates are comparatively low and declining in the United States. Unionization rates are still increasing in many other nations.

represent or negotiate for any particular group of workers but focuses instead on issues of general labor interest. The AFL-CIO acts as an advocate for the labor movement and represents labor's interest in legislative areas. It's the primary vehicle for political action. In addition, the AFL-CIO may render economic assistance to member unions or to groups of workers who wish to organize.

EMPLOYER POWER

The power possessed by labor unions in various occupations and industries seldom exists in a power vacuum. Power exists on the demand side of labor markets, too. The United Auto Workers confront GM, Ford, and Chrysler; the Steelworkers confront U.S. Steel, International Steel Group, and AK Steel; the Teamsters confront the Truckers' Association; the Communications Workers confront AT&T; and so on. An imbalance of power often exists on one side of the market or the other (as with, say, the Carpenters versus individual construction contractors). Labor markets with significant power on both sides, however, are common. To understand how wage rates and employment are determined in such markets, we have to assess the market power possessed by employers.

Monopsony

monopsony: A market in which there's only one buyer.

Power on the demand side of a market belongs to a *buyer* who is able to influence the market price of a good. With respect to labor markets, market power on the demand side implies the ability of a single employer to alter the market wage rate. The extreme case of such power is a **monopsony,** a situation in which one employer is the only buyer in a particular market. The classic example of a monopsony is a company town—that is, a town that depends for its livelihood on the decisions of a single employer.

A Win for the Graduate(s)

Finally, Teaching Assistants Can Unionize

For years, New York University and other private institutions have argued successfully that graduate students who work as research and teaching assistants shouldn't be treated as employees under federal labor law. The money that grad students earn is financial aid, not compensation, universities say. And while critics complain that grad students are exploited as cheap labor, administrators respond that aspiring Ph.D.'s gain vital career training by teaching undergraduate discussion sections and conducting research.

Last week, however, in a case involving NYU graduate assistants, the National Labor Relations Board gave a decisive thumbs down to these claims. Overturning nearly a quarter century of precedent, the federal panel said that graduate research and teaching assistants at private universities are employees who have the right to form unions and bargain collectively. "We will not deprive workers . . . of their fundamental statutory rights to organize and bargain with their employer, simply because they also are students," the ruling said, upholding a decision issued last spring by a regional NLRB director. Grad student unions have already been recognized at a growing number of public universities, which are governed by state labor laws.

—Ben Wildavsky

Source: *U.S. News & World Report*. November 13, 2000. Copyright 2000 U.S. News & World Report, L.P. Reprinted with permission. www.usnews.com

Analysis: Universities have monopsony power in setting wage and workloads for graduate assistants. To counterbalance that power, grad assistants may organize and bargain collectively.

Graduate teaching assistants have complained that the universities that employ them are much like company towns. Once they've started taking graduate classes at one university, it's difficult to transfer to another. As they see it, there is only one local labor market for graduate students. They complain that their monopsony employer compels them to work long hours at low wages. In 1998, University of California graduate students went out on strike to protest those conditions. In 1999, over 10,000 of those graduate students affiliated with the United Auto Workers to gain more power. In November 2000, the National Labor Relations Board decreed that graduate research and teaching assistants are employees with the right to organize and strike (see News).

Before 1976, professional sports teams also had monopsony power. As the News on the next page relates, sports contracts prohibited pro players from moving from one team (employer) to another without permission. This gave team owners a lot of power to set wages and working conditions.

There are many degrees of market power, and they can be defined in terms of *buyer concentration*. When buyers are many and of limited market power, the demand for resources is likely to be competitive. When only one buyer has access to a particular resource market, a monopsony exists. Between the two extremes lie the various degrees of imperfect competition, including the awkward-sounding but empirically important case of *oligopsony*. In an oligopsony (e.g., the auto industry), only a few firms account for most of the industry's employment.

Firms with power in labor markets generally have the same objective as all other firms—to maximize profits. What distinguishes them from competitive (powerless) firms is their ability to attain and keep economic profits. In labor markets, this means using fewer workers and paying them lower wages.

The distinguishing characteristic of labor market monopsonies is that their hiring decisions influence the market wage rate. In a competitive labor market, no single employer has any direct influence on the market wage rate; each firm can hire as much labor as it needs at the prevailing wage. But a monopsonist confronts the *market* labor supply curve. As a result, any increase in the quantity of labor demanded will force the monopsonist to climb up the labor supply curve in search of additional

The Potential Use of Power

Free Agents in Sports: A Threat to Monopsony

Before 1976, the owners of professional baseball, football, and basketball teams enjoyed monopsonistic power. This power was bestowed by the "reserve clause" included in player contracts. Individual players were permitted to negotiate with only one team. Once signed, they couldn't move to another team without their owner's permission. The player's only option was to "take it or leave"—that is, to accept his team's wage offer or quit playing altogether for at least one season. Team owners used the reserve clause to hold down player salaries far below their marginal revenue product.

The reserve clause began to unravel in 1975, when an arbitration panel ruled it was too restrictive. In 1976, baseball players won the right to become free agents—to negotiate and play for any team—after six years of major-league experience. In 1977, pro football players also won the right to become free

agents, but under more restrictive conditions (the team losing a free agent had to be "compensated" with draft choices). Pro basketball players first won limited mobility rights in 1976 and became true free agents in 1980.

The weakening of monopsonistic power led to dramatically higher player salaries. The average baseball salary soared from about $51,000 in 1976 to $900,000 in 1992. Pro basketball players enjoyed the same kind of wage gain, attaining an *average* salary of over $750,000 in 1990. Only pro football players lagged behind. Their more limited free-agent rights kept a lid on average football salaries. Football players went out on strike in 1982 and again in 1987 but failed to achieve free-agent status. In 1992, however, a federal court ruled that reserve clauses were anticompetitive. This decision prompted football owners to offer greater free agency and higher salaries.

Analysis: Because "reserve clauses" limit competing wage offers, they confer monopsony power on team owners. This kept athletes' wages below competitive equilibrium. Free agency changed that.

---

workers. In other words, *a monopsonist can hire additional workers only if it offers a higher wage rate.*

Marginal Factor Cost. Any time the price of a resource (or product) changes as a result of a firm's purchases, a distinction between marginal cost and price (average cost) must be made. Making this distinction is one of the little headaches—and potential sources of profit—of a monopsonist. For labor, we distinguish between the **marginal factor cost (MFC)** of labor and its wage rate.

Suppose that Figure 16.5 accurately described the labor supply schedule confronting a monopsonist. It's evident that the monopsonist will have to pay a wage of at least $2 an hour if it wants any labor. But even at that wage rate (row F of the supply schedule), only 1 worker will be willing to work. If the firm wants more labor, it will have to offer higher wages.

Two things happen when the firm raises its wage offer to $3 an hour (row G). First, the quantity of labor supplied increases (to 2 workers per hour). Second, the total wages paid rise by $4. This high *marginal* cost of labor is attributable to the fact that the first worker's wages rise when the wage rate is increased to attract additional workers. If all the workers perform the same job, the first worker will demand to be paid the new (higher) wage rate. Thus, *the marginal factor cost exceeds the wage rate, because additional workers can be hired only if the wage rate for all workers is increased.*

The Monopsony Firm's Goal. The marginal factor cost curve confronting this monopsonist is shown in the upper half of Figure 16.5. It starts at the bottom of the labor supply curve and rises above it. The monopsonist must now decide how many workers to hire, given the impact of its hiring decision on the market wage rate.

Remember from Chapter 15 that the labor demand curve is a reflection of labor's **marginal revenue product,** that is, the increase in total revenue attributable to the employment of one additional worker.

As we've emphasized, the profit-maximizing producer always seeks to equalize marginal revenue and marginal cost. Accordingly, the monopsonistic employer will

marginal factor cost (MFC): The change in total costs that results from a one-unit increase in the quantity of a factor employed.

marginal revenue product (MRP): The change in total revenue associated with one additional unit of input.

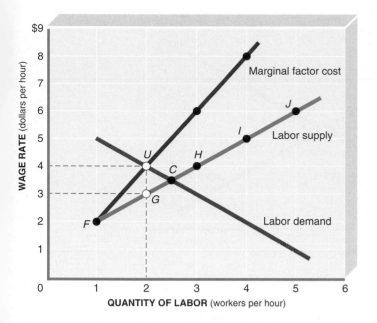

FIGURE 16.5
Marginal Factor Cost

More workers can be attracted only if the wage rate is increased. As it rises, all workers must be paid the higher wage. Consequently, the change in *total* wage costs exceeds the actual wage paid to the last worker. In the table, notice that in row I, for example, the marginal factor cost of the fourth worker ($8) exceeds the wage actually paid to that worker ($5). Thus, the marginal factor cost curve lies above the labor supply curve.

In the graph, the intersection of the marginal factor cost and labor demand curves (point *U*) indicates the quantity of labor a monopsonist will want to hire. The labor supply curve (at point *G*) indicates the wage rate that must be paid to attract the desired number of workers. This is the monopsonist's desired wage ($3). In the absence of market power, an employer would end up at point *C* (the competitive equilibrium), paying a higher wage and employing more workers.

	Wage Rate × (per hour)	Quantity of Labor Supplied = (workers per hour)	Total Wage Cost (per hour)		Marginal Factor Cost (per labor-hour)
D	$0	0	$0		
E	1	0	0		
				>	2
F	2	1	2		
				>	4
G	3	2	6		
				>	6
H	4	3	12		
				>	8
I	5	4	20		
				>	10
J	6	5	30		

seek to hire the amount of labor at which the marginal revenue product of labor equals its marginal factor cost—that is,

$$\text{Profit-maximizing level of input use} : \frac{\text{marginal revenue product of input}}{(MRP)} = \frac{\text{marginal factor cost of input}}{(MFC)}$$

In Figure 16.5, this objective is illustrated by the intersection of the marginal factor cost and labor demand curves at point *U*.

At point *U* the monopsonist is *willing to hire* 2 workers per hour at a wage rate of $4. But the firm doesn't have to pay this much. The labor supply curve informs us that 2 workers are *willing to work* for only $3 an hour. Hence, the firm first decides how many workers it wants to hire (at point *U*) and then looks at the labor supply curve (point *G*) to see what it has to pay them. As we suspected, a monopsonistic employer ends up hiring fewer workers at a lower wage rate than would prevail in a competitive market (point *C*).

COLLECTIVE BARGAINING

The potential for conflict between a powerful employer and a labor union should be evident:

- *The objective of a labor union is to establish a wage rate that's* **higher** *than the competitive wage (Figure 16.3).*
- *A monopsonist employer seeks to establish a wage rate that's* **lower** *than competitive standards (Figure 16.5).*

FIGURE 16.6

The Boundaries of Collective Bargaining

Firms with power in the labor market seek to establish wages and employment levels corresponding to point *G* (from Figure 16.5). Unions, on the other hand, seek to establish an equilibrium at point *U* (from Figure 16.3). The competitive equilibrium is at point *C*. The function of collective bargaining is to identify a compromise between these points—that is, to locate an equilibrium somewhere in the shaded area.

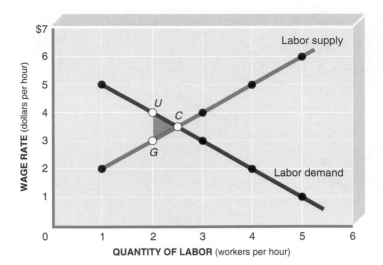

bilateral monopoly: A market with only one buyer (a monopsonist) and one seller (a monopolist).

collective bargaining: Direct negotiations between employers and unions to determine labor market outcomes.

Possible Agreements

The Pressure to Settle

The resultant clash generates intense bargaining that often spills over into politics, the courts, and open conflict.

The confrontation of power on both sides of the labor market is a situation referred to as **bilateral monopoly.** In such a market, wages and employment aren't determined simply by supply and demand. Rather, economic outcomes must be determined by **collective bargaining**—that is, direct negotiations between employers and labor unions for the purpose of determining wages, employment, working conditions, and related issues.

In a typical labor-business confrontation, the two sides begin by stating their preferences for equilibrium wages and employment. The *demands* laid down by the union are likely to revolve around point *U* in Figure 16.6; the *offer* enunciated by management is likely to be at point *G*.[1] Thus the boundaries of a potential settlement—a negotiated final equilibrium—are usually established at the outset of collective bargaining. The accompanying News summarizes the points of contention in the 1991–98 dispute between Caterpillar and the UAW.

The interesting part of collective bargaining isn't the initial bargaining positions but the negotiation of the final settlement. The speed with which a settlement is reached and the terms of the resulting compromise depend on the patience, tactics, and resources of the negotiating parties. ***The fundamental source of negotiating power for either side is its ability to withhold labor or jobs.*** The union can threaten to strike, thereby cutting off the flow of union labor to the employer. The employer can impose a lockout, thereby cutting off jobs and paychecks. The effectiveness of those threats depends on the availability of substitute workers or jobs.

Labor and management both suffer from either a strike or a lockout, no matter who initiates the work stoppage. The strike benefits paid to workers are rarely comparable to wages they would otherwise have received, and the payment of those benefits depletes the union treasury. By the same token, the reduction in labor costs and other expenses rarely compensates the employer for lost profits.

When the UAW was unable to attain its bargaining goals with Caterpillar, it instructed its 12,600 workers to go out on strike. The Caterpillar company, however, held a strong bargaining position. As a result of the 1990–1991 recession, it had a huge inventory of unsold farm equipment and was in no hurry to settle. When inventories got low, Caterpillar found a willing supply of replacement workers. This substitute labor put all the pressure on the union to settle. In 1994, the company actually attained record profits, despite the continuing strike.

[1]Even though points *U* and *G* may not be identical to the initial bargaining positions, they represent the positions of maximum attainable benefit for both sides. Points outside the demand or supply curve will be rejected out of hand by one side or the other.

Caterpillar vs. the UAW

	Company Proposal	Union Proposal
	What Separates the Two Sides	
Wages	One 3% wage hike for 12,800 of Cat's 16,500 union workers	One 3% wage hike for all workers, plus two one-time payments of 3% each
	Lower pay for new hires at parts-distribution centers	Same wage scales for all union workers
Benefits	Medical co-payments and a preferred-provider plan	A traditional plan with no co-payments
Job security	Employment levels can fall by attrition	Guaranteed number of union jobs

Source: Reprinted from the March 23, 1992 issue of *BusinessWeek* by permission. Copyright 1992 by The McGraw-Hill Companies, Inc. www.businessweek.com.

Analysis: Collective bargaining begins with a set of union demands and management offers. The outcome depends on the relative strength and tactics of the two parties.

In 1996, a strike by UAW workers at a GM brake plant caused shutdowns at all of GM's 29 U.S. assembly plants. More than 175,000 workers were idled. GM's 1,600 parts suppliers also had to lay off workers. With heavy inventories of unsold cars, GM had a relatively strong bargaining position. The UAW caved in quickly (17 days later). In 1998, the balance of power was different. Car sales were brisk and inventories were lean. So when the UAW struck a key parts plant in June 1998, GM was under greater pressure to settle. Rather than continuing to lose over $100 million a day, GM relented after 54 days, accepting little more than a UAW promise not to strike again for a year and a half. Ironically, the decline in GM profits due to the UAW strike cost GM autoworkers more that $6,000 apiece in *profit-sharing* bonuses that year.

Because potential income losses are usually high, both labor and management try to avoid a strike or lockout if they can. In fact, over 90 percent of all collective bargaining agreements are concluded without recourse to a strike and often without even the explicit threat of one.

The built-in pressures for settlement help resolve collective bargaining. They don't tell us, however, what the dimensions of that final settlement will be. All we know is that the settlement will be located within the boundaries established in Figure 16.6. The relative pressures on each side will determine whether the final equilibrium is closer to the union or the management position.

In the 1987 National Football League strike, the pressures to settle were very one-sided. The average pro football player was losing $14,375 per missed game. But the team owners were actually making *more* profit during the strike than before it. Although their revenues from ticket sales, parking, and food concessions fell, weekly TV revenues of $1 million per team continued to pour in. Those revenues, together with the sharply lower costs of replacement teams, led to higher profits. It didn't take long for the striking players to capitulate and accept the team owners' offer.

The 1998–99 pro basketball lockout wasn't so one-sided. When the season startup was canceled in November, the players started missing paychecks (an average of $2.6 million per season). But the team owners were also losing ticket revenue and concession sales, and they stood to lose another $465 million in TV revenues if the

The Final Settlement

For information about recent union contracts and strikes, see the U.S. Bureau of Labor Statistics at www.bls.gov. Click on "Collective Bargaining" under the "Wages, Earnings, and Benefits" heading.

season didn't start by January. As that deadline approached, the owners decided to compromise with the players and commence a shortened basketball season.

The 2003–4 strike of Southern California grocery workers ended with a different type of compromise. The 70,000 *existing* members of the United food and commercial workers union would not give up pay or benefits. But they agreed that *new* hires would get less pay ($15.10 an hour verses the existing $17.90) and have to pay health-insurance premiums ($9 per week). By burdening future workers with these costs, the existing union members were able to end their five-month strike without further losses.

The final settlement almost always necessitates hard choices on both sides. The union usually has to choose between an increase in job security or higher pay. A union must also consider how management will react in the long run to higher wages, perhaps by introducing new technology that reduces its dependence on labor. The employer has to worry whether productivity will suffer if workers are dissatisfied with their pay package.

THE IMPACT OF UNIONS

Stepping back from the negotiations that take place between individual unions and companies, we may ask whether the presence of unions has altered broader economic outcomes. We know that unions tend to raise wage rates in individual companies, industries, and occupations. But can we be equally sure that unions have raised wages in general? If the UAW is successful in raising wages in the automobile industry, what, if anything, happens to car prices? If car prices rise in step with UAW wage rates, labor and management in the auto industry will get proportionally larger slices of the economic pie. At the same time, workers in other industries will be burdened with higher car prices.

Relative Wages

One measure of union impact is *relative* wages—the wages of union members in comparison with those of nonunion workers. As we've noted, unions seek to control the supply of labor in a particular industry or occupation and thereby increase union wages. In their efforts to control labor supply, they restrict the number of people who can compete for available jobs. This forces the excluded workers to seek work elsewhere. As a result of this labor supply imbalance, wages tend to be higher in unionized industries than in nonunionized industries. Figure 16.7 illustrates this effect.

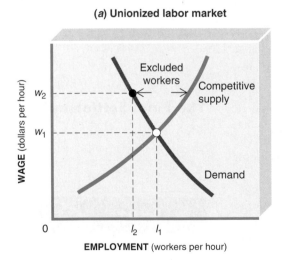

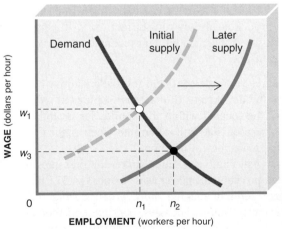

FIGURE 16.7
The Effect of Unions on Relative Wages

In the absence of unions, the average wage rate would be equal to w_1. As unions take control of the market, however, they seek to raise wage rates to w_2, in the process reducing the amount of employment in that market from l_1 to l_2. The workers displaced from the unionized market will seek work in the nonunionized market, thereby shifting the nonunion supply curve to the right. The result will be a reduction of wage rates (to w_3) in the nonunionized market. Thus, union wages end up higher than nonunion wages.

Although the theoretical impact of union exclusionism on relative wages is clear, empirical estimates of that impact are fairly rare. We do know that union wages in general are significantly higher than nonunion wages ($760 versus $599 per week in 2003). But part of this differential is due to the fact that unions are more common in industries that have always been more capital-intensive and paid relatively high wages. When comparisons are made within particular industries or sectors, the differential narrows considerably. Nevertheless, there's a general consensus that unions have managed to increase their relative wages from 15 to 20 percent.

Even though unions have been successful in redistributing some income from nonunion to union workers, the question still remains as to whether they've increased labor's share of *total* income. The *labor share* of total income is the proportion of income received by all workers, in contrast to the share of income received by owners of capital (the *capital share*). The labor share of total income will rise only if the gains to union workers exceed the losses to the (excluded) nonunion workers.

Evidence of unions' impact on labor's share is almost as difficult to assemble as evidence on relative wages, and for much the same reasons. Labor's share has risen dramatically, from only 56 percent in 1919 to 76 percent in 2004. But there have been tremendous changes in the mix of output during that same period. The proportion of output composed of personal services (accountants, teachers, electricians) is much larger now than it was in 1919. The labor share of income derived from personal services is and always was close to 100 percent. Accordingly, *most of the rise in labor's share of total income is due to changes in the structure of the economy rather than to unionization.*

One way firms can protect their profits in the face of rising union wages is to raise product prices. If firms raise prices along with union wages, then consumers end up footing the bill. In that case, profits and the capital share of total income might not be reduced.

The ability of firms to pass along increased union wages depends on the structure of product markets as well as labor markets. If a firm has power in both markets, it's better able to protect itself in this way. There's little evidence, however, that unions have contributed significantly to general cost-push inflation.

Unions also affect prices indirectly, via changes in **productivity**. Unions bargain not only for wages but also for work rules that specify how goods should be produced. Work rules may limit the pace of production, restrict the type of jobs a particular individual can perform, or require a minimum number of workers to accomplish a certain task. A factory carpenter, for example, may not be permitted to change a lightbulb that burns out in his shop area. And the electrician who is summoned may be required to have an apprentice on all work assignments. Such restrictive work rules would make it very costly to change a burned-out lightbulb.

Not all work rules are so restrictive. In general, however, work rules are designed to protect jobs and maximize the level of employment at any given rate of output. From this perspective, work rules directly restrain productivity and thus inflate costs and prices.

Work rules may also have some beneficial effects. The added job security provided by work rules and seniority provisions tends to reduce labor turnover (quitting) and thus saves recruitment and training costs. Protective rules may also make workers more willing to learn new tasks and to train others in specific skills. Richard Freeman of Harvard asserts that unions have actually accelerated advances in productivity and economic growth.

Perhaps more important than any of these specific union effects is the general impact the union movement has had on our economic, social, and political institutions. Unions are a major political force in the United States. They've not only provided critical electoral and financial support for selected political candidates, but they've also fought hard for important legislation. Unions have succeeded in establishing minimum wage

Labor's Share of Total Income

Prices

Productivity

productivity: Output per unit of input, such as output per labor-hour.

Political Impact

laws, work and safety rules, and retirement benefits. They've also actively lobbied for such things as civil rights legislation and health and education programs. Whatever one may think of any particular union or specific union action, it's clear that our institutions and national welfare would be very different in their absence.

THE ECONOMY TOMORROW

Merging to Survive

WEBNOTE

For trends in union membership, see www.aflcio.org/aboutunions/joinunions/whyjoin/uniondifference/uniondiff11.cfm.

Unions have been in retreat for nearly a generation. As shown in Figure 16.4, the unionized share of the labor force has fallen from 35 percent in 1950 to less than 13 percent today. Even that modest share has been maintained only by the spread of unionism among public school teachers and other government employees. In the private sector, the unionization rate is closer to 9 percent and still declining. The Teamsters, the Auto Workers, and the Steelworkers have lost over 1 million members in the last 15 years.

The decline in unionization is explained by three phenomena. Most important is the relative decline in manufacturing, coupled with rapid growth in high-tech service industries (like computer software, accounting, and medical technology). The second force is the downsizing of major corporations and the relatively faster growth of smaller companies. These structural changes have combined to shrink the traditional employment base of labor unions.

The third cause of shrinking unionization is increased global competition. The decline of worldwide trade and investment barriers has made it easier for firms to import products from low-wage nations and even to relocate production plants. With more options, firms can more easily resist noncompetitive wage demands.

The labor-union movement is fully aware of these forces and determined to resist them. To increase their power, unions are merging across craft and industry lines. In 1995, the Rubber Workers merged with the Steelworkers, the two major textile unions combined forces, and the Food Workers and Retail Clerks formed a new union. In 1999, the Grain Millers merged with the Paperworkers Union. By merging, the unions hope to increase representation, gain financial strength, and enhance their political clout. They're also seeking to broaden their appeal by organizing low-wage workers in the service industries. These efforts, together with their political strength, will help unions to play a continuing role in the economy tomorrow, even if their share of total employment continues to shrink.

SUMMARY

- Power in labor markets is the ability to alter market wage rates. Such power is most evident in local labor markets defined by geographical, occupational, or industrial boundaries.
- Power on the supply side of labor markets is manifested by unions, organized along industry or craft lines. The basic function of a union is to evaluate employment offers in terms of the *collective* interest of its members.
- The downward slope of the labor demand curve creates a distinction between the marginal wage and the market wage. The marginal wage is the change in *total* wages

occasioned by employment of one additional worker and is less than the market wage.
- Unions seek to establish that rate of employment at which the marginal wage curve intersects the labor supply curve. The desired union wage is then found on the labor demand curve at that level of employment.
- Power on the demand side of labor market is manifested in buyer concentrations such as monopsony and oligopsony. Such power is usually found among the same firms that exercise market power in product markets.
- By definition, power on the demand side implies some direct influence on market wage rates; additional hiring

by a monopsonist will force up the market wage rate. Hence, a monopsonist must recognize a distinction between the marginal factor cost of labor and its (lower) market wage rate.

- The goal of a monopsonistic employer is to hire the number of workers indicated by the point at which the marginal factor cost of labor equals its marginal revenue product. The employer then looks at the labor supply curve to determine the wage rate that must be paid for that number of workers.

- The desire of unions to establish a wage rate that's higher than competitive wages directly opposes the desire of powerful employers to establish lower wage rates. In bilateral monopolies, in which power exists on both sides of the labor market, unions and employers engage in collective bargaining to negotiate a final settlement.

- The impact of unions on the economy is difficult to measure. It appears, however, that they've increased their own relative wages and contributed to rising prices. They've also had substantial political impact.

Key Terms

market power
labor supply
demand for labor
equilibrium wage
marginal wage

union shop
unionization ratio
monopsony
marginal factor cost (MFC)
marginal revenue product (MRP)

bilateral monopoly
collective bargaining
productivity

Questions for Discussion

1. Collective bargaining sessions often start with unreasonable demands and categorical rejections. Why do unions and employers tend to begin bargaining from extreme positions?

2. Does a strike for a raise of 5 cents an hour make any sense? What kinds of long-term benefits might a union gain from such a strike?

3. Are large and powerful firms easier targets for union organization than small firms? Why or why not?

4. Nonunionized firms tend to offer wage rates that are close to rates paid by unionized firms in the same industry. How do you explain this?

5. Why are farm workers much less successful than airplane machinists in securing higher wages?

6. In 1998, teaching assistants at the University of California struck for higher wages and union recognition, something they had sought for 14 years. How did the availability of replacement workers affect their power?

7. A key issue in the 1998 GM strike involved "peg rates" that allow workers to go home or get paid overtime wages once production reaches a specified level. How do peg rates affect productivity and costs?

8. How will union mergers affect the market power of unions?

ALERT!

PROBLEMS The Student Problem Set at the back of this book contains numerical and graphing problems for this chapter.

WEB ACTIVITIES to accompany this chapter can be found on the Online Learning Center: **http://www.mhhe.com/economics/schiller10**

Financial Markets

Christopher Columbus had a crazy entrepreneurial idea: He was certain he could find a new route to the Indies by sailing not east from Europe but west—around the world. Such a route, he surmised, would give Europe quicker access to the riches of the East Indies. Whoever discovered that western route could become very, very rich.

To find that route, Columbus needed ships, sailors, and tons of provisions. He couldn't afford to supply these resources himself. He needed financial backers who would put up the money. For several years he tried to convince King Ferdinand of Spain to provide the necessary funds. But the king didn't want to risk so much wealth on a single venture. Twice he'd turned Columbus down.

Fortunately, Genoese merchant bankers in Seville came to Columbus's rescue. Convinced that Columbus's "enterprise of the Indies" might bring back "pearls, precious stones, gold, silver, spiceries," and other valuable merchandise, they guaranteed repayment of any funds lent to Columbus. With that guarantee in hand, the Duke of Medina Sidonia, in April 1492, offered to lend 1,000 maravedis (about $5,000 in today's dollars) to Queen Isabella for the purpose of funding Columbus's expedition. With no personal financial risk, King Ferdinand then granted Columbus the funds and authority for a royal expedition.

Columbus's experience in raising funds for his expedition illustrates a critical function of financial markets, namely, the management of *risk*. This chapter examines how financial markets facilitate economic activities (like Columbus's expedition) by managing the risks of failure. Three central questions guide the discussion:

- **What is traded in financial markets?**
- **How do the financial markets affect the economic outcomes of WHO, WHAT, and FOR WHOM?**
- **Why do financial markets fluctuate so much?**

THE ROLE OF FINANCIAL MARKETS

A central question for every economy is WHAT to produce. In 1492, all available resources were employed in farming, fishing, food distribution, metalworking, and other basic services. For Columbus to pursue his quest, he needed some of those resources. To get them, he needed money to bid scarce resources from other pursuits and employ them on his expedition.

Entrepreneurs who don't have great personal wealth must get start-up funds from other people. There are two possibilities: either *borrow* the money, or invite other people to *invest* in the new venture.

How might you pursue these options? You could ask your relatives for a loan or go door-to-door in your neighborhood seeking investors. But such direct fund-raising is

**Financial
Intermediaries**

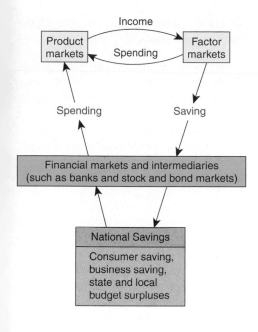

FIGURE 17.1
Mobilizing Savings

The central economic function of financial markets is to channel national savings into new investment and other desired expenditure. Financial intermediaries such as banks, insurance companies, and stockbrokers help transfer purchasing power from savers to spenders.

costly, inefficient, and often unproductive. Columbus went hat in hand to the Spanish royal court twice, but each time he came back empty-handed.

The task of raising start-up funds is made much easier by the existence of **financial intermediaries**—institutions that steer the flow of savings to cash-strapped entrepreneurs and other investors. Funds flow into banks, pension funds, bond markets, stock markets, and other financial intermediaries from businesses, households, and government entities that have some unspent income. This pool of national savings is then passed on to entrepreneurs, expanding businesses, and other borrowers by these same institutions (see Figure 17.1).

Financial intermediaries provide several important services: They greatly reduce the cost of locating loanable funds. Their pool of savings offers a clear economy of scale compared to the alternative of door-to-door solicitations. They also reduce the cost to savers of finding suitable lending or investment opportunities. Few individuals have the time, resources, or interest to do the searching on their own. With huge pools of amassed savings, however, financial intermediaries have the incentive to acquire and analyze information about lending and investment opportunities. Hence, *financial intermediaries reduce search and information costs* in the financial markets. In so doing, they make the allocation of resources more efficient.

Although financial intermediaries make the job of acquiring start-up funds a lot easier, there's no guarantee that the funds needed will be acquired. First, there must be an adequate supply of funds available. Second, financial intermediaries must be convinced that they should allocate some of those funds to a project.

As noted, the supply of loanable funds originates in the decisions of market participants to not spend all their current income. Those saving decisions are influenced by time preferences and interest rates.

Time Preferences. In deciding to *save* rather than *spend,* people effectively reallocate their spending over time. That is, people save *now* in order to spend more *later.* How much to save, then, depends partly on *time preference.* If a person doesn't give any thought to the future, she's likely to save little. If, by contrast, a person wants to buy a car, a vacation, or a house in the future, he's more inclined to save some income now.

Interest Rates. Interest rates also affect saving decisions. If interest rates are high, the future payoff to every dollar saved is greater. A higher return on savings translates

financial intermediary: Institution (e.g., bank or the stock market) that makes savings available to dissavers (e.g., investors).

The Supply of Loanable Funds

into more future income for every dollar of current income saved. Hence, *higher interest rates increase the quantity of available savings (loanable funds).*

Risk. In the early 1990s, banks in Russia were offering interest rates on savings accounts of nearly 100 percent a year. In Latin America, banks have offered even higher interest rates on occasion. Yet few people rushed to deposit their savings in these banks. People worried that the banks might fail, wiping out their savings in the process. In other words, there was a high *risk* attached to those high interest rates.

Anyone who contemplated lending funds to Columbus confronted a similar risk. That was the dilemma King Ferdinand confronted. He had enough funds to finance Columbus's expedition, but he didn't want to risk losing so much on a single venture.

Risk Management. This is why the Genoese bankers were so critical: These financial intermediaries could spread the risk of failure among many individuals. Each investor could put up just a fraction of the needed funds. No one had to put all his eggs in one basket. Once the consortium of bankers agreed to share the risks of Columbus's expedition, the venture had wings. The Genoese merchant bankers could afford to take portions of the expedition's risks because they also financed many less risky projects. By diversifying their portfolios, they could select any degree of average risk they preferred. That is the essence of risk management.

Risk Premiums. Even though diversification permits greater risk management, lenders will want to be compensated for any above-average risks they take. Money lent to local merchants must have seemed a lot less risky than lending funds to Columbus. Thus no one would have stepped forward to finance Columbus if he hadn't been promised an *above-average* return upon the expedition's success. The difference between the rates of return on a safe (certain) investment and a risky (uncertain) one is called the **risk premium.** Risk premiums compensate people who finance risky ventures that succeed. Because these ventures are risky, however, investors often lose their money in such ventures too.

risk premium: The difference in rates of return on risky (uncertain) and safe (certain) investments.

Risk premiums help explain why blue-chip corporations such as Microsoft can borrow money from a bank at the low "prime" rate while ordinary consumers have to pay much higher interest rates on personal loans. Corporate loans are less risky because corporations typically have plenty of revenue and assets to cover their debts. Consumers often get overextended, however, and can't pay all their bills. As a result, there's a greater risk that consumers loans won't be paid back. It may also be more expensive to collect payments from consumers who fall behind. Banks charge higher interest rates on consumer loans to compensate for this risk.

THE PRESENT VALUE OF FUTURE PROFITS

In deciding whether to assume the *risk* of supplying funds to a new venture, financial intermediaries assess the potential *rewards*. People who are *demanding* funds must also have some sense of what the payoff to their venture will be. In Columbus's case, the rewards were the fabled treasures of the East Indies. Even if he found those treasures, however, the rewards would only come long after the expedition was financed. When Columbus proposed his East Indies expedition, he envisioned a round trip that would last at least six months. Were he successful in finding the fabled treasures of the East, he planned subsequent trips to acquire and transport his precious cargoes back home. Although King Ferdinand granted Columbus only one-tenth of any profits from the first expedition, Columbus had a claim on one-eighth of the profits of any subsequent voyages. Hence, even if Columbus succeeded in finding a shortcut to the East, he wouldn't generate any substantial profit for perhaps two years or more.

Suppose for the moment that Columbus expected no profit from the first expedition but a profit of $1,000 at the end of two years from a second voyage. How much was that future profit worth to Columbus?

To assess the value of *future* receipts, we have to consider the *time value* of money. A dollar received today is worth more than a dollar received two years from today. Why? Because a dollar received today can earn *interest.* If you have a dollar today and put it in an interest-bearing account, in two years you'll have your original dollar *plus* accumulated interest.[1] *As long as interest-earning opportunities exist, present dollars are worth more than future dollars.*

In 1492, there were plenty of opportunities to earn interest. Indeed, the Genoese bankers were charging high interest rates on their loans and guarantees. If Columbus had had the cash, he too could have lent money to others and earned interest on his funds.

To calculate the present value of future dollars, this forgone interest must be taken into account. This computation is essentially interest accrual in reverse. *We "discount" future dollars by the opportunity cost of money*—that is, the market rate of interest.

Suppose the market rate of interest in 1492 was 10 percent. To compute the **present discounted value (PDV)** of future payment, we discount as follows:

$$PDV = \frac{\text{future payment}_N}{(1 + \text{interest rate})^N}$$

where N refers to the number of years into the future when a payment is to be made. If the future payment is to be made in 1 year, the N in the equation equals 1, and we have

$$PDV = \frac{\$1,000}{1.10}$$
$$= \$909.09$$

Hence, the present discounted value of $1,000 to be paid one year from today is $909.09. If $909.09 were received today, it could earn interest. In a year's time, the $909.09 would grow to $1,000 with interest accrued at the rate of 10 percent per year.

Suppose it would have taken Columbus two years to complete his expeditions and collect his profits. In that case, the present value of the $1,000 payment would be lower. The N in the formula would be 2 and the present value would be

$$PDV = \frac{\$1,000}{(1.10)^2} = \frac{\$1,000}{1.21} = \$826.45$$

Hence, *the longer one has to wait for a future payment, the less present value it has.*

Lottery winners often have to choose between present and future values. In July 2004, for example, Geraldine Williams, a housekeeper in Lowell, Massachusetts, won a $294 million MegaMillions lottery. The $294 million was payable in 26 annual installments of $11.3 million. If the lucky winner wanted to get her prize sooner, she could accept an immediate but smaller payout rather than 25 future installments.

Table 17.1 shows how the lottery officials figured the present value of the $294 prize. The first installment of $11.3 million would be paid immediately. Mrs. Williams would have had to wait one year for the second check, however. At the then-prevailing interest rate of 4.47 percent, the *present* value of that second $11.3 million check was only $10.82 million. The *last* payoff check had even less value since it wasn't due to be paid for 25 years. With so much time for interest to accrue, that final $11.3 million payment had a present value of only $3.79 million. The calculations in Table 17.1 convinced lottery officials to offer an immediate payout of only $168 million on the $294 million prize. Mrs. Williams wasn't too disappointed.

The winner would have received even less money had interest rates been higher. At the time Mrs. Williams won the lottery, the interest rate on bonds was 4.47 percent.

Time Value of Money

present discounted value (PDV): The value today of future payments, adjusted for interest accrual.

Interest Rate Effects

---

[1]Part of that interest payment will compensate for anticipated inflation; the remainder will compensate for the pure time value of money (postponed spending). Real (inflation-adjusted) interest rates express the time value of money.

TABLE 17.1
Computing Present Value

The present value of a future payment declines the longer one must wait for a payment. At an interest rate of 4.47 percent, $11.3 million payable in 1 year is worth only $10.82 million today. A payout of $11.3 million 25 years from now has a present value of only $3.79 million. A string of $11.3 million payments spread out over 25 years has a present value of $168 million (at 4.47 percent interest).

Years in the Future	Future Payment ($ millions)	Present Value ($ millions)
0	$ 11.3	$ 11.30
1	11.3	10.82
2	11.3	10.35
3	11.3	9.91
4	11.3	9.49
5	11.3	8.04
*	*	*
*	*	*
*	*	*
25	11.3	3.79
	$294.0	$168.0

Note: The general formula for computing present values is $PDV = \Sigma \dfrac{\text{payment in year } N}{(1 + r)^N}$, where r is the prevailing rate.

Had the rate been higher, the discount for immediate payment would have been higher as well. Table 17.2 indicates that Mrs. Williams would have received only $107 million had the prevailing interest rate been 10 percent. What Tables 17.1 and 17.2 illustrate, then, is that *the present discounted value of a future payment declines with*

- *Higher interest rates.*
- *Longer delays in future payment.*

Uncertainty

The valuation of future payments must also consider the possibility of *non*payment. State governments are virtually certain to make promised lottery payouts, so there's little risk in accepting a promised payout of 25 annual installments. But what about the booty from Columbus's expeditions? There was great uncertainty that Columbus would ever return from his expeditions, much less bring back the "pearls, precious stones, gold, silver, spiceries" that people coveted. Investing in those expeditions was far riskier than deferring a lottery payment.

expected value: The probable value of a future payment, including the risk of nonpayment.

Expected Value. Whenever an anticipated future payment is uncertain, a risk factor should be included in present-value computations. This is done by calculating the **expected value** of a future payment. Suppose there was only a 50:50 chance that Columbus would bring back the bacon. In that event, the expected payoff would be

$$\text{Expected value} = (1 - \text{risk factor}) \times \text{present discounted value}$$

TABLE 17.2
Higher Interest Rates Reduce Present Values

Higher interest rates raise the *future* value of current dollars. The rates therefore reduce the *present* value of future payments. Shown here is the present discounted value of the July 2004 MegaMillions lottery prize of $294 million at different interest rates.

Interest Rate (%)	Present Discounted Value of $294 Million Lottery Prize ($ millions)
5.0%	$166.3
6.0	150.8
7.0	137.5
8.0	126.0
9.0	115.9
10.0	107.1

With a 50:50 chance of failure, the expected value of Columbus's first-year profits would have been

$$\text{Expected value} = (1 - 0.5) \times \$909.09$$
$$= \$454.55$$

Expected values also explain why people buy more lottery tickets when the prize is larger. The odds of winning the multistate Powerball lottery are 80 *million*:1. That's about the same odds as getting struck by lightning *14 times* in the same year. So it makes almost no sense to buy a ticket. With a $16 million prize, the *undiscounted* expected value of a $1 lottery ticket is only 20 cents. When the lottery prize increases, however, the expected value of a ticket grows as well (there are still only 80 million possible combinations of numbers). When the grand prize reached $250 million in July 1998, the undiscounted expected value of a lone winning ticket jumped to over $3. Millions of people decided that the expected value was high enough to justify playing the lottery. People took off from work, skipped classes, and drove across state lines to queue up for lottery tickets. So many people bought tickets on the last day that the lottery grand prize swelled to $295 million. (13 machinists from Ohio had the winning ticket and chose the present discounted value of $165.6 million.) When the prize is only $10 million, far fewer people buy tickets.

The Demand for Loanable Funds

People rarely borrow money to buy lottery tickets. But entrepreneurs and other market participants often use other people's funds to finance their ventures. *How much loanable funds are demanded depends on*

- *The expected rate of return.*
- *The cost of funds.*

The higher the expected return, or the lower the cost of funds, the greater will be the amount of loanable funds demanded.

Figure 17.2 offers a general view of the loanable funds market that emerges from these considerations. From the entrepreneur's perspective, the prevailing interest rate represents the cost of funds. From the perspective of savers, the interest rate represents the payoff to savings. When interest rates rise, the quantity of funds supplied goes up and the quantity demanded goes down. The prevailing (equilibrium) interest rate is set by the intersection of these supply and demand curves.

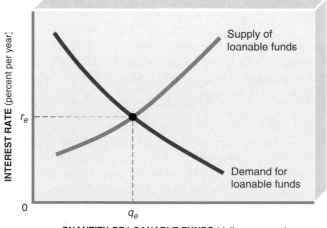

FIGURE 17.2
The Loanable Funds Market

The market rate of interest (r_e) is determined by the intersection of the curves representing supply of and demand for loanable funds. The rate of interest represents the price paid for the use of money.

THE STOCK MARKET

The concept of a loanable funds market sounds a bit alien. But the same principles of supply, demand, and risk management go a long way in explaining the action in stock markets. Suppose you had $1,000 to invest. Should you invest it all in lottery tickets that offer a multimillion-dollar payoff? Put it in a savings account that pays next to nothing? Or how about the stock market? The stock market can reward you handsomely; or it can wipe out your savings if the stocks you own tumble. Hence, stocks offer a higher average return than bank accounts but also entail greater average risk. People who bought Amazon.com stock in May 1997 got a 1,000 percent profit on their stock in only two years. But people who bought Amazon.com stock in December 1999 lost 90 percent of their investment in even less time.

Corporate Stock

When people buy a share of stock, they're buying partial ownership of a corporation. The three legal forms of business entities are

- Corporations
- Partnerships
- Proprietorships

corporation: A business organization having a continuous existence independent of its members (owners) and power and liabilities distinct from those of its members.

Limited Liability. Proprietorships are businesses owned by a single individual. The owner-proprietor is responsible for all the business, including repayment of any debts. Members of a partnership are typically liable for all business debts and activities as well. By contrast, a **corporation** is a limited liability form of business. The corporation itself, not its individual shareholders, is responsible for all business activity and debts. As a result of this limited liability, you can own a piece of a corporation without worrying about being sued for business mishaps (like environmental damage) or nonpayment of debt. This feature significantly reduces the risk of owning corporate stock.

corporate stock: Shares of ownership in a corporation.

Shared Ownership. The ownership of a corporation is defined in terms of stock shares. Each share of **corporate stock** represents partial ownership of the business. Chipmaker Intel, for example, has nearly 7 *billion* shares of stock outstanding (that is, shares held by the public). Hence, each share of Intel stock represents less than one-seventh of one-billionth ownership of the corporation. Potentially, this means that as many as 7 billion people could own the Intel Corporation. In reality, however, many individuals own hundreds of shares, and institutions may own thousands. Indeed, some of the largest pension funds in the United States own over a million shares of Intel.

In principle, the owners of corporate stock collectively run the business. In practice, the shareholders select a board of directors to monitor corporate activity and protect their interests. The day-to-day business of running a corporation is the job of managers who report to the board of directors.

Stock Returns

If shareholders don't have any direct role in running a corporation, why would they want to own a piece of it? Essentially, for the same reason that the Genoese bankers agreed to finance Columbus's expedition: profits. Owners (shareholders) of a corporation hope to share in the profits the corporation earns.

dividend: Amount of corporate profits paid out for each share of stock.

Dividends. Shareholders rarely receive their full share of the company's profits in cash. Corporations typically use some of the profits for investment in new plants or equipment. They may also want to retain some of the profits for operational needs or unforeseen contingencies. *Corporations may choose to retain earnings or pay them out to shareholders as* **dividends.** Any profits not paid to shareholders are referred to as **retained earnings.** Thus,

retained earnings: Amount of corporate profits not paid out in dividends.

$$\text{Dividends} = \text{corporate profits} - \text{retained earnings}$$

In 2004, Intel paid quarterly dividends amounting to 4 cents per share for the year. But the company earned profits equal to $1.11 cents per share. Thus, shareholders received less than 5 percent of their accrued profits in dividend checks; Intel retained the remaining $1.07 per-share profit earned in 2004 for future investments.

Capital Gains. If Intel invests its retained earnings wisely, the corporation may reap even larger profits in the future. As a company grows and prospers, each share of ownership may become more valuable. This increase in value would be reflected in higher market prices for shares of Intel stock. Any increase in the value of a stock represents a **capital gain** for shareholders. Capital gains directly increase shareholder wealth.

capital gain: An increase in the market value of an asset.

Total Return. People who own stocks can thus get two distinct payoffs: dividends and capital gains. Together, these payoffs represent the total return on stock investments. Hence, *the higher the expected total return (future dividends and capital gains), the greater the desire to buy and hold stocks.* If a stock paid no dividends and had no prospects for price appreciation (capital gain, for example) you'd probably hold your savings in a different form (such as another stock or maybe an interest-earning bank account).

When a corporation is formed, its future sales and profits are uncertain. When shares are first offered to the public, the seller of stock is the company itself. By *going public,* the corporation seeks to raise funds for investment and growth. A true *start-up* company may have nothing more than a good idea, a couple of dedicated employees, and Big Plans. To fund these plans, it sells shares of itself in an **initial public offering (IPO).** People who buy the newly issued stock are putting their savings directly into the corporation's accounts.[2] As new owners, they stand to profit from the corporation's business or take their lumps if the corporation fails.

Initial Public Offering

initial public offering (IPO): The first issuance (sale) to the general public of stock in a corporation.

In 1997, Amazon.com Inc. was still a relatively new company. Although the company had been in operation since 1994, its capacity to sell books on the Internet was limited. To expand, it needed more warehouse space, more computers, and additional staff. To finance this expansion, Amazon needed more money. The company could have *borrowed* money from a bank or other financial institution, but that would have saddled the company with debt and forced it to make regular interest payments. Lenders might have even wanted the officers of the company to guarantee repayment of the loan, burdening them with personal liability.

Rather than borrow money, Amazon's directors elected to sell ownership shares in the company. In May 1997, the company raised $54 million in cash by selling 3 million shares for $18 per share in its initial public offering.

Why were people eager to buy shares in Amazon.com Inc.? They certainly weren't buying the stock with expectations of high dividends. The company hadn't earned any profit in its first three years and didn't expect to earn a profit for at least another three years.

Secondary Trading

What might those future profits be worth? Suppose the company expected to earn profits of $1 per share in four years. What current value might those future profits have? In 1997, the prevailing long-term interest rate was close to 6 percent. Thus, the present discounted value of those future profits was

$$PDV = \frac{\$1}{(1 + 0.06)^4} = \frac{\$1}{1.262} = \$0.79$$

[2]In reality, some of the initial proceeds will go to stockbrokers and investment bankers as compensation for their services as financial intermediaries. The entrepreneur who starts the company, other company employees, and any venture capitalists who help fund the company before the public offering may also get some of the IPO receipts by selling shares they acquired before the company went public.

price/earnings (P/E) ratio: The price of a stock share divided by earnings (profit) per share.

If you paid $18 for a share of stock that earned only 79 cents, you'd be paying a reasonable price for a share of company profits. This can be seen by computing the **price/earnings (P/E) ratio:**

$$P/E \text{ ratio} = \frac{\text{price of stock share}}{\text{earnings (profit) per share}}$$

For Amazon.com in 1997,

$$P/E \text{ ratio} = \frac{\$18}{0.79} = 22.8$$

In other words, investors were paying $22.80 for every $1 of discounted future profits. That implies a rate of return of $1 \div \$22.80$, or 4.4 percent. Compared to the interest rates banks were paying on deposit balances, Amazon.com shares looked like a good buy.

Risk Factors. The stock didn't look quite as cheap, however, when the risks of failure were considered. The 79 cents of discounted future profits were far from certain; they were merely a projection. In reality, the road to riches on the Internet is riddled with risks. Other companies (e.g., Barnes and Noble or Borders) also sell books in cyberspace. Still more companies might enter the market if the outlook for profits improves. Technological advances might make Amazon.com's setup obsolete. Marketing and production costs may escalate. Any of these problems could jeopardize Amazon.com's future profits.

In view of these many risks, any projections of future profits must be adjusted for their uncertainty. If there's a 25 percent chance that Amazon.com will fail to hit the profit target, the *expected* value of future profits is

$$\text{Expected value of profit} = (1 - \text{risk factor}) \times \text{PDV}$$
$$= (1 - 0.25) \times 0.79$$
$$= 0.59$$

From this perspective, the IPO price of Amazon.com wasn't quite so cheap. The expected rate of return was

$$\frac{\text{Expected rate}}{\text{of return}} = \frac{\text{expected value of profit}}{\text{purchase price of stock}}$$
$$= \frac{\$0.59}{\$18.00} = 3.2\%$$

This was still better than most bank accounts but hardly exciting.

What *was* exciting about Amazon.com's IPO was the upside potential for growth. If e-commerce really took off, Amazon.com might generate exceptional profits, not a mere dollar or two. As people saw this potential unfold, they would surely want to buy shares of the company. As they did, the share price would increase, generating capital gains for those who bought earlier.

The prospect of such capital gains enticed a lot of stock buyers. On the first day of trading, the price of Amazon.com shares rose from the IPO price of $18 to as high as $30. Within a year the stock was selling for nearly $100. Within two years' time, the stock rose to $200 a share. This meteoric rise in the price of Amazon's stock represented a huge *capital gain* for its shareholders. The people who paid $200 a share were hoping for still higher share prices.

That post-IPO rise in Amazon's stock price had no direct effect on the company. A corporation reaps the proceeds of stock sales only when it sells shares to the public (the initial public offering). After the IPO, the company's stock is traded among individuals in the "after market." Virtually, all the trading activity on major stock exchanges consists of such after-market sales. Mr. Dow sells his Amazon share to Ms. Jones, who may later sell them to Destiny's Child. Such *secondary* trades may

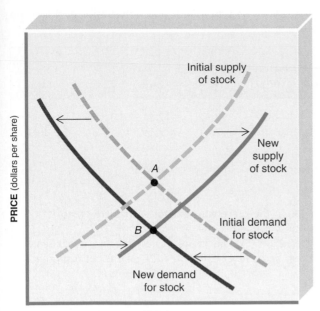

FIGURE 17.3
Changing Expectations

The supply and demand for stocks is fueled in part by expectations of future profits. When investors concluded that Amazon.com's future profit potential wasn't so great, demand for the stock decreased, supply increased, and the share price fell.

take place at the New York Stock Exchange (NYSE) on Wall Street or in the computerized over-the-counter market (e.g., NASDAQ).

The price of a stock at any moment is the outcome of supply-and-demand interactions. I wouldn't mind owning a piece of Amazon.com. But since I think the current share price is too high, I'll buy the stock only if the price falls substantially. Even though I'm not buying any Amazon stock now, I'm part of the *market demand*. That is, all the people who are willing and able to buy Amazon.com stock at *some* price are included in the demand curve in Figure 17.3. The cheaper the stock, the more people will want to buy it, *ceteris paribus*. The opposite is true on the supply side of the market: Everhigher prices are necessary to induce more shareholders to part with their shares.

Changing Expectations. In 2000–2001, investors reevaluated the profit prospects for Amazon.com and other dot.com companies. Several years of experience had shown that earning profits in e-commerce wasn't so easy. Projections of sales growth and future profits were sharply reduced. When Amazon.com failed to meet even those reduced expectations, its stock fell 20 percent in a single day. Figure 17.3 illustrates how this happened. The bad news reduced the demand for Amazon.com stock and increased the willingness of existing shareholders to sell. Such *changes in expectations imply shifts in supply and demand for a company's stock.* As Figure 17.3 illustrates, these combined shifts sent Amazon.com stock plummeting.

As Table 17.3 shows, the share price was $7.64 when the market closed on October 24, 2001. On that day, over 6 million shares of Amazon.com stock were traded. Along the path to the equilibrium closing price—the last trade of the day—the stock price fluctuated between a low ("Lo") of $7.15 and a high ("Hi") of $7.67. The price of Amazon.com stock fluctuated much more than that during the previous 52 weeks. As Table 17.3 documents, the stock traded as high as $40.88 and as low as $5.51 during the year. What accounts for these dramatic price fluctuations?

The Value of Information. The abrupt rise and later plunge in the price of Amazon.com stock highlights a critical dimension of financial markets, namely, the value of information. People who bought Amazon.com shares on the way up were poorly informed about the prospects for e-commerce sales and profits. Had they known profits would be so hard to make, they wouldn't have paid so much for the stock. People who bought Google's IPO in 2004 hoped they wouldn't suffer a similar disappointment (see News).

Market Fluctuations

How is *your* stock doing? Find current and past stock prices at http://finance.yahoo.com.

TABLE 17.3
Reading Stock Quotes

The financial pages of the daily newspaper summarize the trading activity in corporate stocks. The following quotation summarizes trading in AT&T and Amazon.com shares on October 24, 2001.

| 52 Weeks | | | | | | | Vol | | | | Net |
Hi	Lo	Stock	Sym	Div	Yld%	P/E	100s	Hi	Lo	Close	Chg
25.15	14.75	ATT	T	.15	0.8	dd	142327	17.92	17.51	17.75	−.15
27.63	5.51	Amazon	AMZN	—	—	dd	66976	7.67	7.15	7.64	−1.91

The information provided by this quotation includes:

52-Weeks Hi and Lo: The highest and lowest prices paid for a share of stock in the previous year.

Stock: The name of the corporation whose shares are being traded.

Sym: The symbol used as a shorthand description for the stock.

Div: A dividend is the amount of profit paid out by the corporation in the preceding year for each share of stock.

Yld%: The yield is the dividend paid per share divided by the price of a share.

P/E: The price of the stock (P) divided by the earnings (profit) per share (E). This indicates how much a purchaser is effectively paying for each dollar of profits. Because Amazon.com had a loss in 1998, the P/E ratio is not computed.

Vol 100s: The number of shares traded in hundreds.

Hi: The highest price paid for a share of stock on the previous day.

Lo: The lowest price paid for a share of stock on the previous day.

Close: The price paid in the last trade of the day as the market was closing.

Net Chg: The change in the closing price yesterday vs. the previous day's closing price.

IN THE NEWS

Growth Undergirds Google's Pricey IPO But Can It Keep Up?

INVESTORS HAD BETTER be feeling lucky about **Google** Inc.'s growth prospects.

Now that the Internet-search company has trotted out its own $35 billion or so estimate of its value, the challenge for those pondering whether to participate in Google's initial public offering of stock next month is to figure out how much longer the good times will last. Sure, the company is making money hand over fist, and it has juicy margins and profits that are expanding rapidly. But with its IPO shares likely to begin trading at expensive levels, Google is attractive only if it can maintain impressive growth.

In the near term, the acceleration likely will continue, analysts and industry specialists say. But some are concerned that growth in the search business and related advertising is slowing from its heady clip. Fewer people will be going online for the first time, they say, and those already on the Internet probably won't radically increase the number of searches they conduct. In the long run, Google likely will have to prove that it can continue to come up with new ways to profit from its dominant position in the Web-search business for its shares to be big winners.

"It all depends on how fast the growth momentum will come down," says Mark Mahaney, an analyst at American Technology Research, who says investors should put in bids of $115 a share for Google. "The question is how gracefully it exits hyper-growth."

Throughout the search industry there are indications that growth has slowed recently. Rival Internet titan Yahoo Inc., for instance, said earlier this month that the number of search queries was "pretty flattish" during the second quarter compared with the first period. Growth in the current quarter also should be flat, the company indicated. Ask Jeeves Inc., another search company, has seen its share price drop about 30% in the past four months amid investor worries.

—Gregory Zuckerman and Kevin J. Delaney

Analysis: People who buy a company's stock are betting on future sales and profits. If expectations change, the price of the stock will change as well.

The evident value of information raises a question of access. Do some people have better information than others? Do they get their information fairly? Or do they have "inside" sources (such as company technicians, managers, directors) who give them preferential access to information? If so, these insiders would have an unfair advantage in the marketplace and could alter the distribution of income and wealth in their favor. This is the kind of "insider trading" that got Martha Stewart into trouble (and jail).

The value of information also explains the demand for information services. People pay hundreds and even thousands of dollars for newsletters, wire services, and online computer services that provide up-to-date information on companies and markets. They also pay for the services of investment bankers, advisers, and brokers to help keep them informed. These services help disseminate information quickly, thereby helping financial markets operate efficiently (that is, they provide the best possible signal of changing resource values).

Booms and Busts. If stock markets are so efficient at computing the present value of future profits, why does the entire market make abrupt moves every so often? Fundamentally, the same factors that determine the price of a single stock influence the broader stock market averages as well. An increase in interest rates, for example, raises the opportunity cost of holding stocks. Hence, higher interest rates should cause stock prices to fall, *ceteris paribus*. Stocks might decline even further if higher interest rates are expected to curtail investment and consumption, thus reducing future sales and profits. Such a double whammy could cause the whole stock market to tumble.

Other factors also affect the relative desirability of holding stock. Congressional budget and deficit decisions, monetary policy, consumer confidence, business investment plans, international trade patterns, and new inventions are just a few of the factors that may alter present and future profits. These *broad changes in the economic outlook tend to push all stock prices up or down at the same time.*

Broad changes in the economic outlook, however, seldom occur overnight. Moreover, these changes are rarely of a magnitude that could precipitate a stock market boom or bust. In reality, the stock market often changes more abruptly than the economic outlook. These exaggerated movements in the stock market are caused by sudden and widespread changes in expectations. Keep in mind that the value of the stock depends on anticipated *future* profits and expectations for interest rates and the economic outlook. No elements of the future are certain. Instead, people use present clues to try to discern the likely course of future events. In other words, *all information must be filtered through people's expectations.*

The central role of expectations implies that the economy can change more gradually than the stock market. If, for example, interest rates rise, market participants may regard the increase as temporary or inconsequential: Their expectations for the future may not change. If interest rates keep rising, however, investors may have greater doubts. At some point, the market participants may revise their expectations. Stock prices may falter, triggering an adjustment in expectations. A herding instinct may surface, sending expectations for stock prices abruptly lower (see cartoon).

Shocks. The September 11, 2001, terrorist attacks on the World Trade Center and the Pentagon illustrated how much faster expectations can change than does the real economy. The attacks paralyzed the U.S. economy for several days and made people fearful for both their physical and economic security. People wanted to withdraw from the marketplace, taking their assets with them. When the U.S. stock exchanges opened several days after the attacks, stocks tumbled (see News on next page). The Dow Jones industrial average (see Table 17.4) fell 685 points—its biggest loss ever. The NASDAQ Composite (Table 17.4) also plunged by more than 7 percent in one day. Within 10 days, the value of U.S. stocks had declined by more than $1 *trillion*.

The economy didn't fare nearly as bad as the stock market. Although the attacks were tragic in human terms, they made only a tiny dent in the economy's productive

WEBNOTE

You can retrieve the latest news about a company and its stock from various online brokerage and investment-advice services, including cnnfin.com. You can also retrieve charts showing how a stock price has fluctuated during the day or over longer periods. Free charts on individual stocks are available at www.bigcharts.com.

WEBNOTE

Think you can make a profit in the stock market? Try the Stock Market Game, an electronic simulation of Wall Street trading, at www.smg2000.org.

Just a normal day at the nation's most important financial institution . . .

Analysis: Sudden changes in expectations can substantially alter stock prices.

capacity. Quick responses by the government in defending the financial markets also dispelled fears of a financial meltdown. As people's worst fears subsided, the demand for stocks picked up again. Within a month's time, the stock markets had fully recovered their post-attack losses. Along the way, however, changing expectations caused wild gyrations in stock prices.

IN THE NEWS

Market Battered, but Intact

The Dow Jones industrial average suffered its worst one-day point loss ever on Monday as the stock market was swamped with selling on the first day of trading since last week's terrorist attacks.

Forecasts for today's trading were hard to find. In contrast, the market's first-day sell-off was widely expected in the aftermath of terrorists crashing hijacked airliners into the World Trade Center in New York and the Pentagon near Washington.

A sense that "everything had changed" pervaded Wall Street over the four days last week that the market was closed following the Sept. 11 attack. That was the longest market closing since World War I. Monday's session was a technical victory, given the damage to phone lines, computers and other equipment that had to be repaired. By day's end, the system handled a record 2.37 billion New York Stock Exchange shares.

The Dow's plunge of 684.81 points to 8,920.70 in Monday's trading eclipsed its previous one-day record loss of 617.78 points on April 14, 2000, at the beginning of the current bear market. But the percentage loss was not among the 10 worst of all time.

—Tom Walker

Source: *Atlanta Journal-Constitution,* September 18, 2001. Reprinted with permission. www.accessatlanta.com/ajc

Analysis: A sudden change in expectations can cause severe fluctuations in stock market values. The September 11 terrorist attacks created new uncertainties and reduced profit expectations.

TABLE 17.4
Stock Market Averages

Over 1,600 stocks are listed (traded) on the New York Stock Exchange, and many times that number are traded in other stock markets. To gauge changes in so many stocks, people refer to various indices, such as the Dow Jones industrial average. The Dow and similar indexes help us keep track of the market's ups and downs. Some of the most frequently quoted indexes are

Dow Jones

Industrial average: An arithmetic average of the prices of 30 blue-chip industrial stocks traded on the New York Stock Exchange (NYSE) and by computers of the National Association of Securities Dealers (NASD).

Transportation average: An average of 20 transportation stocks traded on the NYSE.

Utilities average: An average of 15 utility stocks traded on the NYSE.

S&P 500: An index compiled by Standard and Poor of 500 stocks drawn from major stock exchanges as well as over-the-counter stocks. The S&P 500 is made up of 400 industrial companies, 40 utilities, 20 transportation companies, and 40 financial institutions.

NASDAQ Composite: Index of stocks traded in the over-the-counter market among securities dealers.

New York Stock Exchange composite index: The "Big Board" index, which includes all 1,600-plus stocks traded on the NYSE.

Nikkei index: An index of 225 stocks traded on the Tokyo stock market.

TABLE 17.4
Stock Market Averages

Resource Allocations

Although it's fascinating and sometimes fun to watch stock market gyrations, we shouldn't lose sight of the *economic* role of financial markets. Columbus needed *real* resources—ships, men, equipment—for his expeditions. Five centuries later, Amazon.com also needed real resources—computers, labor, warehouse space—to get underway. To find the necessary economic resources, both Columbus and Amazon.com had to convince society to reallocate resources from other activities to their new ventures.

Financial markets facilitate resource reallocations. In Columbus's case, the Genoese bankers lent the funds that Columbus used to buy scarce resources. The funds obtained from Amazon.com's 1997 initial public offering served the same purpose. In both cases, the funds obtained in the financial markets helped change the mix of output. If the financial markets hadn't supplied the necessary funding, neither Columbus nor Amazon.com would have been able to get underway. The available resources would have been used to produce other goods.

THE BOND MARKET

The bond market is another mechanism for transferring the pool of national savings into the hands of would-be spenders. It operates much like the stock market. The major difference is the kind of paper traded. *In the stock market, people buy and sell shares of corporate ownership. In the bond market, people buy and sell promissory notes (IOUs).* A **bond** is simply an IOU, a written promise to repay a loan. The bond itself specifies the terms of repayment, noting both the amount of interest to be paid each year and the maturity date (the date on which the borrower is to repay the entire debt). The borrower may be a corporation (corporate bonds), local governments (municipal bonds), the federal government (Treasury bonds), or other institutions.

bond: A certificate acknowledging a debt and the amount of interest to be paid each year until repayment; an IOU.

Bond Issuance

A bond is first issued when an institution wants to borrow money. Recall the situation Amazon.com faced in 1997. The company needed additional funds to expand its Internet operations. Rather than sell equity shares in itself, Amazon.com could have *borrowed* funds. The advantage of borrowing funds rather than issuing stock is that the owners can keep control of their company. ***Lenders aren't owners, but shareholders are.*** The disadvantage of borrowing funds is that the company gets saddled with a repayment schedule. Lenders want to be paid back—with interest. For a new company like Amazon.com, the burden of interest payments may be too great.

Ignoring these problems momentarily, let's assume that Amazon.com decided in 1997 to borrow funds rather than sell stock in itself. To do so, it would have *issued* bonds. This simply means that it would have printed formal IOUs called bonds. Typically, each bond certificate would have a **par value** (face value) of $1,000. The bond certificate would also specify the rate of interest to be paid and the promised date of repayment. An Amazon.com bond issued in 1997, for example, might specify repayment in 10 years, with annual interest payments of $100. The individual who bought the bond from Amazon.com would lend $1,000 for 10 years and receive annual interest payments of $100. Thus, ***the initial bond purchaser lends funds directly to the bond issuer.*** The borrower (such as Amazon.com, General Motors, or the U.S. Treasury) can then use those funds to acquire real resources. Thus, the bond market also functions as a financial intermediary, transferring available savings (wealth) to those who want to acquire more resources (invest).

As in the case of IPOs of stock, the critical issue here is the *price* of the bond. How many people are willing and able to lend funds to the company? What rate of interest will they charge?

As we observed in Figure 17.2, the quantity of loanable funds supplied depends on the interest rate. At low interest rates no one is willing to lend funds to the company. Why lend your savings to a risky venture like Amazon.com when more secure bonds and even banks pay higher interest rates? Amazon.com might not sell enough books and may later **default** (not pay) on its obligations. Potential lenders would want to be compensated for this extra risk with above-average interest rates, that is, a risk premium. Remember that lenders don't share in any profits Amazon.com might earn. Hence, they'd want a hefty premium to compensate them for the risk of default.

Suppose that market participants will lend the desired amount of money to Amazon.com only at 16 percent interest. In this case, Amazon.com may agree to pay an interest rate—the so-called **coupon rate**—of 16 percent to secure start-up funding of $50 million. That means Amazon.com agrees to pay $160 of interest each year for every $1,000 borrowed and to repay the entire $50 million at the end of 10 years.

Bond Trading

Once a bond has been issued, the initial lenders don't have to wait 10 years to get their money back. They can't go back to the company and demand early repayment, but they can sell their bonds to someone else. This **liquidity** is an important consideration for prospective bondholders. If a person had no choice but to wait 10 years for repayment, he or she might be less willing to buy a bond (lend funds). ***By facilitating resales, the bond market increases the availability of funds to new ventures and other borrowers.*** As is the case with stocks, most of the action in the bond markets consists of such after-market trades, that is, the buying and selling of bonds issued at some earlier time. The company that first issued the bonds doesn't participate in these trades.

The portfolio decision in the bond market is motivated by the same factors that influence stock purchases. The *opportunity cost* of buying and selling bonds is the best alternative rate of return—for example, the interest rate on other bonds or money market mutual funds. *Expectations* also play a role, in gauging both likely changes in opportunity costs and the ability of the borrower to redeem (pay off) the bond when

par value: The face value of a bond; the amount to be repaid when the bond is due.

default: Failure to make scheduled payments of interest or principal on a bond.

coupon rate: Interest rate set for a bond at time of issuance.

liquidity: The ability of an asset to be converted into cash.

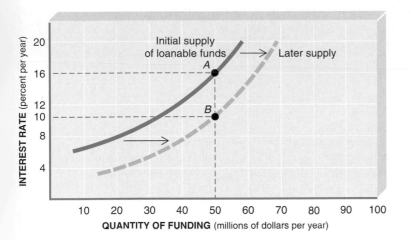

FIGURE 17.4
Shifts in Funds Supply

If lenders decide that a company's future is less risky, they will be more willing to lend it money or hold its bonds. This will raise the market price of existing bonds and lower current yields.

it's due. ***Changes in expectations or opportunity costs shift the bond supply and demand curves,*** thereby altering market interest rates.

We've assumed that Amazon.com would have had to offer 16 percent interest to induce enough people to lend the company (buy bonds worth) $50 million. This was far higher than the 6 percent the U.S. Treasury was paying on its bonds (borrowed funds) because lenders feared that Amazon.com might not be able to convert its great ideas into actual sales in a timely and profitable manner. In lending their funds to Amazon.com, they incur a risk of never getting their wealth back.

Suppose that Amazon.com actually got off to a good start and began selling books on the Web. The risk of a bond default would diminish, and people would be more willing to lend it funds. This change in the availability of loanable funds is illustrated in the rightward shift of the supply curve in Figure 17.4.

According to the new supply curve in Figure 17.4, Amazon.com could now borrow $50 million at 10 percent interest (point *B*) rather than paying 16 percent (point *A*). Unfortunately, Amazon.com already borrowed the funds and is obliged to continue paying $160 per year in interest on each bond. Hence, the company doesn't benefit directly from the supply shift.

The change in the equilibrium value of Amazon.com bonds must show up somewhere, however. People who hold Amazon.com bonds continue to get $160 per year in interest (16 percent of $1,000). Now there are lots of people who would be willing to lend funds to Amazon.com at that rate. These people want to hold Amazon.com bonds themselves. To get them, they'll have to buy the bonds in the market from existing bondholders. Thus, the ***increased willingness to lend funds is reflected in an increased demand for bonds.*** This increased demand will push up the price of Amazon.com bonds. As bond prices rise, their implied effective interest rate **(current yield)** falls. Table 17.5 illustrates this relationship.

Changing bond prices and yields are important market signals for resource allocation. In our example, the rising price of Amazon.com's bonds reflects increased optimism for the company's sales prospects. The collective assessment of the marketplace is that e-commerce will be a profitable venture. The increase in the price of Amazon.com bonds will make it easier and less costly for the company to borrow additional funds. The reverse scenario unfolded in 2000–2001. When investors concluded that e-commerce wasn't going to generate fast profits, the supply of funds to dot.coms dried up. That supply shift made it more difficult for firms to survive, much less expand e-commerce capacity.

Current Yields

current yield: The rate of return on a bond; the annual interest payment divided by the bond's price.

TABLE 17.5
Bond Price and Yields Move in Opposite Directions

Price of Bond	Annual Interest Payment	Current Yield
$ 600	$150	25.0%
800	150	18.8
1,000	150	15.0
1,200	150	12.5

The annual interest payments on a bond are fixed at the time of issuance. Accordingly, only the market (resale) prices of the bond can change. An increase in the price of the bond lowers its *effective* interest rate, or yield. The formula for computing the current yield on a bond is

$$\text{Current yield} = \frac{\text{annual interest payment}}{\text{market (resale) price of bond}}$$

Thus, higher bond prices imply lower yields (effective interest rates), as confirmed in the table above. Bond prices and yields vary with changes in expectations and opportunity costs.

The newspaper quotation below shows how changing bond prices and yields are reported. This General Motors (GM) bond was issued with a coupon rate (nominal interest rate) of 8⅜ percent. Hence, GM promised to pay $83.75 in interest each year until it redeemed (paid off) the $1,000 bond in the year 2033. In July 2004, however, the market price of the bond was $1,032.40 (103.24). This created a yield of 8.08 percent.

Bond	Current Yield	Volume	Close
GM 8⅜ 33	8.083	142	103.24

THE ECONOMY TOMORROW

Venture Capitalists—Financing Tomorrow's Products

One of the proven paths to high incomes and wealth is entrepreneurship. Most of the great American fortunes originated in entrepreneurial ventures, for example, building railroads, mass-producing automobiles, introducing new computers, or perfecting mass-merchandising techniques. These successful ventures all required more than just a great idea. To convert the original idea into actual output requires the investment of real resources.

Recall that Apple Computer started in a garage, with a minimum of resources (Chapter 8). The idea of packaging a personal computer was novel, and few resources were required to demonstrate that it could be done. But Steven Jobs couldn't have become a multimillionaire by building just a few dozen computers a month. To reap huge economic profits from his idea, he needed much greater production capacity. He also needed resources for marketing the new Apples to a broader customer base. In other words, Steven Jobs needed lots of economic resources—land, labor, and capital—to convert his entrepreneurial dream into a profit-making reality.

Steven Jobs and his partner, Steve Wozniak, had few resources of their own. In fact, they'd sold Jobs's Volkswagen and Wozniak's scientific calculator to raise the finances for the first computer. To go any further, they needed financial support from others. Loans were hard to obtain since the company had no assets, no financial history, and no certainty of success. Jobs needed people who were willing to share the *risks* associated with a new venture. He found one such person in A. C. Markkula, who put up $250,000 and became a partner in the new venture. Shortly

Venture Capital Falls 72 Percent from Last Year

SAN FRANCISCO—Venture capitalists, hunkered down because of the dot-com collapse, are tightening the financing spigot even more in the post-terrorist-attack economy.

"What's happened is so significant as to put . . . business on hold," says venture capitalist Richard Kramlich of New Enterprise Associates in Menlo Park.

Third-quarter venture investments totaled $6.7 billion, down 72 percent from the same quarter a year ago, says industry newsletter *VentureWire*. The number of private companies receiving venture capital dropped to 540, down 67 percent from a year earlier and down 39 percent from the second quarter.

—Jim Hopkins

Source: *USA Today,* October 8, 2001. USA TODAY. Copyright 2001. Reprinted with permission. www.usatoday.com

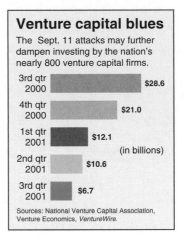

Venture capital blues

The Sept. 11 attacks may further dampen investing by the nation's nearly 800 venture capital firms.

3rd qtr 2000	$28.6
4th qtr 2000	$21.0
1st qtr 2001	$12.1
2nd qtr 2001	$10.6
3rd qtr 2001	$6.7

(in billions)

Sources: National Venture Capital Association, Venture Economics, *VentureWire.*

Analysis: Venture capital is a critical ingredient in entrepreneurship. When the flow of venture capital slows, so does the pace of technology and innovation.

---

thereafter, other venture capitalists provided additional financing. With this start-up financing, Jobs was able to acquire more resources and make the Apple Computer Company a reality.

This is a classic case study in venture capitalism. Venture capitalists provide initial funding for entrepreneurial ventures. In return for their financial backing, the venture capitalists are entitled to a share of any profits that result. If the venture fails, however, they get nothing. Thus, *venture capitalists provide financial support for entrepreneurial ideas and share in the risks and rewards.* Even Christopher Columbus needed venture capitalists to fund his risky expeditions to the New World.

Venture capital is as important to the economy tomorrow as it was to Columbus. In the immediate aftermath of the September 11, 2001, terrorist attacks, venture capitalists briefly withdrew their checkbooks (see News). This slowed the pace of entrepreneurship, innovation, and economic growth. For technology and entrepreneurship to continue growing, market conditions must be amenable to venture capitalists.

SUMMARY

- The primary economic function of financial markets is to help allocate scarce resources to desired uses. They do this by providing access to the pool of national savings for entrepreneurs, investors, and other would-be spenders.

- Financial markets enable individuals to manage risk by holding different kinds of assets. Financial intermediaries also reduce the costs of information and search, thereby increasing market efficiency.

- Future returns on investments must be discounted to present value. The present discounted value (PDV) of a future payment adjusts for forgone interest accrual.

- Future returns are also uncertain. The *expected* value of future payments must also reflect the risk of nonpayment.

- Shares of stock represent ownership in a corporation. The shares are initially issued to raise funds and are then traded on the stock exchanges.
- Changes in the value of a corporation's stock reflect changing expectations and opportunity costs. Share price changes, in turn, act as market signals to direct more or fewer resources to a company.

- Bonds are IOUs issued when a company (or government agency) borrows funds. After issuance, bonds are traded in the after (secondary) market.
- The interest (coupon) rate on a bond is fixed at the time of issuance. The price of the bond itself, however, varies with changes in expectations (perceived risk) and opportunity cost. Yields vary inversely with bond prices.

Key Terms

financial intermediary
risk premium
present discounted value (PDV)
expected value
corporation
corporate stock

dividend
retained earnings
capital gain
initial public offering (IPO)
price/earnings (P/E) ratio
bond

par value
default
coupon rate
liquidity
current yield

Questions for Discussion

1. If there were no organized financial markets, how would an entrepreneur acquire resources to develop and produce a new product?
2. Why would anyone buy shares of a corporation that had no profits and paid no dividends? What's the highest price a person would pay for such a stock?
3. Why would anyone sell a bond for less than its par value?
4. If you could finance a new venture with either a stock issue or bonds, which option would you choose? What are their respective (dis)advantages?

5. Why is it considered riskier to own stock in a software company than to hold U.S. Treasury savings bonds? Which asset will generate a higher return?
6. How does a successful IPO affect WHAT, HOW, and FOR WHOM the economy produces?
7. What considerations might have created the difference between the coupon rate and current yield on GM bonds (Table 17.5)?
8. What is the price of Google stock now? What has caused the change in price since its 2004 IPO at $85 a share (News, p. 362).

PROBLEMS The Student Problem Set at the back of this book contains numerical and graphing problems for this chapter.

WEB ACTIVITIES to accompany this chapter can be found on the Online Learning Center:
http://www.mhhe.com/economics/schiller10

PART 6

Distributional Issues

fficiency and equity are central concerns of every society. Collectively, we seek to get as much output as possible from the resources we use. But we also care about how that output is distributed. We want some sort of fairness in the distribution of goods and services; that is to say, we want both *efficiency* in the production of goods and *equity* in their distribution. Unfortunately, these goals may conflict. If we use taxes to redistribute incomes, incentives to produce may be impaired. Similarly, if we provide income support for the poor, people may choose to work less. Chapters 18 and 19 examine these issues.

Taxes: Equity vs. Efficiency

Insistence on carving the pie into equal slices would shrink the size of the pie.
That fact poses the trade-off between economic equality and economic efficiency.

—Arthur M. Okun

Steve Jobs, chairman of Apple Computer, got a $90 million private jet as a pay bonus in 2001. That would have been enough income to lift nearly 50,000 poor persons out of poverty. But Jobs didn't share his good fortune with those people, and they remained poor.

The market mechanism generated both Steve Jobs's extraordinary income and that of so many poor families. Is this the way we want the basic FOR WHOM question to be settled? Should some people own vast fortunes while others seek shelter in abandoned cars? Or do the inequalities that emerge in product and factor markets violate our notions of equity? If the market's answer to the FOR WHOM question isn't right, some form of government intervention to redistribute incomes may be desired.

The tax system is the government's primary lever for redistributing income. But taxing Peter to pay Paul may affect more than just income shares. If taxed too heavily, Peter may stop producing so much. Paul, too, may work less if assured of government support. The end result may be *less* total income to share. In other words: *Taxes affect production as well as distribution. This creates a potential trade-off between the goal of equity and the goal of efficiency.*

This chapter examines this equity-efficiency trade-off, with the following questions as a guide:

- **How are incomes distributed in the United States?**
- **How do taxes alter that distribution?**
- **How do taxes affect the rate and mix of output?**

After addressing these questions, we examine the allure of a "flat tax."

WHAT IS *INCOME?*

Before examining the distribution of income in the United States, let's decide what to count as *income.* There are several possibilities. The most obvious choice is **personal income (PI)**—the flow of annual income received by households before payment of personal income taxes. Personal income includes wages and salaries, corporate dividends, rent, interest, Social Security benefits, welfare payments, and any other form of money income.

Personal income isn't a complete measure of income, however. Many goods and services are distributed directly as **in-kind income** rather than through market purchases. Many poor people, for example, live in public housing and pay little or no rent. As a consequence, they receive a larger share of total output than their money incomes

Personal Income

personal income (PI): Income received by households before payment of personal taxes.

imply. People with low incomes also receive food stamps that allow them to purchase more food than their money incomes would allow. In this sense, food stamp recipients are better off than the distribution of personal income (which omits food stamps) implies.

In-kind benefits aren't limited to low-income households. Students who attend public schools and colleges consume more goods and services than they directly pay for; public education is subsidized by all taxpayers. People over age 65 also get medical services through Medicare that they don't directly pay for. And middle-class workers get noncash fringe benefits (like health insurance, paid vacations, pension contributions) that don't show up in their paychecks.

So long as some goods and services needn't be purchased in the marketplace, *the distribution of money income isn't synonymous with the distribution of goods and services.* This measurement problem is particularly important when comparisons are made over time. For example, the federal government officially classifies people as "poor" if their money income is below a certain threshold. By this standard, we've made no progress against poverty. The Census Bureau counted nearly 36 million Americans as "poor" in 2003, more than it counted in 1965. In both years the Census Bureau counted only money incomes. In 1965 that approach was acceptable, since little income was transferred in kind. In 2003, however, the federal government spent over $20 billion on Food Stamps, $22 billion on housing subsidies, and $270 billion on Medicaid. Had all this in-kind income been counted, 7 million fewer Americans would have been counted poor in 2003. Although that would still leave a lot of people in poverty, at least more progress in eliminating poverty would be evident.

If our ultimate concern is access to goods and services, the distribution of wealth is also important. **Wealth** refers to the market value of assets (such as houses and bank accounts) people own. Hence, *wealth represents a stock of potential purchasing power; income statistics tell us only how this year's flow of purchasing power (income) is being distributed.* Accordingly, to provide a complete answer to the FOR WHOM question, we have to know how wealth, as well as income, is distributed. In general, wealth tends to be distributed much less equally than income. The Internal Revenue Service estimates that 3 percent of the adult population owns 30 percent of all personal wealth in the United States but gets less than 20 percent of total income.

> **in-kind income:** Goods and services received directly, without payment in a market transaction.

The Census Bureau compiles data on poverty from each year's March household survey. For the most recent data, visit www.census.gov/hhes/ www/poverty.html.

Wealth

> **wealth:** The market value of assets.

THE SIZE DISTRIBUTION OF INCOME

Although incomes aren't a perfect measure of access to goods and services (much less happiness), they're the best single indicator of the FOR WHOM outcomes. The **size distribution of income** tells us how large a share of total personal income is received by various households, grouped by income class. Imagine for the moment that the entire population is lined up in order of income, with lowest-income recipients in front and highest-income recipients at the end of the line. We want to know how much income the people in front get in comparison with those at the back.

We first examined the size distribution of income in Chapter 2. Table 2.1 showed that households in the lowest quintile received less than $18,000 apiece in 2003. As a group, this class received only 3.4 percent of total income, despite the fact that it included 20 percent of all households (the lowest fifth). Thus, the **income share** of the people in the lowest group (3.4 percent) was much smaller than their proportion in the total population (20 percent).

Moving back to the end of the line, we observed that a household needed $87,000 to make it into the highest income class in 2003. Many families in that class made much more than $87,000—some even millions of dollars. But $87,000 was at least enough to get into the top fifth (quintile).

The top quintile ended up with almost half of total U.S. income and, by implication, that much of total output.

> **size distribution of income:** The way total personal income is divided up among households or income classes.

> **income share:** The proportion of total income received by a particular group.

FIGURE 18.1
The Lorenz Curve

The Lorenz curve illustrates the extent of income inequality. If all incomes were equal, each fifth of the population would receive one-fifth of total income. In this case, the diagonal line through point *C* would represent the cumulative size distribution of income. In reality, incomes aren't distributed equally. Point *A*, for example, indicates that the 20 percent of the population with the lowest income receives only 3.4 percent of total income.

Source: Table 2.1.

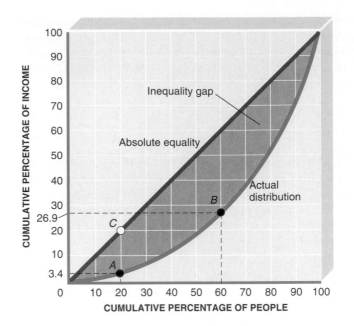

The Lorenz Curve

> **Lorenz curve:** A graphic illustration of the cumulative size distribution of income; contrasts complete equality with the actual distribution of income.

> **Gini coefficient:** A mathematical summary of inequality based on the Lorenz curve.

> **market failure:** An imperfection in the market mechanism that prevents optimal outcomes.

The Call for Intervention

The size distribution of income provides the kind of information we need to determine how total income (and output) is distributed. The **Lorenz curve** is a convenient summary of that information; it is a graphical illustration of the size distribution.

Figure 18.1 is a Lorenz curve for the United States. Our lineup of individuals is on the horizontal axis, with the lowest-income earners on the left. On the vertical axis we depict the cumulative share of income received by people in our income line. Consider the lowest quintile of the distribution again. They're represented on the horizontal axis at 20 percent. If their share of income was identical to their share of population, they'd get 20 percent of total income. This would be represented by point *C* in the figure. In fact, the lowest quintile gets only 3.4 percent, as indicated by point *A*. Point *B* tells us that the *cumulative* share of income received by the lowest *three*-fifths of the population was 26.9 percent.

The really handy feature of the Lorenz curve is the way it contrasts the actual distribution of income with an absolutely equal one. If incomes were distributed equally, the first 20 percent of the people in line would be getting exactly 20 percent of all income. In that case, the Lorenz curve would run through point *C*. Indeed, the Lorenz "curve" would be a straight line along the diagonal. The actual Lorenz curve lies below the diagonal because our national income isn't distributed equally. In fact, the area between the diagonal and the actual Lorenz curve (the shaded area in Figure 18.1) is a convenient measure of the degree of inequality. ***The greater the area between the Lorenz curve and the diagonal, the more inequality exists.***

The visual summary of inequality the Lorenz curve provides is also expressed in a mathematical relationship. The ratio of the shaded area in Figure 18.1 to the area of the triangle formed by the diagonal is called the **Gini coefficient.** The higher the Gini coefficient, the greater the degree of inequality. Between 1980 and 2003, the Gini coefficient rose from 0.403 to 0.462. In other words, the shaded area in Figure 18.1 expanded by about 15 percent, indicating *increased* inequality. Although the size of the economic pie (real GDP) *doubled* between 1980 and 2003, some people's slices got a lot bigger while other people saw little improvement, or even less (see cartoon).

To many people, large and increasing inequality represents a form of **market failure:** The market is generating a suboptimal (unfair) answer to the FOR WHOM question. As in other instances of market failure, the government is called on to intervene. The policy lever in this case is taxes. By levying higher taxes on the rich and providing more generous transfer payments to the poor, the government could promote greater equality.

Robert Graysmith, © Graysmith.

Analysis: An increase in the size of the economic pie doesn't ensure everyone a larger slice. A goal of the tax system is to attain a fairer distribution of the economic pie.

THE FEDERAL INCOME TAX

The federal income tax is designed for this redistributional purpose. Specifically, the federal income tax is designed to be **progressive**—that is, to impose higher tax *rates* on high incomes than on low ones. Progressivity is achieved by imposing increasing **marginal tax rates** on higher incomes. The *marginal* tax rate refers to the tax rate imposed on the last (marginal) dollar of income.

In 2003, the tax code specified the six tax brackets shown in Table 18.1. For an individual with less than $7,000 of income, the tax rate was 10 percent. Any income in excess of $7,000 was taxed at a *higher* rate of 15 percent. If an individual's income rose above $68,800, the amount between $68,800 and $143,500 was taxed at 28 percent. Any income greater than $311,950 was taxed at 35 percent.

To understand the efficiency and equity effects of taxes, we must distinguish between the *marginal* tax rate and the *average* tax rate. A person who earned $350,000 in 2003 paid the 35 percent tax only on the income in excess of $311,950, that is, the last (marginal) $38,050. The first $7,000 was taxed at a marginal rate of only 10 percent.

progressive tax: A tax system in which tax rates rise as incomes rise.

marginal tax rate: The tax rate imposed on the last (marginal) dollar of income.

Tax Bracket	Marginal Tax Rate
$0–7,000	10%
$7,000–28,400	15
$28,400–68,800	25
$68,800–143,500	28
$143,500–311,950	33
Over $311,950	35

Source: Internal Revenue Service (tax rates for single individuals).

TABLE 18.1
Progressive Taxes

The federal income tax is progressive because it levies higher tax rates on higher incomes. The 2003 marginal tax rate started out at 10 percent for incomes below $7,000 and rose to 35 percent for incomes above $311,950.

Current tax rate schedules are available from the Internal Revenue Service at www.irs.gov/formspubs/article/0,,id=109877,oo.html.

Hence this individual's tax bill was

Marginal Tax Rate	Income		Tax
10% of	$ 7,000	=	$ 700
15% of	21,400	=	3,210
25% of	40,400	=	10,100
28% of	74,700	=	20,916
33% of	168,450	=	55,589
35% of	38,050	=	13,318
	$350,000		$93,733

The total tax of $93,733 represented only 26.8 percent of this individual's income. Hence, this person had a

- *Marginal* tax rate of 35 percent.
- *Average* tax rate of 26.8 percent.

The rationale behind this progressive system is to tax ever-larger percentages of higher incomes, thereby restraining inequalities. This makes the *after-tax* distribution of income more equal than the *before-tax* distribution. This is how **progressive taxes reduce inequality.**

Efficiency Concerns

Although the redistributive intent of a progressive tax system is evident, it raises concerns about efficiency. As noted in the chapter-opening quote, attempts to reslice the pie may end up reducing the size of the pie. The central issue here is incentives. Chapter 15 emphasized that the supply of labor is motivated by the pursuit of income. If Uncle Sam takes away ever-larger chunks of income, won't that dampen the desire to work? If so, *the incentive to work more, produce more, or invest more is reduced by higher marginal tax rates.* This suggests that as marginal tax rates increase, total output shrinks, creating a basic conflict between the goals of equity (more progressive taxes) and efficiency (more output).

Tax Elasticity. How great the conflict is between the equity and efficiency depends on how responsive market participants are to higher tax rates. The Rolling Stones left Great Britain off their 1998–99 world tour because the British marginal tax rate was so high (see World View). Many other businesses relocate to low-tax nations for the same reason. For the typical household, however, the response to higher tax rates is limited to reducing hours worked. In all cases we can summarize the response with **the tax elasticity of supply;** that is,

tax elasticity of supply: The percentage change in quantity supplied divided by the percentage change in tax rates.

$$\text{Tax elasticity of supply} = \frac{\text{\% change in quantity supplied}}{\text{\% change in tax rate}}$$

If the tax elasticity of supply were zero, there'd be no conflict between equity and efficiency. But a zero tax elasticity would also imply that people would continue to work, produce, and invest even if Uncle Sam took *all* their income in taxes. In today's range of taxes, the average household's elasticity of labor supply is between 0.15 and 0.30. Hence, if tax rates go up by 20 percent, the quantity of labor supplied would decline by 3 to 6 percent. Figure 18.2 confirms that the top marginal tax rate has changed by more than that in the past.

Equity Concerns

As if the concern about efficiency weren't enough, critics also raise questions about how well the federal income tax promotes equity. What appears to be a fairly progressive tax in theory turns out to be a lot less progressive in practice. Hundreds of people with $1 million incomes pay no taxes. They aren't necessarily breaking any laws, just taking advantage of loopholes in the tax system.

Loopholes. The progressive *tax rates described in the tax code apply to "taxable" income, not to all income.* The so-called loopholes in the system arise from the way

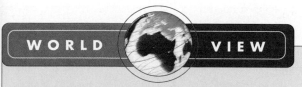

WORLD VIEW

Stones Keep England off '98 Tour to Avoid Tax

MUNICH, Germany, June 11—Mick Jagger said today that the Rolling Stones were disappointed they would not be playing in England this year, but the band looked forward to coming home for a series of concerts in 1999.

Lambasted by the British press for calling off a four-date tour at home because of a new tax law, members of the Stones said they opted out because the band stood to lose $19.6 million in taxes.

Under the previous tax code, Britons who lived and worked abroad for more than a year were exempt from British taxes on their earnings so long as they did not spend more than 62 days on native soil.

But the Labor government elected a year ago has scrapped that arrangement for everyone except some 10,000 seafarers. Now any citizen who works in Britain at all must pay tax on his or her entire year's earnings.

More than 300,000 tickets had been sold for the four British dates, which have been rescheduled for June 1999.

—Dorothee Stoewahse

Source: *The Washington Post*, June 12, 1998. © 1998 *The Washington Post*. Reprinted with permission. www.washingtonpost.com

Analysis: High tax rates deter people from supplying resources—in this case, staging a concert.

Congress defines taxable income. The tax laws permit one to subtract certain exemptions and deductions from gross income in computing taxable income; that is,

$$\frac{\text{Taxable}}{\text{income}} = \frac{\text{gross}}{\text{income}} - \text{exemptions and deductions}$$

Exemptions are permitted for dependent children, spouses, old age, and disabilities. Prior to the 1986 law, deductions were permitted for home mortgage interest, work-related expenses, child care, depreciation of investments, oil exploration, interest payments, union dues, medical expenses, and many other items.

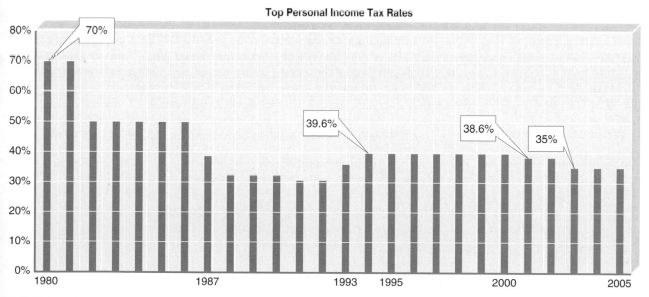

FIGURE 18.2

Changes in Marginal Tax Rates

During the past 25 years, Congress revised the federal income tax system many times. The top marginal tax rates were steadily reduced until 1993, then raised again. The Bush tax cuts of 2001–2004 reduce marginal tax rates again.

Source: Internal Revenue Service.

TABLE 18.2
Vertical Inequity

Tax exemptions and deductions create a gap between total income and *taxable* income. In this case, Mr. Jones has both a higher income and extensive deductions. He ends up with less taxable income than Ms. Smith and so pays less taxes. This vertical inequity is reflected in the lower effective tax rate paid by Mr. Jones.

	Mr. Jones	Ms. Smith
1. Total income	$90,000	$30,000
2. Less exemptions and deductions	−$70,000	−$ 5,000
3. Taxable income	$20,000	$25,000
4. Tax	$ 4,000	$ 5,500
5. Nominal tax rate (= row 4 ÷ row 3)	20%	22%
6. Effective tax rate (= row 4 ÷ row 1)	4.4%	18.3%

The purpose of these many *itemized deductions* was to encourage specific economic activities and reduce potential hardship. The deduction for mortgage interest payments, for example, encourages people to buy their own homes. The deduction for medical expenses helps relieve the financial burden of illness.

Whatever the merits of specific exemptions and deductions, they create potential inequities. People with high incomes can avoid high taxes by claiming large exemptions and deductions. Each year the Internal Revenue Service discovers individuals earning million-dollar incomes and paying little or no taxes. They aren't doing anything illegal, just taking advantage of the many deductions Congress permits. Nevertheless, this means that some people with high incomes could end up paying *less* tax than people with lower incomes. This would violate the principle of **vertical equity,** the progressive intent of taxing people on the basis of their ability to pay.

Table 18.2 illustrates vertical *in*equity. Mr. Jones has an income three times larger than Ms. Smith's. However, Mr. Jones also has huge deductions that reduce his *taxable* income dramatically. In fact, Mr. Jones ends up with less *taxable* income than Ms. Smith. As a result, he also ends up paying lower taxes.

The deductions that create the vertical inequity between Mr. Jones and Ms. Smith could also violate the principle of **horizontal equity**—as people with the *same* incomes end up paying different amounts of income tax. These horizontal *in*equities also contradict basic notions of fairness.

vertical equity: Principle that people with higher incomes should pay more taxes.

horizontal equity: Principle that people with equal incomes should pay equal taxes.

nominal tax rate: Taxes paid divided by taxable income.

effective tax rate: Taxes paid divided by total income.

Nominal vs. Effective Tax Rates. The loopholes exemptions, deductions, and tax credits create form a distinction between gross economic income and taxable income. That distinction, in turn, requires us to distinguish between nominal tax rates and effective tax rates. The term **nominal tax rate** refers to the taxes actually paid as a percentage of *taxable* income. By contrast, the **effective tax rate** is the tax paid divided by *total* economic income without regard to exemptions, deductions, or other intricacies of the tax laws.

As Table 18.2 illustrates, a single individual with a gross income of $90,000 might end up with a very low *taxable* income, thanks to the benefits of various tax deductions and exemptions. Mr. Jones ended up with a taxable income of only $20,000 and a tax bill of merely $4,000. We could then characterize Mr. Jones's tax burden in two ways:

$$\frac{\text{Nominal}}{\text{tax rate}} = \frac{\text{tax paid}}{\text{taxable income}}$$

$$= \frac{\$4,000}{\$20,000} = 20 \text{ percent}$$

or, alternatively,

$$\frac{\text{Effective}}{\text{tax rate}} = \frac{\text{tax paid}}{\text{total economic income}}$$

$$= \frac{\$4,000}{\$90,000} = 4.4 \text{ percent}$$

This huge gap between the nominal tax rate (20 percent) and the effective tax rate (4.4 percent) is a reflection of loopholes in the tax code. It's also the source of the vertical and horizontal inequities discussed earlier. Notice that Ms. Smith, with much less income, ends up with an effective tax rate (18.3 percent) that's more than four times higher than Mr. Jones's (4.4 percent).

Tax-Induced Misallocations. Tax loopholes not only foster inequity but encourage inefficiency as well. The optimal mix of output is the one that balances consumer preferences and opportunity costs. Tax loopholes, however, encourage a different mix of output. By offering preferential treatment for some activities, the tax code reduces their relative accounting cost. In so doing, ***tax preferences induce resource shifts into tax-preferred activities.***

These resource allocations are a principal objective of tax preferences. By 1986, however, the accumulation of exemptions, deductions, and credits had become so unwieldy and complex that tax considerations were overwhelming economic considerations in many investment and consumption decisions. The resulting mix of output, many observers felt, was decidedly inferior to a *pure* market outcome. From this viewpoint, the federal income tax was promoting both inequity and inefficiency.

A Shrinking Tax Base. Loopholes in the tax code create yet another problem. As the **tax base** gets smaller and smaller, it becomes increasingly difficult to sustain, much less increase, tax revenues. The tax arithmetic is simple:

$$\text{Tax revenue} = \frac{\text{average}}{\text{tax rate}} \times \frac{\text{tax}}{\text{base}}$$

As deductions, exemptions, and credits accumulate, the tax base (taxable income) keeps shrinking. To keep tax rates low—or to reduce them further—Congress had to stop this erosion of the tax base.

Rising discontent with a shrinking tax base, horizontal and vertical inequities, and tax-distorted resource allocations led to a major reform of federal taxes in 1986. The basic features of the Tax Reform Act (TRA) of 1986 included

- *Loophole closing.* Major loopholes were closed or reduced.
- *Reductions in marginal tax rates.* The top marginal tax rate was reduced from 50 to 28 percent.
- *Fewer tax brackets.* The number of tax brackets dropped from 16 to 2.
- *Tax relief for the poor.* Increases in the personal exemption and standard deduction removed nearly 5 million poor people from the tax rolls.
- *Shift from personal to corporate taxes.* The direct tax burden on individuals was reduced while the corporate tax burden was increased.

Base Broadening. The elimination or reduction of scores of tax preferences increased the tax base almost 25 percent. By broadening the tax base to encompass more economic income, the TRA eliminated the source of many horizontal and vertical inequities. This loophole closing also made the tax system more progressive, since tax preferences disproportionately benefited higher-income families.

Rate Reductions. By broadening the tax base, the TRA made it possible to reduce tax rates. This was of particular concern to those who feared that high marginal tax rates were inhibiting labor supply, investment, and production. The cut in the top marginal tax rate from 50 to 28 percent was intended to stimulate a greater supply of labor and capital and thus promote efficiency.

Although the 1986 reforms increased the progressivity of the tax system, some critics claimed that the reforms were a "giveaway" to the rich. In 1990, Congress responded to this sentiment by raising the top marginal tax rate from 28 to 31 percent. President Clinton pushed Congress to raise taxes even further in 1993. Two more tax brackets were added, with marginal tax rates of 36 and 39.6 percent. Although these higher marginal tax rates increased progressivity, remaining loopholes left a lot of variation in *effective* tax rates. The following News shows how President George W. Bush used

tax base: The amount of income or property directly subject to nominal tax rates.

The 1986 Tax Reform Act

WEBNOTE

To view tax returns of U.S. presidents and to review the history of tax features, visit www.taxhistory.org. Click on "Presidential Tax Returns."

1990 and 1993 Tax Increases

The President's Taxes

President and Mrs. Bush received over $800,000 of income in 2003. Taxable income was reduced by deductions, however. Their $227,494 tax bill represented 31.3 percent of *taxable* income (the *nominal* tax rate) but only 27.7 percent of *total* income (the *effective* rate).

Income	
Wages	$397,264
Interest	401,803
Dividends	23,471
Capital gain (loss)	−3,000
Partnership gain	2,588
Adjusted gross income	$822,126

Deductions	
Charitable contributions	68,360
Investment expenses	22,990
Tax preparation fee	2,820
Other deductions	873
Total deductions	$ 95,043
Taxable income	$727,083
Tax	$227,494

Source: The White House. www.whitehouse.gov

Analysis: Taxes are levied on *taxable* income, not total income. Various deductions and exemptions reduce taxable income and *effective* tax rates.

The Bush Tax Cuts (2001–2010)

some of these same loopholes to reduce his effective tax rate to 27.7 percent in 2003, despite receiving more than $800,000 of income.

President Bush believed lower tax rates were good for the economy. Cutting marginal tax rates to encourage more production was his top priority in 2001. He also wanted to encourage more education, saving, and family development with an expanded array of tax exemptions, deductions, and credits.

Reduced Marginal Rates. Initially, President Bush wanted the top marginal tax rate of 39.6 percent reduced to 33 percent. Compromises with Congress achieved a smaller rate reduction, however, phased in over several years. As Figure 18.2 illustrated, the 2001 Tax Relief Act reduced the highest marginal tax rate in three steps, to 35 percent in 2006. That Act also reduced the marginal tax rate for the *lowest* income class to only 10 percent (from 15 percent). The goal of this rate cut was to increase the disposable income of low-wage workers (equity) while giving them more incentive to work (efficiency). In 2003, Bush convinced Congress to accelerate the rate cuts to further boost production and employment.

Education Incentives. Aside from encouraging more *work*, President Bush also sought to encourage more *education*. The biggest incentive was a tuition tax deduction of $3,000 per year. This allows students, or their parents, to reduce their taxable income by the amount of tuition payments. In effect, Uncle Sam ends up paying part of the first $3,000 in tuition. In addition, the 2001 legislation allows people to save more money for college in tax-free accounts.

As welcome as these "loopholes" are to college students, they raise the same kind of efficiency and equity concerns as other tax preferences. If most of the students who take the tax deduction would have gone to college anyway, the deduction isn't very efficient in promoting education. Furthermore, most of the deductions go to middle-class families who itemize deductions. Hence, the tuition deduction introduces new vertical inequities. Few students have protested this particular loophole, however.

Family Incentives. President Bush also sought to use the tax code to promote "family values." To encourage marital stability, the "marriage penalty" of the standard

WEBNOTE

Check out the lastest tax deductions for college expenses at http://www.irs.gov. Click on "Tax Info for you" then "Tax Trails."

deduction was phased out (allowing a married couple to have twice the standard deduction of a single person). To defray the cost of raising children, the child tax credit was increased in 2001 and again in 2003.

Saving Incentives. The Tax Relief Act of 2001 also encouraged people to save more by raising the ceiling on deductions for retirement savings accounts (IRA, 401(k) plans). The estate tax was also targeted for phase-out.

The creation of these and other tax preferences raises all the same issues about equity and efficiency. As we noted above, the tuition deduction favors the middle class over the poor. The same can be said of the saving incentives. Although the Bush tax cuts also gave specific tax breaks to the poor, critics said the whole package was tilted toward the rich. Critics also questioned whether the various tax preferences would achieve their efficiency purposes, that is, promoting more college enrollments, more marriages and children, and greater saving.

PAYROLL, STATE, AND LOCAL TAXES

The federal income tax is only one of many taxes the average taxpayer must pay. For many families, in fact, the federal income tax is the smallest of many tax bills. Other tax bills come from the Social Security Administration and from state and local governments. These taxes also affect both efficiency and equity.

Sales taxes are the major source of revenue for state governments. Many local governments also impose sales taxes, but most cities rely on *property taxes* for the bulk of their tax receipts. Both taxes are **regressive:** They impose higher tax rates on lower incomes.

At first glance, a 5 percent sales tax doesn't look very regressive. After all, the same 5 percent tax is imposed on virtually all goods. But we're interested in *people,* not goods and services, so *we gauge tax burdens in relation to people's incomes.* A tax is regressive if it imposes a proportionally *larger* burden on *lower* incomes.

This is exactly what a uniform sales tax does. To understand this concept, we have to look not only at how much tax is levied on each dollar of consumption but also at *what percentage of income* is spent on consumer goods.

Low-income families spend everything they've got (and sometimes more) on basic consumption. As a result, most of their income ends up subject to sales tax. By contrast, higher-income families save more. As a result, a smaller proportion of their income is subject to a sales tax. Table 18.3 illustrates this regressive feature of a sales tax. Notice that the low-income family ends up paying a larger fraction of its income (4.7 percent) than does the high-income family (3 percent).

Property taxes are regressive also and for the same reason. Low-income families spend a higher percentage of their incomes for shelter. A uniform property tax thus ends up taking a larger fraction of their income than it does of the incomes of high-income families.

Tax Incidence. It may sound strange to suggest that low-income families bear the brunt of property taxes. After all, the tax is imposed on the landlords who *own* property, not on people who *rent* apartments and houses. However, here again we have to distinguish between the apparent payee and the individual whose income is actually

Sales and Property Taxes

> **regressive tax:** A tax system in which tax rates fall as incomes rise.

	High-Income Family	Low-Income Family
Income	$50,000	$15,000
Consumption	$30,000	$14,000
Saving	$20,000	$ 1,000
Sales tax paid (5% of consumption)	$ 1,500	$ 700
Effective tax rate (sales tax ÷ income)	3.0%	4.7%

TABLE 18.3
The Regressivity of Sales Taxes

A sales tax is imposed on consumer purchases. Although the sales tax itself is uniform (here at 5 percent), the taxes paid represent different proportions of high and low incomes. In this case, the low-income family's *sales tax* bill equals 4.7 percent of its *income.* The high-income family has a sales tax bill equal to only 3 percent of its income.

tax incidence: Distribution of the real burden of a tax.

reduced by the tax. **Tax incidence** refers to the actual burden of a tax—that is, who really ends up paying it.

In general, people who rent apartments pay higher rents as a result of property taxes. In other words, landlords tend to pass along to tenants any property taxes they must pay. Thus, to a large extent **the burden of property taxes is reflected in higher rents.** Tenants pay property taxes *indirectly* via these higher rents. The incidence of the property tax thus falls on renters, in the form of higher rents, rather than on the landlords who write checks to the local tax authority.

Payroll Taxes

Payroll taxes also impose effective tax burdens quite different from their nominal appearance. Consider, for example, the Social Security payroll tax, the second largest source of federal tax revenue (see Figure 4.6). Every worker sees a Social Security (FICA) tax taken out of his or her paycheck. The nominal tax rate on workers is 7.65 percent. But there's a catch: Only wages below a legislated ceiling are taxable. In 2004, the taxable wage ceiling was $87,900. Hence, a worker earning $200,000 paid no more tax than a worker earning $87,900. As a result, the tax *rate* (tax paid ÷ total wages) is lower for high-income workers than low- and middle-income workers. That's a *regressive* tax.

There is another problem in gauging the impact of the Social Security payroll tax. Nominally, the Social Security payroll tax consists of two parts: half paid by employees and half by employers. But do employers really pay their half? Or do they end up paying lower wages to compensate for their tax share? If so, employees end up paying *both* halves of the Social Security payroll tax.

Figure 18.3 illustrates how the tax incidence of the payroll tax is distributed. The supply of labor reflects the ability and willingness of people to work for various wage rates. Labor demand reflects the **marginal revenue product (MRP)** of labor; it sets a *limit* to the wage an employer is willing to pay.

marginal revenue product (MRP): The change in total revenue associated with one additional unit of input.

The employer's half of the payroll tax increases the nominal cost of labor. Thus, the $S +$ tax curve lies above the labor supply curve. It incorporates the wages that must be paid to workers *plus* the payroll tax that must be paid to the Social Security Administration. This total labor cost is the one that will determine how many workers are hired. Specifically, the intersection of the $S +$ tax curve and the labor demand curve determines the equilibrium level of employment (L_1). The employer will pay the amount w_1 for this much labor. But part of that outlay ($w_1 - w_2$) will go to the public treasury in the form of payroll taxes. Workers will receive only w_2 in wages. This is less than they'd get in the absence of the payroll tax (compare w_0 and w_2). Thus, **fewer workers are employed, and the net wage is reduced when a payroll tax is imposed.**

What Figure 18.3 reveals is how the true incidence of payroll taxes is distributed. The employer share of the Social Security tax is $w_1 - w_2$. This is the amount sent to

FIGURE 18.3
The Incidence of a Payroll Tax

Some portion of a payroll tax imposed on employers may actually be borne by workers. The tax raises the cost of labor and so imposes a tax burdened supply curve ($S +$ tax) on employers. The intersection of this tax-burdened supply curve with the labor demand curve determines a new equilibrium of employment (L_1). At that level, employers pay w_1 in wages and taxes, but workers get only w_2 in wages. The wage reduction from w_0 to w_2 is a real burden of the payroll tax, and it is borne by workers.

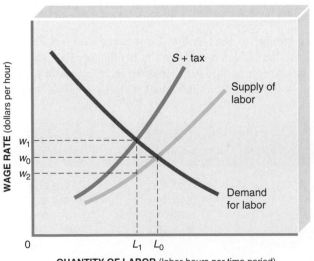

QUANTITY OF LABOR (labor-hours per time period)

the Social Security Administration for every hour of labor. Of this amount, the employer incurs higher labor costs ($w_1 - w_0$) and workers lose ($w_0 - w_2$) in the wage rate. Hence, workers end up paying *their* share (7.65 percent) of the Social Security tax *plus* a sizable part ($w_0 - w_2$) of the employer's share ($w_1 - w_2$).

These reflections on tax incidence don't imply that payroll taxes are necessarily bad. They do emphasize, however, that the apparent taxpayer isn't necessarily the individual who bears the real burden of a tax.

TAXES AND INEQUALITY

The regressivity of the Social Security payroll tax and of many state and local taxes offsets most of the progressivity of the federal income tax. The top 1 percent of income recipients gets 19 percent of total income and pays 37 percent of federal income tax (see Figure 18.4). Hence, the federal income tax is highly progressive, despite rampant loopholes. Other federal taxes (Social Security, excise), however, reduce the tax share of the rich to only 18 percent. State and local tax incidence reduces their tax share still further. The final result is that *the tax system as a whole ends up being nearly proportional.* High-income families end up paying roughly the same percentage of their income in taxes as do low-income families. The tax system does reduce inequality somewhat, but the redistributive impact is quite small.

The tax system tells only half the redistribution story. It tells whose income was taken away. Equally important is who gets the income the government collects. The government completes the redistribution process by *transferring* income to consumers. The **income transfers** may be explicit, as in the case of welfare benefits, Social Security payments, and unemployment insurance. Or the transfers may be indirect, as in the case of public schools, farm subsidies, and student loans. The direct transfers are more likely to be progressive, that is, to increase the income share of lower-income households. This progressivity results from the fact that low-income status is often a requirement for a direct income transfer. By contrast, most indirect transfers are ostensibly designed to fulfill other purposes, such as education and agricultural stability. As a consequence, they're less likely to be progressive and may even be regressive in some cases. We'll look more closely at income transfers in the next chapter.

WHAT IS *FAIR*?

To many people, the apparent ineffectiveness of the tax system in redistributing income is a mark of **government failure.** They want a much more decisive reslicing of the pie—one in which the top quintile gets a *lot* less than half the pie and the poor get more than 4 percent (Figure 2.6). But how much redistribution should we attempt? Rich people can rattle off as many good reasons for preserving income inequalities as poor people can recite for eliminating them.

A Proportional System

The Impact of Transfers

> **Income transfers:** Payments to individuals for which no current goods or services are exchanged, for example, Social Security, welfare, unemployment benefits.

> **government failure:** Government intervention that fails to improve economic outcomes.

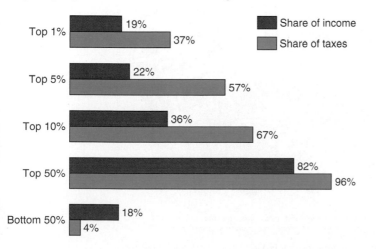

FIGURE 18.4
Income Tax Shares

Despite loopholes, the federal income tax remains highly progressive. The richest 1% of households pay over a third of all federal income taxes, though they receive less than a fifth of all income.

Source: Internal Revenue Service.

Economists aren't uniquely qualified to overcome self-interest, much less to divine what a fair distribution of income might look like. But economists can assess some of the costs and benefits of altering the distribution of income.

The Costs of Greater Equality

The greatest potential cost of a move toward greater equality is the reduced incentives it might leave in its wake. People *are* motivated by income. In factor markets, higher wages call forth more workers and induce them to work longer hours. In fields where earnings are very high, as in the medical and legal professions, people are willing to spend many years and thousands of dollars acquiring the skills such earnings require. Could we really expect people to make such sacrifices in a market that paid everyone the same wage?

The same problem exists in product markets. The willingness of producers to supply goods and services depends on their expectation of profits. Why should they work hard and take risks to produce goods and services if their efforts won't make them any better off? If incomes were distributed equally, producers might just as well sit back and enjoy the fruits of someone else's labor.

The essential economic problem absolute income equality poses is that it breaks the market link between effort and reward. If all incomes were equal, it would no longer pay to make an above-average effort. If people stopped making such efforts, total output would decline, and we'd have less income to share (a smaller pie). Not that all high incomes are attributable to great skill or effort. Such factors as luck, market power, and family connections also influence incomes. It remains true, however, that the promise of higher income encourages work effort. Absolute income equality threatens those conditions.

The argument for preserving income inequalities is thus anchored in a concern for productivity. From this perspective, income inequalities are the driving force behind much of our production. By preserving inequalities, we not only enrich the fortunate few, but also provide incentives to take risks, invest more, and work harder. In so doing, we enlarge the economic pie, including the slices available to lower-income groups. Thus, everyone is potentially better off, even if only a few end up rich. This is the rationale that keeps the top marginal tax rate in the United States below that in most other countries (see World View on the next page).

The Benefits of Greater Equality

Although the potential benefits of inequality are impressive, *there's a trade-off between efficiency and equality.* Moreover, many people are convinced that the terms of the trade-off are exaggerated and the benefits of greater equality are ignored. These rebuttals take the form of economic and noneconomic arguments.

The economic arguments for greater equality also focus on incentives. The first argument is that the present degree of inequality is more than necessary to maintain

"I suppose one could say it favors the rich, but, on the other hand it's a great incentive for everyone to make two hundred grand a year."

Analysis: Inequalities are an incentive for individuals to work and invest more.

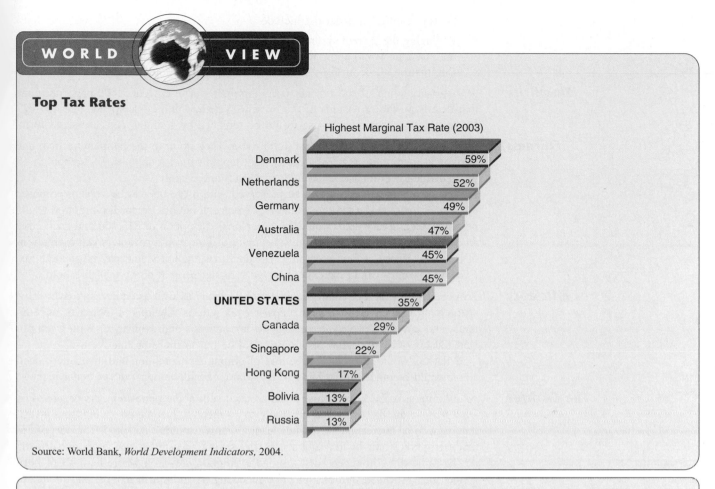

WORLD VIEW

Top Tax Rates

Highest Marginal Tax Rate (2003)

Denmark	59%
Netherlands	52%
Germany	49%
Australia	47%
Venezuela	45%
China	45%
UNITED STATES	35%
Canada	29%
Singapore	22%
Hong Kong	17%
Bolivia	13%
Russia	13%

Source: World Bank, *World Development Indicators*, 2004.

Analysis: The highest marginal tax rate in the United States is lower than in most nations, but still a lot higher than in some countries.

work incentives. Upper-class incomes needn't be 14 times as large as those of the lowest-income classes; perhaps 4 times as large would do as well.

The second argument is that low-income earners might actually work harder if incomes were distributed more fairly. As matters now stand, the low-income worker sees little chance of making it big. Extremely low income can also inhibit workers' ability to work by subjecting them to poor health, malnutrition, or inadequate educational opportunities. Accordingly, some redistribution of income to the poor might improve the productivity of low-income workers and compensate for reduced productivity among the rich.

Finally, we noted that the maze of loopholes that preserves inequality also distorts economic incentives. Labor and investment decisions are influenced by tax considerations, not just economic benefits and costs. If greater equality were achieved via tax simplification, a more efficient allocation of resources might result.

THE ECONOMY TOMORROW

A Flat Tax?

Widespread dissatisfaction with the present tax system has spawned numerous reform proposals. One of the most debated proposals is to replace the current federal income tax with a **flat tax.** First proposed by Nobel Prize winner Milton Friedman in the early 1960s, the flat tax was championed in Congress by former majority leader (and former economics professor) Dick Armey. The concept resurfaced as a political issue in the 2004 presidential election.

flat tax: A single-rate tax system.

The key features of a flat tax include

- Replacing the current system of multiple tax brackets and rates with a single (flat) tax rate that would apply to all taxable income.
- Eliminating all deductions, credits, and most exemptions.

Simplicity

A major attraction of the flat tax is its simplicity. The current 1,400-page tax code that details all the provisions of the present system would be scrapped. The 437 different IRS tax forms now in use would be replaced by a single, postcard-sized form.

Fairness

Flat-tax advocates also emphasize its fairness. They point to the rampant vertical and horizontal inequities created by the current tangle of tax loopholes. By scrapping all those deductions, the flat tax would treat everyone equally.

Some progressivity could also be preserved with a flat tax. In the version proposed by Dick Armey, the flat tax rate would be 17 percent, but one personal exemption would be maintained. Every adult would get a personal exemption of $13,100 and each child an exemption of $5,300. Accordingly, a family of four would have personal exemptions of $36,800. Hence, a family earning less than that amount would pay no income tax. *Effective* tax rates would increase along with rising incomes above that threshold.

Efficiency

Proponents of a flat tax claim it enhances efficiency as well as equity. Taxpayers now spend over a billion hours a year preparing tax returns. Legions of lobbyists, accountants, and lawyers devote their energy to tax analysis and avoidance. With a simplified flat tax, all those labor resources could be put to more productive use.

A flat tax would also change the mix of output. Consumption and investment decisions would be made on the basis of economic considerations, not tax consequences.

The Critique

As alluring as a flat tax appears, it has aroused substantial opposition. As proposed by Dick Armey, the flat tax would not apply to all income. Income on savings and investments (such as interest and dividends, capital gains) wouldn't be taxed. The purpose of that exemption would be to encourage greater saving, investment, and economic growth. At the same time, however, such a broad exemption creates a whole new set of horizontal and vertical inequities. Someone receiving $1 million in interest and dividends could escape all income taxes, while a family earning $50,000 would have to pay.

Critics also object to the wholesale elimination of all deductions and credits. Many of those loopholes are expressly designed to encourage desired economic activity. The Bush tax cuts were explicitly designed to encourage education, family stability, and savings. By discarding all tax preferences, the flat tax significantly reduces the government's ability to alter the mix of output. Even if the current maze of loopholes exceeds the threshold of government failure, complete reliance on the market mechanism isn't necessarily appropriate. A careful pruning of the tax code rather than a complete uprooting might yield better results.

Finally, critics point out that the transition to a flat tax would entail a wholesale reshuffling of wealth and income. Home values would fall precipitously if the tax preference for homeownership were eliminated. That would hit the middle class particularly hard. State and local governments would have greater difficulty raising their own revenues if the federal deduction for state and local taxes were eliminated. Millionaires might benefit by sharply reduced tax burdens. Confronted with such adjustments, many people begin to have second thoughts about the desirability of adopting a flat tax in the economy tomorrow. Taxpayers seem to like the principle of a flat tax more than its actual provisions.

SUMMARY

- The distribution of income is a vital economic issue because incomes largely determine access to the goods and services we produce. Wealth distribution is important for the same reason.

- The size distribution of income tells us how incomes are divided up among individuals. The Lorenz curve is a graphic summary of the cumulative size distribution of income. The Gini coefficient is a mathematical summary.

- Personal incomes are distributed quite unevenly in the United States. At present, the highest quintile (the top 20 percent) gets nearly half of all cash income, and the bottom quintile gets less than 4 percent.
- The trade-off between equity and efficiency is rooted in supply incentives. The tax elasticity of supply measures how the quantity of resources (labor and capital) declines when tax rates rise.
- The progressivity of the federal income tax is weakened by various loopholes (exemptions, deductions, and credits), which create a distinction between nominal and effective tax rates and cause vertical and horizontal inequities.
- The Tax Reform Act of 1986 broadened the tax base (by eliminating many deductions), reduced tax rates, and shifted more of the tax burden onto corporations. The reforms made federal taxes a bit more progressive.
- Tax rates and brackets were increased in 1990 and 1993, reversing earlier trends.

- The 2001–2004 Bush tax cuts reduced marginal tax rates and created new tax preferences for education, marriage, and saving.
- Mildly progressive federal income taxes are offset by regressive payroll, state, and local taxes. Overall, the tax system redistributes little income; most redistribution occurs through transfer payments.
- Tax incidence refers to the real burden of a tax. In many cases, reductions in wages, increases in rent, or other real income changes represent the true burden of a tax.
- There is a trade-off between efficiency and equality. If all incomes are equal, there's no economic reward for superior productivity. On the other hand, a more equal distribution of incomes might increase the productivity of lower income groups and serve important noneconomic goals as well.
- A flat tax is a nominally proportional tax system. A personal exemption and the exclusion of capital income can render a flat tax progressive or regressive, however. A flat tax reduces the government's role in resource allocation (the WHAT and HOW questions).

Key Terms

personal income (PI)	progressive tax	tax base
in-kind income	marginal tax rate	regressive tax
wealth	tax elasticity of supply	tax incidence
size distribution of income	vertical equity	marginal revenue product (MRP)
income share	horizontal equity	income transfers
Lorenz curve	nominal tax rate	government failure
Gini coefficient	effective tax rate	flat tax
market failure		

Questions for Discussion

1. What goods or services do you and your family receive without directly paying for them? How do these goods affect the distribution of economic welfare?
2. Why are incomes distributed so unevenly? Identify and explain three major causes of inequality.
3. Do inequalities stimulate productivity? In what ways? Provide two specific examples.
4. What loopholes reduced the president's tax bill (see News, page 380)? What's the purpose of those loopholes? How else might those purposes be achieved?
5. How might a flat tax affect efficiency? Fairness?
6. If a new tax system encouraged more output but also created greater inequality, would it be desirable?
7. If the tax elasticity of supply were zero, how high could the tax rate go before people reduced their work effort? How do families vary the quantity of labor supplied when tax rates change?
8. Is the new tax deduction for tuition (page 380) likely to increase college enrollments? How will it affect horizontal and vertical equities?
9. If tax breaks for the rich really stimulated investment and growth, wouldn't everyone benefit from them? Why would anyone oppose them?
10. What share of taxes *should* the rich pay (see Figure 18.4)?

PROBLEMS The Student Problem Set at the back of this book contains numerical and graphing problems for this chapter.

WEB ACTIVITIES to accompany this chapter can be found on the Online Learning Center:
http://www.mhhe.com/economics/schiller10

Transfer Payments: Welfare and Social Security

Americans are compassionate. Public opinion polls reveal that an overwhelming majority of the public wants to "help the needy." Most Americans say they're even willing to pay more taxes to help fund aid to the poor. But their compassion is tempered by caution: Taxpayers don't want to be ripped off. They want to be sure their money is helping the "truly needy," not being squandered by deadbeats, drug addicts, shirkers, and "welfare queens."

The conflict between compassion and resentment affects not only welfare programs for the poor but also Social Security for the aged, unemployment insurance benefits for the jobless, and even disability benefits for injured workers. In every one of these programs, people are getting money without working. **Transfer payments** are payments to individuals for which no current goods or services are exchanged. In effect, they're a "free ride." The risk of providing a free ride is that some of the people who take it could have gotten by without it. As the humorist Dave Barry observed, if the government offers $1 million to people with six toes, a lot of people will try to grow a sixth toe or claim they have one. Income transfers create similar incentives: They encourage people to change their behavior in order to get a free ride.

This chapter focuses on how income transfer programs change not only the distribution of income, but also work incentives and behavior. Central questions include

- **How much income do income transfer programs redistribute?**
- **How are transfer benefits computed?**
- **How do transfer payments alter market behavior?**

MAJOR TRANSFER PROGRAMS

Roughly 50 cents out of every federal tax dollar now is devoted to income transfers (see Figure 4.4). That amounts to more than *$1 trillion* a year in transfer payments. Who gets all this money?

The easy answer to this question is that almost every household gets some of the transfer money. There are over 100 federal income transfer programs. Students get tuition grants and subsidized loans. Farmers get crop assistance. Homeowners get disaster relief when their homes are destroyed. Veterans get benefit checks and subsidized health care. People over age 65 get Social Security benefits and subsidized health care. And poor people get welfare checks, food stamps, and subsidized housing.

Although income transfers are widely distributed, not everyone shares equally in the tax-paid bounty. As Figure 19.1 shows, just three of the myriad transfer programs account for nearly 80 percent of total outlays. Social Security, the largest program, alone accounts for 46 percent of the transfer budget. Medicare and Medicaid benefits absorb another 37 percent. By contrast, welfare checks account for only 4 percent of all income transfers.

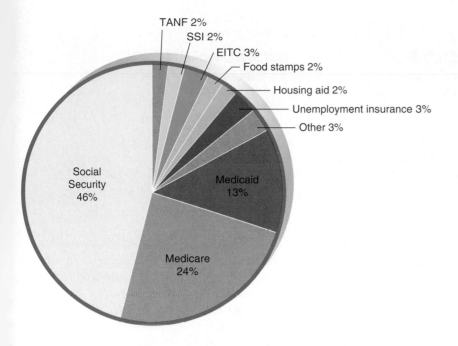

FIGURE 19.1
Income Transfer Program

There are nearly 100 different federal income transfer programs. However, just three programs—Social Security, Medicare and Medicaid—account for nearly 80 percent of all transfers. Cash welfare benefits (TANF, SSI) absorb only 5 percent of all income transfers.

Source: U.S. Office of Management and Budget (FY 2004 data).

Income transfer doesn't always entail cash payments. The Medicare program, for example, is a health insurance subsidy program that pays hospital and doctor bills for people over age 65. The 45 million people who receive Medicare benefits don't get checks from Uncle Sam; instead, Uncle Sam pays the bills for the medical *services* they receive. The same is true for the 43 million people who get Medicaid. Poor people get free health care from the Medicaid program; their benefits are paid *in-kind,* not in cash. Such programs provide **in-kind transfers,** that is, direct transfers of goods and services rather than cash. Food stamps, rent subsidies, legal aid, and subsidized school lunches are all in-kind programs. By contrast, Social Security is a **cash transfer** because it mails benefit checks, not services, to recipients.

The provision of in-kind benefits rather than cash is intended to promote specific objectives. Few taxpayers object to feeding the hungry. But they bristle at the thought that welfare recipients might spend the income they receive on something potentially harmful like liquor or drugs or on nonessentials like cars or fancy clothes. To minimize that risk, taxpayers offer coupons, not cash, thereby limiting the recipient's consumption choices. This helps reassure taxpayers that their assistance is being well spent.

Similar considerations shape the Medicare program. Taxpayers could "cash out" Medicare by simply mailing older people the $275 billion now spent on the program. But then some healthy older Americans would get cash they didn't need. Some sick people might not get as much money as they needed. Or they might choose to spend their new-found income on something other than health care. The end result would be a smaller health care gain than in-kind transfers facilitate.

The **target efficiency** of a transfer program refers to how well income transfers attain their intended purpose. In-kind medical transfers are more target-efficient than cash transfers because recipients would use equivalent cash transfers for other purposes. Food stamps are more target-efficient than cash in reducing hunger for the same reason. If given cash rather than coupons, recipients would spend less than 70 cents of each dollar on food.

You may have noted by now that not all income transfers go to the poor. A lot of student loans go to middle-class college students. And disaster relief helps rebuild both mansions and trailer parks. Such income transfers are triggered by specific *events,* not the recipient's income. By contrast, welfare checks are *means-tested:* They go only to families with little income and fewer assets.

Cash vs. In-Kind Benefits

in-kind transfers: Direct transfers of goods and services rather than cash; examples include food stamps, Medicaid benefits, and housing subsidies.

cash transfers: Income transfers that entail direct cash payments to recipients, for example, Social Security, welfare, and unemployment benefits.

target efficiency: The percentage of income transfers that go to the intended recipients and purposes.

Social Insurance vs. Welfare

FIGURE 19.2
Social Insurance vs. Welfare

Social insurance programs provide *event*-based transfers—for example, upon reaching age 65 or becoming unemployed or disabled. Welfare programs offer benefits only to those in need; they're *means-tested*. Social insurance transfers greatly outnumber welfare transfers.

Source: U.S. Office of Management and Budget.

welfare programs: Means-tested income transfer programs, for example, welfare and food stamps.

social insurance programs: Event-conditioned income transfers intended to reduce the costs of specific problems, for example, Social Security and unemployment insurance.

Transfer Goals

market failure: An imperfection in the market mechanism that prevents optimal outcomes.

Welfare programs always entail some kind of income eligibility test. To receive welfare payments, a family must prove that it has too little income to fend for itself. Medicaid is an in-kind **welfare program** because only poor people are eligible for the health care benefits of that program. To get food stamps, another in-kind welfare program, a family must also pass an income test.

Social Security and Medicare aren't *welfare* programs because recipients don't have to be poor. To get Social Security or Medicare benefits you just have to be old enough. The *event* of reaching age 62 makes people eligible for Social Security retirement benefits. At age 65 everyone—whether rich or poor—gets Medicare benefits. These event-conditioned benefits are the hallmark of **social insurance programs:** They insure people against the costs of old age, illness, disability, unemployment, and other specific problems. As Figure 19.2 illustrates, *most income transfers are for social insurance programs, not welfare.*

If the market sliced up the economic pie in a manner that society deemed fair, there would be no need for all these government-provided income transfers. Hence, the mere existence of such programs implies a **market failure**—an unfair market-generated distribution of income. When the market alone slices up the pie, some people get too much and others get too little. To redress this inequity, we ask the government to play Robin Hood—taking income from the rich and giving it to the poor. Thus, *the basic goal of income transfer programs is to reduce income inequalities.*

FOR WHOM. Transfer programs do in fact significantly change the distribution of income. Social Security alone redistributes $500 billion a year from workers to retirees. Those Social Security checks account for 40 percent of all the income older people receive. Without those checks, nearly half of the elderly population would be poor. More generally, income transfers reduce U.S. inequality by at least 20 percent (as measured by the Gini coefficient).

WHAT to Produce. In the process of redistributing incomes, income transfers also change the mix of output. The goal of food stamps, for example, is to increase food consumption by the poor. The strategy isn't to take food off rich people's plates, however. Instead, it is expected that the additional food purchases of the poor will encourage more food *production,* thereby changing the mix of output. Housing subsidies and free health care have similar effects on the mix of output. So do student loans: If more students end up going to college, the mix of output changes in favor of educational services.

Unintended Consequences

Although income transfers change the distribution of income and mix of output in desired ways, they are not costless interventions. The Law of Unintended Consequences rears its ugly head here: Income transfers often change market behavior and outcomes in unintended (and undesired) ways.

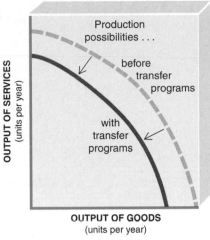

FIGURE 19.3
Reduced Labor Supply and Output

Transfer payments may induce people to supply less labor at any market wage rate. If this happens, the supply of labor shifts to the left and the economy's production possibilities shrink. We end up with less total output.

Reduced Output. First, the provision of transfer payments may dull work incentives. If you can get paid for *not* working (via a transfer payment), why would you go to work? Why endure 40 hours of toil for a paycheck when you can stay home and collect a welfare check, an unemployment check, or Social Security? If the income transfers are large enough, I'll stay home too. When people reduce their **labor supply** in response to income transfers, total output will shrink. Figure 19.3 shows that *attempts to redistribute income may reduce total income.* In other words, the pie shrinks when we try to reslice it.

Undesirable Behavior. A reduction in labor supply isn't the only unintended consequence of income transfer programs. People may also change their *nonwork* behavior. Welfare benefits give women a (small) incentive to have more children and teen moms to establish their own households. Medicare and Medicaid encourage people to overuse health care services and neglect the associated costs. Unemployment benefits encourage workers to stay jobless longer. And, as Dave Berry noted at the beginning of the chapter, disability payments encourage people to grow a sixth toe. Although the actual response to these incentives is hotly debated, the existence of the undesired incentives is unambiguous.

WELFARE PROGRAMS

To understand how income transfer programs change market behavior and outcomes, let's look closer at how welfare programs operate. The largest federal cash welfare program is called Temporary Aid to Needy Families (TANF). The TANF program was created by congressional welfare reforms in 1996 and replaced an earlier program (AFDC) that had operated since 1935. The new program offers states much discretion to decide who gets welfare, under what conditions, and for how long. States can also supplement their federal TANF block grants with their own tax revenues and even establish supplementary programs. However, all such programs confront a central dilemma: how to help the poor without encouraging undesired market behavior.

The first task of the TANF program is to identify potential recipients. In principle, this task is easy: Find out who is poor. To do this, the federal government has established a poverty line that specifies how much cash income families of different sizes need just to buy basic necessities. In 2004, the federal government estimated that a family of four was poor if its income was less than $18,900. Table 19.1 shows how this poverty threshold varies by family size.

labor supply: The willingness and ability to work specific amounts of time at alternative wage rates in a given time period, *ceteris paribus.*

Compare federal welfare programs before and after the major 1996 reform at aspe.os. dhhs.gov/hsp/isp/reform.htm.

Benefit Determination

TABLE 19.1
Poverty Lines

The official definition of poverty relates current income to the minimal needs of a family. Poverty thresholds vary with family size. In 2004, a family of four was considered poor if it had less than $18,900 of income.

Number of Family Members	Family Income
1	$ 9,300
2	12,500
3	15,700
4	18,900
5	22,000
6	25,200
7	28,400
8	31,600

Source: U.S. Department of Commerce, Bureau of the Census (rounded to 100s).

poverty gap: The shortfall between actual income and the poverty threshold.

According to Table 19.1, a four-person family with $16,000 of income in 2004 would have been considered poor. In their case, the **poverty gap**—the shortfall between actual income and the poverty threshold—was $2,900. The Jones family needed at least that much additional income to purchase what the government deems a "minimally adequate" standard of living.

So how much welfare should the government give this family? Should it give $2,900 to this family, thereby closing its poverty gap? As simple as that proposition sounds, it creates some unintended problems.

The Work Incentive Problem

WEBNOTE

Current statistics on poverty are available from the U.S. Census Bureau at www.census.gov/hhes/www/poverty.html.

Suppose we guaranteed all families enough income to reach their respective poverty line. Any family earning less than the poverty line would receive a welfare check in the amount of their poverty gap. In that case, poor people would get enough welfare to escape poverty. No one would be poor.

There are two potential problems with such a welfare policy. First, people who *weren't* poor would have a strong incentive to become poor. Why try to support a family of four with a paycheck of $20,000 when you can quit and get $18,900 in welfare checks? Recall from Chapter 15 that the decision to work is largely a response to both the financial and psychological rewards associated with employment. People in dull, dirty, low-paying jobs get little of either. By quitting their jobs, declaring themselves poor, and accepting a guaranteed income transfer, they would gain much more leisure at little financial or psychological cost. In the process, total output would shrink (Figure 19.3).

The second potential problem affects the work behavior of people who were poor to begin with. We assumed that the Jones family was earning $16,000 before they got a welfare check. The question now is whether the welfare check will change their work behavior.

Suppose that family gets an opportunity to earn an extra $1,000 a year by working overtime. Should they seize that opportunity? Consider the effect of the higher *wages* on the family's *income*. Before working overtime, the Jones family earned

INCOME WITHOUT OVERTIME WAGES

Wages	$16,000
Welfare benefits	2,900
Total income	$18,900

If they now work overtime, their income is

INCOME WITH OVERTIME WAGES

Wages	$17,000
Welfare benefits	1,900
Total income	$18,900

Something is wrong here: Although *wages* have gone up, the family's *income* hasn't.

Marginal Tax Rates. The failure of income to rise with wages is the by-product of how welfare benefits were computed. *If welfare benefits are set equal to the poverty gap, every additional dollar of wages reduces welfare benefits by the same amount.* In effect, the Jones family confronts a **marginal tax rate** of 100 percent: Every dollar of wages results in a lost dollar of benefits. Uncle Sam isn't literally raising the family's taxes by a dollar. By reducing benefits dollar for dollar, however, the end result is the same.

marginal tax rate: The tax rate imposed on the last (marginal) dollar of income.

With a 100 percent marginal tax rate, a family can't improve its income by working more. In fact, this family might as well work *less.* As wages decline, welfare benefits increase by the same amount. Thus, we end up with a conflict between compassion and work incentives. By guaranteeing a poverty-level income, we destroy the economic incentive of low-income workers to support themselves. This creates a **moral hazard** for welfare recipients; that is, we encourage undesirable behavior. The moral hazard here is the temptation not to support oneself by working—choosing welfare checks instead.

moral hazard: An incentive to engage in undesirable behavior.

Less Compassion

To reduce this moral hazard, Congress and the states changed the way benefits are computed. First, they set a much lower ceiling on welfare benefits. States don't offer to close the poverty gap; instead, they set a maximum benefit far below the poverty line. Hence, we have the amended benefit formula:

$$\frac{\text{Welfare}}{\text{benefit}} = \frac{\text{maximum}}{\text{benefit}} - \text{wages}$$

In 2004, the typical state set a maximum benefit of about $8,000 for a family of four. Hence, a family without any other income couldn't get enough money from welfare to stay out of poverty. As a result, *a family totally dependent on welfare is unquestionably poor.* Although the lower benefit ceiling is less compassionate, it reduces the risk of climbing on the welfare wagon for a free ride.

More Incentives

To encourage welfare recipients to lift their own incomes above the poverty line, welfare departments made another change in the benefit formula. As we saw above, *the rate at which benefits are reduced as wages increase is the marginal tax rate.* The dollar-for-dollar benefit cuts illustrated above destroyed the financial incentive to work. To give recipients more incentive to work, the marginal tax rate was cut from 100 to 67 percent. So we now have a new benefit formula:

$$\frac{\text{Welfare}}{\text{benefit}} = \frac{\text{maximum}}{\text{benefit}} - \frac{2}{3} |\text{wages}|$$

Figure 19.4 illustrates how a lower marginal tax rate alters the relationship of total income to wages. The black line in the figure shows the total wages Mrs. Jones could earn at $8 per hour. She could earn nothing by not working or as much as $16,000 per year by working full time (point *F* in the figure).

The red lines in the figure show what happens to her welfare benefits and total income when a 100 percent marginal tax rate is imposed. At point *A* she gets $8,000 in welfare benefits and total income because she's not working at all.

Now consider what happens to the family's total income if Mrs. Jones goes to work. If she works 1,000 hours per year (essentially half-time), she could earn $8,000 (point *B*). But what would happen to her income? If the welfare department cuts her benefit by $1 for every dollar she earns, her benefit check slides down the red "welfare benefits" line to point *C*, where she gets nothing from welfare. By working 1,000 hours per year, all Mrs. Jones has done is replace her welfare check with a paycheck. That might make taxpayers smile, but Mrs. Jones will wonder why she bothered to go to work. With a 100 percent tax rate, her total income doesn't rise above $8,000 until she works more than 1,000 hours.

FIGURE 19.4
Work (Dis)Incentives

If welfare benefits are reduced dollar for dollar as wages increase, the implied marginal tax rate is 100 percent. In that case, total income remains at the benefit limit of $8,000 (point *A*) as work effort increases from 0 to 1,000 hours (point *B*). There is no incentive to work in this range. When the marginal tax rate is reduced to 67 percent, total income starts increasing as soon as the welfare recipient starts working. At 1,000 hours of work, total income is $10,226 (point *G*).

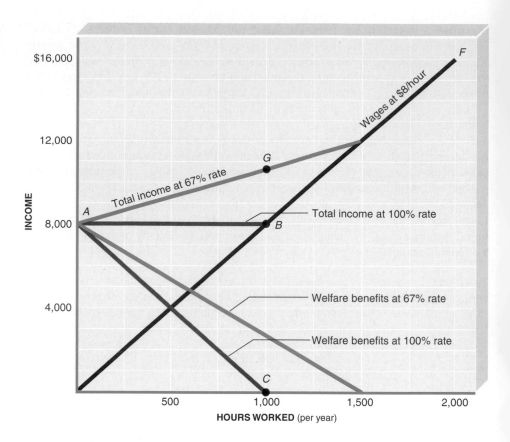

The green lines in Figure 19.4 show how work incentives improve with a lower marginal tax rate. Now welfare benefits are reduced by only 67 cents for every $1 of wages earned. As a result, total income starts rising as soon as Mrs. Jones goes to work. If she works 1,000 hours, her total income will include

Wages	$ 8,000
Welfare benefit	$\underline{2,667}$ = $8,000 − 2/3 ($8,000)
Total income	$10,667

Point *G* on the graph illustrates this outcome.

Incentives vs. Costs

It may be comforting to know that the Jones family can now increase its income to $10,667 by working 1,000 hours per year. But they still face a higher marginal tax rate (67 percent) than rich people (the top marginal tax rate on federal income taxes is 35 percent). Why not lower their marginal tax rate even further, thus increasing both their work incentives and their total income?

Unfortunately, a reduction in the marginal tax rate would also increase welfare costs. Suppose we eliminated the marginal tax rate altogether. Then, the Jones family could earn $8,000 *and* keep welfare benefits of $8,000. That would boost their total income to $16,000. Sounds great, doesn't it? But should we still be providing $8,000 in welfare payments to someone who earns $8,000 on her own? How about someone earning $20,000 or $30,000? Where should we draw the line? Clearly, ***if we don't impose a marginal tax rate at some point, everyone will be eligible for welfare benefits.***

The thought of giving everyone a welfare check might sound like a great idea, but it would turn out to be incredibly expensive. In the end, we'd have to take those checks back, in the form of increased taxes, in order to pay for the vastly expanded program. We must recognize, then, a basic dilemma:

- *Low marginal tax rates encourage more work effort but make more people eligible for welfare.*
- *High marginal tax rates discourage work effort but make fewer people eligible for welfare.*

The conflict between work incentives and the desire to limit welfare costs and eligibility can be summarized in this simple equation:

$$\text{Breakeven level of income} = \frac{\text{basic benefits}}{\text{marginal tax rate}}$$

The **breakeven level of income** is the amount of income a person can earn before losing all welfare benefits. In the Joneses' case, the basic welfare benefit was $8,000 per year and the benefit-reduction (marginal tax) rate was 0.67. Hence, the family could earn as much as

$$\text{Breakeven level of income} = \frac{\$8,000}{0.67} \text{ per year}$$

$$= \$12,000$$

before losing all welfare benefits. Thus, *low marginal tax rates encourage work but make it hard to get completely off welfare.*

If the marginal tax rate were 100 percent, as under the old welfare system, the breakeven point would be $8,000 divided by 1.00. In that case, people who earned $8,000 on their own would get no assistance from welfare. Fewer people would be eligible for welfare, but those who drew benefits would have no incentive to work. If the marginal tax rate were lowered to 0, the breakeven point would rise to infinity ($8,000 divided by 0)—and we'd all be on welfare.

As this arithmetic shows, *there's a basic conflict between work incentives (low marginal tax rates) and welfare containment (smaller welfare rolls and outlays).* We can achieve a lower breakeven level of income (less welfare eligibility) only by sacrificing low marginal tax rates or higher income floors (basic benefits). Hence, welfare costs can be minimized only if we sacrifice income provision or work incentives.

Tax Elasticity of Labor Supply. The terms of the trade off between more welfare and less work depend on how responsive people are to marginal tax rates. As we first noted in Chapter 18, the **tax elasticity of labor supply** measures the response to changes in tax rates; that is,

$$\text{Tax elasticity of labor supply} = \frac{\%\text{ change in quantity of labor supplied}}{\%\text{ change in tax rate}}$$

If the tax elasticity of labor supply were zero, it wouldn't matter how high the marginal tax rate was: People would work for nothing (100 percent tax rate). In reality, the tax elasticity of labor supply among low-wage workers is more in the range of 0.2 to 0.4, so marginal tax rates *do* affect work effort.

Time Limits. The 1996 welfare reforms sidestepped this dilemma by setting time limits on welfare eligibility. TANF recipients must engage in some sort of employment-related activity (e.g., a job, job search, or training) within two years of first receiving benefits. There is also a five-year lifetime limit on welfare eligibility. States, however, can still use their own (nonfederal) funds to extend welfare benefits beyond those time limits.

breakeven level of income: The income level at which welfare eligibility ceases.

tax elasticity of labor supply: The percentage change in quantity of labor supplied divided by the percentage change in tax rates.

SOCIAL SECURITY

Like welfare programs, the Social Security program was developed to redistribute incomes. In the case of Social Security, however, *age,* not low income, is the primary determinant of eligibility. The program seeks to provide a financial prop under retirement incomes. Here again, however, we have to confront policy conflicts between the goals of compassion, work incentives, and program costs.

Program Features

The Social Security program is actually a mix of three separate income transfers. The main program is for retired workers, the second for survivors of deceased workers, and the third for disabled workers. Created in 1935, this combined Old Age Survivors and Disability Insurance (OASDI) program is now so large that it accounts for almost half of all federal income transfers. The monthly benefit checks distributed to 50 million recipients are financed with a payroll tax on workers and employees.

Retirement Age. As Figure 19.5 confirms, the retirement program is by far the largest component of OASDI. Individuals become eligible for Social Security retirement benefits when they reach certain ages. People can choose either "early" retirement (at age 62 to 64) or "normal" retirement (at age 65 to 67). Those who choose early retirement receive a smaller monthly benefit because they're expected to live longer in retirement.

For people born after 1940, the age threshold for "normal" retirement is increasing each year. By the year 2022, the age threshold for normal retirement will be age 67. This delay in benefit eligibility is intended to keep aging baby boomers working longer, thereby curtailing a surge in benefit outlays.

Progressive Benefits. Retirement benefits are based on an individual's wages. In 2004, the median Social Security retirement benefit for an individual was about $12,000. But high-wage workers could get nearly $20,000 and low-wage workers as little as $7,000 a year.

Although high-wage workers receive larger benefit checks than low-wage workers, the *ratio* of benefits to prior wages isn't constant. Instead, the ***Social Security benefits formula is progressive*** because the ratio of benefits to prior wages declines as wages increase. Social Security replaces 90 percent of the first $606 of prior average monthly earnings but only 15 percent of monthly wages above $3,653 (see Table 19.2).

FIGURE 19.5
Social Security Finances

The Social Security retirement, survivor, and disability programs are financed with payroll taxes. Most benefits go to retired workers, who get a median transfer of $12,000 per year.

Source: U.S. Social Security Administration (2003 data).

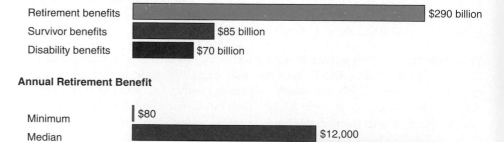

Who Pays Social Security Taxes

Payroll taxes
  7.65% paid by workers
  7.65% paid by employers

Who Gets Social Security Checks

Retirement benefits	$290 billion
Survivor benefits	$85 billion
Disability benefits	$70 billion

Annual Retirement Benefit

Minimum	$80
Median	$12,000
Maximum	$20,000

Wage-Replacement Rate (%)	For Average Monthly Wages of
90%	$1–606
32	606–3,653
15	over $3,653

Source: U.S. Social Security Administration.

TABLE 19.2
Progressive Benefits

Social Security redistributes income progressively by replacing a larger share of low wages than high wages. Shown here are the wage-replacement rates for 2003.

The declining **wage-replacement rate** ensures that low-wage workers receive *proportionately* greater benefits. Thus, retirement benefits end up more equally distributed than wages.

In reality, a worker doesn't have to retire in order to receive Social Security benefits. But the government imposes an *earnings test* to determine how much retirement benefits an older person can collect while still working. The earnings test is very similar to the formula used to compute welfare benefits. The formula establishes a maximum benefit amount and a marginal tax rate that reduces benefits as wages increase:

$$\frac{\text{Benefit}}{\text{amount}} = \frac{\text{maximum}}{\text{award}} - 0.5 \text{ (wages in excess of ceiling)}$$

> **wage-replacement rate:** The percentage of base wages paid out in benefits.

The Earnings Test

Consider the case of Leonard, a 62-year-old worker contemplating retirement. Suppose Leonard's wage history entitles him to a maximum award of $12,000 per year. But he wants to keep working to supplement Social Security benefits with wages. What happens to his benefits if he continues to work?

In 2004, the wage "ceiling" for workers 62 to 64 was $11,640. Hence, the benefit formula was

$$\frac{\text{Benefit}}{\text{amount}} = \$12,000 - 0.5 \text{ (wage} > \$11,640)$$

As a result, a person could earn as much as $11,640 and still get maximum retirement benefits ($12,000), putting the total income at $23,640.

The Work Disincentive

Suppose Leonard wants a bit more income than that. Can he increase his total income by working more? Yes, but not by much. He faces the same kind of work incentives the Jones family had when on welfare. The formula says benefits will drop by 50 cents for every $1 of wages earned over $11,640. Hence, the implicit marginal tax rate is 50 percent. Uncle Sam is effectively getting half of any wages Leonard earns in excess of $11,640 per year. Figure 19.6 illustrates this sorry state of affairs. Notice in particular how *income* rises half as fast as *wages* after point *C*.

In reality, the marginal tax rate on Leonard's wages is even higher. If he works, Leonard will have to pay the Social Security payroll tax (7.65 percent) as well as federal, state, and local income taxes (say, another 15 percent). Hence, the full burden of taxes and benefit losses includes

ITEM	MARGINAL TAX RATE
Social Security benefit loss	50.00%
Payroll tax	7.65
Income taxes	15.00
Total	72.65%

As a consequence, Leonard's income goes up by only 27.35 cents with every $1 he earns.

FIGURE 19.6
The Social Security Work Test

A worker aged 62–64 can earn up to $11,640 (point *A*) without losing any Social Security benefits. If wages increase beyond $11,640 however, Social Security benefits decline by 50 cents for every $1 earned. After point *C*, income rises only half as fast as wages. At the breakeven point *D*, earnings and income are $35,640, and there are no Social Security benefits (point *B*).

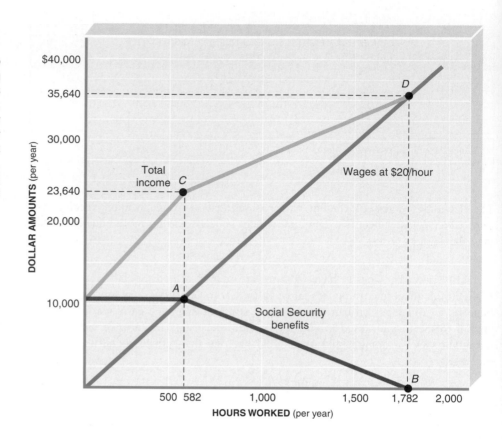

Declining Labor Supply

labor-force participation rate: The percentage of the working-age population working or seeking employment.

Like welfare recipients, older people are quick to realize that work no longer pays. Not surprisingly, they've exited the labor market in droves. The **labor-force participation rate** measures the percentage of the population that is either employed or actively seeking a job (unemployed). Figure 19.7 shows how precipitously the labor-force participation rate has declined among older Americans. As the World View illustrates, this problem isn't unique to the United States. The relative size of the over-65 population is growing everywhere, and more older people are retiring earlier.

Prior to the creation of the Social Security system, most older people had to continue working until advanced age. Many "died with their boots on" because they had no other means of support. Just a generation ago, over 75 percent of men 62 to 64 were working. Today, less than 50 percent of that group are working.

FIGURE 19.7
Declining Labor-Force Participation

In the 1960s and 1970s, the eligibility age for Social Security was lowered for men and benefits were increased. This convinced an increased percentage of older men to leave the labor force and retire. In a single generation the labor-force participation rate of men over age 65 was halved.

Source: U.S. Bureau of Labor Statistics.

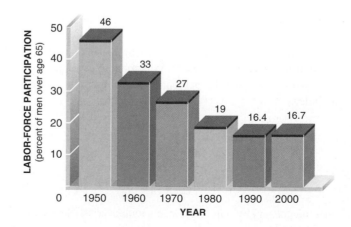

WORLD VIEW

An Aging World

Richer Countries Aging Fastest

The whole world is aging, but the trend is most pronounced in developed countries, where elders will outnumber youths next year.

Percentage 14 and younger
Percentage 60 and older

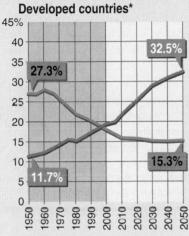

Developed countries*

27.3%
32.5%
11.7%
15.3%

*(Includes North America, Japan, Europe, Australia, New Zealand)

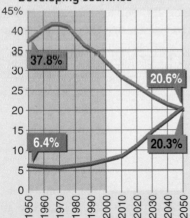

Developing countries

37.8%
20.6%
6.4%
20.3%

Source: *U.S. News & World Report,* March 1, 1999. Copyright 1999 U.S. News & World Report, L. P. Reprinted with permission. www.usnews.com

Workers have been retiring earlier . . .

Average age of retirement for men in industrialized countries

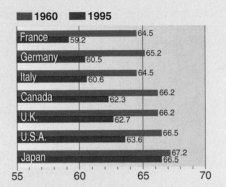

	1960	1995
France	59.2	64.5
Germany	60.5	65.2
Italy	60.6	64.5
Canada	62.3	66.2
U.K.	62.7	66.2
U.S.A.	63.6	66.5
Japan	66.5	67.2

. . . but fewer workers will be supporting retirees in the future . . .

Average number of contributors per retiree in public pension systems

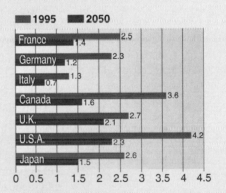

	1995	2050
France	2.5	1.4
Germany	2.3	1.2
Italy	1.3	0.7
Canada	3.6	1.6
U.K.	2.7	2.1
U.S.A.	4.2	2.3
Japan	2.6	1.5

. . . which could lead to higher taxes

Projected payroll tax rates needed to cover all retirees

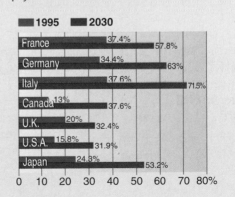

	1995	2030
France	37.4%	57.8%
Germany	34.4%	63%
Italy	37.6%	71.5%
Canada	13%	37.6%
U.K.	20%	32.4%
U.S.A.	15.8%	31.9%
Japan	24.8%	53.2%

Analysis: The aging of the world's population implies an increasing income transfer burden. As older workers choose to retire earlier, the burden increases still further.

Compassion, Incentives, and Cost

WEBNOTE

Read about the future of Social Security as analyzed by the Social Security Administration at www.ssa.gov/qa.htm.

The primary economic cost of the Social Security program isn't the benefits it pays but the reduction in total output that occurs when workers retire early. In the absence of Social Security benefits, millions of older workers would still be on the job, contributing to the output of goods and services. When they instead retire—or simply work less—total output shrinks.

The economic cost of Social Security is increased further by a labor supply reduction among *younger* workers. Recall how all those retirement benefits are *financed* (Figure 19.5). The payroll taxes levied on employees and employers increase the cost of labor and discourage people from working more, which further reduces total output. As the behavior of both older and younger workers changes, *the economic pie shrinks as we try to redistribute it from younger to older workers.*

Trade-Offs. Just because the intergenerational redistribution is expensive doesn't mean we shouldn't do it. Going to college is expensive too, but you're doing it. The real economic issue is benefits versus costs. Compassion for older workers is what motivates Social Security transfers. Presumably, society gains from the more equitable distribution of income that results (a revised FOR WHOM). The economic concern is that we *balance* this gain against the implied costs.

One way of reducing the economic cost of the Social Security program would be to eliminate the work test. The American Association of Retired Persons (AARP) has advocated this option for many years. If the work test were eliminated, the marginal tax rate on the wages of older workers would drop from 50 percent to 0. In a flash, the work disincentive would vanish, and older workers would produce more goods and services.

There's a downside to this reform, however. If the work test were eliminated, all older individuals would get their full retirement benefit, even if they continued to work. This would raise the budgetary cost of the program substantially. To cover that cost, payroll taxes would have to increase. Higher payroll taxes would in turn reduce supply and demand for *younger* workers. Hence, the financial burden of eliminating the work test might actually *increase* the economic cost of Social Security.

There's also an equity issue here. Should we increase payroll taxes on younger low-income workers in order to give higher Social Security benefits to older workers who still command higher salaries? In 2000, Congress gave a very qualified "yes" to this question. The earnings test was eliminated for workers over age 70 and raised to $30,000 for workers aged 65–69. The marginal tax rate for workers aged 65–69 was also reduced to 33.3 percent. The lower earnings test and 50 percent marginal tax rate were left intact, however, for people aged 62–64, the ones for whom the retirement decision is most pressing. The *budget* cost of greater work incentives for "early retirees" was regarded as too high.

THE ECONOMY TOMORROW

Privatize Social Security?

As we saw, all income transfer programs entail a redistribution of income. In the case of Social Security, the redistribution is largely intergenerational: Payroll taxes levied on younger workers finance retirement benefits for older workers. The system is financed on a pay-as-you-go basis; future benefits depend on future taxes. This is very different from private pension plans, whereby you salt away some wages while working to finance your own eventual benefits. Such private plans are advance-*funded.*

Many people say we should run the Social Security system the same way. They want to "privatize" Social Security by permitting workers to establish their own retirement plans. Instead of paying payroll taxes to fund someone else's benefits, you'd make a contribution to your own pension fund.

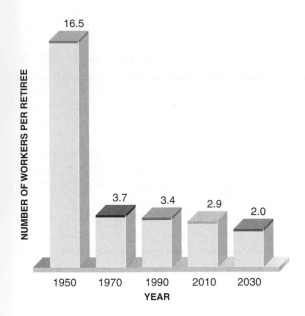

FIGURE 19.8
A Declining Tax Base

Because Social Security benefits are financed by payroll taxes, the ratio of workers to retirees is a basic measure of the program's fiscal health. That ratio has declined dramatically, and it will decline even more when the baby boomers start retiring.

Source: U.S. Social Security Administration.

The case for privatizing Social Security is based on both efficiency and equity. The efficiency argument reflects the core laissez-faire argument that markets know best. In a privatized system, individuals would have the freedom to tailor their consumption and saving choices. The elimination of mandatory payroll taxes and the work test would also lessen work disincentives.

Advocates of privatization also note how inequitable the existing program is for younger workers. The people now retired are getting a great deal: They paid relatively low payroll taxes when young and now receive substantial benefits. In part this high payoff is due to demographics. Thirty years ago there were four workers for every retired person. By the time the post–World War II baby boomers retire, the ratio of workers to retirees will be a lot lower. By the year 2030, there will be only two workers for every retiree (see Figure 19.8). As a result, the tax burden on tomorrow's workers will have to be a lot higher, or the baby boomers will have to accept much lower Social Security benefits. Either way, some generation of workers will get a lot less than everyone else. If Social Security is privatized, tomorrow's workers won't have to bear such a demographic tax burden.

As alluring as these suggestions sound, the privatization of Social Security would foster other inequities. The primary goal of Social Security is to fend off poverty among the aged. Social Security does this in two ways: by (1) transferring income from workers to retirees and (2) redistributing income from high-wage workers to low-wage workers in retirement with progressive wage-replacement rates. In these ways the program changes market outcomes. By contrast, a privatized system would let the market alone determine FOR WHOM goods are produced. Low-income workers and other people who saved little while working would end up poor in their golden years. In a privatized system, even some high earners and savers might end up poor if their investments turned sour. Would we turn our collective backs on these people? If not, then the government would have to intervene with *some* kind of transfer program. The real issue, therefore, may not be whether a privatized Social Security system would work but what kind of *public* transfer program we'd have to create to supplement it. Then the choice would be either (1) Social Security or (2) a privatized retirement system plus a public welfare program for the aged poor. Framed in this context, the choice for the economy tomorrow is a lot more complex.

SUMMARY

- Income transfers are all payments for which no current goods or services are exchanged. They include both cash payments such as welfare checks and in-kind transfers such as food stamps and Medicare.
- Most transfer payments come from social insurance programs that cushion the income effects of specific events, for example, aging, illness, or unemployment. Welfare programs are means-tested; they pay benefits only to the poor.
- The basic goal of transfer programs is to alter the market's FOR WHOM outcome. Attempts to redistribute income may, however, have the unintended effect of reducing total income.
- Welfare programs reduce work incentives in two ways. They offer some income to people who don't work at all,

and they also tax the wages of recipients who do work via offsetting benefit reductions.
- The benefit reduction that occurs when wages increase is an implicit marginal tax. The higher the marginal tax rate, (1) the less the incentive to work but (2) the smaller the welfare caseload.
- The Social Security retirement program creates similar work disincentives. It provides an income floor for people who don't work and imposes a high marginal tax rate on workers aged 62–64.
- The core policy dilemma is to find an optimal balance between compassion (transferring more income) and incentives (keeping people at work contributing to total output).

Key Terms

transfer payment	social insurance programs	moral hazard
in-kind transfers	market failure	breakeven level of income
cash transfers	labor supply	tax elasticity of labor supply
target efficiency	poverty gap	wage-replacement rate
welfare programs	marginal tax rate	labor-force participation rate

Questions for Discussion

1. If we have to choose between compassion and incentives, which should we choose? Do the terms of the trade-off matter?
2. What's so hard about guaranteeing everyone a minimal level of income support? What problems arise?
3. If poor people don't want to work, should they get welfare? What about their children?
4. Once someone has received TANF welfare benefits for a total of five years, they are permanently ineligible for more TANF benefits. Should they receive any further assistance? How will work incentives be affected?
5. In what ways do younger workers pay for Social Security benefits received by retired workers?
6. Should the Social Security earnings test be eliminated? What are the benefits and costs of doing so?
7. How would the distribution of income change if Social Security were privatized?
8. Who pays the economic cost of Social Security? In what ways?

| PROBLEMS | The Student Problem Set at the back of this book contains numerical and graphing problems for this chapter. |
| WEB ACTIVITIES | to accompany this chapter can be found on the Online Learning Center: **http://www.mhhe.com/economics/schiller10** |

PART 7 International Economics

O ur interactions with the rest of the world have a profound impact on the mix of output (WHAT), the methods of production (HOW), and the distribution of income (FOR WHOM). Trade and global money flows can also affect the stability of the macro economy. Chapters 20 and 21 explore the motives, the nature, and the effects of international trade and finance.

International Trade

The 2004 World Series between the Boston Red Sox and the St. Louis Cardinals was played with Japanese gloves, baseballs made in Costa Rica, and Mexican bats. Most of the players were wearing shoes made in Korea or China. And during the regular season, many of the games throughout the league were played on artificial grass made in Taiwan. Baseball, it seems, has become something less than the "all-American" game.

Imported goods have made inroads into other activities as well. All DVDs, VCRs, and video-game machines are imported, as are most televisions, fax machines, personal computers, and cell phones. Most of these imported goods could have been produced in the United States. Why did we purchase them from other countries? For that matter, why does the rest of the world buy computers, tractors, chemicals, airplanes, and wheat from us rather than produce such products for themselves? Wouldn't we all be better off relying on ourselves for the goods we consume (and the jobs we need) rather than buying and selling products in international markets? Or is there some advantage to be gained from international trade?

This chapter begins with a survey of international trade patterns—what goods and services we trade, and with whom. Then we address basic issues related to such trade:

- **What benefit, if any, do we get from international trade?**
- **How much harm do imports cause, and to whom?**
- **Should we protect ourselves from "unfair" trade by limiting imports?**

After examining the arguments for and against international trade, we draw some general conclusions about trade policy. As we'll see, international trade tends to increase *average* incomes, although it may diminish the job and income opportunities for specific industries and workers.

U.S. TRADE PATTERNS

The United States is by far the largest player in global product and resource markets. In 2003, we purchased 20 percent of the world's exports and sold 15 percent of the same total.

In dollar terms, our imports in 2003 exceeded $1.5 trillion. These **imports** included the consumer items mentioned earlier as well as capital equipment, raw materials, and food. Table 20.1 is a sampler of the goods and services we purchase from foreign suppliers.

Although imports represent only 14 percent of total GDP, they account for larger shares of specific product markets. Coffee is a familiar example. Since virtually all coffee is imported (except for a tiny amount produced in Hawaii), Americans would have a harder time staying awake without imports. Likewise, there'd be no aluminum if we didn't import bauxite, no chrome bumpers if we didn't import chromium, no tin cans without imported tin, and a lot fewer computers without

Imports

imports: Goods and services purchased from international sources.

TABLE 20.1
A U.S. Trade Sampler

Country	Imports from	Exports to
Australia	Beef Alumina Autos	Airplanes Computers Auto parts
Belgium	Jewelry Cars Optical glass	Cigarettes Airplanes Diamonds
Canada	Cars Trucks Paper	Auto parts Cars Computers
China	Toys Shoes Clothes	Fertilizer Airplanes Cotton
Germany	Cars Engines Auto parts	Airplanes Computers Cars
Japan	Cars Computers Telephones	Airplanes Computers Timber
Russia	Oil Platinum Artworks	Corn Wheat Oil seeds
South Korea	Shoes Cars Computers	Airplanes Leather Iron ingots and oxides

Source: U.S. Department of Commerce.

The United States imports and exports a staggering array of goods and services. Shown here are the top exports and imports with various countries. Notice that we export many of the same goods we import (such as cars and computers). What's the purpose of trading goods we produce ourselves?

imported components. We couldn't even play the all-American game of baseball without imports, since baseballs are no longer made in the United States.

We import *services* as well as *goods*. If you fly to Europe on Virgin Airways you're importing transportation services. If you stay in a London hotel, you're importing lodging services. When you go to Barclay's Bank to cash traveler's checks, you're importing foreign financial services. These and other services now account for one-sixth of U.S. imports.

While we're buying goods (merchandise) and services from the rest of the world, global consumers are buying our **exports.** In 2003, we exported $726 billion of *goods,* including farm products (wheat, corn, soybeans), tobacco, machinery (computers), aircraft, automobiles and auto parts, raw materials (lumber, iron ore), and chemicals (see Table 20.1 for a sample of U.S. merchandise exports). We also exported $320 billion of services (movies, software licenses, tourism, engineering, financial services, etc.).

Although the United States is the world's largest exporter of goods and services, exports represent a relatively modest fraction of our total output. As the World View illustrates, other nations export much larger proportions of their GDP. Ireland is one of the most export-oriented countries, with tourist services pushing its export ratio to an incredible 98 percent. By contrast, Myanmar (Burma) is basically a closed economy, with few exports (other than opium and other drugs traded in the black market).

The low U.S. export ratio disguises our heavy dependence on exports in specific industries. We export 25 to 50 percent of our rice, corn, and wheat production each year, and still more of our soybeans. Clearly, a decision by international consumers to stop

Exports

exports: Goods and services sold to foreign buyers.

Find the most recent trends in trade statistics at www.whitehouse.gov/fsbr/international.html.

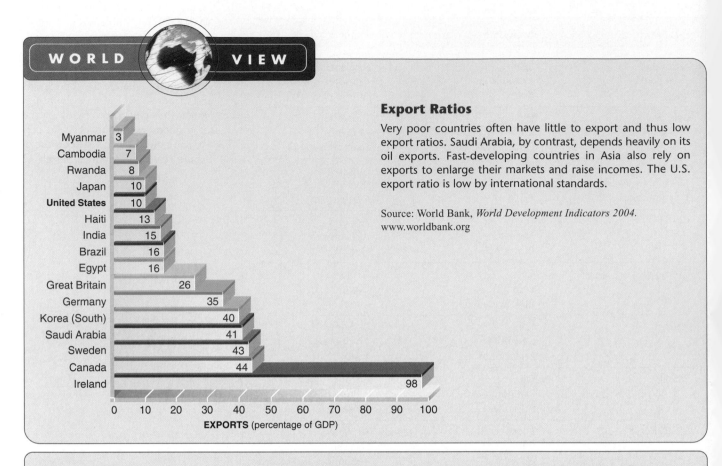

WORLD VIEW

Export Ratios

Very poor countries often have little to export and thus low export ratios. Saudi Arabia, by contrast, depends heavily on its oil exports. Fast-developing countries in Asia also rely on exports to enlarge their markets and raise incomes. The U.S. export ratio is low by international standards.

Source: World Bank, *World Development Indicators 2004.*
www.worldbank.org

Country	Exports (% of GDP)
Myanmar	3
Cambodia	7
Rwanda	8
Japan	10
United States	10
Haiti	13
India	15
Brazil	16
Egypt	16
Great Britain	26
Germany	35
Korea (South)	40
Saudi Arabia	41
Sweden	43
Canada	44
Ireland	98

EXPORTS (percentage of GDP)

Analysis: The relatively low U.S. export ratio reflects the vast size of our domestic market and our relative self-sufficiency in food and resources. European nations are smaller and highly interdependent.

eating U.S. agricultural products could devastate a lot of American farmers. Such companies as Boeing (planes), Caterpillar Tractor (construction and farm machinery), Weyerhaeuser (logs, lumber), Eastman Kodak (film), Dow (chemicals), and Sun Microsystems (computer workstations) sell over one-fourth of their output in foreign markets. McDonald's sells hamburgers to 47 million people a day in 121 countries around the world; to do so, the company exports management and marketing services (as well as frozen food) from the United States. The Walt Disney Company produces the most popular TV shows in Russia and Germany, publishes Italy's best-selling weekly magazine, and has the most popular tourist attraction in Japan (Tokyo Disneyland). The 500,000 foreign students attending U.S. universities are purchasing $5 billion of American educational services. All these activities are part of America's service exports.

Trade Balances

Although we export a lot of products, we often have an imbalance in our trade flows. The trade balance is the difference between the value of exports and imports; that is,

$$\text{Trade balance} = \text{exports} - \text{imports}$$

During 2003, we imported much more than we exported and so had a negative trade balance. A negative trade balance is called a **trade deficit.**

trade deficit: The amount by which the value of imports exceeds the value of exports in a given time period.

Although the overall trade balance includes both goods and services, these flows are usually reported separately, with the *merchandise* trade balance distinguished from the *services* trade balance. As Table 20.2 shows, the United States had a merchandise (goods) trade deficit of $556 billion in 2003 and a *services* trade *surplus* of $58 billion, leaving the overall trade balance in the red.

Product Category	Exports ($ billions)	Imports ($ billions)	Surplus (Deficit) ($ billions)
Merchandise	$ 726	$1,282	$(556)
Services	320	262	58
Total trade	$1,046	$1,544	$(498)

Source: U.S. Department of Commerce.

TABLE 20.2
Trade Balances

Both merchandise (goods) and services are traded between countries. The United States typically has a merchandise deficit and a services surplus. When combined, an overall trade deficit remained in 2003.

When the United States has a trade deficit with the rest of the world, other countries must have an offsetting **trade surplus.** On a global scale, imports must equal exports, since every good exported by one country must be imported by another. Hence, *any imbalance in America's trade must be offset by reverse imbalances elsewhere.*

Whatever the overall balance in our trade accounts, bilateral balances vary greatly. Table 20.3 shows, for example, that our 2003 aggregate trade deficit ($498 billion) incorporated huge bilateral trade deficits with Japan and China. In the same year, however, we had trade surpluses with the Netherlands, Belgium, Australia, Hong Kong, and the United Arab Emirates.

trade surplus: The amount by which the value of exports exceeds the value of imports in a given time period.

MOTIVATION TO TRADE

Many people wonder why we trade so much, particularly since (1) we import many of the things we also export (like computers, airplanes, clothes), (2) we *could* produce many of the other things we import, and (3) we worry so much about trade imbalances. Why not just import those few things that we can't produce ourselves, and export just enough to balance that trade?

Although it might seem strange to be importing goods we could produce ourselves, such trade is entirely rational. Our decision to trade with other countries arises from the same considerations that motivate individuals to specialize in production: satisfying their remaining needs in the marketplace. Why don't you become self-sufficient, growing all your own food, building your own shelter, recording your own songs? Presumably because you've found that you can enjoy a much higher standard of living (and better music) by working at just one job then buying other goods in the

For more data on bilateral trade, visit the U.S. Census Bureau at www.census.gov/foreign-trade.

Specialization

Country	Exports to ($ billions)	Imports from ($ billions)	Trade Balance ($ billions)
Top Deficit Countries			
China	$ 28	$152	−$124
Japan	52	118	−66
Canada	168	222	−54
Mexico	97	138	−41
Germany	68	107	−39
Top Surplus Countries			
Netherlands	21	11	+10
Australia	13	6	+7
Belgium	15	10	+5
Hong Kong	14	9	+5
United Arab Emirates	3	1	+2

Source: U.S. Census Bureau, Foreign Trade Division.

TABLE 20.3
Bilateral Trade Balances

The U.S. trade deficit is the net result of bilateral deficits and surpluses. We had huge trade deficits with Japan and China in 2003, for example, but small trade surpluses with the Netherlands, Belgium, Australia, and Hong Kong. International trade is multinational, with surpluses in some countries being offset by trade deficits elsewhere.

marketplace. When you do so, you're no longer self-sufficient. Instead, you are *specializing* in production, relying on others to produce the array of goods and services you want. When countries trade goods and services, they are doing the same thing—*specializing* in production, then *trading* for other desired goods. Why do they do this? Because **specialization increases total output.**

To see how nations benefit from trade, we'll examine the production possibilities of two countries. We want to demonstrate that two countries that trade can together produce more output than they could in the absence of trade. If they can, *the gain from trade is increased world output and a higher standard of living in all trading countries.* This is the essential message of the *theory of comparative advantage.*

Production and Consumption without Trade

Consider the production and consumption possibilities of just two countries—say, the United States and France. For the sake of illustration, assume that both countries produce only two goods: bread and wine. Let's also set aside worries about the law of diminishing returns and the substitutability of resources, thus transforming the familiar **production possibilities** curve into a straight line, as in Figure 20.1.

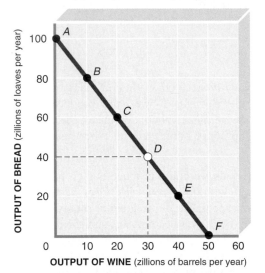

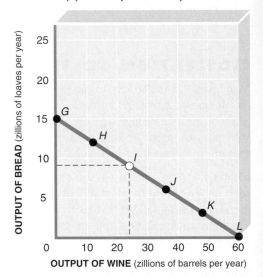

U.S. Production Possibilities		
	Bread (zillions of loaves) +	Wine (zillions of barrels)
A	100 +	0
B	80 +	10
C	60 +	20
D	40 +	30
E	20 +	40
F	0 +	50

French Production Possibilities		
	Bread (zillions of loaves) +	Wine (zillions of barrels)
G	15 +	0
H	12 +	12
I	9 +	24
J	6 +	36
K	3 +	48
L	0 +	60

FIGURE 20.1

Consumption Possibilities without Trade

In the absence of trade, a country's consumption possibilities are identical to its production possibilities. The assumed production possibilities of the United States and France are illustrated in the graphs and the corresponding schedules. Before entering into trade, the United States chose to produce and consume at point *D*, with 40 zillion loaves of bread and 30 zillion barrels of wine. France chose point *I* on its own production possibilities curve. By trading, each country hopes to increase its consumption beyond these levels.

The "curves" in Figure 20.1 suggest that the United States is capable of producing much more bread than France. With our greater abundance of labor, land, and other resources, we assume that the United States is capable of producing up to 100 zillion loaves of bread per year. To do so, we'd have to devote all our resources to that purpose. This capability is indicated by point *A* in Figure 20.1*a* and in row A of the accompanying production possibilities schedule. France (Figure 20.1*b*), on the other hand, confronts a *maximum* bread production of only 15 zillion loaves per year (point *G*) because it has little available land, less fuel, and fewer potential workers.

The capacities of the two countries for wine production are 50 zillion barrels for us (point *F*) and 60 zillion for France (point *L*), largely reflecting France's greater experience in tending vines. Both countries are also capable of producing alternative *combinations* of bread and wine, as evidenced by their respective production possibilities curves (points *A–F* for the United States and *G–L* for France).

In the absence of contact with the outside world, the production possibilities curve for each country would also define its **consumption possibilities.** Without imports, a country cannot consume more than it produces. Thus, the only immediate issue in a closed economy is which mix of output to choose—*what* to produce and consume—out of the domestic choices available.

Assume that Americans choose point *D* on their production possibilities curve, producing and consuming 40 zillion loaves of bread and 30 zillion barrels of wine. The French, on the other hand, prefer the mix of output represented by point *I* on their production possibilities curve. At that point they produce and consume 9 zillion loaves of bread and 24 zillion barrels of wine.

To assess the potential gain from trade, we must focus the *combined* output of the United States and France. In this case, total world output (points *D* and *I*) comes to 49 zillion loaves of bread and 54 zillion barrels of wine. What we want to know is whether world output would increase if France and the United States abandoned their isolation and started trading. Could either country, or both, consume more output by engaging in a little trade?

Because both countries are saddled with limited production possibilities, trying to eke out a little extra wine and bread from this situation might not appear very promising. Such a conclusion is unwarranted, however. Take another look at the production possibilities confronting the United States, as reproduced in Figure 20.2. Suppose the

production possibilities: The alternative combinations of final goods and services that could be produced in a given time period with all available resources and technology.

consumption possibilities: The alternative combinations of goods and services that a country could consume in a given time period.

Production and Consumption with Trade

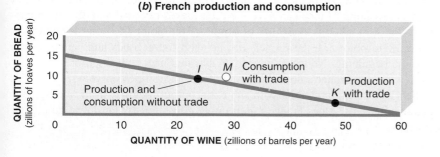

(a) U.S. production and consumption

(b) French production and consumption

FIGURE 20.2
Consumption Possibilities with Trade

A country can increase its consumption possibilities through international trade. Each country alters its mix of domestic output to produce more of the good it produces best. As it does so, total world output increases, and each country enjoys more consumption. In this case, trade allows U.S. consumption to move from point *D* to point *N*. France moves from point *I* to point *M*.

United States were to produce at point *C* rather than point *D*. At point *C* we could produce 60 zillion loaves of bread and 20 zillion barrels of wine. That combination is clearly possible, since it lies on the production possibilities curve. We didn't choose that point earlier because we assumed the mix of output at point *D* was preferable. The mix of output at point *C* could be produced, however.

We could also change the mix of output in France. Assume that France moved from point *I* to point *K*, producing 48 zillion barrels of wine and only 3 zillion loaves of bread.

Two observations are now called for. The first is simply that output mixes have changed in each country. The second, and more interesting, is that total world output has increased. When the United States and France were at points *D* and *I*, their *combined* output consisted of

	Bread (zillions of loaves)	Wine (zillions of barrels)
United States (at point *D*)	40	30
France (at point *I*)	9	24
Total pretrade output	49	54

After moving along their respective production possibilities curves to points *C* and *K*, the combined world output becomes

	Bread (zillions of loaves)	Wine (zillions of barrels)
United States (at point *C*)	60	20
France (at point *K*)	3	48
Total output with trade	63	68

Total world output has increased by 14 zillion loaves of bread and 14 zillion barrels of wine. ***Just by changing the mix of output in each country, we've increased total world output.*** This additional output creates the potential for making both countries better off than they were in the absence of trade.

The United States and France weren't producing at points *C* and *K* before because they simply didn't want to *consume* those particular output combinations. Nevertheless, our discovery that points *C* and *K* allow us to produce *more* output suggests that everybody can consume more goods and services if we change the mix of output in each country. This is our first clue as to how specialization and trade can benefit an economy.

Suppose we're the first to discover the potential benefits from trade. Using Figure 20.2 as our guide, we suggest to the French that they move their mix of output from point *I* to point *K*. As an incentive for making such a move, we promise to give them 6 zillion loaves of bread in exchange for 20 zillion barrels of wine. This would leave them at point *M*, with as much bread to consume as they used to have, plus an extra 4 zillion barrels of wine. At point *I* they had 9 zillion loaves of bread and 24 zillion barrels of wine. At point *M* they can have 9 zillion loaves of bread and 28 zillion barrels of wine. Thus, by altering their mix of output (from point *I* to point *K*) and then trading (point *K* to point *M*), the French end up with more goods and services than they had in the beginning. Notice in particular that this new consumption possibility (point *M*) lies *outside* France's domestic production possibilities curve.

The French will be quite pleased with the extra output they get from trading. But where does this leave us? Does France's gain imply a loss for us? Or do we gain from trade as well?

TABLE 20.4
Gains from Trade

When nations specialize in production, they can export one good and import another and end up with more goods to consume than they had without trade. In this case, the United States specializes in bread production.

	Production and Consumption with Trade							Production and Consumption with No Trade
	Production	+	Imports	−	Exports	=	Consumption	
United States at . . .	Point *C*						Point *N*	Point *D*
Bread	60	+	0	−	6	=	54	40
Wine	20	+	20	−	0	=	40	30
France at . . .	Point *K*						Point *M*	Point *I*
Bread	3	+	6	−	0	=	9	9
Wine	48	+	0	−	20	=	28	24

Mutual Gains

As it turns out, *both* the United States and France gain by trading. The United States, too, ends up consuming a mix of output that lies outside our production possibilities curve.

Note that at point *C* we produce 60 zillion loaves of bread per year and 20 zillion barrels of wine. We then export 6 zillion loaves to France. This leaves us with 54 zillion loaves of bread to consume. In return for our exported bread, the French give us 20 zillion barrels of wine. These imports, plus our domestic production, permit us to *consume* 40 zillion barrels of wine. Hence, we end up consuming at point *N*, enjoying 54 zillion loaves of bread and 40 zillion barrels of wine. Thus, by first changing our mix of output (from point *D* to point *C*), then trading (point *C* to point *N*), we end up with 14 zillion more loaves of bread and 10 zillion more barrels of wine than we started with. International trade has made us better off, too.

Table 20.4 recaps the gains from trade for both countries. Notice that U.S. imports match French exports and vice versa. Also notice how the trade-facilitated consumption in each country exceeds no-trade levels.

There's no sleight of hand going on here; the gains from trade are due to specialization in production. When each country goes it alone, it's a prisoner of its own production possibilities curve; it must make production decisions on the basis of its own consumption desires. When international trade is permitted, however, each country can concentrate on the exploitation of its production capabilities. *Each country produces those goods it makes best and then trades with other countries to acquire the goods it desires to consume.*

The resultant specialization increases total world output. In the process, each country is able to escape the confines of its own production possibilities curve, to reach beyond it for a larger basket of consumption goods. *When a country engages in international trade, its consumption possibilities always exceed its production possibilities.* These enhanced consumption possibilities are emphasized by the positions of points *N* and *M* outside the production possibilities curves (Figure 20.2). If it weren't possible for countries to increase their consumption by trading, there'd be no incentive for trading, and thus no trade.

PURSUIT OF COMPARATIVE ADVANTAGE

Although international trade can make everyone better off, it's not so obvious which goods should be traded, or on what terms. In our previous illustration, the United States ended up trading bread for wine in terms that were decidedly favorable to us. Why did we export bread rather than wine, and how did we end up getting such a good deal?

Opportunity Costs

comparative advantage: The ability of a country to produce a specific good at a lower opportunity cost than its trading partners.

opportunity cost: The most desired goods or services that are forgone in order to obtain something else.

The decision to export bread is based on **comparative advantage,** that is, the *relative* cost of producing different goods. Recall that we can produce a maximum of 100 zillion loaves of bread per year or 50 zillion barrels of wine. Thus, the domestic **opportunity cost** of producing 100 zillion loaves of bread is the 50 zillion barrels of wine we forsake in order to devote our resources to bread production. In fact, at every point on the U.S. production possibilities curve (Figure 20.2*a*), the opportunity cost of a loaf of bread is $\frac{1}{2}$ barrel of wine. We're effectively paying half a barrel of wine to get a loaf of bread.

Although the cost of bread production in the United States might appear outrageous, even higher opportunity costs prevail in France. According to Figure 20.2*b*, the opportunity cost of producing a loaf of bread in France is a staggering 4 barrels of wine. To produce a loaf of bread, the French must use factors of production that could otherwise be used to produce 4 barrels of wine.

Comparative Advantage. A comparison of the opportunity costs prevailing in each country exposes the nature of comparative advantage. The United States has a comparative advantage in bread production because less wine has to be given up to produce bread in the United States than in France. In other words, the opportunity costs of bread production are lower in the United States than in France. *Comparative advantage refers to the relative (opportunity) costs of producing particular goods.*

A country should specialize in what it's *relatively* efficient at producing, that is, goods for which it has the lowest opportunity costs. In this case, the United States should produce bread because its opportunity cost ($\frac{1}{2}$ barrel of wine) is less than France's (4 barrels of wine). Were you the production manager for the whole world, you'd certainly want each country to exploit its relative abilities, thus maximizing world output. Each country can arrive at that same decision itself by comparing its own opportunity costs to those prevailing elsewhere. *World output, and thus the potential gains from trade, will be maximized when each country pursues its comparative advantage.* Each country does so by exporting goods that entail relatively low domestic opportunity costs and importing goods that involve relatively high domestic opportunity costs. That's the kind of situation depicted in Table 20.4.

Absolute Costs Don't Count

absolute advantage: The ability of a country to produce a specific good with fewer resources (per unit of output) than other countries.

In assessing the nature of comparative advantage, notice that we needn't know anything about the actual costs involved in production. Have you seen any data suggesting how much labor, land, or capital is required to produce a loaf of bread in either France or the United States? For all you and I know, the French may be able to produce both a loaf of bread and a barrel of wine with fewer resources than we're using. Such an **absolute advantage** in production might exist because of their much longer experience in cultivating both grapes and wheat or simply because they have more talent.

We can envy such productivity, and even try to emulate it, but it shouldn't alter our production or trade decisions. All we really care about are *opportunity costs*—what *we* have to give up in order to get more of a desired good. If we can get a barrel of wine for less bread in trade than in production, we have a comparative advantage in producing bread. As long as we have a *comparative* advantage in bread production we should exploit it. It doesn't matter to us whether France could produce either good with fewer resources. For that matter, even if France had an absolute advantage in *both* goods, we'd still have a *comparative* advantage in bread production, as we've already confirmed. The absolute costs of production were omitted from the previous illustration because they were irrelevant.

To clarify the distinction between absolute advantage and comparative advantage, consider this example. When Charlie Osgood joined the Willamette Warriors football team, he was the fastest runner ever to play football in Willamette. He could also throw the ball farther than most people could see. In other words, he had an *absolute advantage* in both throwing and running. Charlie would have made the greatest quarterback or the greatest end ever to play football. *Would have.* The problem was that he could play only one position at a time. Thus, the Willamette coach had to play Charlie either as a quarterback or as an end. He reasoned that Charlie could throw only a bit farther than some of the other top quarterbacks but could far outdistance all the other ends. In other words, Charlie had a *comparative advantage* in running and was assigned to play as an end.

TERMS OF TRADE

It definitely pays to pursue one's comparative advantage by specializing in production. It may not yet be clear, however, how we got such a good deal with France. We're clever traders, but beyond that, is there any way to determine the **terms of trade,** the quantity of good A that must be given up in exchange for good B? In our previous illustration, the terms of trade were very favorable to us; we exchanged only 6 zillion loaves of bread for 20 zillion barrels of wine (Table 20.4). The terms of trade were thus 6 loaves = 20 barrels.

terms of trade: The rate at which goods are exchanged; the amount of good A given up for good B in trade.

The terms of trade with France were determined by our offer and France's ready acceptance. But why did France accept those terms? France was willing to accept our offer because the terms of trade permitted France to increase its wine consumption without giving up any bread consumption. Our offer of 6 loaves for 20 barrels was an improvement over France's domestic opportunity costs. France's domestic possibilities required it to give up 24 barrels of wine in order to produce 6 loaves of bread (see Figure 20.2b). Getting bread via trade was simply cheaper for France than producing bread at home. France ended up with an extra 4 zillion barrels of wine (Table 20.4).

Our first clue to the terms of trade, then, lies in each country's domestic opportunity costs. *A country won't trade unless the terms of trade are superior to domestic opportunities.* In our example, the opportunity cost of 1 barrel of wine in the United States is 2 loaves of bread. Accordingly, we won't export bread unless we get at least 1 barrel of wine in exchange for every 2 loaves of bread we ship overseas.

All countries want to gain from trade. Hence, we can predict that *the terms of trade between any two countries will lie somewhere between their respective opportunity costs in production.* That is, a loaf of bread in international trade will be worth at least $\frac{1}{2}$ barrel of wine (the U.S. opportunity cost) but no more than 4 barrels (the French opportunity cost). In our example, the terms of trade ended up at 1 loaf = 3.33 barrels (that is, at 6 loaves = 20 barrels). This represented a very large gain for the United States and a small gain for France. Figure 20.3 illustrates this outcome and several other possibilities.

Limits to the Terms of Trade

Relatively little trade is subject to such direct negotiations between countries. More often than not, the decision to import or export a particular good is left up to the market decisions of individual consumers and producers.

Individual consumers and producers aren't much impressed by such abstractions as comparative advantage. Market participants tend to focus on prices, always trying to allocate their resources in order to maximize profits or personal satisfaction. Consumers tend to buy the products that deliver the most utility per dollar of expenditure, while producers try to get the most output per dollar of cost. Everybody's looking for a bargain.

So what does this have to do with international trade? Well, suppose that Henri, an enterprising Frenchman, visited the United States before the advent of international trade. He observed that bread was relatively cheap while wine was relatively expensive— the opposite of the price relationship prevailing in France. These price comparisons brought to his mind the opportunity for making a fast franc. All he had to do was bring over some French wine and trade it in the United States for a large quantity of bread. Then he could return to France and exchange the bread for a greater quantity of wine. *Alors!* Were he to do this a few times, he'd amass substantial profits.

The Role of Markets and Prices

FIGURE 20.3

Searching for the Terms of Trade

Assume the United States can produce 100 zillion loaves of bread per year (point *A*). If we reduce output to only 85 zillion loaves, we could move to point *X*. At point *X* we have 7.5 zillion barrels of wine and 85 zillion loaves of bread.

Trade increases consumption possibilities. If we continued to produce 100 zillion loaves of bread, we could trade 15 zillion loaves to France in exchange for as much as 60 zillion barrels of wine. This would leave us *producing* at point *A* but *consuming* at point *Y*. At point *Y* we have more wine and no less bread than we had at point *X*.

A country will end up on its consumption possibilities curve only if it gets *all* the gains from trade. It will remain on its production possibilities curve only if it gets *none* of the gains from trade. The terms of trade determine how the gains from trade are distributed, and thus at what point in the shaded area each country ends up.

Note: The kink in the consumption possibilities curve at point *Y* occurs because France is unable to produce more than 60 zillion barrels of wine.

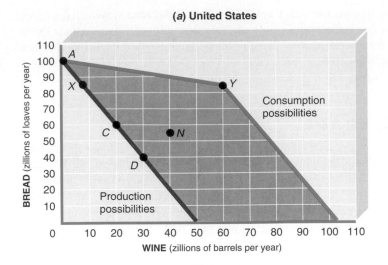

(a) United States

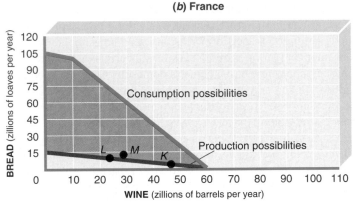

(b) France

Henri's entrepreneurial exploits will not only enrich him but will also move each country toward its comparative advantage. The United States ends up exporting bread to France, and France ends up exporting wine to the United States, exactly as the theory of comparative advantage suggests. The activating agent isn't the Ministry of Trade and its 620 trained economists but simply one enterprising French trader. He's aided and encouraged, of course, by consumers and producers in each country. American consumers are happy to trade their bread for his wines. They thereby end up paying less for wine (in terms of bread) than they'd otherwise have to. In other words, the terms of trade Henri offers are more attractive than the prevailing (domestic) relative prices. On the other side of the Atlantic, Henri's welcome is equally warm. French consumers are able to get a better deal by trading their wine for his imported bread than by trading with the local bakers.

Even some producers are happy. The wheat farmers and bakers in the United States are eager to deal with Henri. He's willing to buy a lot of bread and even to pay a premium price for it. Indeed, bread production has become so profitable in the United States that a lot of people who used to grow and mash grapes are now growing wheat and kneading dough. This alters the mix of U.S. output in the direction of more bread, exactly as suggested in Figure 20.2*a*.

In France, the opposite kind of production shift is taking place. French wheat farmers are planting more grape vines so they can take advantage of Henri's generous purchases. Thus, Henri is able to lead each country in the direction of its comparative advantage while raking in a substantial profit for himself along the way.

Where the terms of trade and the volume of exports and imports end up depends partly on how good a trader Henri is. It will also depend on the behavior of the thousands of individual consumers and producers who participate in the market exchanges. In other words, trade flows depend on both the supply and the demand for bread and wine in each country. ***The terms of trade, like the price of any good, depend on the willingness of market participants to buy or sell at various prices.*** All we know for sure is that the terms of trade will end up somewhere between the limits set by each country's opportunity costs.

PROTECTIONIST PRESSURES

Although the potential gains from world trade are impressive, not everyone will smile at the Franco-American trade celebration. On the contrary, some people will be upset about the trade routes that Henri has established. They'll not only boycott the celebration but actively seek to discourage us from continuing to trade with France.

Consider, for example, the winegrowers in western New York. Do you think they're going to be happy about Henri's entrepreneurship? Americans can now buy wine more cheaply from France than they can from New York. Before long we may hear talk about unfair foreign competition or about the greater nutritional value of American grapes (see News). The New York winegrowers may also emphasize the importance of maintaining an adequate grape supply and a strong wine industry at home, just in case of terrorist attacks.

Microeconomic Pressures

Import-Competing Industries. Joining with the growers will be the farm workers and the other producers and merchants whose livelihood depends on the New York wine industry. If they're clever enough, the growers will also get the governor of the state to join their demonstration. After all, the governor must recognize the needs of his people, and his people definitely don't include the wheat farmers in Kansas who are making a bundle from international trade. New York consumers are of course benefiting from lower wine prices, but they're unlikely to demonstrate over a few cents a bottle. On the other hand, those few extra pennies translate into millions of dollars for domestic wine producers.

The wheat farmers in France are no happier about international trade than are the winegrowers in the United States. They'd dearly love to sink all those boats bringing wheat from America, thereby protecting their own market position.

IN THE NEWS

Whining over Wine

A new type of wine bar has sprung up on Capitol Hill, and it's not likely to tickle the palate of a dedicated oenophile. California wine makers are hawking a bill that could slap higher tariffs on imported wine, and Congress shows some sign of becoming intoxicated with what the wine makers have to offer. First introduced last summer, the Wine Equity Act, as the measure is called, is already sponsored by 345 Congressmen and 60 Senators.

The wine makers aren't putting all their grapes into one bottle. Behind the scenes they have been making common cause with the American Grape Growers Alliance for Fair Trade, a group that represents many of the farmer cooperatives that supply domestic wineries. In a suit they filed with the Commerce Department and International Trade Commission in January, the growers complained that the Europeans, and particularly the Italians, are unfairly subsidizing the wine producers. If their suit is upheld, the ITC could impose stiff duties on the imports. The importers say there is no good evidence of substantial government subsidies.

Source: *Fortune,* February 20, 1984. From FORTUNE. © 1984 Time Inc. All rights reserved. www.fortune.com

Analysis: Although trade increases consumption possibilities, imports typically compete with a domestic industry. The affected industries will try to restrict imports in order to preserve their own jobs and incomes.

If we're to make sense of trade policies, then, we must recognize one central fact of life: Some producers have a vested interest in restricting international trade. In particular, *workers and producers who compete with imported products—who work in import-competing industries—have an economic interest in restricting trade.* This helps explain why GM, Ford, and Chrysler are unhappy about auto imports and why workers in Massachusetts want to end the importation of Italian shoes. It also explains why textile producers in South Carolina think China is behaving irresponsibly when it sells cotton shirts and dresses in the United States.

Export Industries. Although imports typically mean fewer jobs and less income for some domestic industries, exports represent increased jobs and income for other industries. Producers and workers in export industries gain from trade. Thus, on a microeconomic level there are identifiable gainers and losers from international trade. *Trade not only alters the mix of output but also redistributes income from import-competing industries to export industries.* This potential redistribution is the source of political and economic friction.

Net Gain. We must be careful to note, however, that the microeconomic gains from trade are greater than the microeconomic losses. It's not simply a question of robbing Peter to enrich Paul. We must remind ourselves that consumers in general enjoy a higher standard of living as a result of international trade. As we saw earlier, trade increases world efficiency and total output. Accordingly, we end up slicing up a larger pie rather than just reslicing the same old smaller pie.

The gains from trade will mean nothing to workers who end up with a smaller slice of the (larger) pie. It's important to remember, however, that the gains from trade are large enough to make everybody better off. Whether we actually choose to distribute the gains from trade in this way is a separate question, to which we shall return shortly. Note here, however, that *trade restrictions designed to protect specific microeconomic interests reduce the total gains from trade.* Trade restrictions leave us with a smaller pie to split up.

Additional Pressures

Import-competing industries are the principal obstacle to expanded international trade. Selfish micro interests aren't the only source of trade restrictions, however. Other arguments are also used to restrict trade.

National Security. The national security argument for trade restrictions is twofold. We can't depend on foreign suppliers to provide us with essential defense-related goods, it is said, because that would leave us vulnerable in time of war. The machine tool industry used this argument to protect itself from imports. In 1991, the Pentagon again sided with the toolmakers, citing the need for the United States to "gear up military production quickly in case of war," a contingency that couldn't be assured if weapons manufacturers relied on imported lathes, milling machines, and other tools. After the September 11, 2001, terrorist attacks on the World Trade Center and Pentagon, U.S. farmers convinced Congress to safeguard the nation's food supply with additional subsidies (see Chapter 14). The steel industry emphasized the importance of not depending on foreign suppliers.

dumping: The sale of goods in export markets at prices below domestic prices.

Dumping. Another argument against free trade arises from the practice of **dumping.** Foreign producers "dump" their goods when they sell them in the United States at prices lower than those prevailing in their own country, perhaps even below the costs of production.

Dumping may be unfair to import-competing producers, but it isn't necessarily unwelcome to the rest of us. As long as foreign producers continue dumping, we're getting foreign products at low prices. How bad can that be? There's a legitimate worry, however. Foreign producers might hold prices down only until domestic producers are

China Accuses Corning of 'Dumping'

Corning Inc., the big U.S. fiber-optic and glass maker, said the Chinese government has charged it with selling optical-fiber products in China at an unfairly low price that damaged Chinese producers, a practice known as dumping.

Corning denied the charge, which followed a nearly year-long investigation by China's Ministry of Commerce after two Chinese companies alleged that optical-fiber imports were priced below what market conditions justified. . . .

Since it joined the WTO, China has brought about 25 dumping cases against foreign companies, according to a King & Spalding estimate. In that same period, U.S. companies have brought 24 dumping cases against China, according to the International Trade Commission. . . .

Recent U.S. trade actions against China, most notably an antidumping case launched in October against $1 billion worth of Chinese wood and bedroom furniture imports, have likely played a role, too, according to trade experts.

The high-profile U.S. furniture case against China and China's charge against fiber makers such as Corning also exemplify the chief economic concerns in each economy: The U.S. is preoccupied with protecting workers in its hard-hit manufacturing sector, while China is interested in nurturing its technology industry. . . .

With the filing of the Chinese charges, Corning customers in China will have to pay a 16% deposit on the purchase price of the company's products, starting immediately. That money will be held in an escrow account until the matter is resolved.

Source: *The Wall Street Journal*, June 17, 2004. Reprinted by permission of The Wall Street Journal, © 2004 Dow Jones & Company. All rights reserved worldwide.

Analysis: *Dumping* means that a foreign producer is selling exports at prices below cost or below prices in the home market, putting import-competing industries at a competitive disadvantage. *Accusations* of dumping are an effective trade barrier.

driven out of business. Then we might be compelled to pay the foreign producers higher prices for their products. In that case, dumping could consolidate market power and lead to monopoly-type pricing. The fear of dumping, then, is analogous to the fear of predatory pricing.

The potential costs of dumping are serious. It's not always easy to determine when dumping occurs, however. Those who compete with imports have an uncanny ability to associate any and all low prices with predatory dumping. The United States has used dumping *charges* to restrict imports of Chinese shrimp, furniture, lingerie, and other products in which China has an evident comparative advantage. The Chinese have retaliated with dozens of their own dumping investigations, including the 2004 accusation for fiber-optic cable (in which the United States has a comparative advantage), as the accompanying World View explains.

Infant Industries. Actual dumping threatens to damage already established domestic industries. Even normal import prices, however, may make it difficult or impossible for a new domestic industry to develop. Infant industries are often burdened with abnormally high startup costs. These high costs may arise from the need to train a whole workforce and the expenses of establishing new marketing channels. With time to grow, however, an infant industry might experience substantial cost reductions and establish a comparative advantage. When this is the case, trade restrictions might help nurture an industry in its infancy. Trade restrictions are justified, however, only if there's tangible evidence that the industry can develop a comparative advantage reasonably quickly.

Improving the Terms of Trade. A final argument for restricting trade rests on how the gains from trade are distributed. As we observed, the distribution of the gains from trade depends on the terms of trade. If we were to buy fewer imports, foreign producers might lower their prices. If that happened, the terms of trade would move in our favor, and we'd end up with a larger share of the gains from trade.

One way to bring about this sequence of events is to put restrictions on imports, making it more difficult or expensive for Americans to buy foreign products. Such restrictions will reduce the volume of imports, thereby inducing foreign producers to lower their prices. Unfortunately, this strategy can easily backfire: Retaliatory restrictions on imports, each designed to improve the terms of trade, will ultimately eliminate all trade and therewith all the gains people were competing for in the first place.

BARRIERS TO TRADE

The microeconomic losses associated with imports give rise to a constant clamor for trade restrictions. People whose jobs and incomes are threatened by international trade tend to organize quickly and air their grievances. The News depicts the efforts of farmers in Montana and North Dakota to limit imports of Canadian wheat and livestock. They hope to convince Congress to impose restrictions on imports. More often than not, Congress grants the wishes of these well-organized and well-financed special interests.

Embargoes

embargo: A prohibition on exports or imports.

The surefire way to restrict trade is simply to eliminate it. To do so, a country need only impose an embargo on exports or imports, or both. An **embargo** is nothing more than a prohibition against trading particular goods.

In 1951, Senator Joseph McCarthy convinced the U.S. Senate to impose an embargo on Soviet mink, fox, and five other furs. He argued that such imports helped finance world communism. Senator McCarthy also represented the state of Wisconsin, where most U.S. minks are raised. The Reagan administration tried to end the fur embargo in 1987 but met with stiff congressional opposition. By then, U.S. mink ranchers had developed a $120 million per year industry.

The United States has also maintained an embargo on Cuban goods since 1959, when Fidel Castro took power there. This embargo severely damaged Cuba's sugar industry and deprived American smokers of the famed Havana cigars. It also fostered the development of U.S. sugar beet and tobacco farmers, who now have a vested interest in maintaining the embargo.

Tariffs

A more frequent trade restriction is a **tariff,** a special tax imposed on imported goods. Tariffs, also called *customs duties,* were once the principal source of revenue for

IN THE NEWS

Farmers Stage Protests over Import of Products

Farmers claiming that imports of Canadian grain and other agricultural products are depressing U.S. prices threatened on Tuesday more blockades at border crossings unless the U.S. government acts to slow the flow of goods.

Farmers also want Canadian wheat and livestock tested for diseases and additives that are banned here.

Blockades and other protests have appeared at various border crossings in North Dakota and Montana for several days. In Montana, 20 long-haul truckers were ticketed Monday, the first day of a state crackdown on border inspections. And farmers in North Dakota dumped grain on U.S. Highway 281, stopping truck traffic for eight hours.

"We've got an oversupply of wheat, hogs and cattle already," said Curt Trulson, a farmer in Ross, N.D. "We don't need any more foreign commodities."

Source: *USA Today,* September 23, 1998. USA TODAY. © 1998, USA Today. Reprinted with permission. www.usatoday.com

Analysis: Import-competing industries cite lots of reasons for restricting trade. Their primary concern, however, is to protect their own jobs and profits.

governments. In the eighteenth century, tariffs on tea, glass, wine, lead, and paper were imposed on the American colonies to provide extra revenue for the British government. The tariff on tea led to the Boston Tea Party in 1773 and gave added momentum to the American independence movement. In modern times, tariffs have been used primarily as a means to protect specific industries from import competition. The current U.S. tariff code specifies tariffs on over 9,000 different products—nearly 50 percent of all U.S. imports. Although the average tariff is only 5 percent, individual tariffs vary widely. The tariff on cars, for example, is only 2.5 percent, while cotton sweaters confront a 17.8 percent tariff.

The attraction of tariffs to import-competing industries should be obvious. *A tariff on imported goods makes them more expensive to domestic consumers and thus less competitive with domestically produced goods.* Among familiar tariffs in effect in 2004 were $0.50 per gallon on Scotch whiskey and 76 cents per gallon on imported champagne. These tariffs made American-produced spirits look relatively cheap and thus contributed to higher sales and profits for domestic distillers and grape growers. In the same manner, imported baby food is taxed at 34.6 percent, maple sugar at 9.4 percent, golf shoes at 8.5 percent, and imported sailboats at 1.5 percent. In each case, domestic producers in import-competing industries gain. The losers are domestic consumers, who end up paying higher prices. The tariff on orange juice, for example, raises the price of drinking orange juice by $525 million a year. Tariffs also hurt foreign producers, who lose business, and world efficiency, as trade is reduced.

"Beggar Thy Neighbor." Microeconomic interests aren't the only source of pressure for tariff protection. Imports represent leakage from the domestic circular flow and a potential loss of jobs at home. From this perspective, the curtailment of imports looks like an easy solution to the problem of domestic unemployment. Just get people to "buy American" instead of buying imported products, so the argument goes, and domestic output and employment will surely expand. Congressman Willis Hawley used this argument in 1930. He assured his colleagues that higher tariffs would "bring about the growth and development in this country that has followed every other tariff bill, bringing as it does a new prosperity in which all people, in all sections, will increase their comforts, their enjoyment, and their happiness."[1] Congress responded by passing the Smoot-Hawley Tariff Act of 1930, which raised tariffs to an average of nearly 60 percent, effectively cutting off most imports.

Tariffs designed to expand domestic employment are more likely to fail than to succeed. If a tariff wall does stem the flow of imports, it effectively transfers the unemployment problem to other countries, a phenomenon often referred to as "beggar thy neighbor." The resultant loss of business in other countries leaves them less able to purchase our exports. The imported unemployment also creates intense political pressures for retaliatory action. That's exactly what happened in the 1930s. Other countries erected trade barriers to compensate for the effects of the Smoot-Hawley tariff. World trade subsequently fell from $60 billion in 1928 to a mere $25 billion in 1938. This trade contraction increased the severity of the Great Depression (see World View).

Tariffs reduce the flow of imports by raising import prices. The same outcome can be attained more directly by imposing import **quotas,** numerical restrictions on the quantity of a particular good that may be imported. The United States limits the quantity of ice cream imported from Jamaica to 950 gallons a year. Only 1.4 million kilograms of Australian cheddar cheese and no more than 7,730 tons of Haitian sugar can be imported. Textile quotas are imposed on every country that wants to ship textiles to the U.S. market. According to the U.S. Department of State, approximately 12 percent of our imports are subject to import quotas.

tariff: A tax (duty) imposed on imported goods.

WEBNOTE

The harmonized tariff schedule for imported products is available online from the U.S. International Trade Commission. Go to www.usitc.gov, and click on "Publications" then "Harmonized Tariff Schedule."

Quotas

quota: A limit on the quantity of a good that may be imported in a given time period.

[1] *The New York Times,* June 15, 1930, p. 25.

"Beggar-Thy-Neighbor" Policies in the 1930s

President Herbert Hoover, ignoring the pleas of 1,028 economists to veto it, signed the Smoot-Hawley Tariff Act on June 17, 1930. It was a hollow celebration. The day before, anticipating the signing, the stock market suffered its worst collapse since November 1929, and the law quickly helped push the Great Depression deeper.

The new tariffs, which by 1932 rose to an all-time high of 59 percent of the average value of imports (today it's 5 percent), were designed to save American jobs by restricting foreign competition. Economists warned that angry nations would retaliate, and they did.

- Spain passed the Wais tariff in July in reaction to U.S. tariffs on grapes, oranges, cork, and onions.
- Switzerland, objecting to new U.S. tariffs on watches, embroideries, and shoes, boycotted American exports.
- Italy retaliated against tariffs on hats and olive oil with high tariffs on U.S. and French automobiles in June 1930.
- Canada reacted to high duties on many food products, logs, and timber by raising tariffs threefold in August 1932.

- Australia, Cuba, France, Mexico, and New Zealand also joined in the tariff wars.

From 1930 to 1931 U.S. imports dropped 29 percent, but U.S. exports fell even more, 33 percent, and continued their collapse to a modern-day low of $2.4 billion in 1933. World trade contracted by similar proportions, spreading unemployment around the globe.

In 1934 the U.S. Congress passed the Reciprocal Trade Agreements Act to empower the president to reduce tariffs by half the 1930 rates in return for like cuts in foreign duties on U.S. goods. The "beggar-thy-neighbor" policy was dead. Since then, the nations of the world have been reducing tariffs and other trade barriers.

Source: World Bank, *World Development Report 1987;* and *The Wall Street Journal,* April 28, 1989, Reprinted by permission of The Wall Street Journal, © 1989 Dow Jones & Company. All rights reserved. www.worldbank.org; www.wsj.com

Analysis: Tariffs inflict harm on foreign producers. If foreign countries retaliate with tariffs of their own, world trade will shrink and unemployment will increase in all countries.

Comparative Effects

Quotas, like all barriers to trade, reduce world efficiency and invite retaliatory action. Moreover, their impact can be even more damaging than tariffs. To see this, we may compare market outcomes in four different contexts: no trade, free trade, tariff-restricted trade, and quota-restricted trade.

No-Trade Equilibrium. Figure 20.4*a* depicts the supply-and-demand relationships that would prevail in an economy that imposed a trade *embargo* on foreign textiles. In this situation, the **equilibrium price** of textiles is completely determined by domestic demand and supply curves. The no-trade equilibrium price is p_1, and the quantity of textiles consumed is q_1.

> **equilibrium price:** The price at which the quantity of a good demanded in a given time period equals the quantity supplied.

Free-Trade Equilibrium. Suppose now that the embargo is lifted. The immediate effect of this decision will be a rightward shift of the market supply curve, as foreign supplies are added to domestic supplies (Figure 20.4*b*). If an unlimited quantity of textiles can be bought in world markets at a price of p_2, the new supply curve will look like S_2 (infinitely elastic at p_2). The new supply curve (S_2) intersects the old demand curve (D_1) at a new equilibrium price of p_2 and an expanded consumption of q_2. At this new equilibrium, domestic producers are supplying the quantity q_d while foreign producers are supplying the rest ($q_2 - q_d$). Comparing the new equilibrium to the old one, we see that *free trade results in reduced prices and increased consumption.*

Domestic textile producers are unhappy, of course, with their foreign competition. In the absence of trade, the domestic producers would sell more output (q_1) and get higher prices (p_1). Once trade is opened up, the willingness of foreign producers to sell unlimited quantities of textiles at the price p_2 puts a lid on domestic prices.

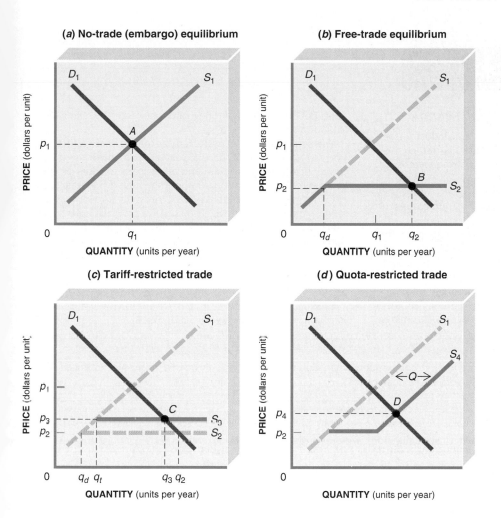

FIGURE 20.4
The Impact of Trade Restrictions

In the *absence of trade,* the domestic price and sales of a good will be determined by domestic supply and demand curves (point *A* in part *a*). Once trade is permitted, the market supply curve will be altered by the availability of imports. With *free trade* and unlimited availability of imports at price p_2, a new market equilibrium will be established at world prices (point *B*).

Tariffs raise domestic prices and reduce the quantity sold (point *C*). *Quotas* put an absolute limit on imported sales and thus give domestic producers a great opportunity to raise the market price (point *D*).

Tariff-Restricted Trade. Figure 20.4*c* illustrates what would happen to prices and sales if the United Textile Producers were successful in persuading the government to impose a tariff. Assume that the tariff raises imported textile prices from p_2 to p_3, making it more difficult for foreign producers to undersell domestic producers. Domestic production expands from q_d to q_1, imports are reduced from $q_2 - q_d$ to $q_3 - q_t$, and the market price of textiles rises. Domestic textile producers are clearly better off, whereas consumers and foreign producers are worse off. In addition, the U.S. Treasury will collect increased tariff revenues.

Quota-Restricted Trade. Now consider the impact of a textile *quota*. Suppose we eliminate tariffs but decree that imports can't exceed the quantity Q. Because the quantity of imports can never exceed Q, the supply curve is effectively shifted to the right by that amount. The new curve S_4 (Figure 20.4*d*) indicates that no imports will occur below the world price p_2 and above that price the quantity Q will be imported. Thus, the *domestic* demand curve determines subsequent prices. Foreign producers are precluded from selling greater quantities as prices rise further. This outcome is in marked contrast to that of tariff-restricted trade (Figure 20.4*c*), which at least permits foreign producers to respond to rising prices. Accordingly, *quotas are a greater threat to competition than tariffs, because quotas preclude additional imports at any price.* The actual quotas on textile imports raise the prices of shirts, towels, and other textile products by 58 percent. As a result, a $10 shirt ends up costing consumers $15.80. All told, U.S. consumers end up paying an extra $25 billion a year for textile products.

Differing views on the cost of sugar quotas are offered by The Foundation for American Communications at www.facsnet.org and by the Sugar Alliance at www.sugaralliance.org and at www.opensecrets.org.

Some See Bush Sheltering Sugar for Votes

The Bush administration is shielding the sugar industry from competition in a new trade pact with Australia, rather than damage the president's re-election hopes in swing states such as Florida and Michigan, industry groups say. . . .

"It all boils down to electoral politics. It's very raw," says Sarah Thorn, a lobbyist at the Grocery Manufacturers of America. . . .

President Bush edged Al Gore four years ago after the Supreme Court ruled on the vote in Florida, the biggest sugar-producing state. Michigan and Minnesota, home to thousands of sugar beet growers, are considered up for grabs this fall.

The industry is among the largest contributors to both parties. Growers and processors, along with makers of corn-based sweetener, made $25.5 million in political action committee contributions and soft money gifts between 1997 and June 2003, Common Cause says.

The sugar industry is protected by quotas that restrict imports to about 15% of the U.S. market. The government also has a price-support program and offers loans to sugar processors, who can repay in sugar rather than cash if prices fall. . . .

Critics of the program say U.S. growers and processors aren't globally competitive. They say the program hurts sugar users such as candymakers and forces consumers to pay inflated prices. U.S. sugar prices last year were 21.4 cents a pound, nearly three times the world price of 7.5 cents a pound.

—James Cox

Source: *USA Today*, February 11, 2004. USA TODAY. Copyright 2004. Reprinted with permission. www.usatoday.com

Analysis: Import quotas preclude increased foreign competition when domestic prices rise. Protected domestic producers enjoy higher prices and profits while consumers pay higher prices.

The sugar industry is one of the greatest beneficiaries of quota restrictions. By limiting imports to 15 percent of domestic consumption, sugar quotas keep U.S. prices artificially high (see News). This costs consumers nearly $2 billion a year in higher prices. Candy and soda producers lose sales and profits. Foreign sugar producers (mainly in poor nations) lose sales and income. Who gains? Domestic sugar producers—who, coincidentally, are highly concentrated in key electoral states.

Voluntary Restraint Agreements

voluntary restraint agreement (VRA): An agreement to reduce the volume of trade in a specific good; a voluntary quota.

A slight variant of quotas has been used in recent years. Rather than impose quotas on imports, the U.S. government asks foreign producers to "voluntarily" limit their exports. These so-called **voluntary restraint agreements** have been negotiated with producers in Japan, South Korea, Taiwan, China, the European Union, and other countries. Korea, for example, agreed to reduce its annual shoe exports to the United States from 44 million pairs to 33 million pairs. Taiwan reduced its shoe exports from 156 million pairs to 122 million pairs per year. In 1989, China agreed to slow its exports of clothing, limiting its sales growth to 3 percent a year. For their part, the Japanese agreed to reduce sales of color TV sets in the United States from 2.8 million to 1.75 million per year. In 1989, President George H. Bush extended voluntary restraint agreements on foreign steel exports, limiting imported steel to 18.4 percent of total U.S. sales. In 1996, President Clinton forced Canada to limit its exports of lumber to the United States, and in 1999, Russia reluctantly agreed to limit steel exports.

All these voluntary export restraints, as they're often called, represent an informal type of quota. The only difference is that they're negotiated rather than imposed. But these differences are lost on consumers, who end up paying higher prices for these goods. The voluntary limit on Japanese auto exports to the United States alone cost consumers $15.7 billion in only four years.

Nontariff Barriers

Tariffs and quotas are the most visible barriers to trade, but they're only the tip of the iceberg. Indeed, the variety of protectionist measures that have been devised is testimony to the ingenuity of the human mind. At the turn of the century, the Germans were committed to a most-favored-nation policy, a policy of extending equal treatment

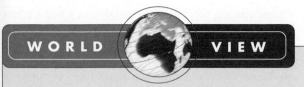

WORLD VIEW

High Court Opens U.S. Roads to Mexican Trucks

The Supreme Court ruled yesterday that the Bush administration can open U.S. roads to Mexican trucks as soon as it wants, overruling a lower court judgment that the government must first study the environmental effects.

Under NAFTA, which went into effect in 1994, the United States was supposed to phase out restrictions on Mexican trucks crossing the border by 2000, provided those trucks meet U.S. safety standards. But under pressure from members of Congress and the Teamsters union, which feared losing jobs to low-wage Mexican drivers, the Clinton administration maintained the existing barriers, citing safety concerns. As a result, Mexican trucks have been confined to a 20-mile zone along the border, where they transfer their loads to U.S. carriers in cities such as San Diego and Laredo, Tex.

The Bush administration vowed to open the border in 2001 after a NAFTA panel held that Washington was violating the agreement.

—Paul Blustein

Source: *The Washington Post*, June 8, 2004. © 2004 The Washington Post. Reprinted with permission.

Analysis: Nontariff barriers like extraordinary safety requirements on Mexican trucks limit import competition.

to all trading partners. The Germans, however, wanted to lower the tariff on cattle imports from Denmark without extending the same break to Switzerland. Such a preferential tariff would have violated the most-favored-nation policy. Accordingly, the Germans created a new and higher tariff on "brown and dappled cows reared at a level of at least 300 meters above sea level and passing at least one month in every summer at an altitude of at least 800 meters." The new tariff was, of course, applied equally to all countries. But Danish cows never climb that high, so they weren't burdened with the new tariff.

With the decline in tariffs over the last 20 years, nontariff barriers have increased. The United States uses product standards, licensing restrictions, restrictive procurement practices, and other nontariff barriers to restrict roughly 15 percent of imports. In 1999–2000, the European Union banned imports of U.S. beef, arguing that the use of hormones on U.S. ranches created a health hazard for European consumers. Although both the U.S. government and the World Trade Organization disputed that claim, the ban was a highly effective nontariff trade barrier. The United States responded by slapping 100 percent tariffs on dozens of European products. In 2001, the U.S. Congress blocked Mexican trucks from open access to U.S. highways. Although the safety of Mexican trucks was spotlighted, the underlying motive was to limit competition in the multibillion-dollar U.S. transport services market. It took a U.S. Supreme Court ruling to open the roads to foreign competition (see World View).

"TELL ME AGAIN HOW THE QUOTAS ON JAPANESE CARS HAVE PROTECTED US"

—from *Herblock at Large* (Pantheon Books, 1987).

Analysis: Trade restrictions that protect import-competing industries also raise consumer prices.

THE ECONOMY TOMORROW

An Increasingly Global Market

Proponents of free trade and representatives of special interests that profit from trade protection are in constant conflict. But most of the time the trade-policy deck seems stacked in favor of the special interests. Because the interests of import-competing firms and workers are highly concentrated, they're quick to mobilize politically. By contrast, the benefits of freer trade are less direct and spread over millions of consumers. As a consequence, the beneficiaries of freer trade are less likely to monitor trade policy—much less lobby actively to change it. Hence, the political odds favor the spread of trade barriers.

Multilateral Trade Pacts

Despite these odds, the long-term trend is toward *lowering* trade barriers, thereby increasing global competition. Two forces encourage this trend. The principal barrier to protectionist policies is worldwide recognition of the gains from freer trade. Since world nations now understand that trade barriers are ultimately self-defeating, they're more willing to rise above the din of protectionist cries and dismantle trade barriers. They diffuse political opposition by creating across-the-board trade pacts that seem to spread the pain (and gain) from freer trade across a broad swath of industries. Such pacts also incorporate multiyear timetables that give affected industries time to adjust.

The opposition of import-competing industries to these multilateral, multiyear trade pacts is countered by a second force: the interests of *export*-oriented industries and other multilateral firms. Barriers to auto imports from Japan may keep out cars produced by General Motors in that country. Tariffs on imported steel raise product costs for U.S.-based auto producers. Foreign retaliation to our trade barriers may hurt our own exports. Increasing awareness of such damage has created a political climate for freer trade.

Global Pacts: GATT and WTO

The granddaddy of the multilateral, multiyear free-trade pacts was the 1947 *General Agreement on Tariffs and Trade (GATT)*. Twenty-three nations pledged to reduce trade barriers and give all GATT nations equal access to their domestic markets.

Since the first GATT pact, seven more "rounds" of negotiations have expanded the scope of GATT: 117 nations signed the 1994 pact. As a result of these GATT pacts, average tariff rates in developed countries have fallen from 40 percent in 1948 to less than 4 percent today.

WTO. The 1994 GATT pact also created the *World Trade Organization (WTO)* to enforce free-trade rules. If a nation feels its exports are being unfairly excluded from another country's market, it can file a complaint with the WTO. This is exactly what the United States did when the European Union (EU) banned U.S. beef imports. The WTO ruled in favor of the United States. When the EU failed to lift its import ban, the WTO authorized the United States to impose retaliatory tariffs on European exports.

The EU turned the tables on the United States in 2003. They complained to the WTO that U.S. tariffs on steel violated trade rules. The WTO agreed and gave the EU permission to impose retaliatory tariffs on $2.2 billion of U.S. exports. That prompted the Bush administration to scale back the tariffs in December 2003.

In effect, the WTO is now the world's trade police force. It is empowered to cite nations that violate trade agreements and even to impose remedial action when violations persist. Why do sovereign nations give the WTO such power? Because they are all convinced that free trade is the surest route to GDP growth.

WTO Protests. Although freer trade clearly boosts economic growth, some people say that it does more harm than good. Environmentalists question the very desirability of continued economic growth. They worry about the depletion of resources, congestion and pollution, and the social friction that growth often promotes. Labor organizations worry that global competition will depress wages and working conditions. And many Third World nations are concerned about playing by trade rules that always seem to benefit rich nations (e.g., copyright protection, import protection, farm subsidies).

Despite some tumultuous street protests (e.g., Seattle in 1999), WTO members continue the difficult process of dismantling trade barriers. The latest round of negotiations began in Daha, Qatar, in 2001. The key issue in the "Daha Round" has been

IN THE NEWS

NAFTA Reallocates Labor: Comparative Advantage at Work

More Jobs in These Industries		but . . .	Few Jobs in These Industries	
Agriculture	+10,600		Construction	−12,800
Metal products	+6,100		Medicine	−6,000
Electrical appliances	+5,200		Apparel	−5,900
Business services	+5,000		Lumber	−1,200
Motor vehicles	+5,000		Furniture	−400

Source: Congressional Budget Office.

The lowering of trade barriers between Mexico and the United States is changing the mix of output in both countries. New export opportunities create jobs in some industries while increased imports eliminate jobs in other industries. (Estimated gains and losses are during the first five years of NAFTA.)

Analysis: The specialization encouraged by free trade creates new jobs in export but reduces employment in import-competing industries. In the process, total world output increases.

farm subsidies in rich nations. Poor nations protest that farm subsidies in the United States and Europe not only limit their exports but also lower global farm prices (hurting farmers in developing nations). By the end of 2004, the WTO had secured pledges to reduce those farm subsidies.

Because worldwide trade pacts are so complex, many nations have also pursued *regional* free-trade agreements. In December 1992, the United States, Canada, and Mexico signed the *North American Free Trade Agreement (NAFTA)*, a 1,000 page document covering more than 9,000 products. The ultimate goal of NAFTA is to eliminate all trade barriers between these three countries. At the time of signing, intraregional tariffs averaged 11 percent in Mexico, 5 percent in Canada, and 4 percent in the United States. NAFTA requires that all tariffs between the three countries be eliminated by 2007. The pact also requires the elimination of specific nontariff barriers.

The NAFTA-initiated reduction in trade barriers substantially increased trade flows between Mexico, Canada, and the United States. It also prompted a wave of foreign investment in Mexico, where both cheap labor and NAFTA access were available. Overall, NAFTA accelerated economic growth and reduced inflationary pressures in all three nations. Some industries (like construction and apparel) suffered from the freer trade, but others (like trucking, farming, and finance) reaped huge gains (see News).

The *European Union* is another regional pact, but one that virtually eliminates national boundaries among 25 countries. The EU not only eliminates trade barriers but also enhances full intercountry mobility of workers and capital. In 1999, the EU nations also created a new currency (the euro) that has replaced the German mark, the French franc, and other national currencies. In effect, Europe has become one large, unified market. As trade barriers continue to fall around the world, the global marketplace is likely to become more like an open bazaar as well. The resulting increase in competition should spur efficiency and growth in the economy tomorrow.

Regional Pacts: NAFTA and EU

To see how detailed a trade pact can be, access the NAFTA pact at www.nafta-sec-alena.org.

SUMMARY

- International trade permits each country to specialize in areas of relative efficiency, increasing world output. For each country, the gains from trade are reflected in consumption possibilities that exceed production possibilities.
- One way to determine where comparative advantage lies is to compare the quantity of good A that must be given up in order to get a given quantity of good B from domestic production. If the same quantity of B can be obtained for less A by engaging in world trade, we have a comparative advantage in the production of good A. Comparative advantage rests on a comparison of relative opportunity costs.
- The terms of trade—the rate at which goods are exchanged—are subject to the forces of international supply and demand. The terms of trade will lie somewhere between the opportunity costs of the trading partners. The terms of trade determine how the gains from trade are shared.

- Resistance to trade emanates from workers and firms that must compete with imports. Even though the country as a whole stands to benefit from trade, these individuals and companies may lose jobs and incomes in the process.
- Trade barriers take many forms. Embargoes are outright prohibitions against import or export of particular goods. Quotas limit the quantity of a good imported or exported. Tariffs discourage imports by making them more expensive. Other nontariff barriers make trade too costly or time-consuming.
- The World Trade Organization (WTO) seeks to reduce worldwide trade barriers and enforce trade rules. Regional accords such as the European Union (EU) and North American Free Trade Agreement (NAFTA) pursue similar objectives among fewer countries.

Key Terms

imports	comparative advantage	tariff
exports	opportunity cost	quota
trade deficit	absolute advantage	equilibrium price
trade surplus	terms of trade	voluntary restraint agreement (VRA)
production possibilities	dumping	
consumption possibilities	embargo	

Questions for Discussion

1. Suppose a lawyer can type faster than any secretary. Should the lawyer do her own typing? Can you demonstrate the validity of your answer?
2. What would be the effects of a law requiring bilateral trade balances?
3. If a nation exported much of its output but imported little, would it be better or worse off? How about the reverse, that is, exporting little but importing a lot?
4. How does international trade restrain the price behavior of domestic firms?
5. Suppose we refused to sell goods to any country that reduced or halted its exports to us. Who would benefit and who would lose from such retaliation? Can you suggest alternative ways to ensure import supplies?

6. Domestic producers often base their claim for import protection on the fact that workers in country X are paid substandard wages. Is this a valid argument for protection?
7. Based on the News on page 425, how do U.S. furniture manufacturers feel about NAFTA? How about farmers?
8. Who would gain or lose from the proposed Wine Equity Act? (See the News, page 415.)
9. Who pays for sugar quotas? (See News, page 422.) How could the quotas be eliminated?
10. Who gains and who loses from restrictions on the access of Mexican trucks to U.S. markets? (See World View, page 423.)

PROBLEMS   The Student Problem Set at the back of this book contains numerical and graphing problems for this chapter.

WEB ACTIVITIES   to accompany this chapter can be found on the Online Learning Center: **http://www.mhhe.com/economics/schiller10**

International Finance

U S. textile, furniture, and shrimp producers want China to increase the value of the yuan. They say China's undervalued currency makes Chinese exports too cheap, undercutting American firms. On the other hand, Wal-Mart thinks a cheap yuan is a good thing, as it keeps prices low for the $12 *billion* of toys, tools, linens, and other goods it buys from China each year. Those low import prices help Wal-Mart keep its prices low and sales volume high.

This chapter examines how currency values affect trade patterns and ultimately the core questions of WHAT, HOW, and FOR WHOM to produce. We focus on the following questions:

- **What determines the value of one country's money as compared to the value of another's?**
- **What causes the international value of currencies to change?**
- **Should governments intervene to limit currency fluctuations?**

EXCHANGE RATES: THE GLOBAL LINK

As we saw in Chapter 20, the United States exports and imports a staggering volume of goods and services. Although we trade with nearly 200 nations around the world, we seldom give much thought to where imports come from and much less to how we acquire them. Most of the time, all we want to know is which products are available and at what price.

Suppose you want to buy a Magnavox DVD player. You don't have to know that Magnavox players are produced by the Dutch company Philips Electronics. And you certainly don't have to fly to the Netherlands to pick it up. All you have to do is drive to the nearest electronics store; or you can just "click and buy" at the Internet's virtual mall.

But you may wonder how the purchase of an imported product was so simple. Dutch companies sell their products in euros, the currency of Europe. But you purchase the DVD player in dollars. How is such an exchange possible?

There's a chain of distribution between your dollar purchase in the United States and the euro-denominated sale in the Netherlands. Somewhere along that chain someone has to convert your dollars into euros. The critical question for everybody concerned is how many euros we can get for our dollars—that is, what the **exchange rate** is. If we can get two euros for every dollar, the exchange rate is 2 euros = 1 dollar. Alternatively, we could note that the price of a euro is 50 U.S. cents when the exchange rate is 2 to 1. Thus, *an exchange rate is the price of one currency in terms of another.*

exchange rate: The price of one country's currency expressed in terms of another's; the domestic price of a foreign currency.

FOREIGN-EXCHANGE MARKETS

Most exchange rates are determined in foreign-exchange markets. Stop thinking of money as some sort of magical substance, and instead view it as a useful commodity that facilitates market exchanges. From that perspective, an exchange rate—the price of money—is subject to the same influences that determine all market prices: demand and supply.

The Demand for Dollars

When Daimler-Benz bought Chrysler in 1998, it paid $36 billion. When the Sony Corporation bought Columbia Pictures, it also needed dollars—over 3 billion of them! In both cases, the objective of the foreign investor was to acquire an American business. To attain their objectives, however, the buyers first had to buy *dollars*. The German and Japanese buyers had to exchange their own currency for American dollars.

Canadian tourists also need American dollars. Few American restaurants or hotels accept Canadian currency as payment for goods and services; they want to be paid in U.S. dollars. Accordingly, Canadian tourists must buy American dollars if they want to see the United States.

Europeans love iPods. The Apple Corporation, however, wants to be paid in U.S. dollars. Hence, European consumers must exchange their currencies for U.S. dollars if they want an iPod. Individual consumers can spend euros at their local electronics store. When they do so, however, they're initiating a series of market transactions that will end when Apple Corporation gets paid in U.S. dollars. In this case, some intermediary exchanges the European currency for American dollars.

Some foreign investors also buy U.S. dollars for speculative purposes. When the ruble collapsed, Russians feared that the value of the ruble would drop further and preferred to hold U.S. dollars. Barclay's Bank also speculates in dollars on occasions when it fears that the value of the British pound will drop.

All these motivations give rise to a demand for U.S. dollars. Specifically, *the market demand for U.S. dollars originates in*

- *Foreign demand for American exports* (including tourism).
- *Foreign demand for American investments.*
- *Speculation.*

Governments may also create a demand for dollars through currency *swaps* and other activities.

The Supply of Dollars

The *supply* of dollars arises from similar sources. On the supply side, however, it's Americans who initiate most of the exchanges. Suppose you take a trip to Mexico. You'll need to buy Mexican pesos at some point. When you do, you'll be offering to *buy* pesos by offering to *sell* dollars. In other words, **the demand *for foreign currency* represents a supply of U.S. dollars.**

When Americans buy BMW cars, they also supply U.S. dollars. American consumers pay for their BMWs in dollars. Somewhere down the road, however, those dollars will be exchanged for European euros. At that exchange, dollars are being *supplied* and euros *demanded.*

American corporations demand foreign exchange too. General Motors builds cars in Germany, Coca-Cola produces Coke in China, Exxon produces and refines oil all over the world. In nearly every such case, the U.S. firm must first build or buy some plant and equipment, using another country's factors of production. This activity requires foreign currency and thus becomes another component of our demand for foreign currency.

We may summarize these market activities by noting that **the supply of dollars originates in**

- *American demand for imports* (including tourism).
- *American investments in foreign countries.*
- *Speculation.*

As on the demand side, government intervention can also contribute to the supply of dollars.

Whether American consumers will choose to buy a BMW depends partly on what the car costs. The price tag isn't always apparent in international transactions. Remember that the BMW producer and workers want to be paid in their own currency. Hence, the *dollar* price of a BMW depends on two factors: (1) the German price of a BMW and (2) the *exchange rate* between U.S. dollars and euros. Specifically, the U.S. price of a BMW is

$$\text{Dollar price of BMW} = \text{euro price of BMW} \times \text{dollar price of euro}$$

Suppose the BMW company is prepared to sell a BMW for 100,000 euros and that the current exchange rate is 2 euros = $1. At these rates, a BMW will cost you

$$\text{Dollar price of BMW} = 100{,}000 \text{ euros} \times \frac{\$1}{2 \text{ euros}}$$

$$= \$50{,}000$$

If you're willing to pay this much for a shiny new BMW, you may do so at current exchange rates.

Now suppose the exchange rate changes from 2 euros = $1 to 1 euro = $1. *A higher dollar price for euros will raise the dollar costs of European goods.* In this case, the dollar price of a euro increases from $0.50 to $1. At this new exchange rate, the BMW plant in Germany is still willing to sell BMWs at 100,000 euros apiece. And German consumers continue to buy BMWs at that price. But this constant euro price now translates into a higher *dollar* price. Thus a BMW now costs you $100,000.

As the dollar price of a BMW rises, the number of BMWs sold in the United States will decline. As BMW sales decline, the quantity of euros demanded may decline as well. Thus, the quantity of foreign currency demanded declines when the exchange rate rises because foreign goods become more expensive and imports decline.[1] When the dollar price of European currencies actually increased in 1992, BMW decided to start producing cars in South Carolina. A year later Mercedes-Benz decided to produce cars in the United States as well. Sales of American-made BMWs and Mercedes no longer depend on the exchange rate of the U.S. dollars.

What's a euro? Read more about the European currency at www.europe-euro.com.

The Supply Curve. These market responses suggest that the supply of dollars is upward-sloping. If the value of the dollar rises, Americans will be able to buy more euros. As a result, the dollar price of imported BMWs will decline. American consumers will respond by demanding more imports, thereby supplying a larger quantity of dollars. The supply curve in Figure 21.1 shows how the quantity of dollars supplied rises as the value of the dollar increases.

The Demand Curve. The demand for dollars can be explained in similar terms. Remember that the demand for dollars arises from the foreign demand for U.S. exports and investments. If the exchange rate moves from 2 euros = $1 to 1 euro = $1, the euro price of dollars falls. As dollars become cheaper for Germans, all American exports effectively fall in price. Germans will buy more American products (including trips to Disney World) and therefore demand a greater quantity of dollars. In addition, foreign investors will perceive in a cheaper dollar the opportunity to buy U.S. stocks, businesses, and property at fire-sale prices. Accordingly, they join foreign consumers in demanding more dollars. Not all these behavioral responses will occur overnight, but they're reasonably predictable over a brief period of time.

---

[1]The extent to which imports decline as the cost of foreign currency rises depends on the *price elasticity of demand*.

FIGURE 21.1

The Foreign-Exchange Market

The foreign-exchange market operates like other markets. In this case, the "good" bought and sold is dollars (foreign exchange). The price and quantity of dollars actually exchanged are determined by the intersection of market supply and demand.

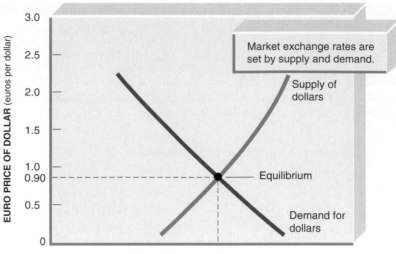

Equilibrium

equilibrium price: The price at which the quantity of a good demanded in a given time period equals the quantity supplied.

Given market demand and supply curves, we can predict the **equilibrium price** of any commodity, that is, the price at which the quantity demanded will equal the quantity supplied. This occurs in Figure 21.1 where the two curves cross. At that equilibrium, the value of the dollar (the exchange rate) is established. In this case, the euro price of the dollar turns out to be 0.90.

The value of the dollar can also be expressed in terms of other currencies. The World View below displays a sampling of dollar exchange rates in August 2004.

Foreign-Exchange Rates

The foreign exchange mid-range rates below apply to trading among banks in amounts of $1 million and more, as quoted at 4 P.M. Eastern time by Reuters and other sources. Retail transactions provide fewer units of foreign currency per dollar.

Country	U.S. Dollar per Unit (dollar price of foreign currency)	Currency per U.S. Dollar (foreign price of U.S. dollar)
Brazil (real)	0.3292	3.0377
Britain (pound)	1.8211	0.5491
Canada (dollar)	0.7523	1.3293
China (renminbi)	0.1208	8.2781
Indonesia (rupiah)	0.0001	9,141.00
Japan (yen)	0.0090	111.20
Mexico (peso)	0.0876	11.4155
Russia (ruble)	0.0344	29.104
Euroland (euro)	1.2024	0.8317

Source: *The Wall Street Journal,* August 2, 2004. Reprinted by permission of *The Wall Street Journal,* © 2004 Dow Jones & Company, Inc. All rights reserved worldwide. www.wsj.com

Analysis: The exchange rates between currencies are determined by supply and demand in foreign-exchange markets. The rates reported here represent the equilibrium exchange rates on a particular day.

(Notice how many Indonesian rupiah you could buy for $1.) The *average* value of the dollar is a weighted mean of the exchange rates between the U.S. dollar and all these currencies. The value of the dollar is "high" when its foreign-exchange price is above recent levels, "low" when it is below recent averages.

The equilibrium depicted in Figure 21.1 determines not only the *price* of the dollar but also a specific *quantity* of international transactions. Those transactions include the exports, imports, international investments, and other sources of dollar supply and demand. A summary of all those international money flows is contained in the **balance of payments**—an accounting statement of all international money flows in a given period of time.

Trade Balance. Table 21.1 depicts the U.S. balance of payments for 2003. Notice first how the millions of separate transactions are classified into a few summary measures. The trade balance is the difference between exports and imports of goods (merchandise) and services. In 2003, the United States imported over $1.5 trillion of goods and services but exported only $1 trillion. This created a **trade deficit** of $498 billion. That trade deficit represents a net outflow of dollars to the rest of the world.

$$\text{Trade balance} = \text{exports} - \text{imports}$$

The excess supply of dollars created by the trade gap widened further by other net outflows. U.S. government grants to foreign nations (line 7 in Table 21.1) contributed $94 billion to the net *supply* of dollars.

Current-Account Balance. The current-account balance is a subtotal in Table 21.1. It includes the merchandise, services, and investment balances as well as government grants and private transfers such as wages sent home by foreign citizens working in the United States.

$$\frac{\text{Current-account}}{\text{balance}} = \frac{\text{trade}}{\text{balance}} + \frac{\text{unilateral}}{\text{transfers}}$$

The current-account balance is the most comprehensive summary of our trade relations. As indicated in Table 21.1, the United States had a current-account deficit of $530 billion in 2003.

Item	Amount ($ billions)
1. Merchandise exports	$713
2. Merchandise imports	(1,261)
3. Service exports	307
4. Service imports	(256)
Trade balance (items 1–4)	−497
5. Income from U.S. overseas investments	188
6. Income outflow for foreign-owned U.S. investments	(69)
7. Net U.S. government grants	(94)
8. Net private transfers and pensions	(57)
Current-account balance (items 1–8)	−530
9. U.S. capital inflow	581
10. U.S. capital outflow	(285)
11. Increase in U.S. official reserves	(2)
12. Increase in foreign official assets in U.S.	249
Capital-account balance (items 9–12)	547
13. Statistical discrepancy	−13
Net balance (items 1–13)	0

Source: U.S. Department of Commerce (2003 data).

The Balance of Payments

balance of payments: A summary record of a country's international economic transactions in a given period of time.

trade deficit: The amount by which the value of imports exceeds the value of exports in a given time period.

TABLE 21.1
The U.S. Balance of Payments

The balance of payments is a summary statement of a country's international transactions. The major components of that activity are the trade balance (merchandise exports minus merchandise imports), the current-account balance (trade, services, and transfers), and the capital-account balance. The net total of these balances must equal zero, since the quantity of dollars paid must equal the quantity received.

Capital-Account Balance. The current-account deficit is offset by the capital-account surplus. The capital-account balance takes into consideration assets bought and sold across international borders; that is,

$$\text{Capital-account balance} = \text{foreign purchases of U.S. assets} - \text{U.S. purchases of foreign assets}$$

As Table 21.1 shows, foreign consumers demanded $581 billion worth of dollars in 2003 to buy farms and factories as well as U.S. bonds, stocks, and other investments (item 9). This exceeded the flow of U.S. dollars going overseas to purchase foreign assets (item 10). In addition, the United States and foreign governments bought and sold dollars, creating an additional outflow of dollars (items 11 and 12).

The net capital inflows were essential in financing the U.S. trade deficit (negative trade balance). As in any market, the number of dollars demanded must equal the number of dollars supplied. Thus, ***the capital-account surplus must equal the current-account deficit.*** In other words, there can't be any dollars left lying around unaccounted for. Item 13 in Table 21.1 reminds us that our accounting system isn't perfect—that we can't identify every transaction. Nevertheless, all the accounts must eventually "balance out":

$$\text{Net balance of payments} = \text{current-account balance} + \text{capital-account balance} = 0$$

That's the character of a market *equilibrium:* The quantity of dollars demanded equals the quantity of dollars supplied.

MARKET DYNAMICS

The interesting thing about markets isn't their character in equilibrium but the fact that prices and quantities are always changing in response to shifts in demand and supply. The U.S. demand for BMWs shifted overnight when Japan introduced a new line of sleek, competitively priced cars (e.g., Lexus). The reduced demand for BMWs shifted the supply of dollars leftward. That supply shift raised the value of the dollar vis-á-vis the euro, as illustrated in Figure 21.2. (It also increased the demand for Japanese yen, causing the yen value of the dollar to *fall.*)

Depreciation and Appreciation

depreciation (currency): A fall in the price of one currency relative to another.

appreciation: A rise in the price of one currency relative to another.

Exchange-rate changes have their own terminology. **Depreciation** of a currency occurs when one currency becomes cheaper in terms of another currency. In our earlier discussion of exchange rates, for example, we assumed that the exchange rate between euros and dollars changed from 2 euros = $1 to 1 euro = $1, making the euro price of a dollar cheaper. In this case, the dollar *depreciated* with respect to the euro.

The other side of depreciation is **appreciation,** an increase in value of one currency as expressed in another country's currency. ***Whenever one currency depreciates, another currency must appreciate.*** When the exchange rate changed from 2 euros = $1 to 1 euro = $1, not only did the euro price of a dollar fall, but also the dollar price of a euro rose. Hence, the euro appreciated as the dollar depreciated.

Figure 21.3 illustrates actual changes in the exchange rate of the U.S. dollar since 1980. The trade-adjusted value of the U.S. dollar is the (weighted) average of all exchange rates for the dollar. Between 1980 and 1985, the U.S. dollar appreciated over 80 percent. This appreciation greatly reduced the price of imports and thus increased their quantity. At the same time, the dollar appreciation raised the foreign price of U.S. exports and so reduced their volume. U.S. farmers, aircraft manufacturers, and tourist services suffered huge sales losses. The trade deficit ballooned.

The value of the dollar reversed course after 1985. This brief dollar depreciation set in motion forces that reduced the trade deficit in the late 1980s. Then the dollar

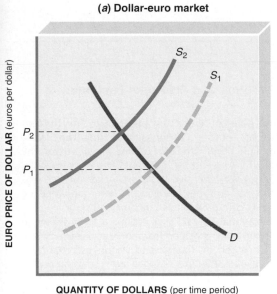

(a) Dollar-euro market

(b) Dollar-yen market

FIGURE 21.2
Shifts in Foreign-Exchange Markets

When the Japanese introduced luxury autos into the United States, the American demand for German cars fell. As a consequence, the supply of dollars in the dollar-euro market (part *a*) shifted to the left and the euro value of the dollar rose. At the same time, the increased American demand for Japanese cars shifted the dollar supply curve in the yen market (part *b*) to the right, reducing the yen price of the dollar.

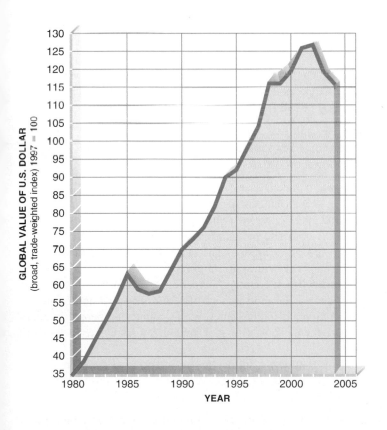

FIGURE 21.3
Changing Values of U.S. Dollar

Since 1973, exchange rates have been flexible. As a result, the value of the U.S. dollar has fluctuated with international differences in inflation, interest rates, and economic growth. U.S. economic stability has given the U.S. dollar increasing value over time.

Weak Dollar Helps U.S. Firms

The dollar's precipitous decline against European currencies has brought overseas customers to Al Lubrano's small Rhode Island manufacturing firm that he hasn't heard from in five years.

Gerry Letendre's manufacturing plant in New Hampshire just hired five employees to keep up with growing European demand, two and a half years after Letendre laid off a quarter of his work force.

The dollar's slide has made U.S. goods far cheaper for European consumers, and European exports considerably more expensive here. Letendre's Diamond Casting and Machine Co. in Hollis, N.H., has already boosted shipments of its circuit board printing equipment and industrial valves to Europe by 30 percent. Lubrano, president of Technical Materials Inc., in Lincoln, R.I., said his export business should jump as much as 25 percent this year.

"On balance, the weak dollar has been tremendous for us," Lubrano said.

—Jonathan Weisman

Source: *The Washington Post*, January 26, 2004. © 2004 The Washington Post. Reprinted with permission.

Dollar's Fall Puts Big Crimp in European Tourism

ROME—As the euro continues to strengthen against the battered U.S. dollar, tourists, businesses and Americans living abroad complain that Europe is pricing itself out of the market.

"It has become so expensive it almost makes me ill," says Nancy Oliveira, 55, an American living in Rome on what she says was once a "comfortable fixed income." . . .

The Italian National Tourist office reports a 15% decline in the number of Americans visiting from 2000 to 2002. . . .

Companies that rely on tourists and visitors estimate business is down 20% to 30%. . . .

Sales at Florence Moon, a leather store in Rome that caters primarily to Americans, are down 50%, says Farshad Shahabadi, whose family owns the store. "If it's bad for us, then it must be bad for everyone else, too," Shahabadi says.

—Ellen Hale

Source: *USA Today*, February 20, 2004. USA TODAY. Copyright 2004. Reprinted with permission. www.usatoday.com.

Analysis: Depreciation of a nation's currency is good for that nation's exporters but bad for that nation's importers (including its tourists).

started appreciating again, slowing export growth and increasing imports throughout the 1990s. After a long steep appreciation, the dollar started losing value in 2003. This was good for U.S. exporters, but bad for U.S. tourists (see World View).

Market Forces

Exchange rates change for the same reasons that any market price changes: The underlying supply or demand (or both) has shifted. Among the more important sources of such shifts are

- *Relative income changes.* If incomes are increasing faster in country A than in country B, consumers in A will tend to spend more, thus increasing the demand for B's exports and currency. B's currency will appreciate.
- *Relative price changes.* If domestic prices are rising rapidly in country A, consumers will seek out lower-priced imports. The demand for B's exports and currency will increase. B's currency will appreciate.
- *Changes in product availability.* If country A experiences a disastrous wheat crop failure, it will have to increase its food imports. B's currency will appreciate.
- *Relative interest rate changes.* If interest rates rise in country A, people in country B will want to move their deposits to A. Demand for A's currency will rise and it will appreciate.
- *Speculation.* If speculators anticipate an increase in the price of A's currency, for the preceding reasons or any other, they'll begin buying it, thus pushing its price up. A's currency will appreciate.

All these various changes are taking place every minute of every day, thus keeping **foreign-exchange markets** active. On an average day, over *$1 trillion* of foreign

foreign-exchange markets:
Places where foreign currencies are bought and sold.

Analysis: When the foreign price of the U.S. dollar rises (dollar appreciation), American exports (including educational services) become more expensive, which causes a decline in enrollments (quantity demanded).

exchange is bought and sold in the market. Significant changes occur in currency values, however, only when several of these forces move in the same direction at the same time. This is what caused the Asian crisis of 1997–98.

In July 1997, the Thai government decided the baht was overvalued and let market forces find a new equilibrium. Within days, the dollar prices of the baht plunged 25 percent. This sharp decline in the value of the Thai baht simultaneously increased the Thai price of the U.S. dollar. As a consequence, Thais could no longer afford to buy as many American products.

The devaluation of the baht had a domino effect on other Asian currencies. The plunge in the baht shook confidence in the Malaysian ringget, the Indonesian rupiah, and even the Korean won. People wanted to hold "hard" currencies like the U.S. dollar. As people rushed to buy U.S. dollars with their local currencies, the value of those currencies plunged. At one point the Indonesian rupiah had lost 80 percent of its dollar value, making U.S. exports five times more expensive for Indonesians. As a result, Indonesians could no longer afford to buy imported rice, machinery, cars, or pork. Indonesian students attending U.S. colleges could no longer afford to pay tuition (see World View). The sudden surge in prices and scarcity of goods led to street demonstrations and a change in government. Similar problems erupted throughout Southeast Asia.

The "Asian contagion" unfortunately wasn't confined to that area of the world. Hog farmers in the United States saw foreign demand for their pork evaporate. Koreans stopped taking vacations in Hawaii. Thai Airways canceled orders for Boeing jets. And Japanese consumers bought fewer Washington state apples and California oranges. This loss of export markets slowed economic growth in the United States, Europe, Japan, and other nations.

The Asian Crisis of 1997–98

Check out the latest exchange rates for the euro and the baht at www.x-rates.com.

RESISTANCE TO EXCHANGE-RATE CHANGES

Given the scope and depth of the Asian crisis of 1997–98, it's easy to understand why people crave *stable* exchange rates. The resistance to exchange-rate fluctuations originates in various micro- and macroeconomic interests.

WORLD VIEW

Nobel Prize Was Nobler in October

STOCKHOLM—Winners of the four Nobel science awards said yesterday that the honor is more important than the money, so it does not matter much that each award has lost $242,000 in value since October.

"If we had been more intelligent, we would have done some hedging," said Gary S. Becker, 61, a University of Chicago professor and a Nobel economics laureate. Sweden's decision last month to let the krona float caused the prizes' value to drop from $1.2 million each when announced in

October to $958,000 when King Carl XVI Gustaf presents them Thursday.

The recipients are Becker; American Rudolph A. Marcus, the chemistry laureate; Frenchman Georges Charpak, the physics laureate; and medicine prize winners Edmond Fischer and Edwin Krebs of the University of Washington in Seattle.

—Associated Press

Source: *Boston Globe*, December 8, 1992. Reprinted with permission of The Associated Press. www.ap.org.

Analysis: Currency depreciation reduces the external value of domestic income and assets. The dollar value of the Nobel Prize fell when the Swedish krona depreciated.

Micro Interests

The microeconomic resistance to changes in the value of the dollar arises from two concerns. First, people who trade or invest in world markets want a solid basis for forecasting future costs, prices, and profits. Forecasts are always uncertain, but they're even less dependable when the value of money is subject to change. An American firm that invests $2 million in a ski factory in Sweden expects not only to make a profit on the production there but also to return that profit to the United States. If the Swedish krona depreciates sharply in the interim, however, the profits amassed in Sweden may dwindle to a mere trickle, or even a loss, when the kronor are exchanged back into dollars. Even the Nobel Prize loses a bit of its luster when the krona depreciates (see World View). From this view, the uncertainty associated with fluctuating exchange rates is an unwanted burden.

Even when the direction of an exchange rate move is certain, those who stand to lose from the change are prone to resist. ***A change in the price of a country's money automatically alters the price of all its exports and imports.*** When the Russian ruble and Japanese yen depreciated in 2000–2001, for example, the dollar price of Russian and Japanese steel declined as well. This prompted U.S. steelmakers to accuse Russia and Japan of "dumping" steel. Steel companies and unions appealed to Washington to protect their sales and jobs.

Even in the country whose currency becomes cheaper, there'll be opposition to exchange-rate movements. When the U.S. dollar appreciates, Americans buy more foreign products. This increased U.S. demand for imports may drive up prices in other countries. In addition, foreign firms may take advantage of the reduced American competition by raising their prices. In either case, some inflation will result. The consumer's insistence that the government "do something" about rising prices may turn into a political force for "correcting" foreign-exchange rates.

Macro Interests

Any microeconomic problem that becomes widespread enough can turn into a macroeconomic problem. The huge U.S. trade deficits of the 1980s effectively exported jobs to foreign nations. Although the U.S. economy expanded rapidly in 1983–85, the unemployment rate stayed high, partly because American consumers were spending more of their income on imports. Yet fear of renewed inflation precluded more stimulative fiscal and monetary policies.

The U.S. trade deficits of the 1980s were offset by huge capital-account surpluses. Foreign investors sought to participate in the U.S. economic expansion by buying land, plant, and equipment and by lending money in U.S. financial markets. These capital inflows complicated monetary policy, however, and greatly increased U.S. foreign debt and interest costs.

The inflow of foreign investment also raised anxieties about "selling off" America. As Japanese and other foreign investors increased their purchases of farmland, factories, and real estate (e.g., Rockefeller Center), many Americans worried that foreign investors were taking control of the U.S. economy.

Fueling these fears was the dramatic change in America's international financial position. From 1914 to 1984, the United States had been a net creditor in the world economy. We owned more assets abroad than foreign investors owned in the United States. Our financial position changed in 1985. Continuing trade deficits and offsetting capital inflows transformed the United States into a net debtor in that year. Since then, foreigners have owned more U.S. assets than Americans own of foreign assets.

America's new debtor status can complicate domestic policy. A sudden flight from U.S. assets could severely weaken the dollar and disrupt the domestic economy. To prevent that from occurring, policymakers must consider the impact of their decisions on foreign investors. This may necessitate difficult policy choices.

There's a silver lining to this cloud, however. The inflow of foreign investment is a reflection of confidence in the U.S. economy. Foreign investors want to share in our growth and profitability. In the process, their investments (like BMW's auto plant) expand America's production possibilities and stimulate still more economic growth.

Foreign investors actually assume substantial risk when they invest in the United States. If the dollar falls, the foreign value of their U.S. investments will decline. Hence, foreigners who've already invested in the United States have no incentive to start a flight from the dollar. On the contrary, a strong dollar protects the value of their U.S. holdings.

EXCHANGE-RATE INTERVENTION

Given the potential opposition to exchange-rate movements, governments often feel compelled to intervene in foreign-exchange markets. The intervention is usually intended to achieve greater exchange-rate stability. But such stability may itself give rise to undesirable micro- and macroeconomic effects.

One way to eliminate fluctuations in exchange rates is to fix the rate's value. To fix exchange rates, each country may simply proclaim that its currency is worth so much in relation to that of other countries. The easiest way to do this is for each country to define the worth of its currency in terms of some common standard. Under a **gold standard,** each country determines that its currency is worth so much gold. In so doing, it implicitly defines the worth of its currency in terms of all other currencies, which also have a fixed gold value. In 1944, the major trading nations met at Bretton Woods, New Hampshire, and agreed that each currency was worth so much gold. The value of the U.S. dollar was defined as being equal to 0.0294 ounce of gold, while the British pound was defined as being worth 0.0823 ounce of gold. Thus, the exchange rate between British pounds and U.S. dollars was effectively fixed at $1 = 0.357 pound, or 1 pound = $2.80 (or $2.80/0.0823 = $1/0.0294).

gold standard: An agreement by countries to fix the price of their currencies in terms of gold; a mechanism for fixing exchange rates.

Balance-of-Payments Problems. It's one thing to proclaim the worth of a country's currency; it's quite another to *maintain* the fixed rate of exchange. As we've observed, foreign-exchange rates are subject to continual and often unpredictable

FIGURE 21.4
Fixed Rates and Market Imbalance

If exchange rates are fixed, they can't adjust to changes in market supply and demand. Suppose the exchange rate is initially fixed at e_1. When the demand for British pounds increases (shifts to the right), an excess demand for pounds emerges. More pounds are demanded (q_D) at the rate e_1 than are supplied (q_S). This causes a balance-of-payments deficit for the United States.

market shortage: The amount by which the quantity demanded exceeds the quantity supplied at a given price; excess demand.

balance-of-payments deficit: An excess demand for foreign currency at current exchange rates.

balance-of-payments surplus: An excess demand for domestic currency at current exchange rates.

foreign-exchange reserves: Holdings of foreign exchange by official government agencies, usually the central bank or treasury.

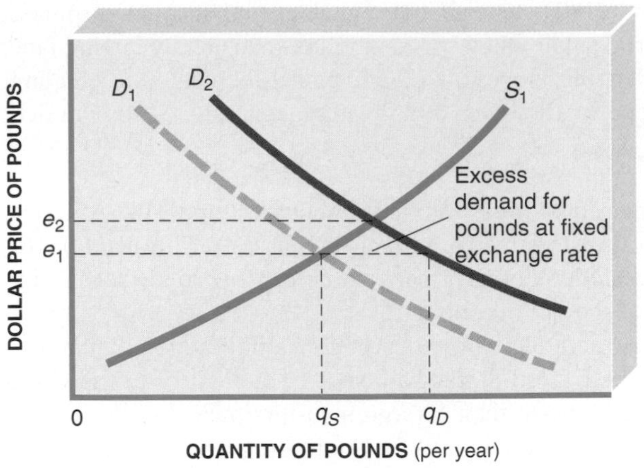

changes in supply and demand. Hence, two countries that seek to stabilize their exchange rate at some fixed value are going to find it necessary to compensate for such foreign-exchange market pressures.

Suppose the exchange rate officially established by the United States and Great Britain is equal to e_1, as illustrated in Figure 21.4. As is apparent, that particular exchange rate is consistent with the then-prevailing demand and supply conditions in the foreign-exchange market (as indicated by curves D_1 and S_1).

Now suppose that Americans suddenly acquire a greater taste for British cars and start spending more income on Jaguars and the like. Although Ford Motor owns Jaguar, the cars are still produced in Great Britain. Hence, as U.S. purchases of British goods increase, the demand for British currency will *shift* from D_1 to D_2 in Figure 21.4. Were exchange rates allowed to respond to market influences, the dollar price of a British pound would rise, in this case to the rate e_2. But we've assumed that government intervention has fixed the exchange rate at e_1. Unfortunately, at e_1, American consumers want to buy more pounds (q_D) than the British are willing to supply (q_s). The difference between the quantity demanded and the quantity supplied in the market at the rate e_1 represents a **market shortage** of British pounds.

The excess demand for pounds implies a **balance-of-payments deficit** for the United States: More dollars are flowing out of the country than into it. The same disequilibrium represents a **balance-of-payments surplus** for Britain, because its outward flow of pounds is less than its incoming flow.

Basically, there are only two solutions to balance-of-payments problems brought about by the attempt to fix exchange rates:

- Allow exchange rates to rise to e_2 (Figure 21.4), thereby eliminating the excess demand for pounds.
- Alter market supply or demand so that they intersect at the fixed rate e_1.

Since fixed exchange rates were the initial objective of policy, only the second alternative is of immediate interest.

The Need for Reserves. One way to alter market conditions would be for someone simply to supply British pounds to American consumers. The U.S. Treasury could have accumulated a reserve of foreign exchange in earlier periods. By selling some of those **foreign-exchange reserves** now, the Treasury could help to stabilize market conditions at the officially established exchange rate. The rightward shift of the pound supply curve in Figure 21.5 illustrates the sale of accumulated British pounds—and related purchase of U.S. dollars—by the U.S. Treasury. (In 2003, the U.S. Treasury increased foreign-exchange reserves by $2 billion; see item 12 in Table 21.1.)

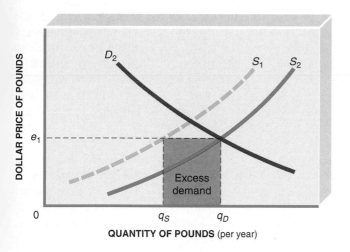

QUANTITY OF POUNDS (per year)

FIGURE 21.5
The Impact of Monetary Intervention

If the U.S. Treasury holds reserves of British pounds, it can use them to buy U.S. dollars in foreign-exchange markets. As it does so, the supply of pounds will shift to the right, to S_2, thereby maintaining the desired exchange rate, e_1. The Bank of England could bring about the same result by offering to buy U.S. dollars with pounds.

Although foreign-exchange reserves can be used to fix exchange rates, such reserves may not be adequate. Indeed, Figure 21.6 should be testimony enough to the fact that today's deficit isn't always offset by tomorrow's surplus. A principal reason that fixed exchange rates didn't live up to their expectations is that the United States had balance-of-payments deficits for 22 consecutive years. This long-term deficit overwhelmed our stock of foreign-exchange reserves.

The Role of Gold. Gold reserves are a potential substitute for foreign-exchange reserves. As long as each country's money has a value defined in terms of gold, we can use gold to buy British pounds, thereby restocking our foreign-exchange reserves. Or we can simply use the gold to purchase U.S. dollars in foreign-exchange markets. In either case, the exchange value of the dollar will tend to rise. However, we must have **gold reserves** available for this purpose. Unfortunately, the continuing U.S. balance-of-payments deficits recorded in Figure 21.6 exceeded even the hoards of gold buried under Fort Knox. As a consequence, our gold reserves lost their credibility as a potential guarantee of fixed exchange rates.

Domestic Adjustments. The supply and demand for foreign exchange can also be shifted by changes in basic fiscal, monetary, or trade policies. With respect to trade

gold reserves: Stocks of gold held by a government to purchase foreign exchange.

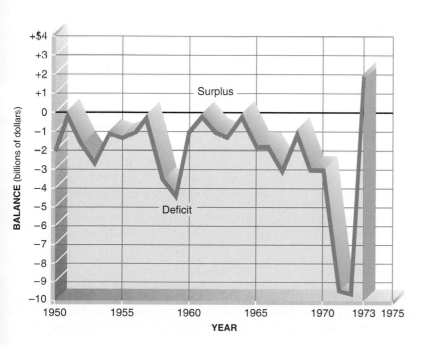

YEAR

FIGURE 21.6
The U.S. Balance of Payments, 1950–1973

The United States had a balance-of-payments deficit for 22 consecutive years. During this period, the foreign-exchange reserves of the U.S. Treasury were sharply reduced. Fixed exchange rates were maintained by the willingness of foreign countries to accumulate large reserves of U.S. dollars. However, neither the Treasury's reserves nor the willingness of foreigners to accumulate dollars was unlimited. In 1973, fixed exchange rates were abandoned.

policy, ***trade protection can be used to prop up fixed exchange rates.*** We could eliminate the excess demand for pounds (Figure 21.4), for example, by imposing quotas and tariffs on British goods. Such trade restrictions would reduce British imports to the United States and thus the demand for British pounds. In August 1971, President Nixon imposed an emergency 10 percent surcharge on all imported goods to help reduce the payments deficit that fixed exchange rates had spawned. Such restrictions on international trade, however, violate the principle of comparative advantage and thus reduce total world output. Trade protection also invites retaliatory trade restrictions.

Fiscal policy is another way out of the imbalance. An increase in U.S. income tax rates will reduce disposable income and have a negative effect on the demand for all goods, including imports. A reduction in government spending will have similar effects. In general, ***deflationary (or restrictive) policies help correct a balance-of-payments deficit by lowering domestic incomes and thus the demand for imports.***

Monetary policies in a deficit country could follow the same restrictive course. A reduction in the money supply will tend to raise interest rates. The balance of payments will benefit in two ways. The resultant slowdown in spending will reduce import demand. In addition, higher interest rates may induce international investors to move some of their funds into the deficit country. Such moves will provide immediate relief to the payments imbalance.[2] Russia tried this strategy in 1998, tripling key interest rates (to as much as 150 percent). But even that wasn't enough to restore confidence in the ruble, which kept depreciating. Within three months of the monetary policy tightening, the ruble lost half its value.

A surplus country could help solve the balance-of-payments problem. By pursuing expansionary—even inflationary—fiscal and monetary policies, a surplus country could stimulate the demand for imports. Moreover, any inflation at home will reduce the competitiveness of exports, thereby helping to restrain the inflow of foreign demand. Taken together, such efforts would help reverse an international payments imbalance.

Even under the best of circumstances, domestic economic adjustments entail significant costs. In effect, ***domestic adjustments to payments imbalances require a deficit country to forsake full employment and a surplus country to forsake price stability.*** China has had to grapple with these domestic consequences of fixing the value of its currency. The artificially low value of the yuan has promoted Chinese exports and accelerated China's GDP growth. It has also caused prices in China to rise faster than the government desires, however. To maintain the yuan's fixed exchange rate, the Chinese government began introducing restrictive monetary and fiscal policies in 2003–4. There's no easy way out of this impasse. Market imbalances caused by fixed exchange rates can be corrected only with abundant supplies of foreign-exchange reserves or deliberate changes in fiscal, monetary, or trade policies.

The Euro Fix. As noted earlier in the chapter, the original 12 nations of the European Monetary Union (EMU) did fix their exchange rates in 1999. They went far beyond the kind of exchange-rate fix we're discussing here. Members of the EMU *eliminated* their national currencies, making the euro the common currency of Euroland. They don't have to worry about reserve balances or domestic adjustments. However, they do have to reconcile their varied national interests to a single monetary authority, which may prove to be difficult politically in times of economic stress.

Flexible Exchange Rates

Balance-of-payments problems wouldn't arise in the first place if exchange rates were allowed to respond to market forces. Under a system of **flexible exchange rates** (often

---

[2]Before 1930, not only were foreign-exchange rates fixed, but domestic monetary supplies were tied to gold stocks as well. Countries experiencing a balance-of-payments deficit were thus forced to contract their money supply, and countries experiencing a payments surplus were forced to expand their money supply by a set amount. Monetary authorities were powerless to control domestic money supplies except by erecting barriers to trade. The system was abandoned when the world economy collapsed into the Great Depression.

called floating exchange rates), the exchange rate moves up or down to choke off any excess supply of or demand for foreign exchange. Notice again in Figure 21.4 that the exchange-rate move from e_1 to e_2 prevents any excess demand from emerging. *With flexible exchange rates, the quantity of foreign exchange demanded always equals the quantity supplied,* and there's no imbalance. For the same reason, there's no need for foreign-exchange reserves.

Although flexible exchange rates eliminate balance-of-payments and foreign-exchange reserves problems, they don't solve all of a country's international trade problems. *Exchange-rate movements associated with flexible rates alter relative prices and may disrupt import and export flows.* As noted before, depreciation of the dollar raises the price of all imported goods. The price increases may contribute to domestic cost-push inflation. Also, domestic businesses that sell imported goods or use them as production inputs may suffer sales losses. On the other hand, appreciation of the dollar raises the foreign price of U.S. goods and reduces the sales of American exporters. Hence, *someone is always hurt, and others are helped, by exchange-rate movements.* The resistance to flexible exchange rates originates in these potential losses. Such resistance creates pressure for official intervention in foreign-exchange markets or increased trade barriers.

The United States and its major trading partners abandoned fixed exchange rates in 1973. Although exchange rates are now able to fluctuate freely, it shouldn't be assumed that they necessarily undergo wild gyrations. On the contrary, experience with flexible rates since 1973 suggests that some semblance of stability is possible even when exchange rates are free to change in response to market forces.

Speculation. One force that often helps maintain stability in a flexible exchange-rate system is speculation. Speculators often counteract short-term changes in foreign-exchange supply and demand. If an exchange rate temporarily rises above its long-term equilibrium, speculators will move in to sell foreign exchange. By selling at high prices and later buying at lower prices, speculators hope to make a profit. In the process, they also help stabilize foreign-exchange rates.

Speculation isn't always stabilizing, however. Speculators may not correctly gauge the long-term equilibrium. Instead, they may move "with the market" and help push exchange rates far out of kilter. This kind of destabilizing speculation sharply lowered the international value of the U.S. dollar in 1987, forcing the Reagan administration to intervene in foreign-exchange markets, borrowing foreign currencies to buy U.S. dollars. In 1997, the Clinton administration intervened for the opposite purpose: stemming the rise in the

"Damn it! How can I relax, knowing that out there, somewhere, somehow, someone's attacking the dollar?"

Analysis: A "weak" dollar reduces the buying power of American tourists.

U.S. dollar. the Bush administration has been more willing to stay on the sidelines, lettin[ ] global markets set the exchange rates for the U.S. dollar.

Managed Exchange Rates. Governments can intervene in foreign-exchange mar[ ] kets without completely fixing exchange rates. That is, they may buy and sell foreig[ ] exchange for the purpose of *narrowing* rather than *eliminating* exchange-rate move[ ] ments. Such limited intervention in foreign-exchange markets is often referred to a[ ] **managed exchange rates,** or, popularly, "dirty floats."

> **managed exchange rates:** A system in which governments intervene in foreign-exchange markets to limit but not eliminate exchange-rate fluctuations; "dirty floats."

The basic objective of exchange-rate management is to provide a stabilizing force[ ] The U.S. Treasury, for example, may use its foreign-exchange reserves to buy dollar[ ] when they're depreciating too much. Or it will buy foreign exchange if the dollar i[ ] rising too fast. From this perspective, exchange-rate management appears as a fai[ ] safe system for the private market. Unfortunately, the motivation for official inter[ ] vention is sometimes suspect. Private speculators buy and sell foreign exchange fo[ ] the sole purpose of making a profit. But government sales and purchases may be moti[ ] vated by other considerations. A falling exchange rate increases the competitive advar[ ] tage of a country's exports. A rising exchange rate makes international investment les[ ] expensive. Hence, a country's efforts to manage exchange-rate movements may arous[ ] suspicion and outright hostility in its trading partners.

Although managed exchange rates would seem to be an ideal compromise betwee[ ] fixed rates and flexible rates, they can work only when some acceptable "rules of th[ ] game" and mutual trust have been established. As Sherman Maisel, a former gove[ ] nor of the Federal Reserve Board, put it, "Monetary systems are based on credit an[ ] faith: If these are lacking, a . . . crisis occurs."[3]

THE ECONOMY TOMORROW

Currency Bailouts

The world has witnessed a string of currency crises, including the one in As[ ] during 1997–98, the Brazilian crisis of 1999, the Argentine crisis of 2001–[ ] recurrent ruble crises in Russia, and periodic panics in Mexico and Sou[ ] America. In every instance, the country in trouble pleads for external help. In mo[ ] cases, a currency "bailout" is arranged, whereby global monetary authorities lend t[ ] troubled nation enough reserves (such as U.S. dollars) to defend its currency. Typicall[ ] the International Monetary Fund (IMF) heads the rescue party, joined by the centr[ ] banks of the strongest economies.

The Case for Bailouts

> **devaluation:** An abrupt depreciation of a currency whose value was fixed or managed by the government.

The argument for currency bailouts typically rests on the domino theory. Weakness[ ] one currency can undermine another. This seemed to be the case during the 1997–[ ] Asian crisis. After the **devaluation** of the Thai baht, global investors began worryi[ ] about currency values in other Asian nations. Choosing to be safe rather than sor[ ] they moved funds out of Korea, Malaysia, and the Philippines and invested in U.S. a[ ] European markets (notice in Figure 21.3 the 1997–98 appreciation of the U.S. dolla[ ]

The initial baht devaluation also weakened the competitive trade position of the[ ] same economies. Thai exports became cheaper, diverting export demand from oth[ ] Asian nations. To prevent loss of export markets, Thailand's neighbors felt they h[ ] to devalue as well. Speculators who foresaw these effects accelerated the domi[ ] effect by selling the region's currencies.

When Brazil devalued its currency (the *real*) in January 1999, global investors worri[ ] that a "samba effect" might sweep across Latin American (see World View). The domi[ ] effect could reach across the ocean and damage U.S. and European exports as well. Henc[ ] the industrial countries often offer a currency bailout as a form of self-defense.

[3]Sherman Maisel, *Managing the Dollar* (New York: W. W. Norton, 1973), p. 196.

WORLD   VIEW

Brazil's Ills Distress Continent
Money Crisis Shakes Investors' Confidence

BUENOS AIRES—Fallout from the continuing currency crisis in Brazil has sparked the most serious financial turmoil in Latin America since the Mexican peso crisis of four years ago, scaring away foreign investors and undermining growth after years of rapid gains.

In the days since Brazil, Latin America's largest nation, devalued its currency on January 12, a number of leading economists have scaled back their forecasts for Latin American growth, predicting it will be flat or negative for the first half of 1999.

The "samba effect," as Brazil's impact on its neighbors is called, is exacerbating regional unemployment rates and sending already high interest rates climbing. Even more significantly, perhaps, it is eroding foreign investment and confidence in the region amid fears that Brazil may default on its foreign debt despite government promises to the contrary.

To encourage investors to keep their money in Brazil, the central bank raised interest rates to stratospheric levels, with dire consequences for Brazilian borrowers. Economists predict that the world's eighth-largest economy will contract by 6 percent this year.

With the Brazilian real's value having fallen sharply, Brazil's neighbors, especially Argentina, are now discovering that one of their biggest markets has been closed off—essentially because of the weaker real, which has raised the price of imported goods in the nation of 165 million people.

—Anthony Faiola

Source: *The Washington Post*, February 1, 1999. © 1999 *The Washington Post*. Reprinted with permission. www.washingtonpost.com

Analysis: When a nation devalues its currency, its imports become more expensive and its exports cheaper. These price changes disrupt trade flows of other nations. Devaluations also shake the confidence of global investors.

The Case against Bailouts

Critics of bailouts argue that such interventions are ultimately self-defeating. They say that once a country knows for sure that currency bailouts are in the wings, it doesn't have to pursue the domestic policy adjustments that might stabilize its currency. A nation can avoid politically unpopular options such as high interest rates, tax hikes, or cutbacks in government spending. It can also turn a blind eye to trade barriers, monopoly power, lax lending policies, and other constraints on productive growth. Hence, the expectation of readily available bailouts may foster the very conditions that cause currency crises.

Future Bailouts?

The decision to bail out a depreciating currency isn't as simple as it appears. To minimize the ill effects of bailouts, the IMF and other institutions typically require the crisis nation to pledge more prudent monetary, fiscal, and trade policies. Usually there's a lot of debate about what kinds of adjustments will be made—and how soon. As long as the crisis nation is confident of an eventual bailout, however, it has a lot of bargaining power to resist policy changes. Only after the IMF finally said no to further bailouts in 2001 did Argentina devalue its currency and pursue more domestic reforms.

SUMMARY

- Money serves the same purposes in international trade as it does in the domestic economy, namely, to facilitate productive specialization and market exchanges. The basic challenge of international finance is to create acceptable standards of value from the various currencies maintained by separate countries.

- Exchange rates are the basic mechanism for translating the value of one national currency into the equivalent value of another. An exchange rate of $1 = 2 euros means that one dollar is worth two euros in foreign-exchange markets.

- Foreign currencies have value because they can be used to acquire goods and resources from other countries. Accordingly, the supply of and demand for foreign currency reflect the demands for imports and exports, for international investment, and for overseas activities of governments.

- The balance of payments summarizes a country's international transactions. Its components are the trade balance, the current-account balance, and the capital-account balance. The current and capital accounts must offset each other.

- The equilibrium exchange rate is subject to any and all shifts of supply and demand for foreign exchange. If relative incomes, prices, or interest rates change, the demand for foreign exchange will be affected. A depreciation is a change in market exchange rates that makes one country's currency cheaper in terms of another currency. An appreciation is the opposite kind of change.

- Changes in exchange rates are often resisted. Producers of export goods don't want their currencies to rise in value (appreciate); importers and people who travel dislike it when their currencies fall in value (depreciate).

- Under a system of fixed exchange rates, changes in the supply and demand for foreign exchange can't be expressed in exchange-rate movements. Instead, such shifts will be reflected in excess demand for or excess supply of foreign exchange. Such market imbalances are referred to as balance-of-payments deficits or surpluses.

- To maintain fixed exchange rates, monetary authorities must enter the market to buy and sell foreign exchange. In order to do so, deficit countries must have foreign-exchange reserves. In the absence of sufficient reserves, a country can maintain fixed exchange rates only if it's willing to alter basic fiscal, monetary, or trade policies.

- Flexible exchange rates eliminate balance-of-payments problems and the crises that accompany them. But complete flexibility can lead to excessive changes. To avoid this contingency, many countries prefer to adopt managed exchange rates, that is, rates determined by the market but subject to government intervention.

Key Terms

exchange rate
equilibrium price
balance of payments
trade deficit
depreciation (currency)
appreciation

foreign-exchange markets
gold standard
market shortage
balance-of-payments deficit
balance-of-payments surplus

foreign-exchange reserves
gold reserves
flexible exchange rates
managed exchange rates
devaluation

Questions for Discussion

1. Why would a decline in the value of the dollar prompt foreign manufacturers such as BMW to build production plants in the United States?

2. How do changes in the foreign value of the U.S. dollar affect foreign enrollments at U.S. colleges? (See World View, page 435.)

3. How would rapid inflation in Canada alter our demand for travel to Canada and for Canadian imports? Does it make any difference whether the exchange rate between Canadian and U.S. dollars is fixed or flexible?

4. Under what conditions would a country welcome a balance-of-payments deficit? When would it *not* want a deficit?

5. In what sense do fixed exchange rates permit a country to "export its inflation"?

6. In the World View on p. 434, who is Farshad Shahabadi referring to as "everyone else"?

7. If a nation's currency depreciates, are the reduced export prices that result "unfair"?

8. How would each of these events affect the supply or demand for Japanese yen?
   (a) Stronger U.S. economic growth.
   (b) A decline in Japanese interest rates.
   (c) Higher inflation in the USA.

9. Is a stronger dollar good or bad for America? Explain.

10. Who will gain and who will lose if China depreciates the yuan?

ALERT!

PROBLEMS The Student Problem Set at the back of this book contains numerical and graphing problems for this chapter.

WEB ACTIVITIES to accompany this chapter can be found on the Online Learning Center:
http://www.mhhe.com/economics/schiller10

GLOSSARY

Note: Numbers in parentheses indicate the chapters in which the definitions appear.

absolute advantage: The ability of a country to produce a specific good with fewer resources (per unit of output) than other countries. (20)

acreage set-aside: Land withdrawn from production as part of policy to increase crop prices. (14)

antitrust: Government intervention to alter market structure or prevent abuse of market power. (4)(9)(10)(12)

appreciation: A rise in the price of one currency relative to another. (21)

average fixed cost (AFC): Total fixed cost divided by the quantity produced in a given time period. (6)

average total cost (ATC): Total cost divided by the quantity produced in a given time period. (6)(8)(9)

average variable cost (AVC): Total variable cost divided by the quantity produced in a given time period. (6)

balance of payments: A summary record of a country's international economic transactions in a given period of time. (21)

balance-of-payments deficit: An excess demand for foreign currency at current exchange rates. (21)

balance-of-payments surplus: An excess demand for domestic currency at current exchange rates. (21)

barriers to entry: Obstacles such as patents that make it difficult or impossible for would-be producers to enter a particular market. (8)(9)(10)(11)(12)(13)(14)

bilateral monopoly: A market with only one buyer (a monopsonist) and one seller (a monopolist). (16)

bond: A certificate acknowledging a debt and the amount of interest to be paid each year until repayment; an IOU. (17)

breakeven level of income: The income level at which welfare eligibility ceases. (19)

budget constraint: A line depicting all combinations of goods that are affordable with a given income and given prices. (5)

capital: Final goods produced for use in the production of other goods, e.g., equipment, structures. (1)

capital gain: An increase in the market value of an asset. (17)

capital-intensive: Production processes that use a high ratio of capital to labor inputs. (2)

cartel: A group of firms with an explicit, formal agreement to fix prices and output shares in a particular market. (10)

cash transfers: Income transfers that entail direct cash payments to recipients, e.g., Social Security, welfare, and unemployment benefits. (19)

categorical grants: Federal grants to state and local governments for specific expenditure purposes. (4)

ceteris paribus: The assumption of nothing else changing. (1)(3)(5)

collective bargaining: Direct negotiations between employers and unions to determine labor market outcomes. (16)

comparative advantage: The ability of a country to produce a specific good at a lower opportunity cost than its trading partners. (2)(20)

competitive firm: A firm without market power, with no ability to alter the market price of the goods it produces. (7)

competitive market: A market in which no buyer or seller has market power. (8)

complementary goods: Goods frequently consumed in combination; when the price of good *x* rises, the demand for good *y* falls, *ceteris paribus.* (3)(5)

concentration ratio: The proportion of total industry output produced by the largest firms (usually the four largest). (10)(11)

constant returns to scale: Increases in plant size do not affect minimum average cost; minimum per-unit costs are identical for small plants and large plants. (6)

consumption possibilities: The alternative combinations of goods and services that a country could consume in a given time period. (20)

contestable market: An imperfectly competitive industry subject to potential entry if prices or profits increase. (9)(10)(12)

corporate stock: Shares of ownership in a corporation. (17)

corporation: A business organization having a continuous existence independent of its members (owners) and power and liabilities distinct from those of its members. (17)

cost efficiency: The amount of output associated with an additional dollar spent on input; the MPP of an input divided by its price (cost). (15)

counter-cyclical payment: Income transfer paid to farmers for difference between target and support prices. (14)

coupon rate: Interest rate set for a bond at time of issuance. (17)

cross-price elasticity of demand: Percentage change in the quantity demanded of *X* divided by percentage change in price of *Y.* (5)

cross-subsidization: Use of high prices and profits on one product to subsidize low prices on another product. (12)

current yield: The rate of return on a bond; the annual interest payment divided by the bond's price. (17)

default: Failure to make scheduled payments of interest or principal on a bond. (17)

demand: The willingness and ability to buy specific quantities of a good at alternative prices in a given time period, *ceteris paribus.* (3)(5)

demand curve: A curve describing the quantities of a good a consumer is willing and able to buy at alternative prices in a given time period, *ceteris paribus.* (3)(5)

demand for labor: The quantities of labor employers are willing and able to hire at alternative wage rates in a given time period, *ceteris paribus.* (15)(16)

demand schedule: A table showing the quantities of a good a consumer is willing and able to buy at alternative prices in a given time period, *ceteris paribus.* (3)

depreciation (currency): A fall in the price of one currency relative to another. (21)

derived demand: The demand for labor and other factors of production results from (depends on) the demand for final goods and services produced by these factors. (15)

devaluation: An abrupt depreciation of a currency whose value was fixed or managed by the government. (21)

dividend: Amount of corporate profits paid out for each share of stock. (17)

dumping: The sale of goods in export markets at prices below domestic prices. (20)

economic cost: The value of all resources used to produce a good or service; opportunity cost. (6)(7)

economic growth: An increase in output (real GDP); an expansion of production possibilities. (1)(2)

economic profit: The difference between total revenues and total economic costs. (7)(8)(11)(12)(14)

economics: The study of how best to allocate scarce resources among competing uses. (1)

economies of scale: Reductions in minimum average costs that come about through increases in the size (scale) of plant and equipment. (6)(9)(12)

effective tax rate: Taxes paid divided by total income. (18)

efficiency: Maximum output of a good from the resources used in production. (1)(6)(8)

efficiency decision: The choice of a production process for any given rate of output. (13)(15)

elasticity of labor supply: The percentage change in the quantity of labor supplied divided by the percentage change in wage rate. (15)

embargo: A prohibition on exports or imports. (20)

emission charge: A fee imposed on polluters, based on the quantity of pollution. (13)

entrepreneurship: The assembling of resources to produce new or improved products and technologies. (1)

equilibrium price: The price at which the quantity of a good demanded in a given time period equals the quantity supplied. (3)(8)(20)(21)

equilibrium wage: The wage rate at which the quantity of labor supplied in a given time period equals the quantity of labor demanded. (15)(16)

exchange rate: The price of one country's currency expressed in terms of another's; the domestic price of a foreign currency. (21)

expected value: The probable value of a future payment, including the risk of nonpayment. (17)

explicit costs: A payment made for the use of a resource. (6)(7)

exports: Goods and services sold to foreign buyers. (2)(20)

external costs: Costs of a market activity borne by a third party; the difference between the social and private costs of a market activity. (13)

externalities: Costs (or benefits) of a market activity borne by a third party; the difference between the social and private costs (benefits) of a market activity. (2)(4)(13)

factor market: Any place where factors of production (e.g., land, labor, capital) are bought and sold. (3)

factors of production: Resource inputs used to produce goods and services, e.g., land, labor, capital, entrepreneurship. (1)(2)(6)

financial intermediary: Institution (e.g., a bank or the stock market) that makes savings available to dissavers (e.g., investors). (17)

fixed costs: Costs of production that don't change when the rate of output is altered, e.g., the cost of basic plant and equipment. (6)(7)

flat tax: A single-rate tax system. (18)

flexible exchange rates: A system in which exchange rates are permitted to vary with market supply-and-demand conditions; floating exchange rates. (21)

foreign-exchange markets: Places where foreign currencies are bought and sold. (21)

foreign-exchange reserves: Holdings of foreign exchange by official government agencies, usually the central bank or treasury. (21)

free rider: An individual who reaps direct benefits from someone else's purchase (consumption) of a public good. (4)

game theory: The study of decision making in situations where strategic interaction (moves and countermoves) occurs between rivals. (10)

Gini coefficient: A mathematical summary of inequality based on the Lorenz curve. (18)

gold reserves: Stocks of gold held by a government to purchase foreign exchange. (21)

gold standard: An agreement by countries to fix the price of their currencies in terms of gold; a mechanism for fixing exchange rates. (21)

government failure: Government intervention that fails to improve economic outcomes. (1)(4)(12)(13)(18)

gross domestic product (GDP): The total market value of all final goods and services produced within a nation's borders in a given time period. (2)

Herfindahl-Hirshman Index (HHI): Measure of industry concentration that accounts for number of firms and size of each. (10)

horizontal equity: Principle that people with equal incomes should pay equal taxes. (18)

human capital: The knowledge and skills possessed by the workforce. (2)

implicit cost: The value of resources used, even when no direct payment is made. (6)(7)

imports: Goods and services purchased from international sources. (2)(20)

income effect of wages: An increased wage rate allows a person to reduce hours worked without losing income. (15)

income elasticity of demand: Percentage change in quantity demanded divided by percentage change in income. (5)(14)

income quintile: One-fifth of the population, rank-ordered by income (e.g., top fifth). (2)

income share: The proportion of total income received by a particular group. (18)

income transfers: Payments to individuals for which no current goods or services are exchanged, e.g., Social Security, welfare, unemployment benefits. (2)(18)

indifference curve: A curve depicting alternative combinations of goods that yield equal satisfaction. (5)

indifference map: The set of indifference curves that depicts all possible levels of utility attainable from various combinations of goods. (5)

inferior good: Good for which demand decreases when income rises. (5)

inflation: An increase in the average level of prices of goods and services. (4)

initial public offering (IPO): The first issuance (sale) to the general public of stock in a corporation. (17)

in-kind income: Goods and services received directly, without payment, in a market transaction. (18)

in-kind transfers: Direct transfers of goods and services rather than cash; examples include food stamps, Medicaid benefits, and housing subsidies. (19)

investment: Expenditures on (production of) new plant, equipment, and structures (capital) in a given time period, plus changes in business inventories. (2)

investment decision: The decision to build, buy, or lease plant and equipment; to enter or exit an industry. (7)(8)

labor-force participation rate: The percentage of the working-age population working or seeking employment. (19)

labor supply: The willingness and ability to work specific amounts of time at alternative wage rates in a given time period, *ceteris paribus.* (15)(16)(19)

laissez faire: The doctrine of "leave it alone," of nonintervention by government in the market mechanism. (1)(12)

law of demand: The quantity of a good demanded in a given time period increases as its price falls, *ceteris paribus.* (3)(5)

law of diminishing marginal utility: The marginal utility of a good declines as more of it is consumed in a given time period. (5)

law of diminishing returns: The marginal physical product of a variable input declines as more of it is employed with a given quantity of other (fixed) inputs. (6)(15)

law of supply: The quantity of a good supplied in a given time period increases as its price increases, *ceteris paribus.* (3)

liquidity: The ability of an asset to be converted into cash. (17)

loan rate: The implicit price paid by the government for surplus crops taken as collateral for loans to farmers. (14)

long run: A period of time long enough for all inputs to be varied (no fixed costs). (6)(7)

long-run competitive equilibrium: $p = \text{MC} = \text{minimum ATC}.$ (8)

Lorenz curve: A graphic illustration of the cumulative size distribution of income; contrasts complete equality with the actual distribution of income. (18)

macroeconomics: The study of aggregate economic behavior, of the economy as a whole. (1)

managed exchange rates: A system in which governments intervene in foreign-exchange markets to limit but not eliminate exchange-rate fluctuations; "dirty floats." (21)

marginal cost (MC): The increase in total cost associated with a one-unit increase in production. (6)(7)(8)

marginal cost pricing: The offer (supply) of goods at prices equal to their marginal cost. (8)(9)(11)(12)

marginal factor cost (MFC): The change in total costs that results from a one-unit increase in the quantity of a factor employed. (16)

marginal physical product (MPP): The change in total output associated with one additional unit of input. (6)(15)

marginal rate of substitution: The rate at which a consumer is willing to exchange one good for another; the relative marginal utilities of two goods. (5)

marginal revenue (MR): The change in total revenue that results from a one-unit increase in the quantity sold. (7)(9)(10)

marginal revenue product (MRP): The change in total revenue associated with one additional unit of input. (15)(16)(18)

marginal tax rate: The tax rate imposed on the last (marginal) dollar of income. (18)(19)

marginal utility: The change in total utility obtained by consuming one additional (marginal) unit of a good or service. (5)

marginal wage: The change in total wages paid associated with a one-unit increase in the quantity of labor employed. (16)

market demand: The total quantities of a good or service people are willing and able to buy at alternative prices in a given time period, the sum of individual demands. (3)

market failure: An imperfection in the market mechanism that prevents optimal outcomes. (1)(4)(10)(12)(13)(18)(19)

market mechanism: The use of market prices and sales to signal desired outputs (or resource allocations). (1)(3)(4)(8)(17)

market power: The ability to alter the market price of a good or service. (4)(7)(9)(11)(14)(16)

market share: The percentage of total market output produced by a single firm. (10)

market shortage: The amount by which the quantity demanded exceeds the quantity supplied at a given price; excess demand. (3)(21)

market structure: The number and relative size of firms in an industry. (7)(10)

market supply: The total quantities of a good that sellers are willing and able to sell at alternative prices in a given time period, *ceteris paribus*. (3)(8)

market supply of labor: The total quantity of labor that workers are willing and able to supply at alternative wage rates in a given time period, *ceteris paribus*. (15)

market surplus: The amount by which the quantity supplied exceeds the quantity demanded at a given price; excess supply. (3)(14)

merit good: A good or service society deems everyone is entitled to some minimal quantity of. (4)

microeconomics: The study of individual behavior in the economy, of the components of the larger economy. (1)

mixed economy: An economy that uses both market signals and government directives to allocate goods and resources. (1)

monopolistic competition: A market in which many firms produce similar goods or services but each maintains some independent control of its own price. (11)

monopoly: A firm that produces the entire market supply of a particular good or service. (2)(4)(7)(9)

monopsony: A market in which there's only one buyer. (16)

moral hazard: An incentive to engage in undesirable behavior. (14)(19)

natural monopoly: An industry in which one firm can achieve economies of scale over the entire range of market supply. (4)(9)(12)

net exports: The value of exports minus the value of imports: $(X - M)$. (2)

nominal tax rate: Taxes paid divided by taxable income. (18)

normal good: Good for which demand increases when income rises. (5)

normal profit: The opportunity cost of capital: zero economic profit. (7)

oligopolist: One of the dominant firms in an oligopoly. (10)

oligopoly: A market in which a few firms produce all or most of the market supply of a particular good or service. (10)

opportunity cost: The most desired goods or services that are forgone in order to obtain something else. (1)(3)(4)(5)(6)(8)(12)(13)(20)

opportunity wage: The highest wage an individual would earn in his or her best alternative job. (15)

optimal consumption: The mix of consumer purchases that maximizes the utility attainable from available income. (5)

optimal mix of output: The most desirable combination of output attainable with existing resources, technology, and social values. (4)

optimal rate of pollution: The rate of pollution that occurs when the marginal social benefit of pollution control equals its marginal social cost. (13)

outsourcing: The relocation of production to foreign countries. (6)(15)

par value: The face value of a bond; the amount to be repaid when the bond is due. (17)

parity: The relative price of farm products in the period 1910–14. (14)

per capita GDP: The dollar value of GDP divided by total population; average GDP. (2)

perfect competition: A market in which no buyer or seller has market power. (7)

personal income (PI): Income received by households before payment of personal taxes. (5)(18)

poverty gap: The shortfall between actual income and the poverty threshold. (19)

predatory pricing: Temporary price reductions designed to alter market shares or drive out competition. (10)

present discounted value (PDV): The value today of future payments, adjusted for interest accrual. (17)

price ceiling: Upper limit imposed on the price of a good. (3)

price discrimination: The sale of an identical good at different prices to different consumers by a single seller. (9)

price/earnings (P/E) ratio: The price of a stock share divided by earnings (profit) per share. (17)

price elasticity of demand: The percentage change in quantity demanded divided by the percentage change in price. (5)(9)(14)

price-fixing: Explicit agreements among producers regarding the price(s) at which a good is to be sold. (10)

price floor: Lower limit set for the price of a good. (3)

price leadership: An oligopolistic pricing pattern that allows one firm to establish the (market) price for all firms in the industry. (10)

private costs: The costs of an economic activity directly borne by the immediate producer or consumer (excluding externalities). (13)

private good: A good or service whose consumption by one person excludes consumption by others. (4)

product differentiation: Features that make one product appear different from competing products in the same market. (10)(11)(12)

product market: Any place where finished goods and services (products) are bought and sold. (3)

production decision: The selection of the short-run rate of output (with existing plant and equipment). (7)(8)(9)(11)(13)

production function: A technological relationship expressing the maximum quantity of a good attainable from different combinations of factor inputs. (6)

production possibilities: The alternative combinations of final goods and services that could be produced in a given time period with all available resources and technology. (1)(20)

production process: A specific combination of resources used to produce a good or service. (15)

productivity: Output per unit of input, e.g., output per labor-hour. (2)(6)(16)

profit: The difference between total revenue and total cost. (6)(7)(14)

profit-maximization rule: Produce at that rate of output where marginal revenue equals marginal cost. (7)(9)(10)

profit per unit: Total profit divided by the quantity produced in a given time period; price minus average total cost. (8)

progressive tax: A tax system in which tax rates rise as incomes rise. (4)(18)

proportional tax: A tax that levies the same rate on every dollar of income. (4)

public choice: Theory of public-sector behavior emphasizing rational self-interest of decision makers and voters. (4)

public good: A good or service whose consumption by one person does not exclude consumption by others. (4)(12)

quota: A limit on the quantity of a good that may be imported in a given time period. (20)

regressive tax: A tax system in which tax rates fall as incomes rise. (4)(18)

regulation: Government intervention to alter the behavior of firms, e.g., in pricing, output, or advertising. (12)

retained earnings: Amount of corporate profits not paid out in dividends. (17)

risk premium: The difference in rates of return on risky (uncertain) and safe (certain) investments. (17)

scarcity: Lack of enough resources to satisfy all desired uses of those resources. (1)

shift in demand: A change in the quantity demanded at any (every) given price. (3)(5)

short run: The period in which the quantity (and quality) of some inputs can't be changed. (6)(7)

short-run competitive equilibrium: $p = $ MC. (8)

shutdown point: The rate of output where price equals minimum AVC. (7)(8)

size distribution of income: The way total personal income is divided up among households or income classes. (18)

social costs: The full resource costs of an economic activity, including externalities. (13)

social insurance programs: Event-conditioned income transfers intended to reduce the cost of specific problems, e.g., Social Security and unemployment insurance. (19)

substitute goods: Goods that substitute for each other; when the price of good x rises, the demand for good y increases, *ceteris paribus*. (3)(5)

substitution effect of wages: An increased wage rate encourages people to work more hours (to substitute labor for leisure). (15)

supply: The ability and willingness to sell (produce) specific quantities of a good at alternative prices in a given time period, *ceteris paribus*. (3)

supply curve: A curve describing the quantities of a good a producer is willing and able to sell (produce) at alternative prices in a given time period, *ceteris paribus*. (7)

target efficiency: The percentage of income transfers that go to the intended recipients and purposes. (19)

tariff: A tax (duty) imposed on imported goods. (20)

tax base: The amount of income or property directly subject to nominal tax rates. (18)

tax elasticity of labor supply: The percentage change in quantity of labor supplied divided by the percentage change in tax rates. (19)

tax elasticity of supply: The percentage change in quantity supplied divided by the percentage change in tax rates. (18)

tax incidence: Distribution of the real burden of a tax. (18)

terms of trade: The rate at which goods are exchanged; the amount of good A given up for good B in trade. (20)

total cost: The market value of all resources used to produce a good or service. (6)

total revenue: The price of a product multiplied by the quantity sold in a given time period: $p \times q$. (5)(7)

total utility: The amount of satisfaction obtained from entire consumption of a product. (5)

trade deficit: The amount by which the value of imports exceeds the value of exports in a given time period (negative net exports). (20)(21)

trade surplus: The amount by which the value of exports exceeds the value of imports in a given time period (positive net exports). (20)

transfer payments: Payments to individuals for which no current goods or services are exchanged, like Social Security, welfare, unemployment benefits. (4)(19)

unemployment: The inability of labor-force participants to find jobs. (4)

union shop: An employment setting in which all workers must join the union within 30 days after being employed. (16)

unionization ratio: The percentage of the labor force belonging to a union. (16)

unit labor cost: Hourly wage rate divided by output per labor-hour. (6)

user charge: Fee paid for the use of a public-sector good or service. (4)

utility: The pleasure or satisfaction obtained from a good or service. (5)

variable costs: Costs of production that change when the rate of output is altered, e.g., labor and material costs. (6)(7)

vertical equity: Principle that people with higher incomes should pay more taxes. (18)

voluntary restraint agreement (VRA): An agreement to reduce the volume of trade in a specific good; a "voluntary" quota. (20)

wage-replacement rate: The percentage of base wages paid out in benefits. (19)

wealth: The market value of assets. (18)

welfare programs: Means-tested income transfer programs, e.g., welfare and food stamps. (19)

INDEX

PRODUCTIVITY AND RELATED DATA, BUSINESS SECTOR 1959–2003 (1992 = 100)

Year	Output per Hour of All Persons	Output	Hours of All Persons	Compensation per Hour	Real Compensation per Hour	Unit Labor Costs
1959	48.6	31.9	65.5	13.3	59.2	27.4
1960	49.5	32.5	65.6	13.9	60.7	28.0
1961	51.3	33.1	64.5	14.4	62.5	28.1
1962	53.6	35.2	65.7	15.1	64.6	28.1
1963	55.7	36.8	66.1	15.6	66.1	28.0
1964	57.6	39.2	68.0	16.2	67.7	28.1
1965	59.7	41.9	70.3	16.8	69.1	28.2
1966	62.1	44.8	72.1	17.9	71.7	28.9
1967	63.5	45.6	71.9	19.0	73.6	29.9
1968	65.5	47.9	73.2	20.4	76.0	31.2
1969	65.8	49.4	75.1	21.9	77.2	33.2
1970	67.1	49.4	73.6	23.6	78.6	35.1
1971	70.0	51.3	73.3	25.0	80.1	35.8
1972	72.2	54.7	75.7	26.6	82.3	36.8
1973	74.5	58.5	78.6	28.8	84.1	38.7
1974	73.2	57.6	78.7	31.6	83.1	43.2
1975	75.8	57.0	75.3	34.8	83.9	46.0
1976	78.4	60.9	77.7	37.9	86.2	48.3
1977	79.7	64.3	80.7	40.9	87.4	51.3
1978	80.6	68.3	84.8	44.5	88.9	55.2
1979	80.5	70.6	87.7	48.8	89.1	60.6
1980	80.3	69.8	86.9	54.1	88.9	67.3
1981	81.9	71.7	87.6	59.2	89.0	72.3
1982	81.6	69.6	85.2	63.7	90.5	78.1
1983	84.5	73.3	86.7	66.3	90.4	78.5
1984	86.8	79.7	91.8	69.2	90.7	79.7
1985	88.5	83.1	93.8	72.6	92.1	82.0
1986	91.2	86.1	94.4	76.4	95.2	83.8
1987	91.0	89.2	97.3	79.3	95.6	86.8
1988	93.0	92.9	99.9	83.4	97.0	89.7
1989	93.9	96.2	102.5	85.7	95.5	91.2
1990	95.3	97.6	102.5	90.7	96.3	95.2
1991	96.4	96.5	100.1	95.0	97.4	98.6
1992	100.0	100.0	100.0	100.0	100.0	100.0
1993	100.5	103.1	102.6	102.4	99.9	101.9
1994	101.7	108.1	106.3	104.4	99.7	102.6
1995	102.3	111.5	108.9	106.5	99.4	104.1
1996	105.1	110.4	110.7	109.9	99.8	104.6
1997	107.4	122.5	114.0	113.2	100.7	105.4
1998	110.2	128.5	116.6	119.4	104.8	108.4
1999	113.0	134.5	119.0	124.8	107.2	110.4
2000	116.5	140.0	120.1	133.5	111.0	114.6
2001	118.8	139.8	117.6	138.6	112.1	116.7
2002	123.7	143.5	115.8	144.5	115.0	116.6
2003	129.5	149.0	115.1	150.5	117.1	116.2

Source: *Economic Report of the President 2004* and U.S. Bureau of Labor Statistics

Stock prices and yields, 1969–2003

Year	Common stock prices — Dow Jones industrial average	Common stock yields — Dividend-price ratio	Common stock yields — Earnings-price ratio	10 year Treasury bond (to yield)
1969	876.72	3.24	6.08	6.67
1970	753.19	3.83	6.45	7.35
1971	884.76	3.14	5.41	6.16
1972	950.71	2.84	5.50	6.21
1973	923.88	3.06	7.12	6.84
1974	759.37	4.47	11.59	7.56
1975	802.49	4.31	9.15	7.99
1976	974.92	3.77	8.90	7.61
1977	894.63	4.62	10.79	7.42
1978	820.23	5.28	12.03	8.41
1979	844.40	5.47	13.46	9.44
1980	891.41	5.26	12.66	11.46
1981	932.92	5.20	11.96	13.91
1982	884.36	5.81	11.60	13.00
1983	1,190.34	4.40	8.03	11.10
1984	1,178.48	4.64	10.02	12.44
1985	1,328.23	4.25	8.12	10.62
1986	1,792.76	3.49	6.09	7.68
1987	2,275.99	3.08	5.48	8.39
1988	2,060.82	3.64	8.01	8.85
1989	2,508.91	3.45	7.42	8.49
1990	2,678.94	3.61	6.47	8.55
1991	2,929.33	3.24	4.79	7.86
1992	3,284.29	2.99	4.22	7.01
1993	3,522.06	2.78	4.46	5.87
1994	3,793.77	2.82	5.83	7.09
1995	4,493.76	2.56	6.09	6.57
1996	5,742.89	2.19	5.24	6.44
1997	7,441.15	1.77	4.57	6.35
1998	8,625.52	1.49	3.46	5.26
1999	10,464.88	1.25	3.17	5.65
2000	10,734.90	1.15	3.63	6.03
2001	10,188.13	1.32	2.95	5.02
2002	9,226.43	1.61	2.92	4.61
2003	8,993.59	1.77	....	4.01

Source: *Economic Report of the President, 2004*

—Corporate profits with inventory valuation and capital consumption adjustments, 1959–2003
(Billions of dollars)

Year	Corporate profits with inventory valuation and capital consumption adjustments	Taxes on corporate income	Corporate profits after tax with inventory valuation and capital consumption adjustments — Total	Corporate profits after tax with inventory valuation and capital consumption adjustments — Net dividends	Undistributed profits with inventory valuation and capital consumption adjustments
1959	55.7	23.7	32.0	12.6	19.4
1960	53.8	22.8	31.0	13.4	17.6
1961	54.9	22.9	32.0	13.9	18.1
1962	63.3	24.1	39.2	15.0	24.1
1963	69.0	26.4	42.6	16.2	26.4
1964	76.5	28.2	48.3	18.2	30.1
1965	87.5	31.1	56.4	20.2	36.2
1966	93.2	33.9	59.3	20.7	38.7
1967	91.3	32.9	58.4	21.5	36.9
1968	98.8	39.6	59.2	23.5	35.6
1969	95.4	40.0	55.4	24.2	31.2
1970	83.6	34.8	48.9	24.3	24.6
1971	98.0	38.2	59.9	25.0	34.8
1972	112.1	42.3	69.7	26.8	42.9
1973	125.5	50.0	75.5	29.9	45.6
1974	115.8	52.8	63.0	33.2	29.8
1975	134.8	51.6	83.2	33.0	50.2
1976	163.3	65.3	98.1	39.0	59.0
1977	192.4	74.4	118.0	44.8	73.2
1978	216.6	84.9	131.8	50.8	81.0
1979	223.2	90.0	133.2	57.5	75.7
1980	201.1	87.2	113.9	64.1	49.9
1981	226.1	84.3	141.8	73.8	68.0
1982	209.7	66.5	143.2	77.7	65.4
1983	264.2	80.6	183.6	83.5	100.1
1984	318.6	97.5	221.1	90.8	130.3
1985	330.3	99.4	230.9	97.6	133.4
1986	319.5	109.7	209.8	106.2	103.7
1987	368.8	130.4	238.4	112.3	126.1
1988	432.6	141.6	291.0	129.9	161.1
1989	426.6	146.1	280.5	158.0	122.6
1990	437.8	145.4	292.4	169.1	123.3
1991	451.2	138.6	312.6	180.7	131.9
1992	479.3	148.7	330.6	187.9	142.7
1993	541.9	171.0	370.9	202.8	168.1
1994	600.3	193.7	406.5	234.7	171.8
1995	696.7	218.7	478.0	254.2	223.8
1996	786.2	231.7	554.5	297.6	256.9
1997	868.5	246.1	622.4	334.5	287.9
1998	801.6	248.3	553.3	351.6	201.7
1999	851.3	258.6	592.6	337.4	255.3
2000	817.9	265.2	552.7	377.9	174.8
2001	770.4	201.1	569.3	373.2	196.0
2002	904.2	195.0	709.1	398.3	310.8

Source: *Economic Report of the President, 2004*

Name: _____

1. According to Table 1.1 (or Figure 1.1), what is the opportunity cost of the

           (*a*) Fourth truck? _____
           (*b*) Fifth truck? _____

2. (*a*) According to Figure 1.2, what is the opportunity cost of North Korea's military force at point *N*? _____
   (*b*) How much of a peace dividend would North Korea get if it cut the military establishment from OD to OH? _____

3. How much of a peace dividend is generated in a $11 trillion economy when defense spending is cut from 3.5 percent to 3.0 percent of total output? $_____

4. What is the opportunity cost (in dollars) to attend an hour-long econ lecture for
   (*a*) A minimum-wage teenager $_____
   (*b*) A $100,000 per year corporate executive $_____

5. Suppose either computers or televisions can be assembled with the following labor inputs:

Units produced	1	2	3	4	5	6	7	8	9	10
Total labor used	3	7	12	18	25	33	42	54	70	90

   (*a*) Draw the production possibilities curve for an economy with 54 units of labor. Label it P54.
   (*b*) What is the opportunity cost of the eighth computer? _____
   (*c*) Suppose immigration brings in 36 more workers. Redraw the production possibilities curve to reflect this added labor. Label the new curve P90.
   (*d*) Suppose advancing technology (e.g., the miniaturization of electronic circuits) increases the productivity of the 90-laborer workforce by 20 percent. Draw a third production possibilities curve (PT) to illustrate this change.

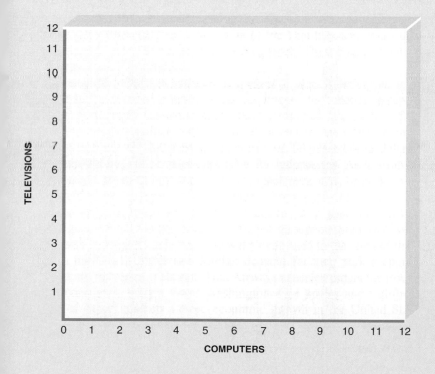

6. Suppose there's a relationship of the following sort between study time and grades:

	(a)	(b)	(c)	(d)	(e)
Study time (hours per week)	0	2	6	12	20
Grade-point average	0	1.0	2.0	3.0	4.0

If you have only 20 hours per week to use for either study time or fun time,
(a) Draw the (linear) production possibilities curve on the graph below that represents the alternative uses of your time.
(b) What is the cost, in lost fun time, of raising your grade-point average from 2.0 to 3.0? Illustrate this effort on the graph (point C to point D).   _____
(c) What is the opportunity cost of increasing your grades from 3.0 to 4.0? Illustrate as point D to point E.   _____
(d) Why does the opportunity cost change? _____

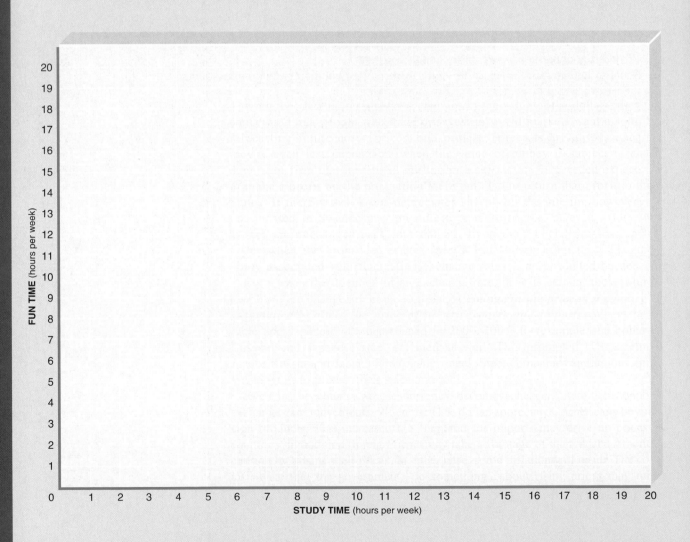

Problems for Chapter 2

Name: _____

1. In 2002, the worlds' total output (real GDP) was roughly $46 trillion. What percent of this total was produced by the three largest economies (World View, p. 28)?

_____%

2. According to the World View on p. 29, what percentage of America's GDP per capita is available to the average citizen of

    (a) Mexico   _____%

    (b) China   _____%

    (c) Ethiopia   _____%

3. If Haiti's per capita GDP of roughly $1,280 increases by an exceptionally fast 5 percent a year, what will its per capita GDP be in

    (a) 10 years? $_____

    (b) 20 years? $_____

    (c) In 20 years, what percent of America's 2002 per capita income would it attain at that rate?   _____%

4. According to Table 2.1, how fast does total output have to grow in order to raise per capita GDP in

    (a) France?   _____

    (b) Nigeria?   _____

5. U.S. real gross domestic product increased from $3.8 trillion in 1980 to $4.8 trillion in 1990. During that same decade the share of durable goods (e.g., cars, appliances) fell from 18.5 percent to 17.0 percent. What was the value of durable-goods output

    (a) In 1980? $_____

    (b) In 1990? $_____

    (c) By how much did durable output change?   _____%

6. Using the data in Figure 2.6,

    (a) Compute the average income of U.S. households. $_____

    (b) If all incomes were equalized by government taxes and transfer payments, how much would the average household in each income quintile gain (via transfers) or lose (via taxes)?

        (i) Highest fifth $_____

        (ii) Second fifth $_____

        (iii) Third fifth $_____

        (iv) Fourth fifth $_____

        (v) Lowest fifth $_____

    (c) What is the implied tax rate on the highest quintile?   _____%

7. What percent of U.S. exports go to

    (a) China?   _____%

    (b) Canada?   _____%

What percent of U.S. imports come from

    (a) China?   _____%

    (b) Canada?   _____%

8. How much more output (income) per year will have to be produced in the world

    (a) Just to reduce the "extreme poverty" (less than $2 per day) of 3 billion people by $1 per day? $_____

    (b) To raise the incomes of the world's "extremely poor" population to the official threshold of U.S. poverty (roughly $5,000 per year)? $_____

9. **(Macro course only)** Using the data from the endpapers of this book, complete the following table.

Sector	Share of Total Output	
	1950	2000
Consumption	_____	_____
Investment	_____	_____
Government purchases	_____	_____
Exports	_____	_____
Imports	_____	_____

   (*a*) Which sector share has increased the most?   _____

   (*b*) Which sector share has decreased the most?   _____

10. **(Macro course only)** Using data from the endpapers, illustrate on the graph below
   (*a*) The federal government's share of the total output.
   (*b*) The state/local government's share of total output.

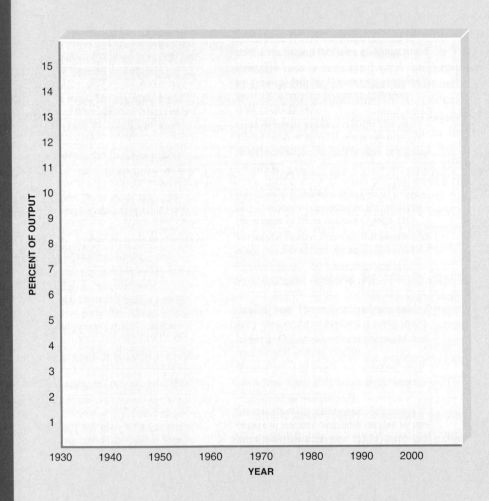

Problems for Chapter 3

Name: _____

1. According to Figure 3.3, at what price would Tom buy 15 hours of web tutoring?

        (*a*) Without a lottery win.   _____

        (*b*) With a lottery win.   _____

2. According to Figures 3.5 and 3.6, what would the new equilibrium price of tutoring services be if Ann decided to stop tutoring?   _____

3. Given the following data, identify the amount of shortage or surplus that would exist at a price of

        (*a*) $5.00   _____

        (*b*) $3.00   _____

        (*c*) $1.00   _____

A. Price	$5.00	$4.00	$3.00	$2.00	$1.00			$5.00	$4.00	$3.00	$2.00	$1.00
B. Quantity demanded							C. Quantity supplied					
Al	1	2	3	4	5		Alice	3	3	3	3	3
Betsy	0	1	1	1	2		Butch	7	5	4	4	2
Casey	2	2	3	3	4		Connie	6	4	3	3	1
Daisy	1	3	4	4	6		Dutch	6	5	4	3	0
Eddie	1	2	2	3	5		Ellen	4	2	2	2	1
Market total	__	__	__	__	__		Market total	__	__	__	__	__

4. Graph the official and equilibrium prices for the U2 rock concert (see News, page 61).

PRICE (dollars per ticket)

QUANTITY (tickets per show)

5. In the World View on page 64, menu prices are continuously adjusted. Graph the initial and final (adjusted) prices for the following situations. Be sure to label axes and graph completely.

(*a*) Customers are ordering too little haddock.

(*b*) The kitchen is running out of beef ribs.

6. What factors caused the supply and demand shifts in the California electricity market (see "Economy Tomorrow" p. 65–67)?

Demand Shift Factors	**Supply Shift Factors**
_____	_____
_____	_____
_____	_____
_____	_____

7. In Figure 3.8, when a price ceiling is imposed on the "new" market by how much does
   (a) The quantity of electricity demanded increase?   _____
   (b) The quantity of electricity supplied decrease?   _____
   (c) How large is the resulting shortage?   _____

8. In the California electricity market (Figure 3.8),
   (a) What is the "new" equilibrium price?   _____
   (b) How large is the market shortage at that price?   _____

9. What is the relationship of Idaho power to California power? (circle one)
   (a) Complementary good   (b) Substitute good
   Illustrate on the graphs below the impacts of a California price ceiling (at P_c) on the California and Idaho electricity markets.
   (c) Which determinant of demand for Idaho electricity changes in this case?   _____

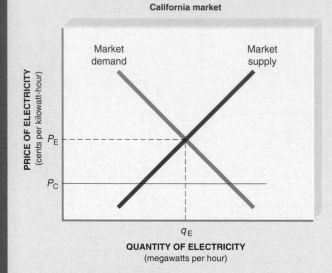

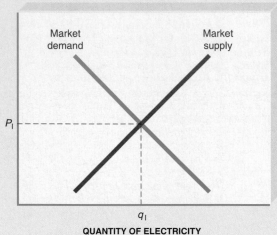

10. Use the following data to draw supply and demand curves on the accompanying graph.

Price	$ 8	7	6	5	4	3	2	1
Quantity demanded	2	3	4	5	6	7	8	9
Quantity supplied	10	9	8	7	6	5	4	3

   (a) What is the equilibrium price?   _____
   (b) If a *minimum* price (price floor) of $6 is set, what disequilibrium results?   _____
   (c) If a *maximum* price (price ceiling) of $3 is set, what disequilibrium results?   _____

   Illustrate these answers.

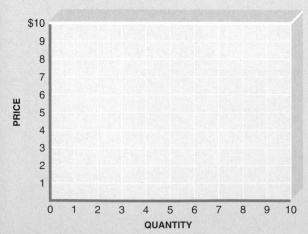

Problems for Chapter 4

Name: _____

1. In Figure 4.2, by how much is the market
   (a) Overproducing private goods? _____
   (b) Underproducing public goods? _____

2. Use Figure 4.3 to illustrate on the accompanying production possibilities curve
   (a) The market mix of output (M).
   (b) The optimal mix of output (X).

3. Assume that the product depicted below generates external costs in consumption of $5 per unit.
   (a) Draw the social demand curve.

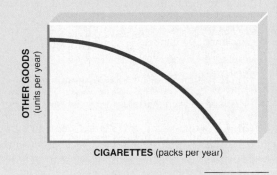

CIGARETTES (packs per year)

   (b) What is the socially optimal output? _____
   (c) By how much does the market overproduce this good? _____

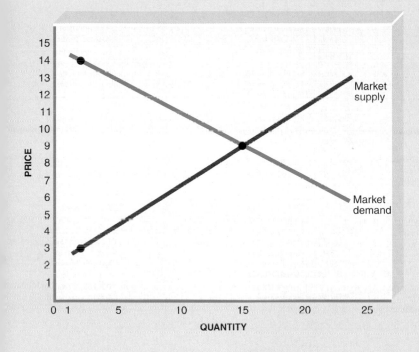

4. In the previous problem's market equilibrium, what is
   (a) The market value of the good? _____
   (b) The social value of the good? _____

5. (a) Assuming a 10 percent sales tax is levied on all consumption, complete the following table:

Income	Consumption	Sales Tax	Percent of Income Paid in Taxes
$10,000	$10,000	_____	_____
20,000	19,000	_____	_____
40,000	36,000	_____	_____
80,000	68,000	_____	_____

   (b) Is the sales tax progressive or regressive? _____

6. If a new home can be constructed for $120,000, what is the opportunity cost of federal defense spending, measured in terms of private housing? (Assume a defense budget of $400 billion.)   _____

7. Suppose the following data represent the market demand for college education:

Tuition (per year)	$1,000	2,000	3,000	4,000	5,000	6,000	7,000	8,000
Enrollment demanded (in millions per year)	8	7	6	5	4	3	2	1

(*a*) If tuition is set at $5,000, how many students will enroll?   _____

Now suppose that society gets an external benefit of $1,000 for every enrolled student.

(*b*) Draw the social and market demand curves for this situation on the graph below (left).
(*c*) What is the socially optimal level of enrollments at the same tuition price of $5,000?   _____
(*d*) How can this optimal enrollment level be achieved? _____

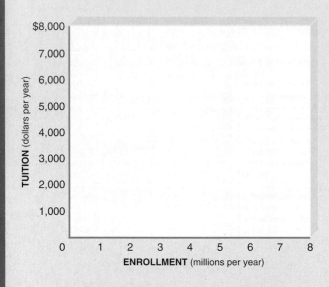

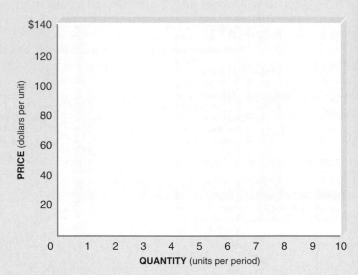

8. Suppose the following data represent the prices that each of three consumers is willing to pay:

Quantity	Consumer A	Consumer B	Consumer C
1	$50	$40	$30
2	30	20	20
3	20	15	10

(*a*) Construct the market demand curve for this good on the graph above (right).
(*b*) If this good were priced in the market at $40, how many units would be demanded?   _____
(*c*) Now suppose that this is a public good, in the sense that all consumers receive satisfaction from the good even if only one person buys it. Under these conditions, what is the social value of the
   (*i*) First unit?   _____
   (*ii*) Second unit?   _____

9. According to the News on p. 84, what percent of income is spent on lottery tickets by
(*a*) A poor family with income of $18,000 per year?   _____
(*b*) An affluent family with income of $80,000 per year?   _____

Problems for Chapter 5

Name: _____

1. Illustrate the following demand on the accompanying graph:

Price (per pair)	$100	$80	$60	$40	$20
Quantity demanded (pairs per day)	10	14	18	22	26

(*a*) How many pairs will be demanded when the price is $70? _____

(*b*) How much money will be spent on shoes at a price of $50? _____

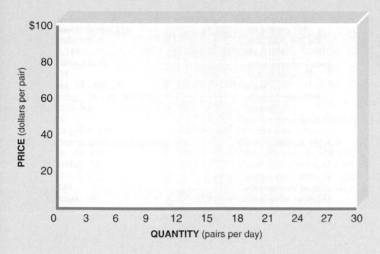

2. According to the News stories on pages 103 and 105, by how much would cigarette prices have to rise to get a 50 percent reduction in smoking by

          (*a*) Teenagers? _____%

          (*b*) Adults (short-run)? _____%

3. Suppose consumers buy 10 million packs of cigarettes per month at a price of $2 per pack. If a $1 tax is added to that price,

(*a*) By what percent does price change? (Use midpoint formula on p. 101.) _____%

(*b*) By what percent will cigarette sales decline in the short run? (See Table 5.1 for clue.) _____%

(*c*) According to Gary Becker, by how much will sales decline in the long run? (See News, page 105.) _____%

4. From Figure 5.1, compute (*a*) the price elasticity between each of the following points and (*b*) the total revenue at each point.

	Price Elasticity		Total Revenue
Point *D* to *E*	_____	At point *D*	_____
		E	_____
G to *H*	_____	*G*	_____
		H	_____

5. What is the price elasticity of demand for New York City cigarettes? (See News, page 104.) _____

6. According to the calculation on p. 109, by how much will popcorn sales increase if average income goes up by 2.0 percent? _____%

7. Use the following table to compute the income elasticity of the demand for air travel:

	Income (per year)	Vacations (per year)		Income Elasticity of Demand
a.	$ 20,000	0		
b.	50,000	1	*b* to *c*	_____
c.	100,000	3	*c* to *d*	_____
d.	200,000	5		

8. Suppose the following table reflects the total satisfaction derived from consumption of pizza slices and Pepsis. Assume that pizza costs $1 per slice and a large Pepsi costs $2. With $20 to spend, what consumption mix will maximize satisfaction?   _____

Quantity consumed	1	2	3	4	5	6	7	8	9	10	11	12	13	14
Total units of pleasure from pizza slices	47	92	132	166	196	224	251	271	288	303	313	315	312	300
Total units of pleasure from Pepsis	111	200	272	336	386	426	452	456	444	408	340	217	92	−17

9. Use the following data to illustrate the (a) demand curve and (b) total revenue curve:

Price	$ 1	2	3	4	5	6	7	8	9	10
Quantity	18	16	14	12	10	8	6	4	2	0

(a) At what price is total revenue maximized? $_____

(b) At that price what is the elasticity of demand? $E =$ _____

(c) Indicate the elastic and inelastic regions of each curve on the graphs.

(a) Demand curve

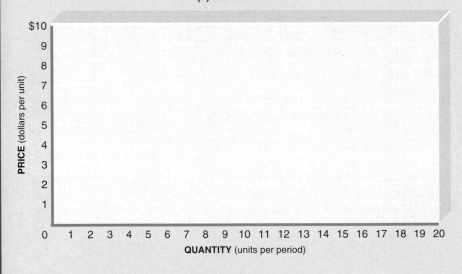

(b) Total revenue curve

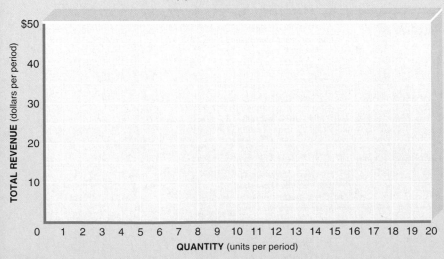

Problems for Chapter 6

Name: _____

1. (*a*) Complete the following cost schedule:

Rate of Output	Total Cost	Marginal Cost	Average Fixed Cost	Average Variable Cost	Average Total Cost
0	$100	_____	_____	_____	_____
1	110	_____	_____	_____	_____
2	130	_____	_____	_____	_____
3	165	_____	_____	_____	_____
4	220	_____	_____	_____	_____
5	300	_____	_____	_____	_____

(*b*) Use the cost data to plot the ATC and MC curves on the accompanying graph.

(*c*) At what output rate is ATC minimized? _____

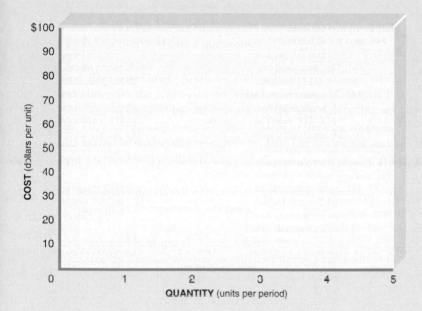

2. Based on the News on page 145, what is the ATC per dollar of sales at a

    (*a*) Large funeral home? _____

    (*b*) Small funeral home? _____

3. Suppose a company incurs the following costs: labor, $400; equipment, $300; and materials, $100. The company owns the building, so it doesn't have to pay the usual $800 in rent.

(*a*) What is the total accounting cost? _____

(*b*) What is the total economic cost? _____

(*c*) How would accounting and economic costs change if the company sold the building and then leased it back? _____

4. Refer to the production table for jeans (Table 6.1). Suppose a firm had three sewing machines and could vary only the amount of labor input.

(*a*) Graph the production function for jeans given the three sewing machines.

(*b*) Compute and graph the marginal physical product curve.

(*c*) At what amount of labor input does the law of diminishing returns first become apparent in your graph of marginal physical product? _____

(*d*) Is total output still increasing when MPP begins to diminish? _____

(*e*) When total output stops increasing what is the value of MPP? _____

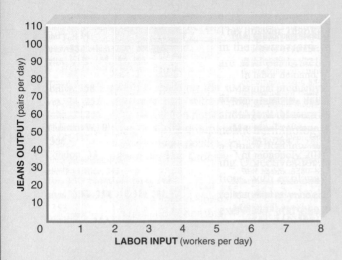

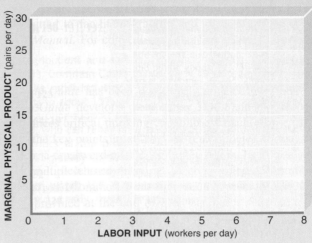

5. The following table indicates the average total cost of producing varying quantities of output from three different plants:

Rate of output	10	20	30	40	50	60	70	80	90	100
Average total cost										
Small firm	$ 600	$500	$400	$500	$600	$700	$800	$900	$1,000	$1,100
Medium firm	800	650	500	350	200	300	400	500	600	700
Large firm	1,000	900	800	700	600	500	400	300	400	500

(a) Plot the ATC curves for all three firms on the graph.
(b) Which plant(s) should be used to produce 40 units?   _____
(c) Which plant(s) should be used to produce 100 units?   _____
(d) Are there economies of scale in these plant-size choices?   _____

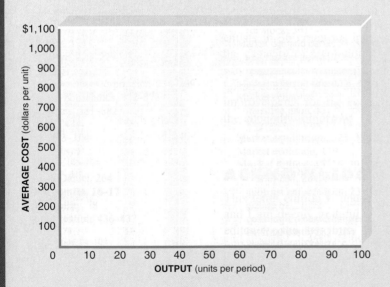

6. According to the World View on page 148, which nation had the biggest loss of competitive position in years 1990–2002?   _____

7. Suppose (A) the hourly wage rate is $15 in the United States and $1 in China, and (B) productivity is 20 units per hour in the U.S. and 1 unit per hour in China. What are unit labor costs in
(a) The United States?   _____
(b) China?   _____

Problems for Chapter 7

Name: _____

1. If the owner of the Table 7.1 drugstore hired a manager for $10 an hour to take his place, how much of a change would show up in

    (a) Accounting profits?   _____

    (b) Economic profits?   _____

2. If the price of catfish fell from $13 to $7 per bushel, use Figure 7.7 to determine the

    (a) Profit-maximizing output.   _____

    (b) Profit or loss per bushel.   _____

    (c) Total profit or loss.   _____

3. (a) Complete the following cost and revenue schedules:

Quantity	Price	Total Revenue	Total Cost	Marginal Cost
0	$80	_____	$ 50	_____
1	80	_____	70	_____
2	80	_____	110	_____
3	80	_____	170	_____
4	80	_____	250	_____
5	80	_____	350	_____

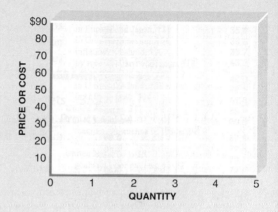

(b) Graph MC and P.

(c) What rate of output maximizes profit?   _____

(d) What is MC at that rate of output?   _____

4. Complete the following cost schedule:

Quantity	0	1	2	3	4	5	6	7
Total cost	$10	$12	$16	$21	$30	$40	$52	$66
ATC	___	___	___	___	___	___	___	___
MC	___	___	___	___	___	___	___	___

Assuming the price of this product is $12, at what output rate is

    (a) Total revenue maximized?   _____

    (b) ATC minimized?   _____

    (c) Profit per unit maximized?   _____

    (d) Total profit maximized?   _____

5. Assume that the price of silk ties in a perfectly competitive market is $15 and that the typical firm confronts the following costs:

Quantity (ties per day)	0	1	2	3	4	5	6	7	8	9	10
Total cost	$10	$17	$26	$37	$50	$65	$82	$101	$122	$145	$170

(a) What is the profit-maximizing rate of output for the firm?   _____

(b) How much profit does the firm earn at that rate of output?   _____

(c) If the price of ties fell to $11, how many ties should the firm produce?   _____

(d) At what price should the firm shut down?   _____

6. Using the data from Problem 5 (at the original price of $15), determine how many ties the producer would supply if

    (a) A tax of $2 per tie were collected from the producer.   _____

    (b) A property tax of $2 was levied.   _____

    (c) Profits were taxed at 50 percent.   _____

7. Suppose labor is the only variable cost in fish farming and that a new minimum-wage law increases wages by 40 percent.
   (*a*) What will the new output rate be for the firm in Figure 7.7?   _____
   (*b*) How much profit will it make?   _____

8. Complete the following table:

Output	Total Cost	Marginal Cost	Average Total Cost	Average Variable Cost
0	$100	_____	_____	_____
5	110	_____	_____	_____
10	130	_____	_____	_____
15	170	_____	_____	_____
20	220	_____	_____	_____
25	290	_____	_____	_____
30	380	_____	_____	_____
35	490	_____	_____	_____

   According to the table above,
   (*a*) If the price is $8, how much output will the firm supply?   _____
   (*b*) How much profit or loss will it make?   _____
   (*c*) At what price will the firm shut down?   _____

9. A firm has leased plant and equipment to produce video game cartridges, which can be sold in unlimited quantities at $21 each. The following figures describe the associated costs of production:

Rate of output (per day)	0	1	2	3	4	5	6	7	8
Total cost (per day)	$50	$55	$62	$75	$96	$125	$162	$203	$248

   (*a*) How much are fixed costs?   _____
   (*b*) Draw total revenue and cost curves on the graphs below.
   (*c*) Draw the average total cost (ATC), marginal cost (MC), and demand curves of the firm.
   (*d*) What is the profit-maximizing rate of output?   _____
   (*e*) Should the producer stay in business?   _____
   (*f*) What is the size of the loss if production continues?   _____
   (*g*) How much is lost if the firm shuts down?   _____

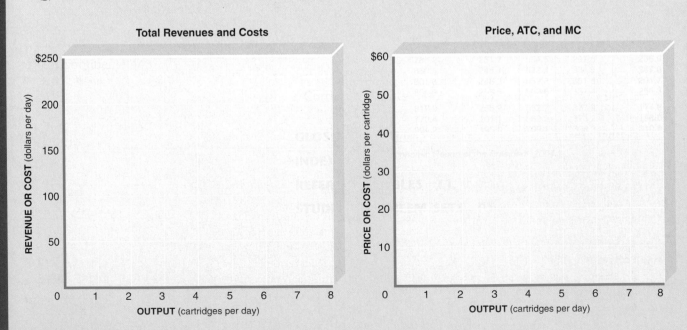

Problems for Chapter 8

Name: _____

1. According to Table 8.1,
   (a) What were the fixed costs of production for the firm? _____
   (b) At what rate of output was profit per computer maximized? _____
   (c) At what output rate was total profit maximized? _____

2. Suppose the following data summarize the costs of a perfectly competitive firm:

Quantity	0	1	2	3	4	5	6	7	8
Total cost	$100	102	105	109	114	120	127	135	144

   (a) Draw the firm's MC curve on the graph on the left below.
   (b) Draw the market supply curve on the right graph, assuming 8 firms identical to the one above.
   (c) What is the equilibrium price in this market? _____

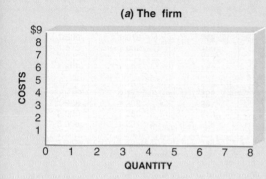

3. Suppose the following data describe the demand for liquid-diet beverages:

Price	$11	$10	$9	$8	$7	$6	$5	$4	$3	$2
Quantity demanded	9	12	15	18	21	24	27	30	33	36

Four identical, perfectly competitive firms are producing these beverages. The cost of producing these beverages at each firm are the following:

Quantity produced	0	1	2	3	4	5	6	7	8	9	10
Total cost	$5	$8	$10	$13	$17	$22	$28	$36	$45	$55	$67

   (a) What price will prevail in this market? _____
   (b) What quantity is produced? _____
   (c) How much profit (loss) does each firm make? _____
   (d) What happens to price if two more identical firms enter the market? _____

4. Suppose the typical catfish farmer was incurring an economic loss at the prevailing price p_1.
   (a) Illustrate these losses on the firm and market graphs. (b) What forces would raise the price? What price would prevail in long-term equilibrium? Illustrate your answers on the graphs.

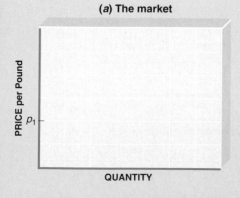

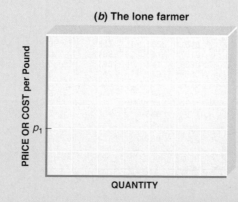

5. According to Table 8.1,
   (a) What was the prevailing computer price in 1978?   _____
   (b) How much total profit did the typical firm earn?   _____
   (c) At what price would profits have been zero?   _____
   (d) At what price would the firm have shut down?   _____

6. Suppose that the monthly market demand schedule for Frisbees is

Price	$8	$7	$6	$5	$4	$3	$2	$1
Quantity demanded	1,000	2,000	4,000	8,000	16,000	32,000	64,000	128,000

Suppose further that the marginal and average costs of Frisbee production for every competitive firm are

Rate of output	100	200	300	400	500	600
Marginal cost	$2.00	$3.00	$4.00	$5.00	$6.00	$7.00
Average total cost	2.00	2.50	3.00	3.50	4.00	4.50

Finally, assume that the equilibrium market price is $6 per Frisbee.
   (a) Draw the cost curves of the typical firm and identify its profit-maximizing rate of output and
        its total profits.
   (b) Draw the market demand curve and identify market equilibrium.
   (c) How many Frisbees are being sold?   _____
   (d) How many (identical) firms are initially producing Frisbees?   _____
   (e) How much profit is the typical firm making?   _____
   (f) In view of the profits being made, more firms will want to get into Frisbee production. In the
        long run, these new firms will shift the market supply curve to the right and push price down
        to average total cost, thereby eliminating profits. At what equilibrium price are all profits
        eliminated?   _____
   (g) How many firms will be producing Frisbees at this price?   _____

(a) The firm

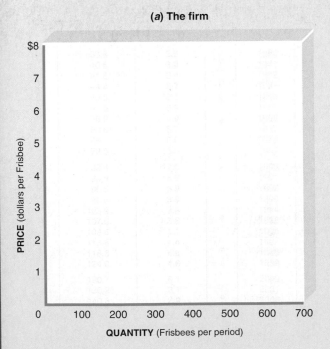

(b) The market

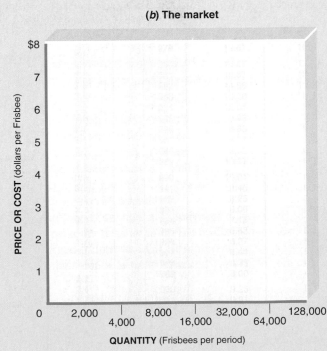

Problems for Chapter 9

Name: _____

1. Use Figures 9.2 and 9.3 to answer the following questions:
   (a) What is the highest price the monopolist could charge and still sell fish? _____
   (b) What is total revenue at that highest price? _____
   (c) What rate of output maximizes total revenue? _____
   (d) What is marginal revenue at that rate of output? _____
   (e) What is price at that rate of output? _____
   (f) What rate of output maximizes total profit? _____
   (g) What is MR at that rate of output? _____
   (h) What is price? _____

2. (a) Complete the following table:

Price	$15	$13	$11	$9	$7	$5	$3	$1
Quantity demanded	1	2	3	4	5	6	7	8
Marginal revenue	___	___	___	___	___	___	___	___

   (b) If marginal cost is constant at $7, what is the profit-maximizing rate of output? _____
   (c) What price should be charged at that rate of output? _____

3. The following table indicates the prices various buyers are willing to pay for a Miata sports car:

Buyer	Maximum Price	Buyer	Maximum Price
Buyer A	$50,000	Buyer D	$20,000
Buyer B	40,000	Buyer E	10,000
Buyer C	30,000		

   The cost of producing the cars includes $50,000 of fixed costs and a constant marginal cost of $10,000.
   (a) Graph below the demand, marginal revenue, and marginal cost curves.
   (b) What is the profit-maximizing rate of output and price for a monopolist? How much profit does the monopolist make?

   Output _____
   Price _____
   Profit _____

   (c) If the monopolist can price-discriminate, how many cars will he sell? _____
   (d) How much profit will he make? _____

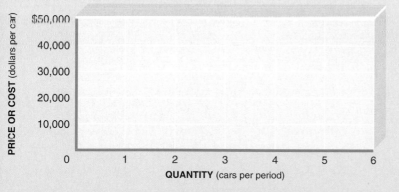

4. If the on-campus demand for soda is as follows:

Price (per can)	$0.25	0.50	0.75	1.00	1.25	1.50	1.75	2.00
Quantity demanded (per day)	100	90	80	70	60	50	40	30

   and the marginal cost of supplying a soda is 50 cents, what price will students end up paying in
   (a) A perfectly competitive market? _____
   (b) A monopolized market? _____

Name: _____

5. The following table summarizes the weekly sales and cost situation confronting a monopolist:

Price	Quantity Demanded	Total Revenue	Marginal Revenue	Total Cost	Marginal Cost	Average Total Cost
$20	0			$ 8		
18	1			14		
16	2			22		
14	3			32		
12	4			44		
10	5			58		
8	6			74		
6	7			92		
4	8			112		
2	9			147		

(a) Complete the table.
(b) Graph the demand, MR, and MC curves on the graph below.
(c) At what rate of output is total revenue maximized within this range? _____
(d) What are the values of MR and MC at the revenue-maximizing rate of output?   MR _____
  MC _____

(e) At what rate of output are profits maximized within this range? _____
(f) What are the values of MR and MC at the profit-maximizing rate of output?   MR _____
  MC _____

(g) What are total profits at that output rate? _____
(h) If a competitive industry confronted the same demand and costs, how much output would it produce in the short run? _____
(i) What would happen to long-run price if the market became perfectly competitive?

_____

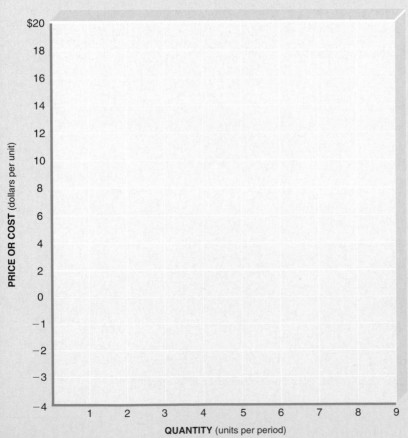

Name: _____

1. According to Table 10.2, in which markets do fewer than 4 firms produce at least 90 percent of total output?

   _____   _____   _____

   _____   _____   _____

   _____   _____   _____

2. According to the News on page 224,
   (*a*) What is the concentration ratio in the U.S. soda market? _____
   (*b*) What is the *maximum* value of the Herfindahl-Hirshman Index? _____

3. Assume an oligopolist confronts *two* possible demand curves for its own output, as illustrated below. The first (*A*) prevails if other oligopolists don't match price changes. The second (*B*) prevails if rivals *do* match price changes.

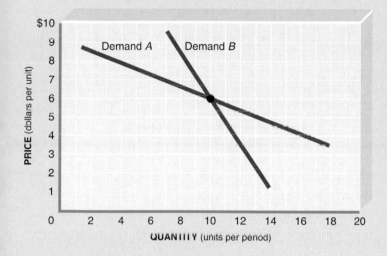

   (*a*) By how much does quantity demanded change if price is reduced from $6 to $4 and
       (*i*) Rivals match price cut? _____
       (*ii*) Rivals don't match price cut? _____
   (*b*) By how much does quantity demanded change when price is raised from $6 to $8 and
       (*i*) Rivals match price hike? _____
       (*ii*) Rivals don't match price hike? _____

4. How large would the probability of a "don't match" outcome have to be to make a universal price cut statistically worthwhile? (See expected payoff, p. 228.) _____

5. Suppose the payoffs to each of four strategic interactions is as follows:

	Rival Response	
Action	Reduce Price	Don't Reduce Price
Reduce price	Loss = $200	Gain = $20,000
Don't reduce price	Loss = $5,000	No loss or gain

   (*a*) If the probability of rivals matching a price reduction is 99 percent, what is the expected payoff to a price cut? _____
   (*b*) If the probability of rivals reducing price even though you don't is 5 percent, what is the expected payoff to *not* reducing price? _____
   (*c*) What should you do? _____

6. Suppose that the following schedule summarizes the sales (demand) situation confronting an oligopolist:

Price (per unit)	$8	$10	$12	$14	$16	$17	$18	$19	$20
Quantity demanded (units per period)	9	8	7	6	5	4	3	2	1

Using the graph below,
(*a*) Draw the demand and marginal revenue curves facing the firm.
(*b*) Identify the profit-maximizing rate of output in a situation where marginal cost is constant at $10 per unit. _____

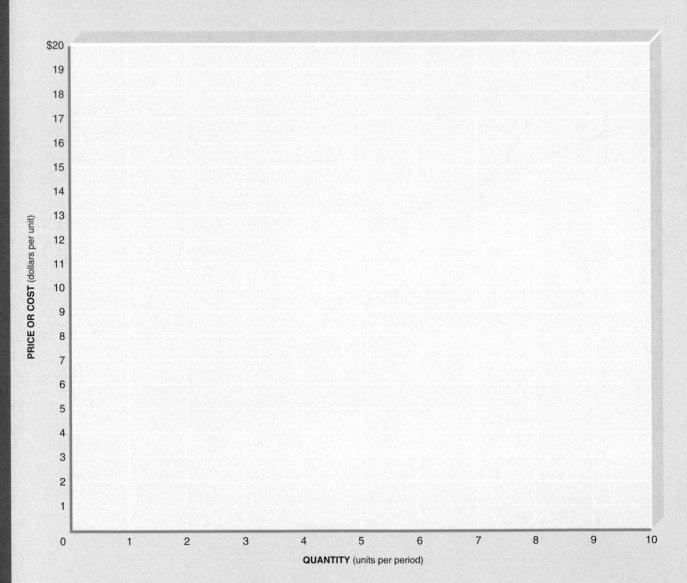

7. What is the price elasticity of demand in Figure 10.2? _____

Problems for Chapter 11

Name: _____

1. In Figure 11.1(b),
   (*a*) At what output rate is economic profit equal zero? _____
   (*b*) At what output rate(s) are positive economic profits available? _____
   (*c*) At what output rate(s) do economic losses occur? _____

2. (*a*) Use the accompanying graph to illustrate the short-run equilibrium of a monopolistically competitive firm.
   (*b*) At that equilibrium, what is
              (*i*) Price? _____
              (*ii*) Output? _____
              (*iii*) Total profit? _____

   (*c*) Identify the long-run equilibrium of the same firm.
   (*d*) In long-run equilibrium, what is
              (*i*) Price? _____
              (*ii*) Output? _____
              (*iii*) Total profit? _____

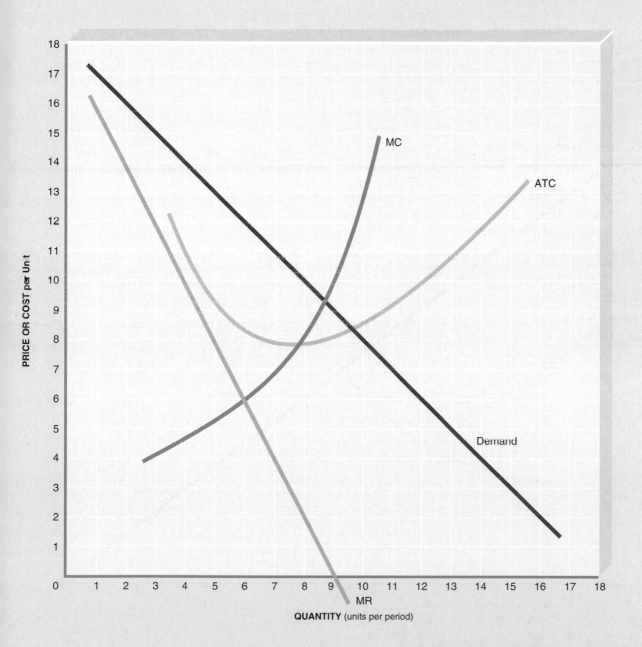

3. (*a*) In the *short*-run equilibrium of the previous problem, what is
    (*i*) The price of the product?   _____
    (*ii*) The opportunity cost of producing the last unit?   _____
  (*b*) In *long*-run equilibrium what is
    (*i*) The price of the product?   _____
    (*ii*) The opportunity cost of producing the last unit?   _____

4. According to the News on p. 246,
  (*a*) By how much could unit sales at Starbucks decline after the 2004 price increase without
    reducing total revenue?   _____%
  (*b*) If the price elasticity of demand for Starbucks is 0.10, by how much would unit sales have
    fallen?   _____%

5. On the accompanying graph, identify each of the following *market* outcomes:
  (*a*) Short-run equilibrium output in competition.
  (*b*) Long-run equilibrium output in competition.
  (*c*) Long-run equilibrium output in monopoly.
  (*d*) Long-run equilibrium output in monopolistic competition.

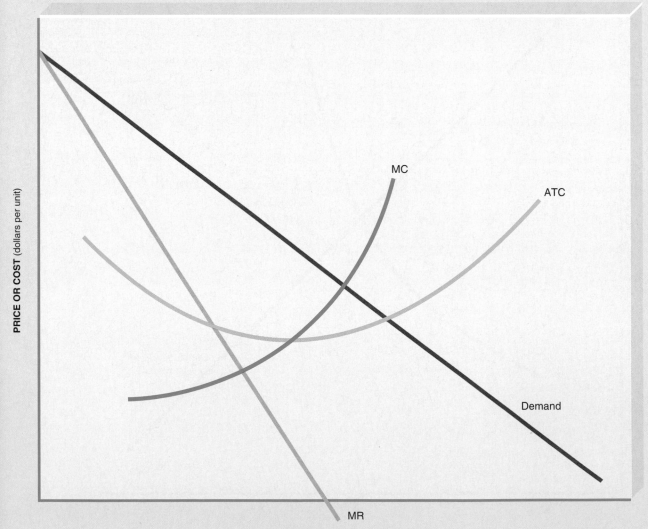

Name: _____

1. In Figure 12.1,
   (*a*) How much profit does an unregulated monopolist earn?   _____
   (*b*) How much profit would be earned if MC pricing was imposed?   _____

2. What happens to total profits when new technology reduces average total costs (shifts ATC downward in Figure 12.1) in
   (*a*) An unregulated natural monopoly?   _____
   (*b*) A price-regulated natural monopoly?   _____
   (*c*) A profit-regulated natural monopoly?   _____

3. Suppose a natural monopolist has fixed costs of $30 and a constant marginal cost of $2. The demand for the product is as follows:

Price (per unit)	$10	$9	$8	$7	$6	$5	$4	$3	$2	$1
Quantity demanded (units per day)	0	2	4	6	8	10	12	14	16	18

Under these conditions,
   (*a*) What price and quantity will prevail if the monopolist isn't regulated?   _____
   (*b*) What price-output combination would exist with efficient pricing (MC = p)?   _____
   (*c*) What price-output combination would exist with profit regulation (zero economic profits)?   _____
   Illustrate your answers on the graph below.

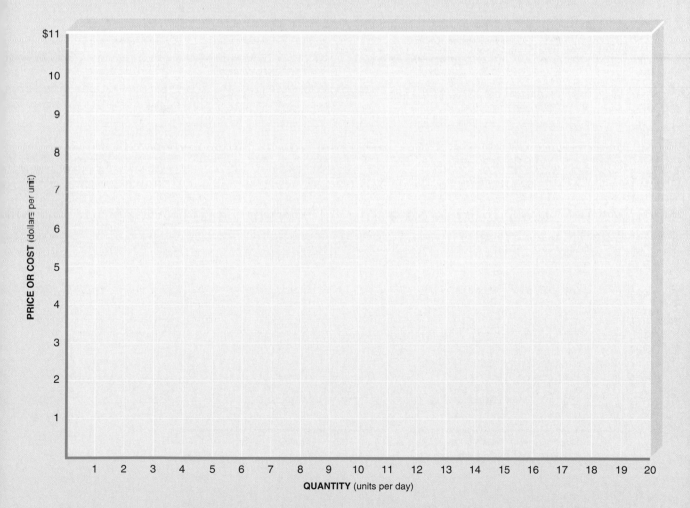

4. According to the News on p. 264, how much will annual shipping costs increase for each saved life?   _____

5. In the long-distance telephone industry, three new transmission technologies—microwaves, satellites, and fiber-optic cable—have replaced the traditional coaxial cable made of copper. The following schedule indicates the costs of the different technologies. (Although similar to the actual figures, the data have been altered to ease calculation and graphing.) Voice circuits indicate the number of phone conversations that can be carried simultaneously. Costs are given in thousands of dollars per month.

Number of voice circuits	50	100	500	1,000	1,500
Total cost of					
Fiber-optic cable	$60	$100	$250	$300	$337
Microwave	40	45	150	250	375
Satellite	35	50	200	350	525

(*a*) Compute and graph (in a single diagram) the average costs of each technology.

(*b*) Draw the long-run average cost curve facing a long-distance telecommunication company that's deciding what transmission technology to use.

(*c*) Are there economies, diseconomies, or constant returns to scale? _____

(*d*) In the long run, how many firms would you expect to provide long-distance service over any given route between two cities? (Base your answer on the long-run average cost curve you drew.) _____

(*e*) With microwave technology, what would be the smallest number of voice circuits that a company could provide and still achieve minimum average cost? _____

(*f*) What kind of technology would be most appropriate if only 50 voice circuits were needed between two towns? _____

(*g*) What if between 100 and 1,000 voice circuits were needed? _____

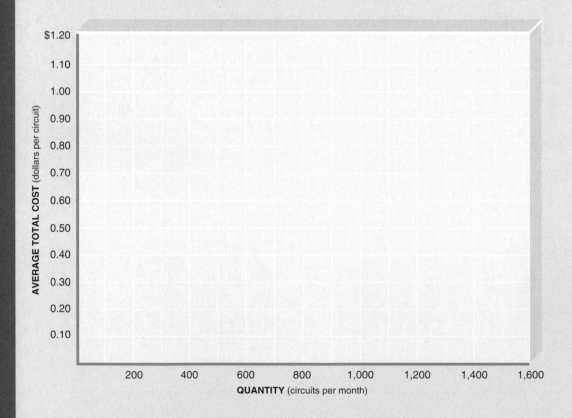

Problems for Chapter 13

Name: _____

1. How many tons of SO_2 emissions did the Carolina Power and Light Company buy in 1993? See News, page 288. _____

2. In some states, mining for coal leaves large mounds of rubble, which poses flooding problems, causes land damage, and is unsightly. The following table shows the estimated annual social benefits and costs of restoring various amounts of such land:

Land restored (in acres)	0	100	200	300	400	500
Social benefits of restoring land	0	$70	$120	$160	$190	$220
Social costs of restoring land	0	$10	$40	$80	$140	$230

(a) Compute the marginal social benefits and the marginal social costs for each restoration level.

Land restored (in acres)	0	100	200	300	400	500
Marginal benefit	___	___	___	___	___	___
Marginal cost	___	___	___	___	___	___

(b) What is the optimal rate of restoration? _____

3. Most people pay nothing for each extra pound of garbage they create. Yet the garbage imposes external costs on a community. In view of this factor, what's an appropriate price for garbage collection? Answer the questions based on the following graph.
   (a) What is the quantity of garbage collection now demanded? _____
   (b) IIow much would be demanded if a fee of $2 per pound were charged? _____
   (c) Draw the social demand curve when an external benefit of $3 per pound exists.
   (d) If the marginal cost of collecting garbage were constant at $5 per pound, what would be the optimal level of garbage collection? _____

Garbage-collection Service

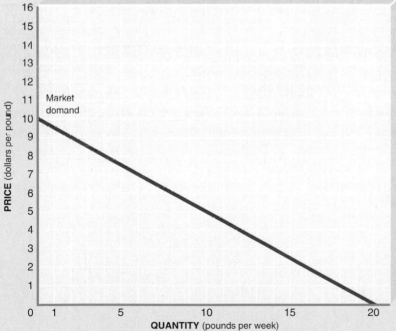

4. Using the *high* estimate of costs and *low* estimate of benefits for pollution controls (News, bottom of p. 291), what is the average benefit per dollar spent? _____

5. How much more per ton is New York City paying to recycle rather than just dump its garbage (News, p. 292)? _____

6. Suppose three firms confront the following costs for pollution control:

Emissions Reduction (tons per year)	Total Costs of Control		
	Firm A	Firm B	Firm C
1	$ 50	$ 60	$ 40
2	100	140	150
3	180	230	300
4	300	350	600

(a) If each firm must reduce emissions by 1 ton, how much will be spent?   _____

(b) If the firms can trade pollution rights, what would be the cheapest way of attaining a net
3-ton reduction?   _____

(c) How much would a pollution permit trade for?   _____

Now suppose the goal is to reduce pollution by 6 tons.

(d) If each firm must reduce emissions by 2 tons, how much will be spent?   _____

(e) If the firms can trade permits, what is the cheapest way of attaining a 6-ton reduction?   _____

(f) How much will a permit cost?   _____

7. The following cost schedule depicts the private and social costs associated with the daily
production of apacum, a highly toxic fertilizer. The sales price of apacum is $18 per ton.

Output (in tons)	0	1	2	3	4	5	6	7	8
Total private cost	$5	7	13	23	37	55	77	103	133
Total social cost	$7	13	31	61	103	157	223	301	391

Answer the questions using this schedule, and graph on the figure below.

(a) Graph the private and social marginal costs associated with apacum production.

(b) What is the profit-maximizing rate of output?   _____

(c) How much profit is earned at that output level?   _____

(d) What is the socially optimal rate of output?   _____

(e) How much profit is there at that output level?   _____

(f) How much of a "green tax" per ton would have to be levied to induce the firm to produce
the socially optimal rate of output?   _____

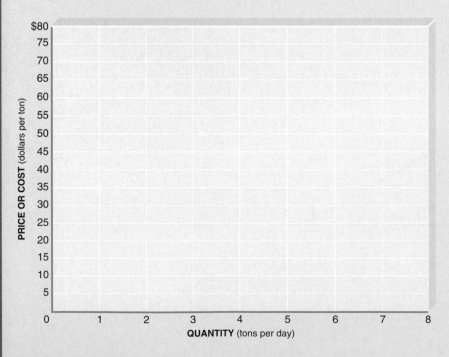

Problems for Chapter 14

Name: _____

1. Suppose the market price of wheat was $3 per bushel.
   (*a*) Would a farmer have sold wheat to the market or to the government (CCC)? (See Table 14.2.) _____
   (*b*) How much of a counter-cyclical payment would the farmer have received? (See Table 14.3.) _____
   (*c*) If the market price fell to $2.50, what would the farmer do with his wheat? _____

2. Suppose that consumers' incomes fall 20 percent, which results in a 2 percent drop in consumption of farm goods without change in prices. What is the income elasticity of demand for farm goods? _____

3. Assume that the unregulated supply schedule for milk is the following:

Price (per pound)	5¢	7¢	8¢	10¢	14¢
Quantity supplied (billions of pounds per year)	42	53	63	76	103

   (*a*) Draw the supply and demand curves for milk, assuming that the demand for milk is perfectly inelastic and consumers will buy 53 billion pounds of it. What is the equilibrium price? _____

   (*b*) Suppose that the farmers' response to the government's offer to pay them for not producing milk results in the following supply schedule:

Price (per pound)	5¢	7¢	8¢	10¢	14¢
Quantity supplied (billions of pounds per year)	19	30	40	53	80

   (*c*) Draw this new supply curve on the same set of axes as the supply curve prior to the government's action. What is the equilibrium price following the government's action? _____
   (*d*) How much more money would consumers pay for the 53 billion pounds of milk because of the higher equilibrium price? _____
   (*e*) Shade in the area in your diagram that represents how much more consumers will pay because of the government-sponsored cutbacks.

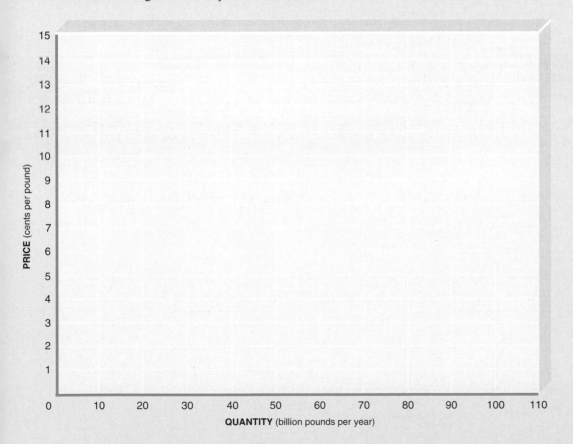

4. Suppose there are 100 grain farmers, each with identical cost structures as shown in the following table:

Production Costs (per farm)		Demand	
Output (bushels per day)	Total Cost (per day)	Price (per bushel)	Quantity Demanded (bushels per day)
0	$ 5	$1	600
1	7	2	500
2	10	3	400
3	14	4	300
4	19	5	200
5	25	6	100
6	33	7	50

Under these circumstances, graph the market supply and demand.
(a) What is the equilibrium price for grain?   _____
(b) How much grain will be produced at the equilibrium price?   _____
(c) How much profit will each farmer earn at that price?   _____
(d) If the government gives farmers a cost subsidy equal to $1 a bushel, what will happen to
                                                                                (i) Output?   _____
                                                                                (ii) Price?   _____
                                                                                (iii) Profit?   _____
(e) What will happen to total output if the government additionally guarantees a price of $5 per bushel?   _____
(f) What price is required to sell this output?   _____
(g) What is the cost to the government in d?   _____
(h) Show your answers on the graph below.

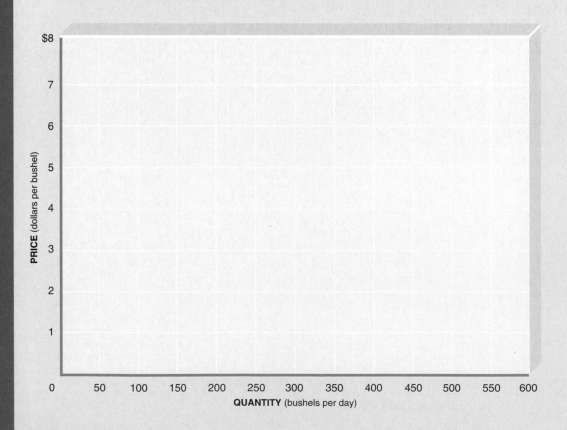

Problems for Chapter 15

Name: _____

1. (a) What was the federal minimum wage the year you were born? _____
   (b) What is it now? _____

2. (a) In Figure 15.8, how many workers are unemployed at the equilibrium wage? _____
   (b) How many workers are unemployed at the minimum wage? _____

3. Suppose a wage increase from $10 to $12 an hour increases the number of job applicants from 42 to 56. What is the price elasticity of labor supply? _____

4. According to the News on page 324, how much more ticket revenue are the Yankees bringing in since signing A-Rod? _____

5. If the price of strawberries doubled, how many pickers would be hired at $4 an hour, according to Table 15.1? _____

6. Apples can be harvested by hand or machine. Handpicking yields 40 pounds per hour, mechanical pickers yield 70 pounds per hour. If the wage rate of human pickers is $6 an hour and the rental on a mechanical picker is $15 an hour,
   (a) Which is more cost-effective? _____
   (b) If the wage rate increased to $8 an hour, which would be more cost-effective? _____

7. Assume that the following data describe labor-market conditions:

Wage rate (per hour)	$3	$4	$5	$6	$7	$8	$9	$10
Labor demanded	50	45	40	35	30	25	20	15
Labor supplied	20	30	40	50	60	70	80	90

On the graph below, illustrate
(a) The equilibrium wage.
(b) A government-set minimum wage of $6 per hour when the minimum wage is implemented.
(c) How many workers lose jobs? _____
(d) How many additional workers seek jobs? _____
(e) How many workers end up unemployed? _____

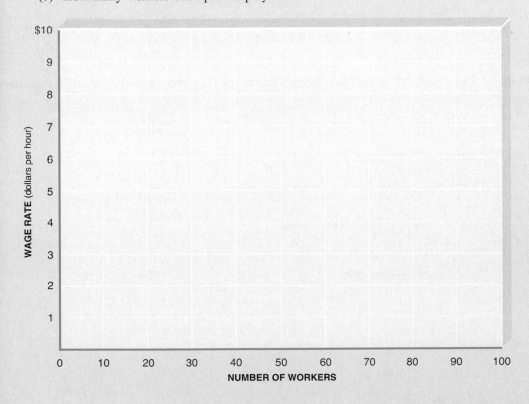

8. The following table depicts the number of grapes that can be picked in an hour with varying amounts of labor:

Number of pickers (per hour)	1	2	3	4	5	6	7	8
Output of grapes (in flats)	20	38	53	64	71	74	74	70

(a) Illustrate the supply and demand of labor for a single farmer, assuming that the local wage rate is $6 an hour and a flat of grapes sells for $2.

(b) How many pickers will be hired?   _____

(c) If the wage rate doubles, how many pickers will be hired?   _____

(d) If the productivity of all workers doubles, how many pickers will be hired at a wage of $12 an hour?   _____

(e) Illustrate your answers on the graph below.

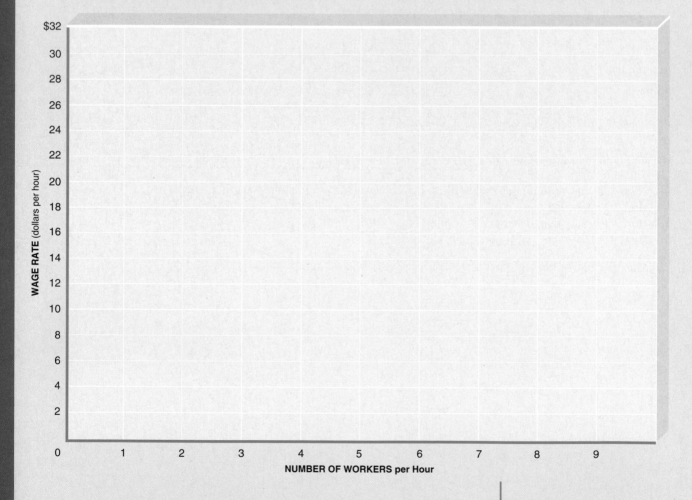

9. Illustrate the change in the U.S. labor supply between 1890 and 2004, as discussed on page 316.

Problems for Chapter 16

Name: _____

1. Complete the following table:

Wage rate	$12	$11	$10	$9	$8	$7	$6	$5
Quantity of labor demanded	0	5	20	50	75	95	110	120
Marginal wage		___	___	___	___	___	___	___

(a) At what wage rate(s) is the marginal wage below the nominal wage? _____

(b) At what wage rate does the marginal wage first become negative? _____

2. Complete the following table:

Wage rate	$4	$5	$6	$7	$8	$9	$10
Quantity of labor supplied	80	120	155	180	200	210	215
Marginal factor cost		___	___	___	___	___	___

3. Based on the data in problems (1) and (2) above,

(a) What is the competitive wage rate? _____

(b) Approximately what wage will the union seek? _____

(c) How many workers will the union have to exclude in order to get that wage? _____

4. At the time of the National Football League strike in 1987, the football owners made available the following data:

	Revenue	
Source of Revenue	Before the Strike	During the Strike
Television	$973,000	$973,000
Stadium gate	526,000	126,000
Luxury box seats	255,000	200,000
Concessions	60,000	12,000
Radio	40,000	40,000
Players' salaries and costs	854,000	230,000
Nonplayer costs (coaches' salaries)	200,000	200,000

(a) Compute total revenues, total expenses, and profits both before and during the strike.

	Before Strike	During Strike
Total revenue	_____	_____
Total expense	_____	_____
Total profit	_____	_____

(b) Why would the owners ever agree to settle the strike under these conditions?

Name: _____

5. Suppose the following supply-and-demand schedules apply in a particular labor market:

Wage rate (per hour)	$4	$5	$6	$7	$8	$9	$10
Quantity of labor supplied (workers per hour)	2	3	4	5	6	7	8
Quantity of labor demanded (workers per hour)	6	5	4	3	2	1	0

Graph the relevant curves and identify the
  (a) Competitive wage rate.   _____
  (b) Union wage rate.   _____
  (c) Monopsonist's wage rate.   _____

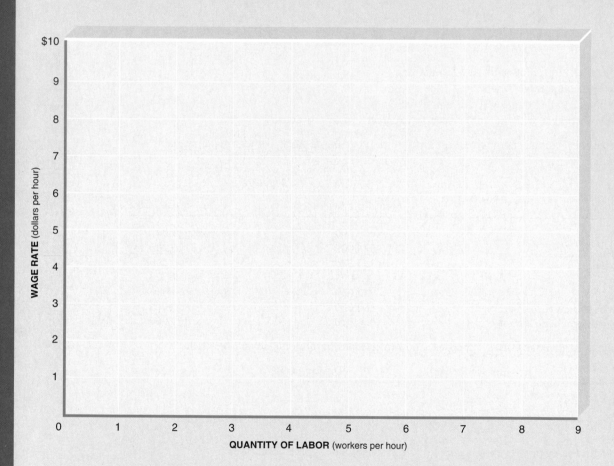

Problems for Chapter 17

Name: _____

1. If a $48 stock pays a quarterly dividend of $1, what is the implied rate of return? _____

2. If a $32 per share stock has a P/E ratio of 20 and pays out 40 percent of its profits in dividends, what is the implied rate of (dividend) return on the stock? _____

3. If the market rate of interest is 5 percent, what is the present discounted value of $1,000 that will be paid in

        (*a*) 1 year? _____
        (*b*) 5 years? _____
        (*c*) 10 years? _____

4. What is the present discounted value of $10,000 that is to be received in 5 years if the market rate of interest is

        (*a*) 0 percent? _____
        (*b*) 5 percent? _____
        (*c*) 10 percent? _____

5. Compute the expected return on Columbus's expedition assuming that he had a 50 percent chance of discovering valuables worth $1 million, a 25 percent chance of bringing home only $10,000, and a 25 percent chance of sinking. _____

6. Locate the stock quotation for General Motors Corporation in today's newspaper (traded on the New York Stock Exchange). From the information provided, determine
(*a*) Yesterday's percentage change in the price of GM stock. _____
(*b*) How much profit (earnings) GM made last year for each share of stock. _____
(*c*) How much of that profit was paid out in dividends. _____
(*d*) How much profit GM retained for investment. _____

7. Compute the market price of the GM bonds described in Table 17.5 if the yield goes to 9 percent. _____

8. What is the current yield on a $1,000 bond with a 6 percent coupon if its market price is

        (*a*) $900? _____
        (*b*) $1,000? _____
        (*c*) $1,100? _____

9. How much interest accrued each day on the cash payoff of the MegaMillions jackpot? (See Table 17.1.)

10. Illustrate the impact of the following events on stock prices:

   (*a*) A federal court finds Microsoft guilty of antitrust violations.

   Microsoft stock

   PRICE (dollars per share)

   QUANTITY (shares per day)

   (*b*) Intel announces a new and faster processor.

   Intel stock

   PRICE (dollars per share)

   QUANTITY (shares per day)

   (*c*) Corporate executives announce they intend to sell a large block of stock.

   Company stock

   PRICE (dollars per share)

   QUANTITY (shares per day)

   (*d*) AOL's competitors cut Internet-access prices.

   AOL stock

   PRICE (dollars per share)

   QUANTITY (shares per day)

Problems for Chapter 18

Name: _____

1. How much income tax would President Bush have paid in 2003 (News, p. 380) if there were no tax deductions? (Use tax rates in Table 18.1.) _____

2. Use Table 18.1 to compute the taxes on a taxable income of $150,000.
   (a) What is the marginal tax rate? _____
   (b) What is the average tax rate? _____

3. Using Table 18.1, compute the taxable income and taxes for the following taxpayers:

Taxpayer	Gross Income	Exemptions and Deductions	Taxable Income	Tax
A	$ 20,000	$ 7,000	_____	_____
B	30,000	4,000	_____	_____
C	40,000	28,000	_____	_____
D	70,000	32,000	_____	_____
E	200,000	80,000	_____	_____

   Which taxpayer has
   (a) The highest nominal tax rate? _____
   (b) The highest effective tax rate? _____
   (c) The highest marginal tax rate? _____

4. If the tax elasticity of supply is 0.30, by how much will the quantity supplied decrease when the marginal tax rate increases from 40 to 50 percent? _____

5. By how much would the quantity of labor supplied have increased from the Bush tax cuts of 2001–3 if the tax elasticity of supply is 0.15 and the marginal tax rate fell from 22 to 19 percent?

6. If the tax elasticity of labor supply was 0.15, by how much would the quantity of labor supplied increase among people in the top U.S. tax bracket if the highest marginal tax rate in the United States were reduced to the level of Hong Kong's (World View, p. 385)? _____

7. What percentage of income is paid in Social Security taxes by a worker earning
   (a) $20,000? _____
   (b) $100,000? _____
   (c) $200,000? _____
   (d) What kind of tax is this? _____

8. What is the effective tax rate with Dick Armey's proposed flat tax for a family of four with earnings of
   (a) $30,000? _____
   (b) $60,000? _____
   (c) $90,000? _____

9. Following are hypothetical data on the size distribution of income and wealth for each quintile (one-fifth) of a population:

Quintile	Lowest	Second	Third	Fourth	Highest
Income	5%	10%	15%	25%	45%
Wealth	2%	8%	12%	20%	58%

   (a) On the graph on the next page, draw the line of absolute equity; then draw a Lorenz curve for income, and shade the area between the two curves.
   (b) In the same diagram, draw a Lorenz curve for wealth. Is there more inequality in the distribution of wealth than of income, or less? How do you know?
   (c) The difference in inequality between income and wealth is quite typical of most economies. What might be the reason? _____

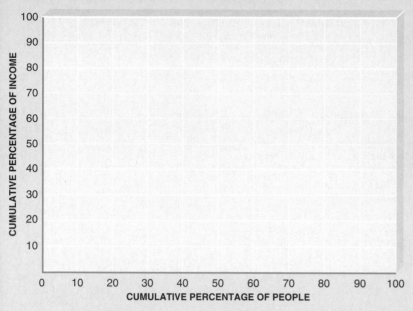

10. (a) On the graph below, draw the supply and demand for labor represented by the following data:

Wage	$1	2	3	4	5	6	7	8	9	10	11	12
Quantity of labor												
Supplied	1	2	3	4	5	6	8	10	12	14	17	20
Demanded	20	18	16	14	12	10	8	6	5	4	3	2

(b) How many workers are employed in equilibrium? _____

(c) What wage are they paid? _____

(d) Now suppose a payroll tax of $2 per worker is imposed on the employer. Draw the "supply + tax" graph that results.

(e) How many workers are now employed? _____

(f) How much is the employer paying for each worker? _____

(g) How much is each worker receiving? _____

For the incidence of this tax,

(h) What is the increase in unit labor cost to the employer? _____

(i) What is the reduction in the wage paid to labor? _____

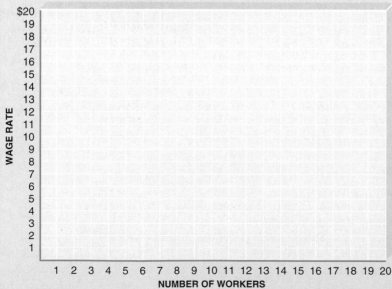

Problems for Chapter 19

Name: _____

1. Suppose the welfare benefit formula is

$$\text{Benefit} = \$6{,}000 - 2/3\,(\text{wages} > \$4{,}000)$$

(a) What is the marginal tax rate? _____

(b) How large is the benefit if wages equal

                                                       (i) $0? _____

                                                       (ii) $4,000? _____

                                                       (iii) $9,000? _____

(c) What is the breakeven level of income in this case? _____

2. A welfare recipient can receive food stamps as well as cash welfare benefits. If the food stamp allotment is set as follows,

$$\text{Food stamps} = \$5{,}000 - 0.30\,(\text{wages})$$

(a) How high can wages rise before all food stamps are eliminated? _____

(b) If the welfare check formula in Problem 1 applies, what is the *combined* marginal tax rate of both welfare and food stamps for wages above $4,000? _____

3. Draw a graph showing how benefits, total income, and wages change under the following conditions:

$$\text{Wage rate} = \$10 \text{ per hour}$$

$$\text{Welfare benefit} = \$6{,}000 - 0.5\,(\text{wages} > \$3{,}000)$$

Label the following points:
A—welfare benefit when wages = 0
B—welfare benefit when wages = $10,000
C—breakeven level of income

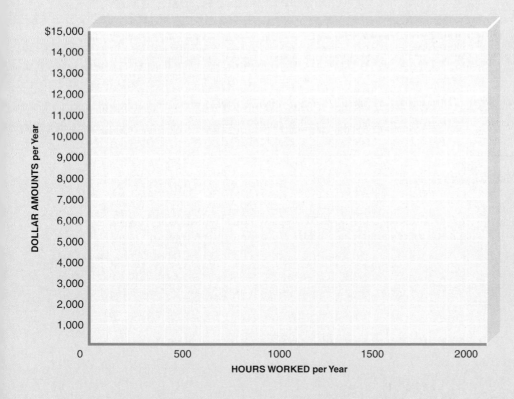

4. What is the breakeven level of income for Social Security as depicted in Figure 19.6?   _____

5. According to the benefit formula in Table 19.2, how large will the Social Security benefit be for a worker who had earned

        (*a*) $16,000 a year?   _____
        (*b*) $60,000 a year?   _____

  What is the implied wage replacement rate for

        (*c*) The $16,000 per year worker?   _____
        (*d*) The $60,000 per year worker?   _____

6. How large a monthly Social Security check will a retiree get if her maximum benefit is $1,600 per month and she continues working for wages of $2,000 per month?   _____

7. (*a*) On the graph below, depict the wages income and Social Security benefits at different hours of work for a worker aged 62–64 who earns $15 per hour and is eligible for $12,000 in Social Security benefits.
   (*b*) What is total income if the person works 1,000 hours per year?   _____
   (*c*) What is the breakeven level of income?   _____

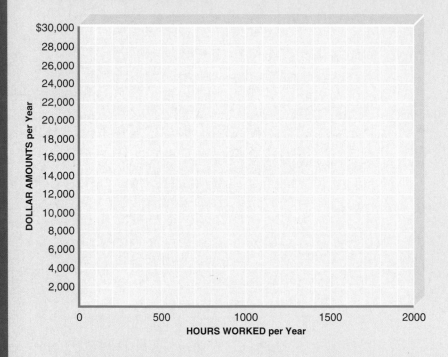

8. If older workers have a tax elasticity of labor supply equal to 0.20, by how much will their work activity decline when they hit the Social Security earnings-test limit? (Assume explicit taxes of 30 percent below that limit)   _____%

Problems for Chapter 20

Name: _____

1. Which countries are the two largest export markets for the United States? (See Table 20.3.)

   1. _____

   2. _____

2. Suppose a country can produce a maximum of 1,000 jumbo airliners or 800 aircraft carriers.
   (*a*) What is the opportunity cost of an aircraft carrier?   _____
   (*b*) If another country offers to trade six planes for four aircraft carriers, should the offer be accepted?   _____
   (*c*) What are the implied terms of trade?   _____

3. If it takes 64 farm workers to harvest one ton of strawberries and 16 farm workers to harvest one ton of wheat, what is the opportunity cost of five tons of strawberries?   _____

4. Alpha and Beta, two tiny islands off the east coast of Tricoli, produce pearls and pineapples. The following production possibilities schedules describe their potential output in tons per year.

Alpha		Beta	
Pearls	**Pineapples**	**Pearls**	**Pineapples**
0	30	0	20
2	25	10	16
4	20	20	12
6	15	30	8
8	10	40	4
10	5	45	2
12	0	50	0

   (*a*) Graph the production possibilities confronting each island.

   (*b*) What is the opportunity cost of pineapples on each island (before trade)?

      Alpha: _____

      Beta: _____

   (*c*) Which island has a comparative advantage in pearl production?   _____

   (*d*) Graph the consumption possibilities of each island with free trade.

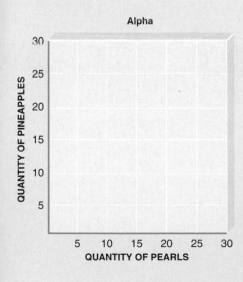

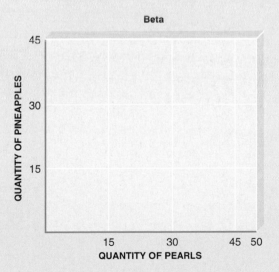

5. (*a*) How much more are U.S. consumers paying for the 20 billion pounds of sugar they consume each year as a result of the quotas on sugar imports? (See News, p. 422.)   _____
   (*b*) How much sales revenue are foreign sugar producers losing as a result of those same quotas?   _____

6. Suppose the two islands in Problem 4 agree that the terms of trade will be one for one and exchange 10 pearls for 10 pineapples.

   (a) If Alpha produced 6 pearls and 15 pineapples while Beta produced 30 pearls and 8 pineapples before they decided to trade, how much would each be producing after trade? Assume that the two countries specialize just enough to maintain their consumption of the item they export, and make sure each island follows its comparative advantage.

   (b) How much would each island be consuming after specializing and trading?   Alpha: _____

   (c) How much would the combined production of pineapples increase for the two islands due to   Beta: _____
   trade? _____

   (d) How much would the combined production of pearls increase? _____

   (e) How could both countries produce and consume even more? _____
   _____

   (f) Assume the two islands are able to trade as much as they want with the rest of the world, with the terms of trade at one pineapple for one pearl. Draw the ultimate consumption possibilities curve for each island.

7. Suppose the following table reflects the domestic supply and demand for compact disks (CDs):

Price ($)	16	14	12	10	8	6	4	2
Quantity supplied	8	7	6	5	4	3	2	1
Quantity demanded	2	4	6	8	10	12	14	16

   (a) Graph these market conditions and identify the equilibrium price and sales.   Price/sales: _____

   (b) Now suppose that foreigners enter the market, offering to sell an unlimited supply of CDs for $6 apiece. Illustrate and identify
      (i) The market price   _____
      (ii) Domestic consumption   _____
      (iii) Domestic production   _____

   (c) If a tariff of $2 per CD is imposed, what will happen to
      (i) The market price?   _____
      (ii) Domestic consumption?   _____
      (iii) Domestic production?   _____
   Graph your answers.

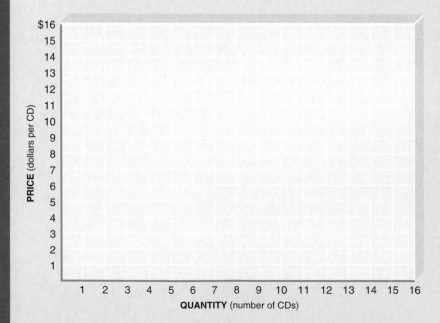

Problems for Chapter 21

Name: _____

1. If a euro is worth $1.25, what is the euro price of a dollar? _____

2. If a pound of U.S. pork cost 40 rupiah in Indonesia before the Asian crisis, how much did it cost during the crisis? See World View on page 435 for clues. _____

3. If a PlayStation 2 costs 20,000 yen in Japan, how much will it cost in U.S. dollars if the exchange rate is

                                           (a) 120 yen = $1? _____
                                           (b) 1 yen = $0.00833? _____
                                           (c) 100 yen = $1? _____

4. Between 1980 and 2000,
    (a) By how much did the dollar appreciate (Figure 21.3)? _____%
    (b) How did that appreciation affect the relative price of U.S. exports? _____

5. If inflation raises U.S. prices by 3 percent and the U.S. dollar appreciates by 2 percent, by how much does the foreign price of U.S. exports change? _____%

6. According to the World View on p. 430, what was the peso price of a euro in August 2004? _____

7. For each of the following possible events, indicate whether the demand or supply curve for dollars would shift, the direction of the shift, the determinant of the change, the inflow or outflow effect on the balance of payments (and the specific account that would be affected), and the resulting movement of the equilibrium exchange rate for the value of the dollar.

    (a) American cars become suddenly more popular abroad. _____

    (b) Inflation rates in the United States accelerate. _____

    (c) The United States falls into a depression. _____

    (d) Interest rates in the United States drop. _____

    (e) The United States suddenly experiences rapid increases in productivity. _____

    (f) Anticipating a return to the gold standard, Americans suddenly rush to buy gold from the two big producers, South Africa and the Soviet Union. _____

    (g) War is declared in the Middle East. _____

    (h) The stock markets in the United States suddenly collapse. _____

8. The following schedules summarize the supply and demand for trifflings, the national currency of Tricoli:

Triffling price (U.S. dollars per triffling)	0	$4	$8	$12	$16	$20	$24
Quantity demanded (per year)	40	38	36	34	32	30	28
Quantity supplied (per year)	1	11	21	31	41	51	61

Use the above schedules for the following:

(a) Graph the supply and demand curves.

(b) Determine the equilibrium exchange rate.   _____

(c) Determine the size of the excess supply or excess demand that would exist if the Tricolian government fixed the exchange rate $22 = 1 triffling.   _____

(d) How might this imbalance be remedied?

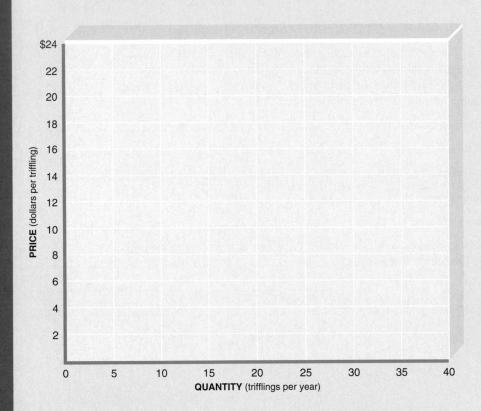